AF767287

Blackstone's Police Manual

General Police Duties

Blackstone's Police Manual

Volume 3

General Police Duties

2027

Glenn Hutton

BA, MPhil, FCIPD

Elliot Gold KC

LLB (Hons), Barrister-at-Law

Andy Cox

M.St.

and

Paul Connor

Cert Ed (FE), PG Cert Ed (ODE), LLB

Consultant Editor: Paul Connor

OXFORD
UNIVERSITY PRESS

OXFORD
UNIVERSITY PRESS

Great Clarendon Street, Oxford, OX2 6DP,
United Kingdom

Oxford University Press is a department of the University of Oxford.
It furthers the University's objective of excellence in research, scholarship,
and education by publishing worldwide. Oxford is a registered trade mark of
Oxford University Press in the UK and in certain other countries.

First Edition published in 1998
Twenty-ninth Edition published in 2026

Published in the United States of America by Oxford University Press
546 Fifth Avenue, New York, NY 10036, United States of America

British Library Cataloguing in Publication Data
Data available

ISBN 978–0–19–791806–7

DOI: 10.1093/law/9780197918067.001.0001

Printed in the UK by
Bell & Bain Ltd., Glasgow

The manufacturer's authorized representative in the EU for product safety is
Oxford University Press España S.A. of Parque Empresarial San Fernando de Henares,
Avenida de Castilla, 2 – 28830 Madrid (www.oup.es/en or product.safety@oup.com).
OUP España S.A. also acts as importer into Spain of products made by the manufacturer.

MIX
Paper | Supporting responsible forestry
FSC www.fsc.org FSC® C007785

Foreword for 2027 Blackstone's Police Manuals

As the Chief Executive of the College of Policing, the professional body for policing, I am pleased to provide the foreword for *Blackstone's Police Manuals 2027*.

The role of the College is to set standards, provide training and share good practice for policing nationally. Practitioner knowledge is at the heart of everything we do, and we use evidence of what works, to make a difference in fighting crime and protecting the public.

Policing continues to be the focus of intense political, public and media scrutiny not least of which because of the challenges we face on trust, confidence and our performance in tackling crime and disorder that impacts upon the communities we serve. I know from the many officers, staff and volunteers that I meet in policing that they do what they do and go the extra mile so often because they care and they want to make a difference. With this in mind, we should welcome the intense scrutiny because it validates that what we do is important and matters. To succeed in our mission, it has never been more important than now that knowledge and standards are the cornerstones of the policing profession. Blackstone's Manuals are the definitive reference source for all who are involved in police law and procedure and those seeking to progress to a specialised role. They are widely used in the professional development of police officers and staff in a variety of roles.

Whilst Oxford University Press produces these titles independently, the College develops, maintains and tests standards to ensure suitability for promotion by producing a comprehensive and relevant syllabus. Blackstone's Manuals are the official study guide for the College's National Police Promotion Framework that underpins the national legal examination, which candidates must pass, to be promoted to the ranks of Sergeant and Inspector.

If you are using these Manuals as a reference guide for continuous professional development, thank you for your commitment. If you are using Blackstone's Manuals as a professional reference to ensure your work is of the highest possible standards, thank you for your dedication and, finally, if you are referencing these books to study for promotion or progression into a specialist role, I wish you every success.

Chief Constable Sir Andy Marsh QPM
Chief Executive, College of Policing

Preface

The *Blackstone's Police Manuals* are the only official study guides for the Police Promotion Examinations—if the law is not in the Manuals, it will not be in the exams.

All the Manuals include explanatory Keynotes and case law examples, providing clear and incisive analysis of important areas. They can also be used as a training resource for police probationers, special constables and PCSOs, or as an invaluable reference tool for police staff of all ranks and positions.

The 2027 edition has been edited and updated to incorporate all recent legislative changes and a number of recent criminal cases decided by the appellate courts.

The aim of this Manual is to take this shifting and growing body of law and analyse the essential elements in a practical and pragmatic context—without losing the specific meaning and applicability along the way. If we have achieved that, it is thanks to the contributions of the many police officers and staff, lawyers and practitioners who have helped in the development of this Manual, now in its twenty-ninth edition; if we haven't, it is not for the want of trying.

Oxford University Press are always happy to receive any useful written feedback from any reader on the content and style of the Manual, especially from those involved in or with the criminal justice system. Please email this address with any comments or queries: police@oup.com.

The law is stated as at 1 June 2026.

Acknowledgements

Blackstone's Police Manuals have become firmly established as a 'household name' in the context of police law for which they are the leading text in England and Wales. Their growth and refinement year on year is a result, not simply of Parliament and the legislators, but also of the many and varied contributions of the Manuals' wide readership.

Thanks are due to all (except perhaps the legislators) and there is never space to mention everyone individually.

In particular, thanks to the staff of the Legal Services Department of the College of Policing (CoP) and Examinations and Assessment.

Our thanks, as always, to all the staff involved in the production of the Manual in the Academic and Professional Law Department at Oxford University Press. Special thanks also to Sonal, Priya, Jayna, Selina and Rosalie for their continued support and forbearance.

Glenn Hutton, Elliot Gold KC, Andy Cox and Paul Connor

Contents

Table of Cases

Table of Statutes

Table of Statutory Instruments

Table of Codes of Practice

Table of Home Office Circulars

Table of International Treaties and Conventions

How to use this Manual

Volume numbers for the Manuals

The 2027 *Blackstone's Police Manuals* each have a volume number as follows:

Volume 1: *Crime*
Volume 2: *Evidence and Procedure*
Volume 3: *General Police Duties*

The first digit of each paragraph number in the text of the Manuals denotes the Manual number. For example, chapter 2.3 is chapter 3 of the *Evidence and Procedure Manual* and chapter 3.3 is chapter 3 of the *General Police Duties Manual*.

All index entries and references in the Tables of Legislation and the Table of Cases, etc. refer to paragraph numbers instead of page numbers, making information easier to find.

Material outside the scope of the police promotion examinations syllabus—blacklining

These Manuals contain some information which is outside the scope of the police promotion examinations. A full black line down the margin indicates that the text beside it is excluded from Inspectors' examinations.

PACE Code chapters

The PACE Codes of Practice have been taken out of the appendices and are now incorporated within chapters in the main body of the *Blackstone's Police Manuals*. A thick grey line down the margin is used to denote text that is an extract of the PACE Code itself (i.e. the actual wording of the legislation) and does not form part of the general commentary of the chapter.

The PACE Codes of Practice form an important part of the police promotion examinations syllabus and are examinable for both Sergeants and Inspectors. They are not to be confused with 'blacklined' content that is excluded from the syllabus for Inspectors' examinations (see 'Material outside the scope of the police promotion examinations syllabus—blacklining').

Length of sentence for an offence

Where a length of sentence for an offence is stated in this Manual, please note that the number of months or years stated is the maximum number and will not be exceeded.

Any feedback regarding content or other editorial matters in the Manuals can be emailed to police@oup.com.

NPPF Step Two Legal Examinations Candidate Handbook Information

The rules and syllabus for the police promotion examinations system are defined within the Candidate Handbook published by College of Policing (Career and Assessment) on behalf of the Police Promotion Examinations Board (PPEB).

The document provides details of the law and procedure to be tested within the National Police Promotion Framework Step 2 Legal Examination, and also outlines the rules underpinning the police promotion examination system.

All candidates who are taking a police promotion examination are strongly encouraged to familiarise themselves with the Candidate Handbook during their preparation. The police promotion examination rules apply to candidates undertaking the National Police Promotion Framework.

The document can be downloaded from the Development Section of the College of Policing website, which can be found at <https://www.college.police.uk>. Electronic versions are also supplied to all force examination officers.

If you have any problems obtaining the Candidate Handbook from the above source, please contact your force examination officer.

In exceptional circumstances, the College of Policing (on behalf of the PPEB) reserves the right to issue an amended syllabus prior to the next scheduled annual publication date.

For example, a major change to a key area of legislation or procedure (e.g. the Codes of Practice) during the lifespan of the current Candidate Handbook would render a significant part of the current syllabus content obsolete. In such circumstances, it may be necessary for an update to the syllabus to be issued, which would provide guidance to candidates on any additional material which would be examinable within their police promotion examinations.

In such circumstances, an update to the Candidate Handbook would be made available through the College of Policing website, and would be distributed to all force examination contacts. The College of Policing will ensure that any syllabus update is distributed well in advance of the examination date, to ensure that candidates have sufficient time to familiarise themselves with any additional examinable material. Where possible, any additional study materials would be provided to candidates free of charge.

Please note that syllabus updates will only be made in *exceptional* circumstances; an update will not be made for every change to legislation included within the syllabus. For further guidance on this issue, candidates are advised to check regularly the College of Policing website, or consult their force examination officer, during their preparation period.

Useful Reference Tables

Inspector and Superintendent Authorisations in the NPPF Syllabus

The table below sets out the situations in the NPPF syllabus when the authorisation of an officer of the rank of Inspector or above or Superintendent or above is required.

INSP	SUPT
Information about guests at hotels s. 116 Anti-social Behaviour, Crime & Police Act 2014 *Crime*, para. 1.12.11.3	Further extension of bail (6 to 9 months) s. 47ZDA PACE84 *Evidence and Procedure*, para. 2.2.3.2
Extend bail in standard case 3 to 6 months s. 47ZD PACE84 *Evidence and Procedure*, para. 2.2.3.2	Delay access to legal advice Code C–6 and Annex B/s. 58 PACE84 *Evidence and Procedure*, paras 2.6.11, 2.6.23
Incommunicado/Whereabouts on arrest/phone call/letter Code C–5 and Annex B/s. 56 PACE84 *Evidence and Procedure*, paras 2.6.10, 2.6.23	Authorisation of continued detention (24 to 36 hours) s. 42 PACE84 *Evidence and Procedure*, para. 2.6.18
Interview goes ahead after detainee changes mind about legal advice Code C–6.6(d)(iv) *Evidence and Procedure*, para. 2.6.11	Acting Ranks s. 107 PACE84 Various Codes (Code B–2.7, Code C–1.9A, Code D–2.9) *General Police Duties*, para. 3.2.3
Test for Class A drugs Code C–17.3(b)–Arrest condition *Evidence and Procedure*, para. 2.6.21	Urgent interview at police station–Vulnerable Suspects Code C–11.18 *Evidence and Procedure*, para. 2.8.3
Test for Class A drugs Code C–17.4(b)–Charge condition *Evidence and Procedure*, para. 2.6.21	Authorise extension of s. 60 search power by 24hrs Code A–2.8/s. 60(3) Criminal Justice and Public Order Act 1994 *General Police Duties*, para. 3.1.4
Intimate Search Code C–Annex A *Evidence and Procedure*, para. 2.6.22	Authorise extension of s. 60AA remove face coverings etc. by 24hrs Code A–2.8/s. 60AA(4) Criminal Justice and Public Order Act 1994 *General Police Duties*, para. 3.1.4
X-ray or Ultrasound Scan Code C–Annex K/s. 55A PACE84 *Evidence and Procedure*, para. 2.6.27	Authorise extension of s. 11 search for additional 24hrs Code A–2.42/s. 11(5) Public Order Act 2023 *General Police Duties*, para. 3.1.4
Authorise live-link interpretation Code C–Annex N, para. 5 *Evidence and Procedure*, para. 2.6.30	Signed authority for a search warrant or production order under sch. 5 to the Terrorism Act 2000 Code B–3.4(b) *General Police Duties*, para. 3.2.4
Authorise fingerprints without consent Code D–4.3(c)/s. 61(4A) PACE84 *Evidence and Procedure*, para. 2.7.5	Give a closure order to premises where a person persistently sells alcohol to children s. 169A Licensing Act 2003 *General Police Duties*, para. 3.6.6.4
Authorise fingerprints without consent Code D–4.3(d)/s. 61(6) PACE84 *Evidence and Procedure*, para. 2.7.5	Removal of truants to designated premises/school s. 16(2) Crime and Disorder Act 1998 *General Police Duties*, para. 3.7.10
Authorise fingerprints without consent Code D–4.3(f)/s. 61(6D) PACE84 *Evidence and Procedure*, para. 2.7.5	Issue a Domestic Violence Protection Order (DVPN) s. 24 Crime and Security Act 2010 *General Police Duties*, para. 3.11.4

Required to attend police station for fingerprints Code D–4.4/sch. 2A (para. 6) PACE84 *Evidence and Procedure*, para. 2.7.5	Ordinary or Urgent CHIS Authorisation RIPA 2000 *General Police Duties*, para. 3.13.5.4
Search and/or examination to find marks Code D–5.2/s. 54A(1) PACE84 *Evidence and Procedure*, para. 2.7.6	Urgent 'Relevant Source' authorisation RIPA 2000 *General Police Duties*, para. 3.13.5.4
Search or examination to assist in establishing identity Code D–5.3/s. 54A(1)(b) PACE84 *Evidence and Procedure*, para. 2.7.6	Ordinary or Urgent Directed Surveillance Authorisation RIPA 2000 *General Police Duties*, para. 3.13.5.8
To take intimate samples from a person in police detention Code D–6.2(a)/s. 62(1) PACE84 *Evidence and Procedure*, para. 2.7.7.1	Power to Designate an Area (Cordons) s. 34 Terrorism Act 2000 *General Police Duties*, para. 3.15.7.2
To take intimate samples from a person not in police detention (samples taken but insufficient) Code D–6.2(b)/s. 62(1A) PACE84 *Evidence and Procedure*, para. 2.7.7.1	Authorise a Road Check s. 4 PACE84 *General Police Duties*, para. 3.20.3
To take intimate samples from a person convicted o/s E&W etc. Code D–6.2(c)/s. 62(2A) PACE84 *Evidence and Procedure*, para. 2.7.7.1	
To take non-intimate samples from a person held in custody by the police on the authority of a court Code D–6.6(b)/s. 63(3) PACE84 *Evidence and Procedure*, para. 2.7.7.2	
To take non-intimate samples from a person convicted o/s E&W etc. Code D–6.6(g)/s. 63(3E) PACE84 *Evidence and Procedure*, para. 2.7.7.2	
Required to attend police station for non-intimate samples Code D–6.6A/sch. 2A (para. 14) PACE84 *Evidence and Procedure*, para. 2.7.7.2	
Authorise 'live-link' interview Code C–12.9A(d) *Evidence and Procedure*, para. 2.8.4	
Authorise s. 60 search power Code A–2.13/s. 60(1) Criminal Justice and Public Order Act 1994 *General Police Duties*, para. 3.1.4	
Authorise s. 60AA remove face coverings etc. Code A–2.17/s. 60AA(3) Criminal Justice and Public Order Act 1994 *General Police Duties*, para. 3.1.4	

Authorise s. 11 search s. 11 Public Order Act 2023 Code A–2.40 *General Police Duties*, para. 3.1.4
Signed authority for a search warrant or production order Code B–3.4(a) *General Police Duties*, para. 3.2.4
Enter & search premises for 2nd or more time under a warrant authorising multiple entry s. 16(3B) PACE84 *General Police Duties*, para. 3.2.6
Authorising search of premises under s. 18 PACE84 Code B–4.3 *General Police Duties*, para. 3.2.7
Authorise an adult be kept at a place of safety that is a police station reg. 2(1) Mental Health Act 1983 *General Police Duties*, para. 3.4.2
Dispersal Order of no more than 48hrs under s. 35 s. 34 Anti-social Behaviour, Crime and Policing Act 2014 General Police Duties, para. 3.7.5.1
Closure Notice–Premises associated with nuisance or disorder s. 76 Anti-social Behaviour, Crime and Policing Act 2014 *General Police Duties*, para. 3.7.8
Detain for 6 hours (football banning orders) s. 21A(3) Football Spectators Act 1989 *General Police Duties*, para. 3.10.4.3
Reference to a Court (football banning orders) s. 21B Football Spectators Act 1989 *General Police Duties*, para. 3.10.4.4
Urgent CHIS Authorisation RIPA 2000 *General Police Duties*, para. 3.13.5.4
Urgent Directed Surveillance Authorisation RIPA 2000 *General Police Duties*, para. 3.13.5.8

When considering PACE84 authorities alone (there are 20 of these in the table/syllabus), it might assist to remember that Superintendents authorise six of them and they can be remembered by using the mnemonic FRAUD:

F	Further extend (bail 6 to 9/detention 24 to 36)
R	Road checks
A	Acting ranks
U	Urgent interview
D	Delay access to legal advice

Powers Requiring a Constable to be in Uniform

What is a 'Constable in Uniform'?

Whether a constable (which includes an officer of any rank, including special constables) was in uniform at the time is a matter of fact for a court to determine. What counts as 'uniform' is unclear but, if constables can be easily identified from their manner of dress as police officers, the requirement has probably been met (*Wallwork* v *Giles* [1970] RTR 117; officer without a helmet held to be 'in uniform'). The wearing of an 'ordinary' raincoat over a police uniform (*Taylor* v *Baldwin* [1976] RTR 265) did not affect the conclusion that the officer was still in uniform. Justices are also able to rely on their knowledge of how the local constabulary operates (*Cooper* v *Rowlands* [1971] RTR 291, in relation to a motorway patrol officer, and *Richards* v *West* [1980] RTR 215, in relation to special constables) and, in the absence of evidence to the contrary, they are entitled to infer or assume from the surrounding circumstances that a constable is in uniform (*Gage* v *Jones* [1983] RTR 508).

A Constable MUST be in Uniform to Stop a Vehicle for a Search

Section 2(9)(b) of the Police and Criminal Evidence Act 1984 states that neither the power conferred by section 1 *nor any other power to detain and search a vehicle without making an arrest* is to be construed as authorising a constable not in uniform to stop a vehicle. In other words, to stop a vehicle for the purposes of a search the constable stopping the vehicle must be in uniform. So, for example, an officer wishing to use the power to search a vehicle under s. 23(2)(b) of the Misuse of Drugs Act 1971 (***Crime*, para. 1.6.15.1**) or s. 47(4) of the Firearms Act 1968 (***Crime*, para. 1.7.11**) must be in uniform to stop the vehicle they wish to search.

The NPPF Uniform Powers/Functions

ACT/SECTION	POWER	BLACKSTONE'S REF
s. 60 Criminal Justice and Public Order Act 1994	Stop and search persons and vehicles for offensive weapons/dangerous instruments and to prevent serious violence	3.1.4
s. 60AA Criminal Justice and Public Order Act 1994	To require the removal of disguises and to seize them	3.1.4
s. 11 Public Order Act 2023	Stop and search persons and vehicles for prohibited objects or that protest-related offences may be committed in their police area	3.1.4
s. 17 PACE84	Enter & search premises for the purpose of arresting a person for: Any enactment contained in ss. 6 to 8 or 10 of the Criminal Law Act 1977 (offences relating to entering and remaining on property). For information, only one of those Criminal Law Act 1977 offences is contained in NPPF syllabus and that is the offence under s. 8 of the Criminal Law Act 1977 (trespassing with a weapon of offence (*Crime*, para. 1.8.6)); An offence under s. 76 of the Criminal Justice and Public Order Act 1994 (failure to comply with interim possession order). For information, this offence is not in the NPPF syllabus; or an offence under s. 144 of the Legal Aid, Sentencing and Punishment of Offenders Act 2012 (squatting in a residential building (*General Police Duties*, para. 3.5.7))	3.2.7
s. 35 Anti-social Behaviour, Crime and Policing Act 2014	Direct a person in a public place in an area subject to a dispersal order under s. 35 to leave and not return for up to 48hrs	3.7.5.1
s. 14C Public Order Act 1986	Stop a person on their way to a trespassory assembly and direct that person not to proceed to the assembly	3.8.4.7
s. 21A Football Spectators Act 1989	Detain a person (for a max. of 4 hours) until the constable has decided whether or not to issue a notice under s. 21B of the Act	3.10.4.3
s. 21B Football Spectators Act 1989	*If authorised to do so by an officer of at least the rank of Inspector*, give a person a notice under s. 21B of the Act (relates to reporting to a court and banning orders)	3.10.4.4
s. 47A Terrorism Act 2000	To stop and search pedestrians and vehicles in a specified area or place to discover whether anything that constitutes evidence the vehicle is being used for terrorism/the person is a terrorist	3.15.6.4
s. 36 Terrorism Act 2000	Use powers associated with cordons	3.15.7.3
s. 163 Road Traffic Act 1988	Stop a mechanically propelled vehicle or cycle on a road	3.20.2
s. 165A Road Traffic Act 1988	Power to seize vehicles driven without a licence or insurance	3.20.6

s. 6(7) Road Traffic Act 1988	To administer a preliminary breath/impairment/drug test the officer MUST be in uniform *NOTE that when the test is administered following an accident (s. 6(5) Road Traffic Act 1988), the officer DOES NOT need to be in uniform*	3.22.4.2
s. 7(2)(c) Road Traffic Act 1988	This entry is included to provide a comprehensive list of situations where a police officer is required to be in uniform to exercise a power. However, it is important to stress that this scenario only exists on paper and could not occur in any policing reality **THEORY SCENARIO** Section 7(2) of the Road Traffic Act 1988 states that a requirement for an evidential specimen of breath may only be made if: the requirement is made at a police station or hospital, the requirement is imposed in circumstances where s. 6(5) of the Road Traffic Act 1988 applies, or the officer is in UNIFORM The law is set out so that it provides for scenarios where the police have access to a machine that enables *evidential specimens of breath* to be obtained using a mobile device (so this could be used at the roadside or elsewhere (e.g. a hospital)). NO SUCH MACHINE EXISTS. But, if it did, then let's say a person was subject to a roadside preliminary test procedure under s. 6(7) of the Road Traffic Act 1988 by an officer in UNIFORM who suspected the driver was 'drink driving'. The driver fails the preliminary breath test causing the officer to suspect the person is over the prescribed limit regarding alcohol. In reality, the driver may be arrested and taken to a police station where evidential breath specimens can be required but, in this theory scenario, the 'roadside evidential specimen machine' could be produced at the scene where the driver failed the preliminary screening test. The officer could now make the requirement for *evidential breath specimens* at the roadside. In such a situation, s. 7(2)(c) applies and the officer making the requirement would have to be in UNIFORM.	3.22.5.1

3.1 Stop and Search

A thick grey line down the margin denotes text that is an extract of the PACE Code itself (i.e. the actual wording of the Code of Practice).

3.1.1 Introduction

This chapter uses the elements of the December 2023 version of the PACE Code of Practice for the Exercise by Police Officers of Statutory Powers of Stop and Search (hereafter referred to as 'Code A') as a framework to explain this area of the syllabus and incorporates relevant law (particularly the Police and Criminal Evidence Act 1984 (hereafter referred to as 'PACE84')) within the keynotes where appropriate. This permits additional useful and explanatory detail to be presented to candidates that would not ordinarily be mentioned in any standard version of the code.

3.1.2 Code A—1.0 General

1.01 This Code of Practice must be readily available at all police stations for consultation by police officers, police staff, detained persons and members of the public.

1.02 The notes for guidance [included within the Keynotes of this chapter] are not provisions of this code, but are guidance to police officers and others about its application and interpretation. Provisions in the annexes to the code are provisions of this code.

1.03 This code governs the exercise by police officers of statutory powers to search a person or a vehicle without first making an arrest. The main stop and search powers to which this code applies are set out in Annex A [which can be found at **the end of this chapter**], but that list should not be regarded as definitive. In addition, it covers requirements on police officers and police staff to record encounters not governed by statutory powers. This code does not apply to:

(a) the powers of stop and search under;
  (i) Aviation Security Act 1982, section 27(2);
  (ii) Police and Criminal Evidence Act 1984, section 6(1) (which relates specifically to powers of constables employed by statutory undertakers on the premises of the statutory undertakers).

(b) searches carried out for the purposes of examination under Schedule 7 to the Terrorism Act 2000 and to which the Code of Practice issued under paragraph 6 of Schedule 14 to the Terrorism Act 2000 applies.

(c) the powers to search persons and vehicles and to stop and search in specified locations to which the Code of Practice issued under section 47AB of the Terrorism Act 2000 applies.

3.1.3 Code A—1 Principles governing stop and search

1.1 Powers to stop and search must be used fairly, responsibly, with respect for people being searched and without unlawful discrimination. Under the Equality Act 2010, section 149, when police officers are carrying out their functions, they also have a duty to have due regard to the need to eliminate unlawful discrimination, harassment and victimisation, to advance equality of opportunity between people who share a relevant protected characteristic and people who do not share it, and to take steps to foster good relations between those persons. The Children Act 2004, section 11, also requires chief police officers and other specified persons and bodies to ensure that in the discharge of their functions they have regard to the need to safeguard and promote the welfare of all persons under the age of 18.

KEYNOTE

The 'relevant protected characteristics' include: age, disability, gender reassignment, pregnancy and maternity, race, religion or belief, sex and sexual orientation.

1.2 The intrusion on the liberty of the person stopped or searched must be brief and detention for the purposes of a search must take place at or near the location of the stop.

1.3 If these fundamental principles are not observed the use of powers to stop and search may be drawn into question. Failure to use the powers in the proper manner reduces their effectiveness. Stop and search can play an important role in the detection and prevention of crime, and using the powers fairly makes them more effective.

1.4 The primary purpose of stop and search powers is to enable officers to allay or confirm suspicions about individuals without exercising their power of arrest. Officers may be required to justify the use or authorisation of such powers, in relation both to individual searches and the overall pattern of their activity in this regard, to their supervisory officers or in court. Any misuse of the powers is likely to be harmful to policing and lead to mistrust of the police. Officers must also be able to explain their actions to the member of the public searched. The misuse of these powers can lead to disciplinary action.

KEYNOTE

This Code does not affect the ability of an officer to speak to or question a person in the ordinary course of the officer's duties without detaining the person or exercising any element of compulsion. It is not the purpose of the Code to prohibit such encounters between the police and the community with the cooperation of the person concerned and neither does it affect the principle that all citizens have a duty to help police officers to prevent crime and discover offenders. This is a civic rather than a legal duty; but when a police officer is trying to discover whether, or by whom, an offence has been committed he/she may question any person from whom useful information might be obtained, subject to the restrictions imposed by Code C. A person's unwillingness to reply does not alter this entitlement, but in the absence of a power to arrest, or to detain in order to search, the person is free to leave at will and cannot be compelled to remain with the officer.

1.5 An officer must not search a person, even with his or her consent, where no power to search is applicable. Even where a person is prepared to submit to a search voluntarily, the person must not be searched unless the necessary legal power exists, and the search must be in accordance with the relevant power and the provisions of this Code. The only exception, where an officer does not require a specific power, applies to searches of persons entering sports grounds or other premises carried out with their consent given as a condition of entry.

KEYNOTE

This means the practice of conducting 'voluntary' searches in the street or other public places is not permitted.

1.6 Evidence obtained from a search to which this Code applies may be open to challenge if the provisions of this Code are not observed.

3.1.4 **Code A—2 Types of stop and search powers**

2.1 This code applies, subject to paragraph 1.03, to powers of stop and search as follows:

(a) powers which require reasonable grounds for suspicion, before they may be exercised; that articles unlawfully obtained or possessed are being carried such as section 10 of the Public Order Act 2023 for articles used to commit protest-related offences, section 1 of PACE for stolen and prohibited articles and section 23 of the Misuse of Drugs Act 1971 for controlled drugs;

(b) authorised under section 60 of the Criminal Justice and Public Order Act 1994, based upon a reasonable belief that incidents involving serious violence may take place or that people are carrying dangerous instruments or offensive weapons within any locality in the police area or that it is expedient to use the powers to find such instruments or weapons that have been used in incidents of serious violence, and

(c) authorised under section 11 of the Public Order Act 2023, based upon a reasonable belief that individuals are carrying prohibited items for the purpose of, or in connection with, protest-related offences listed in section 11 of the Act, such as locking causing serious disruption by tunnelling;

(d) the powers in Schedule 5 to the Terrorism Prevention and Investigation Measures (TPIM) Act 2011 to search an individual who has not been arrested, conferred by:

(i) paragraph 6(2)(a) at the time of serving a TPIM notice;

(ii) paragraph 8(2)(a) under a search warrant for compliance purposes; and

(iii) paragraph 10 for public safety purposes.

See *paragraph 2.18A*.

(e) powers to search a person who has not been arrested in the exercise of a power to search premises (see Code B *paragraph 2.4*).

KEYNOTE

It is important to emphasise that Code A applies to any search by a police officer, i.e. the principles and processes created by Code A must be followed in all searches (there are exceptions for certain powers under the Aviation Security Act 1982 and those exercised by statutory undertakers).

Section 1 PACE 1984

There are many specific statutory authorities providing the police (and others) with powers to stop people and vehicles and search them (**see Annex A at the end of this chapter**). One of the most significant is the general power for police officers to stop and search people and vehicles under s. 1 of PACE84 referred to at para. 2.1(a).

A summary of s. 1 of PACE84 is that it provides a constable with the power to stop, detain and search a person and/or a vehicle (or anything in or on a vehicle) for stolen articles, prohibited articles, bladed or sharply pointed articles and for fireworks. While such a summary is useful, a more detailed analysis of the power is required.

PACE84, s. 1 states:

(1) A constable may exercise any power conferred by this section—
   (a) in any place to which at the time when he proposes to exercise the power the public or any section of the public has access, on payment or otherwise, as of right or by virtue of express or implied permission; or
   (b) in any other place to which people have ready access at the time when he proposes to exercise the power but which is not a dwelling.

KEYNOTE

The power is restricted to those places set out in s. 1(1)(a) or (b) of PACE84. This does not mean that the search itself must be carried out there; in fact Code A, paras 3.6 and 3.7 require certain searches to be carried out away from public view.

(2) Subject to subsection (3) to (5) below, a constable—
   (a) may search—
      (i) any person or vehicle;
      (ii) anything which is in or on a vehicle, for stolen or prohibited articles, any article to which subsection (8A) below applies, any substance to which subsection (8AA) below applies or any firework to which subsection (8B) below applies; and
   (b) may detain a person or vehicle for the purpose of such a search.

KEYNOTE

A constable must be in uniform to stop a vehicle for the purposes of a search (whether that is a search under s. 1 of PACE84 or when using other search powers, e.g. under s. 23 of the Misuse of Drugs Act 1971 or s. 47 of the Firearms Act 1968 (s. 2(9)(b)).

(3) This section does not give a constable power to search a person or vehicle or anything in or on a vehicle unless he has reasonable grounds for suspecting that he will find stolen or prohibited articles, any article to which subsection (8A) below applies, any substance to which subsection (8AA)) below applies or any firework to which subsection (8B) below applies.
(4) If a person is in a garden or yard occupied with and used for the purposes of a dwelling or on other land so occupied and used, a constable may not search him in the exercise of the power conferred by this section unless the constable has reasonable grounds for believing—
   (a) that he does not reside in the dwelling; and
   (b) that he is not in the place in question with the express or implied permission of a person who resides in the dwelling.
(5) If a vehicle is in a garden or yard occupied with and used for the purposes of a dwelling or on other land so occupied and used, a constable may not search the vehicle or anything in or on it in the exercise of the power conferred by this section unless he has reasonable grounds for believing—
   (a) that the person in charge of the vehicle does not reside in the dwelling; and
   (b) that the vehicle is not in the place in question with the express or implied permission of a person who resides in the dwelling.

KEYNOTE

If the garden or yard is attached to a house that is not so 'occupied', the restriction at ss. 1(4) and 1(5) would not apply.

Section 1 Searches—Where?

When considering the question of where a s. 1 search can take place, it is useful to reverse the question and ask where such a search cannot take place. In effect, the only places where a constable cannot exercise the s. 1 stop and search power are:

- dwellings;
- the garden, yard or other land of a dwelling if the person is there lawfully (because they live there or have permission to be there from someone who resides in the dwelling); or
- any other place which is secure and does not permit 'ready access'.

(6) If in the course of such a search a constable discovers an article which he has reasonable grounds for suspecting to be stolen or a prohibited article, an article to which subsection (8A) below applies, a substance to which subsection (8AA) below applies or a firework to which subsection (8B) below applies, he may seize it.

(7) An article is prohibited for the purposes of this Part of this Act if it is—
- (a) an offensive weapon; or
- (b) an article—
  - (i) made or adapted for use in the course of or in connection with an offence to which this sub-paragraph applies; or
  - (ii) intended by the person having it with him for such use by him or by some other person.

(8) The offences to which subsection (7)(b)(i) above applies are—
- (a) burglary;
- (b) theft;
- (c) offences under section 12 of the Theft Act 1968 (taking motor vehicle or other conveyance without authority);
- (d) fraud (contrary to section 1 of the Fraud Act 2006); and
- (e) offences under section 1 of the Criminal Damage Act 1971 (destroying or damaging property)
- (f) an offence under section 137 of the Highways Act 1980 (wilful obstruction) involving activity which causes or is capable of causing serious disruption to two or more individuals or to an organisation;
- (g) an offence under section 78 of the Police, Crime, Sentencing and Courts Act 2022 (intentionally or recklessly causing public nuisance);
- (h) an offence under section 1 of the Public Order Act 2023 (offence of locking on);
- (i) an offence under section 3 of that Act (offence of causing serious disruption by tunnelling);
- (j) an offence under section 4 of that Act (offence of causing serious disruption by being present in a tunnel);
- (k) an offence under section 6 of that Act (obstruction etc of major transport works); and
- (l) an offence under section 7 of that Act (interference with use or operation of key national infrastructure).

(8A) This subsection applies to any article in relation to which a person has committed, or is committing or is going to commit an offence under section 139 or 139AA of the Criminal Justice Act 1988.

(8AA) This subsection applies to any substance in relation to which a person has committed, or is committing or is going to commit an offence under section 6 of the Offensive Weapons Act 2019 (offence of having a corrosive substance in a public place).

(8AB) In this section references to such a substance include an article which contains such a substance.

(8B) This subsection applies to any firework which a person possesses in contravention of a prohibition imposed by fireworks regulations.

(8C) In this section—
- (a) 'firework' shall be construed in accordance with the definition of 'fireworks' in section 1(1) of the Fireworks Act 2003; and
- (b) 'fireworks regulations' has the same meaning as in that Act.

(9) In this Part of this Act 'offensive weapon' means any article—
- (a) made or adapted for use for causing injury to persons; or
- (b) intended by the person having it with him for such use by him or by some other person.

KEYNOTE

A firearm, as defined by s. 57 of the Firearms Act 1968, would fall within the definition of offensive weapon if any of the criteria above apply.

Reasonable Suspicion

The existence of 'reasonable grounds for suspicion' is at the heart of the power under s. 1 (and a number of other stop and search powers) and, for that reason, Code A devotes considerable attention to the concept.

(a) Stop and search powers requiring reasonable grounds for suspicion—explanation

General

2.2 Reasonable grounds for suspicion is the legal test which a police officer must satisfy before they can stop and detain individuals or vehicles to search them under powers such as section 1 of PACE (to find stolen or prohibited articles) and section 23 of the Misuse of Drugs Act 1971 (to find controlled drugs). This test must be applied to the particular circumstances in each case and is in two parts:

(i) *Firstly*, the officer must have formed a *genuine suspicion* in their own mind that they will find the object for which the search power being exercised allows them to search (see Annex A, second column, for examples); and

(ii) *Secondly*, the suspicion that the object will be found must be *reasonable*. This means that there must be an *objective* basis for that suspicion based on facts, information and/or intelligence which are relevant to the likelihood that the object in question will be found, so that a reasonable person would be entitled to reach the same conclusion based on the same facts and information and/or intelligence.

Officers must therefore be able to explain the basis for their suspicion by reference to intelligence or information about, or some specific behaviour by, the person concerned (see *paragraphs 3.8(d), 4.6* and *5.5*).

KEYNOTE

'Suspicion' requires a lower degree of certainty than 'belief'. A statutory requirement for 'belief' imposes a greater degree of certainty on the officers concerned (*Baker* v *Oxford* [1980] RTR 315). Accordingly, police officers using powers that impose such an extra requirement must be prepared to justify their belief. Suspicion can be based on any evidence, even if the evidence itself would be inadmissible at trial (e.g. because it is hearsay).

The courts have accepted that reasonable grounds for suspicion can arise from information given to the officer by a colleague, an informant or even anonymously (*O'Hara* v *Chief Constable of the Royal Ulster Constabulary* [1997] AC 286).

The courts have held that it must be shown that any such grounds on which an officer acted would have been enough to give rise to that suspicion in a 'reasonable person' (*Nakkuda Ali* v *Jayaratne* [1951] AC 66).

However, the mere existence of such circumstances or evidence is not enough. The officer must actually have a 'reasonable suspicion' that the relevant articles will be found. If, in fact, the officer knows that there is little or no likelihood of finding the articles, the power cannot be used (*R* v *Harrison* [1938] 3 All ER 134).

2.2A The exercise of these stop and search powers depends on the likelihood that the person searched is in possession of an item for which they may be searched; it does not depend on the person concerned being suspected of committing an offence in relation to the object of the search. A police officer who has reasonable grounds to suspect that a person is in *innocent possession* of a stolen or prohibited article, controlled drug or other item for which the officer is empowered to search, may stop and search the person even though there would be no power of arrest. This would apply when a child under the age of criminal responsibility (10 years) is suspected of carrying any such item, even if they knew they had it.

KEYNOTE

Innocent possession means that the person does not have the guilty knowledge that they are carrying an unlawful item which is required before an arrest on suspicion that the person has committed an offence in respect of the item sought (if arrest is necessary—see PACE Code G) and/or a criminal prosecution can be considered. It is not uncommon for children under the age of criminal responsibility to be used by older children and adults to carry stolen property, drugs and weapons and, in some cases, firearms, for the criminal benefit of others, either:

- in the hope that police may not suspect they are being used for carrying the items; or
- knowing that if they are suspected of being couriers and are stopped and searched, they cannot be arrested or prosecuted for any criminal offence.

Stop and search powers therefore allow the police to intervene effectively to break up criminal gangs and groups that use young children to further their criminal activities.

Whenever a child under 10 is suspected of carrying unlawful items for someone else, or is found in circumstances which suggest that their welfare and safety may be at risk, the facts should be reported and actioned in accordance with established force safeguarding procedures. This will be in addition to treating the child as a potentially vulnerable or intimidated witness in respect of their status as a witness to the serious criminal offence(s) committed by those using them as couriers. Safeguarding considerations will also apply to other persons aged under 18 who are stopped and searched under any of the powers to which this Code applies.

Personal factors can never support reasonable grounds for suspicion

2.2B Reasonable suspicion can never be supported on the basis of personal factors. This means that unless the police have information or intelligence which *provides a description* of a person suspected of carrying an article for which there is a power to stop and search, the following *cannot be used*, alone or in combination with each other, or in combination with any other factor, as the reason for stopping and searching any individual, including any vehicle which they are driving or are being carried in:

(a) A person's physical appearance with regard, for example, to any of the 'relevant protected characteristics' set out in the Equality Act 2010, section 149, which are age, disability, gender reassignment, pregnancy and maternity, race, religion or belief, sex and sexual orientation (see *paragraph 1.1*), or the fact that the person is known to have a previous conviction; and

(b) Generalisations or stereotypical images that certain groups or categories of people are more likely to be involved in criminal activity.

2.3 *Not used.*

Reasonable grounds for suspicion based on information and/or intelligence

2.4 Reasonable grounds for suspicion should normally be linked to accurate and current intelligence or information, relating to articles for which there is a power to stop and search, being carried by individuals or being in vehicles in any locality. This would include reports from members of the public or other officers describing:

- a person who has been seen carrying such an article or a vehicle in which such an article has been seen.
- crimes committed in relation to which such an article would constitute relevant evidence, for example, property stolen in a theft or burglary, an offensive weapon or bladed or sharply pointed article used to assault or threaten someone or an article used to cause criminal damage to property.

2.4A Searches based on accurate and current intelligence or information are more likely to be effective. Targeting searches in a particular area at specified crime problems not only increases their effectiveness but also minimises inconvenience to law-abiding members of the public. It also helps in justifying the use of searches both to those who are searched and to the public. This does not, however, prevent stop and search powers being exercised in other locations where such powers may be exercised and reasonable suspicion exists.

2.5 *Not used.*

Reasonable grounds for suspicion and searching groups

2.6 Where there is reliable information or intelligence that members of a group or gang habitually carry knives unlawfully or weapons or controlled drugs, and wear a distinctive item of clothing or other means of identification in order to identify themselves as members of that group or gang, that distinctive item of clothing or other means of identification may provide reasonable grounds to stop and search any person believed to be a member of that group or gang.

KEYNOTE

Other means of identification might include jewellery, insignias, tattoos or other features which are known to identify members of the particular gang or group.

2.6A A similar approach would apply to particular organised protest groups where there is reliable information or intelligence:

(a) that the group in question arranges meetings and marches to which one or more members bring articles intended to be used to cause criminal damage and/or injury to others in support of the group's aims;

(b) that at one or more *previous* meetings or marches arranged by that group, such articles have been used and resulted in damage and/or injury; and

(c) that on the subsequent occasion in question, one or more members of the group have brought with them such articles with similar intentions.

These circumstances may provide reasonable grounds to stop and search any members of the group to find such articles. See also *paragraphs 2.12* to *2.18*, '*Searches authorised under section 60 of the Criminal Justice and Public Order Act 1994*', when serious violence is anticipated at meetings and marches.

KEYNOTE

A decision to search individuals believed to be members of a particular group or gang must be judged on a case-by-case basis according to the circumstances applicable at the time of the proposed searches and in particular having regard to: (a) the number of items suspected of being carried; (b) the nature of those items and the risk they pose; and (c) the number of individuals to be searched. A group search will only be justified if it is a necessary and proportionate approach based on the facts and having regard to the nature of the suspicion in these cases. The extent and thoroughness of the searches must not be excessive. The size of the group and the number of individuals it is proposed to search will be a key factor and steps should be taken to identify those who are to be searched to avoid unnecessary inconvenience to unconnected members of the public who are also present. The onus is on the police to be satisfied and to demonstrate that their approach to the decision to search is in pursuit of a legitimate aim, necessary and proportionate.

Reasonable grounds for suspicion based on behaviour, time and location

2.6B Reasonable suspicion may also exist without specific information or intelligence and on the basis of the behaviour of a person. For example, if an officer encounters someone on the street at night who is obviously trying to hide something, the officer may (depending on the other surrounding circumstances) base such suspicion on the fact that this kind of behaviour is often linked to stolen or prohibited articles being carried. An officer who forms the opinion that a person is acting suspiciously or that they appear to be nervous must be able to explain, with reference to specific aspects of the person's behaviour or conduct which they have observed, why they formed that opinion. A hunch or instinct which cannot be explained or justified to an objective observer can never amount to reasonable grounds.

2.7 *Not used.*

2.8 *Not used.*

Securing public confidence and promoting community relations

2.8A All police officers must recognise that searches are more likely to be effective, legitimate and secure public confidence when their reasonable grounds for suspicion are based on a range of objective factors. The overall use of these powers is more likely to be effective when up-to-date and accurate intelligence or information is communicated to officers and they are well-informed about local crime patterns. Local senior officers have a duty to ensure that those under their command who exercise stop and search powers have access to such information, and the officers exercising the powers have a duty to acquaint themselves with that information (see *paragraphs 5.1* to *5.6*).

Questioning to decide whether to carry out a search

2.9 An officer who has reasonable grounds for suspicion may detain the person concerned in order to carry out a search. Before carrying out the search the officer may ask questions about the person's behaviour or presence in circumstances which gave rise to the suspicion. As a result of questioning the detained person, the reasonable grounds for suspicion necessary to detain that person may be confirmed or, because of a satisfactory explanation, be dispelled. Questioning may also reveal reasonable grounds to suspect the possession of a different kind of unlawful article from that originally suspected. Reasonable grounds for suspicion however cannot be provided retrospectively by such questioning during a person's detention or by refusal to answer any questions asked.

2.10 If, as a result of questioning before a search, or other circumstances which come to the attention of the officer, there cease to be reasonable grounds for suspecting that an article of a kind for which there is a power to stop and search is being carried, no search may take place. In the absence of any other lawful power to detain, the person is free to leave at will and must be so informed.

2.11 There is no power to stop or detain a person in order to find grounds for a search. Police officers have many encounters with members of the public which do not involve detaining people against their will and do not require any statutory power for an officer to speak to a person (see *paragraph 4.12*). However, if reasonable grounds for suspicion emerge during such an encounter, the officer may detain the person to search them, even though no grounds existed when the encounter began. As soon as detention begins, and before searching, the officer must inform the person that they are being detained for the purpose of a search and take action in accordance with *paragraphs 3.8* to *3.11* under *'Steps to be taken prior to a search'*.

KEYNOTE

In some circumstances, preparatory questioning may be unnecessary, but in general a brief conversation or exchange will be desirable not only as a means of avoiding unsuccessful searches, but to explain the grounds for the stop/search, to gain cooperation and reduce any tension there might be surrounding the stop/search process. Where a person is lawfully detained for the purpose of a search, but no search in the event takes place, the detention will not thereby have been rendered unlawful.

(b) Searches authorised under section 60 of the Criminal Justice and Public Order Act 1994

2.12 Authority for a constable in uniform to stop and search under section 60 of the Criminal Justice and Public Order Act 1994 may be given if the authorising officer reasonably believes:

(a) that incidents involving serious violence may take place in any locality in the officer's police area, and it is expedient to use these powers to prevent their occurrence;

(b) that persons are carrying dangerous instruments or offensive weapons without good reason in any locality in the officer's police area; or

(c) that an incident involving serious violence has taken place in the officer's police area, a dangerous instrument or offensive weapon used in the incident is being carried by a person in any locality in that police area, and it is expedient to use these powers to find that instrument or weapon.

KEYNOTE

A 'Uniform' Power

The power under s. 60 confers on any constable in uniform the power:

(a) to stop any pedestrian and search him or anything carried by him for offensive weapons or dangerous instruments;

(b) to stop any vehicle and search the vehicle, its driver and any passenger for offensive weapons or dangerous instruments.

'Vehicles' includes caravans, aircraft, vessels and hovercraft.

If a dangerous instrument or anything reasonably suspected to be an 'offensive weapon' is found during the search, the officer may seize it (s. 60(6)).

An Additional Power

The powers under s. 60 are separate from and additional to the normal stop and search powers which require reasonable grounds to suspect an individual of carrying an offensive weapon (or other article). Their overall purpose is to prevent serious violence and the widespread carrying of weapons which might lead to persons being seriously injured by disarming potential offenders or finding weapons that have been used in circumstances where other powers would not be sufficient. They should not therefore be used to replace or circumvent the normal powers for dealing with routine crime problems. A particular example might be an authorisation to prevent serious violence or the carrying of offensive weapons at a sports event by rival team supporters when the expected general appearance and age range of those likely to be responsible, alone, would not be sufficiently distinctive to support reasonable suspicion (see Code A, para. 2.6).

Reasonable Belief and Necessity

The reasonable belief on the part of the officer authorising the use of the power under s. 60 must have an objective basis, for example: intelligence or relevant information such as a history of antagonism and violence between particular groups; previous incidents of violence at, or connected with, particular events or locations; a significant increase in knife-point robberies in a limited area; reports that individuals are regularly carrying weapons in a particular locality or information following an incident in which weapons were used about where the weapons might be found.

Any authorisation made under s. 60 must be made only when the officer believes it is necessary. In practice, in addition to expediency, which is explicit in the 1994 Act, the authorising officer must also have considered the authorisation necessary to prevent serious violence or to find dangerous instruments or weapons after an incident involving serious violence, or to apprehend persons carrying weapons.

Interpretation

'Serious violence' is not defined in the 1994 Act but, although violence could relate to property, the whole tenor of the section suggests that it is aimed at tackling violence against people. 'Dangerous instruments' are bladed or sharply pointed instruments, while offensive weapons have the same meaning as that under s. 1(9) of PACE84. For the purposes of s. 60, 'carrying' will mean 'having in your possession' (s. 60(11A)), a much wider meaning than carrying usually conveys.

2.13 An authorisation under section 60 may only be given by an officer of the rank of inspector or above and in writing, or orally if paragraph 2.12(c) applies and it is not practicable to give the authorisation in writing. The authorisation (whether written or oral) must specify the grounds on which it was given, the locality in which the powers may be exercised and the period of time for which they are in force. The period authorised shall be no longer than appears reasonably necessary to prevent, or seek to prevent incidents of serious violence, or to deal with the problem of carrying dangerous instruments or offensive weapons or to find a dangerous instrument or offensive weapon that has been used. It may not exceed 24 hours. An oral authorisation given where paragraph 2.12(c) applies must be recorded in writing as soon as practicable.

2.14 An inspector who gives an authorisation must, as soon as practicable, inform an officer of or above the rank of superintendent. This officer may direct that the authorisation shall be extended for a further 24 hours, if violence or the carrying of dangerous instruments or offensive weapons has occurred, or is suspected to have occurred, and the continued use of the powers is considered necessary to prevent or deal with further such activity or to find a dangerous instrument or offensive weapon that has been used. That direction must be given in writing unless it is not practicable to do so, in which case it must be recorded in writing as soon as practicable afterwards.

KEYNOTE

Time Frame

It is for the authorising officer to determine the period of time during which the power may be exercised and in any event must not exceed 24 hours. The officer should set the minimum period he/she considers necessary to deal with the risk of violence, the carrying of knives or offensive weapons or to find dangerous instruments or weapons that have been used. A direction to extend the period authorised under the power may be given only once (by a superintendent or above for a further period not exceeding 24 hours). So the maximum period a s. 60 authorisation could last for would be 48 hours—thereafter further use of the powers requires a new authorisation.

Geographical Area

It is for the authorising officer to determine the geographical area in which the use of the powers is to be authorised. In doing so, the officer may wish to take into account factors such as the nature and venue of the anticipated incident or the incident which has taken place, the number of people who may be in the immediate area of that incident, their access to surrounding areas and the anticipated level of violence. The officer should not set a geographical area which is wider than he/she believes necessary for the purpose of preventing anticipated violence, the carrying of knives or offensive weapons or for finding a dangerous instrument or weapon that has been used. It is particularly important to ensure that constables exercising such powers are fully aware of where they may be used. If the area specified is smaller than the whole force area, the officer giving the authorisation should specify either the streets which form the boundary of the area or a divisional boundary within the force area. If the power is to be used in response to a threat or incident that straddles police force areas, an officer from each of the forces concerned will need to give an authorisation.

Continuing the Authorisation

If it appears to an officer of or above the rank of superintendent that:

- having regard to offences that have been, or are reasonably suspected to have been, committed;
- in connection with any activity falling within the authorisation; and
- it is expedient to do so;

he/she may authorise the continuation of the authority to exercise the powers under s. 60(1) for a further period of 24 hours (s. 60(3) and Code A, para. 2.14).

This authorisation must be in writing, signed by the officer giving it, and must specify:

- the grounds on which it is given;
- the locality in which it is to operate; and
- the period during which the powers are exercisable;

and any direction for the authorisation to continue must also be given in writing at the time or reduced into writing as soon as it is practicable to do so (s. 60(9)).

2.14A The selection of persons and vehicles under s. 60 to be stopped and, if appropriate searched should reflect an objective assessment of the nature of the incident or weapon in question and the individuals and vehicles thought likely to be associated with that incident or those weapons. The powers must not be used to stop and search persons and vehicles for reasons unconnected with the purpose of the authorisation. When selecting persons and vehicles to be stopped in response to a specific threat or incident, officers must take care not to discriminate unlawfully against anyone on the grounds of any of the protected characteristics set out in the Equality Act 2010 (see *paragraph 1.1*).

KEYNOTE

A significant difference between this power and the general powers of stop and search (which are not affected by the granting of this power (s. 60(12))) is that it does not require any grounds at all for the officer to suspect that the person/vehicle is carrying offensive weapons or dangerous instruments (s. 60(5)). However, para. 2.14A is clear in that it states that the stopping of people and/or vehicles should reflect the purpose of the authorisation and should be capable of 'objective assessment'. A further difference is that the power under s. 60 authorises officers in uniform to stop vehicles in order to search them and their occupants.

2.14B The driver of a vehicle which is stopped under section 60 and any person who is searched under section 60 are entitled to a written statement to that effect if they apply within twelve months from the day the vehicle was stopped or the person was searched. This statement is a record which states that the vehicle was stopped or (as the case may be) that the person was searched under s. 60 and it may form part of the search record or be supplied as a separate record.

2.14C An inspector who gives an authorisation must communicate their decision to the public as soon as possible and where it is operationally beneficial to do so. This information must include the reason, time limit and geographical location of the authorisation.

KEYNOTE

The general requirements governing searches imposed by Code A apply to this power.

Failing to stop (or to stop a vehicle) when required to do so under this power is a summary offence punishable with one month's imprisonment and/or a fine (s. 60(8)(a)).

Section 60 of the Criminal Justice and Public Order Act 1994
(Power to stop and search in anticipation of, or after, violence)

Officer of the rank of **INSPECTOR** or above

Reasonably **BELIEVES**

SITUATION 1	SITUATION 2	SITUATION 3
Serious violence may take place and it is expedient to give an authorisation to prevent it	Persons are carrying dangerous instruments or offensive weapons without good reason	An incident involving serious violence has taken place where a dangerous instrument or offensive weapon was used and it is expedient to use s. 60 to find the instrument or weapon

The officer may authorise the power in **THEIR POLICE AREA**

For a period **NOT EXCEEDING 24 HOURS**

SITUATION 1	SITUATION 2	SITUATION 3
Authorisation in writing	Authorisation in writing	Authorisation in writing Can be oral

If an **INSPECTOR** authorises they must, ASAP, inform an officer of the rank of **SUPERINTENDENT** or above

Section 60 authorises a constable **IN UNIFORM** to stop and search persons and vehicles for dangerous instruments or offensive weapons

SUPERINTENDENT or above can authorise an extension

If it appears to the **SUPERINTENDENT** that having regard to offences that have, or are reasonably **SUSPECTED** to have, been committed in connection with activity within the authorisation and it is expedient to do so

For a further period of **24 HOURS**
(s. 60s last a **MAXIMUM of 48 HOURS**)

Authorisation for extension can be oral or written

Figure 3.1 Section 60 of the Criminal Justice and Public Order Act 1994 (Power to stop and search in anticipation of, or after, violence)
Source: © Oxford University Press 2025.

Powers to require removal of face coverings

2.15 Section 60AA of the Criminal Justice and Public Order Act 1994 also provides a power to demand the removal of disguises. The officer exercising the power must reasonably believe that someone is wearing an item wholly or mainly for the purpose of concealing identity. There is also a power to seize such items where the officer believes that a person intends to wear them for this purpose. There is no power to stop and search for disguises. An officer may seize any such item which is discovered when exercising a power of search for something else, or which is being carried, and which the officer reasonably believes is intended to be used for concealing anyone's identity. This power can only be used if an authorisation under section 60 or an authorisation under section 60AA is in force.

KEYNOTE

These provisions are wider than those under s. 60 in that they are not restricted to anticipated outbreaks of serious violence. This is not simply a preventive power and can be used where the 'activities' are already under way.

A 'Uniform' Power

The power under s. 60AA is only available to officers in uniform.

Using the Power Requires 'Belief'

Any officer exercising these powers must reasonably believe that the person wearing the item is doing so wholly or mainly for the purpose of concealing his/her identity or he/she intends to wear it wholly or mainly for that purpose. Therefore if the person is a cyclist wearing a face mask to prevent the inhalation of traffic fumes, or a motorcyclist wearing a crash helmet, the fact that its effect is to conceal his/her identity will not be enough—concealing his/her identity has to be the whole purpose/main purpose of the wearer.

Wearing an Item

The expression 'item' is wide and would include balaclavas, scarves and crash helmets (if the officer believes that such items are being worn wholly or mainly to conceal identity). It is not specifically restricted to face coverings and extends to anything that could be worn wholly or mainly for the purpose of concealing identity (e.g. where offenders swap clothing after an offence). The purpose of the legislation is primarily to ensure that people are not allowed to commit offences anonymously in situations of public disorder.

Religious Sensitivities

Specific guidance in relation to religious sensitivities is provided by Code A. Many people customarily cover their heads or faces for religious reasons, e.g. Muslim women, Sikh men, Sikh or Hindu women or Rastafarian men or women. A police officer cannot order the removal of a head or face covering except where there is reason to believe that the item is being worn by the individual wholly or mainly for the purpose of disguising identity, not simply because it disguises identity. Where there may be religious sensitivities about ordering the removal of such an item, the officer should permit the item to be removed out of public view (perhaps in a police van or a police station if there is one nearby). Where practicable, the item should be removed in the presence of an officer of the same sex as the person and out of sight of anyone of the opposite sex. This approach is a general principle of Code A and would apply to all searches the Code relates to.

Not a Power to Search

There is no power to search for face coverings etc. under this power. Clearly, if an item is found during a lawful search for other articles (say under s. 60(4)) which does not require any 'reasonable belief' by the officer, face coverings and masks could then be seized under subs. (b). The procedure to be followed in relation to the retention and disposal of items seized under s. 60 is set out in the Police (Retention and Disposal of Items Seized) Regulations 2002 (SI 2002/1372).

Not a Power to Stop Vehicles

Unlike s. 60, there is no specific power under this section to stop vehicles but, given that this is a power for police officers in uniform, the general power under s. 163 of the Road Traffic Act 1988 could be used.

It is a summary only offence (punishable by one month's imprisonment and/or a fine) to fail to comply with a requirement to remove items when required to do so by a constable in the exercise of the power under s. 60AA. The wording of this offence is absolute. There is no requirement that the person failed without reasonable excuse or without good reason etc.; simply that he/she failed to remove an item worn by him/her. However, it must be shown that:

- the requirement was made (and presumably understood);
- it was made by a police officer in uniform;
- in the exercise of powers authorised under s. 60;

in the reasonable belief that the person was wearing the item wholly or mainly for the purpose of concealing identity.

2.16 Authority for a constable in uniform to require the removal of disguises and to seize them under section 60AA may be given if the authorising officer reasonably believes that activities may take place in any locality in the officer's police area that are likely to involve the commission of offences and it is expedient to use these powers to prevent or control these activities.

2.17 An authorisation under section 60AA may only be given by an officer of the rank of inspector or above, in writing, specifying the grounds on which it was given, the locality in which the powers may be exercised and the period of time for which they are in force. The period authorised shall be no longer than appears reasonably necessary to prevent, or seek to prevent the commission of offences. It may not exceed 24 hours.

2.18 If an inspector gives an authorisation, he or she must, as soon as practicable, inform an officer of or above the rank of superintendent. This officer may direct that the authorisation shall be extended for a further 24 hours, if crimes have been committed, or is suspected to have been committed, and the continued use of the powers is considered necessary to prevent or deal with further such activity. This direction must also be given in writing at the time or as soon as practicable afterwards.

KEYNOTE

Initial Authorisation

The powers under s. 60AA are accessible in one of two ways:

- an authorisation is given under s. 60 of the Act—such an authorisation automatically engages the powers under s. 60AA in addition to the powers authorised under s. 60; or
- a 'stand-alone' authorisation under s. 60AA engages the s. 60AA powers.

The authorisation process closely follows that of an authorisation under s. 60 of the Act, i.e. the authorising officer reasonably believes that activities may take place in any locality in his/her police area that are likely (if they take place) to involve the commission of offences. This reasonable belief must have an objective basis, for example where the authorising officer is aware of previous incidents of crimes being committed while wearing face coverings to conceal identity. If an inspector gives an authorisation, they must, as soon as is practicable to do so, cause an officer of or above the rank of superintendent to be informed (s. 60AA(3)).

Continuing the Authorisation

If it appears to an officer of or above the rank of superintendent that it is expedient to do so, having regard to offences which have been committed in connection with the activities in respect of which the authorisation was given, or are reasonably suspected to have been so committed, he/she may direct that the authorisation shall continue in force for a further 24 hours (s. 60AA(4)).

An authorisation (whether to grant the use of the power or to extend it) shall be in writing unless it is not practicable to do so. An oral authorisation will state the matters which would otherwise have been specified in a written authorisation (grounds for the search, locality and time period) and be recorded in writing as soon as it is practicable to do so.

The limitations and requirements as to the time and geographical extent of any authorisation are the same as an authorisation given under s. 60 of the Act.

Section 60AA of the Criminal Justice and Public Order Act 1994
(Power to require the removal of disguises)

The power is accessible in one of two ways

SITUATION 1	SITUATION 2
An authorisation has been given under s. 60 This **AUTOMATICALLY** engages the powers under s. 60AA in addition to the s. 60 powers	A 'stand-alone' authorisation for s. 60AA

'STAND-ALONE' AUTHORISATION

⇩

Officer of the rank of **INSPECTOR** or above

⇩

Reasonably **BELIEVES**

⇩

That activities may take place in the locality of **THEIR POLICE AREA** that are likely to involve the commission of offences

⇩

The officer may authorise the power in **THEIR POLICE AREA**

⇩

For a period **NOT EXCEEDING 24 HOURS**

⇩

Authorisation in writing—can be oral

⇩

If an **INSPECTOR** authorises they must, ASAP, inform an officer of the rank of **SUPERINTENDENT** or above

⇩

Section 60 authorises a constable **IN UNIFORM** to demand the removal of any item the officer **REASONABLY BELIEVES** the person is wearing or will wear wholly or mainly to **CONCEAL THEIR IDENTITY**

⇩

SUPERINTENDENT or above can authorise an extension

⇩

If it appears to the **SUPERINTENDENT** that having regard to offences that have, or are reasonably **SUSPECTED** to have, been committed in connection with activity within the authorisation and it is expedient to do so

⇩

For a further period of **24 HOURS**
(s. 60s last a **MAXIMUM of 48 HOURS)**

⇩

Authorisation for extension in writing—can be oral

Figure 3.2 Section 60AA of Criminal Justice and Public Order Act 1994 (Power to require the removal of disguises)

(c) *Not used*

(d) Searches under Schedule 5 to the Terrorism Prevention and Investigation Measures Act 2011 and Schedule 11 of the National Security Act 2023

2.18A Paragraph 3 of Schedule 5 to the TPIM Act 2011 and Paragraph 3 of Schedule 11 to the National Security Act 2023 allows a constable to detain an individual to be searched under the following powers:

(i) paragraph 6(2)(a) in the above Schedules, when a TPIM or State Threats Prevention and Investigation Measures ('STPIM') notice is being, or has just been, served on the individual for the purpose of ascertaining whether there is anything on the individual that contravenes measures specified in the notice;

(ii) paragraph 8(2)(a) in the above Schedules, in accordance with a warrant to search the individual issued by a justice of the peace in England and Wales, a sheriff in Scotland or a lay magistrate in Northern Ireland who is satisfied that a search is necessary for the purpose of determining whether an individual in respect of whom a TPIM or STPIM notice is in force is complying with measures specified in the notice (see *paragraph 2.20*); and

(iii) paragraph 10 in the above Schedules, to ascertain whether an individual in respect of whom a TPIM or STPIM notice is in force is in possession of anything that could be used to threaten or harm any person.

See paragraph 2.1(e).

2.19 The exercise of the powers mentioned in *paragraph 2.18A* does not require the constable to have reasonable grounds to suspect that the individual:

(a) has been, or is, contravening any of the measures specified in the TPIM or STPIM notice; or

(b) has on them anything which:

- in the case of the power in sub-paragraph (i), contravenes measures specified in the TPIM or STPIM notice;
- in the case of the power in sub-paragraph (ii) is not complying with measures specified in the TPIM or STPIM notice; or
- in the case of the power in sub-paragraph (iii), could be used to threaten or harm any person.

2.20 A search of an individual on warrant under the power mentioned in paragraph 2.18A(ii) must carried out within 28 days of the issue of the warrant and:

- the individual may be searched on one occasion only within that period;
- the search must take place at a reasonable hour unless it appears that this would frustrate the purposes of the search.

2.21 *Not used.*

2.22 *Not used.*

2.23 *Not used.*

2.24 *Not used.*

2.24A *Not used.*

2.25 *Not used.*

2.26 The powers under Schedule 5 to the Terrorism Prevention and Investigation Measures Act 2011 and Schedule 11 to the National Security Act 2023 allow a constable to conduct a search of an individual only for specified purposes relating to a TPIM or STPIM notice as set out above. However, anything found may be seized and retained if there are reasonable grounds for believing that it is or it contains evidence of any offence for use at a trial for that offence or to prevent it being concealed, lost, damaged, altered, or destroyed.

However, this would not prevent a search being carried out under other search powers if, in the course of exercising these powers, the officer formed reasonable grounds for suspicion.

(e) Powers to search persons in the exercise of a power to search premises

2.27 The following powers to search premises also authorise the search of a person, not under arrest, who is found on the premises during the course of the search:

(a) section 139B of the Criminal Justice Act 1988 under which a constable may enter school premises and search the premises and any person on those premises for any bladed or pointed article or offensive weapon;

(b) under a warrant issued under section 23(3) of the Misuse of Drugs Act 1971 to search premises for drugs or documents but only of the warrant specifically authorises the search of persons found on the premises; and

(c) under a search warrant or order issued under paragraph 1, 3 or 11 of Schedule 5 to the Terrorism Act 2000 to search premises and any person found there for material likely to be of substantial value to a terrorist investigation;

(ca) under a search warrant or order issued under paragraph 2, 9 or 12 of Schedule 2 to the National Security Act 2023 to search premises and any person found there for material likely to be of substantial value to the investigation.

2.28 Before the power under section 139B of the Criminal Justice Act 1988 may be exercised, the constable must have reasonable grounds to suspect that an offence under section 139A or 139AA of the Criminal Justice Act 1988 (having a bladed or pointed article or offensive weapon on school premises) has been or is being committed. A warrant to search premises and persons found therein may be issued under section 23(3) of the Misuse of Drugs Act 1971 if there are reasonable grounds to suspect that controlled drugs or certain documents are in the possession of a person on the premises.

2.29 The powers in paragraph 2.34 do not require prior specific grounds to suspect that the person to be searched is in possession of an item for which there is an existing power to search. However, it is still necessary to ensure that the selection and treatment of those searched under these powers is based upon objective factors connected with the search of the premises, and not upon personal prejudice.

(f) *Not used*

2.30 *Not used*
2.31 *Not used*
2.32 *Not used*
2.33 *Not used*
2.34 *Not used*
2.35 *Not used*
2.36 *Not used*
2.37 *Not used*
2.38 *Not used*
2.39 *Not used*

(g) Searches authorised under section 11 of the Public Order Act 2023

2.40 Authority for a constable in uniform to stop and search under section 11 of the Public Order Act 2023 may be given if the authorising officer reasonably believes that persons are carrying prohibited objects or that any of the following protest related offences may be committed in their police area:

I. **Wilful obstruction** (section 137 of the Highways Act 1980). This involves activity which causes or is capable of causing serious disruption to two or more individuals or to an organisation.
II. **Intentionally or recklessly causing public nuisance** (section 78 of the Police, Crime, Sentencing and Courts Act 2022)
III. **Locking on** (Section 1 of the Public Order Act 2023)
IV. **Causing serious disruption by tunnelling** (section 3 of the Public Order Act 2023)
V. **Causing serious disruption by being present in a tunnel** (section 4 of the Public Order Act 2023)
VI. **Obstruction etc of major transport works** (section 6 of the Public Order Act 2023)
VII. **Interference with use or operation of key national infrastructure** (section 7 of the Public Order Act 2023).

KEYNOTE

Section 11 Offences

There are a number of offences contained in s. 11; the offences may be remembered by using the mnemonic PILOT:

P Public nuisance
I Interference with use/operation of key national infrastructure
L Locking on
O Obstruction (causing or capable of causing serious disruption to two or more individuals/an organisation or obstruction of major transport works)
T Tunnelling (causing serious disruption by tunnelling/being present in a tunnel)

A 'Uniform' Power

The power under s. 11 confers on any constable in uniform the power:
(a) to stop any person and search them or anything carried by them for a prohibited object;
(b) to stop any vehicle and search the vehicle, its driver and any passenger for a prohibited object.

'Vehicle' includes a caravan.

If in the course of a search under this section a constable discovers an object which the constable has reasonable grounds for suspecting to be a prohibited object, the constable may seize it (s. 11(8)).

'Prohibited Object'

A 'prohibited object' means an object which:

- is made or adapted for use in the course or in connection with an offence listed between I and VII above; or
- is intended by the person having it with them for such use by them or some other person.

A person 'carries' a prohibited object if they have it in their possession (s. 11(2)).

2.40A That an officer has, by a reasonable and legitimate source, access to intelligence that would justify the use of suspicion-less powers to prevent the commission of offences listed in part [sic] 2.40.

2.41 An authorisation under section 11 of the Public Order Act 2023 may only be given by an officer of the rank of inspector or above and in writing by the authorising officer. The authorisation must specify the grounds on which it was given, the locality in which the powers may be exercised and the period of time for which it is in force. The period authorised shall be no longer than appears reasonably necessary to prevent protest-related offences in 2.40 being committed or prohibited objects being carried. It may not exceed 24 hours.

KEYNOTE

Similarities to Section 60 of the Criminal Justice and Public Order Act 1994

Like s. 60, the power under s. 11 of the Public Order Act 2023 is a 'uniform'-only power and an 'additional' power (separate from and additional to the normal stop and search powers).

The Purpose of Section 11

The overall purpose of the powers in s. 11 is to prevent the carrying out of offences listed in para. 2.40 (I–VII). A particular example might be an authorisation to prevent protest-related offences or the carrying of prohibited items (such items may include glue, locking devices, shovels etc.) used for locking-on at a protest where the named protest group have engaged in locking-on in previous instances, at similar locations (e.g. art galleries). In these cases, an authorising officer may have been made aware of evidence or intelligence which shows that the named protest group actively encourages members to employ locking-on as a protest tactic.

Reasonable Belief and Necessity

Authorisations under s. 11 of the Public Order Act 2023 require a reasonable belief on the part of the authorising officer. This must have an objective basis, taking into account the information known by the authorising officer at the time, for example: intelligence or relevant information such as a history of antagonism and commission of protest-related offences by specific protest groups, previous incidents of serious disruption at, or connected with, particular events or locations; a significant increase in protest-related criminal activity in a limited area; reports that individuals are regularly carrying prohibited objects in a particular locality.

In addition to the authorising officer's reasonable belief regarding the offences between I to VII being committed and that persons are carrying prohibited items in his/her locality, the authorising officer must reasonably believe:

- the authorisation is necessary to prevent the commission of offences I to VII or the carrying of prohibited objects (as the case may be);
- the specified locality is no greater than necessary to prevent such activity; and
- the specified period is no longer than is necessary to prevent such activity.

(s. 11(4))

Time Frame

It is for the authorising officer to determine the period of time during which the powers mentioned in para. 2.40 may be exercised. The officer should set the minimum period he/she considers necessary to deal with the risk of serious disruption, the carrying of prohibited objects mentioned in para. 2.40 or to find objects that have been used in the course of a protest-related offence. A direction to extend the period authorised under the powers mentioned in para. 2.42 may be given only once. Thereafter, further use of the powers requires a new authorisation.

Geographical Area

It is for the authorising officer to determine the period of time during which the powers mentioned in para. 2.40 may be exercised. The officer should set the minimum period he/she considers necessary to deal with the risk of serious disruption, the carrying of prohibited objects mentioned in para. 2.40 or to find objects that have been used in the course of a protest-related offence.

2.42 An inspector who gives an authorisation must, as soon as practicable, inform an officer of or above the rank of superintendent. This officer may direct that the authorisation shall be extended for a further 24 hours if it is considered necessary to prevent or deal with further such activity or to find a prohibited item mentioned in 2.40. That direction must be given in writing unless it is not practicable to do so, in which case it must be recorded in writing as soon as practicable afterwards.

KEYNOTE

Initial Authorisation

Section 12(2) states that an authorisation under s. 11 will:

- be given in writing and signed by the officer giving it;
- specify the grounds on which it is given; and
- specify the locality in which and period during which the powers conferred by that section are exercisable.

The initial authorisation is for a period not exceeding 24 hours.

Continuing the Authorisation

Section 11(5) states that if it appears to a police officer of or above the rank of superintendent that it is necessary to do so to prevent the commission of offences listed between I to VIII or the carrying of prohibited objects, the officer may direct that the authorisation is to continue in force for a further period not exceeding 24 hours. Section 12(3) states that such an authorisation must be given in writing or, where it is not practicable to do so, be recorded in writing as soon as it is practicable to do so.

The maximum period the power can be authorised for is therefore 48 hours (an initial 24 hours followed by an extended 24 hours) as a direction to extend the period authorised under the powers mentioned in para. 2.42 may be given only once. Thereafter, further use of the powers requires a new authorisation.

2.42A The selection of persons and vehicles to be stopped under section 11 of the Public Order Act 2023 and, if appropriate, searched should reflect an objective assessment of the nature of activity in the locality or items in question and the individuals and vehicles thought likely to be associated with that local activity or those items. The powers must not be used to stop and search persons and vehicles for reasons unconnected with the purpose of the authorisation.

2.42B The driver of a vehicle which is stopped under section 11 of the Public Order Act 2023 and any person who is searched under section 11 are entitled to a written statement to that effect if they apply within twelve months from the day the vehicle was stopped or the person was searched. This statement is a record which states that the vehicle was stopped or (as the case may be) that the person was searched under section 11 and it may form part of the search record or be supplied as a separate record.

2.43 An inspector who gives an authorisation must communicate their decision to the public as soon as possible and where it is operationally beneficial to do so. This information must include the reason, time limit and geographical location of the authorisation.

2.44 Officers who use stop and search powers during a protest, namely those referred to in section 10 and 11 of the Public Order Act 2023 must act compatibly with the rights to freedom of expression and the freedom of assembly and association under Articles 10 and 11 of the ECHR (European Convention on Human Rights). Officers must be clear that the act of protesting is not an offence. The intrusion on the liberty of the person stopped and searched must be brief and detention for the purposes of a stop and search must take place near or at the location of the stop.

Section 11 of the Public Order Act 2023
(Powers to stop and search without suspicion)

↓

Officer of the rank of **INSPECTOR** or above

↓

Reasonably **BELIEVES**

↓

SITUATION 1	SITUATION 2
That a **PILOT** offence may be committed in **THEIR POLICE AREA**	That persons are carrying anything made, adapted or intended for use in the course of or in connection with a **PILOT** offence in **THEIR AREA**

↓

And it is **NECESSARY** to prevent the commission of **PILOT** offences/people carrying **PILOT** objects

↓

The power can be authorised for a period **NOT EXCEEDING 24 HOURS**

↓

Authorisation in writing

↓

If an **INSPECTOR** authorises they must, ASAP, inform an officer of the rank of **SUPERINTENDENT** or above

↓

Section 11 authorises a constable **IN UNIFORM** to stop and search any person or anything carried by them and to stop and search any vehicle, the driver and passengers for **PILOT** items

↓

SUPERINTENDENT or above can authorise an extension

↓

If it appears to the **SUPERINTENDENT** that it is **NECESSARY** to prevent the commission of **PILOT** offences/carrying of **PILOT** items

↓

For a further period of **24 HOURS**
(s. 11 lasts a **MAXIMUM of 48 HOURS**)

↓

Authorisation for extension can be oral or written

Figure 3.3 Section 11 of the Public Order Act 2023 (Powers to stop and search without suspicion)
Source: Oxford University Press 2025.

3.1.5 Code A—3 Conduct of searches

3.1 All stops and searches must be carried out with courtesy, consideration and respect for the person concerned. This has a significant impact on public confidence in the police. Every reasonable effort must be made to minimise the embarrassment that a person being searched may experience.

3.2 The cooperation of the person to be searched must be sought in every case, even if the person initially objects to the search. A forcible search may be made only if it has been established that the person is unwilling to co-operate or resists. Reasonable force may be used as a last resort if necessary to conduct a search or to detain a person or vehicle for the purposes of a search.

3.3 The length of time for which a person or vehicle may be detained must be reasonable and kept to a minimum. Where the exercise of the power requires reasonable suspicion, the thoroughness and extent of a search must depend on what is suspected of being carried, and by whom. If the suspicion relates to a particular article which is seen to be slipped into a person's pocket, then, in the absence of other grounds for suspicion or an opportunity for the article to be moved elsewhere, the search must be confined to that pocket. In the case of a small article which can readily be concealed, such as a drug, and which might be concealed anywhere on the person, a more extensive search may be necessary. In the case of searches mentioned in *paragraph 2.1(b)* and *(d)*, which do not require reasonable grounds for suspicion, officers may make any reasonable search to look for items for which they are empowered to search.

3.4 The search must be carried out at or near the place where the person or vehicle was first detained.

3.5 There is no power to require a person to remove any clothing in public other than an outer coat, jacket or gloves except under section 60AA of the Criminal Justice and Public Order Act 1994 (which empowers a constable to require a person to remove any item worn to conceal identity). A search in public of a person's clothing which has not been removed must be restricted to superficial examination of outer garments. This does not, however, prevent an officer from placing his or her hand inside the pockets of the outer clothing, or feeling round the inside of collars, socks and shoes if this is reasonably necessary in the circumstances to look for the object of the search or to remove and examine any item reasonably suspected to be the object of the search. For the same reasons, subject to the restrictions on the removal of headgear, a person's hair may also be searched in public (see *paragraphs 3.1* and *3.3*).

3.6 Where on reasonable grounds it is considered necessary to conduct a more thorough search (e.g. by requiring a person to take off a T-shirt), this must be done out of public view, for example, in a police van unless *paragraph 3.7* applies, or police station if there is one nearby. Any search involving the removal of more than an outer coat, jacket, gloves, headgear or footwear, or any other item concealing identity, may only be made by an officer of the same sex as the person searched and may not be made in the presence of anyone of the opposite sex unless the person being searched specifically requests it (see *Code C, Annex L*).

3.7 Searches involving exposure of intimate parts of the body must not be conducted as a routine extension of a less thorough search, simply because nothing is found in the course of the initial search. Searches involving exposure of intimate parts of the body may be carried out only at a nearby police station or other nearby location which is out of public view (but not a police vehicle). These searches must be conducted in accordance with paragraph 11 of Annex A to Code C except that an intimate search mentioned in *paragraph 11(f) of Annex A* to Code C may not be authorised or carried out under any stop and search powers. The other provisions of Code C do not apply to the conduct and recording of searches of persons detained at police stations in the exercise of stop and search powers.

KEYNOTE

A person may be detained under a stop and search power at a place other than where the person was first detained only if that place, be it a police station or elsewhere, is nearby. Such a place should be located within a reasonable travelling distance using whatever mode of travel (on foot or by car) is appropriate. This applies to all searches under stop and search powers, whether or not they involve the removal of clothing or exposure of intimate parts of the body (see Code A, paras 3.6 and 3.7) or take place in or out of public view. It means, for example, that a search under the stop and search power in s. 23 of the Misuse of Drugs Act 1971 which involves the compulsory removal of more than a person's outer coat, jacket or gloves cannot be carried out unless a place which is both nearby the place he/she was first detained and out of public view, is available. If a search involves exposure of intimate parts of the body and a police station is not nearby, particular care must be taken to ensure that the location is suitable in that it enables the search to be conducted in accordance with the requirements of para. 11 of Annex A to Code C.

A search in the street itself should be regarded as being in public for the purposes of paras 3.6 and 3.7, even though it may be empty at the time a search begins.

Although there is no power to require a person to do so, there is nothing to prevent an officer from asking a person *voluntarily to remove* more than an outer coat, jacket or gloves.

Conduct of a Search—Summary Chart

In public, the officer can require the person to be searched to remove their **JOG**

↓

A search of clothing not removed must be restricted to a superficial examination

↓

This does not prevent an officer from placing their hand inside the pockets of the outer clothing, or feeling round the inside of collars, socks and shoes if necessary. Subject to the restrictions on the removal of headgear (see below), a person's hair may also be searched in public

SAME-SEX SEARCH

↓

If the person to be searched **VOLUNTEERS** to remove additional items of clothing, this is permissible but if that means they remove **MORE THAN** headgear and footwear, additional items **CANNOT** be removed in the presence of a person/officer of the opposite sex (unless the person being searched specifically requests it)

↓

If the person to be searched **WILL NOT** volunteer to remove more than the **JOG** in public and a more thorough search is required, the person to be searched must be removed from the public arena (into a police vehicle/taken to a police station or elsewhere)

↓

Once removed from the public arena, they can be required to remove additional items of clothing even to the extent of exposing intimate body parts but a search exposing intimate body parts **CANNOT** take place in a police vehicle (a search exposing intimate body parts would take place in a police station or elsewhere)

↓

A search that exposes intimate body parts taking place at a police station or elsewhere is subject to the same rules you would apply to a strip search (under Code C)

OPPOSITE-SEX SEARCH

↓

If the person to be searched **VOLUNTEERS** to remove additional items of clothing, this is permissible but they can only remove headgear and footwear—opposite-sex searches are limited to the removal of the **JOG, HEADGEAR** and **FOOTWEAR**—if the search involves the removal of **MORE THAN** those items, it **MUST** be carried out by an **OFFICER OF THE SAME SEX** as the person being searched

↓

If the person to be searched **WILL NOT** volunteer to remove more than the **JOG** in public (we are talking about headgear and footwear here) and a more thorough search is required, the person to be searched must be removed from the public arena (into a police vehicle/taken to a police station or elsewhere)

↓

Once removed from the public arena, they can be required to remove additional items of clothing—the additional items of clothing being limited to headgear and footwear. If the search requires the removal of **MORE THAN** those items, it **MUST** be carried out by an **OFFICER OF THE SAME SEX** as the person being searched

Figure 3.4 Conduct of a search—summary chart

Steps to be taken prior to a search

3.8 Before any search of a detained person or attended vehicle takes place the officer must take reasonable steps, if not in uniform (see *paragraph 3.9*), to show their warrant card to the person to be searched or in charge of the vehicle to be searched and whether or not in uniform, to give that person the following information:

(a) that they are being detained for the purposes of a search;

(b) the officer's name (except in the case of enquiries linked to National Security including terrorism, or otherwise where the officer reasonably believes that giving their name might put him or her in danger, in which case a warrant or other identification number shall be given) and the name of the police station to which the officer is attached;

(c) the legal search power which is being exercised; and

(d) a clear explanation of:

(i) the object of the search in terms of the articles or articles for which there is a power to search; and

(ii) in the case of

- the power under section 60 of the Criminal Justice and Public Order Act 1994 (see *paragraph 2.1(b)*), the nature of the power, the authorisation and the fact that it has been given;
- the powers under Schedule 5 to the Terrorism Prevention and Investigation Measures Act 2011 and Schedule 11 to the National Security Act 2023 (see *paragraph 2.1(e)* and *2.18A*):
  - ~ the fact that a TPIM or STPIM notice is in force or, (in the case of paragraph 6(2)(a) to those Schedules) that a TPIM or STPIM notice is being served;
  - ~ the nature of the power being exercised.

  For a search under paragraph 8 of Schedule 5 or paragraph 8 Schedule 11 above, the warrant must be produced and the person be provided with a copy of it.
- all other powers requiring reasonable suspicion (see *paragraph 2.1(a)*), the grounds for that suspicion. This means explaining the basis for the suspicion by reference to information and/or intelligence about, or some specific behaviour by, the person concerned (see *paragraph 2.2*).

KEYNOTE

The officer carrying out the search must take reasonable steps to bring the matters at s. 2(3)(a)–(d) to the person's attention before starting the search. This information must be given whether it is requested or not. Whether reasonable steps have been taken to communicate information will ultimately be a question of fact for the court to decide and what is 'reasonable' will vary with the particular circumstances of each search (e.g. what is reasonable outside a busy city centre nightclub may well be different from that which is required on a rural public footpath). The courts have taken a firm position in interpreting and applying these requirements. For example, the requirements for officers to provide details of their names and police stations still apply even though that information is discernible from the officers' uniform; failure to provide the information in such circumstances will make any subsequent search unlawful and will mean that the person being searched may use reasonable force to resist it (*Osman* v *DPP* (1999) 163 JP 725).

The requirement to provide the name of the officer concerned applies even if the officer conducting the search and the person who is subject to the search are well known to each other (*R (Michaels)* v *Highbury Corner Magistrates' Court* [2009] EWHC 2928 (Admin)). In a further case, the Divisional Court held that the officers conducting the stop and search had not informed the suspect of their intention to search him at an early enough stage before laying their hands on him. The suspect, who was standing with his hands in his pockets and who was suspected of drugs offences, had struggled with the officers when they took hold of him and had been arrested. The magistrates' court held that where it was obvious that the people apprehending a suspect were police officers and where an officer was genuinely concerned for the safety of a fellow officer, it was not essential to comply with all the requirements of s. 2(3). However, the Divisional Court disagreed, quashing the conviction and holding that where police officers contemplated a statutory search, they were required (by s. 2(2)) to comply with s. 2(3) before commencing the search (*Bonner* v *DPP* [2004] EWHC 2415 (Admin)).

(e) that they are entitled to a copy of the record of the search if one is made (see section 4 below) if they ask within 3 months from the date of the search and:

(i) if they are not arrested and taken to a police station as a result of the search and it is practicable to make a record on the spot, that immediately after the search is completed they will be given, if they request, either:

- a copy of the record, or

- a receipt which explains how they can obtain a copy of the full record or access to an electronic copy of the record, or

(ii) if they are arrested and taken to a police station as a result of the search, that the record will be made at the station as part of their custody record and they will be given, if they request, a copy of their custody record which includes a record of the search as soon as practicable whilst they are at the station.

KEYNOTE

These Code A requirements (para. 3.8(a)–(e)), are mirrored by the specific requirements of s. 2 of PACE84.

3.9 Stops and searches under the power mentioned in *paragraph 2.1(b)* may be undertaken only by a constable in uniform.

3.10 The person should also be given information about police powers to stop and search and the individual's rights in these circumstances.

3.11 If the person to be searched, or in charge of a vehicle to be searched, does not appear to understand what is being said, or there is any doubt about the person's ability to understand English, the officer must take reasonable steps to bring information regarding the person's rights and any relevant provisions of this Code to his or her attention. If the person is deaf or cannot understand English and is accompanied by someone, then the officer must try to establish whether that person can interpret or otherwise help the officer to give the required information.

3.1.6 Code A—4 Recording requirements

(a) Searches which do not result in an arrest

4.1 When an officer carries out a search in the exercise of any power to which this Code applies, and the search does not result in the person searched or person in charge of the vehicle searched being arrested and taken to a police station, a record must be made of it, electronically or on paper, unless there are exceptional circumstances which make this wholly impracticable (e.g. in situations involving public disorder or where the recording officer's presence is urgently required elsewhere). If a record is to be made, the officer carrying out the search must make the record on the spot unless this is not practicable, in which case, the officer must make the record as soon as practicable after the search is completed.

4.2 If the record is made at the time, the person who has been searched or who is in charge of the vehicle that has been searched must be asked if they want a copy and if they do, they must be given immediately, either:

- a copy of the record, or
- a receipt which explains how they can obtain a copy of the full record or access to an electronic copy of the record.

KEYNOTE

If a record of the search under s. 1 of PACE84 has been made, then the person who was searched shall be entitled to a copy of the record if he/she asks for one (s. 3(7)).

If a vehicle is searched and a record of the search has been made, then the owner of the vehicle which was searched or the person who was in charge of the vehicle at the time when it was searched is entitled to a copy of the record of search if they ask for one (s. 3(8)).

In both of the above cases, the entitlement to a copy of the search record will run for three months beginning on the date on which the search was made (s. 3(9)).

4.2A An officer is not required to provide a copy of the full record or a receipt at the time if they are called to an incident of higher priority.

KEYNOTE

It has been held that a failure to make a record of a search does not thereby render the search unlawful (*Basher* v *DPP* [1993] COD 372). However, it is not only the lawfulness of a search that is of concern to police officers and the general principles set out in Code A should be borne in mind at all times.

In situations where it is not practicable to provide a written copy of the record or immediate access to an electronic copy of the record or a receipt of the search at the time (see para. 4.2A), the officer should consider providing the person with details of the station at which the person may attend for a record. A receipt may take the form of a simple business card which includes sufficient information to locate the record should the person ask for the copy, e.g. the date and place of the search, a reference number or the name of the officer who carried out the search (unless para. 4.4 applies).

(b) Searches which result in an arrest

4.2B If a search in the exercise of any power to which this Code applies results in a person being arrested and taken to a police station, the officer carrying out the search is responsible for ensuring that a record of the search is made as a part of their custody record. The custody officer must then ensure that the person is asked if they want a copy of the record and if they do, that they are given a copy as soon as practicable.

KEYNOTE

When the search results in the person searched or in charge of a vehicle which is searched being arrested, the requirement to make the record of search part of the person's custody record does not apply if the person is granted 'street bail' after arrest (s. 30A of PACE84) to attend a police station and is not taken in custody to the police station. An arrested person's entitlement to a copy of the search record which is made as part of his/her custody record does not affect his/her entitlement to a copy of his/her custody record or any other provisions of Code C, section 2 (Custody Records).

(c) Record of search

4.3 The record of a search must always include the following information:

(a) A note of the self-defined ethnicity, and if different, the ethnicity as perceived by the officer making the search, of the person searched or of the person in charge of the vehicle (as the case may be);

KEYNOTE

Officers should record the self-defined ethnicity of every person stopped according to the categories used in the 2001 census question listed in Annex B. The person should be asked to select one of the five main categories representing broad ethnic groups and then a more specific cultural background from within this group. The ethnic classification should be coded for recording purposes using the coding system in Annex B. An additional 'Not stated' box is available but should not be offered to respondents explicitly. Officers should be aware and explain to members of the public, especially where concerns are raised, that this information is required to obtain a true picture of stop and search activity and to help improve ethnic monitoring, tackle discriminatory practice and promote effective use of the powers. If the person gives what appears to the officer to be an 'incorrect' answer (e.g. a person who appears to be white states that he/she is black), the officer should record the response that has been given and then record his/her own perception of the ethnic background by using the PNC classification system. If the 'Not stated' category is used the reason for this must be recorded on the form.

(b) The date, time and place the person or vehicle was searched;
(c) The object of the search in terms of the article or articles for which there is a power to search;
(d) In the case of:
  - the power under section 60 of the Criminal Justice and Public Order Act 1994 (see *paragraph 2.1(b)*), the nature of the power, the authorisation and the fact that it has been given;
  - the power under section 11 of the Public Order Act 2023, the nature of the power, the authorisation and the fact that it has been given;

KEYNOTE

It is important for monitoring purposes to specify when authority is given for exercising the stop and search power under s. 60 of the Criminal Justice and Public Order Act 1994 or the stop and search power under s. 11 of the Public Order Act 2023.

  - the powers under Schedule 5 to the Terrorism Prevention and Investigation Measures Act 2011 and Schedule 11 to the National Security Act 2023 (see *paragraphs 2.1(e)* and *2.18A*):
    - ~ the fact that a TPIM or STPIM notice is in force or, (in the case of paragraph 6(2)(a)), that a TPIM or STPIM notice is being served;
    - ~ the nature of the power, and
    - ~ for a search under paragraph 8 of either of the above Schedules, the date the search warrant was issued, the fact that the warrant was produced and a copy of it provided and the warrant must also be endorsed by the constable executing it to state whether anything was found and whether anything was seized, and
  - all other powers requiring reasonable suspicion (see *paragraph 2.1(a)*), the grounds for that suspicion.

(e) subject to paragraph 3.8(b), the identity of the officer carrying out the search.

4.3A For the purposes of completing the search record, there is no requirement to record the name, address and date of birth of the person searched or the person in charge of a vehicle which is searched and the person is under no obligation to provide this information.

4.4 Nothing in *paragraph 4.3* requires the names of police officers to be shown on the search record or any other record required to be made under this code in the case of enquiries linked to the investigation of terrorism or otherwise where an officer reasonably believes that recording names might endanger the officers. In such cases the record must show the officers' warrant or other identification number and duty station.

KEYNOTE

Where a stop and search is conducted by more than one officer, the identity of all the officers engaged in the search must be recorded on the record. Nothing prevents an officer who is present but not directly involved in searching from completing the record during the course of the encounter.

4.5 A record is required for each person and each vehicle searched. However, if a person is in a vehicle and both are searched, and the object and grounds of the search are the same, only one record need be completed. If more than one person in a vehicle is searched, separate records for each search of a person must be made. If only a vehicle is searched, the self-defined ethnic background of the person in charge of the vehicle must be recorded, unless the vehicle is unattended.

4.6 The record of the grounds for making a search must, briefly but informatively, explain the reason for suspecting the person concerned, by reference to information and/or intelligence about, or some specific behaviour by, the person concerned (see *paragraph 2.2*).

KEYNOTE

Once again, the requirements of Code A (paras 4.3 to 4.6) are mirrored by the requirements of s. 3 of PACE84. The requirements of s. 3 will apply to the searches of vehicles, vessels, aircraft and hovercraft (s. 3(10)).

4.7 Where officers detain an individual with a view to performing a search, but the need to search is eliminated as a result of questioning the person detained, a search should not be carried out and a record is not required. (See *paragraph 2.10*).

KEYNOTE

Where a person is lawfully detained for the purpose of a search, but no search in the event takes place, the detention will not thereby have been rendered unlawful.

4.8 After searching an unattended vehicle, or anything in or on it, an officer must leave a notice in it (or on it, if things on it have been searched without opening it) recording the fact that it has been searched.

4.9 The notice must include the name of the police station to which the officer concerned is attached and state where a copy of the record of the search may be obtained and how (if applicable) an electronic copy may be accessed and where any application for compensation should be directed.

4.10 The vehicle must if practicable be left secure.

4.10A *Not used.*

4.10B *Not used.*

Searching Unattended Vehicles

In the case of unattended vehicles, s. 2 of PACE84 states:

(6) On completing a search of an unattended vehicle or anything in or on such a vehicle in the exercise of any such power as is mentioned in subsection (2) above a constable shall leave a notice—
  (a) stating that he has searched it;
  (b) giving the name of the police station to which he is attached;
  (c) stating that an application for compensation for any damage caused by the search may be made to that police station; and
  (d) stating the effect of section 3(8) below.

(7) The constable shall leave the notice inside the vehicle unless it is not reasonably practicable to do so without damaging the vehicle.

Recording of encounters not governed by Statutory Powers

4.11 *Not used.*

4.12 There is no national requirement for an officer who requests a person in a public place to account for themselves, i.e. their actions, behaviour, presence in an area or possession of anything, to make a record of the encounter or to give the person a receipt (see *paragraph 2.11*).

4.12A *Not used.*

4.13 *Not used.*

4.14 *Not used.*

4.15 *Not used.*

4.16 *Not used.*

4.17 *Not used.*

4.18 *Not used.*

4.19 *Not used.*

4.20 *Not used.*

KEYNOTE

Where there are concerns which make it necessary to monitor any local disproportionality, forces have discretion to direct officers to record the self-defined ethnicity of persons they request to account for themselves in a public place or who they detain with a view to searching but do not search. Guidance should be provided locally and efforts made to minimise the bureaucracy involved. Records should be closely monitored and supervised in line with paras 5.1 to 5.4 and forces can suspend or reinstate recording of these encounters as appropriate.

A person who is asked to account for him/herself should, if he/she requests, be given information about how to report his/her dissatisfaction about how he/she has been treated.

3.1.7

Code A—5 Monitoring and supervising the use of stop and search powers

General

5.1 Any misuse of stop and search powers is likely to be harmful to policing and lead to mistrust of the police by the local community and by the public in general. Supervising officers must monitor the use of stop and search powers and should consider in particular whether there is any evidence that they are being exercised on the basis of stereotyped images or inappropriate generalisations. Supervising officers must satisfy themselves that the practice of officers under their supervision in stopping, searching and recording is fully in accordance with this Code. Supervisors must also examine whether the records reveal any trends or patterns which give cause for concern and, if so, take appropriate action to address this. (See *paragraph 2.8A*.)

5.2 Senior officers with area or force-wide responsibilities must also monitor the broader use of stop and search powers and, where necessary, take action at the relevant level.

5.3 Supervision and monitoring must be supported by the compilation of comprehensive statistical records of stops and searches at force, area and local level. Any apparently disproportionate use of the powers by particular officers or groups of officers or in relation to specific sections of the community should be identified and investigated.

5.4 In order to promote public confidence in the use of the powers, forces in consultation with police and crime commissioners must make arrangements for the records to be scrutinised by representatives of the community, and to explain the use of the powers at a local level.

5.4A Forces must make arrangements to send records of all stop and search interactions to the Home Office for national publication in accordance with section 44 of the Police Act 1996 and as part of the Annual Data Requirement (ADR) process.

Suspected misuse of powers by individual officers

5.6 Police supervisors must monitor the use of stop and search powers by individual officers to ensure that they are being applied appropriately and lawfully. Monitoring takes many forms, such as direct supervision of the exercise of the powers, examining stop and search records (particularly examining the officer's documented reasonable grounds for suspicion) and asking the officer to account for the way in which they conducted and recorded particular searches or through complaints about a stop and search that an officer has carried out.

5.7 Where a supervisor identifies issues with the way that an officer has used a stop and search power, the facts of the case will determine whether the standards of professional behaviour as set out in the Code of Ethics (see https://www.college.police.uk/ethics/code-of-ethics) have been breached and which formal action is pursued. Improper use might be a result of poor performance or a conduct matter, which will require the supervisor to take appropriate action such as performance or misconduct procedures. It is imperative that supervisors take both timely and appropriate action to deal with all such cases that come to their notice.

KEYNOTE

Arrangements for public scrutiny of records should take account of the right to confidentiality of those stopped and searched. Anonymised forms and/or statistics generated from records should be the focus of the examinations by members of the public.

3.1.8 Code A—Annexes A–C

ANNEX A—SUMMARY OF MAIN STOP AND SEARCH POWERS

THIS TABLE RELATES TO STOP AND SEARCH POWERS ONLY. INDIVIDUAL STATUTES BELOW MAY CONTAIN OTHER POLICE POWERS OF ENTRY, SEARCH AND SEIZURE

Power	Object of Search	Extent of Search	Where Exercisable
Unlawful articles general			
1. Public Stores Act 1875, s. 6.	HM Stores stolen or unlawfully obtained.	Persons, vehicles and vessels.	Anywhere where the constabulary powers are exercisable.
2. Firearms Act 1968, s. 47.	Firearms.	Persons and vehicles.	A public place, or anywhere in the case of reasonable suspicion of offences of carrying firearms with criminal intent or trespassing with firearms.
3. Misuse of Drugs Act 1971, s. 23.	Controlled drugs.	Persons and vehicles.	Anywhere.
4. Customs and Excise Management Act 1979, s. 163.	Goods: (a) on which duty has not been paid; (b) being unlawfully removed, imported or exported; (c) otherwise liable to forfeiture to HM Revenue and Customs.	Vehicles and vessels only.	Anywhere.
5. Aviation Security Act 1982, s. 24B. Note: This power applies throughout the UK but the provisions of this Code will apply only when the power is exercised at an aerodrome situation in England and Wales.	Stolen articles or articles made, adapted or intended for use in the course of/in connection with conduct which constitutes an offence in the part of the UK where the aerodrome is situated or would so do, if it occurred there.	Persons, vehicles and aircraft. Anything in or on a vehicle or aircraft.	Any part of an aerodrome.

Power	Object of Search	Extent of Search	Where Exercisable
6. Police and Criminal Evidence Act 1984, s. 1. This includes section 10 of the Public Order Act 2023, which broadened the range of circumstances in which the power to stop and search under section 1 of PACE can be exercised.	Stolen goods.	Persons and vehicles.	Where there is public access.
	Articles made, adapted or intended for use in the course of or in connection with, certain offences under the Public Order Act 2023, the Theft Act 1968, Fraud Act 2006 and Criminal Damage Act 1971;	Persons and vehicles.	Where there is public access.
	Offensive weapons, Bladed or sharply-pointed articles (except folding pocket knives with a bladed cutting edge not exceeding 3 inches);	Persons and vehicles.	Where there is public access.
	Fireworks: Category 4 (display grade) fireworks if possession prohibited, Adult fireworks in possession of a person under 18 in a public place.	Persons and vehicles.	Where there is public access.
7. Sporting events (Control of Alcohol etc.) Act 1985, s. 7.	Intoxicating liquor.	Persons, coaches and trains.	Designated sports grounds or coaches and trains travelling to or from a designated sporting event.
8. Crossbows Act 1987, s. 4.	Crossbows or parts of crossbows (except crossbows with a draw weight of less than 1.4 kilograms).	Persons and vehicles.	Anywhere except dwellings.
9. Criminal Justice Act 1988 s. 139B.	Offensive weapons, bladed or sharply pointed article.	Persons.	School premises.
Evidence of game and wildlife offences			
10. Poaching Prevention Act 1862, s. 2.	Game or poaching equipment.	Persons and vehicles.	A public place.
11. Deer Act 1991, s. 12.	Evidence of offences under the Act.	Persons and vehicles.	Anywhere except dwellings.
12. Conservation of Seals Act 1970, s. 4.	Seals or hunting equipment.	Vehicles only.	Anywhere.
13. Protection of Badgers Act 1992, s. 11.	Evidence of offences under the Act.	Persons and vehicles.	Anywhere.
14. Wildlife and Countryside Act 1981, s. 19.	Evidence of wildlife offences.	Persons and vehicles.	Anywhere except dwellings.
Other			
15. Paragraphs 6 & 8 of Schedule 5 to the Terrorism Prevention and Investigation Measures Act 2011.	Anything that contravenes measures specified in a TPIM notice.	Persons in respect of whom a TPIM notice is being served or is in force.	Anywhere.

Power	Object of Search	Extent of Search	Where Exercisable
16. Paragraph 10 of Schedule 5 to the Terrorism Prevention and Investigation Measures Act 2011.	Anything that could be used to threaten or harm any person.	Persons in respect of whom a TPIM notice is in force.	Anywhere.
17. ***Not used***			
18. ***Not used***			
19. Section 60 Criminal Justice and Public Order Act 1994.	Offensive weapons or dangerous instruments to prevent incidents of serious violence or to deal with the carrying of such items or find such items which have been used in incidents of serious violence.	Persons and vehicles.	Anywhere within a locality authorised under subsection (1).
19A Paragraphs 6 & 8 of Schedule 11 to the National Security Act 2023	Anything that contravenes measures specified in an STPIM notice.	Persons in respects of whom a STPIM notice is being served or is in force.	Anywhere.
19B Paragraph 10 of Schedule 11 of the National Security Act 2023	Anything that could be used to threaten or harm any person.	Persons in respect of whom an STPIM notice is in force.	Anywhere.

ANNEX B—SELF-DEFINED ETHNIC CLASSIFICATION CATEGORIES

White	**W**
A. White–British	W1
B. White–Irish	W2
C. Any other White background	W9
Mixed	**M**
D. White and Black Caribbean	M1
E. White and Black African	M2
F. White and Asian	M3
G. Any other Mixed Background	M9
Asian/Asian–British	**A**
H. Asian–Indian	A1
I. Asian–Pakistani	A2
J. Asian–Bangladeshi	A3
K. Any other Asian background	A9
Black/Black-British	**B**
L. Black–Caribbean	B1
M. Black African	B2
N. Any other Black background	B9
Other	**O**
O. Chinese	O1
P. Any other	O9
Not Stated	**NS**

ANNEX C—SUMMARY OF POWERS OF COMMUNITY SUPPORT OFFICERS TO SEARCH AND SEIZE

The following is a summary of the search and seizure powers that may be exercised by a community support officer (CSO) who has been designated with the relevant powers in accordance with Part 4 of the Police Reform Act 2002.

When exercising any of these powers, a CSO must have regard to any relevant provisions of this Code, including section 3 governing the conduct of searches and the steps to be taken prior to a search.

1. *Not used*
2. Powers to search requiring the consent of the person and seizure

A CSO may detain a person using reasonable force where necessary as set out in Part 1 of Schedule 4 to the Police Reform Act 2002. If the person has been lawfully detained, the CSO may search the person provided that person gives consent to such a search in relation to the following:

Designation	Powers conferred	Object of Search	Extent of Search	Where Exercisable
Police Reform Act 2002, Schedule 4, paragraphs 7 and 7A.	(a) Criminal Justice and Police Act 2001, s. 12(2).	(a) Alcohol or a container for alcohol.	(a) Persons.	(a) Designated public place.
	(b) Confiscation of Alcohol (Young Persons) Act 1997, s. 1.	(b) Alcohol.	(b) Persons under 18 years old.	(b) Public place.
	(c) Children and Young Persons Act 1933, s. 7(3).	(c) Tobacco or cigarette papers.	(c) Persons under 16 years old found smoking.	(c) Public place.

3. Powers to search not requiring the consent of the person and seizure

A CSO may detain a person using reasonable force where necessary as set out in Part 1 of Schedule 4 to the Police Reform Act 2002. If the person has been lawfully detained, the CSO may search the person without the need for that person's consent in relation to the following:

Designation	Power conferred	Object of Search	Extent of Search	Where Exercisable
Police Reform Act 2002, Schedule 4, paragraph 2A.	Police and Criminal Evidence Act 1984, s. 32.	(a) Objects that might be used to cause physical injury to the person or the CSO. (b) Items that might be used to assist escape.	Persons made subject to a requirement to wait.	Any place where the requirement to wait has been made.

4. Powers to seize without consent

This power applies when drugs are found in the course of any search mentioned above.

Designation	Power conferred	Object of Search	Where Exercisable
Police Reform Act 2002, Schedule 4, paragraph 7B.	Police Reform Act 2002, Schedule 4, paragraph 7B.	Controlled drugs in a person's possession.	Any place where the person is in possession of the drug.

3.2 Entry, Search and Seizure

A thick grey line down the margin denotes text that is an extract of the PACE Code itself (i.e. the actual wording of the Code of Practice).

3.2.1 Introduction

The main police powers dealing with entry to premises, searching them and seizing evidence from them, are contained within the Police and Criminal Evidence Act 1984 (hereafter referred to as 'PACE84') and the PACE Code of Practice for searches of premises by police officers and the seizure of property found by police officers on persons or premises (hereafter referred to as 'Code B').

This chapter uses the December 2023 version of the Code as a framework to explain this area of the syllabus and incorporates relevant law within the keynotes where appropriate.

3.2.2 Code B—1 Introduction

1.1 This Code of Practice deals with police powers to:

- search premises
- seize and retain property found on premises and persons

1.1A These powers may be used to find:

- property and material relating to a crime
- wanted persons
- children who abscond from local authority accommodation where they have been remanded or committed by a court

1.2 A justice of the peace may issue a search warrant granting powers of entry, search and seizure, e.g. warrants to search for stolen property, drugs, firearms and evidence of serious offences. Police also have powers without a search warrant. The main ones provided by the Police and Criminal Evidence Act 1984 (PACE) include powers to search premises:

- to make an arrest
- after an arrest

1.3 The right to privacy and respect for personal property are key principles of the Human Rights Act 1998. Powers of entry, search and seizure should be fully and clearly justified before use because they may significantly interfere with the occupier's privacy. Officers should consider if the necessary objectives can be met by less intrusive means.

1.3A Powers to search and seize must be used fairly, responsibly, with respect for people who occupy premises being searched or are in charge of property being seized and without unlawful discrimination. Under the Equality Act 2010, section 149, when police officers are carrying out their functions, they also have a duty to have due regard to the need to eliminate unlawful discrimination, harassment and victimisation, to advance equality of opportunity between people who share a relevant protected characteristic and people who do not share it, and to take steps to foster good relations.

KEYNOTE

In para. 1.3A, 'relevant protected characteristic' includes: age, disability, gender reassignment, pregnancy and maternity, race, religion or belief, sex and sexual orientation.

1.4 In all cases, police should therefore:

- exercise their powers courteously and with respect for persons and property
- only use reasonable force when this is considered necessary and proportionate to the circumstances.

1.5 If the provisions of PACE and this Code are not observed, evidence obtained from a search may be open to question.

3.2.3 Code B—2 General

2.1 This Code must be readily available at all police stations for consultation by:

- police officers
- police staff
- detained persons
- members of the public

2.2 The *Notes for Guidance* [presented as Keynotes in this chapter] are not provisions of this Code.

2.3 This Code applies to searches of premises:

(a) by police for the purposes of an investigation into an alleged offence, with the occupier's consent, other than:
- routine scene of crime searches;
- calls to a fire or burglary made by or on behalf of an occupier or searches following the activation of fire or burglar alarms or discovery of insecure premises;
- searches when *paragraph 5.4* applies;
- bomb threat calls;

(b) under powers conferred on police officers by PACE, sections 17, 18 and 32;

(c) undertaken in pursuance of search warrants issued to and executed by constables in accordance with PACE, sections 15 and 16;

KEYNOTE

Sections 15 and 16 of PACE84 apply to all search warrants issued to and executed by constables under any enactment, e.g. search warrants issued by:

(a) a justice of the peace under:
- Theft Act 1968, s. 26—stolen property;
- Misuse of Drugs Act 1971, s. 23—controlled drugs;
- PACE84, s. 8—evidence of an indictable offence;
- Terrorism Act 2000, sch. 5, para. 1;
- Terrorism Prevention and Investigation Measures Act 2011, sch. 5, para. 8(2)(b)—search of premises for compliance purposes;

(b) a Circuit judge under:
- PACE84, sch. 1;
- Terrorism Act 2000, sch. 5, para. 11;

(ba) a judge entitled to exercise the jurisdiction of the Crown Court under the National Security Act 2023, sch. 2, para. 9(1).

(d) subject to *paragraph 2.6*, under any other power given to police to enter premises with or without a search warrant for any purpose connected with the investigation into an alleged, suspected or anticipated offence.

For the purposes of this Code, 'premises' as defined in PACE, section 23, includes any place, vehicle, vessel, aircraft, hovercraft, tent or movable structure and any offshore installation as defined in the Mineral Workings (Offshore Installations) Act 1971, section 1.

KEYNOTE

Examples of the other powers in para. 2.3(d) include:

(a) Road Traffic Act 1988, s. 6E(1) giving police power to enter premises under s. 6E(1) to:
- require a person to provide a specimen of breath; or
- arrest a person following
  - a positive breath test;
  - failure to provide a specimen of breath;

(b) Transport and Works Act 1992, s. 30(4) giving police powers to enter premises mirroring the powers in (a) in relation to specified persons working on transport systems to which the Act applies;

(c) Criminal Justice Act 1988, s. 139B giving police power to enter and search school premises for offensive weapons, bladed or pointed articles;

(d) Terrorism Act 2000, sch. 5, paras 3 and 15 empowering a superintendent in urgent cases to give written authority for police to enter and search premises for the purposes of a terrorist investigation;

(da) National Security Act 2023, sch. 2, para. 12 empowering a superintendent in urgent cases to give written authority for police to enter and search a premises for the purposes of state threats investigation;

(e) Explosives Act 1875, s. 73(b) empowering a superintendent to give written authority for police to enter premises, examine and search them for explosives;

(f) search warrants and production orders or the equivalent issued in Scotland or Northern Ireland endorsed under the Summary Jurisdiction (Process) Act 1881 or the Petty Sessions (Ireland) Act 1851 respectively for execution in England and Wales;

(g) Terrorism Prevention and Investigation Measures Act 2011, sch. 5, paras 5(1), 6(2)(b) and 7(2), searches relating to TPIM notices (**see para. 10.1**).

(ga) National Security Act 2023, sch. 11, paras 5(1), 6(2)(b) and 8(2)(b) searches relating to STPIM notices.

2.4 A person who has not been arrested but is searched during a search of premises should be searched in accordance with Code A.

KEYNOTE

Search of Persons

The Criminal Justice Act 1988, s. 139B provides that a constable who has reasonable grounds for suspecting that an offence under the Criminal Justice Act 1988, s. 139A or 139AA has been or is being committed may enter school premises and search the premises and any persons on the premises for any bladed or pointed article or offensive weapon. Persons may be searched under a warrant issued under the Misuse of Drugs Act 1971, s. 23(3) to search premises for drugs or documents only if the warrant specifically authorises the search of persons on the premises. Powers to search premises under certain national security provisions also authorise the search of persons on the premises, e.g. under paras 1, 2, 11 and 15 of sch. 5 to the Terrorism Act 2000, s. 52 of the Anti-terrorism, Crime and Security Act 2001 and paras 2, 9 and 12 of the National Security Act 2023.

2.5 This Code does not apply to the exercise of a statutory power to enter premises or to inspect goods, equipment or procedures if the exercise of that power is not dependent on the existence of grounds for suspecting that an offence may have been committed and the person exercising the power has no reasonable grounds for such suspicion.

2.6 This Code does not affect any directions or requirements of a search warrant, order or other power to search and seize lawfully exercised in England or Wales that any item or evidence seized under that warrant, order or power be handed over to a police force, court, tribunal, or other authority outside England or Wales. For example, warrants and orders issued in Scotland or Northern Ireland, and search warrants and powers provided for in sections 14 to 17 of the Crime (International Co-operation) Act 2003.

2.7 When this Code requires the prior authority or agreement of an officer of at least inspector or superintendent rank, that authority may be given by a sergeant or chief inspector authorised to perform the functions of the higher rank under PACE, section 107.

KEYNOTE

Police Officers Performing Duties of Higher Rank

Paragraph 2.7 refers to PACE84, s. 107 which states:

(1) For the purpose of any provision of this Act or any other Act under which a power in respect of the investigation of offences or the treatment of persons in police custody is exercisable only by or with the authority of a police officer of at least the rank of superintendent, an officer of the rank of chief inspector shall be treated as holding the rank of superintendent if:

(a) he has been authorised by an officer holding a rank above the rank of superintendent to exercise the power or, as the case may be, to give his authority for its exercise, or

(b) he is acting during the absence of an officer holding the rank of superintendent who has authorised him, for the duration of that absence, to exercise the power or, as the case may be, to give his authority for its exercise.

(2) For the purpose of any provision of this Act or any other Act under which such a power is exercisable only by or with the authority of an officer of at least the rank of inspector, an officer of the rank of sergeant shall be treated as holding the rank of inspector if he has been authorised by an officer of at least the rank of superintendent to exercise the power or, as the case may be, to give his authority for its exercise.

2.8 Written records required under this Code not made in the search record shall, unless otherwise specified, be made:

- in the recording officer's pocket book ('pocket book' includes any official report book issued to police officers) or
- on forms provided for the purpose.

2.9 Nothing in this Code requires the identity of officers, or anyone accompanying them during a search of premises, to be recorded or disclosed:

(a) in the case of enquiries linked to the investigation of terrorism; or

(b) if officers reasonably believe recording or disclosing their names might put them in danger.

In these cases officers should use warrant or other identification numbers and the name of their police station. Police staff should use any identification number provided to them by the police force.

KEYNOTE

The purpose of para. 2.9(b) of Code B is to protect those involved in serious organised crime investigations or arrests of particularly violent suspects when there is reliable information that those arrested or their associates may threaten or cause harm to the officers or anyone accompanying them during a search of premises. In cases of doubt, an officer of inspector rank or above should be consulted.

2.10 The 'officer in charge of the search' means the officer assigned specific duties and responsibilities under this Code. Whenever there is a search of premises to which this Code applies one officer must act as the officer in charge of the search.

KEYNOTE

For the purposes of para. 2.10, the officer in charge of the search should normally be the most senior officer present. Some exceptions are:

(a) a supervising officer who attends or assists at the scene of a premises search may appoint an officer of lower rank as officer in charge of the search if that officer is:
- more conversant with the facts;
- a more appropriate officer to be in charge of the search;

(b) when all officers in a premises search are the same rank. The supervising officer if available must make sure one of them is appointed officer in charge of the search, otherwise the officers themselves must nominate one of their number as the officer in charge;

(c) a senior officer assisting in a specialist role. This officer need not be regarded as having a general supervisory role over the conduct of the search or be appointed or expected to act as the officer in charge of the search.

Except in (c), nothing in this Keynote diminishes the role and responsibilities of a supervisory officer who is present at the search or knows of a search taking place.

2.11 In this Code:

(a) 'designated person' means a person other than a police officer, designated under the Police Reform Act 2002, Part 4 who has specified powers and duties of police officers conferred or imposed on them;

(b) any reference to a police officer includes a designated person acting in the exercise or performance of the powers and duties conferred or imposed on them by their designation;

(c) a person authorised to accompany police officers or designated persons in the execution of a warrant has the same powers as a constable in the execution of the warrant and the search and seizure of anything related to the warrant. These powers must be exercised in the company and under the supervision of a police officer.

KEYNOTE

In relation to para. 2.11(a), an officer of the rank of inspector or above may direct a designated investigating officer not to wear a uniform for the purposes of a specific operation.

Paragraph 2.11(c) connects to s. 16(2) of PACE84, which states that a search warrant may authorise persons other than police officers to accompany the constable who executes the warrant. This includes, for example, any suitably qualified or skilled person or an expert in a particular field whose presence is needed to help accurately identify the material sought or to advise where certain evidence is most likely to be found and how it should be dealt with. It does not give them any right to force entry, but it gives them the right to be on the premises during the search and to search for or seize property without the occupier's permission.

2.12 If a power conferred on a designated person:

(a) allows reasonable force to be used when exercised by a police officer, a designated person exercising that power has the same entitlement to use force;

(b) includes power to use force to enter any premises, that power is not exercisable by that designated person except:

(i) in the company and under the supervision of a police officer; or

(ii) for the purpose of:
- saving life or limb; or
- preventing serious damage to property.

2.13 Designated persons must have regard to any relevant provisions of the Codes of Practice.

3.2.4 Code B—3 Search warrants and production orders

(a) Before making an application

3.1 When information appears to justify an application, the officer must take reasonable steps to check the information is accurate, recent and not provided maliciously or irresponsibly. An application may not be made on the basis of information from an anonymous source if corroboration has not been sought.

KEYNOTE

The identity of an informant need not be disclosed when making an application, but the officer should be prepared to answer any questions the magistrate or judge may have about:

- the accuracy of previous information from that source;
- any other related matters.

3.2 The officer shall ascertain as specifically as possible the nature of the articles concerned and their location.

3.3 The officer shall make reasonable enquiries to:

(i) establish if:

- anything is known about the likely occupier of the premises and the nature of the premises themselves;
- the premises have been searched previously and how recently;

(ii) obtain any other relevant information.

3.4 An application:

(a) to a justice of the peace for a search warrant or to a Circuit judge for a search warrant or production order under PACE, Schedule 1 must be supported by a signed written authority from an officer of inspector rank or above:

Note: *If the case is an urgent application to a justice of the peace and an inspector or above is not readily available, the next most senior officer on duty can give the written authority.*

(b) to a circuit judge under the Terrorism Act 2000, Schedule 5 or a judge under the National Security Act 2023, Schedule 2 for

- a production order;
- search warrant; or
- an order requiring an explanation of material seized or produced under such a warrant or production order

must be supported by a signed written authority from an officer of superintendent rank or above.

3.5 Except in a case of urgency, if there is reason to believe a search might have an adverse effect on relations between the police and the community, the officer in charge shall consult the local police/community liaison officer:

- before the search; or
- in urgent cases, as soon as practicable after the search.

(b) Making an application

3.6 A search warrant application must be supported in writing, specifying:

(a) the enactment under which the application is made;

(b)

(i) whether the warrant is to authorise entry and search of:

- one set of premises; or
- if the application is under PACE section 8, or Schedule 1, paragraph 12, NSA 2023 Schedule 2, paragraphs 2 or 9; or TACT 2000 Schedule 5 paragraphs 1 or 11, more

than one set of specified premises or all premises occupied or controlled by a specified person; and

(ii) the premises to be searched;

(c) the object of the search;

(d) the grounds for the application, including, when the purpose of the proposed search is to find evidence of an alleged offence, an indication of how the evidence relates to the investigation;

(da) Where the application is under PACE section 8, or Schedule 1, paragraph 12; NSA 2023 Schedule 2, paragraphs 2 or 9; or TACT Schedule 5 paragraphs 1 or 11; for a single warrant to enter and search:

(i) more than one set of specified premises, the officer must specify each set of premises which it is desired to enter and search

(ii) all premises occupied or controlled by a specified person, the officer must specify:

- as many sets of premises which it is desired to enter and search as it is reasonably practicable to specify;
- the person who is in occupation or control of those premises and any others which it is desired to search;
- why it is necessary to search more premises than those which can be specified;
- why it is not reasonably practicable to specify all the premises which it is desired to enter and search;

(db) Whether an application under PACE section 8 is for a warrant authorising entry and search on more than one occasion, and if so, the officer must state the grounds for this and whether the desired number of entries authorised is unlimited or a specified maximum;

(e) That there are no reasonable grounds to believe the material to be sought, when making application to a:

(i) justice of the peace or a Circuit judge consists of or includes items subject to legal privilege;

(ii) justice of the peace, consists of or includes excluded material or special procedure material;

(ea) That, in the case of applications under powers in the National Security Act 2023, there are no reasonable grounds to suspect the material to be sought, when making an application to a:

(i) justice of the peace consists of or includes confidential material;

(ii) judge entitled to exercise the jurisdiction of the Crown Court includes items subject to legal privilege;

Note: this does not affect the additional powers of seizure in the Criminal Justice and Police Act 2001, Part 2 covered in *paragraph 7.7;*

(f) if applicable, a request for the warrant to authorise a person or persons to accompany the officer who executes the warrant.

KEYNOTE

In relation to para. 3.6(c) (the object of the search), the information supporting a search warrant application should be as specific as possible, particularly in relation to the articles or persons being sought and where in the premises it is suspected they may be found.

Items Subject to Legal Privilege

Material which falls within the definition in s. 10 of the 1984 Act is subject to legal privilege which means that it cannot be searched for or seized.

PACE84, s. 10 states:

(1) Subject to subsection (2) below, in this Act 'items subject to legal privilege' means—

(a) communications between a professional legal adviser and his client or any person representing his client made in connection with the giving of legal advice to the client;

(b) communications between a professional legal adviser and his client or any person representing his client or between such an adviser or his client or any such representative and any other person made in connection with or in contemplation of legal proceedings and for the purposes of such proceedings; and

(c) items enclosed with or referred to in such communications and made—

(i) in connection with the giving of legal advice; or

(ii) in connection with or in contemplation of legal proceedings and for the purposes of such proceedings,

when they are in the possession of a person who is entitled to possession of them.

Items held with the intention of furthering a criminal purpose are not subject to this privilege (s. 10(2)). When making an application for a warrant to search for and seize such material the procedure under sch. 1 should be used. Occasions where this will happen are rare and would include instances where a solicitor's firm is the subject of a criminal investigation (*R* v *Leeds Crown Court, ex parte Switalski* [1991] Crim LR 559). However, it may be possible during a search to ascertain which material is subject to legal privilege and which might be lawfully seized under the warrant being executed. Therefore, although a warrant cannot authorise a search for legally privileged material, the fact that such material is inadvertently seized in the course of a search authorised by a proper warrant does not render the search unlawful (*R* v *HM Customs and Excise, ex parte Popely* [2000] Crim LR 388).

Excluded Material

Access to 'excluded material' can generally only be gained by applying to a judge for a production order under the procedure set out in s. 9 of, and sch. 1 to PACE84 and Code B. That strict statutory procedure also applies to the application for and execution of warrants by investigating officers designated under sch. 4 to the Police Reform Act 2002.

PACE84, s. 11 states:

(1) Subject to the following provisions of this section, in this Act 'excluded material' means—

(a) personal records which a person has acquired or created in the course of any trade, business, profession or other occupation or for the purposes of any paid or unpaid office and which he holds in confidence;

(b) human tissue or tissue fluid which has been taken for the purposes of diagnosis or medical treatment and which a person holds in confidence;

(c) journalistic material which a person holds in confidence and which consists—

(i) of documents; or

(ii) of records other than documents.

(2) A person holds material other than journalistic material in confidence for the purposes of this section if he holds it subject—

(a) to an express or implied undertaking to hold it in confidence; or

(b) to a restriction on disclosure or an obligation of secrecy contained in any enactment, including an enactment contained in an Act passed after this Act.

(3) A person holds journalistic material in confidence for the purposes of this section if—

(a) he holds it subject to such an undertaking, restriction or obligation; and

(b) it has been continuously held (by one or more persons) subject to such an undertaking, restriction or obligation since it was first acquired or created for the purposes of journalism.

Medical records and dental records would fall into this category, as might records made by priests or religious advisers.

'Personal records' are defined under s. 12 of the 1984 Act and include records relating to the physical or mental health, counselling or assistance given to an individual who can be identified by those records.

'Journalistic material' is defined under s. 13 as material acquired or created for the purposes of journalism.

Special Procedure Material

Special procedure material can be gained by applying for a search warrant or a production order under sch. 1 to PACE84.

PACE84, s. 14 states:

(1) In this Act 'special procedure material' means—

(a) material to which subsection (2) below applies; and

(b) journalistic material, other than excluded material.

(2) Subject to the following provisions of this section, this subsection applies to material, other than items subject to legal privilege and excluded material, in the possession of a person who—

(a) acquired or created it in the course of any trade, business, profession or other occupation or for the purpose of any paid or unpaid office; and

(b) holds it subject—
(i) to an express or implied undertaking to hold it in confidence; or
(ii) to a restriction or obligation such as is mentioned in section 11(2)(b) above.

The person believed to be in possession of the material must have come by it under the circumstances set out at s. 14(2)(a) and must hold it under the undertakings or obligations set out at s. 14(2)(b).

3.7 A search warrant application under PACE, Schedule 1, paragraph 12(a), shall if appropriate indicate why it is believed service of notice of an application for a production order may seriously prejudice the investigation. Applications for search warrants under the Terrorism Act 2000, Schedule 5, paragraph 11 must indicate why a production order would not be appropriate.

3.8 If a search warrant application is refused, a further application may not be made for those premises unless supported by additional grounds.

KEYNOTE

Connection to s. 15 PACE84

Section 3 of Code B mirrors the content of s. 15 of PACE84 (dealing with the application for a search warrant and the safeguards associated with that application). It should be noted that s. 15 of PACE84 (and therefore section 3 of Code B) applies to all search warrants issued to and executed by constables under any enactment.

An application for a warrant will be made 'ex parte' (in private (s. 15(3)).

The details of the extent of the proposed search should be made clear in the application and the officer swearing the warrant out must be prepared to answer any questions put to him/her on oath under s. 15(4). Courts will go into background detail about the particular premises, or part of the premises, and who is likely to be present on the premises at the time the warrant is executed (e.g. children).

A warrant shall specify:

- the name of the person who applies for it;
- the date on which it is issued;
- the enactment under which it is issued;
- each set of premises to be searched, or (in the case of an all premises warrant) the person who is in occupation or control of premises to be searched, together with any premises under their occupation or control which can be specified and which are to be searched; and
- shall identify, so far as is practicable, of the articles or persons to be sought.

(s. 15(6))

Two copies shall be made of a warrant which specifies only one set of premises and does not authorise multiple entries; and as many copies as are reasonably required may be made of any other kind of warrant (s. 15(7)); the copies shall be clearly certified as copies (s. 15(8)).

3.2.5 Search Warrants for Indictable Offences

Section 8 of PACE84 provides a power to a justice of the peace to issue a warrant authorising the search and entry into premises connected to indictable offences.

PACE84, s. 8 states:

(1) If on an application made by a constable a justice of the peace is satisfied that there are reasonable grounds for believing—
(a) that an indictable offence has been committed; and
(b) that there is material on premises mentioned in subsection (1A) below which is likely to be of substantial value (whether by itself or together with other material) to the investigation of the offence; and
(c) that the material is likely to be relevant evidence; and

(d) that it does not consist of or include items subject to legal privilege, excluded material or special procedure material; and

(e) that any of the conditions specified in subsection (3) below applies in relation to each set of premises specified in the application,

he may issue a warrant authorising a constable to enter and search the premises.

(1A) The premises referred to in subsection (1)(b) above are—

(a) one or more sets of premises specified in the application (in which case the application is for a 'specific premises warrant'); or

(b) any premises occupied or controlled by a person specified in the application, including such sets of premises as are so specified (in which case the application is for an 'all premises warrant').

(1B) If the application is for an all premises warrant, the justice of the peace must also be satisfied—

(a) that because of the particulars of the offence referred to in paragraph (a) of subsection (1) above, there are reasonable grounds for believing that it is necessary to search premises occupied or controlled by the person in question which are not specified in the application in order to find the material referred to in paragraph (b) of that subsection; and

(b) that it is not reasonably practicable to specify in the application all the premises which he occupies or controls and which might need to be searched.

(1C) The warrant may authorise entry to and search of premises on more than one occasion if, on the application, the justice of the peace is satisfied that it is necessary to authorise multiple entries in order to achieve the purpose for which he issues the warrant.

(1D) If it authorises multiple entries, the number of entries authorised may be unlimited, or limited to a maximum.

(2) A constable may seize and retain anything for which a search has been authorised under subsection (1) above.

(3) The conditions mentioned in subsection (1)(e) above are—

(a) that it is not practicable to communicate with any person entitled to grant entry to the premises;

(b) that it is practicable to communicate with a person entitled to grant entry to the premises but it is not practicable to communicate with any person entitled to grant access to the evidence;

(c) that entry to the premises will not be granted unless a warrant is produced;

(d) that the purpose of a search may be frustrated or seriously prejudiced unless a constable arriving at the premises can secure immediate entry to them.

(4) In this Act 'relevant evidence', in relation to an offence, means anything that would be admissible in evidence at a trial for the offence.

(5) The power to issue a warrant conferred by this section is in addition to any such power otherwise conferred.

KEYNOTE

There must be reasonable grounds for believing that material which is likely to be of substantial value to the investigation of the offence is on the premises specified. Therefore, when executing such a warrant, the officer must be able to show that any material seized thereunder fell within that description (*R* v *Chief Constable of the Warwickshire Constabulary, ex parte Fitzpatrick* [1999] 1 WLR 564).

Possession of a warrant under s. 8 does not authorise police officers to seize all material found on the relevant premises to be taken away and 'sifted' somewhere else (*R* v *Chesterfield Justices, ex parte Bramley* [2000] QB 576) (see s. 50 of the Criminal Justice and Police Act 2001 for the power to 'seize and sift'). This means that material which is solely of value for intelligence purposes may not be seized under a s. 8 warrant.

The power to apply for and execute a warrant under s. 8 and to carry out the actions under s. 8(2) are among those powers that can be conferred on a person designated as an investigating officer under sch. 4 to the Police Reform Act 2002.

The conditions set out under s. 8(1)(e) are part of the application process, not part of the general execution process (which is set out at s. 16 (**see para. 3.2.6**)). Therefore the officer swearing out a s. 8 warrant will have to satisfy the court that any of those conditions apply.

3.2.6 Execution of a Warrant

Execution of a Warrant—s. 16 PACE84

The procedures connected to the execution of a search warrant are contained in s. 16 of PACE84—they apply to all search warrants executed by constables under any enactment.

PACE84, s. 16 states:

(1) A warrant to enter and search premises may be executed by any constable.
(2) Such a warrant may authorise persons to accompany any constable who is executing it.
(2A) A person so authorised has the same powers as the constable whom he accompanies in respect of—
  (a) the execution of the warrant, and
  (b) the seizure of anything to which the warrant relates.
(2B) But he may exercise those powers only in the company, and under the supervision, of a constable.
(3) Entry and search under a warrant must be within three months from the date of its issue.
(3A) If the warrant is an all premises warrant, no premises which are not specified in it may be entered or searched unless a police officer of at least the rank of inspector has in writing authorised them to be entered.
(3B) No premises may be entered or searched for the second or any subsequent time under a warrant which authorises multiple entries unless a police officer of at least the rank of inspector has in writing authorised that entry to those premises.
(4) Entry and search under a warrant must be at a reasonable hour unless it appears to the constable executing it that the purpose of a search may be frustrated on an entry at a reasonable hour.
(5) Where the occupier of premises which are to be entered and searched is present at the time when a constable seeks to execute a warrant to enter and search them, the constable—
  (a) shall identify himself to the occupier and, if not in uniform, shall produce to him documentary evidence that he is a constable;
  (b) shall produce the warrant to him; and
  (c) shall supply him with a copy of it.
(6) Where—
  (a) the occupier of such premises is not present at the time when a constable seeks to execute such a warrant; but
  (b) some other person who appears to the constable to be in charge of the premises is present,
  subsection (5) above shall have effect as if any reference to the occupier were a reference to that other person.
(7) If there is no person present who appears to the constable to be in charge of the premises, he shall leave a copy of the warrant in a prominent place on the premises.
(8) A search under a warrant may only be a search to the extent required for the purpose for which the warrant was issued.
(9) A constable executing the warrant shall make an endorsement on it stating—
  (a) whether the articles or persons sought were found; and
  (b) whether any articles were seized, other than articles which were sought;
  and unless the warrant is a warrant specifying one set of premises only, he shall do so separately in respect of each set of premises entered and searched, which he shall in each case state in the endorsement.
(10) A warrant shall be returned to the appropriate person mentioned in subsection (10A) below—
  (a) when it has been executed; or
  (b) in the case of a specific premises warrant which has not been executed, or an all premises warrant, or any warrant authorising multiple entries, upon the expiry of the period of three months referred to in subsection (3) above or sooner.
(10A) The appropriate person is—
  (a) if the warrant was issued by a justice of the peace, the designated officer for the local justice area in which the justice was acting when he issued the warrant;
  (b) if it was issued by a judge, the appropriate officer of the court from which he issued it.
(11) A warrant which is returned under subsection (10) above shall be retained for 12 months from its return—
  (a) by the designated officer for the local justice area, if it was returned under paragraph (i) of that subsection; and
  (b) by the appropriate officer, if it was returned under paragraph (ii).

(12) If during the period for which a warrant is to be retained the occupier of premises to which it relates asks to inspect it, he shall be allowed to do so.

KEYNOTE

Entry and search under a warrant must be within three months from date of issue (s. 16(3)) except for warrants under s. 23 of the Misuse of Drugs Act 1971 where the time frame for entry and search is *one month.*

If the provisions of ss. 15 and 16 of PACE84 are not fully complied with, any entry and search made under a warrant will be unlawful. Although the officers executing the warrant may have some protection from personal liability where there has been a defect in the procedure by which the warrant was issued, failure to follow the requirements of ss. 15 and 16 may result in the exclusion of any evidence obtained under the warrant. Therefore, where officers failed to provide the occupier of the searched premises with a copy of the warrant (under s.16(5)(c)), they were obliged to return the property seized during the search (*R* v *Chief Constable of Lancashire, ex parte Parker* [1993] QB 577).

If a warrant itself is invalid for some reason, any entry and subsequent seizure made under it are unlawful (*R* v *Central Criminal Court and British Railways Board, ex parte AJD Holdings Ltd* [1992] Crim LR 669).

Very minor departures from the letter of the warrant, however, will not render any search unlawful (*Attorney-General of Jamaica* v *Williams* [1998] AC 351).

3.2.7

Code B—4 Entry without warrant—particular powers

(a) Making an arrest etc.

4.1 The conditions under which an officer may enter and search premises without a warrant are set out in PACE, section 17. It should be noted that this section does not create or confer any powers of arrest.

KEYNOTE

Power of Entry—s.17 PACE84

PACE84, s. 17 states:

(1) Subject to the following provisions of this section, and without prejudice to any other enactment, a constable may enter and search any premises for the purpose—
- (a) of executing—
  - (i) a warrant of arrest issued in connection with or arising out of criminal proceedings; or
  - (ii) a warrant of commitment issued under section 76 of the Magistrates' Courts Act 1980;
- (b) of arresting a person for an indictable offence;
- (c) of arresting a person for an offence under—
  - (i) section 1 (prohibition of uniforms in connection with political objectives) of the Public Order Act 1936;
  - (ii) any enactment contained in sections 6 to 8 or 10 of the Criminal Law Act 1977 (offences relating to entering and remaining on property);
  - (iii) section 4 of the Public Order Act 1986 (fear or provocation of violence);
  - (iiia) section 4 (driving etc. when under influence of drink or drugs) or 163 (failure to stop when required to do so by constable in uniform) of the Road Traffic Act 1988;
  - (iiib) section 27 of the Transport and Works Act 1992 (which relates to offences involving drink or drugs);
  - (iv) section 76 of the Criminal Justice and Public Order Act 1994 (failure to comply with interim possession order);
  - (v) any of sections 4, 5, 6(1) and (2), 7 and 8(1) and (2) of the Animal Welfare Act 2006 (offences relating to the prevention of harm to animals);
  - (vi) section 144 of the Legal Aid, Sentencing and Punishment of Offenders Act 2012 (squatting in a residential building);
- (ca) of arresting, in pursuance of section 32(1A) of the Children and Young Persons Act 1969, any child or young person who has been remanded or committed to local authority accommodation or youth detention accommodation under section 91 of the Legal Aid, Sentencing and Punishment of Offenders Act 2012;
- (caa) of arresting a person for an offence to which section 61 of the Animal Health Act 1981 applies;

(cab) of arresting a person under any of the following provisions—
   (i) section 30D(1) or (2A);
   (ii) section 46A(1) or (1A);
   (iii) section 5B(7) of the Bail Act 1976 (arrest where a person fails to surrender to custody in accordance with a court order);
   (iv) section 7(3) of the Bail Act 1976 (arrest where a person is not likely to surrender to custody etc.);
   (v) section 97(1) of the Legal Aid, Sentencing and Punishment of Offenders Act 2012 (arrest where a child is suspected of breaking conditions of remand);
(cb) of recapturing any person who is, or is deemed for any purpose to be, unlawfully at large while liable to be detained—
   (i) in a prison, young offender institution, secure training centre or secure college, or
   (ii) in pursuance of section 92 of the Powers of Criminal Courts (Sentencing) Act 2000 or section 260 of the Sentencing Code (dealing with children and young persons guilty of grave crimes), in any other place;
(d) of recapturing any person whatever who is unlawfully at large and whom he is pursuing; or
(e) of saving life or limb or preventing serious damage to property.

(2) Except for the purpose specified in paragraph (e) of subsection (1) above, the powers of entry and search conferred by this section—
   (a) are only exercisable if the constable has reasonable grounds for believing that the person whom he is seeking is on the premises; and
   (b) are limited, in relation to premises consisting of two or more separate dwellings, to powers to enter and search—
      (i) any parts of the premises which the occupiers of any dwelling comprised in the premises use in common with the occupiers of any other such dwelling; and
      (ii) any such dwelling in which the constable has reasonable grounds for believing that the person whom he is seeking may be.

(3) The powers of entry and search conferred by this section are only exercisable for the purposes specified in subsection (1)(c)(ii), (iv) or (vi) above by a constable in uniform.

(4) The power of search conferred by this section is only a power to search to the extent that is reasonably required for the purpose for which the power of entry is exercised.

(5) Subject to subsection (6) below, all the rules of common law under which a constable has power to enter premises without a warrant are hereby abolished.

(6) Nothing in subsection (5) above affects any power of entry to deal with or prevent a breach of the peace.

Use of Force

Force may be used in exercising the power of entry where it is necessary to do so. In a case where police had been called to an address by an abandoned 999 call, the officers had to move a man away from the front door in order to gain entry under s. 17. It was held that the officers had the power to use reasonable force in order to do so under s. 117 of PACE84 (*Smith (Peter John)* v *DPP* [2001] EWHC Admin 55). Generally, the officer should first attempt to communicate with the occupier of the premises, explaining by what authority and for what purpose entry is to be made, before making a forcible entry. Clearly though, there will be occasions where such communication is impossible, impracticable or unnecessary; in those cases there is no need for the officer to enter into such an explanation (*O'Loughlin* v *Chief Constable of Essex* [1998] 1 WLR 374).

Unlawfully at Large

The term 'unlawfully at large' (used at s. 17(1)(cb)) does not have a statutory meaning and can apply to someone who is subject to an order under the Mental Health Act 1983 or someone who has escaped from custody. The pursuit of the person who is unlawfully at large must be 'fresh' and entry must effectively be contemporaneous with that pursuit (the power will only be available while the officer is actually 'pursuing' the person concerned (*D'Souza* v *DPP* [1992] 1 WLR 1073)).

Saving Life and Limb or Preventing Serious Damage to Property

The officer must have reasonable grounds to believe that the person is on the premises in all cases except saving life and limb at s. 17(1)(e). In *Syed* v *DPP* [2010] EWHC 81 (Admin), the court stated that 'concern for the welfare' of a person was not sufficient to enter properties using the power under s. 17(1)(e), it was too low a threshold. The power to enter and search any premises in the relevant police area for the purpose of saving life or limb or preventing serious damage to property as above is among those that can be conferred on a designated person under sch. 4 to the Police Reform Act 2002.

(b) Search of premises where arrest takes place or the arrested person was immediately before arrest

4.2 When a person has been arrested for an indictable offence, a police officer has power under PACE, section 32 to search the premises where the person was arrested or where the person was immediately before being arrested.

KEYNOTE

Search upon Arrest—s. 32 PACE84

PACE84, s. 32 states:

(1) A constable may search an arrested person, in any case where the person to be searched has been arrested at a place other than a police station, if the constable has reasonable grounds for believing that the arrested person may present a danger to himself or others.
(2) Subject to subsections (3) to (5) below, a constable shall also have power in any such case—
  (a) to search the arrested person for anything—
    (i) which he might use to assist him to escape from lawful custody; or
    (ii) which might be evidence relating to an offence; and
  (b) if the offence for which he has been arrested is an indictable offence, to enter and search any premises in which he was when arrested or immediately before he was arrested for evidence relating to the offence.
(3) The power to search conferred by subsection (2) above is only a power to search to the extent that is reasonably required for the purpose of discovering any such thing or any such evidence.
(4) The powers conferred by this section to search a person are not to be construed as authorising a constable to require a person to remove any of his clothing in public other than an outer coat, jacket or gloves but they do authorise a search of a person's mouth.
(5) A constable may not search a person in the exercise of the power conferred by subsection (2)(a) above unless he has reasonable grounds for believing that the person to be searched may have concealed on him anything for which a search is permitted under that paragraph.
(6) A constable may not search premises in the exercise of the power conferred by subsection (2)(b) above unless he has reasonable grounds for believing that there is evidence for which a search is permitted under that paragraph on the premises.
(7) In so far as the power of search conferred by subsection (2)(b) above relates to premises consisting of two or more separate dwellings, it is limited to a power to search—
  (a) any dwelling in which the arrest took place or in which the person arrested was immediately before his arrest; and
  (b) any parts of the premises which the occupier of any such dwelling uses in common with the occupiers of any other dwellings comprised in the premises.
(8) A constable searching a person in the exercise of the power conferred by subsection (1) above may seize and retain anything he finds, if he has reasonable grounds for believing that the person searched might use it to cause physical injury to himself or to any other person.
(9) A constable searching a person in the exercise of the power conferred by subsection (2)(a) above may seize and retain anything he finds, other than an item subject to legal privilege, if he has reasonable grounds for believing—
  (a) that he might use it to assist him to escape from lawful custody; or
  (b) that it is evidence of an offence or has been obtained in consequence of the commission of an offence.
(10) Nothing in this section shall be taken to affect the power conferred by section 43 of the Terrorism Act 2000.

Search of Persons under s. 32 PACE84

The power under s. 32(1) *does not* authorise a search of a person arrested at a police station; if a person is arrested at a police station, the search must be authorised by the custody officer under s. 54 of PACE84.

Search of Premises under s. 32 PACE84

The power under s. 32(2)(b) is one for use *at the time of arrest* and should not be used to return to the relevant premises some time after the arrest in the way that s. 18 of PACE84 may be used (*R* v *Badham* [1987] Crim LR 202). Officers exercising their power to enter and search under s. 32 must have a genuine belief that there is evidence on the premises; it is not a licence for a general fishing expedition (*R* v *Beckford* [1992] 94 Cr App R 43). The Divisional Court has refused to allow s. 32 to be used in a situation where the arrested person had not been in the relevant premises (where he did not live) for a period of over two hours preceding his arrest and where there were no reasonable grounds for believing that he presented a danger to himself or others (*Hewitson* v *Chief Constable of Dorset Police* [2003] EWHC 3296 (QB)).

Common Law Power of Search and Seizure after Arrest

The House of Lords has confirmed that the police have a common law power to search for and seize property after a lawful arrest (*R* v *Governor of Pentonville Prison, ex parte Osman* [1990] 1 WLR 277). This decision was confirmed by the House of Lords in *R (On the Application of Rottman)* v *Commissioner of Police of the Metropolis* [2002] UKHL 20. In *Rottman*, it was held that it was a well-established principle of the common law that an arresting officer had the power to search a room in which a person had been arrested (per *Ghani* v *Jones* [1970] 1 QB 693). This extended power is not limited to purely 'domestic' offences, but also applies to cases involving extradition offences.

(c) Search of premises occupied or controlled by the arrested person

4.3 The specific powers to search premises which are occupied or controlled by a person arrested for an indictable offence are set out in PACE, section 18. They may not be exercised, except if section 18(5) applies, unless an officer of inspector rank or above has given written authority. That authority should only be given when the authorising officer is satisfied that the premises are occupied or controlled by the arrested person and that the necessary grounds exist. If possible the authorising officer should record the authority on the Notice of Powers and Rights and, subject to *paragraph 2.9*, sign the Notice. The record of the grounds for the search and the nature of the evidence sought as required by section 18(7) of the Act should be made in:

- the custody record if there is one, otherwise
- the officer's pocket book, or
- the search record.

KEYNOTE

Entry and Search after Arrest—s. 18 PACE84

PACE84, s. 18 states:

(1) Subject to the following provisions of this section, a constable may enter and search any premises occupied or controlled by a person who is under arrest for an indictable offence, if he has reasonable grounds for suspecting that there is on the premises evidence, other than items subject to legal privilege, that relates—
  (a) to that offence; or
  (b) to some other indictable offence which is connected with or similar to that offence.

(2) A constable may seize and retain anything for which he may search under subsection (1) above.

(3) The power to search conferred by subsection (1) above is only a power to search to the extent that is reasonably required for the purpose of discovering such evidence.

(4) Subject to subsection (5) below, the powers conferred by this section may not be exercised unless an officer of the rank of inspector or above has authorised them in writing.

(5) A constable may conduct a search under subsection (1)—
  (a) before the person is taken to a police station or released on bail under section 30A; and
  (b) without obtaining an authorisation under subsection (4), if the condition in subsection (5A) is satisfied.

(5A) The condition is that the presence of the person at a place (other than a police station) is necessary for the effective investigation of the offence.

(6) If a constable conducts a search by virtue of subsection (5) above, he shall inform an officer of the rank of inspector or above that he has made the search as soon as practicable after he has made it.

(7) An officer who—
  (a) authorises a search; or
  (b) is informed of a search under subsection (6) above, shall make a record in writing—
    (i) of the grounds for the search; and
    (ii) of the nature of the evidence that was sought.

(8) If the person who was in occupation or control of the premises at the time of the search is in police detention at the time the record is to be made, the officer shall make the record as part of his custody record.

Are

Paragraph 4.3 of Code B emphasises that the power under s. 18 only applies to premises which are occupied or controlled by a person under arrest for an indictable offence; reasonable *suspicion* that the person occupies or controls the premises *is not sufficient*. A short stay may be sufficient to amount to 'occupation', but it must be such as to support the belief that it will have caused or contributed to the evidence sought being on the premises (*R (AB and CD)* v *Huddersfield Magistrates' Court and Chief Constable of West Yorkshire Police* [2014] 2 Cr App R 409 (25)).

Limits of the Search

The search is limited to evidence relating to the indictable offence for which the person has been arrested or another indictable offence which is similar or connected; it does not authorise a general search for anything that might be of use for other purposes (e.g. for intelligence reports). The extent of the search is limited by s. 18(3). If you are looking for a stolen fridge-freezer, you would not be empowered to search through drawers or small cupboards. You would be able to, however, if you were looking for packaging, receipts or other documents relating to the fridge-freezer.

Searching Premises before the Person is Taken to a Police Station

The provision under s. 18(5) relates to cases where the presence of the person *is necessary* for the effective investigation of the offence. If such a search is made, the searching officer must inform an inspector (or above) as soon as practicable after the search. If such a search is carried out and is lawful in every respect apart from the failure of the authorising officer to make a record in writing of the search (as required to by s. 18(7)), that failure by the authorising officer will not render the search illegal (*Krohn* v *DPP* [1997] COD 345).

Communication with the Occupier

Where officers carry out a search under s. 18 they must, so far as is possible in the circumstances, explain to the occupier(s) the reason for it. If officers attempt to carry out an authorised search under s. 18 without attempting to explain to an occupier the reason, it may mean that the officers are not acting in the execution of their duty and their entry may be lawfully resisted (*Lineham* v *DPP* [2000] Crim LR 861).

Re-arrest = Renew the Power

If the person is in police detention after the arrest, the facts concerning the search must be recorded in the custody record. Where a person is re-arrested under s. 31 of the 1984 Act for an indictable offence, the powers to search under s. 18 begin again, that is, a new power to search is created in respect of each indictable offence.

3.2.8 Code B—5 Search with consent

5.1 Subject to *paragraph 5.4*, if it is proposed to search premises with the consent of a person entitled to grant entry the consent must, if practicable, be given in writing on the Notice of Powers and Rights before the search. The officer must make any necessary enquiries to be satisfied the person is in a position to give such consent.

KEYNOTE

In a lodging house or similar accommodation, every reasonable effort should be made to obtain the consent of the tenant, lodger or occupier. A search should not be made solely on the basis of the landlord's consent.

If the intention is to search premises under the authority of a warrant or a power of entry and search without warrant, and the occupier of the premises cooperates in accordance with para. 6.4, there is no need to obtain written consent.

5.2 Before seeking consent the officer in charge of the search shall state the purpose of the proposed search and its extent. This information must be as specific as possible, particularly regarding the articles or persons being sought and the parts of the premises to be searched. The person concerned must be clearly informed they are not obliged to consent, that any consent can be withdrawn at any time, including before the search starts or while it is underway and anything seized may be produced in evidence. If at the time the person is not suspected of an offence, the officer shall say this when stating the purpose of the search.

5.3 An officer cannot enter and search or continue to search premises under *paragraph 5.1* if consent is given under duress or withdrawn before the search is completed.

5.4 It is unnecessary to seek consent under *paragraphs 5.1* and *5.2* if this would cause disproportionate inconvenience to the person concerned.

KEYNOTE

Paragraph 5.4 is intended to apply when it is reasonable to assume innocent occupiers would agree to, and expect, police to take the proposed action, e.g. if:

- a suspect has fled the scene of a crime or to evade arrest and it is necessary quickly to check surrounding gardens and readily accessible places to see if the suspect is hiding or;
- police have arrested someone in the night after a pursuit and it is necessary to make a brief check of gardens along the pursuit route to see if stolen or incriminating articles have been discarded.

3.2.9 Code B—6 Searching premises—general considerations

(a) Time of searches

6.1 Searches made under warrant must be made within three calendar months of the date of the warrant is issued or within the period specified in the enactment under which the warrant is issued if this is shorter.

6.2 Searches must be made at a reasonable hour unless this might frustrate the purpose of the search.

6.3 When the extent or complexity of a search mean it is likely to take a long time, the officer in charge of the search may consider using the seize and sift powers referred to in *section 7*.

6.3A A warrant under PACE, section 8 may authorise entry to and search of premises on more than one occasion if, on the application, the justice of the peace is satisfied that it is necessary to authorise multiple entries in order to achieve the purpose for which the warrant is issued. No premises may be entered or searched on any subsequent occasions without the prior written authority of an officer of the rank of inspector who is not involved in the investigation. All other warrants authorise entry on one occasion only.

6.3B Where a warrant under PACE section 8, or Schedule 1, paragraph 12; NSA 2023 Schedule 2, paragraphs 2 or 9; or TACT 2000 Schedule 5 paragraphs 1 or 11, authorises entry to and search of all premises occupied or controlled by a specified person, no premises which are not specified in the warrant may be entered and searched without the prior written authority of an officer of the rank of inspector who is not involved in the investigation.

(b) Entry other than with consent

6.4 The officer in charge of the search shall first try to communicate with the occupier, or any other person entitled to grant access to the premises, explain the authority under which entry is sought and ask the occupier to allow entry, unless:

(i) the search premises are unoccupied;

(ii) the occupier and any other person entitled to grant access are absent;

(iii) there are reasonable grounds for believing that alerting the occupier or any other person entitled to grant access would frustrate the object of the search or endanger officers or other people.

6.5 Unless *sub-paragraph 6.4(iii)* applies, if the premises are occupied the officer, subject to *paragraph 2.9*, shall, before the search begins:

(i) identify him or herself, show their warrant card (if not in uniform) and state the purpose of, and grounds for, the search, and

(ii) identify and introduce any person accompanying the officer on the search (such persons should carry identification for production on request) and briefly describe that person's role in the process.

6.6 Reasonable and proportionate force may be used if necessary to enter premises if the officer in charge of the search is satisfied the premises are those specified in any warrant, or in exercise of the powers described in *paragraphs 4.1* to *4.3*, and if:

(i) the occupier or any other person entitled to grant access has refused entry;

(ii) it is impossible to communicate with the occupier or any other person entitled to grant access; or

(iii) any of the provisions of *paragraph 6.4* apply.

(c) Notice of Powers and Rights

6.7 If an officer conducts a search to which this Code applies the officer shall, unless it is impracticable to do so, provide the occupier with a copy of a Notice in a standard format:

(i) specifying if the search is made under warrant, with consent, or in the exercise of the powers described in *paragraphs 4.1* to *4.3*. Note: the notice format shall provide for authority or consent to be indicated (see *paragraphs 4.3* and *5.1*);

(ii) summarising the extent of the powers of search and seizure conferred by PACE and other relevant legislation as appropriate;

(iii) explaining the rights of the occupier, and the owner of the property seized;

(iv) explaining compensation may be payable in appropriate cases for damages caused entering and searching premises, and giving the address to send a compensation application, and

(v) stating this Code is available at any police station.

KEYNOTE

Whether compensation is appropriate depends on the circumstances in each case. Compensation for damage caused when effecting entry is unlikely to be appropriate if the search was lawful, and the force used can be shown to be reasonable, proportionate and necessary to effect entry. If the wrong premises are searched by mistake everything possible should be done at the earliest opportunity to allay any sense of grievance and there should normally be a strong presumption in favour of paying compensation.

6.8 If the occupier is:

- present, copies of the Notice and warrant shall, if practicable, be given to them before the search begins, unless the officer in charge of the search reasonably believes this would frustrate the object of the search or endanger officers or other people
- not present, copies of the Notice and warrant shall be left in a prominent place on the premises or appropriate part of the premises and endorsed, subject to *paragraph 2.9* with the name of the officer in charge of the search, the date and time of the search the warrant shall be endorsed to show this has been done.

(d) Conduct of searches

6.9 Premises may be searched only to the extent necessary to achieve the object of the search, having regard to the size and nature of whatever is sought.

6.9A A search may not continue under:

- a warrant's authority once all the things specified in that warrant have been found
- any other power once the object of that search has been achieved.

6.9B No search may continue once the officer in charge of the search is satisfied whatever is being sought is not on the premises. This does not prevent a further search of the same premises if additional grounds come to light supporting a further application for a search warrant or exercise or further exercise of another power. For example, when, as a result of new information, it is believed articles previously not found or additional articles are on the premises.

KEYNOTE

It is important that, when possible, all those involved in a search are fully briefed about any powers to be exercised and the extent and limits within which it should be conducted.

6.10 Searches must be conducted with due consideration for the property and privacy of the occupier and with no more disturbance than necessary. Reasonable force may be used only when necessary and proportionate because the cooperation of the occupier cannot be obtained or is insufficient for the purpose.

KEYNOTE

In all cases the number of officers and other persons involved in executing the warrant should be determined by what is reasonable and necessary according to the particular circumstances.

6.11 A friend, neighbour or other person must be allowed to witness the search if the occupier wishes unless the officer in charge of the search has reasonable grounds for believing the presence of the person asked for would seriously hinder the investigation or endanger officers or other people. A search need not be unreasonably delayed for this purpose. A record of the action taken should be made on the premises search record including the grounds for refusing the occupier's request.

6.12 A person is not required to be cautioned prior to being asked questions that are solely necessary for the purpose of furthering the proper and effective conduct of a search, see Code C, *paragraph 10.1(c)*. For example, questions to discover the occupier of specified premises, to find a key to open a locked drawer or cupboard or to otherwise seek cooperation during the search or to determine if a particular item is liable to be seized.

6.12A If questioning goes beyond what is necessary for the purpose of the exemption in Code C, the exchange is likely to constitute an interview as defined by Code C, *paragraph 11.1A* and would require the associated safeguards included in Code C, *section 10*.

(e) Leaving premises

6.13 If premises have been entered by force, before leaving the officer in charge of the search must make sure they are secure by:

- arranging for the occupier or their agent to be present
- any other appropriate means.

(f) Searches under PACE Schedule 1 or the Terrorism Act 2000, Schedule 5 or the National Security Act 2023, Schedule 2

6.14 An officer shall be appointed as the officer in charge of the search, see *paragraph 2.10*, in respect of any search made under a warrant issued under PACE Act 1984, Schedule 1, the Terrorism Act 2000, Schedule 5 or the National Security Act 2023, Schedule 2. They are responsible for making sure the search is conducted with discretion and in a manner that causes the least possible disruption to any business or other activities carried out on the premises.

6.15 Once the officer in charge of the search is satisfied material may not be taken from the premises without their knowledge, they shall ask for the documents or other records concerned. The officer in charge of the search may also ask to see the index to files held on the premises, and the officers conducting the search may inspect any files which, according to the index, appear to contain the material sought. A more extensive search of the premises may be made only if:

- the person responsible for them refuses to:
  - produce the material sought, or
  - allow access to the index
- it appears the index is:
  - inaccurate, or
  - incomplete
- for any other reason the officer in charge of the search has reasonable grounds for believing such a search is necessary in order to find the material sought.

3.2.10

Code B—7 Seizure and retention of property

(a) Seizure

7.1 Subject to *paragraph 7.2*, an officer who is searching any person or premises under any statutory power or with the consent of the occupier may seize anything:

(a) covered by a warrant

(b) the officer has reasonable grounds for believing is evidence of an offence or has been obtained in consequence of the commission of an offence but only if seizure is necessary to prevent the items being concealed, lost, disposed of, altered, damaged, destroyed or tampered with

(c) covered by the powers in the Criminal Justice and Police Act 2001, Part 2 allowing an officer to seize property from persons or premises and retain it for sifting or examination elsewhere.

KEYNOTE

General Power of Seizure—s. 19 PACE84

Paragraph 7.1 refers to 'searching premises' under a statutory power or with the consent of the owner. Whilst s. 19 of PACE84 *is not a power to enter and search premises*, it is relevant as it provides *a power of seizure* (specifically under s. 19(3)) if the officer concerned is lawfully on the premises, for example:

- a lawful search of premises is being carried out under s. 32(2)(b) of PACE84 (searching premises where the arrested person was when arrested or immediately before being arrested). During the search, the officer carrying out the search discovers property which he/she reasonably believes is evidence in relation to the offence. Section 32 does not provide a power of seizure in such circumstances but, because the officer is lawfully on the premises carrying out a search using a statutory power, the officer may seize the evidence under s. 19 of PACE84;

- an officer is making inquiries in relation to a robbery and, with the consent of the owner, is searching a garage the offender ran through to escape. During the search, the officer discovers property he/she reasonably believes was stolen in the robbery—the officer may seize the property under s. 19 of PACE84;
- an officer is carrying out house-to-house inquires regarding a murder and is invited into a house by the owner. Once in the house, the officer sees an item of property he/she believes is evidence in relation to the offence—the officer may seize the property under s. 19 of PACE84.

'Lawfully' on Premises—s. 19(1) PACE84

Section 19 of PACE84 will only apply when the officers concerned are on the premises *lawfully* (s. 19(1)). If officers are on premises only with the consent of the occupier or some other person entitled to grant access to the premises, they become trespassers the instant that consent has been withdrawn—they are no longer 'lawfully' on the premises (unless they have a power to be there) and the person may remove them by force (*Robson* v *Hallett* [1967] 2 QB 939). If that consent is terminated, the person needs to communicate that clearly to the officer; merely telling officers to 'fuck off' is not necessarily sufficient (*Snook* v *Mannion* [1982] RTR 321). The officers must be given a reasonable opportunity to leave but, as they are now 'trespassers', they cannot seize any property that they may find on the premises (they are on the premises unlawfully). For this reason, it is far safer to exercise a power where one exists, albeit that the *cooperation* of the relevant person should be sought.

If the warrant under which entry or seizure was made is invalid, the officers will not be on the premises lawfully.

Reason for Seizure—ss. 19(2) and (3) PACE84

The reasons for seizure are contained in ss. 19(2) and (3)—they are both driven by an officer's reasonable belief.

Section	Why Seize?	Necessity for Seizure?
19(2)	That it has been obtained in *consequence of the commission* of an offence	In order to prevent it from being concealed, lost, *damaged*, altered or destroyed
19(3)	That it is *evidence* in relation to an offence	In order to prevent it from being concealed, lost, altered or destroyed

Unless the elements above are satisfied, the power under s. 19 will not apply. Therefore, the power does not authorise the seizure of property purely for intelligence purposes.

Seizing 'Premises' under s. 19 PACE84

The powers of seizure conferred by s. 19(3) (and also s. 18(2)) of PACE84 extend to the seizure of the whole premises when it is physically possible to seize and retain the premises in their totality and practical considerations make seizure desirable. The police may remove premises such as tents, vehicles or caravans to a police station for the purpose of preserving evidence (e.g. in *Cowan* v *Commissioner of Police for the Metropolis* [2000] 1 WLR 254, the 'premises' seized was a vehicle). However, it does not extend to seizing things that are not on the premises, such as a car parked in a car park adjacent to the premises (*Wood* v *North Avon Magistrates' Court* [2009] EWHC 3614 (Admin)).

Common Law Power of Seizure

Section 19(5) of PACE84 expressly preserves any common law power of search and seizure. The conditions required to use the common law power of seizure were set out in the case of *Ghani* v *Jones* [1969] 3 All ER 1700, they are:

(1) the police must have reasonable grounds for believing that a serious crime has been committed; and
(2) the police must have reasonable grounds for believing that the article in question is either the fruit of the crime (as in the case of stolen goods) or is the instrument by which the crime was committed (as in the

case of an axe used by the murderer) or is material evidence to prove the commission of the crime (as is the case of the car used by the bank robber); and

(3) the police must have reasonable grounds for believing that the person in possession of it has him/herself committed the crime, or is implicated in it, or is an accessory to it, or at any rate his/her refusal must be quite unreasonable; and

(4) the police must not keep the article, nor prevent its removal, for any longer than is reasonably necessary to complete their investigations or preserve it for evidence. If a copy will suffice, it should be made and the original returned. As soon as the case is over, or it is decided not to go on with it, the article should be returned; and

(5) the lawfulness of the conduct of the police must be judged at the time, and not by what happens afterwards.

7.2 No item may be seized which an officer has reasonable grounds for believing to be subject to legal privilege, as defined in PACE, section 10, other than under the Criminal Justice and Police Act 2001, Part 2.

7.3 Officers must be aware of the provisions in the Criminal Justice and Police Act 2001, section 59, allowing for applications to a judicial authority for the return of property seized and the subsequent duty to secure in section 60. (See *paragraph 7.12(iii)*.)

7.4 An officer may decide it is not appropriate to seize property because of an explanation from the person holding it but may nevertheless have reasonable grounds for believing it was obtained in consequence of an offence by some person. In these circumstances, the officer should identify the property to the holder, inform the holder of their suspicions and explain the holder may be liable to civil or criminal proceedings if they dispose of, alter or destroy the property.

7.5 An officer may arrange to photograph, image or copy, any document or other article they have the power to seize in accordance with *paragraph 7.1*. This is subject to specific restrictions on the examination, imaging or copying of certain property seized under the Criminal Justice and Police Act 2001, Part 2. An officer must have regard to their statutory obligation to retain an original document or other article only when a photograph or copy is not sufficient.

7.6 If an officer considers information stored in any electronic form and accessible from the premises could be used in evidence, they may require the information to be produced in a form:

- which can be taken away and in which it is visible and legible; or
- from which it can readily be produced in a visible and legible form.

KEYNOTE

Paragraph 7.6 of Code B reflects the provisions of s. 20 of PACE84 (extension of powers of seizure to computerised information). This states that where a power of seizure exists under any enactment, there will also be a power to require any information stored in any electronic form and accessible from the premises to be produced in a form in which it can be taken away and in which it is visible and legible or from which it can readily be produced in a visible and legible form (s. 20(1)). This provision applies to:

- powers conferred under pre-PACE84 statutes;
- powers exercised under a s. 8 warrant (for 'indictable offences');
- powers exercised under s. 18 (following arrest for an indictable offence);
- powers under sch. 1 ('excluded' or 'special procedure material');
- powers exercised under s. 19 (officers lawfully on premises);
- powers of seizure exercised by investigating officers designated under sch. 4 to the Police Reform Act 2002.

(b) Criminal Justice and Police Act 2001: Specific procedures for seize and sift powers

7.7 The Criminal Justice and Police Act 2001, Part 2 gives officers limited powers to seize property from premises or persons so they can sift or examine it elsewhere. Officers must be careful they only exercise these powers when it is essential and they do not remove any more material than necessary. The removal of large volumes of material, much of which may not ultimately be retainable, may have serious implications for the owners, particularly when they are involved in business or activities such as journalism or the provision of medical services. Officers must carefully consider if removing copies or images of relevant material or data would be a satisfactory alternative to removing originals. When originals are taken, officers must be prepared to facilitate the provision of copies or images for the owners when reasonably practicable.

KEYNOTE

Clarifying the Nature of the Seize and Sift Power

These seize and sift powers extend the scope of some other existing powers. They *do not provide* free-standing powers to seize property—rather, they supplement other powers of search and seizure where the relevant conditions and circumstances apply. The full list of these powers is set out in sch. 1 to the Act and includes all the relevant powers under PACE84, along with those under other key statutes such as the Firearms Act 1968 and the Misuse of Drugs Act 1971. If there is no existing power of seizure other than the Criminal Justice and Police Act 2001, then there is no power.

Why Use the Power?

Section 50 of the 2001 Act provides the extended powers to seize material where it is not reasonably practicable to sort through it at the scene of the search. The factors that can be taken into account in considering whether or not it is reasonably practicable for something to be determined, or for relevant material to be separated from other materials, are set out in s. 50(3); these include the length of time and number of people that would be required to carry out the determination or separation on those premises within a reasonable period, whether that would involve damage to property, any apparatus or equipment that would be needed and (in the case of separation of materials) whether the separation would be likely to prejudice the use of some or all of the separated seizable property. Section 50 also allows for the seizure of material that is reasonably believed to be legally privileged where it is not reasonably practicable to separate it. In some cases, the power to 'seize' will be read as a power to take copies (s. 63).

Section 51 provides for extended seizure of materials in the same vein as above but where the material is found on people who are being lawfully searched.

Simplifying Access

Officers should consider reaching agreement with owners and/or other interested parties on the procedures for examining a specific set of property, rather than awaiting the judicial authority's determination. Agreement can sometimes give a quicker and more satisfactory route for all concerned and minimise costs and legal complexities.

7.8 Property seized under the Criminal Justice and Police Act 2001, sections 50 or 51 must be kept securely and separately from any material seized under other powers. An examination under section 53 to determine which elements may be retained must be carried out at the earliest practicable time, having due regard to the desirability of allowing the person from whom the property was seized, or a person with an interest in the property, an opportunity of being present or represented at the examination.

7.8A All reasonable steps should be taken to accommodate an interested person's request to be present, provided the request is reasonable and subject to the need to prevent harm to, interference with, or unreasonable delay to the investigatory process. If an examination proceeds in the absence of an interested person who asked to attend or their representative, the officer who exercised the relevant seizure power must give that person a written notice of why the examination was carried out in those circumstances. If it is necessary for security reasons or to maintain confidentiality officers may exclude interested persons from decryption or other processes which facilitate the examination but do not form part of it.

KEYNOTE

What constitutes a relevant interest in specific material may depend on the nature of that material and the circumstances in which it is seized. Anyone with a reasonable claim to ownership of the material and anyone entrusted with its safe keeping by the owner should be considered.

7.9 It is the responsibility of the officer in charge of the investigation to make sure property is returned in accordance with sections 53 to 55. Material which there is no power to retain must be:

- separated from the rest of the seized property
- returned as soon as reasonably practicable after examination of all the seized property.

7.9A Delay is only warranted if very clear and compelling reasons exist, e.g. the:

- unavailability of the person to whom the material is to be returned
- need to agree a convenient time to return a large volume of material.

7.9B Legally privileged, excluded or special procedure material (or in the case the National Security Act 2023, confidential material) which cannot be retained must be returned:

- as soon as reasonably practicable
- without waiting for the whole examination.

7.9C As set out in section 58, material must be returned to the person from whom it was seized, except when it is clear some other person has a better right to it.

KEYNOTE

Requirements to secure and return property apply equally to all copies, images or other material created because of seizure of the original property.

7.10 When an officer involved in the investigation has reasonable grounds to believe a person with a relevant interest in property seized under section 50 or 51 intends to make an application under section 59 for the return of any legally privileged, special procedure or excluded material, the officer in charge of the investigation should be informed as soon as practicable and the material seized should be kept secure in accordance with section 61.

7.11 The officer in charge of the investigation is responsible for making sure property is properly secured. Securing involves making sure the property is not examined, copied, imaged or put to any other use except at the request, or with the consent, of the applicant or in accordance with the directions of the appropriate judicial authority. Any request, consent or directions must be recorded in writing and signed by both the initiator and the officer in charge of the investigation.

KEYNOTE

The mechanics of securing property vary according to the circumstances; 'bagging up', i.e. placing material in sealed bags or containers, and strict subsequent control of access is the appropriate procedure in many cases.

When material is seized under the powers of seizure conferred by PACE84, the duty to retain it under the Code of Practice issued under the Criminal Procedure and Investigations Act 1996 is subject to the provisions on retention of seized material in s. 22 of PACE84.

7.12 When an officer exercises a power of seizure conferred by sections 50 or 51 they shall provide the occupier of the premises or the person from whom the property is being seized with a written notice:

(i) specifying what has been seized under the powers conferred by that section;

(ii) specifying the grounds for those powers;

(iii) setting out the effect of sections 59 to 61 covering the grounds for a person with a relevant interest in seized property to apply to a judicial authority for its return and the duty of officers to secure property in certain circumstances when an application is made;

(iv) specifying the name and address of the person to whom:

- notice of an application to the appropriate judicial authority in respect of any of the seized property must be given;
- an application may be made to allow attendance at the initial examination of the property.

7.13 If the occupier is not present but there is someone in charge of the premises, the notice shall be given to them. If no suitable person is available, so the notice will easily be found it should either be:

- left in a prominent place on the premises
- attached to the exterior of the premises.

(c) Retention

7.14 Subject to *paragraph 7.15*, anything seized in accordance with the above provisions may be retained only for as long as is necessary. It may be retained, among other purposes:

(i) for use as evidence at a trial for an offence;

(ii) to facilitate the use in any investigation or proceedings of anything to which it is inextricably linked;

(iii) for forensic examination or other investigation in connection with an offence;

(iv) in order to establish its lawful owner when there are reasonable grounds for believing it has been stolen or obtained by the commission of an offence.

KEYNOTE

Inextricably Linked Material

Paragraph 7.14(ii) applies if inextricably linked material is seized under the Criminal Justice and Police Act 2001, s. 50 or 51. Inextricably linked material is material it is not reasonably practicable to separate from other linked material without prejudicing the use of that other material in any investigation or proceedings. For example, it may not be possible to separate items of data held on computer disk without damaging their evidential integrity. There are very strict limits on what use can be made of this material—it must not be examined, imaged, copied or used for any purpose other than for proving the source and/or integrity of the linked material (s. 62).

7.15 Property shall not be retained under *paragraph 7.14(i), (ii)* or *(iii)* if a copy or image would be sufficient.

7.15A An order given under the urgent case premises search power found in paragraph 15 of Schedule 5 to the Terrorism Act 2000, or paragraph 12 of Schedule 2 to the National Security Act 2023 does not authorise a constable to retain confidential journalistic material. If confidential journalistic material is seized during a search conducted under such an order, a constable may apply to a Circuit Judge as soon as reasonably practicable after the material is seized for the issue of a warrant authorising the retention of the confidential journalistic material. A warrant issued by the court may impose conditions on the retention and use of the material.

KEYNOTE

Retention of Property—s. 22 PACE84

Section 22 of PACE84 makes provision for the retention of seized property. Section 22(1) provides that anything seized may be retained for as long as necessary in all the circumstances. However, s. 22(2) allows for property to be retained for use as evidence in a trial, forensic examination or further investigation *unless a photograph or copy would suffice*. Seized property may be retained in order to establish its lawful owner (s. 22(2)(b)). Once this power to retain property is exhausted, a person claiming it can rely on his/her right to possession at the time the property was seized as giving sufficient title to recover the property from the police. This situation was confirmed by the Court of Appeal in a case where the purchaser of a stolen car was allowed to rely upon his possession of the car at the time it was seized. As it could not be established that anyone else was entitled to the vehicle, the court allowed the claimant's action for return of the car to him (*Costello* v *Chief Constable of Derbyshire Constabulary* [2001] EWCA Civ 381). Clearly any claim based on previous possession where it would be unlawful for the police to return the property (e.g. a controlled drug) could not be enforced. There is no specific provision under s. 22 for the retention of property for purely intelligence purposes.

The importance of police officers being able to point clearly to the need for retaining property either in order to establish its owner or as a necessary part of the investigative or law enforcement process when relying on the above powers, was highlighted by the Court of Appeal in *Gough* v *Chief Constable of the West Midlands Police* [2004] EWCA Civ 206. In that case, it was clear that neither of these purposes was being served and therefore the officers could not rely on the statutory power for retaining the property.

Property seized simply to prevent an arrested person from using it to escape or to cause injury, damage etc. cannot be retained for those purposes once the person has been released (s. 22(3)). This includes car keys belonging to someone who is released from police detention having been detained under the relevant drink driving legislation.

The provisions of s. 21 of PACE84 apply to powers of seizure exercised by investigating officers designated under sch. 4 of the Police Reform Act 2002.

Disposal of Property in Police Possession

Any person claiming property seized by the police may apply to a magistrates' court under the Police (Property) Act 1897 for its possession and should, if appropriate, be advised of this procedure.

(d) Rights of owners etc.

7.16 If property is retained, the person who had custody or control of it immediately before seizure must, on request, be provided with a list or description of the property within a reasonable time.

7.17 That person or their representative must be allowed supervised access to the property to examine it or have it photographed or copied, or must be provided with a photograph or copy, in either case within a reasonable time of any request and at their own expense, unless the officer in charge of an investigation has reasonable grounds for believing this would:

(i) prejudice the investigation of any offence or criminal proceedings; or

(ii) lead to the commission of an offence by providing access to unlawful material such as pornography.

A record of the grounds shall be made when access is denied.

KEYNOTE

Paragraphs 7.16 and 7.17 summarise the law contained in s. 22 of PACE84 which sets out the rights certain people have in respect of access to and/or copies of property seized. The provisions of s. 22 of PACE84 apply to powers of seizure exercised by investigating officers designated under sch. 4 of the Police Reform Act 2002.

3.2.11 Code B—8 Action after searches

8.1 If premises are searched in circumstances where this Code applies, unless the exceptions in *paragraph 2.3(a)* apply, on arrival at a police station the officer in charge of the search shall make or have made a record of the search, to include:

(i) the address of the searched premises;

(ii) the date, time and duration of the search;

(iii) the authority used for the search:

- if the search was made in exercise of a statutory power to search premises without warrant, the power which was used for the search:
- if the search was made under a warrant or with written consent;
  - a copy of the warrant and the written authority to apply for it, see *paragraph 3.4*; or
  - the written consent;

shall be appended to the record or the record shall show the location of the copy warrant or consent.

(iv) subject to *paragraph 2.9*, the names of:

- the officer(s) in charge of the search;
- all other officers and any authorised persons who conducted the search;

(v) the names of any people on the premises if they are known;

(vi) any grounds for refusing the occupier's request to have someone present during the search, see *paragraph 6.11*;

(vii) a list of any articles seized or the location of a list and, if not covered by a warrant, the grounds for their seizure;

(viii) whether force was used, and the reason;

(ix) details of any damage caused during the search, and the circumstances;

(x) if applicable, the reason it was not practicable;

(a) to give the occupier a copy of the Notice of Powers and Rights, see *paragraph 6.7*;

(b) before the search to give the occupier a copy of the Notice, see *paragraph 6.8*;

(xi) when the occupier was not present, the place where copies of the Notice of Powers and Rights and search warrant were left on the premises, *see paragraph 6.8*.

8.2 On each occasion when premises are searched under warrant, the warrant authorising the search on that occasion shall be endorsed to show:

(i) if any articles specified in the warrant were found and the address where found;

(ii) if any other articles were seized;

(iii) the date and time it was executed and if present, the name of the occupier or if the occupier is not present the name of the person in charge of the premises;

(iv) subject to *paragraph 2.9*, the names of the officers who executed it and any authorised persons who accompanied them;

(v) if a copy, together with a copy of the Notice of Powers and Rights was:

- handed to the occupier; or
- endorsed as required by *paragraph 6.8*; and left on the premises and where.

8.3 Any warrant shall be returned within three calendar months of its issue or sooner on completion of the search(es) authorised by that warrant, if it was issued by a:

- justice of the peace, to the designated officer for the local justice area in which the justice was acting when issuing the warrant; or
- judge, to the appropriate officer of the court concerned.

3.2.12 Code B—9 Search registers

9.1 A search register will be maintained at each sub-divisional or equivalent police station. All search records required under *paragraph 8.1* shall be made, copied, or referred to in the register.

KEYNOTE

Paragraph 9.1 also applies to search records made by immigration officers. In these cases, a search register must also be maintained at an immigration office.

3.2.13 Code B—10 Searches under Schedule 5 to the Terrorism Prevention and Investigation Measures Act 2011 and Schedule 11 to the National Security Act 2023

10.1 This Code applies to the powers of constables under Schedule 5 to the Terrorism Prevention and Investigation Measures Act 2011 and Schedule 11 to the National Security Act 2023 relating to TPIM and State Threats Prevention and Investigation Measures (STPIM) notices to enter and search premises subject to the modifications in the following paragraphs.

10.2 In paragraph 2.3(d), the reference to the investigation into an alleged or suspected offence include the enforcement of TPIM and STPIM measures which may be imposed on an individual by a TPIM or STPIM notice in accordance with the Terrorism Prevention and Investigation Measures Act 2011 or National Security Act 2023.

10.3 References to the purpose and object of the entry and search of premises, the nature of articles sought and what may be seized and retained include (as appropriate):

(a) in relation to the power to search *without a search warrant in paragraph 5* (for purposes of serving a TPIM or STPIM notice), finding the individual on whom the notice is to be served.

(b) in relation to the power to search *without a search warrant in paragraph 6* (at time of serving TPIM or STPIM notice), ascertaining whether there is anything in the premises, that contravenes measures specified in the notice.

(c) in relation to the power to search *without a search warrant under paragraph 7* (suspected absconding), ascertaining whether a person has absconded or if there is anything on the premises which will assist in the pursuit or arrest of an individual in respect of whom a TPIM or STPIM notice is in force who is reasonably suspected of having absconded.

(d) in relation to the power to search *under a search warrant* issued under *paragraph 8* (for compliance purposes), determining whether an individual in respect of whom a TPIM or STPIM notice is in force is complying with measures specified in the notice.

KEYNOTE

Searches of individuals under paras 6(2)(a) (at time of serving a notice) and 8(2)(a) (for compliance purposes) of sch. 5 to the Terrorism Prevention and Investigation Measures Act 2011 or sch. 11 to the National Security Act 2023, must be conducted and recorded in accordance with Code A. See Code A, para. 2.18A for details.

3.3 Powers of Arrest

A thick grey line down the margin denotes text that is an extract of the PACE Code itself (i.e. the actual wording of the Code).

3.3.1 Introduction

This chapter considers several key features that are relevant to powers of arrest before examining specific provisions in detail (particularly powers of arrest under ss. 24 and 24A of the Police and Criminal Evidence Act 1984 (hereafter referred to as 'PACE84')) and the PACE Code of Practice for the Statutory Powers of Arrest by Police Officers (hereafter referred to as 'Code G' (November 2012 version)).

3.3.2 Legal Characteristics of an Arrest

'Arrest' is not defined by PACE84 or other legislation—it is an ordinary English word, and whether or not a person has been arrested depends not only on the legality of the arrest but on whether the person has been deprived of liberty to go where he/she pleases (*Lewis* v *Chief Constable of South Wales Constabulary* [1991] 1 All ER 206). An arrest begins at the time when the arresting officer informs the person of it or when his/her words or actions suggest that the person is under arrest (*Murray* v *Ministry of Defence* [1988] 1 WLR 692).

Where a power of arrest exists, any lawful arrest must be made for a proper purpose. In the past, the courts have allowed the police some latitude in what amounts to a proper purpose, including bringing the person to a police station (*Holgate-Mohammed* v *Duke* [1984] AC 437) and to obtain a confession even after a complainant has withdrawn his/her initial complaint (*Plange* v *Chief Constable of Humberside* (1992) *The Times*, 23 March). The courts have even accepted an arrest based on force policy (*Al Fayed* v *Commissioner of Police of the Metropolis* [2004] EWCA Civ 1579).

The practice of arresting someone on a 'holding' offence was accepted by the Court of Appeal in *R* v *Chalkley* [1998] QB 848, provided the arresting officers had reasonable grounds for suspecting that the person had actually committed that offence. If that suspicion is present, then the fact that the officers making the arrest are doing so with the intention of investigating another more serious offence does not render the arrest unlawful. If, however, there are no such grounds to suspect that the person had in fact committed the offence, or the officers know at the time of the arrest that there is no possibility of the person actually being charged with it, the arrest will be unlawful.

Section 117 of PACE84 allows the use of reasonable force when making an arrest as does s. 3 of the Criminal Law Act 1967 (allowing the use of such force as is reasonably necessary in the arrest of people and the prevention of crime). Whether any force used is 'reasonable' will be determined in the light of all the circumstances, including the circumstances as the arresting officer believed them to be at the time. Such force may even be lethal to the defendant. Where serious harm is caused by an arrest, the courts will consider the time that was available to the officer to reflect on his/her actions and whether or not he/she believed that the danger presented to others by failing to arrest the person outweighed the harm caused to the person by the arrest (*Attorney-General for Northern Ireland's Reference (No. 1 of 1975)* [1977] AC 105). Use of excessive force, while amounting to possible misconduct and assault, does not render an otherwise lawful arrest unlawful (*Simpson* v *Chief Constable of South Yorkshire* (1991) 135 SJ 383).

3.3.3 Code G—1 Introduction

1.1 This Code of Practice deals with statutory power of police to arrest a person who is involved, or suspected of being involved, in a criminal offence. The power of arrest must be used fairly, responsibly, with respect for people suspected of committing offences and without unlawful discrimination. The Equality Act 2010 makes it unlawful for police officers to discriminate against, harass or victimise any person on the grounds of the 'protected characteristics' of age, disability, gender reassignment, race, religion or belief, sex and sexual orientation, marriage and civil partnership, pregnancy and maternity when using their powers. When police forces are carrying out their functions they also have a duty to have regard to the need to eliminate unlawful discrimination, harassment and victimisation and to take steps to foster good relations.

KEYNOTE

Criminal 'Offence'

For the purposes of this Code, 'offence' means any statutory or common law offence for which a person may be tried by a magistrates' court or the Crown Court and punished if convicted. Examples of statutory offences include assault, rape and offences under road traffic and immigration legislation and local government byelaws. Examples of common law offences include murder, manslaughter and kidnapping.

Applicability of Code G

This Code *does not apply* to powers of arrest conferred on constables under any arrest warrant, for example a warrant issued under the Magistrates' Courts Act 1980, s. 1 or 13, or the Bail Act 1976, s. 7(1), or to the powers of constables to arrest without warrant *other than* under s. 24 of PACE84 for an offence.

These other powers to arrest without warrant *do not* depend on the arrested person committing any specific offence and include:

- PACE84, s. 46A, arrest of a person who fails to answer police bail to attend a police station or is suspected of breaching any condition of that bail for the custody officer to decide whether they should be kept in police detention which applies whether or not the person commits an offence under s. 6 of the Bail Act 1976 (e.g. failing without reasonable cause to surrender to custody);
- Bail Act 1976, s. 7(3), arrest of a person bailed to attend court who is suspected of breaching, or is believed to be likely to breach, any condition of bail to take them to court for bail to be reconsidered;
- Children and Young Persons Act 1969, s. 32(1A) (absconding)—arrest to return the person to the place where they are required to reside;
- Mental Health Act 1983, s. 136 to remove a person suffering from mental disorder to a place of safety for assessment;
- Road Traffic Act 1988, s. 6D arrest of a driver following the outcome of a preliminary roadside test requirement to enable the driver to be required to provide an evidential sample;
- the common law power to stop or prevent a breach of the peace—after arrest, a person aged 18 or over may be brought before a justice of the peace court to show cause why they should not be bound over to keep the peace—not criminal proceedings.

1.2 The exercise of the power of arrest represents an obvious and significant interference with the Right to Liberty and Security under Article 5 of the European Convention on Human Rights set out in Part I of Schedule 1 to the Human Rights Act 1998.

KEYNOTE

Article 5—The Right to Liberty and Security

Article 5 *does not* provide any power to arrest or detain; it simply sets out certain circumstances where the general right to liberty may be interfered with by some existing lawful means.

Article 5 of the Convention states:

1. Everyone has the right to liberty and security of person. No one shall be deprived of his liberty save in the following cases and in accordance with a procedure prescribed by law:
   (a) the lawful detention of a person after conviction by a competent court;
   (b) the lawful arrest or detention of a person for non-compliance with the lawful order of a court or in order to secure the fulfilment of any obligation prescribed by law;
   (c) the lawful arrest or detention of a person effected for the purpose of bringing him before the competent legal authority on reasonable suspicion of having committed an offence or when it is reasonably considered necessary to prevent his committing an offence or fleeing after having done so;
   (d) the detention of a minor by lawful order for the purpose of educational supervision or his lawful detention for the purpose of bringing him before the competent legal authority;
   (e) the lawful detention of persons for the prevention of the spreading of infectious diseases, of persons of unsound mind, alcoholics or drug addicts or vagrants;
   (f) the lawful arrest or detention of a person to prevent his effecting an unauthorised entry into the country or of a person against whom action is being taken with a view to deportation or extradition.
2. Everyone who is arrested shall be informed promptly, in a language which he understands, of the reasons for his arrest and of any charge against him.
3. Everyone arrested or detained in accordance with the provisions of paragraph 1(c) of this Article shall be brought promptly before a judge or other officer authorised by law to exercise judicial power and shall be entitled to trial within a reasonable time or to release pending trial. Release may be conditioned by guarantees to appear for trial.
4. Everyone who is deprived of his liberty by arrest or detention shall be entitled to take proceedings by which the lawfulness of his detention shall be decided speedily by a court and his release ordered if the detention is not lawful.
5. Everyone who has been the victim of arrest or detention in contravention of the provisions of this Article shall have an enforceable right to compensation.

Article 5(1)—'Procedure'

The 'procedure' in Article 5(1) must be set out in the domestic law of the country and be recorded in such a way that people can appreciate the possible consequences of their actions and adapt their behaviour accordingly. If the legal authority used to deprive a person of his/her liberty is ambiguous or unclear, that may provide grounds for challenge under Article 5.

Article 5(1)(a)—Lawful Detention after Conviction

This allows a person to be detained after their conviction by a 'competent court', i.e. a court having the jurisdiction to try that particular case.

Article 5(1)(b)—Lawful Arrest or Detention for Non-compliance

This allows for the detention or arrest of a person who has failed to comply with the *lawful* order of a court. Failing to pay a fine or to observe the conditions of an injunction would be examples of such non-compliance. It extends to arrest or detention in order to secure the fulfilment of any obligation prescribed by law, such as an obligation to provide a roadside breath specimen. The circumstances of any arrest or detention will be examined by the courts which will need to consider whether the person was given a reasonable opportunity to comply with the order/obligation and whether the arrest or detention was a reasonable way to make sure that the order/obligation was met.

Article 5(1)(c)—Lawful Arrest/Detention in Relation to an Offence

The arrest/detention must first be lawful in itself. Any arrest/detention that is later shown to have been *unlawful* cannot be saved under any of the other headings. Where a person has been lawfully arrested for the purpose of bringing him/her before a competent legal authority, it is not necessary to show that he/she actually *was brought* before that authority (*Brogan* v *United Kingdom* (1989) 11 EHRR 117). It is the *purpose* of the arrest at the time that is relevant as opposed to its ultimate achievement. This matches the provisions of s. 30(7) of PACE84 which require an arrested person to be released if the grounds for detaining him/her cease to exist.

Article 5(1)(d)—Lawful Detention of Minors

This ground refers solely to lawful 'detention' rather than arrest; a minor for these purposes is a person who has not attained the age of 18.

Article 5(1)(e)—Lawful Detention of Others

The reasoning behind Article 5(1)(e) is that those who have physical and mental ailments may need to be detained in their own interests, a good example being the detention of people under the Mental Health Act 1983. Although there is a power under s. 34 of the Criminal Justice Act 1972 for a person to be taken after arrest to an approved alcohol treatment centre, Article 5(1)(e) would apply as there is no further power to detain such a person once he/she arrives at the centre. In such cases, the permitted grounds under Article 5(1)(c) would be more appropriate. The mere fact that an individual has, for example, an infectious disease will not of itself justify his/her 'detention'.

Article 5(1)(f)—Lawful Arrest/Detention for Deportation or Extradition

Article 5(1)(f) does not require the detention to be necessary in order to be justified (*R (On the Application of Saadi)* v *Secretary of State for the Home Department* [2002] UKHL 41).

Article 5(2)—Reason for Arrest

The wording of Article 5(2) strengthens the requirement that exists under s. 28 of PACE84 (the right to be informed of the reason for arrest) by specifying that the information must be given in a language that the person understands. This is to allow the arrested person to challenge the arrest and subsequent detention (*X* v *United Kingdom* (1982) 4 EHRR 188).

1.3 The use of the power must be fully justified and officers exercising the power should consider if the necessary objectives can be met by other, less intrusive means. Absence of justification for exercising the powers of arrest may lead to challenges should the case proceed to court. It could also lead to civil claims against the police for unlawful arrest and false imprisonment. When the power of arrest is exercised it is essential that it is exercised in a non-discriminatory and proportionate manner which is compatible with the Right to Liberty under Article 5.

KEYNOTE

Juveniles should not be arrested at their place of education unless this is unavoidable. When a juvenile is arrested at their place of education, the principal or their nominee must be informed.

1.4 Section 24 of the Police and Criminal Evidence Act 1984 (as substituted by section 110 of the Serious Organised Crime and Police Act 2005) provides the statutory power for a constable to arrest without warrant for all offences. If the provisions of the Act and this Code are not observed, both the arrest and the conduct of any subsequent investigation may be open to question.

1.5 This Code of Practice must be readily available at all police stations for consultation by police officers and police staff, detained persons and members of the public.

1.6 The *Notes for Guidance* [presented as Keynotes in this chapter] are not provisions of the Code.

3.3.4 Code G—2 Elements of Arrest under section 24 PACE

2.1 A lawful arrest requires two elements:

A person's involvement or suspected involvement or attempted involvement in the commission of a criminal offence;

AND

Reasonable grounds for *believing* that the person's arrest is necessary.

- both elements must be satisfied, and
- it can never be necessary to arrest a person unless there are reasonable grounds to suspect them of committing an offence.

2.2 The arrested person must be informed that they have been arrested, even if this fact is obvious, and of the relevant circumstances of the arrest in relation to both the above elements. The custody officer must be informed of these matters on arrival at the police station. See *Code C paragraph 3.4.*

(a) Involvement 'in the commission of an offence'

2.3 A constable may arrest without warrant in relation to any offence anyone:

- who is about to commit an offence or is in the act of committing an offence
- whom the officer has reasonable grounds for suspecting is about to commit an offence or to be committing an offence
- whom the officer has reasonable grounds to suspect of being guilty of an offence which he or she has reasonable grounds for suspecting has been committed
- anyone who is guilty of an offence which has been committed or anyone whom the officer has reasonable grounds for suspecting to be guilty of that offence.

KEYNOTE

Seven 'Constable's Arrest' Powers—s. 24 PACE84

Paragraph 2.3 of Code G reflects the law contained in s. 24(1)–(3) of PACE84 which sets out seven situations where *a constable* may arrest a person—these can be separated using the time frame of the offence in question:

Offence Time Frame	Police Powers of Arrest under s. 24 PACE84
PAST	1. If a constable has reasonable grounds for suspecting that an offence *has been committed*, he may arrest without a warrant anyone whom he has reasonable grounds to suspect of being guilty of it (s. 24(2)). 2. If an offence *has been committed*, a constable may arrest anyone without a warrant who is guilty of the offence (s. 24(3)(a)). 3. If an offence *has been committed*, a constable may arrest anyone without warrant whom he/she has reasonable grounds for suspecting to be guilty of it (s. 24(3)(b)).
PRESENT	4. A constable may arrest without warrant anyone *who is in the act of committing* an offence (s. 24(1)(b)). 5. A constable may arrest without warrant anyone whom he/she has reasonable grounds for suspecting *to be committing* an offence (s. 24(1)(d)).
FUTURE	6. A constable may arrest without warrant anyone who is *about to commit* an offence (s. 24(1)(a)). 7. A constable may arrest without warrant anyone whom he has reasonable grounds for suspecting to be *about to commit* an offence (s. 24(1(c)).

2.3A There must be some reasonable, objective grounds for the suspicion, based on known facts and information which are relevant to the likelihood the offence has been committed and the person liable to arrest committed it.

KEYNOTE

Reasonable Suspicion

In *Hussien* v *Chong Fook Kam* (1970) AC 942, it was said that 'suspicion' in its ordinary meaning is a state of conjecture or surmise where proof is lacking; 'I suspect but I cannot prove'. The concept has been the subject of numerous case law decisions, *Castorina* v *Chief Constable of Surrey* (1996) 160 LG Rev 241 being one of those. In *Castorina*, the court set out a three-stage test for establishing whether there are reasonable grounds for suspicion to justify an arrest without warrant:

(1) Did the arresting officer suspect that the person who was arrested was guilty of the offence (or committing/about to commit an offence)?
(2) If so, was there reasonable cause (i.e. reasonable grounds) for the arresting officer's suspicion?
(3) If the answer to the two previous questions is in the affirmative, then the officer has a discretion which entitles him/her to make an arrest—was the arresting officer's exercise of his/her discretion reasonable in all the circumstances?

The first stage in the *Castorina* test is a subjective one in that it depends entirely on what was in the officer's mind at the time. The second stage of the *Castorina* test is a purely objective one to be determined by the judge on facts found by the jury/court. This element means that it is not enough for the officer to claim reasonable suspicion in his/her own mind. A court will go on to look at whether there were reasonable grounds to suspect that an offence had been committed and that the person had committed it.

It is not uncommon for police officers to be called to a situation where, while there might be only one or two people responsible for an offence, it is unclear which of a group of people is the culprit. The Court of Appeal has confirmed that where an offence has been committed and one of only a small number of people could have committed it, there is no reason why each member or all the group members cannot be arrested (*Cumming* v *Chief Constable of Northumbria Police* [2003] EWCA Civ 1844). In the absence of any information that could or should enable the police to reduce the number further, the fact that a person is in a small group, one of whom must have committed the offence, can amount to reasonable grounds for suspecting him/her.

Where only one person had the opportunity to commit the offence, that 'opportunity' alone is enough to justify reasonable grounds for suspicion (*Al Fayed* v *Commissioner of Police for the Metropolis* [2004] EWCA Civ 1579). Indeed, in some circumstances opportunity may be sufficient to found a conviction.

However, merely being told to arrest someone by a more senior officer is not a reasonable ground for doing so (*O'Hara* v *Chief Constable of the Royal Ulster Constabulary* [1997] AC 286).

Facts and Information

Facts and information relevant to a person's suspected involvement in an offence should not be confined to those which tend to indicate that the person has committed or attempted to commit the offence. Before making a decision to arrest, a constable should take account of any facts and information that are available, including claims of innocence made by the person, which might dispel the suspicion. Examples of facts and information which might point to a person's innocence and dispel suspicion include those which relate to the statutory defence provided by the Criminal Law Act 1967, s. 3(1) which allows the use of reasonable force in the prevention of crime or making an arrest and the common law of self-defence. This may be relevant when a person appears, or claims, to have been acting reasonably in defence of themselves or others or to prevent their property or the property of others from being stolen, destroyed or damaged, particularly if the offence alleged is based on the use of unlawful force, e.g. a criminal assault. When investigating allegations involving the use of force by school staff, the power given to all school staff under the Education and Inspections Act 2006, s. 93, to use reasonable force to prevent their pupils from committing any offence, injuring persons, damaging property or prejudicing the maintenance of good order and discipline may be similarly relevant. Failing to follow up an obvious line of inquiry (e.g. as to the ownership of property found in the possession of the defendant) may well provide grounds for challenging the exercise of a power of arrest (*Castorina*). There is no need, however, for the officer to discount every possible defence or to seek complete proof of the relevant facts or circumstances before effecting an arrest (*Ward* v *Chief Constable of Avon and Somerset Constabulary* (1986) *The Times*, 26 June).

(b) Necessity criteria

2.4 The power of arrest is only exercisable if the constable has reasonable grounds for *believing* that it is necessary to arrest the person. The statutory criteria for what may constitute necessity are set out in paragraph 2.9 and it remains an operational decision at the discretion of the constable as to:

- which one or more of the necessity criteria (if any) applies to the individual; and
- if any of the criteria do apply, whether to arrest, grant street bail after arrest, report for summons or for charging by post, issue a fixed penalty notice or take any other action that is open to the officer.

2.5 In applying the criteria, the arresting officer has to be satisfied that at least one of the reasons supporting the need for arrest is satisfied.

2.6 Extending the power of arrest to all offences provides a constable with the ability to use that power to deal with any situation. However applying the necessity criteria requires the constable to examine and justify the reason or reasons why a person needs to be arrested or (as the case may be) further arrested, for an offence for the custody officer to decide whether to authorise their detention for that offence.

KEYNOTE

For a constable to have reasonable grounds for *believing* it *necessary* to arrest, he/she is not required to be satisfied that there is no viable alternative to arrest. However, it does mean that in all cases the officer should consider that arrest is the practical, sensible and proportionate option in all the circumstances at the time the decision is made. This applies to a person in police detention after being arrested for an offence who is suspected of involvement in a further offence and where the necessity to arrest them for that further offence is being considered.

2.7 The criteria in paragraph 2.9 below which are set out in section 24 of PACE as substituted by section 110 of the Serious Organised Crime and Police Act 2005 **are** exhaustive. However, the circumstances that may satisfy those criteria remain a matter for the operational discretion of individual officers. Some examples are given to illustrate what those circumstances may be and what officers might consider when deciding whether an arrest is necessary.

2.8 In considering the individual circumstances, the constable must take into account the situation of the victim, the nature of the offence, the circumstances of the suspect and the needs of the investigative process.

2.9 When it is practicable to tell a person why their arrest is necessary (as required by paragraphs 2.2 and 3.3), the constable should outline the facts, information and other circumstances which provide the grounds for believing that their arrest is necessary and which the officer considers satisfy one or more of the statutory criteria in sub-paragraphs (a) to (f) namely:

(a) to enable the name of the person in question to be ascertained (in the case where the constable does not know, and cannot readily ascertain, the person's name, or has reasonable grounds for doubting whether a name given by the person as his name is his real name):

An officer might decide that a person's name cannot be readily ascertained if they fail or refuse to give it when asked, particularly after being warned that failure or refusal is likely to make their arrest necessary. Grounds to doubt a name given may arise if the person appears reluctant or hesitant when asked to give their name or to verify the name they have given.

Where mobile fingerprinting is available and the suspect's name cannot be ascertained or is doubted, the officer should consider using the power under section 61(6A) of PACE (see *Code D paragraph 4.3(e)*) to take and check the fingerprints of a suspect as this may avoid the need to arrest solely to enable their name to be ascertained.

(b) correspondingly as regards the person's address:

An officer might decide that a person's address cannot be readily ascertained if they fail or refuse to give it when asked, particularly after being warned that such a failure or refusal is likely to make their arrest necessary. Grounds to doubt an address given may arise if the person appears reluctant or hesitant when asked to give their address or is unable to provide verifiable details of the locality they claim to live in.

When considering reporting to consider summons or charging by post as alternatives to arrest, an address would be satisfactory if the person will be at it for a sufficiently long period for it to be possible to serve them with the summons or requisition and charge; or, that some other person at that address specified by the person will accept service on their behalf. When considering issuing a penalty notice, the address should be one where the person will be in the event of enforcement action if the person does not pay the penalty or is convicted and fined after a court hearing.

(c) to prevent the person in question—

(i) causing physical injury to himself or any other person;

This might apply where the suspect has already used or threatened violence against others and it is thought likely that they may assault others if they are not arrested.

(ii) suffering physical injury;

This might apply where the suspect's behaviour and actions are believed likely to provoke, or have provoked, others to want to assault the suspect unless the suspect is arrested for their own protection.

(iii) causing loss or damage to property;

This might apply where the suspect is a known persistent offender with a history of serial offending against property (theft and criminal damage) and it is thought likely that they may continue offending if they are not arrested.

(iv) committing an offence against public decency (only applies where members of the public going about their normal business cannot reasonably be expected to avoid the person in question);

This might apply when an offence against public decency is being committed in a place to which the public have access and is likely to be repeated in that or some other public place at a time when the public are likely to encounter the suspect.

(v) causing an unlawful obstruction of the highway;

This might apply to any offence where its commission causes an unlawful obstruction which it is believed may continue or be repeated if the person is not arrested, particularly if the person has been warned that they are causing an obstruction.

KEYNOTE

Paragraph 2.9(a), (b) and (c)

Although a warning is not expressly required, officers should, if practicable, consider whether to issue a warning which points out the person's offending behaviour and explains why, if the person does not stop, the resulting consequences may make his/her arrest necessary. Such a warning might:

- if heeded, avoid the need to arrest; or
- if ignored, support the need to arrest and also help to prove the mental element of certain offences, e.g. the person's intent or awareness, or help to rebut a defence that he/she was acting reasonably.

A person who is warned that he/she may be liable to arrest if his/her real name and address cannot be ascertained should be given a reasonable opportunity to establish his/her real name and address before deciding that either or both are unknown and cannot be readily ascertained or that there are reasonable grounds to doubt that a name and address the person has given is his/her real name and address. He/she should be told why his/her name is not known and cannot be readily ascertained and (as the case may be) of the grounds for doubting that a name and address he/she has given is his/her real name and address, including, for example, the reason why a particular document the person has produced to verify his/her real name and/or address is not sufficient.

(d) to protect a child or other vulnerable person from the person in question.
This might apply when the health (physical or mental) or welfare of a child or vulnerable person is likely to be harmed or is at risk of being harmed, if the person is not arrested in cases where it is not practicable and appropriate to make alternative arrangements to prevent the suspect from having any harmful or potentially harmful contact with the child or vulnerable person.

(e) to allow the prompt and effective investigation of the offence or of the conduct of the person in question.

KEYNOTE

Paragraph 2.9(e)

The meaning of 'prompt' should be considered on a case-by-case basis taking account of all the circumstances. It indicates that the progress of the investigation should not be delayed to the extent that it would adversely affect the effectiveness of the investigation. The arresting officer also has discretion to release the arrested person on 'street bail' as an alternative to taking the person directly to the station. Having determined that the necessity criteria have been met and having made the arrest, the officer can then consider the use of street bail on the basis of the effective and efficient progress of the investigation of the offence in question. It gives the officer discretion to compel the person to attend a police station at a date/time that best suits the overall needs of the particular investigation. Its use is not confined to dealing with child-care issues or allowing officers to attend to more urgent operational duties, and granting street bail does not retrospectively negate the need to arrest.

In *DE* v *Chief Constable of West Midlands Police* [2023] EWHC 146 (KB), it was held that an arrest could be necessary for the purposes of the 'prompt and effective investigation' criterion where the arresting officer's sole reason for believing the arrest to be necessary was the imposition of specific bail conditions, such as to protect a witness from intimidation. However, a general wish to impose bail conditions without considering what they might be could fall foul of s. 25(5)(e) of PACE84.

This may arise when it is thought likely that unless the person is arrested and then either taken in custody to the police station or granted 'street bail' to attend the station later, further action considered necessary to properly investigate their involvement in the offence would be frustrated, unreasonably delayed or otherwise hindered and therefore be impracticable. Examples of such actions include:

(i) *interviewing the suspect* on occasions when the person's voluntary attendance is not considered to be a practicable alternative to arrest, because for example:
- it is thought unlikely that the person would attend the police station voluntarily to be interviewed.
- it is necessary to interview the suspect about the outcome of other investigative action for which their arrest is necessary, see (ii) to (v) below.
- arrest would enable the special warning to be given in accordance with Code C paragraphs 10.10 and 10.11 when the suspect is found:
  - ~ in possession of incriminating objects, or at a place where such objects are found;
  - ~ at or near the scene of the crime at or about the time it was committed.
- the person has made false statements and/or presented false evidence;

- it is thought likely that the person:
  - ~ may steal or destroy evidence;
  - ~ may collude or make contact with, co-suspects or conspirators;
  - ~ may intimidate or threaten or make contact with, witnesses.

KEYNOTE

Paragraph 2.9(e)(i)

An officer who believes that it is necessary to interview the person suspected of committing the offence must then consider whether his/her arrest is necessary in order to carry out the interview. The officer is not required to interrogate the suspect to determine whether he/she will attend a police station voluntarily to be interviewed but the officer must consider whether the suspect's voluntary attendance is a practicable alternative for carrying out the interview. If it is, then arrest would not be necessary. Conversely, an officer who considers this option but is not satisfied that it is a practicable alternative may have reasonable grounds for deciding that the arrest is necessary at the outset 'on the street'. Without such considerations, the officer would not be able to establish that arrest was necessary in order to interview.

Circumstances which suggest that a person's arrest 'on the street' would not be necessary to interview him/her might be where the officer:

- is satisfied as to the person's identity and address and that he/she will attend the police station voluntarily to be interviewed, either immediately or by arrangement at a future date and time; and
- is not aware of any other circumstances which indicate that voluntary attendance would not be a practicable alternative. See para. 2.9(e)(i)–(v).

When making arrangements for the person's voluntary attendance, the officer should tell the person:

- that to properly investigate his/her suspected involvement in the offence, he/she must be interviewed under caution at the police station, but in the circumstances his/her arrest for this purpose will not be necessary if he/she attends the police station voluntarily to be interviewed;
- that if he/she attends voluntarily, he/she will be entitled to free legal advice before, and to have a solicitor present at, the interview;
- that the date and time of the interview will take account of the person's circumstances and the needs of the investigation; and
- that if the person does not agree to attend voluntarily at a time which meets the needs of the investigation, or having so agreed fails to attend, or having attended fails to remain for the interview to be completed, his/her arrest will be necessary to enable him/her to be interviewed.

When the person attends the police station voluntarily for interview by arrangement (as above), his/her arrest on arrival at the station prior to interview will only be justified if:

- new information coming to light after the arrangements were made indicates that, from that time, voluntary attendance ceased to be a practicable alternative and the person's arrest became necessary; and
- it was not reasonably practicable for the person to be arrested before he/she attended the station.

If a person who attends the police station voluntarily to be interviewed decides to leave before the interview is complete, the police would at that point be entitled to consider whether the person's arrest was necessary to carry out the interview. The possibility that the person might decide to leave during the interview is therefore not a valid reason for arresting him/her before the interview has commenced. See Code C, para. 3.21.

(ii) when considering arrest in connection with the investigation of an *indictable offence*, there is a need:

- to enter and search without a search warrant any premises occupied or controlled by the arrested person or where the person was when arrested or immediately before arrest;
- to prevent the arrested person from having contact with others;
- to detain the arrested person for more than 24 hours before charge.

KEYNOTE

Paragraph 2.9(e)(ii)

It should be remembered that certain powers available as the result of an arrest (e.g. entry and search of premises, detention without charge beyond 24 hours, holding a person incommunicado and delaying access to legal advice) only apply in respect of indictable offences and are subject to the specific requirements on authorisation as set out in PACE84 and the relevant Code of Practice.

(iii) when considering arrest in connection with any *recordable offence* and it is necessary to secure or preserve evidence of that offence by taking fingerprints, footwear impressions or samples from the suspect for evidential comparison or matching with other material relating to that offence, for example, from the crime scene.

(iv) when considering arrest in connection with any offence and it is necessary to search, examine or photograph the person to obtain evidence.

KEYNOTE

Paragraph 2.9(e)(iii) and (iv)

The necessity criteria do not permit arrest solely to enable the routine taking, checking (speculative searching) and retention of fingerprints, samples, footwear impressions and photographs when there are no prior grounds to believe that checking and comparing the fingerprints etc. or taking a photograph would provide relevant evidence of the person's involvement in the offence concerned or would help to ascertain or verify his/her real identity.

(v) when considering arrest in connection with an offence to which the statutory Class A drug testing requirements in Code C section 17 apply, to enable testing when it is thought that drug misuse might have caused or contributed to the offence.

KEYNOTE

Paragraph 2.9(e)(v)

The necessity criteria do not permit arrest for an offence solely because it happens to be one of the statutory drug testing 'trigger offences' when there is no suspicion that Class A drug misuse might have caused or contributed to the offence.

(f) to prevent any prosecution for the offence from being hindered by the disappearance of the person in question.

This may arise when it is thought that:

- if the person is not arrested they are unlikely to attend court if they are prosecuted;
- the address given is not a satisfactory address for service of a summons or a written charge and requisition to appear at court because the person will not be at it for a sufficiently long period for the summons or charge and requisition to be served and no other person at that specified address will accept service on their behalf.

KEYNOTE

Section 24(4)–(6) of PACE84 sets out the necessity criteria—para. 2.9 of Code G repeats and expands on the law.

3.3.5 ## Code G—3 Information to be given on Arrest

(a) Cautions—when a caution must be given

3.1 Code C paragraphs 10.1 and 10.2 set out the requirement for a person whom there are grounds to suspect of an offence to be cautioned before being questioned or further questioned about an offence.

3.2 *Not used.*

3.3 A person who is arrested, or further arrested, must be informed at the time if practicable, or if not, as soon as it becomes practicable thereafter, that they are under arrest and the grounds and reasons for their arrest.

KEYNOTE

Information to be Given on Arrest—s. 28 PACE84

Paragraph 3.3 summarises the requirements set out in s. 28 of PACE84 which states:

(1) Subject to subsection (5) below, where a person is arrested, otherwise than by being informed that he is under arrest, the arrest is not lawful unless the person arrested is informed that he is under arrest as soon as is practicable after his arrest.
(2) Where a person is arrested by a constable, subsection (1) above applies regardless of whether the fact of the arrest is obvious.
(3) Subject to subsection (5) below, no arrest is lawful unless the person arrested is informed of the ground for the arrest at the time of, or as soon as is practicable after, the arrest.
(4) Where a person is arrested by a constable, subsection (3) above applies regardless of whether the ground for the arrest is obvious.
(5) Nothing in this section is to be taken to require a person to be informed—
 (a) that he is under arrest; or
 (b) of the ground for the arrest,
 if it was not reasonably practicable for him to be so informed by reason of his having escaped from arrest before the information could be given.

Arrest and Reason(s) For It

Arrested persons must be given sufficient information to enable them to understand they have been deprived of their liberty and the reason they have been arrested, as soon as practicable after the arrest, e.g. when persons are arrested on suspicion of committing an offence, they must be informed of the nature of the suspected offence and when and where it was committed.

In relation to the arrest itself, in *R* v *Fiak* [2005] EWCA Crim 2381 it was held that an arrest had not been rendered unlawful by the police officer's failure to use the word 'arrest'—this requirement might be met by using a colloquialism, provided that the person is familiar with it and understands its meaning (e.g. 'you're locked up' or 'you're nicked' (*Christie* v *Leachinsky* [1947] AC 573)).

In relation to the reason for arrest, each case will be decided in relation to individual circumstances. For example, in *Taylor* v *Chief Constable of Thames Valley* [2004] EWCA Civ 858, the court stated that the words 'I am arresting you on suspicion of violent disorder on 18 April 1998 at Hillgrove Farm' were sufficient, whereas in *Wilson* v *Chief Constable of Lancashire Constabulary* (2000) Po LR 367, the words 'You're under arrest for theft' were insufficient. In essence, vague or technical language should be avoided (*Fox* v *United Kingdom* (1991) 13 EHRR 157). It does not matter that the words describe more than one offence (e.g. 'burglary' or 'fraud'), provided that they adequately describe the offence for which the person has been arrested (*Abbassy* v *Metropolitan Police Commissioner* [1990] 1 WLR 385). An arresting officer may not, however, lead a person to think that the officer is arresting him/her for one offence when in truth the officer wishes to arrest the person for another offence (*Christie*).

When explaining why one or more of the arrest criteria apply, it is not necessary to disclose any specific details that might undermine or otherwise adversely affect any investigative processes. For example, the conduct of a formal interview when prior disclosure of such details might give the suspect an opportunity to fabricate an innocent explanation or to otherwise conceal lies from the interviewer.

Suspects must also be informed of the reason or reasons why arrest is considered necessary.

3.4 A person who is arrested, or further arrested, must also be cautioned unless:

(a) it is impracticable to do so by reason of their condition or behaviour at the time;

(b) they have already been cautioned immediately prior to arrest as in *paragraph 3.1.*

(b) Terms of the cautions (Taken from Code C section 10)

3.5 The caution, which must be given on arrest, should be in the following terms:

'You do not have to say anything. But it may harm your defence if you do not mention when questioned something which you later rely on in Court. Anything you do say may be given in evidence.'

Where the use of the Welsh Language is appropriate, a constable may provide the caution directly in Welsh in the following terms:

'Does dim rhaid i chi ddweud dim byd. Ond gall niweidio eich amddiffyniad os na fyddwch chi'n sôn, wrth gael eich holi, am rywbeth y byddwch chi'n dibynnu arno nes ymlaen yn y Llys. Gall unrhyw beth yr ydych yn ei ddweud gael ei roi fel tystiolaeth.'

KEYNOTE

Nothing in this Code requires a caution to be given or repeated when informing a person not under arrest that he/she may be prosecuted for an offence. However, a court will not be able to draw any inferences under the Criminal Justice and Public Order Act 1994, s. 34, if the person was not cautioned.

3.6 Minor deviations from the words of any caution given in accordance with this Code do not constitute a breach of this Code, provided the sense of the relevant caution is preserved.

KEYNOTE

If it appears that a person does not understand the caution, the people giving it should explain it in their own words.

3.7 *Not used.*

3.3.6 Code G—4 Records of Arrest

(a) General

4.1 The arresting officer is required to record in his pocket book or by other methods used for recording information:

- the nature and circumstances of the offence leading to the arrest
- the reason or reasons why arrest was necessary
- the giving of the caution
- anything said by the person at the time of arrest.

4.2 Such a record should be made at the time of the arrest unless impracticable to do. If not made at that time, the record should then be completed as soon as possible thereafter.

4.3 On arrival at the police station or after being first arrested at the police station, the arrested person must be brought before the custody officer as soon as practicable and a custody record must be opened in accordance with section 2 of Code C. The information given by the arresting officer on the circumstances and reason or reasons for arrest shall be recorded as part of the custody record. Alternatively, a copy of the record made by the officer in accordance with paragraph 4.1 above shall be attached as part of the custody record. See *paragraph 2.2* and *Code C paragraphs 3.4 and 10.3.*

4.4 The custody record will serve as a record of the arrest. Copies of the custody record will be provided in accordance with paragraphs 2.4 and 2.4A of Code C and access for inspection of the original record in accordance with paragraph 2.5 of Code C.

(b) Interviews and arrests

4.5 Records of interview, significant statements or silences will be treated in the same way as set out in sections 11 and 12 of Code C and in Codes E and F (audio and visual recording of interviews).

3.3.7 Arrest without Warrant—'Citizen's Arrest'

Section 24A of PACE84 provides a more restricted scheme of powers of arrest for *a person other than a constable* (sometimes referred to as the 'citizen's arrest').

PACE84, s. 24A states:

(1) A person other than a constable may arrest without a warrant—
 (a) anyone who is in the act of committing an indictable offence;
 (b) anyone whom he has reasonable grounds for suspecting to be committing an indictable offence.

(2) Where an indictable offence has been committed, a person other than a constable may arrest without a warrant—
 (a) anyone who is guilty of the offence;
 (b) anyone whom he has reasonable grounds for suspecting to be guilty of it.

KEYNOTE

Four 'Citizen's Arrest' Scenarios—s. 24A PACE84

Section 24A(1)–(2) of PACE84 sets out four arrest powers—these can be separated using the time frame of the offence in question:

Offence Time Frame	Citizen's Powers of Arrest under s. 24A PACE84
PAST	1. Where an indictable offence *has been committed*, a person other than a constable may arrest without warrant anyone who is guilty of the offence (s. 24A(2)(a)). 2. Where an indictable offence *has been committed*, a person other than a constable may arrest without warrant anyone whom he/she has reasonable grounds for suspecting to be guilty of it (s. 24A(2)(b)).
PRESENT	3. A person other than a constable may arrest without warrant anyone who is *in the act of committing* an indictable offence (s. 24A(1)(a)). 4. A person other than a constable may arrest without warrant anyone whom he/she has reasonable grounds for suspecting *to be committing* an indictable offence (s. 24A(1)(b)).

'Citizen's Arrest' Facts

1. These powers *only apply to indictable offences*. An 'indictable offence' means an offence which, if committed by an adult, is triable on indictment, whether it is exclusively so triable or triable either way, i.e. a citizen cannot arrest a person in relation to a summary only offence (s. 64 of the Criminal Law Act 1977).
2. Unlike a constable, a citizen *cannot arrest a person for an* anticipated (future) offence.
3. 'Reasonable suspicion' operates in the same way as it does for a constable (**see para. 3.3.4**).
4. If a citizen arrests a person under s. 24A(2) for an offence the citizen believes has been committed, the arrest *will be unlawful* if it cannot be established that an indictable offence was in fact committed (*R* v *Self* [1992] 1 WLR 657).

5. Where an arrest is carried out under s. 24A(1)(b), there is *no requirement* that an indictable offence has actually been committed (*Sowande* v *CPS* [2017] EWHC 1234 (Admin)).
6. A citizen *cannot arrest* a person for an offence under part 3 or 3A of the Public Order Act 1986 (these are offence relating to racial, religious and sexual orientation hatred (**see para. 3.12.2**)). *Only constables* will have the power to arrest persons in the context of these offences (s. 24A(5)).

Necessity

A citizen cannot arrest a person unless the necessity criteria (set out in s. 24A(3) and (4)) are satisfied.

The citizen making the arrest has *reasonable grounds for believing* that for *any* of the below reasons it is necessary to arrest the person in question:

↓

To prevent the person:
Causing physical injury to him/herself or any other person;
Suffering physical injury;
Causing loss of or damage to property;
Making off before a constable can assume responsibility for him/her

↓

AND
It appears to the person making the arrest that it is not reasonably practicable for a constable to make it instead

3.3.8 Arrest without Warrant—Other Powers of Arrest

Apart from the general power of arrest under s. 24 of PACE84, several other powers of arrest exist.

3.3.8.1 Preserved Powers of Arrest

Section 26 of PACE84 repealed all other powers of arrest without warrant which existed before the 1984 Act except those listed in sch. 2.

The common law power of arrest for breach of the peace has been preserved by s. 26 of the 1984 Act (*DPP* v *Orum* [1989] 1 WLR 88).

3.3.8.2 Fingerprinting

Section 27 of PACE84 provides a power of arrest to take a person's fingerprints.

3.3.8.3 Failure to Answer Police Bail

Section 46A of PACE84 provides a power of arrest when a person fails to answer police bail.

3.3.8.4 Arrest to Take Samples

Section 63A of PACE84 provides a power of arrest without warrant in respect of people:

- who have been charged with/reported for a recordable offence and who have not had a sample taken or the sample was unsuitable/insufficient for analysis;
- who have been convicted of a recordable offence and have not had a sample taken since conviction;

- who have been so convicted and have had a sample taken before or since conviction but the sample was unsuitable/insufficient for analysis.

This is simply a summary of s. 63A and reference should be made to the 1984 Act for the exact wording.

3.3.8.5 Cross-border Arrest without Warrant

The Criminal Justice and Public Order Act 1994 makes provision for officers from one part of the United Kingdom to go into another part of the United Kingdom to arrest someone there in connection with an offence committed within their jurisdiction.

KEYNOTE

Three situations are catered for under s. 137 of the Act.

1. *A police officer from an English or Welsh police force may arrest a person in Scotland or Northern Ireland.* If it appears to the constable that it would have been lawful for him/her to have exercised the powers had the suspected person been in England or Wales (s. 137(4)), a constable of a police force in England or Wales who has reasonable grounds for suspecting that an offence has been committed or attempted in England or Wales and that the suspected person is in Scotland or Northern Ireland may arrest without warrant the suspected person wherever he/she is in Scotland or Northern Ireland (s. 137(1)).
2. *A police officer from a Scottish police force may arrest a person in England, Wales or Northern Ireland.* If it appears to the constable that it would have been lawful for him/her to have exercised the powers had the suspected person been in Scotland (s. 137(5)), any constable of a police force in Scotland who has reasonable grounds for suspecting that an offence has been committed or attempted in Scotland and that the suspected person is in England or Wales or in Northern Ireland may, as regards the suspected person, wherever he/she is in England or Wales or in Northern Ireland, exercise the same powers of arrest as it would be competent for him/her to exercise were the person in Scotland (s. 137(2)).
3. *A police officer from a police force in Northern Ireland may arrest a person in England, Wales or Scotland.* If it appears to the constable that it would have been lawful for him/her to have exercised the powers had the suspected person been in Northern Ireland (s. 137(6)), any constable of a police force in Northern Ireland who has reasonable grounds for suspecting that an offence has been committed or attempted in Northern Ireland and that the suspected person is in England or Wales or in Scotland may arrest without a warrant the suspected person wherever he/she is in England or Wales or in Scotland (s. 137(3)).

The 1994 Act sets out where a person arrested outside the relevant country should be taken on arrest (s. 137(7)). The Act also provides wide powers of search in connection with arrests (s. 139).

3.3.9 Arrest under Warrant

The law and procedures associated with the issue and execution of warrants is dealt with in ***Evidence and Procedure*, paras 2.1.5 to 2.1.6.2**.

3.3.10 Voluntary Attendance at a Police Station or Elsewhere

There are a variety of situations where a person attends at a police station or elsewhere in a voluntary capacity. For example, where the person is a suspect, by pre-arrangement with the officers in the case or where the person learns that the police want to speak to him/her or perhaps where a person has elected to accompany a Police Community Support Officer to a police station rather than awaiting the arrival of a constable. Code C, paras 3.21 to 3.22B set out how such a person should be treated (**see *Evidence and Procedure*, para. 2.6.8**).

There is no distinction between a person being arrested at a police station after attending voluntarily and a person arrested elsewhere, provided the arresting officers acted appropriately and reasonably (*Al Fayed*). However, there are certain statutory provisions with regard to the entitlements and treatment of people who are 'voluntary attendees' and these are set out below.

PACE84, s. 29 states:

> Where for the purpose of assisting with an investigation a person attends voluntarily at a police station or at any other place where a constable is present or accompanies a constable to a police station or any such other place without having been arrested—
> (a) he shall be entitled to leave at will unless he is placed under arrest;
> (b) he shall be informed at once that he is under arrest if a decision is taken by a constable to prevent him from leaving at will.

KEYNOTE

The person's attendance at a police station or other place must be for the purpose of 'assisting with an investigation', which would, on a strict interpretation, encompass witnesses and victims. The principle behind s. 29 (and also Code C, paras 3.2.1 to 3.22B) is to avoid the situation where people find themselves at a police station (or any other place where there is a police officer present) and feel compelled to remain there but without the attendant procedural protection that follows a formal arrest. Section 29(b) is unusual in that it (along with s. 31 below) imposes an obligation on a police officer to make an arrest, an activity that is usually entirely within his/her discretion. The time when the need to arrest the person arises is when the officer takes the decision to prevent the person from leaving (e.g. the time when the officer decides him/herself). It is not the time when the person is actually prevented from leaving or even when he/she is told of the decision.

The PACE84, s. 31 states:

> Where—
> (a) a person—
> (i) has been arrested for an offence; and
> (ii) is at a police station in consequence of that arrest; and
> (b) it appears to a constable that, if he were released from that arrest, he would be liable to arrest for some other offence, he shall be arrested for that other offence.

The purpose of the s. 31 requirement is to prevent the release and immediate re-arrest of an offender. Therefore, s. 31 does not prevent any further arrest from being delayed until the release of the prisoner for the initial arrest is imminent (*R* v *Samuel* [1988] QB 615). It has been held that where officers who had arrested a man for a breach of the peace failed to arrest him formally for the further offence of assault on the police, their omission did not impact on the magistrates' decision that there was a case to answer in respect of the assault charge (*Blench* v *DPP* [2004] EWHC 2717 (Admin)).

The power (though not, on the strict wording, the *obligation*) to arrest a person at a police station for a further offence under s. 31 is among those that can be conferred on an investigating officer designated under sch. 4 to the Police Reform Act 2002. Where this power is exercised by a designated investigating officer, the provisions of s. 36 of the Criminal Justice and Public Order Act 1994 (failing to account for objects etc.) will apply.

3.3.11 Arrest Elsewhere than at a Police Station

PACE84, s. 30 provides for the procedure to be adopted when a person has been arrested at any place other than a police station. Section 30 states:

> (1) Subsection (1A) applies where a person is, at any place other than a police station—
> (a) arrested by a constable for an offence, or
> (b) taken into custody by a constable after being arrested for an offence by a person other than a constable.

(1A) The person must be taken by a constable to a police station as soon as practicable after the arrest.

(1B) Subsection (1A) has effect subject to section 30A (release on bail) and subsection (7) (release without bail).

(2) Subject to subsections (3) and (5) below, the police station to which an arrested person is taken under subsection (1A) above shall be a designated police station.

(3) A constable to whom this subsection applies may take an arrested person to any police station unless it appears to the constable that it may be necessary to keep the arrested person in police detention for more than six hours.

(4) Subsection (3) above applies—
  (a) to a constable who is working in a locality covered by a police station which is not a designated police station; and
  (b) to a constable belonging to a body of constables maintained by an authority other than a police authority.

(5) Any constable may take an arrested person to any police station if—
  (a) either of the following conditions is satisfied—
    (i) the constable has arrested him without the assistance of any other constable and no other constable is available to assist him;
    (ii) the constable has taken him into custody from a person other than a constable without the assistance of any other constable and no other constable is available to assist him; and
  (b) it appears to the constable that he will be unable to take the arrested person to a designated police station without the arrested person injuring himself, the constable or some other person.

(6) If the first police station to which an arrested person is taken after his arrest is not a designated police station, he shall be taken to a designated police station not more than six hours after his arrival at the first police station unless he is released previously.

(7) A person arrested by a constable at any place other than a police station must be released without bail if the condition in subsection (7A) is satisfied.

(7A) The condition is that, at any time before the person arrested reaches a police station, a constable is satisfied that there are no grounds for keeping him under arrest or releasing him on bail under section 30A.

KEYNOTE

Summary

When a person is arrested by a constable for an offence/taken into custody after having been arrested by a person other than a constable (i.e. a 'citizen's arrest'), that person must be taken to a designated police station as soon as possible after arrest (unless he/she is given 'street bail'/de-arrested or the s. 30(10) 'delay' applies).

The person can be taken to *any* police station if:

The arrest was made without the assistance of any other constable/the person was taken into custody from a citizen and no other constable is available to assist

+

it appears to the constable that he/she will be unable to take the arrested person to a designated police station without the arrested person injuring him/herself or some other person.

If the first station the arrested person is taken to is not a designated police station, he/she shall be taken to a designated police station ***not more than six hours*** after his/her arrival at the first police station unless released previously.

De-arrest

Under s. 30(7) and (7A), the officer must de-arrest a person if he/she is satisfied, before reaching the police station, that there are no grounds for detaining that person. This may happen where the person has been arrested under one of the general arrest conditions and the particular condition has ceased to apply (e.g. the person gives a suitable name and address having originally failed to do so). An officer who releases a prisoner under s. 30(7) and (7A) must record the fact that he/she has done so and must make that record as soon as practicable after the release (s. 30(8) and (9)).

Delay

Under s. 30(10), the arresting officer can delay taking the arrested person to a police station if the arrested person's presence elsewhere is necessary to carry out such investigations as it is reasonable to carry out immediately (immediately means immediately—otherwise they must be taken to a police station. Where there is such a delay, the reasons for it must be recorded when the person first arrives at the police station (s. 30(11)). The delay permitted under s. 30(10) and (11) will only apply if the matter requires immediate investigation; if it can wait, the exception will not apply and the person must be taken straight to a police station (*R* v *Kerawalla* [1991] Crim LR 451). Checking out an alibi is an example of such a justified delay (*Dallison* v *Caffery* [1965] 1 QB 348)).

Escort Officers

Escort officers designated under sch. 4 to the Police Reform Act 2002 may be authorised to take people who have been arrested by a constable in the relevant police area to a police station under the provisions of s. 30(1). The provisions for taking a detainee to a non-designated police station (s. 30(3) and 4(a)), and also the provisions allowing a delay in taking the prisoner to a police station (s. 30(10)), will also apply to any exercise of the powers by a designated escort officer (Police Reform Act 2002, sch. 4, part 4). Other exceptions in the application of s. 30(1) to terrorism and immigration are made by s. 30(12).

3.4 Protection of People Suffering from Mental Disorders

3.4.1 Introduction

The Mental Health Act 1983 provides for the detention, care and treatment of people suffering from mental disorders and includes powers for enforcing some of its provisions. This chapter focuses on the law regarding the power to remove a person to a place of safety (under s. 136), executing warrants to search for and remove patients (under s. 135) and powers to retake patients after their escape (under s. 138). If those powers are executed in good faith, the 1983 Act also provides some protection against criminal and civil liability for the police officers and care workers who use them (s. 139).

3.4.2 Removal etc. of Mentally Disordered Persons Without a Warrant

The Mental Health Act 1983 creates a power for police officers to remove a person who appears to be suffering from a mental disorder under certain conditions.

Section 136 states:

(1) If a person appears to a constable to be suffering from mental disorder and to be in immediate need of care or control, the constable may, if he thinks it necessary to do so in the interests of that person or for the protection of other persons—
- (a) remove the person to a place of safety within the meaning of section 135, or
- (b) if the person is already at a place of safety within the meaning of that section, keep the person at that place or remove the person to another place of safety.

(1A) The power of a constable under subsection (1) may be exercised where the mentally disordered person is at any place, other than—
- (a) any house, flat or room where that person, or any other person, is living, or
- (b) any yard, garden, garage or outhouse that is used in connection with the house, flat or room, other than one that is also used in connection with one or more other houses, flats or rooms.

(1B) For the purpose of exercising the power under subsection (1), a constable may enter any place where the power may be exercised, if need be by force.

(1C) Before deciding to remove a person to, or to keep a person at, a place of safety under subsection (1), the constable must, if it is practicable to do so, consult—
- (a) a registered medical practitioner,
- (b) a registered nurse,
- (c) an approved mental health professional, or
- (d) a person of a description specified in regulations made by the Secretary of State.

(2) A person removed to, or kept at a place of safety under this section may be detained there for a period not exceeding the permitted period of detention for the purpose of enabling him to be examined by a registered medical practitioner and to be interviewed by an approved mental health professional and of making any necessary arrangements for his treatment or care.

(2A) In subsection (2), 'the permitted period of detention' means—
- (a) the period of 24 hours beginning with—
  - (i) in a case where the person is removed to a place of safety, the time when the person arrives at that place;
  - (ii) in a case where the person is kept at a place of safety, the time when the constable decides to keep the person at that place; or

(b) where an authorisation is given in relation to the person under section 136B, that period of 24 hours and such further period as is specified in the authorisation.

(3) A constable, an approved mental health professional or a person authorised by either of them for the purposes of this subsection may, before the end of the period of the permitted period of detention mentioned in subsection (2) above, take a person detained in a place of safety under that subsection to one or more other places of safety.

(4) A person taken to a place of safety under subsection (3) above may be detained there for a purpose mentioned in subsection (2) above for a period ending no later than at the end of the period of the permitted period of detention mentioned in that subsection.

(5) This section is subject to section 136A which makes provision about the removal and taking of persons to a police station, and the keeping of persons at a police station, under this section.

KEYNOTE

The power places a lot of responsibility and latitude on the officer who must decide whether:

- the person is suffering from mental disorder (see below),
- the person is in immediate need of care or control, and
- it is necessary in the person's interest or for someone else's protection that he/she be removed to a place of safety,

before the power is applicable.

For the purposes of this Act, 'mental disorder' means any disorder or disability of the mind; and 'mentally disordered' shall be construed accordingly (s. 1(2)).

Section 135(6) defines a 'place of safety' as:

- residential accommodation provided by a local social services authority;
- a hospital;
- a police station;
- an independent hospital or care home for mentally disordered persons; or
- any other suitable place the occupier of which is willing temporarily to receive the patient.

For the purpose of subs. (6), a house, flat or room where a person is living may not be regarded as a suitable place unless the person believed to be suffering from a mental disorder is the sole occupier of the place, and that person agrees to the use of the place as a place of safety, or any other occupier or person responsible for the management of the property agrees to such use (s. 135(7)).

The use of police stations as places of safety is subject to s. 136A of the Act. This provides that a child (a person aged under 18) may not be removed to, kept at or taken to a place of safety that is a police station (subs. (1A)).

However, an adult may be removed to, kept at or taken to a place of safety that is a police station but only in circumstances specified in the Mental Health Act 1983 (Places of Safety) Regulations 2017 (SI 2017/1036).

Regulation 2(1) states:

> An adult ('A') may only be removed to, kept at, or taken to, a place of safety that is a police station in the exercise of a power to which section 136A of the Act applies where—
>
> (a) the decision-maker is satisfied that—
>
> (i) the behaviour of A poses an imminent risk of serious injury or death to A, or to another person,
>
> (ii) because of that risk, no place of safety other than a police station in the relevant police area can reasonably be expected to detain A, and
>
> (iii) the requirement in sub-paragraph (b) of regulation 4(1) will be met, and
>
> (b) where the decision-maker is not an officer of the rank of inspector or above, an officer of that rank or above authorises that A may be removed to, kept at, or taken to a place of safety that is a police station.

Regulation 4(1) referred to in reg. 2(1)(a)(iii) refers to the duty of a custody officer in relation to the welfare of a detained adult (see *Evidence and Procedure*, para. 2.6.7).

Before determining that the circumstances in paras (i) to (iii) of reg. 2(1)(a) exist, a decision-maker must, if it is reasonably practicable to do so, consult a registered medical practitioner, a registered nurse, an approved mental health professional, an occupational therapist or a paramedic (para. 2(2)).

A 'decision maker' means, in relation to the exercise of a power under a warrant issued under s. 135(1) or a power under s. 136(1) of the Act, the constable exercising that power, or in relation to the exercise of a power under a warrant issued under s. 135(3A) or a power under s. 136(3) of the Act, the constable or approved mental health professional who exercises that power or authorises a person to exercise that power (reg. 2(3)).

Any person being conveyed to a place of safety or detained at such a place will be deemed to be in legal custody (s. 137(1)). Such a person will not be in 'police detention' for the purposes of s. 118 of the Police and Criminal Evidence Act 1984 even where the place of safety is a police station.

The registered medical practitioner who is responsible for the examination of a person detained, at any time before the expiry of the period of 24 hours, may authorise the detention of the person for a further period not exceeding 12 hours (beginning immediately at the end of the period of 24 hours). This authorisation may be given only if the registered medical practitioner considers that the extension is necessary because the condition of the person detained is such that it would not be practicable for the assessment of the person to be carried out before the end of the period of 24 hours (s. 136B). Where the maximum period of detention is due to expire, the police may make an application to the High Court for an order of further detention to be made. In *Surrey Police* v *PC* [2024] EWHC 1274 (Fam), it was held that such an application should be supported by evidence setting out the chronology, the steps that have been taken to locate an alternative place of safety, details of what care and support the person will/has received while in police custody and the relevant legal framework. Where a person is detained under a warrant issued under s. 135(1) or (2) or a power under s. 136(2) or (4), a constable may search the person, at any time while the person is so detained, if the constable has reasonable grounds for believing that the person may present a danger to themself or to others and is concealing on their person an item that could be used to cause physical injury to themself or to others. The power to search is only a power to search to the extent that is reasonably required for the purpose of discovering the item that the constable believes the person to be concealing. It does not authorise a constable to require a person to remove any of their clothing other than an outer coat, jacket or gloves, but does authorise a search of a person's mouth (s. 136C(5)).

3.4.3 Warrant to Search for and Remove Patients

Where there is reasonable cause to suspect that a person believed to be suffering from a mental disorder has been, or is being, ill-treated, neglected or kept otherwise than under proper control, or being unable to care for themself, is living alone, an information on oath may be laid by an approved mental health professional and a warrant issued by a justice of the peace (s. 135(1)).

The warrant authorises any constable to enter, if need be by force, any premises specified in the warrant in which that person is believed to be and, if thought fit, to remove them to a place of safety. The constable must be accompanied by an approved mental health professional and by a registered medical practitioner (s. 135(4)). Where the premises specified in the warrant are a place of safety, the constable executing the warrant may, instead of removing the person to another place of safety, keep the person at those premises for the purpose mentioned in subs. (1) (s. 135(1A)).

A warrant may also be issued in respect of a patient ordered to be detained by a court (s. 135(2)). The constable executing the warrant may be accompanied by a registered medical practitioner or any person authorised by or under the Act to take or retake the patient (s. 135(4)).

The power to conduct a protective search of a person detained under the above provisions is contained in s. 136C of the Act (**see para. 3.4.2, Keynote**).

3.4.4 Retaking of Patients Escaping from Custody

Section 138 of the 1983 Act provides a power to retake people who have been legally detained.

Where a person escapes while being removed to a place of safety in the execution of a warrant under s. 135(1) or under s. 136(1), they shall not be retaken after the end of the period of 24 hours *beginning with the escape* (s. 138(3)(a)). In the case of a person where detention (24 hours) or further detention (a total of 36 hours) has been authorised, they shall not be retaken after the end of the period of 24 hours or 36 hours as the case may be, *beginning with the time detention is authorised* (s. 138(3)(b)).

Section 18 of the Act deals with the return and readmission of patients absent without leave. This provides occasions where a constable may take a person into custody and return them to hospital where they are a patient who is the subject of a hospital order authorising their detention.

KEYNOTE

Examples to illustrate the above 'escape and retake' situations under s. 138 of the Act can be seen below:

Situation 1 (Escape Time)

A police officer detains a person under s. 136(1) at 13.30hrs Saturday 2 January 2027. The person escapes from the police vehicle they are being transported in to a place of safety at 13.45hrs Saturday 2 January 2027. That person can be retaken up to 24 hours later (13.45hrs Sunday 3 January 2027).

Situation 2 (Detention Time—Initial 24 Hrs Authorised)

A police officer takes a person to a place of safety and they are detained there—an authorisation for detention for 24 hours is given starting at 15.30hrs Saturday 2 January 2027. The person escapes at 16.00hrs Saturday 2 January 2027. That person cannot be retaken after 15.30hrs Sunday 3 January 2027.

Situation 3 (Detention Time—12 Hrs Extension Authorised)

A person is detained at a place of safety for the 'permitted period' of 24 hours starting at 16.30hrs Saturday 2 January 2027. An extension of detention is authorised for 12 hours (beginning immediately after the initial 24-hour period and starting at 16.30hrs Sunday 3 January 2027 so detention is extended until 04.30hrs Monday 4 January 2027). If the person escapes, they cannot be retaken after 04.30hrs Monday 4 January 2027.

3.4.5 Assisting Patients to Absent Themselves Without Leave, etc.

The following three offences are created under the 1983 Act and s. 128 states:

(1) Where any person induces or knowingly assists another person who is liable to be detained in a hospital within the meaning of Part II of this Act or is subject to guardianship under this Act or is a community patient to absent himself without leave he shall be guilty of an offence.

(2) Where any person induces or knowingly assists another person who is in legal custody by virtue of section 137 below to escape from such custody he shall be guilty of an offence.

(3) Where any person knowingly harbours a patient who is absent without leave or is otherwise at large and liable to be retaken under this Act or gives him any assistance with intent to prevent, hinder or interfere with his being taken into custody or returned to the hospital or other place where he ought to be he shall be guilty of an offence.

KEYNOTE

Any person required or authorised by or by virtue of this Act to be conveyed to any place or to be kept in custody or detained in a place of safety is deemed to be in legal custody (s. 137(1)). A constable or authorised person required to take any person into custody, or to convey or detain any person, has all the powers, authorities, protection and privileges of a constable (s. 137(2)).

A person guilty of any of the above offences is liable on summary conviction to six months' imprisonment and/or a fine, and on indictment to two years' imprisonment and/or a fine (s. 128(4)). Additionally, a court may issue a warrant for the arrest of a convicted mental patient who is unlawfully at large (Criminal Justice Act 1967, s. 72(3)).

3.4.6 Mental Health Units (Use of Force): Police Body Cameras

This legislation was primarily introduced following the death of a person being restrained on a mental health ward by 11 police officers. An inquest found that the restraint used was excessive and disproportionate.

The Mental Health Units (Use of Force) Act 2018, s. 12 states:

Police body cameras

(1) If a police officer is going to a mental health unit on duty that involves assisting staff who work in that unit, the officer must take a body camera if reasonably practicable.

(2) While in a mental health unit on duty that involves assisting staff who work in that unit, a police officer who has a body camera there must wear it and keep it operating at all times when reasonably practicable.

(3) Subsection (2) does not apply if there are special circumstances at the time that justify not wearing the camera or keeping it operating.

(4) A failure by a police officer to comply with the requirements of subsection (1) or (2) does not of itself make the officer liable to criminal or civil proceedings.

(5) But if those requirements appear to the court or tribunal to be relevant to any question arising in criminal or civil proceedings, they must take account in determining that question.

KEYNOTE

Statutory guidance has been published by the Department of Health and Social Care (December 2021). The aim of the Act and statutory guidance is to clearly set out the measures that are needed to both reduce the use of force and to ensure accountability and transparency about the use of force in mental health units.

In this section 'body camera' means a device that operates so as to make a continuous audio and video recording while being worn (s. 12(6)).

'Mental health unit' means a health service hospital in England providing inpatient mental health care, or an independent hospital providing such treatment on behalf of the NHS (s. 1(3)).

3.5 Offences Relating to Land and Premises

3.5.1 Introduction

The Criminal Justice and Public Order Act 1994 sets out a number of offences associated with trespassing and trespassing with vehicles and provides the police with a series of powers to direct persons and vehicles associated with these offences to leave the land. This chapter examines those offences and powers along with legislation dealing with squatting in residential premises and nuisance in educational and NHS premises.

3.5.2 Aggravated Trespass

OFFENCE: **Trespass Intending to Obstruct, Disrupt or Intimidate—*Criminal Justice and Public Order Act 1994, s. 68***

- Triable summarily • Three months' imprisonment and/or a fine

The Criminal Justice and Public Order Act 1994, s. 68 states:

(1) A person commits the offence of aggravated trespass if he trespasses on land and, in relation to any lawful activity which persons are engaging in or are about to engage in on that or adjoining land, does there anything which is intended by him to have the effect—

(a) of intimidating those persons or any of them so as to deter them or any of them from engaging in that activity,

(b) of obstructing that activity, or

(c) of disrupting that activity.

(2) Activity on any occasion on the part of a person or persons on land is 'lawful' for the purposes of this section if he or they may engage in the activity on the land on that occasion without committing an offence or trespassing on the land.

KEYNOTE

Trespass, as a concept in civil law, is concerned with the interference with *possession* of land, not ownership. It is common ground that for the purposes of section 68 of the 1994 Act 'trespass' is not intended to be given a different and novel meaning from the meaning it has at common law. Thus, the trespass element of the offence contrary to section 68 of the 1994 Act is by its nature against another's possession of land. It is not legally necessary for the prosecution to establish legal ownership of the land to prove whether a defendant has trespassed upon it. To disclose a case to answer, the prosecution needed only adduce sufficient evidence to prove that the accused was present on land (as defined by the 1994 Act) without legal right; that is to say, otherwise than with the consent of the possessor/occupier, or by authority of law or any other justification in law (*DPP* v *Cannon* [2025] EWHC 520 (Admin)).

In *DPP* v *Bailey* [2022] EWHC 3302 (Admin), the court determined that for the offence to be committed it was not necessary to prove that a person intended to trespass on the land or was reckless as to whether they were trespassing on the land. To disclose a case to answer, the prosecution need only adduce evidence sufficient to prove that the accused was present on land without legal right, namely without the consent of the possessor/occupier, or by authority of law or any other justification in law (*DPP* v *Cannon* [2025] EWHC 520 (Admin).

In relation to subs. (1), the persons engaging in any lawful activity do not need to be physically present on the land provided they have a right to possess, or occupy, the land, and they are about to carry out a lawful activity on the land (*DPP* v *Highbury Corner Magistrates' Court* [2022] EWHC 3207 (Admin)).

Examples of the sort of conduct envisaged would be environmental activists disrupting a building programme or disrupting the planting of genetically modified crops (*DPP* v *Bayer* [2003] EWHC 2567 (Admin)).

It must be shown that the defendant intended to bring about the effects set out at s. 68(1)(a)–(c). There is no need to specify which of the intended activities (i.e. deterring, obstructing or disrupting) in any charge and use of all three expressions is not bad for duplicity (*Nelder* v *DPP* (1988) *The Times*, 11 June). However, proof is required of both the trespassing on land and of some overt act, other than the trespassing, which was intended to have the effects set out at s. 68(1)(a)–(c) (*DPP* v *Barnard* [2000] Crim LR 371; *Peppersharp* v *DPP* [2012] EWHC 474 (Admin)).

In *Bauer* v *DPP* [2013] EWHC 634 (Admin), it was held that a large group of protesters, known as 'UK Uncut', protesting against tax avoidance, who occupied Fortnum and Mason's store in London for a period of nearly two and a half hours were guilty of aggravated trespass by virtue of their presence which had the intention to intimidate staff and customers within the store. It was also held that if the facts showed that people were part of the group which had committed the aggravated trespass then they were as guilty as the rest as a joint principal.

In the following case, s. 68 was successfully used in a matter that did not include dealing with protesters. At a cricket test match between England and India, the defendant dressed as an Indian player, entered the playing field while the match was in progress, bowling a ball to a batsman and colliding with a player. Croydon Magistrates' Court found him guilty of aggravated trespass (*R* v *Jarvis* (2003) 14 September, unreported).

In *DPP* v *Cuciurean* [2022] EWHC 736 (Admin), it was held that there was no requirement for the prosecution to prove that a conviction for aggravated trespass would be a proportionate interference with a person's rights under Article 10 or 11 of the European Convention on Human Rights. This reasoning was approved by the Supreme Court in *Re Abortion Services (Self Access Zones) (Northern Ireland) Bill* [2022] UKSC 32.

Under s. 68(5), land does not include a highway unless it is a footpath, bridleway or byway open to all traffic within the meaning of part 3 of the Wildlife and Countryside Act 1981, is a restricted byway within the meaning of part 2 of the Countryside and Rights of Way Act 2000 or is a cycle track under the Highways Act 1980 or the Cycle Tracks Act 1984.

'Lawful' activity is defined at s. 68(2) and is a very wide concept. This point has been determined in the context of anti-war protestors where it was argued that the war against Iraq was illegal and therefore the activities carried out by staff at airbases were also unlawful. The House of Lords determined that for the purposes of s. 68(2), an act of aggression against another State or a general crime against peace did not constitute an offence contrary to the law of England and Wales (*R* v *Jones* [2006] UKHL 16; *Ayliffe* v *DPP* [2005] EWHC 684 (Admin); *Nero* v *DPP* [2012] EWHC 1238 (Admin); *Richardson* v *DPP* [2014] UKSC 8).

3.5.2.1 Aggravated Trespass: Power to Remove Persons

The Criminal Justice and Public Order Act 1994, s. 69 states:

(1) If the senior police officer present at the scene reasonably believes—
   (a) that a person is committing, has committed or intends to commit the offence of aggravated trespass on land; or
   (b) that two or more persons are trespassing on land and are present there with the common purpose of intimidating persons so as to deter them from engaging in a lawful activity or of obstructing or disrupting a lawful activity,

   he may direct that person or (as the case may be) those persons (or any of them) to leave the land.

(2) A direction under subsection (1) above, if not communicated to the persons referred to in subsection (1) by the police officer giving the direction, may be communicated to them by any constable at the scene.

KEYNOTE

Although this power requires the senior officer present at the scene to have a reasonable belief as to the circumstances set out at s. 69(1)(a) or (b), the power is available as a preventive measure and as a means of dealing with the incident after it has happened.

The direction to leave the land may be communicated to the relevant people by any police officer at the scene and there is no requirement for either officer to be in uniform.

3.5.3 Failure to Leave Land or Re-entry to Land when Directed to Leave

OFFENCE: **Failure to Leave or Re-entry when Directed to Leave—*Criminal Justice and Public Order Act 1994, s. 69(3)***

- Triable summarily • Three months' imprisonment and/or a fine

The Criminal Justice and Public Order Act 1994, s. 69 states:

(3) If a person knowing that a direction under subsection (1) above has been given which applies to him—

(a) fails to leave the land as soon as practicable, or

(b) having left again enters the land as a trespasser within the period of three months beginning with the day on which the direction was given,

he commits an offence ...

KEYNOTE

In order to prove this offence it must be shown that the person knew of the direction and that it applied to him/her. Clearly, the easiest way of ensuring both elements would be to serve a written notice on the person at the same time as communicating the direction to leave and to record any response.

It is a defence for the accused to show that he/she was not trespassing on the land, or had a reasonable excuse for failing to leave the land as soon as practicable or for again entering the land as a trespasser (s. 69(4)). When the legal burden is on the accused, the standard required is proof on a balance of probabilities.

In *Nero* v *DPP* [2012] EWHC 1238 (Admin), the court quashed the appellants' convictions for failing to leave the premises as soon as practicable when so directed by the police because they were physically unable to move until they had been unchained, and had left as soon as this was done. What they did was designed to disrupt the shop's trade, not to frustrate the operation of s. 69: the fact that they had voluntarily (and deliberately) placed themselves in a situation in which they could not leave when directed was held to be irrelevant. Likewise, in *Richardson* v *DPP* [2012] EWHC 1238 (Admin), it was held that protesters tying themselves together who could not leave until untied left 'as soon as practicable'.

3.5.4 Residing on Land Without Consent in or with a Vehicle

OFFENCE: **Residing on Land Without Consent in or with a Vehicle—*Criminal Justice and Public Order Act 1994, s. 60C***

- Triable summarily • Three months' imprisonment and/or a fine

The Criminal Justice and Public Order Act 1994, s. 60C states:

(1) Subsection (2) applies where—

(a) a person aged 18 or over ('P') is residing, or intending to reside, on land without the consent of the occupier of the land,

(b) P has, or intends to have, at least one vehicle with them on the land,

(c) one or more of the conditions mentioned in subsection (4) is satisfied, and

(d) the occupier, a representative of the occupier or a constable requests P to do either or both of the following—
    (i) leave the land;
    (ii) remove from the land property that is in P's possession or under P's control.

(2) P commits an offence if—
  (a) P fails to comply with the request as soon as reasonably practicable, or
  (b) P—
    (i) enters (or having left, re-enters) the land within the prohibited period with the intention of residing there without the consent of the occupier of the land, and
    (ii) has, or intends to have, at least one vehicle with them on the land.

(3) The prohibited period is the period of 12 months beginning with the day on which the request was made.

(4) The conditions are—
  (a) in a case where P is residing on the land, significant damage or significant disruption has been caused or is likely to be caused as a result of P's residence;
  (b) in a case where P is not yet residing on the land, it is likely that significant damage or significant disruption would be caused as a result of P's residence if P were to reside on the land;
  (c) that significant damage or significant disruption has been caused or is likely to be caused as a result of conduct carried on, or likely to be carried on, by P while P is on the land;
  (d) that significant distress has been caused or is likely to be caused as a result of offensive conduct carried on, or likely to be carried on, by P while P is on the land.

KEYNOTE

This offence is designed to target trespassers who intend to reside on any private or public land in vehicles without permission, and where they are causing significant disruption, distress or harm to local communities. It provides the police with powers to seize vehicles and arrest offenders.

The criminal offence is tightly defined and only applies in cases where:

- a person is aged 18 or over and they are using vehicles to reside on the land—this ensures occasional campers are not affected;
- they are residing or intending to reside on land without the consent of the occupier—this will ensure unintentional instances of trespass are not affected, such as ramblers or hikers;
- one or more of the conditions mentioned in s. 60C(4) is satisfied;
- they fail to respond to a request from the occupier or police to leave the land and remove their property;
- they return to the land within 12 months with an intention to reside with a vehicle, following that request.

If a constable reasonably suspects that an offence has been committed under s. 60C, the constable may seize and remove any relevant property that appears to the constable: (a) to belong to the person who the constable suspects has committed the offence ('P'); (b) to be in P's possession; or (c) to be under P's control (s. 60D(1)).

'Relevant property' means a vehicle (wherever located) which, for the purposes of s. 60C(1)(b) (in the case of an offence under s. 60C(2)(a)) or for the purposes of s. 60C(2)(b)(ii) (in the case of an offence under s. 60C(2)(b)), the constable suspects P had or intended to have with them, or any other property that is on the relevant land.

It is a defence for the accused to show that he/she had a reasonable excuse for failing to comply with a request as soon as practicable, or after receiving such a request had a reasonable excuse for entering (or re-entering) the land with the intention of residing there without the consent of the occupier of the land (s. 60C(6)).

3.5.5 Power to Remove Trespassers on Land

OFFENCE: **Power to Remove Trespassers on Land—*Criminal Justice and Public Order Act 1994, s. 61***

- Triable summarily • Three months' imprisonment and/or a fine

The Criminal Justice and Public Order Act 1994, s. 61 states:

(1) If the senior police officer present at the scene reasonably believes that two or more persons are trespassing on land and are present there with the common purpose of residing there for any period, that reasonable steps have been taken by or on behalf of the occupier to ask them to leave and—
 (a) that any of those persons
  (i) in the case of persons trespassing on land in England and Wales, has caused damage, disruption or distress (see subsection (10));
  (ii) in the case of persons trespassing on land in Scotland, and has caused damage to the land or to property on the land or used threatening, abusive or insulting words or behaviour towards the occupier, a member of his family or an employee or agent of his, or
 (b) in either case, that those persons have between them six or more vehicles on the land,
he may direct those persons, or any of them, to leave the land and to remove any vehicles or other property they have with them on the land.
(2) Where the persons in question are reasonably believed by the senior police officer to be persons who were not originally trespassers but have become trespassers on the land, the officer must reasonably believe that the other conditions specified in subsection (1) are satisfied after those persons became trespassers before he can exercise the power conferred by that subsection.
(3) A direction under subsection (1) above, if not communicated to the persons referred to in subsection (1) by the police officer giving the direction, may be communicated to them by any constable at the scene.
(4) If a person knowing that a direction under subsection (1) above has been given which applies to him—
 (a) fails to leave the land as soon as reasonably practicable, or
 (b) having left again enters the land as a trespasser within the prohibited period
he commits an offence ...

KEYNOTE

Setting aside the provisions that relate to Scotland in s. 61(1)(a)(ii), the key features of this section can be broken down into two parts. First, the senior officer present at the scene must have a reasonable belief that:

- at least two people *are trespassing* on land; and
- that they are there with the common purpose of residing there; *and*
- that reasonable steps have been taken by/on behalf of the occupier to ask them to leave.

Secondly, the senior officer must also have a reasonable belief that:

- *any* of those people have caused damage, disruption or distress to the land or to property on the land; *or*
- *any* of those people have between them six or more vehicles on the land.

Damage, Disruption or Distress

The Criminal Justice and Public Order Act 1994, s. 61(10) states that for the purposes of s. (1)(a)(i):

'damage' includes—
(a) damage to the land;
(b) damage to any property on the land not belonging to the persons trespassing;
(c) damage to the environment (including excessive noise, smells, litter or deposits of waste);

'disruption' includes an interference with—
(a) a person's ability to access any services or facilities located on the land or otherwise make lawful use of the land, or
(b) a supply of water, energy or fuel;

'distress' means distress caused by—
(a) the use of threatening, abusive or insulting words or behaviour, or disorderly behaviour, or
(b) the display of any writing, sign, or other visible representation that is threatening, abusive or insulting.

Vehicle

A 'vehicle' includes:

- any vehicle whether or not it is in a fit state for use on roads, and includes any chassis or body, with or without wheels, appearing to have formed part of such a vehicle, and any load carried by, and anything attached to, such a vehicle; and

- a caravan as defined in s. 29(1) of the Caravan Sites and Control Development Act 1960.

If all the conditions under the first heading, together with EITHER of the conditions under the second are met, the officer may direct the people to leave the land and to take their vehicles and other property with them.

'Land' does not include buildings other than agricultural buildings or scheduled monuments. It also has the same restrictions in relation to highways as those set out under s. 68 (see para. 3.5.2).

The 'prohibited period' (subs. (4)(b)), in the case of a person trespassing, is the period of 12 months beginning with the day on which the direction was given (s. 61(4ZA)).

It is a defence to show that the person was not trespassing on the land or had a reasonable excuse for failing to leave as soon as reasonably practicable or for re-entering the land as a trespasser (s. 61(6)).

A person may be regarded as having a purpose of residing in a place notwithstanding that he/she has a home elsewhere (s. 61(9)).

3.5.6 Power to Remove Trespassers: Alternative Site Available

Section 62A of the Criminal Justice and Public Order Act 1994 creates a power for a senior police officer to direct people to leave land and remove any vehicle or other property with them on that land.

Section 62A states:

(1) If the senior police officer present at a scene reasonably believes that the conditions in subsection (2) are satisfied in relation to a person and land, he may direct the person—
  (a) to leave the land;
  (b) to remove any vehicle and other property he has with him on the land.

(2) The conditions are—
  (a) that the person and one or more others ('the trespassers') are trespassing on the land;
  (b) that the trespassers have between them at least one vehicle on the land;
  (c) that the trespassers are present on the land with the common purpose of residing there for any period;
  (d) if it appears to the officer that the person has one or more caravans in his possession or under his control on the land, that there is a suitable pitch on a relevant caravan site for that caravan or each of those caravans;
  (e) that the occupier of the land or a person acting on his behalf has asked the police to remove the trespassers from the land.

KEYNOTE

This effectively creates two situations in which the power can be exercised—one excluding the element at s. 62(2)(d) and one including it. The table below illustrates the relevant circumstances; in order for a direction to be given under s. 62A, the senior officer present at the scene must have a reasonable belief that:

Situation 1	Situation 2
at least two people are trespassing on the land; and	at least two people are trespassing on the land;
↓	↓
that they have at least one vehicle between them; and	that they have at least one vehicle between them; and
↓	↓
that they are there with the common purpose of residing there for any period; and	that they are there with the common purpose of residing there for any period; and
↓	↓
	it appears to the officer that the person has one or more caravans in their possession or under their control on the land and that there are relevant caravan sites with suitable pitches available for the trespassers to move to; and
↓	↓
that the occupier (or person acting on the occupier's behalf) has asked the police to remove the trespassers from the land.	that the occupier (or person acting on the occupier's behalf) has asked the police to remove the trespassers from the land.

A person commits a summary offence punishable by three months' imprisonment and/or a fine if he/she knows that a direction has been given and he/she fails to leave the land as soon as reasonably practicable or enters any land in the area of the relevant local authority as a trespasser before the end of the relevant period with the intention of residing there (s. 62B). The relevant period is the period of 12 months starting with the day on which the direction is given (s. 62B(2)).

It is a defence to show that the person:

- was not trespassing on the land in respect of which he/she is alleged to have committed the offence; or
- had a reasonable excuse for failing to leave the relevant land as soon as reasonably practicable; or
- entered land in the area of the relevant local authority as a trespasser with the intention of residing there; or
- at the time the direction was given was under the age of 18 years and was residing with his/her parent or guardian

(s. 62B(5))

Local authorities also have the power to direct people to leave land and remove any vehicle or other property (s. 77).

3.5.7 Squatting in a Residential Building

OFFENCE: **Squatting in a Residential Building—*Legal Aid, Sentencing and Punishment of Offenders Act 2012, s. 144***

- Six months' imprisonment and/or a fine summarily

The Legal Aid, Sentencing and Punishment of Offenders Act 2012, s. 144 states:

(1) A person commits an offence if—
  (a) the person is in a residential building as a trespasser having entered it as a trespasser,
  (b) the person knows or ought to know that he or she is a trespasser, and
  (c) the person is living in the building or intends to live there for any period.

(2) The offence is not committed by a person holding over after the end of a lease or licence (even if the person leaves and re-enters the building).

KEYNOTE

'Building' includes any structure or part of a structure (including a temporary or moveable structure), and a building is 'residential' if it is designed or adapted, before the time of entry, for use as a place to live (s. 144(3)).

For the purposes of this section the fact that a person derives title from a trespasser, or has the permission of a trespasser, does not prevent the person from being a trespasser (s. 144(4)).

Section 17 of the Police and Criminal Evidence Act 1984 gives police officers the power to enter and search premises for the purpose of arresting a person for the offence of squatting in a residential building.

3.5.8 Nuisance on Educational Premises

In relation to nuisances on educational premises, the Education Act 1996 applies to premises that provide primary or secondary education (or both) and which are maintained by a local education authority or are grant-maintained.

OFFENCE **Causing or Permitting Nuisance—*Education Act 1996, s. 547(1)***

- Triable summarily • Fine

The Education Act 1996, s. 547 states:

(1) Any person who without lawful authority is present on premises to which this section applies and causes or permits nuisance or disturbance to the annoyance of persons who lawfully use those premises (whether or not any such persons are present at the time) is guilty of an offence.

KEYNOTE

This offence is designed to deal with many types of nuisance, from using school playing fields inappropriately (this provision applies to playing fields and other premises for outdoor recreation of the relevant institution including playgrounds (s. 547(2)), to interrupting lessons and lectures.

To be guilty of the above offence, the defendant must be on the relevant premises without lawful authority and have caused (been directly responsible for bringing about) or permitted a nuisance or disturbance.

If a police constable, or a person whom the appropriate authority has authorised to exercise the power conferred by this section, has reasonable cause to suspect that any person is committing or has committed an offence under this section they may remove them from the premises in question.

3.5.9 Causing Nuisance or Disturbance on NHS Premises

OFFENCE: **Causing a Nuisance or Disturbance on NHS Premises—*Criminal Justice and Immigration Act 2008, s. 119***

- Triable summarily • Fine

The Criminal Justice and Immigration Act 2008, s. 119 states:

(1) A person commits an offence if—

(a) the person causes, without reasonable excuse and while on NHS premises, a nuisance or disturbance to an NHS staff member who is working there or otherwise there in connection with work,

(b) the person refuses, without reasonable excuse, to leave the NHS premises when asked to do so by a constable or an NHS staff member, and

(c) the person is not on the NHS premises for the purpose of obtaining medical advice, treatment or care for himself or herself.

KEYNOTE

A person ceases to be on NHS premises for the purpose of obtaining medical advice, treatment or care for him/herself once the person has received the advice, treatment or care. Also, a person is not on NHS premises for the purpose of obtaining medical advice, treatment or care for him/herself if the person has been refused the advice, treatment or care during the last eight hours (s. 119(3)).

If a constable reasonably suspects that a person is committing or has committed an offence under s. 119, the constable may remove the person from the NHS premises concerned (s. 120(1)).

If an authorised officer reasonably suspects that a person is committing or has committed an offence, he/she may remove the person from the NHS premises concerned, or authorise an appropriate NHS staff member to do so (s. 120(2)).

Any person removing another person from NHS premises under this section may, if necessary, use reasonable force (s. 120(3)).

An authorised officer cannot remove the person or authorise another person to do so if it is reasonably believed he/she is in need of medical advice etc. or that such removal would endanger his/her mental or physical health (s. 120(4)). An authorised officer is a duly authorised NHS staff member (s. 120(5)).

It will be a defence for a person to show they had a reasonable excuse for causing a nuisance or disturbance or refusing to leave the premises, for instance where a person's behaviour was consequent upon a bereavement.

3.6 Offences and Powers Relating to Alcohol

3.6.1 Introduction

This chapter is concerned with offences in relation to drunkenness and offences under the Licensing Act 2003 relating to alcohol and children. The chapter also sets out a variety of powers available to the police and briefly examines the powers of the courts to grant exclusion orders and closure orders.

3.6.2 Power of Entry to Investigate Licensable Activities or Offences

Sections 179 and 180 of the Licensing Act 2003 Act provide rights of entry regarding 'licensable activities'. 'Licensable activities' include, for example, the sale by retail of alcohol and the supply of alcohol by or on behalf of a club to, or to the order of, a member of the club (s. 1 of the Licensing 2003). Where a constable, an authorised person or an immigration officer has reason to believe that any premises are being, or are about to be, used for a licensable activity, he/she may enter the premises with a view to seeing whether the activity is being, or is to be, carried on under and in accordance with an authorisation (s. 179(1)). An authorised person exercising the power must, if so requested, produce evidence of his/her authority to exercise the power (s. 179(2)).

A person exercising the power conferred by this section may, if necessary, use reasonable force (s. 179(3)) and a person commits an offence if he/she intentionally obstructs an authorised person exercising a power conferred by this section (s. 179(4)).

A constable may enter and search any premises in respect of which he/she has reason to believe that an offence under this Act has been, is being or is about to be committed (s. 180(1)) and may, if necessary, use reasonable force (s. 180(2)).

3.6.3 Drunk and Disorderly

OFFENCE: **Drunk and Disorderly—*Criminal Justice Act 1967, s. 91(1)***

- Triable summarily • Fine

The Criminal Justice Act 1967, s. 91 states:

(1) Any person who in any public place is guilty, while drunk, of disorderly behaviour shall be liable ...

KEYNOTE

In *Carroll* v *DPP* [2009] EWHC 554 (Admin), the court stated that drunk and disorderly was one of the most basic of offences and that it required proof of three elements: the accused was drunk; he/she was in a public place; and he/she was guilty of disorderly behaviour.

The drunkenness must be as a result of excessive consumption of alcohol; if the person's state is caused by some other intoxicant (e.g. glue solvents), the offence is not made out (*Neale* v *R.M.I.E. (a minor)* (1985) 80 Cr App R 20). The same ruling applies to a person 'found drunk' in a public place (*Lanham* v *Rickwood* (1984) 148 JP 737).

'Drunkenness' here means where the defendant has taken intoxicating liquor (alcohol) to an extent that affects his/her steady self-control (per Goff LJ in *Neale*).

Where there are several causes of a person's incapacitated state, one of which is alcohol, a court can find that the person was in fact 'drunk' even though some additional intoxicant had an exacerbating effect on his/her loss of 'steady self-control'.

In *McMillan* v *CPS* [2008] EWHC 1457 (Admin), it was held that where a police officer took hold of a drunken person by the arm, to steady her for her own safety, it was not an arrest. The circumstances entailed the officer leading the drunken person from a private garden to a public place. It was then legitimate for the officer to arrest for this offence where the accused displayed disorderly behaviour. However, this offence is not committed where a person did not commit any disorderly act until after the arrest (*H* v *DPP* [2005] EWHC 2459 (Admin)).

This offence is a 'penalty offence' for the purposes of s. 1 of the Criminal Justice and Police Act 2001. Note that a penalty notice for s. 91(1) cannot be given to a person aged under 18 and a constable giving a notice to a person other than at a police station does not need to be in uniform (Legal Aid, Sentencing and Punishment of Offenders Act 2012 (Consequential Amendments) Regulations 2013 (SI 2013/903)).

Where a person is arrested for committing this offence, under the powers contained within s. 24 of the Police and Criminal Evidence Act 1984, a constable may take him/her to an approved treatment centre for alcoholism (a 'detoxification' centre) and he/she will be treated as being in lawful custody for the purposes of that journey (see s. 34(1) of the Criminal Justice Act 1972). This course of action does not preclude the person being charged with any offence (s. 34(2)).

The Air Navigation Order 2016 (SI 2016/765), part 10, art. 242 provides that a person must not enter any aircraft when drunk or be drunk in any aircraft (art. 242(1)) and a person must not, when acting as a member of the crew of any aircraft or being carried in any aircraft for the purpose of acting as a member of the crew, be under the influence of drink or a drug to such an extent as to impair his/her capacity so to act (art. 242(2)). Both offences are triable either way. The penalty for conviction on indictment is two years' imprisonment and or a fine and on summary conviction an unlimited fine (art. 265(7) and sch. 13, part 3)).

3.6.4 Found Drunk

OFFENCE: **Being Found Drunk—*Licensing Act 1872, s. 12***

- Triable summarily • Fine

The Licensing Act 1872, s. 12 states:

> Every person found drunk in any highway or other public place, whether a building or not, or on any licensed premises, shall be liable ...
>
> Every person who is drunk while in charge on any highway or other public place of any carriage, horse, cattle, or steam engine, or who is drunk when in possession of any loaded firearms, shall be liable to a penalty not exceeding level 1 on the standard scale or in the discretion of the court to imprisonment for any term not exceeding one month.

KEYNOTE

This offence is committed if a person is on the highway or public place and shown to be drunk. It does not matter that the person is there only briefly or of his/her own volition.

'Other public place' will include all places to which the public have access (whether on payment or otherwise).

The offence has been held to apply to the licensee when found drunk on the licensed premises even when those premises were not open to the public (*Evans* v *Fletcher* (1926) 135 LT 153).

This offence is a 'penalty offence' for the purposes of s. 1 of the Criminal Justice and Police Act 2001.

The power of a constable to take a drunken offender to a treatment centre under s. 34 of the Criminal Justice Act 1972 is the same as that for a person arrested for being drunk and disorderly (see para. 3.6.3).

3.6.5 Children—Offences under the Licensing Act 2003

The Licensing Act 2003 makes provision for offences and breaches of the regulatory framework with the protection of children as one of its primary objectives. In summary, the key offences under the 2003 Act are:

Unaccompanied children prohibited from certain premises (s. 145). Allowing an unaccompanied child, aged under 16, on relevant premises at a time when they are open for the purposes of being used for the supply of alcohol for consumption on the premises.

Sale of alcohol to children (s. 146). The 'selling' of alcohol to a person aged under 18 *anywhere* (not just on licensed premises). It is a defence where the person charged believed that the individual was 18 or over, had taken all reasonable steps to establish the individual's age or nobody could reasonably have suspected from the individual's appearance that they were aged under 18.

Allowing the sale of alcohol to children (s. 147). Where a person, who works at relevant premises in a paid or unpaid capacity which authorises them to prevent the sale, knowingly allows the sale of alcohol on the premises to an individual under 18.

Persistently selling alcohol to children (s. 147A). If, on two or more different occasions within a period of three consecutive months, alcohol is unlawfully sold on the same premises to an individual aged under 18. It is 'unlawfully sold' if the person making the sale believed the individual to be under 18 or did not have reasonable grounds for believing them to be 18 or over.

Purchase of alcohol by or on behalf of children (s. 149). This covers all forms of under-18s buying (or trying to buy) alcohol or someone else doing it on their behalf.

Consumption of alcohol by children (s. 150). A person aged under 18 knowingly consumes alcohol on relevant premises and a person working at the premises knowingly allows the consumption of alcohol. However, no offences are committed where the individual is aged 16 or 17, the alcohol is beer, wine or cider, the consumption is at a table meal and the individual is accompanied by a person aged 18 or over.

Delivering alcohol to children (s. 151). A person working on relevant premises knowingly delivering alcohol sold on the premises to a person aged under 18. For example, circumstances where a child takes delivery of a consignment of alcohol bought by a parent from an off-licence.

Sending a child to obtain alcohol (s. 152). A person knowingly sending an individual aged under 18 to obtain alcohol that is sold on relevant premises for consumption off the premises. For example, where a parent sends their child to an off-licence to collect some alcohol which had been bought over the telephone. The offence will be committed regardless of whether the child is sent to the actual premises from where the alcohol is sold or supplied or whether the child is sent to other premises to which the alcohol has been sent.

Prohibition of unsupervised sales by children (s. 153). A premises licence holder, designated premises supervisor or someone over 18 authorised by them, to knowingly allow an individual aged under 18 to make on the relevant premises any sale of alcohol or, in the case of a club, any supply of alcohol to members of the club. This does not apply to the sale or supply of alcohol to persons having table meals.

KEYNOTE

All of the offences listed above are triable summarily and punishable by a fine.

In relation to *allowing the sale of alcohol to children* (s. 147), *purchase of alcohol by or on behalf of children* (s. 149) and *sending a child to obtain alcohol* (s. 152), an offence will not be committed where the individual buys or attempts to buy the alcohol at the request of a constable or a weights and measures inspector who is acting in the course of his/her duty.

With the exceptions of ss. 146, 147A and 149, all the other offences listed refer to the offence occurring on 'relevant premises'. This means premises that are exclusively or primarily used for the supply of alcohol for consumption on the premises and include premises operating with a temporary event notice.

3.6.6 Children—Other Offences

In addition to the offences outlined above, other legislation creates specific offences in relation to children.

3.6.6.1 Being Drunk While in Charge of Child

OFFENCE: **Being Drunk While in Charge of Child—*Licensing Act 1902, s. 2***

- One month's imprisonment and/or a fine summarily

The Licensing Act 1902, s. 2 states:

(1) If any person is found drunk in any highway or other public place, whether a building or not, or on any licensed premises, while having the charge of a child apparently under the age of seven years, he shall, if the child is under that age, be liable ...

(2) If the child appears to the court to be under the age of seven, the child shall, for the purposes of this section, be deemed to be under that age unless the contrary is proved.

KEYNOTE

This is used for its specific purpose, i.e. the safety of young children (*R (On the Application of A)* v *Lowestoft Magistrates' Court* [2013] EWHC 659 (Admin)).

3.6.6.2 Persistently Possessing Alcohol in a Public Place

OFFENCE: **Persistently Possessing Alcohol in a Public Place—*Policing and Crime Act 2009, s. 30***

- Triable summarily • Fine

The Policing and Crime Act 2009, s. 30 states:

(1) A person under the age of 18 is guilty of an offence if, without reasonable excuse, the person is in possession of alcohol in any relevant place on 3 or more occasions within a period of 12 consecutive months.

(2) 'Relevant place', in relation to a person, means—
  (a) any public place, other than excluded premises, or
  (b) any place, other than a public place, to which the person has unlawfully gained access.

...

(4) For the purposes of subsection (2) a place is a public place if at the material time the public or any section of the public has access to it, on payment or otherwise, as of right or by virtue of express or implied permission.

KEYNOTE

In relation to s. 30(2)(a), 'excluded premises' means premises with a premises licence or permitted temporary activity used for the supply of alcohol, and premises with a club premises certificate used for the supply of alcohol to members or guests.

The original Home Office guidance set out the steps to be taken to deter young people from drinking and possessing alcohol in public places, including engagement with their parents or guardians. It was intended that this offence be used in conjunction with s. 1 of the Confiscation of Alcohol (Young Persons) Act 1997 (see para. 3.6.6.3) to enable a constable to confiscate alcohol from those under 18 years of age and to ensure that the young person was required to give his/her name and address to the constable.

3.6.6.3 Confiscation of Intoxicating Liquor

The Confiscation of Alcohol (Young Persons) Act 1997, s. 1 states:

(1) Where a constable reasonably suspects that a person in a relevant place is in possession of alcohol, and that either—
  (a) he is under the age of 18; or
  (b) he intends that any of the alcohol should be consumed by a person under the age of 18 in that or any other relevant place; or
  (c) a person under the age of 18 who is, or has recently been, with him has recently consumed alcohol in that or any other relevant place,

  the constable may require him to surrender anything in his possession which is, or which the constable reasonably believes to be, alcohol or a container for alcohol.

(1AA) A constable who imposes a requirement on a person under subsection (1) shall also require the person to state the person's name and address.

(1AB) A constable who imposes a requirement on a person under subsection (1) may, if the constable reasonably suspects that the person is under the age of 16, remove the person to the person's place of residence or a place of safety.

KEYNOTE

A 'relevant place' is: any public place, other than licensed premises; or any place, other than a public place, to which that person has unlawfully gained access (s. 1(6)).

The power may be exercised in any public place where the public have access on payment or otherwise but this does not include licensed premises.

This is a discretionary power for police officers to exercise as they deem fit.

It is unusual that the wording of the section says 'either', then goes on to give three instances where the power will be available. However, if one of the instances at s. 1(1)(a)–(c) applies, the police officer may require the person concerned to surrender anything that is, or that the officer reasonably believes to be, alcohol or a container for such alcohol.

Subsection (1AA) states that the constable shall require the person to state his/her name and address. Although a 'place of safety' is not defined, this may be a relative or friend or, where necessary, a police station or social services accommodation.

There is no requirement for the officer to be in uniform.

Under s. 1(2), the officer may dispose of anything surrendered to him/her in answer to the making of such a requirement.

It is a summary offence for a person to fail without reasonable excuse to comply with a requirement imposed under subs. (1) or (1AA) (s. 1(3)). A constable may arrest without warrant a person who fails to comply with a requirement imposed on him/her under subs. (1) (s. 1(5)).

Also available in dealing with the control of alcohol are Public Spaces Protection Orders where such orders may be made to prohibit the consumption of alcohol in designated public places together with its surrender and disposal (see para. 3.7.6).

3.6.6.4 Closure Notices for Persistently Selling Alcohol to Children

Section 169A of the Licensing Act 2003 provides that a senior police officer (of the rank of superintendent or higher), or an inspector of weights and measures, may give a closure notice where there is evidence that a person has committed the offence of persistently selling alcohol to children at the premises in question and he/she considers that the evidence is such that there would be a realistic prospect of conviction if the offender was prosecuted for it. A closure notice can only be given within three months of the last offence (s. 169A(9)).

A closure notice will propose a prohibition on sales of alcohol at the premises in question for at least 48 hours but not more than 336 hours (s. 169A(4)) and will offer the opportunity to discharge all criminal liability in respect of the alleged offence by the acceptance of the prohibition proposed in the notice (s. 169A(2)). The premises licence holder will have 14 days to decide whether or not to accept the proposed prohibition or to elect to be tried for the offence (s. 169A(4)). Where the licence holder decides to accept the prohibition, it must take effect not less than 14 days after the date on which the notice was served at a time specified in the closure notice (s. 169A(5)).

A closure notice may be served on the premises to which it applies only by being handed by a constable or trading standards officer to a person on the premises who appears to the constable or trading standards officer to have control of or responsibility for the premises (s. 169A(7)). The closure notice can only be served at a time when licensable activities are being carried on at the premises.

3.6.7 Licensed Premises: Exclusion Orders

The Licensed Premises (Exclusion of Certain Persons) Act 1980, s. 1 states:

> (1) Where a court by or before which a person is convicted of an offence committed on licensed premises is satisfied that in committing that offence he resorted to violence or offered or threatened to resort to violence, the court may, subject to subsection (2) below, make an order (in this Act referred to as an 'exclusion order') prohibiting him from entering those premises or any other specified premises, without the express consent of the licensee of the premises or his servant or agent.

KEYNOTE

An exclusion order shall have effect for such period, being not less than three months or more than two years (s. 1(3)).

In *R* v *Arrowsmith* [2003] EWCA Crim 701, the court made an exclusion order relating to 165 specified licensed premises near to where the accused resided. A copy of the exclusion order must be sent by the court to the licensee of the premises concerned (s. 4(3)).

A person who enters any premises in breach of an exclusion order is guilty of an offence and shall be liable on summary conviction to imprisonment for a term not exceeding one month, to a fine or both (s. 2(1)).

A licensee or their servant or agent has the power to expel a person subject to an exclusion order and a constable shall on the demand of the licensee or their servant or agent help to expel from licensed premises any person whom the constable reasonably suspects of having entered in breach of an exclusion order (s. 3).

'Licensed premises' means premises in respect of which there is in force a premises licence and 'licensee' in relation to any licensed premises means the holder of the licence granted in respect of those premises (s. 4).

3.6.8 Orders to Close Premises in Area Experiencing Disorder

The Licensing Act 2003, s. 160 states:

(1) Where there is or is expected to be disorder in any local justice area, a magistrates' court acting in the area may make an order requiring all premises—
 (a) which are situated at or near the place of the disorder or expected disorder, and
 (b) in respect of which a premises licence or a temporary event notice has effect, to be closed for a period, not exceeding 24 hours, specified in the order.

(2) A magistrates' court may make an order under this section only on the application of a police officer who is of the rank of superintendent or above.

(3) A magistrates' court may not make such an order unless it is satisfied that it is necessary to prevent disorder.

KEYNOTE

This provision can be used where disorder is taking place in an area or where it is expected to take place.

A constable may use such force as may be necessary for the purpose of closing premises ordered to be closed under this section (s. 160(7)).

Where an order is made under this section, any manager of the premises, holder of a premises licence in respect of the premises and the designated premises supervisor (if any) under such a licence, and the premises user in relation to a temporary event notice, commits an offence if they knowingly allow the premises to be kept open (s. 160(4) and (5)).

3.6.9 Closure Notices and Orders for Unlicensed Premises

The Criminal Justice and Police Act 2001, s. 19 states:

(1) Where a constable is satisfied that any premises are being, or within the last 24 hours have been, used for the unauthorised sale of alcohol for consumption on, or in the vicinity of, the premises, he may serve under subsection (3) a notice in respect of the premises.

(2) Where a local authority is satisfied that any premises in the area of the authority are being, or within the last 24 hours have been, used for the unauthorised sale of alcohol for consumption on, or in the vicinity of, the premises, the authority may serve under subsection (3) a notice in respect of the premises.

(3) A notice under subsection (1) or (2) ('a closure notice') shall be served by the constable or local authority concerned on a person having control of, or responsibility for, the activities carried on at the premises.

(4) A closure notice shall also be served by the constable or local authority concerned on any person occupying another part of any building or other structure of which the premises form part if the constable or (as the case may be) the local authority concerned reasonably believes, at the time of serving notice under subsection (3), that the person's access to the other part of the building or other structure would be impeded if an order under section 21 providing for the closure of the premises were made.

(5) A closure notice may also be served by a constable or the local authority concerned on—
 (a) any other person having control of, or responsibility for, the activities carried on at the premises;
 (b) any person who has an interest in the premises.

KEYNOTE

The power provided by this section is available to any police officer irrespective of rank.

The closure notice must specify the alleged use of the premises, the grounds on which it has been issued, the steps that are required to be taken to ensure that the alleged use of the premises ceases or does not recur and state the effects of s. 20 (s. 19(6)).

Where a closure notice has been served under s. 19(3), a constable or the local authority concerned may make a complaint to a justice of the peace for a closure order (s. 20(1)). The complaint must be made not less than seven days, and not more than six months, after the service of the closure notice (s. 20(2)). However, a complaint cannot be made under this subsection if the constable or the local authority is satisfied that the use of the premises for the unauthorised sale of alcohol for consumption on, or in the vicinity of, the premises has ceased and there is no reasonable likelihood that the premises will be so used in the future (s. 20(3)).

Where a closure order is made by the court, a constable or authorised person may enter the premises, if necessary using reasonable force, at any reasonable time to do anything necessary to secure compliance with the order (s. 25(1)). The constable or authorised person must produce identification if so required by the owner, occupier or person in charge of the premises (s. 25(2)). Intentionally obstructing a constable or authorised person is a summary offence (s. 25(3)). Permitting premises to be open in contravention of the order is an offence (s. 25(4), as is failing to comply with a closure order generally (s. 25(5)).

Closure orders and closure notices must be 'policeable' in the sense that they must be clear and comprehensible to the defendant, the police and the public (*R* v *Maguire* [2019] EWCA Crim 1193).

3.7 Protecting Citizens and the Community: Injunctions, Orders and Police Powers

3.7.1 Introduction

This chapter covers a variety of preventative and protective measures available to the courts, local authorities and the police under the following legislation: the Policing and Crime Act 2009 (injunctions to prevent gang-related violence and drug-dealing activity); the Anti-social Behaviour, Crime and Policing Act 2014 (anti-social behaviour injunctions, dispersal powers, community protection notices and closure of premises associated with nuisance or disorder); the Sentencing Act 2020 (criminal behaviour orders); and the Crime and Disorder Act 1998 (parenting orders and the power to remove truants and excluded pupils to designated premises).

3.7.2 Injunctions to Prevent Gang-related Violence and Drug Dealing Activity

The Policing and Crime Act 2009 provides courts with the power to grant injunctions to prevent gang-related violence and drug dealing activity.

Section 34 of the 2009 Act, as amended, states:

(1) A court may grant an injunction under this section against a respondent aged 14 or over if the first and second conditions are met.

(2) The first condition is that the court is satisfied on the balance of probabilities that the respondent has engaged in or has encouraged or assisted—
  (a) gang-related violence, or
  (b) gang-related drug-dealing activity.

(3) The second condition is that the court thinks it is necessary to grant the injunction for either or both of the following purposes—
  (a) to prevent the respondent from engaging in, or encouraging or assisting, gang-related violence or gang-related drug-dealing activity;
  (b) to protect the respondent from gang-related violence or gang-related drug-dealing activity.

(4) An injunction under this section may (for either or both of those purposes)—
  (a) prohibit the respondent from doing anything described in the injunction;
  (b) require the respondent to do anything described in the injunction.

(5) For the purposes of this section, something is 'gang-related' if it occurs in the course of, or is otherwise related to, the activities of a group that—
  (a) consists of at least three people, and
  (b) has one or more characteristics that enable its members to be identified by others as a group.

(6) In this section 'violence' includes a threat of violence.

(7) In this Part 'drug-dealing activity' means—
  (a) the unlawful production, supply, importation or exportation of a controlled drug, or
  (b) the unlawful production, supply, importation or exportation of a psychoactive substance.

KEYNOTE

These injunctions are a civil tool allowing the police or local authority to apply to the High Court, a county court or, in the case of juveniles, a youth court (sitting in a civil capacity), for an injunction against an individual who has been involved in gang-related violence or drug dealing activity. A range of prohibitions and requirements on the behaviour and activities of a person can be included in an injunction, such as prohibiting someone from being in a particular place or requiring them to participate in rehabilitative activities (s. 35).

The court may attach a power of arrest in relation to (a) any prohibition in the injunction, or (b) any requirement in the injunction other than one which has the effect of requiring the respondent to participate in particular activities (s. 36). Where a power of arrest is attached to a provision, a constable may arrest without warrant a person whom the constable has reasonable cause to suspect to be in breach of the provision. The constable must inform the person who applied for the injunction of the arrest, and the person arrested must be brought before a judge of the court that granted the injunction within 24 hours of the arrest (s. 43).

An injunction preventing a person allegedly involved in gang-related activities from entering a large part of a city centre was held not to be incompatible with Article 6(1) of the European Convention on Human Rights (ECHR) (right to a fair trial) (*Jones* v *Birmingham City Council* [2018] EWCA Civ 1189).

In relation to subs. (7)(a), 'controlled drug' has the meaning given by s. 37(1) of the Misuse of Drugs Act 1971, and for subs. (7)(b) 'psychoactive substance' has the meaning given by s. 59 of the Psychoactive Substances Act 2016 (s. 34(8)).

3.7.3 Injunctions under the Anti-social Behaviour, Crime and Policing Act 2014

An application for a civil injunction for dealing with anti-social behaviour must be made to a youth court where the respondent is under 18 years of age or to the High Court or county court in any other case (s. 1(8)(a) and (b)). Such an application can only be made by the police, the local authority and other specified bodies (s. 5(1)).

A youth court may give permission for an application for an injunction against a person aged 18 or over to be made to the youth court if an application to the youth court has been made, or is to be made, for an injunction against a person aged under 18, and the youth court thinks that it would be in the interests of justice for the applications to be heard together (s. 18(2)).

3.7.3.1 Power to Grant Injunctions

A written application must be made to the court by way of complaint and be supported by evidence of the matters of which the court must be satisfied under s. 1 of the Act and state the terms of the injunction applied for.

The Anti-social Behaviour, Crime and Policing Act 2014, s. 1 provides a regime of injunctions for dealing with anti-social behaviour and states:

(1) A court may grant an injunction under this section against a person aged 10 or over ('the respondent') if two conditions are met.
(2) The first condition is that the court is satisfied, on the balance of probabilities, that the respondent has engaged or threatens to engage in anti-social behaviour.
(3) The second condition is that the court considers it just and convenient to grant the injunction for the purpose of preventing the respondent from engaging in anti-social behaviour.
(4) An injunction under this section may for the purpose of preventing the respondent from engaging in anti-social behaviour—
 (a) prohibit the respondent from doing anything described in the injunction;
 (b) require the respondent to do anything described in the injunction.

(5) Prohibitions and requirements in an injunction under this section must, so far as practicable, be such as to avoid—
   (a) any interference with the times, if any, at which the respondent normally works or attends school or any other educational establishment;
   (b) any conflict with the requirements of any other court order or injunction to which the respondent may be subject.
(6) An injunction under this section must—
   (a) specify the period for which it has effect, or
   (b) state that it has effect until further order.
   In the case of an injunction granted before the respondent has reached the age of 18, a period must be specified and it must be no more than 12 months.
(7) An injunction under this section may specify periods for which particular prohibitions or requirements have effect.

KEYNOTE

In relation to the first condition (s. 1(2)), the Supreme Court held that Article 6 of the ECHR (right to a fair trial) did not require the application of the criminal standard of proof (*Jones* v *Birmingham City Council* [2023] UKSC 27).

A person who breaches the terms of an injunction does not commit a criminal offence though the court may make a supervision order or detention order (sch. 2).

The Youth Justice and Criminal Evidence Act 1999, in relation to special measures directions in the case of vulnerable and intimidated witnesses, applies to proceedings under this part of the 2014 Act as it applies to criminal proceedings (s. 16). This might include giving evidence behind a screen, by video link or in private.

Before making an application for an injunction in the youth court there is a formal requirement for the applicant to consult with the local youth offending team and to inform any other body or individual considered appropriate (s. 14). This could include a social landlord (when an application is made by another body against one of its tenants) or a mental health team.

3.7.3.2 Anti-social Behaviour

'Anti-social behaviour' is defined by s. 2 of the Act which states:

(1) In this Part 'anti-social behaviour' means—
   (a) conduct that has caused, or is likely to cause, harassment, alarm or distress to any person,
   (b) conduct capable of causing nuisance or annoyance to a person in relation to that person's occupation of residential premises, or
   (c) conduct capable of causing housing-related nuisance or annoyance to any person.

KEYNOTE

In relation to 'likely to cause' (s. 2(1)(a)), it was held that the prosecution was not required to prove that the offending behaviour was actually witnessed but that it took place in circumstances where it was likely to be witnessed and likely, if witnessed, to cause harassment, alarm or distress (*R (On the Application of Gosport Borough Council* v *Fareham Magistrates' Court* [2006] EWHC 3047 (Admin)).

'Likely' means more probable than not (*Chief Constable of Lancashire* v *Potter* [2003] EWHC 2272 (Admin)).

In *Birmingham City Council* v *Afsar* [2019] EWHC 1560 (QB), the court held that an injunction could be granted for protests thereby prohibiting anti-social utterances and assemblies where it was shown to be necessary and proportionate.

The definition does not capture 'trivial conduct' and in order to prove that anti-social behaviour has taken place the court should expect more by way of evidence than general assertions to that effect (*Swindon Borough Council* v *Abrook* [2024] EWCA Civ 230).

3.7.3.3 Requirements Included in Injunctions

The Anti-social Behaviour, Crime and Policing Act 2014, s. 3 states:

(1) An injunction under section 1 that includes a requirement must specify the person who is to be responsible for supervising compliance with the requirement.

The person may be an individual or an organisation.

(2) Before including a requirement, the court must receive evidence about its suitability and enforceability from—
 (a) the individual to be specified under subsection (1), if an individual is to be specified;
 (b) an individual representing the organisation to be specified under subsection (1), if an organisation is to be specified.

(3) Before including two or more requirements, the court must consider their compatibility with each other.

(4) It is the duty of a person specified under subsection (1)—
 (a) to make any necessary arrangements in connection with the requirements for which the person has responsibility (the 'relevant requirements');
 (b) to promote the respondent's compliance with the relevant requirements;
 (c) if the person considers that the respondent—
  (i) has complied with all the relevant requirements, or
  (ii) has failed to comply with a relevant requirement,
 to inform the person who applied for the injunction and the appropriate chief officer of police.

3.7.3.4 Power of Arrest

Section 4 provides officers with a power of arrest in certain circumstances:

(1) A court granting an injunction under section 1 may attach a power of arrest to a prohibition or requirement of the injunction if the court thinks that—
 (a) the anti-social behaviour in which the respondent has engaged or threatens to engage consists of or includes the use or threatened use of violence against other persons, or
 (b) there is a significant risk of harm to other persons from the respondent.
 'Requirement' here does not include one that has the effect of requiring the respondent to participate in particular activities.

(2) If the court attaches a power of arrest, the injunction may specify a period for which the power is to have effect which is shorter than that of the prohibition or requirement to which it relates.

A power of arrest attached to an injunction allows a police officer to arrest the respondent without a warrant if the respondent breached a condition in the injunction, that is, a prohibition or a requirement (s. 9). Where no power of arrest is attached to the injunction, the applicant may apply to the court to issue a warrant of arrest of a respondent if the applicant thinks that the respondent has breached the injunction (s. 10). Section 11 and sch. 1 make provision for the remand, whether on bail or in custody, of a person arrested for breach of an injunction.

3.7.4 Criminal Behaviour Orders

The Sentencing Code (Sentencing Act 2020, s. 330) states:

In this Code 'criminal behaviour order' means an order which, for the purpose of preventing an offender from engaging in behaviour that is likely to cause harassment, alarm or distress to any person—
(a) prohibits the offender from doing anything described in the order;
(b) requires the offender to do anything described in the order.

The Crown Court, the magistrates' court and the youth court are able to make a criminal behaviour order (CBO) for the most serious and persistent offenders where they have been convicted of an offence (s. 331(1)).

3.7.4.1 Power to Make a Criminal Behaviour Order

The Sentencing Act 2020, s. 331 states:

> (1) This section applies where—
> (a) a person is convicted of an offence, and
> (b) the prosecution makes an application to the court for a criminal behaviour order to be made against the offender.
> (2) The court may make a criminal behaviour order against the offender if it—
> (a) is satisfied that the offender has engaged in behaviour that caused or was likely to cause harassment, alarm or distress to any person, and
> (b) considers that making the order will help in preventing the offender from engaging in such behaviour.
> (3) But the court may make a criminal behaviour order only if it—
> (a) does so in addition to dealing with the offender for the offence, and
> (b) does not make an order for absolute discharge under section 79 in respect of the offence.
> (4) Prohibitions and requirements in a criminal behaviour order must, so far as practicable, be such as to avoid—
> (a) any interference with the times, if any, at which the offender normally works or attends school or any other educational establishment, and
> (b) any conflict with the requirements of any other court order to which the offender may be subject.

KEYNOTE

If the offender is under the age of 18, the prosecution must find out the views of the local youth offending team before applying for a criminal behaviour order to be made (s. 331(5)).

For a person under the age of 18, a criminal behaviour order (CBO) must be made for not less than one year and not more than three years (s. 334(4)). In any other case, a CBO must be either for a fixed period of not less than two years or for an indefinite period (s. 334(5)).

The decision to publicise the granting of a CBO may be taken by the police or council unless the court has made an order prohibiting publication (s. 39 of the Children and Young Persons Act 1933). Making the public aware of the offender and the terms of the CBO is an important part of the process in dealing with anti-social behaviour.

An offender who without reasonable excuse does anything he/she is prohibited from doing by a CBO, or fails to do anything required by a CBO, commits an offence (s. 339(1)). The sentence is six months' imprisonment and/or a fine summarily or five years' imprisonment and/or a fine on indictment (s. 339(2)).

The Youth Justice and Criminal Evidence Act 1999, in relation to special measures directions in the case of vulnerable and intimidated witnesses, applies to proceedings under this part of the Act as it applies to criminal proceedings (s. 340). This might include giving evidence behind a screen, by video link or in private.

3.7.5 Dispersal Powers

The Anti-social Behaviour, Crime and Policing Act 2014 provides the police with a dispersal power enabling constables in uniform and Police Community Support Officers to direct a person who has committed, or is likely to commit, anti-social behaviour to leave a specified area and not return for a period of up to 48 hours.

3.7.5.1 Authorisations to use Powers Under Section 35

The Anti-social Behaviour, Crime and Policing Act 2014, s. 34 states:

(1) A police officer of at least the rank of inspector may authorise the use in a specified locality, during a specified period of not more than 48 hours, of the powers given by section 35.

'Specified' means specified in the authorisation.

(2) An officer may give such an authorisation only if satisfied on reasonable grounds that the use of those powers in the locality during that period may be necessary for the purpose of removing or reducing the likelihood of—
(a) members of the public in the locality being harassed, alarmed or distressed, or
(b) the occurrence in the locality of crime or disorder.

KEYNOTE

In deciding whether to give such an authorisation, an officer must have regard to the rights of freedom of expression and freedom of assembly set out in Articles 10 and 11 of the ECHR (s. 34(3)).

An authorisation must be in writing, must be signed by the officer giving it and must specify the grounds on which it is given (s. 34(4)).

3.7.5.2 Directions Excluding a Person from an Area

The Anti-social Behaviour, Crime and Policing Act 2014, s. 35 states:

(1) If the conditions in subsections (2) and (3) are met and an authorisation is in force under section 34, a constable in uniform may direct a person who is in a public place in the locality specified in the authorisation—
(a) to leave the locality (or part of the locality), and
(b) not to return to the locality (or part of the locality) for the period specified in the direction ('the exclusion period').

(2) The first condition is that the constable has reasonable grounds to suspect that the behaviour of the person in the locality has contributed or is likely to contribute to—
(a) members of the public in the locality being harassed, alarmed or distressed, or
(b) the occurrence in the locality of crime or disorder.

(3) The second condition is that the constable considers that giving a direction to the person is necessary for the purpose of removing or reducing the likelihood of the events mentioned in subsection (2)(a) or (b).

(4) The exclusion period may not exceed 48 hours.

The period may expire after (as long as it begins during) the period specified in the authorisation under section 34.

KEYNOTE

A direction under this section must be given in writing, unless that is not reasonably practicable, must specify the area to which it relates and may impose requirements as to the time by which the person must leave the area and the manner in which the person must do so (including the route) (s. 35(5)). The person must be told that failing without reasonable excuse to comply with the direction is an offence (s. 35(6)).

Where a constable reasonably believes that the person to whom the direction is given is under the age of 16, the constable may remove the person to a place where the person lives or a place of safety (s. 35(7)).

Any constable may withdraw or vary a direction under this section but a variation must not extend beyond 48 hours and any variation should, where reasonably practicable, be in writing (s. 35(8) and (9)).

'Public place' means a place to which at the material time the public or a section of the public has access, on payment or otherwise, as of right or by virtue of express or implied permission (s. 35(10)).

3.7.6 Community Protection Notices

The community protection notice (CPN) is intended to deal with unreasonable, ongoing problems or nuisances which negatively affect the community's quality of life by targeting the person responsible. The notice can direct any individual over the age of 16, business or organisation responsible to stop causing the problem and it could also require the person or body responsible to take reasonable steps to ensure that it does not occur again.

3.7.6.1 Power to Issue Community Protection Notices

The power to issue a community protection notice is provided by s. 43 of the Anti-social Behaviour, Crime and Policing 2014 Act that states:

(1) An authorised person may issue a community protection notice to an individual aged 16 or over, or a body, if satisfied on reasonable grounds that—
  (a) the conduct of the individual or body is having a detrimental effect, of a persistent or continuing nature, on the quality of life of those in the locality, and
  (b) the conduct is unreasonable.

KEYNOTE

In many areas, councils take the lead in dealing with these kinds of issues but the power to issue a notice is also available to the police and PCSOs, if designated by the chief constable (s. 53(5); under s. 53(6), a PCSO will also be able to issue a fixed penalty notice for the offence of breaching a community protection notice, if designated for that).

The notice should be issued to someone who can be held responsible for the anti-social behaviour (s. 44). For instance, if a small shop were allowing litter to be deposited outside the property and not dealing with the issue, a notice could be issued to the business owner, whereas if a large national supermarket were to cause a similar issue, the company itself or the store manager could be issued with a notice.

It is not necessary to prove that the conduct of the individual or body is criminal or tortuous (*R (On the Application of Hacking)* v *Stratford Magistrates' Court* [2022] EWHC 2733 (Admin)).

A CPN cannot be issued in the name of a parent concerning the anti-social behaviour of their child (*Staffordshire Moorlands District Council* v *Sanderson* [2020] EWHC 962 (Admin)). Before issuing a notice, an authorised person is required to inform whatever agencies or persons he/she considered appropriate (e.g. the landlord of the person in question, or the local authority), partly in order to avoid duplication (s. 43(6)). The person would also have to have issued a written warning in advance and allowed an appropriate amount of time to pass (s. 43(5)). This is to ensure that the perpetrator is aware of their behaviour and allows them time to rectify the situation. It will be for the person issuing the written warning to decide how long is appropriate before serving a notice. In the example where a dog owner's fence needs to be fixed, this could be days or weeks, in order to allow the individual to address the problem. However, it could be minutes or hours in a case where, for example, someone was persistently playing loud music in a park.

Wherever possible, the notice should be issued in person. However, where this is not possible, it can be posted or left at the proper address (s. 55(1)). In the case of the latter when it relates to a business, the address may be different from the location of the anti-social behaviour.

A person guilty of failing to comply with a CPN is liable on summary conviction to a fine. However, an offence is not committed if a person took all reasonable steps to comply with the notice or there is some other reasonable excuse for the failure to comply with it (s. 48).

Where a person is convicted of an offence, the magistrates' court may order forfeiture or destruction of any item used in the commission of the offence (s. 50), or where necessary issue a warrant for the seizure of such items (s. 51(1)).

3.7.7 Public Spaces Protection Orders

The power to make a public spaces protection order is contained in s. 59 of the Anti-social Behaviour, Crime and Policing Act 2014. It provides local authorities with the power to make an order to deal with nuisances or problems which harm the local community's quality of life. An order will specify an area where activities are taking place that are detrimental to the quality of life of those in the area and can impose conditions and restrictions on people using the specified area. An expedited public spaces protection order under s. 59A is also available where detrimental activities are taking place in the vicinity of schools and sites providing vaccination or test-and-trace services.

3.7.7.1 Power to make Public Spaces Protection Order

The Anti-social Behaviour, Crime and Policing Act 2014, s. 59 states:

(1) A local authority may make a public spaces protection order if satisfied on reasonable grounds that two conditions are met.

(2) The first condition is that—
  (a) activities carried on in a public place within the authority's area have had a detrimental effect on the quality of life of those in the locality, or
  (b) it is likely that activities will be carried on in a public place within that area and that they will have such an effect.

(3) The second condition is that the effect, or likely effect, of the activities—
  (a) is, or is likely to be, of a persistent or continuing nature,
  (b) is, or is likely to be, such as to make the activities unreasonable, and
  (c) justifies the restrictions imposed by the notice.

(4) A public spaces protection order is an order that identifies the public place referred to in subsection (2) ('the restricted area') and—
  (a) prohibits specified things being done in the restricted area,
  (b) requires specified things to be done by persons carrying on specified activities in that area, or
  (c) does both of those things.

(5) The only prohibitions or requirements that may be imposed are ones that are reasonable to impose in order—
  (a) to prevent the detrimental effect referred to in subsection (2) from continuing, occurring or recurring, or
  (b) to reduce that detrimental effect or to reduce the risk of its continuance, occurrence or recurrence.

KEYNOTE

An expedited order under s. 59A allows for rapid action to be taken in order to protect those who work and use the essential services at the identified sites from the harm that some protests targeting those sites may cause. An expedited order may not have effect for a period of more than six months and may be extended or reduced more than once (s. 60A).

In relation to an order under s. 59, these may be used to prohibit the consumption of alcohol in a public place. The breach of such an order is an offence where an individual does not cease drinking or surrender alcoholic drinks when challenged by an enforcement officer which includes a constable, PCSO or local authority officer (s. 63(6)). A constable or authorised person may dispose of anything surrendered in whatever way is considered appropriate (s. 63(5)).

An order may not have effect for a period of more than three years, but this may be extended for another period of three years and extended more than once (s. 60).

It is a summary offence punishable by a fine for a person without reasonable excuse to do anything that the person is prohibited from doing by a public spaces protection order or an expedited order, or to fail to comply with a requirement to which the person is subject under a public spaces protection order or an expedited order (s. 67). A person failing to comply with an order may be subject to a Fixed Penalty Notice or prosecution (s. 68).

3.7.8 Closure of Premises Associated with Nuisance or Disorder

The Anti-social Behaviour, Crime and Policing Act 2014 provides the police and local authorities with a regime for issuing closure notices and making closure orders to provide a fast and flexible power that can be used to protect victims and communities by quickly closing premises that are causing nuisance or disorder.

3.7.8.1 Closure Notice and Order

The Anti-social Behaviour, Crime and Policing Act 2014, s. 76 states:

Power to issue closure notices

(1) A police officer of at least the rank of inspector, or the local authority, may issue a closure notice if satisfied on reasonable grounds—

(a) that the use of particular premises has resulted, or (if the notice is not issued) is likely soon to result, in nuisance to members of the public, or

(b) that there has been, or (if the notice is not issued) is likely soon to be, disorder near those premises associated with the use of those premises,

and that the notice is necessary to prevent the nuisance or disorder from continuing, recurring or occurring.

(2) A closure notice is a notice prohibiting access to the premises for a period specified in the notice.

KEYNOTE

In *Leeds City Council* v *Persons Unknown* [2023] EWHC 1504 (Admin), it was held that 'premises' had to be somewhere objectively identifiable as a distinct property and could not include an area marked on a map, or a highway or any other locality.

The maximum period that may be specified in a closure notice is 24 hours (s. 77(1)). However, this may be extended to a maximum of 48 hours by an officer of at least the rank of superintendent (s. 77(2)) but must be cancelled where it is no longer required with a cancellation notice (s. 78(2)).

A closure notice may prohibit: access by all persons except those specified or by all persons except those of a specified description; at all times, or at all times except those specified; in all circumstances or in all circumstances except those specified (s. 76(3)). A closure notice may not prohibit access by people who habitually live on the premises or by the owner of the premises (s. 76(4)).

An application for a closure order must be heard by the magistrates' court within 48 hours of a closure notice being issued (s. 80(3)). The court can make a closure order for a maximum period of three months (s. 80(6)) if it is satisfied that: a person has engaged in disorder, anti-social or criminal behaviour on the premises (or that such behaviour is likely if the order is not made) or the use of the premises is associated with the occurrence of disorder or serious nuisance to members of the public (or that such disorder or serious nuisance is likely if the order is not made); and that the order is necessary to prevent the continuation or occurrence or reoccurrence of such disorder or behaviour (s. 80(5)). Unlike the closure notice, a closure order can prohibit access to anyone, including the landlord, owner or habitual residents (s. 80(7)).

The offences committed in relation to closure notices and orders are provided by s. 86 of the Act and include:

- where a person without reasonable excuse remains on or enters premises in contravention of a closure notice (subs. (1));
- where a person without reasonable excuse remains on or enters premises in contravention of a closure order and commits an offence (subs. (2));
- where a person who without reasonable excuse obstructs a person in the act of closing a property (subs. (3)).

A person guilty of an offence under subs. (1) or (3) is liable on summary conviction to imprisonment for three months and/or a fine (subs. (4)). A person guilty of an offence under subs. (2) is liable on summary conviction to imprisonment for a period not exceeding 51 weeks and/or a fine (subs. (5)).

3.7.9 Orders Against Parents

These orders are about influencing parental responsibility and control. The orders are designed to give parents more help and support to change the criminal and/or anti-social behaviour of their children in providing a framework where parents participate in their child's supervision. The strategy here is one of prevention in attempting to dissuade a recurrence of criminality or truancy.

3.7.9.1 Parenting Orders

Parenting orders are provided by the Crime and Disorder Act 1998, s. 8 of which states:

(1) This section applies where, in any court proceedings—
  (a) a child safety order is made in respect of a child, or the court determines on an application under section 12(6) below that a child has failed to comply with any requirement included in such an order;
  (aa) a parental compensation order is made in relation to a child's behaviour;
  (b) an injunction is granted under section 1 of the Anti-social Behaviour, Crime and Policing Act 2014 or a criminal behaviour order or a sexual harm prevention order is made in respect of a child or young person;
(2) Subject to subsection (3) and section 9(1) below, if in the proceedings the court is satisfied that the relevant condition is fulfilled, it may make a parenting order in respect of a person who is a parent or guardian of the child or young person ('the parent').
(3) ...
(4) A parenting order is an order which requires the parent—
  (a) to comply, for a period not exceeding twelve months, with such requirements as are specified in the order; and
  (b) subject to subsection (5) below, to attend, for a concurrent period not exceeding three months and not more than once in any week, such counselling or guidance sessions as may be specified in directions given by the responsible officer.
(5) A parenting order may, but need not, include such a requirement as is mentioned in subsection (4)(b) above in any case where a parenting order under this section or any other enactment has been made in respect of the parent on a previous occasion.
(6) The relevant condition is that the parenting order would be desirable in the interests of preventing—
  (a) in a case falling within paragraph (a), (aa) or (b) of subsection (1) above, any repetition of the kind of behaviour which led to the order being made or the injunction granted
(7) The requirements that may be specified under subsection (4)(a) above are those which the court considers desirable in the interests of preventing any such repetition.

KEYNOTE

The Sentencing Act 2020 provides that a parenting order is available to a court by or before which an offender under 18 is convicted of an offence (s. 366(1)). As with an order under the Crime and Disorder Act, the court may place requirements on the parent(s) for a period of 12 months (s. 366(6)). In *R (On the Application of M)* v *Inner London Crown Court* [2003] EWHC 301 (Admin), the court held that the making of a parenting order did not contravene Article 8 of the ECHR (respect for private and family life).

In relation to subs. (1)(a), child safety orders are made by the family court on the application of a local authority. They are designed to help prevent children under 10 years of age from turning to crime (s. 11).

A parenting order may be made against one or both biological parents (this would include an order against a father who may not be married to the mother), and a person who is a guardian. Guardians are defined as any person who, in the opinion of the court, has for the time being the care of a child or young person (Children and Young Persons Act 1933, s. 107(1)).

A court may bind over a parent or guardian of a person under 18 who is convicted of an offence. The parent or guardian must consent to enter into a recognisance to take proper care of the offender and exercise proper control over them. If he/she does not consent, or the court consider the refusal unreasonable, it may order him/her to pay a fine not exceeding £1,000 (s. 376 of the Sentencing Act 2020).

A parent or guardian commits a summary offence, punishable by a fine, if without reasonable excuse he/she fails to comply with any requirement included within a parenting order or specified in directions given by the responsible officer (s. 9(7)).

3.7.10 Removal of Truants and Excluded Pupils to Designated Premises, etc.

The Crime and Disorder Act 1998, s. 16 states:

(1) This section applies where a local authority—
  (a) designates premises in a police area ('designated premises') as premises to which children and young persons of compulsory school age may be removed under this section; and
  (b) notifies the chief officer of police for that area of the designation.

(2) A police officer of or above the rank of superintendent may direct that the powers conferred on a constable by subsection (3) and (3ZA) below—
  (a) shall be exercisable as respects any area falling within the police area and specified in the direction; and
  (b) shall be so exercisable during a period specified;

and references in each of those subsections to a specified area and a specified period shall be construed accordingly.

(3) If a constable has reasonable cause to believe that a child or young person found by him in a public place in a specified area during a specified period—
  (a) is of compulsory school age; and
  (b) is absent from school without lawful authority,

the constable may remove the child or young person to designated premises, or to the school from which he is so absent.

(3ZA) If a constable has reasonable cause to believe that a child or young person found by him in a public place in a specified area during a specified period and during school hours—
  (a) is of compulsory school age;
  (b) has been excluded on disciplinary grounds from a relevant school for a fixed period or permanently;
  (c) remains excluded from that school;
  (d) has not subsequently been admitted as a pupil to any other school; and
  (e) has no reasonable justification for being in the public place;

the constable may remove the child or young person to designated premises.

KEYNOTE

'Designated premises' are not defined but will generally be a child's own school. 'Public place' means any highway, or any place to which at the material time the public or any section of the public has access, on payment or otherwise (Public Order Act 1986, s. 16).

'Without lawful authority' is qualified by s. 16(4) in that lawful authority will be that which falls within s. 444 of the Education Act 1996—leave, sickness, unavoidable cause or day set apart for religious observation.

In s. 16(3ZA), 'school hours' means any time during a school session of the school referred to in para. (b) of that subsection or during a break between sessions of that school on the same day (s. 16(3B)).

The power of a constable to remove a child or young person to 'designated premises' is not an arrest in the traditional sense of detention, and statutory powers relating to arrests will not apply. However, the duty to explain the reason for a person's 'seizure' may well apply in such cases.

As with the powers conferred in relation to curfew notices, it appears probable that the common law rule entitling a constable to use reasonable force would apply. The requirement for the officer to have 'reasonable cause to believe' that the person meets the criteria at (a) and (b) is more stringent than mere suspicion.

The Education Act 1996 provides that penalty notices can be issued to parents or guardians who fail to ensure the regular attendance of their child of compulsory school age (5–16) who is registered at a state school, or fail to ensure that their excluded child is not found in a public place during school hours without a justifiable reason. If a child is found in such circumstances, designated local authority officers, headteachers (and authorised deputy headteachers and assistant headteachers), police officers and community support officers can issue a fixed penalty notice (ss. 444A and 444B).

3.8 Policing Processions, Assemblies and Protests: Offences and Powers

3.8.1 Introduction

The law controlling processions and assemblies is primarily contained in the Public Order Act 1986. The Public Order Act 2023 is aimed at protesters and criminalises specific forms of protest with the creation of several offences. It also significantly expands police powers of stop and search, including searches without suspicion.

The European Convention on Human Rights has a significant impact on a number of the areas concerned within this chapter and especially Article 10 (Freedom of Expression) and Article 11 (Freedom of Assembly and Association). These two Articles are discussed in the following paragraphs.

3.8.2 Article 10—Freedom of Expression

Article 10 of the Convention states:

1. Everyone has the right to freedom of expression. This right shall include freedom to hold opinions and to receive and impart information and ideas without interference by public authority and regardless of frontiers. This Article shall not prevent States from requiring the licensing of broadcasting, television or cinema enterprises.
2. The exercise of these freedoms, since it carries with it duties and responsibilities, may be subject to such formalities, conditions, restrictions or penalties as are prescribed by law and are necessary in a democratic society, in the interests of national security, territorial integrity or public safety, for the prevention of disorder or crime, for the protection of health or morals, for the protection of the reputation or rights of others, for preventing the disclosure of information received in confidence, or for maintaining the authority and impartiality of the judiciary.

KEYNOTE

Article 10 protects the freedom:

- of expression;
- to hold opinions; and
- to receive and impart information and ideas;

in each case without interference by a public authority.

'Expression' here includes the creation of pictures and images (*Stevens* v *United Kingdom* (1986) 46 DR 245).

Although not providing a general 'right to freedom of expression', Article 10 has been used in a number of different settings including the protection of artistic, political and economic expression. It has been used to protect journalists' sources (*Goodwin* v *United Kingdom* (1996) 22 EHRR 123).

As the right to express freely has to be balanced against the rights of others and the needs of democratic society generally, this area of Convention rights has generated some considerable problems and is often intermingled with issues of freedom of thought, conscience and religion (under Article 9).

In a case where the defendant damaged the perimeter fence of a Trident defence base, the Divisional Court held that her acts could be characterised as an expression of her opinion under Article 10 but that the Convention required the expression of that opinion to be proportionate. There were other ways in which the defendant could have expressed her opinion without committing a crime and therefore her conviction for criminal damage was upheld (*Hutchinson* v *DPP* (2000) *The Independent*, 20 November).

Article 10(1) is drafted to allow for State licensing of broadcasts, television and cinema performances but, as you might expect, the courts will be unlikely to tolerate interference with the freedom of expression without compelling reasons. Once again, the courts will look for a 'pressing social need' and, indeed, one of the main cases setting out the requirement for proportionality (*Handyside* v *United Kingdom* (1979–80) 1 EHRR 737) involved an action under Article 10.

Article 10(2) clearly allows for an individual's freedom of expression to be curtailed under a number of circumstances including the prevention of disorder or crime and the protection of morals. Balancing these competing needs is one area where the European Court of Human Rights has allowed a reasonable 'margin of appreciation'. Nevertheless, any restrictions on an individual's freedom of expression will be narrowly construed and closely scrutinised. It has been held that the exercise of the right to free speech could fall within the concept of harassment for the purposes of the Protection from Harassment Act 1997 where the ingredients for the offence were present (*Howlett* v *Harding* [2006] EWHC 41 (QB)).

3.8.3 Article 11—Freedom of Assembly and Association

Article 11 of the Convention states:

1. Everyone has the right to freedom of peaceful assembly and to freedom of association with others, including the right to form and to join trade unions for the protection of his interests.
2. No restrictions shall be placed on the exercise of these rights other than such as are prescribed by law and are necessary in a democratic society in the interests of national security or public safety, for the prevention of disorder or crime, for the protection of health or morals or for the protection of the rights and freedoms of others. This Article shall not prevent the imposition of lawful restrictions on the exercise of these rights by members of the armed forces, of the police or of the administration of the State.

KEYNOTE

Article 11 is closely related to Article 10 and is often raised in conjunction with it, particularly in situations involving the arrest of demonstrators and protestors. In addition to refraining from interference with the individual's right to peaceful assembly, the State is also under a positive duty to prevent others from doing so. The assembly must, however, be *peaceful* and any intention to use violence or to cause disorder may take the individual's actions outside the protection of Article 11.

As with Article 10, there are allowances for reducing rights of assembly etc. under certain conditions including the prevention of disorder and crime and the interests of national security and public safety.

The right to freedom of association and to join trade unions means, among other things, that trade unions may be victims for the purposes of bringing an action under this Article. The State can impose 'lawful restrictions' on the exercise of these rights.

3.8.4 Public Processions and Assemblies

Chief officers, 'senior police officers' and constables have powers in respect of processions and assemblies.

3.8.4.1 Advance Notice of Public Processions

The Public Order Act 1986, s. 11 states:

(1) Written notice shall be given in accordance with this section of any proposal to hold a public procession intended—
   (a) to demonstrate support for or opposition to the views or actions of any person or body of persons,
   (b) to publicise a cause or campaign, or
   (c) to mark or commemorate an event,

   unless it is not reasonably practicable to give any advance notice of the procession.

(2) Subsection (1) does not apply where the procession is one commonly or customarily held in the police area (or areas) in which it is proposed to be held or is a funeral procession organised by a funeral director acting in the normal course of his business.

(3) The notice must specify the date when it is intended to hold the procession, the time when it is intended to start it, its proposed route, and the name and address of the person (or of one of the persons) proposing to organise it.

(4) Notice must be delivered to a police station—
   (a) in the police area in which it is proposed the procession will start, or
   (b) where it is proposed the procession will start in Scotland and cross into England, in the first police area in England on the proposed route.

KEYNOTE

In relation to s. 11(2) it was held that an organised cycle ride that started at the same time and place on the last Friday of every month, even though there was no fixed, settled or predetermined route, end-time or destination, was a commonly or customarily held procession (*R (On the Application of Kay)* v *Commissioner of Police of the Metropolis* [2008] UKHL 69).

If the notice is delivered not less than six clear days before the date when the procession is intended to be held, the notice may be delivered by post by the recorded delivery service (s. 11(5)). Otherwise, the notice must be delivered by hand not less than six clear days before the date when the procession is intended to be held or, if that is not reasonably practicable, as soon as delivery is reasonably practicable (s. 11(6)).

Where a public procession is held, each of the persons organising it commits a summary offence and is liable to a fine if the requirements of this section as to notice have not been satisfied, or the date when it is held, the time when it starts, or its route, differs from the date, time or route specified in the notice (s. 11(7)).

It is a defence for the accused to prove that he/she did not know of, and neither suspected nor had reason to suspect, the failure to satisfy the requirements or (as the case may be) the difference of date, time or route (s. 11(8)). To the extent that an alleged offence turns on a difference of date, time or route, it is a defence for the accused to prove that the difference arose from circumstances beyond his/her control or from something done with the agreement of a police officer or by the officer's direction (s. 11(9)).

3.8.4.2 Imposing Conditions on Public Processions

The Public Order Act 1986, s. 12 states:

(1) If the senior police officer, having regard to the time or place at which and the circumstances in which any public procession is being held or is intended to be held and to its route or proposed route, reasonably believes that—
   (a) it may result in serious public disorder, serious damage to property or serious disruption to the life of the community,
   (aa) in the case of a procession in England and Wales, the noise generated by persons taking part in the procession may result in serious disruption to the activities of an organisation which are carried on in the vicinity of the procession,
   (ab) in the case of a procession in England and Wales—
      (i) the noise generated by persons taking part in the procession may have a relevant impact on persons in the vicinity of the procession, and
      (ii) that impact may be significant, or

(b) the purpose of the persons organising it is the intimidation of others with a view to compelling them not to do an act they have a right to do, or to do an act they have a right not to do,

he may give directions imposing on the persons organising or taking part in the procession such conditions as appear to him necessary to prevent such disorder, damage, disruption, impact or intimidation, including conditions as to the route of the procession or prohibiting it from entering any public place specified in the directions.

(2) In subsection (1) 'the senior police officer' means—

(a) in relation to a procession being held, or to a procession intended to be held in a case where persons are assembling with a view to taking part in it, the most senior in rank of the police officers present at the scene, and

(b) in relation to a procession intended to be held in a case where paragraph (a) does not apply, the chief officer of police.

(2A) For the purposes of subsection (1)—

(a) the cases in which a public procession in England and Wales may result in serious disruption to the life of the community include, in particular, where it may, by way of physical obstruction, result in—

(i) the prevention of, or a hindrance that is more than minor to, the carrying out of day-to-day activities (including in particular the making of a journey),

(ii) the prevention of, or a delay that is more than minor to, the delivery of a time-sensitive product to consumers of that product, or

(iii) the prevention of, or a disruption that is more than minor to, access to any essential goods or any essential service,

(b) in considering whether a public procession in England and Wales may result in serious disruption to the life of the community, the senior police officer—

(i) must take into account all relevant disruption, and

(ii) may take into account any relevant cumulative disruption, and

(c) 'community', in relation to a public procession in England and Wales, means any group of persons that may be affected by the procession, whether or not all or any of those persons live or work in the vicinity of the procession.

(2B) In subsection (2A) and this subsection—

'access to any essential goods or any essential service' includes, in particular, access to—

(a) the supply of money, food, water, or fuel,

(b) a system of communication,

(c) a place of worship,

(d) a transport facility,

(e) an educational institution, or

(f) a service relating to health;

'area', in relation to a public procession or public assembly, means such area as the senior police officer considers appropriate, having regard to the nature and extent of the disruption that may result from the procession or assembly;

'relevant cumulative disruption', in relation to a public procession in England and Wales, means the cumulative disruption to the life of the community resulting from—

(a) the procession,

(b) any other public procession in England and Wales that was held, is being held or is intended to be held in the same area as the area in which the procession mentioned in paragraph (a) is being held or is intended to be held (whether or not directions have been given under subsection (1) in relation to that other procession), and

(c) any public assembly in England and Wales that was held, is being held or is to be held in the same area in which the procession mentioned in paragraph (a) is being or is intended to be held (whether or not directions have been given under section 14(1A) in relation to that assembly),

and it does not matter whether or not the procession mentioned in paragraph (a) and any procession or assembly within paragraph (b) or (c) are organised by the same person, are attended by any of the same persons or are held or are intended to be held at the same time;

'relevant disruption', in relation to a public procession in England and Wales, means all disruption to the life of the community—

(a) that may result from the procession, or

(b) that may occur regardless of whether the procession is held (including in particular normal traffic congestion);

'time-sensitive product' means a product whose value or use to its consumers may be significantly reduced by a delay in the supply of the product to them.

KEYNOTE

For the purposes of subs. (1)(aa), the cases in which the noise generated by persons taking part in a public procession may result in serious disruption to the activities of an organisation which are carried on in the vicinity of the procession include, in particular, where it may result in persons connected with the organisation not being reasonably able, for a prolonged period of time, to carry on in that vicinity the activities or any one of them (s. 12(2C)).

In relation to subs. (1)(ab)(i), the noise generated by persons taking part in a public procession may have a relevant impact on persons in the vicinity of the procession if—

(a) it may result in the intimidation or harassment of persons of reasonable firmness with the characteristics of persons likely to be in the vicinity; or
(b) it may cause such persons to suffer alarm or distress (s. 12(2D)).

Section 12(2E) provides that in considering for the purposes of subs. (1)(ab)(ii) whether the noise generated by persons taking part in a public procession may have a significant impact on persons in the vicinity of the procession, the senior police officer must have regard to:

(a) the likely number of persons of the kind mentioned in paragraph (a) of subsection (2D) who may experience an impact of the kind mentioned in paragraph (a) or (b) of that subsection;
(b) the likely duration of that impact on such persons; and
(c) the likely intensity of that impact on such persons.

(s. 12(2E))

A direction given by a chief officer of police by virtue of subs. (2)(b) shall be given in writing (subs. (3)).

Conditions may be applied where a public procession may result in the serious disruption to the life of the community by way of a physical obstruction resulting in certain outcomes. These outcomes include hindering day-to-day activities, such as people prevented from making a journey, delaying the delivery of time-sensitive products and preventing access to any essential goods or service. Such 'hinderance' must have more than a minor effect. Where conditions are imposed as to the route of a procession, these must be communicated to those involved either days before the procession, at the point of assembly or during the procession itself. Wherever conditions are given, these must be a preventative measure (*Powlesland* v *DPP* [2013] EWHC 3846 (Admin)).

Subject to subs. (5A), a person who organises a public procession and fails to comply with a condition imposed under this section is guilty of a summary offence, but it is a defence for him/her to prove that the failure arose from circumstances beyond his/her control (subs. (4)). A person guilty of an offence under subs. (4) is liable to 51 weeks' imprisonment and/or a fine (subs. (8)).

Subject to subs. (5A), a person who takes part in a public procession and fails to comply with a condition imposed under this section is guilty of a summary offence, but it is a defence for him/her to prove that the failure arose from circumstances beyond his/her control (subs. (5)). A person guilty of an offence under subs. (5) is liable to a fine (subs. (9)).

A person is guilty of an offence under subs. (4) or (5) only if at the time the person fails to comply with the condition, the person knows or ought to know that the condition has been imposed (subs. (5A)).

A person who incites another to commit an offence under subs. (5) is guilty of a summary offence (subs. (6)). A person guilty of an offence under subs. (6) is liable to 51 weeks' imprisonment and/or a fine (subs. 10)).

3.8.4.3 Prohibiting Public Processions

The Public Order Act 1986, s. 13 states:

(1) If at any time the chief officer of police reasonably believes that, because of particular circumstances existing in any district or part of a district, the powers under section 12 will not be sufficient to prevent the holding of public processions in that district or part from resulting in serious public disorder, he shall apply to the council of the district for an order prohibiting for such period not exceeding 3 months as may be specified in the application the holding of all public processions (or of any class of public procession so specified) in the district or part concerned.

(2) On receiving such an application, a council may with the consent of the Secretary of State make an order either in the terms of the application or with such modifications as may be approved by the Secretary of State.
(3) Subsection (1) does not apply in the City of London or the metropolitan police district.

KEYNOTE

A person who organises a public procession the holding of which he/she knows is prohibited by virtue of an order under this section is guilty of a summary offence (s. 13(7)). A person who takes part in a public procession the holding of which he/she knows is prohibited by virtue of an order under this section is guilty of a summary offence (s. 13(8)), and a person who incites another to commit an offence under s. 13(8) is guilty of a summary offence (s. 13(9)). An offence under s. 13(7) and (9) is punishable by three months' imprisonment and/or a fine (s. 13(11) and (13)), and an offence under s. 13(8) is punishable by a fine (s. 13(12)).

3.8.4.4 Imposing Conditions on Public Assemblies

The Public Order Act 1986, s. 14 states:

(1) Subsection (1A) applies if the senior police officer, having regard to the time or place at which and the circumstances in which any public assembly is being held or is intended to be held, reasonably believes that—
   (a) it may result in serious public disorder, serious damage to property or serious disruption to the life of the community,
   (aa) in the case of an assembly in England and Wales, the noise generated by persons taking part in the assembly may result in serious disruption to the activities of an organisation which are carried on in the vicinity of the assembly,
   (ab) in the case of an assembly in England and Wales—
      (i) the noise generated by persons taking part in the assembly may have a relevant impact on persons in the vicinity of the assembly, and
      (ii) that impact may be significant, or
   (b) the purpose of the persons organising it is the intimidation of others with a view to compelling them not to do an act they have a right to do, or to do an act they have a right not to do.
(1A) The senior police officer may give directions imposing on the persons organising or taking part in the assembly—
   (a) in the case of an assembly in England and Wales, such conditions as appear to the officer necessary to prevent the disorder, damage, disruption, impact or intimidation mentioned in subsection (1);
   (b) in the case of an assembly in Scotland, such conditions as to the place at which the assembly may be (or continue to be) held, its maximum duration, or the maximum number of persons who may constitute it, as appear to the officer necessary to prevent the disorder, damage, disruption or intimidation mentioned in subsection (1)(a) or (b).
(2) In this section 'the senior police officer' means—
   (a) in relation to an assembly being held, the most senior in rank of the police officers present at the scene, and
   (b) in relation to an assembly intended to be held, the chief officer of police.
(3) A direction given by a chief officer of police by virtue of subsection (2)(b) shall be given in writing.

KEYNOTE

In *DPP* v *Eastburn* [2023] EWHC 1063 (Admin), it was held that an offence under this section is an example of an offence-creating statute where the ingredients of the offence in themselves ensure the compatibility of a conviction with a person's rights under Articles 10 and 11 of the European Convention on Human Rights.

Sections 14(2A) to 14(2E) replicate those subsections contained in s. 12 above concerning prolonged disruption of access to any essential goods or any essential service and other considerations. In *Jones* v *The*

Commissioner of Police for the Metropolis [2019] EWHC 2026 (QB), it was held that separate gatherings of Extinction Rebellion protesters, separated both in time and by many miles, even if coordinated under the umbrella of one body, was not a public assembly under the meaning of s. 14(1).

Where a chief officer gives a direction he/she must identify what limb of s. 14(1) was being relied upon and in sufficient detail to enable demonstrators to understand why the decision was made and for a court to understand if a decision was reasonable or not (*R (On the Application of Brehony)* v *Chief Constable of Greater Manchester Police* [2005] EWHC 640 (Admin)).

A direction under this section was lawful where a senior police officer imposed a condition that a Climate Camp protest against the G20 Summit in London must stop. The demonstration had lasted the best part of 12 hours—quite long enough for the protestors to take advantage of their human rights under Article 10 (Freedom of Expression) and Article 11 (Freedom of Assembly and Association)—and those wishing to remain were intent on continuing to block the highway, the main thoroughfare into and out of the City. There was no justification to prolong the demonstration and its continuation would cause serious disturbances and disruption to traffic and pedestrians wishing to use the highway. The police had a duty to clear the highway that could not be done without removing the protestors by force if necessary (*R (On the Application of Moos)* v *Commissioner of Police of the Metropolis* [2011] EWHC 957 (Admin)).

In *R* v *Lucas* (2014) 17 April, unreported, an assembly was already taking place and the notice under s. 14 was signed by a chief officer who was not present at the scene. It was held that the notice was invalid as the police officer giving it was not the authorised officer as required by s. 2(a).

The necessity for imposing a condition must genuinely appear to the relevant senior police officer and must be proportional to the circumstances in which the public assembly is being held (*James* v *DPP* [2015] EWHC 3296 (Admin)).

The offences committed by organisers, participants and persons who incite another to commit an offence in relation to public assemblies are identical to those for public processions (**see para. 3.8.4.2**).

The distinction between this section and s. 12 concerns the conditions that may be imposed under each section. In *DPP* v *Jones* [2002] EWHC 110 (Admin), demonstrators against the Huntingdon Life Sciences Centre were prosecuted for failing to comply with a condition set out in a police notice issued under s. 14. It was held that some of the conditions imposed were more properly concerned with a public procession and therefore were beyond the police powers under s. 14. The offending parts of the police notice were 'severed' leaving the enforceable parts intact. However it may be safer for the police to issue two separate notices, in appropriate circumstances, one relating to the conditions to be observed by participants in the 'procession' element of an operation and the other imposing conditions on the 'assembly' element.

The reference in subs. (2)(a) to a police officer includes a constable of the British Transport Police Force and a member of the Ministry of Defence Police (subs. (2ZA)). The reference in subs. (2)(b) to a chief officer of police includes the chief constable of the British Transport Police Force and the chief constable of the Ministry of Defence Police (subs. (2ZB)).

3.8.4.5 Imposing Conditions on One-person Protests

The Public Order Act 1986, s. 14ZA states:

(1) Subsection (2) applies if the senior police officer, having regard to the time or place at which and the circumstances in which any one-person protest in England and Wales is being carried on or is intended to be carried on, reasonably believes—
  (a) that the noise generated by the person carrying on the protest may result in serious disruption to the activities of an organisation which are carried on in the vicinity of the protest, or
  (b) that—
    (i) the noise generated by the person carrying on the protest may have a relevant impact on persons in the vicinity of the protest, and
    (ii) that impact may be significant.

(2) The senior police officer may give directions imposing on the person organising or carrying on the protest such conditions as appear to the officer necessary to prevent such disruption or impact.

(3) Where the one-person protest is moving, or is intended to move, from place to place—
   (a) the senior police officer must also have regard under subsection (1) to its route or proposed route, and
   (b) the conditions which may be imposed under subsection (2) include conditions as to the route of the protest or prohibiting the person carrying on the protest from entering any public place specified in the direction while the person is carrying it on.

(4) In this section 'one-person protest' means a protest which, at any one time, is carried on by one person in a public place.

KEYNOTE

The 'senior police officer' means, in relation to a one-person protest being held or to a one-person protest intended to be held in a case where a person is in a place with a view to carrying on such a protest, the most senior in rank of the police officers present at the scene, or in any other the chief officer of police (s. 14ZA(5)).

For the purposes of subs. (1)(a), the cases in which the noise generated by a person taking part in a one-person protest may result in serious disruption to the activities of an organisation which are carried on in the vicinity of the protest include, in particular, where it may result in persons connected with the organisation not being reasonably able, for a prolonged period of time, to carry on in that vicinity the activities or any one of them (s. 14ZA(6)).

In relation to subs. (1)(b)(i), the noise generated by a person carrying on a one-person protest may have a relevant impact on persons in the vicinity of the protest if: (a) it may result in the intimidation or harassment of persons of reasonable firmness with the characteristics of persons likely to be in the vicinity, or (b) it may cause such persons to suffer alarm or distress (s. 14ZA(7)).

Subsection (8) provides that in considering for the purposes of subs. (1)(b)(ii) whether the noise generated by a person carrying on a one-person protest may have a significant impact on persons in the vicinity of the protest, the senior police officer must have regard to (a) the likely number of persons of the kind mentioned in para. (a) of subs. (7) who may experience an impact of the kind mentioned in para. (a) or (b) of that sub-section; (b) the likely duration of that impact on such persons, and (c) the likely intensity of that impact on such persons.

A person is guilty of a summary offence and is liable to a fine if he/she organises or carries on a one-person protest, fails to comply with a condition imposed under this section, and at the time fails to comply with a condition that they ought to know has been imposed (s. 14ZA(10) and (13)). It is a defence for a person charged with an offence under subs. 10 to prove that the failure arose from circumstances beyond the person's control. A person who incites another to commit an offence under this subsection commits a summary offence and is liable to a term of imprisonment for 51 weeks and/or a fine (s. 47ZA(12) and (14)).

3.8.4.6 Prohibiting Trespassory Assemblies

The provisions of s. 14 (**see para. 3.8.4.4**) apply to public assemblies. However, occasions have arisen where the assembly has been *trespassory*, that is, on land which is either private or where there is only a limited right of public access and the permission of the relevant landowner has not been granted. In such instances, s. 14A of the Public Order Act 1986 provides the police with certain powers.

The Public Order Act 1986, s. 14A states:

(1) If at any time the chief officer of police reasonably believes that an assembly is intended to be held in any district at a place on land to which the public has no right of access or only a limited right of access and that the assembly—
   (a) is likely to be held without the permission of the occupier of the land or to conduct itself in such a way as to exceed the limits of any permission of his or the limits of the public's right of access, and
   (b) may result—
      (i) in serious disruption to the life of the community, or

(ii) where the land, or a building or monument on it, is of historical, architectural, archaeological or scientific importance, in significant damage to the land, building or monument,

he may apply to the council of the district for an order prohibiting for a specified period the holding of all trespassory assemblies in the district or a part of it, as specified.

KEYNOTE

An 'assembly' for the purpose of this section means 20 or more people, 'land' means land in the open air, and 'public' includes a section of the public (s. 14A(9)).

A classic example of a trespassory assembly might be found at sites such as Stonehenge.

An order prohibiting the holding of trespassory assemblies operates to prohibit any assembly which: (a) is held on land to which the public has no right of access or only a limited right of access, and (b) takes place in the prohibited circumstances, that is to say, without the permission of the occupier of the land or so as to exceed the limits of any of his/her permission or the limits of the public's right of access (subs. (5)).

On receiving an application from a chief officer, the council may make an order either in the terms of the application, or with modifications, either of which must be approved by the Secretary of State (s. 14A(2)(a)), and the order must be in writing or reduced to writing as soon as practicable after being made (s. 14A(8)).

An order must not last for more than four days, nor must it apply to an area beyond a radius of five miles from a specified centre (s. 14A(6)).

A person who organises an assembly the holding of which he/she knows is prohibited by an order under s. 14A is guilty of a summary offence and is liable to a term of three months' imprisonment and/or a fine (s. 14B(1) and (5)). A person who takes part in an assembly which he/she knows is prohibited by an order under s. 14A is guilty of a summary offence and is liable to a fine (s. 14B(2) and (6)), and a person who incites another to commit an offence under s. 14B(2) is guilty of a summary offence and is liable to a term of three months' imprisonment and/or a fine (s. 14B(3) and (7)).

Even where an order has been made, there will be a need to show that the assembly was obstructive of the highway or at least that it exceeded the public's general right of access (*DPP* v *Jones* [1999] 2 AC 240).

3.8.4.7 Stopping Persons from Proceeding to Trespassory Assemblies

The Public Order Act 1986, s. 14C states:

(1) If a constable in uniform reasonably believes that a person is on his way to an assembly within the area to which an order under section 14A applies which the constable reasonably believes is likely to be an assembly which is prohibited by that order, he may, subject to subsection (2) below—
   (a) stop that person, and
   (b) direct him not to proceed in the direction of the assembly.

(2) The power conferred by subsection (1) may only be exercised within the area to which the order applies.

(3) A person who fails to comply with a direction under subsection (1) which he knows has been given to him is guilty of an offence.

KEYNOTE

A person guilty of an offence under subs. (3) is liable on summary conviction to a fine (subs. (5)).

This power allows officers to stop people, though not, it would seem, vehicles (in which case the general power under s. 163 of the Road Traffic Act 1988 must be used).

3.8.5 Locking On

OFFENCE: **Locking On—*Public Order Act 2023, s. 1***

- Triable summarily • Six months' imprisonment and/or a fine

The Public Order Act 2023, s. 1 states:

(1) A person commits an offence if—
   (a) they—
      (i) attach themselves to another person, to an object or to land,
      (ii) attach a person to another person, to an object or to land, or
      (iii) attach an object to another object or to land,
   (b) that act causes, or is capable of causing, serious disruption to—
      (i) two or more individuals, or
      (ii) an organisation, in a place other than in a dwelling, and
   (c) they intend that act to have a consequence mentioned in paragraph (b) or are reckless as to whether it will have such a consequence.

(2) It is a defence for a person charged with an offence under subsection (1) to prove that they had a reasonable excuse for the act mentioned in paragraph (a) of that subsection.

KEYNOTE

In this section, 'dwelling' means (a) a building or structure which is used as a dwelling, or (b) a part of a building or structure, if the part is used as a dwelling, and includes any yard, garden, grounds, garage or outhouse belonging to and used with a dwelling (s. 1(5)).

The Public Order Act 2023 amended s. 1 of the Police and Criminal Evidence Act 1984 allowing a constable to stop and search a person or vehicle if he/she has reasonable grounds for suspecting that he/she will find an article made, or adapted or intended, for use in the course of or in connection with the 'protest' offences, including locking on, causing serious disruption by tunnelling, causing serious disruption by tunnelling by being present in a tunnel, obstruction etc., of major transport works and interference with use or operation of key national infrastructure. In addition, the 2023 Act provides powers to stop and search without suspicion where a senior police officer may give an authorisation that allows a constable to stop and search a person or vehicle for an object made, adapted or intended for use in the course of or in connection with a specified protest-related offence (**see chapter 3.2**).

3.8.5.1 Meaning of Serious Disruption

The Public Order Act 2023, s. 34 states:

(1) For the purposes of this Act, the cases in which individuals or an organisation may suffer serious disruption include, in particular, where the individuals or the organisation—
   (a) carrying out—
      (i) their day-to-day activities (including in particular the making of a journey),
      (ii) construction or maintenance works, or
      (iii) activities related to such works,
   (b) are prevented from making or receiving, or suffer a delay that is more than minor to the making or receiving of, a delivery of a time-sensitive product, or
   (c) are prevented from accessing, or suffer a disruption that is more than minor to the accessing of, any essential goods or any essential service.

KEYNOTE

A 'time-sensitive product' means a product whose value or use to its consumers may be significantly reduced by a delay in the supply of the product to them. A reference to accessing essential goods or essential services includes a reference to accessing the supply of money, food, water, energy or fuel, or a system of communication, a place of worship, a transport facility, an educational institution or a service relating to health (s. 34(2)).

3.8.5.2 Being Equipped for Locking On

OFFENCE: **Being Equipped for Locking On—*Public Order Act 2023, s. 2***
- Triable summarily • Fine

The Public Order Act 2023, s. 2 states:

(1) A person commits an offence if they have an object with them in a place other than a dwelling with the intention that it may be used in the course of or in connection with the commission by any person of an offence under section 1(1) (offence of locking on).
(2) ...
(3) In this section 'dwelling' has the same meaning as in section 1.

3.8.6 Causing Serious Disruption by Tunnelling

OFFENCE: **Causing Serious Disruption by Tunnelling—*Public Order Act 2023, s. 3***
- Triable either way • Three years' imprisonment and/or a fine on indictment
- 12 months' imprisonment and/or a fine summarily

The Public Order Act 2023, s. 3 states:

(1) A person commits an offence if—
 (a) they create, or participate in the creation of, a tunnel,
 (b) the creation or existence of the tunnel causes, or is capable of causing, serious disruption to—
  (i) two or more individuals, or
  (ii) an organisation,
 in a place other than a dwelling, and
 (c) they intend the creation or existence of the tunnel to have a consequence mentioned in paragraph (b) or are reckless as to whether its creation or existence will have such a consequence.
(2) It is a defence for a person charged with an offence under subsection (1) to prove that they had a reasonable excuse for creating, or participating in the creation of, the tunnel.

KEYNOTE

In relation to the defence contained in subs. (2), a person is to be treated as having a reasonable excuse if the creation of the tunnel was authorised by a person with an interest in land which entitled them to authorise its creation (subs. (3)).

Subsection (5) provides that for the purposes of this section:

(a) 'tunnel' means an excavation that extends beneath land, whether or not—
 (i) it is big enough to permit the entry or passage of an individual, or
 (ii) it leads to a particular destination;
(b) an excavation which is created with the intention that it will become or connect with a tunnel is to be treated as a tunnel, whether or not—
 (i) any tunnel with which it is intended to connect has already been created, or
 (ii) it is big enough to permit the entry or passage of an individual.

References to the creation of an excavation include: (a) the extension or enlargement of an excavation, and (b) the alteration of a natural or artificial underground feature (subs. (6)).

This section does not apply in relation to a tunnel if or to the extent that it is in or under a dwelling (subs. (7)), and 'dwelling' has the same meaning as in the offence of locking on (subs. (8)).

3.8.6.1 Causing Serious Disruption by Being Present in a Tunnel

OFFENCE: **Causing Serious Disruption by Being Present in a Tunnel—*Public Order Act 2023, s. 4***

- Triable either way • Three years' imprisonment and/or a fine on indictment
- 12 months' imprisonment and/or a fine summarily

The Public Order Act 2023, s. 4 states:

(1) A person commits an offence if—
(a) they are present in a relevant tunnel having entered it after the coming into force of this section,
(b) their presence in the tunnel causes, or is capable of causing, serious disruption to—
(i) two or more individuals, or
(ii) an organisation,
in a place other than a dwelling, and
(c) they intend their presence in the tunnel to have a consequence mentioned in paragraph (b) or are reckless as to whether their presence there will have such a consequence.

KEYNOTE

The defence of reasonable excuse replicates that provided for the offence under s. 3, as do the meanings of 'tunnel' and 'dwelling'.

'Relevant tunnel' means a tunnel that was created for the purposes of, or in connection with, a protest and it does not matter whether an offence has been committed under s. 3 in relation to the creation of the tunnel (subs. (6)).

In this section, the creation of an excavation includes: (a) the extension or enlargement of an excavation, and (b) the alteration of a natural or artificial underground feature (subs. (7)).

3.8.6.2 Being Equipped for Tunnelling

OFFENCE: **Being Equipped for Tunnelling—*Public Order Act 2023, s. 5***

- Triable summarily • Six months' imprisonment and/or a fine

The Public Order Act 2023, s. 5 states:

(1) A person commits an offence if they have an object with them in a place other than a dwelling with the intention that it may be used in the course of or in connection with the commission by any person of an offence under section 3(1) or 4(1) (offences relating to tunnelling).
(2) ...
(3) ...
(4) In this section 'dwelling' has the same meaning as in section 1 (offence of locking on).

3.8.7 Obstruction of Major Transport Works

OFFENCE: **Obstruction of Major Transport Works—*Public Order Act 2023, s. 6***

- Triable summarily • Six months' imprisonment and/or a fine

The Public Order Act 2023, s. 6 states:

(1) A person commits an offence if the person—
(a) obstructs the undertaker or a person acting under the authority of the undertaker—
(i) in setting out the lines of any major transport works,
(ii) in constructing or maintaining any major transport works, or
(iii) in taking any steps that are reasonably necessary for the purposes of facilitating, or in connection with, the construction or maintenance of any major transport works, or

(b) interferes with, moves or removes any apparatus which—
(i) relates to the construction or maintenance of any major transport works, and
(ii) belongs to a person within subsection (5).
(2) It is a defence for a person charged with an offence under subsection (1) to prove that—
(a) they had a reasonable excuse for the act mentioned in paragraph (a) or (b) of that subsection, or
(b) the act mentioned in paragraph (a) or (b) of that subsection was done wholly or mainly in contemplation or furtherance of a trade dispute.

KEYNOTE

In relation to subs. (1)(b)(ii), subs. (5) provides that the person includes:

- the undertaker;
- a person acting under the authority of the undertaker;
- a statutory undertaker;
- a person acting under the authority of a statutory undertaker.

'Major transport works' covers transport infrastructure authorised by an Act of Parliament, for example the High Speed Rail (London–West Midlands) Act 2017, and transport works granted development consent by an order made under s. 114 of the Planning Act 2008 that cover nationally significant infrastructure projects, including new airports, airport extensions and major road projects (subs. (6)).

'Undertaker' essentially mean a person who is authorised to construct or maintain any of the works (subs. (8)).

3.8.8 Interference With Use or Operation of Key National Infrastructure

OFFENCE: **Interference With Use or Operation of Key National Infrastructure—*Public Order Act 2023, s. 7***
- Triable either way • 12 months' imprisonment and/or a fine on indictment
- Imprisonment to a term not exceeding the general limit in a magistrates' court and/or a fine summarily

The Public Order Act 2023, s. 7 states:

(1) A person commits an offence if—
(a) they do an act which interferes with the use or operation of any key national infrastructure in England and Wales, and
(b) they intend that act to interfere with the use or operation of such infrastructure or are reckless as to whether it will do so.
(2) It is a defence for a person charged with an offence under subsection (1) to prove that—
(a) they had a reasonable excuse for the act mentioned in paragraph (a) of that subsection, or
(b) the act mentioned in paragraph (a) of that subsection was done wholly or mainly in contemplation or furtherance of a trade dispute.

KEYNOTE

A person's act interferes with the use or operation of key national infrastructure if it prevents the infrastructure from being used or operated to any extent for any of its intended purposes (s. 7(4)) and cases in which infrastructure is prevented from being used or operated for any of its intended purposes include where its use or operation for any of those purposes is significantly delayed (s. 7(5)).

'Key national infrastructure' means:

(a) road transport infrastructure,
(b) rail infrastructure,
(c) air transport infrastructure,

(d) harbour infrastructure,
(e) downstream oil infrastructure,
(f) downstream gas infrastructure,
(g) onshore oil and gas exploration and production infrastructure,
(h) onshore electricity generation infrastructure,
(i) newspaper printing infrastructure, or
(j) life sciences infrastructure.

(s. 7(6))

Section 8 makes further provision about these kinds of infrastructure.

In *Sarti* v *R* [2025] EWCA Crim 61, offences under this section arose in the context of a protest organised to campaign against the use of fossil fuels. The appellants and 61 others had gathered outside Earl's Court Underground station and proceeded to walk down roads designated as A roads. The definition of 'road transport infrastructure' in s. 8(2) has the aim of identifying the roads where obstruction or delay is likely to have the greatest impact on the rights of the travelling public. The definition includes 'special roads' (principally motorways) and A and B roads. The protesters were walking very slowly in a procession large enough to block the entire carriageway. Police officers observed significant disruption and frustration amongst motorists. Warnings given to the protesters went unheeded even when told that they were committing offences under section 7 and that if they did not leave the road, they could be arrested. The court held that once the ingredients of the s. 7 offence are made out, s. 7(2)(a) does not require a court to consider whether a conviction would be a proportionate interference with the defendant's Article 10 or 11 rights.

3.8.9 Serious Disruption Prevention Order

A court may make a serious disruption prevention order (SDPO) upon conviction where a person is aged 18 or over, the current offence is a protest-related offence and the person has been convicted of a protest-related offence (or committed a protest-related breach of an injunction), when they were aged 16 or over, in the previous five years (s. 20 of the Public Order Act 2023).

The court must consider it necessary to make the order for a purpose specified in subs. (5). Those purposes are to:

- prevent the person from committing a protest-related offence or a protest-related breach of an injunction;
- prevent the person from carrying out activities related to protests that result, or are likely to result, in serious disruption to two or more individuals or an organisation;
- prevent the person from causing or contributing to the commission by another person of the acts set out at (a) or (b) above (e.g. where the person was responsible for organising protests);
- protect two or more individuals or an organisation from the risk of serious disruption caused by a protest-related offence, a protest-related breach of an injunction or activities related to a protest.

The SDPO under this section is an order which imposes any requirement or prohibition necessary to achieve one of the purposes specified in subs. (5).

The requirements placed on a person might include that they present themselves to a particular person at a particular place at, or between, particular times on particular days or to remain at a particular place for particular periods.

The prohibitions imposed might include being in or entering a particular place or area; being in or entering a particular place or area between particular times on any day; and using the internet to facilitate or encourage persons to commit a protest-related offence or a protest-related breach of an injunction. Further examples of possible requirements or prohibitions that may be imposed are contained in s. 22 of the 2023 Act.

An SDPO can also be made by a magistrates' court on application by a chief officer of the police where the prospective subject of the order lives or is intending to come to reside (s. 21). The conditions that must be met are identical to those contained is s. 20 above as are the purposes for making such an order.

The maximum duration of an SDPO must be for a fixed period of not less than one week and not more than two years (s. 25). Breach of such an order is a summary offence punishable by 51 weeks' imprisonment and/or a fine (s. 27).

3.8.10 Offence of Interference with Access to or Provision of Abortion Services

OFFENCE: **Offence of Interference with Access to or Provision of Abortion Services—*Public Order Act 2023, s. 9***

- Triable summarily • Fine

The Public Order Act 2023, s. 9 states:

(1) It is an offence for a person who is within a safe access zone to do an act with the intent of, or reckless as to whether it has the effect of—
  (a) influencing any person's decision to access, provide or facilitate the provision of abortion services at an abortion clinic,
  (b) obstructing or impeding any person accessing, providing, or facilitating the provision of abortion services at an abortion clinic, or
  (c) causing harassment, alarm or distress to any person in connection with a decision to access, provide, or facilitate the provision of abortion services at an abortion clinic,

  where the person mentioned in paragraph (a), (b) or (c) is within the safe access zone for the abortion clinic.

(2) A 'safe access zone' means an area which is within a boundary which is 150 metres from any part of an abortion clinic or any access point to any building or site that contains an abortion clinic and is—
  (a) on or adjacent to a public highway or public right of way,
  (b) in an open space to which the public has access,
  (c) within the curtilage of an abortion clinic, or building or site which contains an abortion clinic, or
  (d) in any location that is visible from a public highway, public right of way, open space to which the public have access, or the curtilage of an abortion clinic.

KEYNOTE

No offence is committed under subs. (1) by a person inside a dwelling where the person affected is also in that or another dwelling or a person inside a building or site used as a place of worship where the person affected is also in that building or site (subs. (3)).

This section does not apply to anything done while providing or facilitating abortion services in an abortion clinic, anything done while providing medical care in a health care facility, any action by a person accompanying with consent, persons accessing, providing or facilitating abortion services or the operation of a camera if its coverage of persons accessing a clinic is incidental (subs. (5)).

An 'abortion clinic' means a place approved for the purposes of s. 1 of the Abortion Act 1967 or a hospital identified in a notification to the Chief Medical Officer under s. 2(1) of the Abortion Act 1967. 'Abortion services' means any treatment for the termination of pregnancy and 'dwelling' has the same meaning as in the offence of locking on (**see para. 3.8.5**) (subs. (6)).

3.8.11 Public Meetings

It is an offence to attempt to break up a public meeting.

OFFENCE: **Trying to Break up a Public Meeting—*Public Meeting Act 1908, s. 1***

• Triable summarily • Six months' imprisonment and/or a fine *(No specific power of arrest)*

The Public Meeting Act 1908, s. 1 states:

(1) Any person who at a lawful public meeting acts in a disorderly manner for the purpose of preventing the transaction of the business for which the meeting was called together shall be guilty of an offence ...

(2) Any person who incites others to commit an offence under this section shall be guilty of a like offence.

KEYNOTE

'Public meeting' is not defined in the 1908 Act. There appears to be no requirement for the meeting to be lawfully assembled.

In relation to s. 1(2), the offence is a summary offence punishable by a fine.

This offence does not apply to meetings held in relation to s. 97 of the Representation of the People Act 1983 (meetings concerned with public national and local elections). Under this section, a person who, at a lawful public meeting, acts, or incites others to act, in a disorderly manner for the purpose of preventing the transaction of the business for which the meeting was called together shall be guilty of an illegal practice (s. 97(1)). If a constable reasonably suspects any person of committing an offence under subs. (1) above, he/she may, if requested so to do by the chairman of the meeting, require that person to declare immediately their name and address and, if that person refuses or fails to do so or gives a false name and address, the person shall be liable on summary conviction to a fine. Where a person refuses or fails to give their name and address or if the constable reasonably suspects them of giving a false name and address, the constable may without warrant arrest the person (s. 97(3)).

3.9 Public Order Offences

3.9.1 Introduction

The principal piece of legislation dealing with public order is the Public Order Act 1986. While this chapter examines some of the more well-known elements of this legislation, it also looks at the common law offence of breach of the peace and the statutory offence of intentionally or recklessly causing a public nuisance.

3.9.2 Breach of the Peace

A breach of the peace is defined specifically in *R* v *Howell* [1982] QB 416. A breach of the peace generally occurs when an act is done, or threatened to be done:

- which harms a person or, in his/her presence, his/her property; or
- which is likely to cause such harm; or
- which puts someone in fear of such harm.

The common law provides a power of arrest and also the power to intervene and/or detain by force, in order to prevent any action likely to result in a breach of the peace in either public or private places.

Breach of the peace is dealt with by way of complaint and is not a criminal offence (*R* v *County of London Quarter Sessions Appeals Committee, ex parte Metropolitan Police Commissioner* [1948] 1 KB 670). Although not a criminal offence in domestic law, it may be treated as such for the purposes of the European Convention on Human Rights (ECHR) (*Steel* v *UK* (1999) 28 EHRR 603). In *Williamson* v *Chief Constable of West Midlands Police* [2003] EWCA Civ 337, the Court of Appeal held that a person arrested for a breach of the peace is not, strictly speaking, in police detention for the purposes of s. 118 of the Police and Criminal Evidence Act 1984 and the provisions in relation to bail do not apply. A person may be detained and placed before the next available court, or detained until there is no further likelihood of a reoccurrence of the breach of the peace. In *Williamson*, it was considered good practice for people arrested and detained for breach of the peace to be treated in accordance with the provisions of PACE, and that they should also be cautioned.

It is an offence at common law for a person to refuse to assist a constable who calls for assistance in dealing with a breach of the peace (*R* v *Brown* (1841) Car & M 314; *Waugh* (1976), *The Times*, 1 October).

3.9.2.1 Breach of the Peace on Private Premises

A breach of the peace may take place on private premises as well as in public places (*R* v *Chief Constable of Devon and Cornwall, ex parte Central Electricity Generating Board* [1982] QB 458). The police are entitled to enter premises to prevent a breach of the peace and to remain there in order to do so (*Thomas* v *Sawkins* [1935] 2 KB 249). This power has not been affected by the general powers of entry provided by the Police and Criminal Evidence Act 1984 (**see chapter 3.2** and s. 17(6) of the 1984 Act).

Where a breach of the peace takes place on private property, there is no requirement to show that the resulting disturbance affected members of the public outside that property—*McQuade* v *Chief Constable of Humberside Police* [2001] EWCA Civ 1330. The presence of a member (or members) of the public is, however, a highly relevant factor when dealing with a breach of the peace (*McConnell* v *Chief Constable of Greater Manchester Police* [1990] 1 WLR 364).

3.9.2.2 Police Powers are Discretionary

Although the police have a general duty to preserve the King's peace, and enjoy common law powers to carry out that duty, they also have a wide discretion as to how they go about that function. The common law powers of the police allow them, where appropriate, to prevent people from travelling to certain locations (e.g. striking miners heading for a working coalfield where their presence would give reasonable grounds to apprehend a breach of the peace (*Moss* v *McLachlan* [1985] IRLR 76)). Such an 'anticipatory' power is, however, exceptional (*Foulkes* v *Chief Constable of Merseyside Police* [1998] 3 All ER 705) and requires a balancing of the individual rights of the people involved against the wider interests of public safety, the maintenance of public order and the prevention of crime. Such exceptional powers to impose anticipatory restrictions on the movement of individuals, falling short of arrest, only arise if there is an imminent threat to public order.

The practicalities involved in this balancing exercise were considered in *R (On the Application of Laporte)* v *Chief Constable of Gloucestershire* [2006] UKHL 55. In *Laporte*, a lawful assembly had been arranged under the provisions of ss. 12 and 14 of the Public Order Act 1986 in connection with protests against the war in Iraq. As the result of a stop and search order made under s. 60 of the Criminal Justice and Public Order Act 1994 (**see para. 3.1.4**) the police stopped a number of coaches en route to the lawful assembly at Fairford US Air Force base, and then escorted them back to London. Intelligence had been received that the passengers would cause disorder at the base. The House of Lords ruled that the police had acted unlawfully because a breach of the peace was not imminent when the coaches were stopped. This action interfered with the passengers' rights under Articles 10 (freedom of expression) and 11 (freedom of assembly and association) of the ECHR and was disproportionate.

3.9.2.3 Which Parties are Likely to Present Actual Threat?

When exercising discretionary powers to prevent disorder, police officers will be expected to focus their attention on those who are likely to present the actual threat of violence or disorder. In *Redmond-Bate* v *DPP* [1999] Crim LR 998, people preaching on the steps of a church were warned by police that they were antagonising passers-by. Despite the warning, the preachers continued and, as there was an imminent likelihood of a recently gathered crowd attacking them, the preachers were arrested. The Divisional Court felt that the approach taken by the police was incompatible with Article 10 of the ECHR and that the officers' attention should have been directed at the crowd from whom the threat to the 'peace' was emanating. The individuals preaching were simply exercising their right to freedom of expression. It was the crowd who, in the court's view, ought to have received the warning and who should have been arrested in the event of their continuing to represent a threat to public order.

However, it will not always be practicable to separate those who are directly and individually presenting a threat to the peace and those who are part of a larger crowd. In *Austin* v *Commissioner of Police of the Metropolis* [2009] UKHL 5, it was held that in extreme and exceptional circumstances it would be lawful for the police to contain demonstrators and members of the public caught up in that demonstration, even though they themselves did not appear to be about to commit a breach of the peace. This would be the case where it was necessary to prevent an imminent breach of the peace by others, and no other means would achieve that. In *Austin* v *United Kingdom* (2012) 55 EHRR 14, the European Court of Human Rights decided, by a majority, that there had been no violation of Article 5 (right to liberty and security) of the ECHR. *Austin* [2009] was followed in *R (On the Application of Moos)* v *Commissioner of Police of the Metropolis* [2011] EWHC 957 (Admin) which related to a Climate Camp protest against the G20 Summit in London. It is only when the police reasonably believe that there is no other means whatsoever to prevent an imminent breach of the peace that they can as a matter of necessity curtail the lawful exercise of their rights of freedom of expression by third parties. The test of necessity is met only in truly extreme and exceptional circumstances. The action taken has to be both reasonably necessary and proportionate and taken in good faith. In *R (On the Application of McClure)* v *Commissioner of Police of the Metropolis* [2012] EWCA Civ 12, the Court of Appeal concluded that a decision to contain a substantial crowd of demonstrators whose behaviour, though at times unruly and somewhat violent, did not of itself justify containment was, however, justifiable on the ground that containment was the least drastic way of preventing what the police officer responsible for the decision reasonably apprehended would be imminent and serious breaches of the peace.

Where demonstrators were contained in a police pen, in a demonstration against Israel and its Head of State, it was held that the police may deploy reasonable force to prevent a breach of the peace that they reasonably apprehend as imminent (*Wright* v *Commissioner of Police for the Metropolis* [2013] EWHC 2739 (QB)).

Where officers were directed by senior officers to arrest persons for breach of the peace, it was held to be lawful where those senior officers had good reason to believe that had those persons been allowed to proceed to a nearby demonstration point there would have been a strong likelihood of a breach of the peace occurring (*R (On the Application of Hicks)* v *Commissioner of Police of the Metropolis* [2014] EWCA Civ 3; see also *Eiseman-Renyard* v *United Kingdom* (Application no. 57884/17, ECtHR, 5 March 2019)).

Guidance on 'immediacy' in relation to conduct in a domestic setting is contained in *Wragg* v *DPP* [2005] EWHC 1389 (Admin). Police officers attending a domestic dispute found one of the parties, who had been in a heated argument with a relative also living in the house, to have consumed a large amount of alcohol. In relation to the immediacy or imminence test, the police officers believed that a breach of the peace could take place in the house after they departed that night in so far as the other household member was at risk of immediate assault while the accused was still in drink. The arrest of the accused was held to be lawful. In *Demetriou* v *DPP* [2012] EWHC 2443 (Admin), it was also held that an arrest was lawful if a person willing to leave premises but who an officer believed would return to cause violence gave rise to a reasonable basis for fearing imminent violence.

3.9.2.4 Power of Arrest

Any person, whether constable or civilian, has a common law power of arrest where:

(a) a breach of the peace is committed in his/her presence,
(b) the person effecting the arrest reasonably believes that such a breach will be committed in the immediate future by the person arrested, or
(c) a breach of the peace has been committed or the person effecting the arrest reasonably believes that a breach of the peace has occurred and that a further breach is threatened.

KEYNOTE

In order to comply with Article 5(1)(c) of the ECHR (right to liberty), an arrest must be for the purpose of bringing the person before a competent legal authority. However, in *R (On the Application of Hicks)* v *Metropolitan Police Commissioner* [2017] UKSC 9 it was held that an arrest is lawful notwithstanding that the person is released before he/she could practically be brought before a court.

There is an element of pre-emptive risk assessment involved in application of the test as to whether or not a breach of the peace is actually occurring even before moving on to consider whether such a breach, if not occurring, is imminent (*Laporte* v *Commissioner of Police of the Metropolis* [2014] EWHC 3574 (QB)).

This power of arrest may be exercised on private premises, even where there is no other member of the public present (*R* v *Howell* [1982] QB 416).

In *Bibby* v *Chief Constable of Essex Police* (2000) 164 JP 297, the Court of Appeal held that the power of arrest for breach of the peace was wholly exceptional and set out the conditions that must be met before this power should be used. These conditions are:

- there must be the clearest of circumstances and a real and present threat to the peace to justify the arrest;
- the threat must be coming from the person who is ultimately arrested;
- his/her conduct must be clearly interfering with the rights of another;
- that conduct must be unreasonable.

In *Howell*, it was held that where a breach of the peace has not yet occurred it is sufficient that a constable uses the wording and sets out the conditions that must be met before this power should be used.

3.9.3 Riot

OFFENCE: **Riot—*Public Order Act 1986, s. 1***

- Triable on indictment • 10 years' imprisonment and/or a fine

The Public Order Act 1986, s. 1 states:

(1) Where 12 or more persons who are present together use or threaten unlawful violence for a common purpose and the conduct of them (taken together) is such as would cause a person of reasonable firmness present at the scene to fear for his personal safety, each of the persons using unlawful violence for the common purpose is guilty of riot.
(2) It is immaterial whether or not the 12 or more use or threaten unlawful violence simultaneously.
(3) The common purpose may be inferred from conduct.
(4) No person of reasonable firmness need actually be, or be likely to be, present at the scene.
(5) Riot may be committed in private as well as in public places.

KEYNOTE

This offence requires the consent of the DPP before a prosecution can be brought.

It is not necessary that all 12 people concerned use or threaten unlawful violence at the same time. However, the courts have held that each defendant must be shown to have used unlawful violence and not merely threatened to do so (*R* v *Jefferson* [1994] 1 All ER 270). A defendant must be shown to have *intended* to use/threaten violence or to have been aware that his/her conduct may have been violent (s. 6(1)).

Although there must be a common purpose, this need not be part of a pre-determined plan, nor be unlawful in itself. A common purpose to get into a rock concert or even the January sales at a high street store could therefore be enough, provided all other elements are present.

3.9.3.1 Unlawful Violence

The Public Order Act 1986, s. 8 states:

'violence' means any violent conduct, so that—
(a) except in the context of affray, it includes violent conduct towards property as well as violent conduct towards persons, and
(b) it is not restricted to conduct causing or intended to cause injury or damage but includes any other violent conduct (for example, throwing at or towards a person a missile of a kind capable of causing injury which does not hit or falls short).

KEYNOTE

The term 'unlawful' was included in the Act to allow for the general defences such as self-defence to be applicable (*R* v *Rothwell* [1993] Crim LR 626).

3.9.3.2 Intoxication

Parliament has specifically catered for self-induced intoxication, not just for the offence of riot, but in relation to other offences under the 1986 Act, by s. 6 which states:

> (5) For the purposes of this section a person whose awareness is impaired by intoxication shall be taken to be aware of that of which he would be aware if not intoxicated, unless he shows either that his intoxication was not self-induced or that it was caused solely by the taking or administration of a substance in the course of medical treatment.
>
> (6) In subsection (5) 'intoxication' means any intoxication, whether caused by drink, drugs or other means, or by a combination of means.

3.9.4 Violent Disorder

OFFENCE: **Violent Disorder—*Public Order Act 1986, s. 2***

- Triable either way • Five years' imprisonment and/or a fine on indictment
- 12 months' imprisonment and/or a fine summarily

The Public Order Act 1986, s. 2 states:

> (1) Where 3 or more persons who are present together use or threaten unlawful violence and the conduct of them (taken together) is such as would cause a person of reasonable firmness present at the scene to fear for his personal safety, each of the persons using or threatening unlawful violence is guilty of violent disorder.
>
> (2) It is immaterial whether or not the 3 or more use or threaten unlawful violence simultaneously.
>
> (3) No person of reasonable firmness need actually be, or be likely to be, present at the scene.
>
> (4) Violent disorder may be committed in private as well as in public places.

KEYNOTE

In order to convict a defendant of this offence, you must show that there were three or more people using or threatening unlawful violence. However, while three or more persons must have been present and used or threatened unlawful violence, it is not necessary that three or more persons should actually be charged or prosecuted with the offence. Further, where there are three defendants and two are acquitted of the charge, the remaining defendant can still be convicted of violent disorder (*R* v *Mahroof* (1989) 88 Cr App R 317) as long as *it can be proved that there were three or more people using or threatening violence* (perhaps from CCTV evidence of the incident). If it cannot be proved that there were three or more people using or threatening unlawful violence the court should acquit each defendant (*R* v *McGuigan* [1991] Crim LR 719).

In *R* v *NW* [2010] EWCA Crim 404, the circumstances of the case were that a person was violently resisting arrest by a police officer, during which time a crowd gathered and various members of the crowd used or threatened violence. The Court of Appeal held that for the purposes of this section it was not necessary for a person to act deliberately in combination with at least two other people present at the scene, but that it is sufficient that at least three people be present, each separately using or threatening unlawful violence. The court's view was that the phrase, 'where 3 or more persons who are present together use or threaten violence ...' consists of ordinary words which must be given their ordinary meaning.

There is no requirement to prove a common purpose.

Again, a defendant must be shown to have intended to use/threaten violence or to have been aware that his/her conduct may have been violent (s. 6(2)). 'Violence' for these purposes can include violent conduct towards property (s. 8).

3.9.5 Affray

OFFENCE: **Affray—*Public Order Act 1986, s. 3***

- Triable either way • Three years' imprisonment and/or a fine on indictment
- 12 months' imprisonment and/or a fine summarily

The Public Order Act 1986, s. 3 states:

(1) A person is guilty of affray if he uses or threatens unlawful violence towards another and his conduct is such as would cause a person of reasonable firmness present at the scene to fear for his personal safety.
(2) Where 2 or more persons use or threaten the unlawful violence, it is the conduct of them taken together that must be considered for the purposes of subsection (1).
(3) For the purposes of this section a threat cannot be made by the use of words alone.
(4) No person of reasonable firmness need actually be, or be likely to be, present at the scene.
(5) Affray may be committed in private as well as in public places.

KEYNOTE

The House of Lords held that, in order to prove the offence of affray, the threat of unlawful violence has to be towards a person(s) present at the scene (*I* v *DPP* [2001] UKHL 10). Once this element has been proved, it will be necessary to prove the second element, namely, whether the defendant's conduct would have caused a hypothetical person present at the scene to fear for his/her personal safety (*R* v *Sanchez* (1996) 160 JP 321 and *R* v *Carey* [2006] EWCA Crim 17). However, where the likelihood of a hypothetical person of reasonable firmness being present was low this element of the offence was not satisfied. In *R (On the Application of Leeson)* v *DPP* [2010] EWHC 994 (Admin), a woman had issued a drunken threat to kill her long-term partner while holding a knife, in a bathroom, in an otherwise unoccupied house. In these circumstances, the court held that there was no possibility of hypothetical bystanders fearing for their safety.

Where the accused is one of a number of people who use or threaten unlawful violence, in deciding whether the person of reasonable firmness present at the scene would be caused to fear for his personal safety, it is the conduct of the entire group taken as a whole that counts and so there is no need in such a situation for the court to attribute individual roles to the participants (*Dragjoshi* v *Croydon Magistrates' Court* [2017] EWHC 2840 (QB)).

The threat cannot be made by words alone (s. 3(3)), therefore there must be some action by the defendant—even if that 'action' consists of utilising something else such as a dog to threaten the violence (*R* v *Dixon* [1993] Crim LR 579).

The effect of s. 3(4) is that it is not necessary to show that the defendant's behaviour either was or could have been seen by someone at the time.

Although violence is 'not restricted to conduct causing or intended to cause injury or damage but includes any other violent conduct' (s. 8), the expression does not include conduct towards property as it does with the offences under ss. 1 and 2.

Once more, a defendant must be shown to have *intended* to use/threaten violence or to have been aware that his/her conduct may have been violent (s. 6(2)).

3.9.6 Fear or Provocation of Violence

OFFENCE: **Fear or Provocation of Violence—*Public Order Act 1986, s. 4***

- Triable summarily • Six months' imprisonment and/or a fine

OFFENCE: **Racially or Religiously Aggravated—*Crime and Disorder Act 1998, s. 31(1)(a)***

- Triable either way • Two years' imprisonment and/or a fine on indictment
- Six months' imprisonment and/or a fine summarily

The Public Order Act 1986, s. 4 states:

(1) A person is guilty of an offence if he—
  (a) uses towards another person threatening, abusive or insulting words or behaviour, or
  (b) distributes or displays to another person any writing, sign or other visible representation which is threatening, abusive or insulting,

  with intent to cause that person to believe that immediate unlawful violence will be used against him or another by any person, or to provoke the immediate use of unlawful violence by that person or another, or whereby that person is likely to believe that such violence will be used or it is likely that such violence will be provoked.

(2) An offence under this section may be committed in a public or a private place, except that no offence is committed where the words or behaviour are used, or the writing, sign or other visible representation is distributed or displayed, by a person inside a dwelling and the other person is also inside that or another dwelling.

KEYNOTE

The meaning of 'racially or religiously aggravated' in relation to s. 31(1)(a) of the 1998 Act is discussed in *Crime*, chapter 1.9.

'Immediate' unlawful violence does not have to be instantaneous but it must be shown that the defendant's conduct was likely to lead to more than some form of violence at some later date. 'Immediate' here requires some close proximity between the acts of the defendant and the apprehended violence, with no intervening occurrence.

There are a number of ways in which this offence can be committed (see below). In all of these, however, there must be the use of threatening/abusive/insulting words or behaviour (or distribution/display of writing, signs etc.). This must be carried out with the requisite state of mind set out at s. 6(3) which states:

(3) A person is guilty of an offence under section 4 only if he intends his words or behaviour, or the writing, sign or other visible representation, to be threatening, abusive or insulting, or is aware that it may be threatening, abusive or insulting.

In addition, it must be shown that the person further intended to bring about the consequences set out below (at (a) and (b)) or that the consequences (at (c) and (d)) were likely.

In relation to s. 4(1)(b), 'writing' includes typing, printing, lithography, photography and other modes of presenting or reproducing words in a visible form (Interpretation Act 1978, s. 5 and sch. 1).

The offence was broken down into four component parts in *Winn* v *DPP* (1992) 156 JP 881. For each of these parts it must be shown:

(a) that the defendant:
- intended the person against whom the conduct was directed
- to believe
- that immediate unlawful violence would be used
- either against him/her or against anyone else
- by the defendant or anyone else; *or*

(b) that he/she:
- intended to provoke the immediate use of unlawful violence
- by that person or anyone else; *or*

(c) that:
- the person against whom the words or behaviour (or distribution/display of writing etc.) were directed
- was likely to believe
- that immediate unlawful violence would be used; *or*

(d) that it was likely that immediate unlawful violence would be provoked.

In the case at (a) above, it does not have to be shown that the other person *actually believed* that immediate violence would be used; it has to be shown that the defendant *intended to cause* him/her to believe it (*Swanston* v *DPP* (1997) 161 JP 203).

The person in whom the defendant intends to create that belief must be the same person at whom the conduct is directed (*Loade* v *DPP* [1990] 1 QB 1052).

Section 4(2) provides that this offence cannot be committed by persons inside a dwelling. 'Dwelling' is defined as any structure or part of a structure occupied as a person's home or as other living accommodation (whether the occupation is separate or shared with others) but does not include any part not so occupied, and for this purpose 'structure' includes a tent, caravan, vehicle, vessel or other temporary movable structure (s. 8). A person who shouted a racially aggravated comment from her garden at a person in a neighbouring garden had not been 'inside a dwelling' (*DPP* v *Distill* [2017] EWHC 2244 (Admin)).

3.9.7 Intentional Harassment, Alarm or Distress

OFFENCE: **Intentionally Causing Harassment, Alarm or Distress—*Public Order Act 1986, s. 4A***

- Triable summarily • Six months' imprisonment and/or a fine

OFFENCE: **Racially or Religiously Aggravated—*Crime and Disorder Act 1998, s. 31(1)(b)***

- Triable either way • Two years' imprisonment and/or a fine on indictment
- Six months' imprisonment and/or a fine summarily

The Public Order Act 1986, s. 4A states:

(1) A person is guilty of an offence if, with intent to cause a person harassment, alarm or distress, he—
  (a) uses threatening or abusive or insulting words or behaviour, or disorderly behaviour, or
  (b) displays any writing, sign or other visible representation which is threatening, abusive or insulting,

thereby causing that or another person harassment, alarm or distress.

(2) An offence under this section may be committed in a public or a private place, except that no offence is committed where the words or behaviour are used, or the writing, sign or other visible representation is displayed, by a person inside a dwelling and the person who is harassed, alarmed or distressed is also inside that or another dwelling.

(3) It is a defence for the accused to prove—
  (a) that he was inside a dwelling and had no reason to believe that the words or behaviour used, or the writing, sign or other visible representation displayed, would be heard or seen by a person outside that or any other dwelling, or
  (b) that his conduct was reasonable.

KEYNOTE

For the purpose of the racially or religiously aggravated form of causing fear or provocation of violence, any words used by the defendant have to be construed within the meaning that they are given in England and Wales. In construing those words, the courts should not have any regard to the *defendant's* own racial, national or ethnic origins—or presumably their religious beliefs or lack of such (*R* v *White (Anthony Delroy)* [2001] EWCA Crim 216).

In order to prove this offence you must show that the defendant intended to cause harassment, alarm or distress and, it seems, that by so doing, the defendant actually caused some harassment, alarm or distress. In *Steele* v *DPP* [2008] EWHC 438 (Admin), the defendant took a digital photograph of the complainant and posted it on the internet with a speech bubble and text alleging the complainant had previous convictions for violence. It was several months later that the photograph was shown to the complainant by the police and the Divisional Court held that the time and the circumstances in which it had been brought fully to the attention of the complainant were immaterial.

Harassment, alarm or distress are not defined and it would appear that they are to be given their ordinary everyday meaning. A police officer can be caused such harassment, alarm or distress (*DPP* v *Orum* [1989] 1 WLR 88), and can also be the victim of the racially aggravated form of the offence (*R* v *Jacobs* [2001] 2 Cr App R(S) 38), and he/she can feel that harassment, alarm or distress for someone else present (e.g. a child (*Lodge* v *DPP* [1989] COD 179)). Police officers are expected to display a degree of fortitude and, for an officer to be caused harassment, alarm or distress, the conduct complained of must go beyond that which he/she would regularly come across in the ordinary course of police duties.

In *R* v *Habibi* [2025] EWCA Crim 1523, an accused was found guilty of racially aggravated harassment. Following assaults on two police officers, the accused was taken to a police station where he continued to be aggressive and non-compliant. Whilst in a cell, the appellant racially abused a black police officer using the deeply offensive word 'nigger' twice. The officer stated that the racial abuse had left him upset and made him question his role as an officer in the Metropolitan Police and that he did not join the police force to be racially abused.

Police officers are expected to display a degree of fortitude and, for an officer to be caused harassment, alarm or distress, the conduct complained of must go beyond that which he/she would regularly come across in the ordinary course of police duties.

Whether the use of a particular phrase, in the context and circumstances in which it was used, was intended to cause harassment, alarm or distress for the offences above is a question of fact for the relevant magistrate/jury to decide (*DPP* v *Weeks* (2000) *The Independent*, 17 July). Consequently, in that case where the defendant was alleged to have called the victim a 'black bastard' during a heated argument over a business transaction, the magistrates were still entitled to find him not guilty of the aggravated s. 4A offence if they were satisfied that the relevant intention was not present.

In *R* v *Valentine* [2017] EWCA Crim 207 the Court of Appeal held that where racial hostility was directed at someone who was not the victim, the elements of 'racially aggravated' were not made out.

Posting a threatening, abusive or insulting letter through someone's letter box is not an offence under this section (*Chappell* v *DPP* (1989) 89 Cr App R 82).

It is a defence for a person to prove that he was inside a dwelling and had no reason to believe that the words or behaviour used, or the writing, sign or other visible representation displayed, would be heard or seen by a person outside that or any other building or that his conduct was reasonable (s. 4A(3)). For the definition of dwelling, **see para. 3.9.6**. A person's conduct will be reasonable if a person is exercising a right under the European Convention on Human Rights in circumstances in which an interference with that exercise would not be justified (*R (On the Application of DPP)* v *Manchester City Magistrates' Court* [2023] EWHC 2938 (Admin)).

It is for the defendant to prove that one of the elements existed at the time of the offence. The standard of proof here will be that of the balance of probabilities, i.e. that it was more likely than not.

3.9.7.1 Intentional harassment, alarm or distress on account of sex

OFFENCE: **Intentional Harassment, alarm or distress on account of sex**

- Triable either way • Two years' imprisonment and/or a fine on indictment
- 12 months' imprisonment and or a fine summarily

The Public Order Act 1986 s. 4B states:

(1) A person (A) is guilty of an offence under this section if—
  (a) A commits an offence under section 4A (intentional harassment, alarm or distress), and
  (b) A carried out the conduct referred to in section 4A(1) because of the relevant person's sex (or presumed sex).

(2) In subsection (1)—
  'presumed' means presumed by A;
  'the relevant person' means the person to whom A intended to cause harassment, alarm or distress.

(3) For the purposes of subsection (1)(b) it does not matter whether or not—
  (a) A also carried out the conduct referred to in section 4A(1) because of any other factor not mentioned in subsection (1)(b), or
  (b) A carried out the conduct referred to in section 4A(1) for the purposes of sexual gratification.

KEYNOTE

This section was inserted by the Protection from Sex-based Harassment in Public Act 2023.

If, on the trial on indictment of a person charged with an offence under this section, the jury find the person not guilty of the offence charged, they may find the person guilty of the offence in section 4A (subs. (5)).

3.9.8 Harassment, Alarm or Distress

OFFENCE: **Harassment, Alarm or Distress—*Public Order Act 1986, s. 5***
- Triable summarily • Fine

OFFENCE: **Racially or Religiously Aggravated—*Crime and Disorder Act 1998, s. 31(1)(c)***
- Triable summarily • Fine

The Public Order Act 1986, s. 5 states:

(1) A person is guilty of an offence if he—
(a) uses threatening or abusive words or behaviour, or disorderly behaviour, or
(b) displays any writing, sign or other visible representation which is threatening or abusive, within the hearing or sight of a person likely to be caused harassment, alarm or distress thereby.

(2) An offence under this section may be committed in a public or a private place, except that no offence is committed where the words or behaviour are used, or the writing, sign or other visible representation is displayed, by a person inside a dwelling and the other person is also inside that or another dwelling.

KEYNOTE

Unlike the other racially or religiously aggravated forms of public order offences, the offence under s. 5 remains triable summarily, even if aggravated by the conditions set out in s. 28 of the Crime and Disorder Act 1998 (s. 31(5)).

In a case where the defendant used the words 'You're fucking Islam' in an aggressive manner towards a Sikh police officer of Asian appearance, the Divisional Court held that the expression itself was almost undeniably abusive if not insulting (*R (On the Application of DPP)* v *Humphrey* [2005] EWHC 822 (Admin)). In *Kendall* v *DPP* [2008] EWHC 1848 (Admin), British National Party posters showing a photograph of three black men with the caption 'Illegal Immigrant Murder Scum' were found to be threatening, abusive and insulting and racially aggravated. In *Abdul* v *DPP* [2011] EWHC 247 (Admin), it was held that a prosecution under this section was a proportionate response to a group of protesters carrying placards and chanting slogans such as 'British soldiers burn in hell' and calling the soldiers murderers, rapists and baby killers, during a parade to celebrate soldiers returning from Afghanistan.

In *Cain* v *DPP* [2022] EWHC 1466 (Admin), it was held that a male accused who was black was guilty of a racially aggravated public order offence where the accused called a police officer of mixed race a 'nigger'. In the circumstances of the case, the court held that the use of the word 'nigger' demonstrated hostility towards the officer on the basis of his membership of a black social group.

Note that 'disorderly' is not defined and ought to be given its ordinary everyday meaning. It need not be shown that the disorderly behaviour is itself threatening, abusive or insulting, nor that it brought about any feelings of apprehension in the person to whom it was directed (*Chambers and Edwards* v *DPP* [1995] Crim LR 896). The wording of s. 5 is not limited to rowdy behaviour and will extend to any behaviour that could be construed as threatening or abusive.

There must be evidence that there was someone present who could see or hear what the accused was doing, though there was no requirement for the prosecution to call evidence to this effect (*Taylor* v *DPP* [2006] EWHC 1202 (Admin)).

In *Overd* v *Chief Constable of Avon and Somerset Constabulary* [2021] EWHC 3100 (QB), members of the public complained to the police about a group of four evangelical Christians causing a disturbance by preaching racist and anti-Islamic statements. The court held that because of the complaints made to the police, the hostile crowd, the preaching of hate by the group and ongoing preaching, there were reasonable grounds for suspecting that there had been anti-social behaviour capable of falling within s. 5.

As with the offence under s. 4A (**see para. 3.9.7**), there is nothing to stop the person likely to have felt harassment, alarm or distress from being a police officer acting in the course of his/her duty, but of course one has to be cautious about making such a finding, because police officers are expected to show a certain degree of resilience (*Williams* v *CPS* [2018] EWHC 2869 (Admin)).

A person is only guilty of an offence under this section if he/she intends his/her words or behaviour, or the writing, sign or other visible representation, to be threatening or abusive, or is aware that it may be threatening or abusive or (as the case may be) he/she intends his/her behaviour to be or is aware that it may be disorderly (s. 6(4)). In *R* v *Casserly* [2024] EWCA Crim 25, the Court of Appeal noted that 'some forms of self-expression will fall outside the scope of the free speech right because they amount to no more than vulgar abuse and convey no ideas and no meaningful information or for other reasons'.

This offence is a 'penalty offence' for the purposes of s. 1 of the Criminal Justice and Police Act 2001.

This offence can be committed in a public or private place but not where the words or behaviour are used by a person inside a dwelling and the other person is inside that or another dwelling (s. 5(2)). For the definition of dwelling, see para. 3.9.6.

3.9.8.1 Defences

The Public Order Act 1986, s. 5 states:

(3) It is a defence for the accused to prove—
  (a) that he had no reason to believe that there was any person within hearing or sight who was likely to be caused harassment, alarm or distress, or
  (b) that he was inside a dwelling and had no reason to believe that the words or behaviour used, or the writing sign or other visible representation displayed, would be heard or seen by a person outside that or any other dwelling, or
  (c) that his conduct was reasonable.

KEYNOTE

It is for the defendant to prove that one of the elements existed at the time of the offence. The standard of proof here will be that of the balance of probabilities, i.e. that it was more likely than not.

In deciding whether a defendant's conduct was reasonable under s. 5(3)(c) an objective test will be applied (*DPP* v *Clarke* (1992) 94 Cr App R 359).

The relationship between the Public Order Act 1986, s. 5(1), Article 10 of the ECHR (freedom of expression) and the supposed 'right' to go naked in public was considered in the naked rambler' case (*Gough* v *DPP* [2013] EWHC 3267 (Admin)). It was held that the appellant foresaw the consequence of his voluntary decision to walk naked through a town centre and was at least aware that his behaviour may have been threatening, abusive, insulting or disorderly. Thus the intent required by the legislation was proved.

3.9.9 Intentionally or Recklessly Causing Public Nuisance

OFFENCE: **Intentionally or Recklessly Causing Public Nuisance—*Police, Crime, Sentencing and Courts Act 2022, s. 78***

• Triable either way • 10 years' imprisonment and/or a fine • 12 months' imprisonment and/or a fine summarily

The Police, Crime, Sentencing and Courts Act 2022, s. 78 states:

(1) A person commits an offence if—
  (a) the person—
    (i) does an act, or
    (ii) omits to do an act that they are required to do by any enactment or rule of law,
  (b) the person's act or omission—
    (i) creates a risk of, or causes, serious harm to the public or a section of the public, or
    (ii) obstructs the public or a section of the public in the exercise or enjoyment of a right that may be exercised or enjoyed by the public at large, and
  (c) the person intends that their act or omission will have a consequence mentioned in paragraph (b) or is reckless as to whether it will have such a consequence.

(2) In subsection (1)(b)(i) 'serious harm' means—
   (a) death, personal injury or disease,
   (b) loss of, or damage to, property, or
   (c) serious distress, serious annoyance, serious inconvenience or serious loss of amenity.

(3) It is a defence for a person charged with an offence under subsection (1) to prove that they had a reasonable excuse for the act or omission mentioned in paragraph (a) of that subsection.

KEYNOTE

This legislation is part of measures intended to improve the police's ability to manage protests that have included halting public transport networks, the obstruction of roads and blocking ambulances from reaching hospitals. The measures are designed to balance the rights of protesters against the rights of others to go about their daily business, and for the police to dedicate their resources to ensure public safety. The offence captures conduct which causes serious harm, endangers the life, health, property or comfort of the public, or obstructs the public in the exercise or enjoyment of rights common to the public.

An act or omission is considered to cause serious harm if as a result, a person suffers serious distress, serious annoyance, serious inconvenience or serious loss of amenity. Conduct might include nuisances such as producing excessive noise or offensive or dangerous behaviour in public.

In *Smith* v *R* [2024] EWCA Crim 1040, the appellants were protestors with the movement Just Stop Oil who staged a protest by invading the track at the British Grand Prix Formula 1 motor race held at Silverstone. Part of their defence was that there was no risk of harm or personal injury faced by 'a section of the public' as required in s. 78(1)(b)(i)). In upholding the decision of the trial jury, the Court of Appeal held that it is necessary for a jury to determine the offences 'to distinguish a "section of the public" from a series of individuals'. In addition, the court commented that whilst risk of harm is sufficient for the commission of the offence, that risk must be real, not fanciful.

In relation to the defence under s. 78(3), the burden of proof is placed on the defendant as the facts as to whether they have a reasonable excuse will be within their knowledge.

In *R* v *Brown* [2022] EWCA Crim 6, the accused had glued himself to the top of a commercial passenger aircraft with the intention of causing as much disruption as possible to draw attention to climate change and the contribution that air travel makes to the emissions which cause it. It was held that the right to protest does not entitle a person to cause major widespread disruption with the inevitable impact that has on the lives of hundreds of people simply because it is considered the right thing to do. The defence of reasonable excuse was not accepted and nor did the ECHR rights in Articles 10 (freedom of expression) and 11 (freedom of assembly) provide a defence to the offence of public nuisance as a matter of substantive criminal law.

In *R* v *Trowland* [2023] EWCA Crim 919, two accused scaled the Queen Elizabeth II bridge on the M25 carriageway and hoisted a 'Just Stop Oil' banner across the bridge, resulting in the bridge being closed for 40 hours, causing extreme disruption to many members of the public. The court held that the protesters' activities were carried out on a place from which the public were excluded and amounted to trespass. Articles 10 and 11 of the ECHR did not provide unlimited freedom to exercise protest rights in any forum or location. The protesters had no right to be on the bridge, let alone 60 metres aloft. The defence provided by Articles 10 and 11 were not available to them and nor was the defence of 'reasonable excuse' as provided by s. 78(3).

3.10 Offences and Powers Relating to Football Matches

3.10.1 Introduction

This chapter is concerned with one sport—football. The chapter deals with offences and powers under the Football (Offences) Act 1991, the Football Spectators Act 1989 and the Sporting Events (Control of Alcohol etc.) Act 1985; the offences concern behaviour at football matches, alcohol on vehicles and possession of fireworks and flares as well as powers to impose banning orders and apply detention periods associated with them. The offence of sales of tickets by unauthorised persons (ticket touting) is also discussed.

3.10.2 Designated and Regulated Football Matches

Many of the offences and powers relating to football fixtures apply to 'designated' or 'regulated' football matches. Generally, this will relate to an association football match in which one or both of the participating teams represent a club which is for the time being a member (whether a full or associate member) of the Football League, the Football Association Premier League, the Football Conference, Football Association Women's Super League, the Football Association Women's Championship, the Scottish Professional Football League, the Welsh Premier League, the National League, the Women's Super League, the Women's Super League 2 and the Cymru Premier, or whose home ground is for the time being situated outside England and Wales, or represents a country or territory. This will include an association football match in competition for the Football Association Cup (Football (Offences) (Designation of Football Matches) Order 2004 (SI 2004/2410), as amended by the Football (Offences) (Designation of Football Matches) (Amendment) Order 2011 (SI 2011/1187) and the Football (Offences) (Designation of Football Matches) (Amendment) Order 2025 (SI 2025/876)).

Section 1A of the Football (Offences) Act 1991 provides a specific offence of unauthorised entry to designated football matches (triable summarily and punishable by a fine).

The Football (Offences) Act 1991, s. 1A states:

(1) A person ('P') commits an offence if—
- (a) P enters, or attempts to enter, premises for the purpose of attending a designated football match, and
- (b) at the time of entry or attempted entry, P does not have a match ticket for the match that P is eligible to use.

(2) It is a defence to prove that P had lawful authority or lawful excuse for entering, or attempting to enter, the premises.

(3) It is a defence to prove that—
- (a) P entered, or attempted to enter, the premises through an entry point normally used by spectators,
- (b) at the time of entry or attempted entry, P had something that they reasonably believed was a match ticket for the match, and
- (c) the thing that P had—
  - (i) was not a match ticket for the match, or
  - (ii) was a match ticket for the match but P was not eligible to use it.

(4) In this section—

- 'match ticket' means a ticket or other thing (whether in physical or electronic form) which authorises a person to enter premises for the purpose of attending a designated football match;
- 'premises' includes any place.

KEYNOTE

Defence under s. 1A(2)

Section 1A(2) provides for a defence where a person has lawful authority or lawful excuse for entering (or attempting to enter) the premises for the specified purpose, despite not having a ticket authorising them to do so. For example, persons such as employees, journalists and emergency workers who enter the premises for a legitimate purpose are not in scope of this offence.

Defence under s. 1A(3)

Section 1A(3) sets out that it is a defence if a person can prove that they entered (or attempted to enter) the premises through a standard entry point used by spectators, and at the time of entry or attempted entry, the person had something that they reasonably believed was a match ticket for the match, and the thing that the person had was either not a match ticket for the match, or was a match ticket for the match but the person was not eligible to use it.

In practice this means that if an individual inadvertently purchases a counterfeit ticket in good faith (but, in reality, the ticket is a replica of an original genuine ticket), the individual in question would be able to rely on the defence under subsection (3)(c)(i).

Furthermore, individuals utilising genuine tickets, but not fulfilling the terms and conditions of these tickets, would also not be in scope of this offence. For example, a 17-year-old using an under-16s ticket would typically be in breach of the terms and conditions of the ticket. Such a person would not have a ticket that they were eligible to use for the purposes of subsection (1)(b) but would be able to rely on the defence under subsection (3)(c)(ii).

A person using a season ticket issued in someone else's name would also not have a ticket that they were eligible to use for the purposes of subsection (1)(b) on the assumption that the ticket only authorises the named person. However, the person using it would be able to rely on the defence under subsection (3)(c)(ii).

Match Ticket

This covers the various forms of match tickets, including season tickets and hospitality passes, whether in electronic, plastic card, paper or any other format. A match ticket that has already been used is not valid for further entry.

Premises

The concept of 'premises' is defined as including any place. In practice, this will include football stadia and for some high-profile matches this may also include an area of private land in close proximity to the stadium that persons can only enter by showing a valid match ticket. For example, an event organiser may control entry to private land by using an outer cordon ticket check before the stadium turnstiles. The term may also encompass concourses, bars, and car parks to which a person is required to show a valid match ticket in order to gain entrance.

3.10.3 The Football (Offences) Act 1991

OFFENCE: **Misbehaviour at Designated Football Match—*Football (Offences) Act 1991, ss. 2, 3 and 4***

- Triable summarily • Fine

The Football (Offences) Act 1991 states:

2. **Throwing of missiles**
   It is an offence for a person at a designated football match to throw anything at or towards—
   (a) the playing area, or any area adjacent to the playing area to which spectators are not generally admitted, or
   (b) any area in which spectators or other persons are or may be present,
   without lawful authority or lawful excuse (which shall be for him to prove).
3. **Indecent or racialist chanting**
   (1) It is an offence to engage or take part in chanting of an indecent or racialist nature at a designated football match.
   (2) For this purpose—
      (a) 'chanting' means the repeated uttering of any words or sounds (whether alone or in concert with one or more others); and
      (b) 'of a racialist' nature means consisting of or including matter which is threatening, abusive or insulting to a person by reason of his colour, race, nationality (including citizenship) or ethnic or national origins.
4. **Going onto the playing area**
   It is an offence for a person at a designated football match to go onto the playing area, or any area adjacent to the playing area to which spectators are not generally admitted, without lawful authority or lawful excuse (which shall be for him to prove).

KEYNOTE

Section 1(2) of the 1991 Act provides that references to things done at a 'designated football match' include anything done at the ground:

- within the period beginning two hours before the start of the match or (if earlier) two hours before the time at which it is advertised to start and ending one hour after the end of the match;
- where the match is advertised to start at a particular time on a particular day but does not take place, within the period beginning two hours before and ending one hour after the advertised starting time.

These offences can be separated into those affecting the playing area and adjacent parts of the ground (ss. 2 and 4) and the offence of indecent or racialist chanting (s. 3).

In the case of the first offence (s. 2), throwing anything at or towards the playing area etc., there is a defence of having lawful authority or lawful excuse (which presumably would cover returning the ball to the field of play). Generally there seem to be few occasions on which a defendant would have lawful authority/reasonable excuse for the behaviour prohibited by s. 2.

Section 4 makes the same savings in relation to lawful authority/reasonable excuse and, in both cases, the burden of proof falls on the defendant. (The *standard* of proof will be that of the balance of probabilities.)

For the offence under s. 3, the defendant must be shown to have *repeated* the words or sounds before it can be classed as 'chanting'.

The wording of s. 3(2)(b) requires that the chanting is, rather than, *might be*, threatening, abusive or insulting. Although not expressly required, the best way to prove this element of the offence would be the evidence of a person who was threatened, abused or insulted. In relation to chants 'of a racialist' nature, shouting 'You're just a town full of Pakis' at supporters from Oldham fell squarely within the definition (*DPP v Stoke on Trent Magistrates' Court* [2003] EWHC 1593 (Admin)).

'Indecent' is not defined and will be a question of fact for the court to decide in all the circumstances.

3.10.4 Banning Orders and Detention

The Football Spectators Act 1989 contains the powers to impose banning orders that exclude offenders from attendance at regulated football matches in England, Wales, Scotland and Northern Ireland and football matches outside the United Kingdom.

There are two ways in which a banning order can be made, first where a person is convicted of a relevant offence (s. 14A), and secondly, by way of complaint by the relevant chief officer, or the DPP (s. 14B(1)).

For a banning order to be made, the offending must relate to a regulated football match (*Chapman* v *R* [2024] EWCA Crim 1072).

3.10.4.1 Banning Orders Made on Conviction of an Offence

The Football Spectators Act 1989, s. 14A states:

(1) This section applies where a person (the 'offender') is convicted of a relevant offence.
(2) The court must make a banning order in respect of the offender unless the court considers that there are particular circumstances relating to the offence or to the offender which would make it unjust in all the circumstances to do so.
(3) Where the court does not make a banning order it must state in open court the reasons for not doing so.
(3A) For the purpose of deciding whether to make an order under this section the court may consider evidence led by the prosecution and the defence.
(3B) It is immaterial whether evidence led in pursuance of subsection (3A) would have been admissible in the proceedings in which the offender was convicted.
(4) A banning order may only be made under this section—
  (a) in addition to a sentence imposed in respect of the relevant offence, or
  (b) in addition to an order discharging him conditionally.

KEYNOTE

Courts are under a statutory duty to impose a banning order if they are satisfied that there are reasonable grounds to believe that the order would help prevent violence or disorder.

'Violence' means violence against persons or property and includes threatening violence and doing anything which endangers the life of any person (s. 14C(1)).

'Disorder' includes: (a) stirring up hatred against a group of persons defined by reference to colour, race, nationality (including citizenship) or ethnic or national origins, or against an individual as a member of such a group; (b) using threatening, abusive or insulting words or behaviour or disorderly behaviour; and (c) displaying any writing or other thing which is threatening, abusive or insulting (s. 14C(2)).

'Relevant offence' in subs. (1) means an offence to which sch. 1 to the Act applies (s. 14(8)). These include offences relating to drunkenness, violence or the threat of violence, public order offences, possession of an offensive weapon or firearm, or possession or control of a Class A drug added by the Football Spectators (Relevant Offences) Regulations 2022 (SI 2022/1168). The commission of an offence contained in the schedule must be related to a football match or be in connection with a football organisation.

Banning orders made under s. 14A, in addition to an immediate sentence of imprisonment, will have a minimum duration of six years and a maximum duration of 10 years (s. 14F(3)). Other banning orders, where they do not accompany a sentence of immediate imprisonment, have a minimum duration of three years and a maximum duration of five years (s. 14F(4)).

A person subject to a banning order who fails to comply with: (a) any requirement imposed by the order; or (b) any requirement imposed under s. 19(2B) or (2C) is guilty of an offence (s. 14J(1)) and is liable on summary conviction to six months' imprisonment and/or a fine (s. 14J(2)). Section 19(2B) and (2C) relate to written notices requiring a person to report to a police station and the surrender of passports in advance of certain football matches.

3.10.4.2 Complaint by Chief Officer or DPP

Under s. 14B of the Act, a banning order can be made on complaint by a chief officer or the DPP. On such an application, a magistrates' court can make an order if the person has at any time caused or contributed to any violence or disorder in the United Kingdom or elsewhere (s. 14B(2)). The court may impose conditions on banning orders and must require the surrender of the person's passport in connection with regulated football matches outside the United Kingdom (s. 14E(3)). Where proceedings are adjourned, as with the first way of obtaining a banning order, the offender may be remanded and, where bailed, be required to surrender his/her passport (s. 14B(5)). Again, where the magistrates have failed to make a banning order, the prosecution have a right of appeal to the Crown Court (s. 14D(1A)).

The effect of a banning order, unless a person is detained in legal custody, is that he/she must initially report to a specified police station in England, Wales, Scotland or Northern Ireland, within five days of the order being made (s. 14E(2)). He/she must also notify the enforcing authority of specified changes to his/her personal circumstances within seven days of the occurrence of any such changes (s. 14E(2B) and (2C)).

KEYNOTE

Banning orders made under s. 14B (on complaint by a chief officer of police) have a minimum of three and a maximum of five years' duration (s. 14F(5)).

3.10.4.3 Summary Measures: Detention

The Football Spectators Act 1989, s. 21A states:

(1) This section and section 21B below apply during any control period in relation to a regulated football match outside the United Kingdom or an external tournament if a constable in uniform—
  (a) has reasonable grounds for suspecting that the condition in section 14B(2) above is met in the case of a person present before him, and
  (b) has reasonable grounds to believe that making a banning order in his case would help to prevent violence or disorder at or in connection with any regulated football matches.

(2) The constable may detain the person in his custody (whether there or elsewhere) until he has decided whether or not to issue a notice under section 21B below, and shall give the person his reasons for detaining him in writing.
This is without prejudice to any power of the constable apart from this section to arrest the person.

(3) A person may not be detained under subsection (2) above for more than four hours or, with the authority of an officer of at least the rank of inspector, six hours.

KEYNOTE

'Control period' means, in relation to a regulated football match outside the United Kingdom, the period:

(a) beginning five days before the day of the match; and
(b) ending when the match is finished or cancelled (s. 14(5));

and in relation to an external tournament, means any period described in an order made by the Secretary of State:

(a) beginning five days before the day of the first football match outside the United Kingdom which is included in the tournament; and
(b) ending when the last football match outside the United Kingdom which is included in the tournament is finished or cancelled (s. 14(6)),

but, for the purposes of para. (a), any football match included in the qualifying or pre-qualifying stages of the tournament is to be ignored (s. 14(5) and (6)). An example of a specified 'control period' is the Football Spectators (2022 World Cup Control Period) Order 2022 (SI 2022/977), which commenced 10 days before the first match in the tournament, and ended when the last match in the tournament was finished or cancelled.

The power under s. 21A requires the police officer to be in uniform and may be exercised only in relation to a person who is a British citizen (see s. 21C(1)).

The initial period of detention allowed is a *maximum* of four hours, extendable to a further maximum of six hours by an inspector. There is no requirement under this section that the inspector be either present or in uniform. The purpose of the detention is for the officer to decide whether or not to issue a notice (**see para. 3.10.4.4**).

The condition under s. 14B(2) referred to is that the person has at any time caused or contributed to any violence or disorder in the United Kingdom or elsewhere.

References to football matches include matches intended to be played (s. 14(7)). A person who has been detained under s. 21A(2) may only be further detained under that subsection in the same control period in reliance on information which was not available to the constable who previously detained him/her; and a person on whom a notice has been served under s. 21B(2) may not be detained under s. 21A(2) in the same control period (s. 21A(4)).

3.10.4.4 Summary Measures: Reference to a Court

The Football Spectators Act 1989, s. 21B states:

(1) A constable in uniform may exercise the power in subsection (2) below if authorised to do so by an officer of at least the rank of inspector.
(2) The constable may give the person a notice in writing requiring him—
  (a) to appear before a magistrates' court at a time, or between the times, specified in the notice,
  (b) not to leave England and Wales before that time (or the later of those times), and
  (c) if the control period relates to a regulated football match outside the United Kingdom or to an external tournament which includes such matches, to surrender his passport to the constable,

  and stating the grounds referred to in section 21A(1) above.
(3) The times for appearance before the magistrates' court must be within the period of 24 hours beginning with—
  (a) the giving of the notice, or
  (b) the person's detention under section 21A(2) above, whichever is the earlier.

KEYNOTE

The power applies during any control period in relation to a regulated football match outside England and Wales or an external tournament (as to which, **see para. 3.10.4.3, Keynote**).

A constable may arrest a person to whom he/she is giving a notice if he/she has reasonable grounds to believe that it is *necessary* to do so in order to ensure that the person complies with the notice (s. 21B(5)).

For the purposes of s. 14B, the notice is to be treated as an application for a banning order made by complaint (s. 21B(4)).

As with the provision for detention under s. 21A, the powers conferred by s. 21B may be exercised only in relation to a person who is a British citizen (s. 21C(1)).

A person who fails to comply with a notice given under s. 21B is guilty of an offence and liable on summary conviction to imprisonment for a term not exceeding six months, or a fine or both (s. 21C(2)).

3.10.5 The Sporting Events (Control of Alcohol etc.) Act 1985

This Act applies to sports grounds and sporting events designated by the Secretary of State. Only football grounds and football matches have been designated at this time. The classes of football matches differ slightly from those contained in the Football Spectators Act 1989 and are contained in the Sports Grounds and Sporting Events (Designation) Order 2005 (SI 2005/3204). The 1985 Act creates a number of offences that are outlined below.

3.10.5.1 Offences in Connection with Alcohol on Coaches and Trains

OFFENCE: **Alcohol on Coaches and Trains—*Sporting Events (Control of Alcohol etc.) Act 1985, s. 1***

- Triable summarily • Three months' imprisonment and/or a fine (s. 1(3))
- Fine (s. 1(2) and (4))

The Sporting Events (Control of Alcohol etc.) Act 1985, s. 1 states:

(1) This section applies to a vehicle which—
  (a) is a public service vehicle or railway passenger vehicle, and
  (b) is being used for the principal purpose of carrying passengers for the whole or part of a journey to or from a designated sporting event.
(2) A person who knowingly causes or permits alcohol to be carried on a vehicle to which the section applies is guilty of an offence—
  (a) if the vehicle is a public service vehicle and he is the operator of the vehicle or the servant or agent of the operator, or
  (b) if the vehicle is a hired vehicle and he is the person to whom it is hired or the servant or agent of that person.
(3) A person who has alcohol in his possession while on a vehicle to which this section applies is guilty of an offence.
(4) A person who is drunk on a vehicle to which this section applies is guilty of an offence.

KEYNOTE

Section 1 creates a number of offences in relation to public service vehicles and trains being used principally (though not exclusively) to carry passengers for the whole or part of a journey, to or from a designated sporting event.

The offences can be committed by the vehicle operator/hirer or his/her servant or agent provided there is evidence of *knowingly* causing or permitting the carrying of alcohol.

The other offences are committed by people who have alcohol in their 'possession' and by people who are drunk on a relevant vehicle. Generally, any mature and competent witness may give evidence as to drunkenness.

Section 7(3) provides a power for a constable to stop a public service vehicle in order to search it where he/she has reasonable grounds to suspect that an offence under this section *is being or has been committed* in respect of that vehicle. It also provides a power to search a railway carriage (though not to stop the train) under the same circumstances. The power to search people in those vehicles comes from s. 7(2). The PACE Code of Practice for the Exercise by Police Officers of Statutory Powers of Stop and Search (Code A) (2014) (**see para. 3.1.4**) applies to searches under s. 7, i.e. searches of persons, coaches and trains at designated sports grounds or coaches and trains travelling to or from a designated sporting event.

The Licensing Act 2003, s. 157, provides that a magistrates' court may make an order to prohibit the sale of alcohol on trains where it is satisfied that the order is necessary to prevent disorder where an application has been made to the court by a police officer of, or above, the rank of inspector. There is no specific restriction on the period over which such an order may be made. It is a summary offence to knowingly sell, attempt to sell or allow the sale of alcohol in contravention of an order (s. 157(5)).

3.10.5.2 Alcohol on Certain Other Vehicles

OFFENCE: **Alcohol on Other Vehicles—*Sporting Events (Control of Alcohol etc.) Act 1985, s. 1A***

- Triable summarily • Three months' imprisonment and/or a fine (s. 1A(3))
- Fine (s. 1A(2) and (4))

The Sporting Events (Control of Alcohol etc.) Act 1985, s. 1A states:

(1) This section applies to a motor vehicle which—
  (a) is not a public service vehicle but is adapted to carry more than 8 passengers, and
  (b) is being used for the principal purpose of carrying two or more passengers for the whole or part of a journey to or from a designated sporting event.
(2) A person who knowingly causes or permits alcohol to be carried on a motor vehicle to which this section applies is guilty of an offence—
  (a) if he is its driver, or

(b) if he is not its driver but is its keeper, the servant or agent of its keeper, a person to whom it is made available (by hire, loan or otherwise) by its keeper or the keeper's servant or agent, or the servant or agent of a person to whom it is so made available.

(3) A person who has alcohol in his possession while on a motor vehicle to which this section applies is guilty of an offence.

(4) A person who is drunk on a motor vehicle to which this section applies is guilty of an offence.

KEYNOTE

A motor vehicle under s. 1(1) means a mechanically propelled vehicle intended or adapted for use on roads, and a vehicle's keeper is the person having the duty to take out a licence for it under the Vehicle Excise and Registration Act 1984 (s. 1A(5)).

The power to stop and search vehicles and their occupants under s. 7(3) above also applies to an offence under this section.

3.10.5.3 Offences in Connection with Alcohol, Containers etc. at Sports Grounds

OFFENCE: **Alcohol at Sports Grounds—*Sporting Events (Control of Alcohol etc.) Act 1985, s. 2***

- Triable summarily • Three months' imprisonment and/or a fine (s. 2(1))
- Fine (s. 2(2))

The Sporting Events (Control of Alcohol etc.) Act 1985, s. 2 states:

(1) A person who has alcohol or an article to which this section applies in his possession—

(a) at any time during the period of a designated sporting event when he is in any area of a designated sports ground from which the event may be directly viewed, or

(b) while entering or trying to enter a designated sports ground at any time during the period of a designated sporting event at that ground, is guilty of an offence.

(1A) Subsection (1)(a) above has effect subject to section 5A(1) of this Act.

(2) A person who is drunk in a designated sports ground at any time during the period of a designated sporting event at that ground or is drunk while entering or trying to enter such a ground at any time during the period of a designated sporting event at that ground is guilty of an offence.

KEYNOTE

The articles to which s. 2 applies are:

- articles capable of causing injury to a person struck by them; being
- bottles, cans or other portable containers (including ones that are crushed or broken); which
- are for holding any drink; and
- are of a kind which are normally discarded or returned to/left to be recovered by the supplier when empty, and include parts of those articles.

Any such article that is for holding any medicinal product (within the meaning of the Medicines Act 1968) or any veterinary medicinal product (within the meaning of the Veterinary Medicines Regulations 2006) is excluded from this definition (s. 2(3)).

In relation to s. 2(1) 'the period of a designated sporting event' is provided by s. 9(4) of the Act which states that the period begins two hours before the start of the event or (if earlier) two hours before the time at which it is advertised to start and ending one hour after the end of the event.

In relation to subs. (1A) above, special provision is made by s. 5A(1) for private rooms from which the sporting event can be viewed.

A constable may, at any time during the period of a designated sporting event at any designated sports ground, enter any part of the ground for the purpose of enforcing the provisions of this Act, and search a person he/she has reasonable grounds to suspect is committing or has committed an offence under this Act (s. 7(1) and (2)).

Where a person is convicted of an offence under either s. 2(1) or (2) the court must consider imposing a banning order.

3.10.5.4 Fireworks, Flares and Similar Objects at Sports Grounds and Events

OFFENCE: **Having Fireworks, Flares etc.—*Sporting Events (Control of Alcohol etc.) Act 1985, s. 2A***

- Triable summarily • Three months' imprisonment and/or a fine

The Sporting Events (Control of Alcohol etc.) Act 1985, s. 2A states:

(1) A person is guilty of an offence if he has an article or substance to which this section applies in his possession—
  (a) at any time during the period of a designated sporting event when he is in any area of a designated sports ground from which the event may be directly viewed, or
  (b) while entering or trying to enter a designated sports ground at any time during the period of a designated sporting event at the ground.

(2) ...

(3) This section applies to any article or substance whose main purpose is the emission of a flare for purposes of illuminating or signalling (as opposed to igniting or heating) or the emission of smoke or a visible gas; and in particular it applies to distress flares, fog signals, and pellets and capsules intended to be used as fumigators or for testing pipes, but not to matches, cigarette lighters or heaters.

(4) This section also applies to any article which is a firework.

KEYNOTE

There is a defence under s. 2A(2) for the person to prove that he/she had possession of the article or substance with lawful authority. 'Possession' is quite a broad concept going beyond 'carrying'.

As with the offence under s. 2 (see para. 3.10.5.3), the powers of entry, search and arrest under s. 7 also apply to this offence as does the time period under s. 9(4).

3.10.6 Sale of Tickets by Unauthorised Persons

OFFENCE: **Sale of Tickets by Unauthorised Persons—*Criminal Justice and Public Order Act 1994, s. 166***

- Triable summarily • Fine

The Criminal Justice and Public Order Act 1994, s. 166 states:

(1) It is an offence for an unauthorised person to—
  (a) sell a ticket for a designated football match, or
  (b) otherwise to dispose of such a ticket to another person.

(2) For this purpose—
  (a) a person is 'unauthorised' unless he is authorised in writing to sell or otherwise dispose of tickets for the match by the organisers of the match;
  (aa) a reference to selling a ticket includes a reference to—
    (i) offering to sell a ticket;
    (ii) exposing a ticket for sale;
    (iii) making a ticket available for sale by another;
    (iv) advertising that a ticket is available for purchase; and
    (v) giving a ticket to a person who pays or agrees to pay for some other goods or services or offering to do so.

KEYNOTE

This offence is often described as 'ticket touting'.

A 'ticket' means anything which purports to be a ticket (subs. (2)(b)) and the meaning of a designated football match is contained in the Ticket Touting (Designation of Football Matches) Order 2007 (SI 2007/790).

Section 32 of the Police and Criminal Evidence Act 1984 (search of persons and premises (including vehicles) upon arrest) shall have effect, in its application in relation to an offence under this section, as if the power conferred on a constable to enter and search any vehicle extended to any vehicle which the constable has reasonable grounds for believing was being used for any purpose connected with the offence (s. 166(5)).

The Breaching of Limits on Ticket Sales Regulations 2018 (SI 2018/735) provide for a criminal offence of purchasing tickets for a recreational, sporting or cultural event using 'bots' (a web robot) in excess of conditions made by the event organiser that set a maximum number of tickets that a purchaser may buy. It is also an offence for a person to use software that is designed to enable or facilitate completion of any part of the process, with intent to obtain tickets in excess of the sales limit and with a view to any person obtaining financial gain. The offence is committed whether the offer of tickets is made, or anything is done, to obtain the tickets, in or outside the UK. The offences under these Regulations are triable summarily and punishable by a fine (reg. 5(1)).

3.11 Domestic Violence and Abuse

3.11.1 Introduction

This chapter provides an overview of the measures available to deal with domestic violence and abuse as contained in the Domestic Abuse Act 2021, the offence of controlling or coercive behaviour in an intimate or family relationship contained in the Serious Crime Act 2015 and the application of non-molestation orders when dealing with such cases.

3.11.2 Definition of Domestic Abuse

The Domestic Abuse Act 2021 provides a statutory definition of domestic abuse and s. 1 states:

(1) This section defines 'domestic abuse' for the purposes of this Act.
(2) Behaviour of a person ('A') towards another person ('B') is 'domestic abuse' if—
  (a) A and B are each aged 16 or over and are personally connected to each other, and
  (b) the behaviour is abusive.
(3) Behaviour is 'abusive' if it consists of any of the following—
  (a) physical or sexual abuse;
  (b) violent or threatening behaviour;
  (c) controlling or coercive behaviour;
  (d) economic abuse (see subsection (4));
  (e) psychological, emotional or other abuse;
  and it does not matter whether the behaviour consists of a single incident or a course of conduct.

KEYNOTE

'Personally Connected'

Section 2 of the Act states that for the purposes of this Act, two people are 'personally connected' to each other if any of the following applies:

- they are, or have been, married to each other;
- they are, or have been, civil partners of each other;
- they have agreed to marry one another (whether or not the agreement has been terminated);
- they have entered into a civil partnership agreement (whether or not the agreement has been terminated);
- they are, or have been, in an intimate personal relationship with each other;
- they each have, or there has been a time when they each have had, a parental relationship in relation to the same child (a person has a parental relationship in relation to a child if the person is a parent of the child or the person has parental responsibility for the child); or
- they are relatives.

'Controlling Behaviour'

This is defined as: a range of acts designed to make a person subordinate and/or dependent by isolating them from sources of support, exploiting their resources and capacities for personal gain, depriving them of the means needed for independence, resistance and escape and regulating their everyday behaviour.

'Coercive Behaviour'

'Coercive behaviour' is an act or a pattern of acts of assault, threats, humiliation and intimidation or other abuse that is used to harm, punish or frighten the victim. This definition, which is not a legal definition, includes so-called 'honour'-based violence, female genital mutilation (FGM) and forced marriage, and it is clear that victims are not confined to one gender or ethnic group.

'Economic Abuse'

'Economic abuse' means any behaviour that has a substantial adverse effect on a person's ability to acquire, use or maintain money or other property, or obtain goods or services (s. 1(4)). This behaviour may be behaviour consisting of conduct directed at another person, for example the complainant's child (s. 1(5)).

Children as Victims of Domestic Abuse

Section 3 of the Act recognises that domestic abuse can impact on a child (a person under the age of 18). Where the behaviour of a person ('A') towards another person ('B') is domestic abuse, any reference to a victim of domestic abuse includes a child who:

- sees or hears, or experiences the effects of, the abuse; and
- is related to A or B.

A child is related to a person if the person is a parent of, or has parental responsibility for, the child or the child and the person are relatives.

Section 49A of the 2021 Act requires all police forces to have arrangements in place to ensure that, where a member of a force has reasonable grounds to believe a child (a person under 18) may be a victim of domestic abuse, educational establishments that the child attends are notified as soon as is reasonably practicable.

Harassment and Stalking

Where harassment or stalking occurs, and the perpetrator and victim are 16 or over and 'personally connected', this behaviour falls within the scope of the statutory definition of domestic abuse.

Domestic Abuse and Firearms Certificates

Where police forces have serious concerns about a certificate holder's continued access to firearms or shotguns, prompt action must be taken to ensure no preventable harm is caused to public safety (Home Office, *Guidance on Firearms Licensing Law* (November 2022), paras 10.39 (firearms) and 11.18 (shotguns)). Evidence of domestic abuse will usually mean that the certificate is refused or revoked unless exceptional circumstances can be demonstrated (Home Office, *Firearms Licensing: Statutory Guidance for Chief Officers of Police* (December 2021), para. 3.25).

3.11.3 Controlling or Coercive Behaviour in an Intimate or Family Relationship

OFFENCE: **Controlling or Coercive Behaviour in an Intimate or Family Relationship—*Serious Crime Act 2015, s. 76***

- Triable either way • Five years' imprisonment and/or a fine on indictment
- 12 months' imprisonment

The Serious Crime Act 2015, s. 76 states:

(1) A person (A) commits an offence if—
  (a) A repeatedly or continuously engages in behaviour towards another person (B) that is controlling or coercive,
  (b) at the time of the behaviour, A and B are personally connected (see subsection (6)),
  (c) the behaviour has a serious effect on B, and
  (d) A knows or ought to know that the behaviour will have a serious effect on B.

(2) ...

(3) But A does not commit an offence under this section if at the time of the behaviour in question—
   (a) A has responsibility for B, for the purposes of Part 1 of the Children and Young Persons Act 1933 (see section 17 of that Act), and
   (b) B is under 16.

(4) A's behaviour has a 'serious effect' on B if—
   (a) it causes B to fear, on at least two occasions, that violence will be used against B, or
   (b) it causes B serious alarm or distress which has a substantial adverse effect on B's usual day-to-day activities.

(5) For the purposes of subsection (1)(d) A 'ought to know' that which a reasonable person in possession of the same information would know.

(6) A and B are 'personally connected' if any of the following applies—
   (a) they are, or have been, married to each other;
   (b) they are, or have been, civil partners of each other;
   (c) they have agreed to marry one another (whether or not the agreement has been terminated);
   (d) they have entered into a civil partnership agreement (whether or not the agreement has been terminated);
   (e) they are, or have been, in an intimate personal relationship with each other;
   (f) they each have, or there has been a time when they each have had, a parental relationship in relation to the same child (see subsection (6A));
   (g) they are relatives.

(6A) For the purposes of subsection (6)(f) a person has a parental relationship in relation to a child if—
   (a) the person is a parent of the child, or
   (b) the person has parental responsibility for the child.

KEYNOTE

In relation to subss. (6) and (6A) above, 'civil partnership agreement' has the meaning given by s. 73 of the Civil Partnership Act 2004; 'child' means a person under the age of 18 years; 'parental responsibility' has the same meaning as in the Children Act 1989; 'relative' has the meaning given by s. 63(1) of the Family Law Act 1996 (s. 76(7)).

It is a defence for A to show that: (a) in engaging in the behaviour in question, A believed that he/she was acting in B's best interests, and (b) the behaviour was in all the circumstances reasonable (s. 76(8)). For this defence to be successful, sufficient evidence of the facts is adduced to raise an issue with respect to them, and the contrary is not proved beyond reasonable doubt (s. 76(9)). The defence in subs. is not available to A in relation to behaviour that causes B to fear that violence will be used against B (s. 76(10)).

The Domestic Abuse Act 2021 extended the offence of controlling or coercive behaviour in an intimate or family relationship to cover post-separation abuse.

In addition to this 'domestic abuse' offence, an offence of strangulation and suffocation was inserted under s. 75A of the 2021 Act by the Serious Crime Act 2015. This was due in part to strangulation being a common factor reported by survivors of domestic abuse and that it was a measure often used by an abuser to instil fear, power and control over their victim, rather than being a failed homicide attempt (see *Crime Manual*).

3.11.4 Domestic Violence Protection Notices and Orders

A domestic violence protection notice (DVPN) is the initial notice issued by the police to provide emergency protection to an individual believed to be the victim of domestic violence and abuse.

The power to issue a domestic violence protection notice is provided by s. 24 of the Crime and Security Act 2010, which states:

(1) A member of a police force not below the rank of superintendent ('the authorising officer') may issue a domestic violence protection notice ('a DVPN') under this section.

(2) A DVPN may be issued to a person ('P') aged 18 years or over if the authorising officer has reasonable grounds for believing that—
   (a) P has been violent towards, or has threatened violence towards, an associated person, and

(b) the issue of the DVPN is necessary to protect that person from violence or a threat of violence by P.

(3) Before issuing a DVPN, the authorising officer must, in particular, consider—

(a) the welfare of any person under the age of 18 whose interests the officer considers relevant to the issuing of the DVPN (whether or not that person is an associated person),

(b) the opinion of the person for whose protection the DVPN would be issued as to the issuing of the DVPN,

(c) any representations made by P as to the issuing of the DVPN, and

(d) in the case of provision included by virtue of subsection (8), the opinion of any other associated person who lives in the premises to which the provision would relate.

(4) The authorising officer must take reasonable steps to discover the opinions mentioned in subsection (3).

(5) But the authorising officer may issue a DVPN in circumstances where the person for whose protection it is issued does not consent to the issuing of the DVPN.

KEYNOTE

The purpose of a DVPN is to secure the immediate protection of a victim of domestic violence and abuse (V) from future violence or a threat of violence from a suspected perpetrator (P). A DVPN prohibits P from molesting V and, where they cohabit, may require P to leave those premises.

Where a DVPN has been issued, a constable must apply to a magistrates' court for a domestic violence protection order (DVPO). The application must be heard by the magistrates' court not later than 48 hours after the DVPN was served (s. 27). The DVPO is an order lasting between 14 and 28 days, which prohibits P from molesting V and may also make provision about access to shared accommodation (s. 28).

A person who breaches a DVPN may be arrested without warrant (s. 25(1)(b)) and must be held in custody to appear before a magistrates' court within 24 hours when an application for a DVPO can be heard (s. 26).

New domestic abuse protection notices (DAPN) and orders (DAPO) are to replace the current notices and orders. These new notices are currently being piloted in specific areas (the Domestic Abuse Act 2021 (Commencement No. 6, 8 and 9 and Saving Provisions) (Amendment) Regulations 2026 (SI 2026/342) and the Domestic Abuse Act 2021 (Commencement No. 6, 8 and 9 and Saving Provisions) (Amendment) Regulations 2026 (SI 2026/344)).

3.11.5 Domestic Violence Disclosure Scheme

The Domestic Violence Disclosure Scheme, also known as Clare's Law, gained momentum following the tragic case of Clare Wood, who was murdered by her former partner in 2009. Her partner had three previous convictions under the Protection from Harassment Act 1997.

Details of the scheme are provided by the Domestic Violence Disclosure Scheme (DVDS) Statutory Guidance (April 2023) and the following is an extract from ch. 2 of that statutory guidance:

11. The police have common law powers to disclose information, broadly where there is a pressing need to protect people. In this context, these powers form the basis of disclosures under the DVDS, meaning in practice that information can be shared about a person's known history of violence or abuse, normally relating to previous convictions or charges, to members of the public where there is a pressing need for disclosure of the information in order to prevent further crime. The principal aim of the DVDS is to introduce recognised and consistent procedures for the exercise of this power in this context, to enable the police to make a disclosure of information where it would protect a member of the public who may be at risk of harm from domestic abuse. Critical to the success of the scheme is the need for ongoing safety planning throughout the process and the need for a formal risk assessment to be reviewed at every stage in the disclosure process, as this will inform the practical actions necessary to safeguard the potential victim(s), and, any relevant children.

12. The DVDS recognises two procedures for disclosing information:
'Right to ask' is triggered by a member of the public applying to the police for a disclosure.
'Right to know' is triggered by the police making a proactive decision to disclose information to protect a potential victim(s).
For the purpose of this guidance:
   - Individual A: the person potentially at risk, which includes intimate partners and previous intimate partners. The person potentially at risk might also be the applicant.
   - Individual B: the person about whom a request is being made.
   - Individual C: a person who may request information about B on behalf of or out of concern for A, such as a friend or relative, or a professional such as an IDVA. Any disclosure should be made to the person best placed to safeguard A, which may or may not be C.
   - Third Party: a person to whom a disclosure can be made if deemed by safety planning as the person best placed to safeguard A (e.g. parent, third-sector worker, healthcare professional) and in some instances could be C.
13. The DVDS provides the following benefits:
   a. introduces recognised and consistent procedures for disclosing information that enables an individual (A) who is or was in an intimate personal relationship with an individual who has previously been violent or abusive (B) to make informed choices about that relationship or about their personal safety;
   b. under 'right to ask', individual members of the public, whether A or C, can proactively seek information, with an expectation that the agencies responsible for safeguarding victims of domestic abuse will check to see whether relevant information exists and if it does, that consideration using the three-stage disclosure test will be given to its disclosure, where necessary to protect A;
   c. under 'right to know', where the police come into the possession of information about the previous violent and abusive behaviour of B that may cause harm to A, members of the public can expect the police to consider using the three-stage disclosure test whether any disclosure should be made and to disclose information if it is lawful, i.e. if it is necessary and proportionate to protect the potential victim from crime;
   d. encourages the police and allows members of the public to take responsibility for the safety of the potential victim and their family.
14. The DVDS is focused on disclosure, safety planning and risk management where B is identified as having a conviction, caution, reprimand, or final warning for domestic abuse or related offences; and/or information held about B's behaviour which may not include domestic abuse-related matters but reasonably leads the police and other safeguarding agencies if involved to believe that B poses a risk of harm to A. There is a non-exhaustive list of the relevant offences at Annex B.

KEYNOTE

The DVDS does not replace arrangements for Disclosure and Barring Service (DBS) checks, the 'right of access' by individuals to their personal data (which used to be known as Subject Access Request) or Freedom of Information (FOI) requests. Also, the DVDS may overlap with and complement other disclosure processes, such as the Child Sex Offender Disclosure Scheme (CSODS, also known as 'Sarah's Law'). Consideration should be given to which process is the most appropriate in each case.

Disclosures under the scheme are determined by local multi-agency forums consisting of the police, probation services, social services and other agencies who decide whether any disclosure is lawful, necessary and proportionate. Ultimately, it will be the police, as owners of the information, who will make the final decision as to whether to disclose the information.

3.11.6 Court Orders

Any court having jurisdiction over family law matters can make an order under the Family Law Act 1996 and part IV of the Act makes provisions relating to family homes and domestic violence.

3.11.6.1 Non-molestation Order

The Family Law Act 1996, s. 42 states:

(1) In this Part a 'non-molestation order' means an order containing either or both of the following provisions—
  (a) provision prohibiting a person ('the respondent') from molesting another person who is associated with the respondent;
  (b) provision prohibiting the respondent from molesting a relevant child.

(2) The court may make a non-molestation order—
  (a) if an application for the order has been made (whether in other family proceedings or without any other family proceedings being instituted) by a person who is associated with the respondent; or
  (b) if in any family proceedings to which the respondent is a party the court considers that the order should be made for the benefit of any other party to the proceedings or any relevant child even though no such application has been made.

KEYNOTE

Non-molestation orders can be applied for even though no other proceedings have been commenced. Such orders do not relate just to spouses or former partners; they apply to anyone who is 'associated' with the respondent.

In deciding whether or not to make such an order, the court must consider all the circumstances, including the need to secure the health, safety and well-being of the applicant or any relevant child (s. 42(5)).

A person who without reasonable excuse does anything in contravention of a prohibition contained in a non-molestation order commits an offence liable on indictment to a term of five years' imprisonment and/or a fine and summarily to a term of imprisonment not exceeding the general limit in a magistrates' court and/or a fine (s. 42A).

The Family Law Act 1996 also provides for those experiencing domestic violence and abuse to apply for an occupation order. These orders are essentially short term and determine who has 'home rights' in relation to a particular property (ss. 33 to 42).

The Domestic Abuse Act 2021, ss. 65 and 66 have amended the Matrimonial and Family Proceedings Act 1984 providing in family and civil proceedings for the prohibition of cross-examination in person by a witness or a party to the proceedings in domestic abuse cases (s. 31T(1) and (2)). 'Domestic abuse' has the meaning given by s. 1 of the 2021 Act (s. 31T(3)). Any court having jurisdiction over family law matters can make a non-molestation order.

In addition to non-molestation orders, there are orders or injunctions contained in other legislation that may be considered when dealing with domestic violence and abuse. These might include: restraining orders (s. 5A of the Protection from Harassment Act 1997 (**see para. 3.12.4.11**)); anti-social behaviour injunctions (s. 1 of the Anti-social Behaviour, Crime and Policing Act 2014 (**see para. 3.7.3**)); criminal behaviour orders (s. 331 of the Sentencing Act 2020 (**see para. 3.7.4**)); stalking protection orders (s. 1 of the Stalking Protection Act 2019 (**see para. 3.12.6.3**)); community protection notices (s. 43 of the Anti-social Behaviour, Crime and Policing Act 2014 (**see para. 3.7.6**)); and public spaces protection orders (s. 59 of the Anti-social Behaviour, Crime and Policing Act 2014 (**see para. 3.7.7**)).

3.12 Hatred, Harassment and Stalking

3.12.1 Introduction

Offences involving racial, religious or sexual orientation hatred are dealt with by the Public Order Act 1986. This chapter provides a summary of these offences which are aimed at addressing incidents specifically motivated by racial hatred, religious hatred or hatred on the grounds of sexual orientation. The chapter also deals with offences of harassment and stalking under the Protection from Harassment Act 1997 and associated injunctions and orders. This chapter additionally sets out police powers under the Criminal Justice and Police Act 2001 in relation to preventing intimidation and harassment.

3.12.2 Offences Involving Racial, Religious or Sexual Orientation Hatred

For the purposes of the offences contrary to ss. 18 to 23 of the 1986 Act, 'racial hatred' means hatred against a group of persons defined by reference to colour, race, nationality (including citizenship) or ethnic or national origins (s. 17).

For the purposes of offences contrary to ss. 29B to 29C of the 1986 Act, 'religious hatred' means hatred against a group of persons defined by reference to religious belief or lack of religious belief (s. 29A).

Section 29AB of the 1986 Act defines 'hatred on the grounds of sexual orientation'. The definition covers hatred against a group of persons defined by reference to their sexual orientation, be they heterosexual, homosexual or bi-sexual.

3.12.2.1 Use of Words, Behaviour or Display of Written Material

OFFENCE: **Use of Words or Behaviour or Display of Written Material—*Public Order Act 1986, s. 18***

- Triable either way • Seven years' imprisonment and/or a fine on indictment
- Six months' imprisonment and/or a fine summarily

The Public Order Act 1986, s. 18 states:

(1) A person who uses threatening, abusive or insulting words or behaviour, or displays any written material which is threatening, abusive or insulting, is guilty of an offence if—
   (a) he intends thereby to stir up racial hatred, or
   (b) having regard to all the circumstances racial hatred is likely to be stirred up thereby.

(2) An offence under this section may be committed in a public or a private place, except that no offence is committed where the words or behaviour are used, or the written material is displayed, by a person inside a dwelling and are not heard or seen except by other persons in that or another dwelling.

KEYNOTE

This, and the other offences under ss. 19, 29B and 29C, may not be prosecuted without the consent of the Attorney General (or Solicitor General).

This offence does not apply to broadcasts in a programme (but **see para. 3.12.3**) and there are exemptions in the case of fair and accurate reports of parliamentary or court proceedings.

3.12.2.2 Defence

The Public Order Act 1986, s. 18 states:

(4) In proceedings for an offence under this section it is a defence for the accused to prove that he was inside a dwelling and had no reason to believe that the words or behaviour used, or the written material displayed, would be heard or seen by a person outside that or any other dwelling.

3.12.2.3 Publishing or Distributing Written Material

OFFENCE: **Publishing or Distributing Written Material—*Public Order Act 1986, s. 19***

- Triable either way • Seven years' imprisonment and/or a fine on indictment
- Six months' imprisonment and/or a fine summarily

The Public Order Act 1986, s. 19 states:

(1) A person who publishes or distributes written material which is threatening, abusive or insulting is guilty of an offence if—
(a) he intends thereby to stir up racial hatred, or
(b) having regard to all the circumstances racial hatred is likely to be stirred up thereby.
(2) ...
(3) References in this Part to the publication or distribution of written material are to its publication or distribution to the public or a section of the public.

3.12.2.4 Defence

The Public Order Act 1986, s. 19 states:

(2) In proceedings for an offence under this section it is a defence for an accused who is not shown to have intended to stir up racial hatred to prove that he was not aware of the content of the material and did not suspect, and had no reason to suspect, that it was threatening, abusive or insulting.

3.12.2.5 Use of Words, Behaviour or Display of Written Material

OFFENCE: **Use of Words or Behaviour or Display of Written Material—*Public Order Act 1986, s. 29B***

• Triable either way • Not exceeding seven years' imprisonment and/or a fine on indictment • Not exceeding six months' imprisonment and/or a fine summarily

The Public Order Act 1986, s. 29B states:

(1) A person who uses threatening words or behaviour, or displays any written material which is threatening, is guilty of an offence if he intends thereby to stir up religious hatred or hatred on the grounds of sexual orientation.
(2) An offence under this section is committed in a public or private place, except that no offence is committed where the words or behaviour are used, or the written material is displayed, by a person inside a dwelling and are not heard or seen except by other persons in that or another dwelling.

KEYNOTE

The defences available to the offence under s. 18 apply to this particular section (no reason to believe the words or behaviour etc. would be heard or seen outside the dwelling (s. 29B(4)), or where used solely for the purpose of being included in a programming service (s. 29B(5)).

Section 29J of the Act provides that the offences of stirring up religious hatred are not intended to limit or restrict discussion, criticism or expressions of antipathy, dislike, ridicule or insult or abuse of particular religions or belief systems or lack of religion or of the beliefs and practices of those who hold such beliefs or to apply to persons newly converted to a religious faith, evangelism or the seeking to convert people to a particular belief or to cease holding a belief.

In relation to the sexual orientation element of these offences, the relevant act (namely, words, behaviour, written material or recordings or programme) must be threatening, and the offender must intend thereby to stir up hatred on the grounds of sexual orientation.

3.12.2.6 Publishing or Distributing Material

OFFENCE: **Publishing or Distributing Written Material—*Public Order Act 1986, s. 29C***

- Triable either way • Not exceeding seven years' imprisonment and/or a fine on indictment • Not exceeding six months' imprisonment and/or a fine summarily

The Public Order Act 1986, s. 29C states:

(1) A person who publishes or distributes written material which is threatening is guilty of an offence if he intends thereby to stir up religious hatred or hatred on the grounds of sexual orientation.

(2) References in this Part to the publication or distribution of written material are to its publication or distribution to the public or a section of the public.

KEYNOTE

The offences under ss. 29B and 29C differ from the offences of stirring up racial hatred in part 3 of the 1986 Act, in two respects. First, the offences apply only to 'threatening' words or behaviour, rather than 'threatening, abusive or insulting' words or behaviour. Secondly, the offences apply only to words or behaviour if the accused 'intends' to stir up religious hatred or hatred on grounds of sexual orientation, rather than if hatred is either intentional or 'likely' to be stirred up.

3.12.3 Harassment and Stalking

Offences and powers relating to harassment and stalking are contained in the Protection from Harassment Act 1997. To aid understanding, the offences have been broken down into their component parts and follow the order below:

- Harassment contrary to ss. 1 and 2 of the Act (**see para. 3.12.4**). This section includes the law in relation to injunctions and restraining orders.
- Putting people in fear of violence contrary to s. 4 of the Act (**see para. 3.12.5**). This section includes the law in relation to stalking protection orders.
- Stalking contrary to s. 2A of the Act and stalking involving fear of violence etc. contrary to s. 4A of the Act (**see para. 3.12.6**). This section includes the law in relation to stalking protection orders.

3.12.4 Harassment Offences

OFFENCE: **Harassment—*Protection from Harassment Act 1997, ss. 1 and 2***

- Triable summarily • Six months' imprisonment and/or a fine

OFFENCE: **Racially or Religiously Aggravated Harassment—*Crime and Disorder Act 1998, s. 32(1)(a)***

- Triable either way • Two years' imprisonment and/or a fine on indictment
- Six months' imprisonment and/or a fine summarily

The Protection from Harassment Act 1997, ss. 1 and 2 state:

1.—(1) A person must not pursue a course of conduct—
(a) which amounts to harassment of another, and
(b) which he knows or ought to know amounts to harassment of the other.
(1A) A person must not pursue a course of conduct—
(a) which involves harassment of two or more persons, and
(b) which he knows or ought to know involves harassment of those persons, and
(c) by which he intends to persuade any person (whether or not one of those mentioned above)—
(i) not to do something that he is entitled or required to do, or
(ii) to do something that he is not under any obligation to do.

...

2.—(1) A person who pursues a course of conduct in breach of section 1(1) or (1A) is guilty of an offence.

3.12.4.1 'Person' and Companies

'Person' here does not include companies or corporate bodies and therefore they cannot be the 'direct' *victim* of harassment or apply for injunctions as a 'victim' of harassment under this part of the legislation (it is a requirement that there must be evidence of harassment of an individual ('natural') person(s) and not just a corporate body (s. 7(5)). However, an individual employee of a company or a clearly defined group of individuals could be such a victim (*DPP* v *Dziurzynski* [2002] EWHC 1380 (Admin)) and as such they can apply for injunctions (*Daiichi UK Ltd* v *(1) Stop Huntingdon Cruelty, and (2) Animal Liberation Front* [2003] EWHC 2337 (QB)). For companies taking out injunctions *on behalf of* others, **see para. 3.12.4.8**.

In *Majrowski* v *Guy's and St Thomas' NHS Trust* [2005] EWCA Civ 251, the Court of Appeal held that a company could be a 'person' capable of harassing 'another' within the meaning of the Act. Where it can be shown that the conduct was carried out in the course of employment, the employer could be held to be vicariously liable for that conduct.

3.12.4.2 'Course of Conduct'

The 'course of conduct' by a person is defined under s. 7 of the Act which states:

(3) A 'course of conduct' must involve—
(a) in the case of conduct in relation to a single person (see section 1(1)), conduct on at least two occasions in relation to that person, or
(b) in the case of conduct in relation to two or more persons (see section 1(1A)), conduct on at least one occasion in relation to each of those persons.
(3A) A person's conduct on any occasion shall be taken, if aided, abetted, counselled or procured by another—
(a) to be conduct on that occasion of the other (as well as conduct of the person whose conduct it is); and
(b) to be conduct in relation to which the other's knowledge and purpose, and what he ought to have known, are the same as they were in relation to what was contemplated or reasonably foreseeable at the time of the aiding, abetting, counselling or procuring.

(4) 'Conduct' includes speech.
(5) References to a person, in the context of the harassment of a person, are references to a person who is an individual.

KEYNOTE

Establishing a course of conduct, rather than a series of unrelated acts, is crucial to the success of any prosecution for harassment, and '*it is the course of conduct which has to have the quality of amounting to harassment, rather than the individual instances of conduct*' (*Iqbal* v *Dean Manson (Solicitors)* [2011] EWCA Civ 123). The matters said to constitute a course of conduct amounting to harassment must be properly particularised in the information laid or the indictment (*C* v *CPS* [2008] EWHC 148 (Admin)) and must be so connected in type and in context as to justify the conclusion that they amount to a course of conduct. The fewer and further apart the incidents, the less likely it is that they will be so regarded but circumstances can be conceived '*where instances, as far apart as a year, could constitute a course of conduct*' (*Lau* v *DPP* [2000] Crim LR 580). In *Baron* v *CPS* (2000) 13 June, unreported, the defendant wrote two threatening letters to a member of the Benefits Agency staff; he was convicted of harassment even though there had been an interval of four and a half months between the two letters. At the other end of the scale, it was held in *Kelly* v *DPP* [2002] EWHC 1428 (Admin) that three telephone calls made over the space of five minutes could amount to a 'course of conduct', taking into account the separate and distinct nature of the calls. A course of conduct that may initially take the form of a legitimate inquiry or complaint may descend into harassment if unreasonably prolonged or persisted in, as in *DPP* v *Hardy* [2008] EWHC 2874 (Admin), where the defendant made 95 telephone calls over a 90-minute period and threatened to keep calling all night.

There are some incidents that do not amount to harassment. Where a defendant approached a victim to strike up conversations and had sent her a gift, this was insufficient to constitute harassment. However, such incidents could provide a background to later behaviour that included covertly filming the victim and rummaging through her rubbish (*King* v *DPP* [2001] ACD 7).

There is no specific requirement that the activity making up the course of conduct be of the same nature. Therefore, two distinctly different types of behaviour by a defendant (e.g. making a telephone call on one occasion and damaging the victim's property on another) may suffice.

In a case involving the racially or religiously aggravated offence, the aggravating element will need to be proved in relation to both instances of the defendant's conduct.

It appears that doing something remotely which has the desired effect on the victim, such as deliberately making a dog bark at someone, could form part of a 'course of conduct' for the purposes of an offence under the 1997 Act (*R (On the Application of Taffurelli)* v *DPP* [2004] EWHC 2791 (Admin)).

3.12.4.3 'Harassment'

'Harassment' includes alarming the person or causing him/her distress (s. 7(2) of the 1997 Act). The inclusion of alarm and distress is significant as it has been held that a person, in this case a police officer, can be alarmed for the safety of another (*Lodge* v *DPP* [1989] COD 179). Although the words used in s. 7 are 'alarm *and* distress', the Divisional Court has held that they should be taken disjunctively and not conjunctively, that is, the court need only be satisfied that the behaviour involved one or the other; alarm *or* distress (*DPP* v *Ramsdale* [2001] EWHC Admin 106).

3.12.4.4 The s. 1(1A) Offence

The s. 1(1A) offence was introduced specifically to protect employees working for certain companies from harassment by animal rights protestors. Because of the courts' strict interpretation of the elements of the s. 1 offence (as discussed above) it was unclear how far such employees could be protected by this provision when they had not previously been harassed *individually* even where fellow employees had been. Section 1(1A) makes it an offence for a person to pursue a course of conduct involving the harassment of two or more people on separate occasions which the defendant knows or ought to know involves harassment. The purpose of such harassment is to persuade *any person* (not necessarily one of the people being harassed) not to do something he/she is entitled to do (such as going to work) or to do something he/she is not under any obligation to do (such as releasing animals or passing on confidential information).

The sort of behaviour envisaged by the offence would be the making of threats and intimidation which forces an individual or individuals to stop doing lawful business with another company or with another person. The subsection is not intended to outlaw peaceful protesting or lobbying. For instance, a person simply distributing leaflets outside a shop would not commit this offence unless they threatened or intimidated the people to whom they were handing their leaflets and that person felt harassed, alarmed or distressed. There would also need to be at least two separate incidents amounting to 'a course of conduct'.

KEYNOTE

Examples of 'course of conduct' in relation to s. 1(1A) are provided in Home Office Circular 34/2005 and include:

- Where an animal rights extremist sends a threatening letter on one occasion to an individual who works for a company and the same extremist sends a threatening email on another occasion to another individual who works for the same company, and his/her intention is to persuade the individuals that they should not work for that company because of the work that company does, or the contract that it has with other companies, he/she would commit an offence.
- Where an animal rights extremist sends a threatening letter on one occasion to an individual who works for company A and the same extremist sends a threatening email on another occasion to another individual who works for company B, and his/her intention is to persuade the individuals that they should not work for these companies because both companies supply company C, or he/she intends by his/her actions to persuade companies A and B not to supply company C, he/she would commit an offence. In both these examples, if the letters or emails were sent by separate extremists, yet it could be proved that they were acting together, they both would be guilty of an offence. Additionally, under the new s. 3A both an individual employee or a company can apply for an injunction (see para. 3.12.4.8).

3.12.4.5 What a Reasonable Person Would Think Amounts to Harassment

In addition, s. 1 of the 1997 Act states:

> (2) For the purposes of this section, the person whose course of conduct is in question ought to know that it amounts to or involves harassment of another if a reasonable person in possession of the same information would think the course of conduct amounted to or involved harassment of the other.

KEYNOTE

Section 1(2) requires the jury/court to consider whether the defendant ought to have known that his/her conduct amounted to or involved harassment by the objective test of what a 'reasonable person' would think. Section 1(3)(c) also imposes an objective test as to whether that conduct was reasonable in the judgement of the jury/court. As a result, the Court of Appeal has held that no characteristics of the defendant can be attached to the word 'reasonable' (*R* v *Colohan* [2001] EWCA Crim 1251).

Although the defendant's mental illness may be relevant to sentence, the protective and preventive nature of the Act together with the objective nature of the tests above means that such illness does not provide a defence.

3.12.4.6 Aiding and Abetting

If someone aids, abets, counsels or procures another to commit an offence under the 1997 Act, the conduct of the 'primary' defendant will be taken to be the conduct of the aider, abettor, counsellor or procurer of the offence. This does not prevent the primary defendant's conduct from being relevant; what it does is to make the aider, abettor etc. of the offence liable for the conduct which he/she has facilitated. The Act also makes provision for determining the knowledge and intention of aiders, abettors etc. and, although this is referred to as 'collective harassment', it overlaps with the concept of incomplete offences (**see *Crime*, chapter 1.3**).

3.12.4.7 Defences

If the person concerned in the course of conduct can show that he/she did so:

- for the purpose of preventing or detecting crime; or
- under any enactment or rule of law to comply with a particular condition or requirement; or
- in circumstances whereby the course of conduct was reasonable;

the offence under s. 1(1) and (1A) will not apply (s. 1(3)).

The burden of proving any of these features or circumstances lies with the defendant (on the balance of probabilities). Examples might be police or DSS surveillance teams, or court officers serving summonses.

KEYNOTE

In *KD* v *Chief Constable of Hampshire* [2005] EWHC 2550 (QB), a police officer obtained from a female interviewee, over the course of several visits to her home, detailed explicit information about her sexual conduct. The interviewee was the mother of a complainant who had been allegedly raped and assaulted. The court held that the information obtained was not for the purpose of preventing or detecting crime under s. 1(3)(a) but to satisfy the officer's lewd interest.

3.12.4.8 Injunctions to Protect Persons from Harassment

Under ss. 3 and 3A of the Protection from Harassment Act 1997, the High Court or a county court may issue an injunction in respect of civil proceedings brought in respect of an actual or apprehended breach of s. 1(1) and (1A). The effect of this is that a defendant may be made the subject of an injunction even though his/her behaviour has not amounted to an offence under the 1997 Act.

Section 3 also states:

> (3) Where—
> (a) in such proceedings the High Court or a county court grants an injunction for the purpose of restraining the defendant from pursuing any conduct which amounts to harassment, and
> (b) the plaintiff considers that the defendant has done anything which he is prohibited from doing by the injunction, the plaintiff may apply for the issue of a warrant for the arrest of the defendant.

KEYNOTE

The person who is the victim of the offence under s. 1(1A) or any person at whom the persuasion is aimed, may apply for an injunction. Whilst a company cannot be the 'direct' victim of harassment, a company could apply for an injunction on behalf of the employees of the company as 'indirect' victims of the harassment. For example, where people who work for a life science or fur company are being harassed in order to persuade them not to work for that company, or in order to persuade the company not to supply another company, either the employees themselves (the 'direct' victims) or the company in question (the 'indirect' victim) could apply for an injunction.

Section 3A states:

(1) This section applies where there is an actual or apprehended breach of section 1(1A) by any person ('the relevant person').
(2) In such a case—
 (a) any person who is or may be a victim of the course of conduct in question, or
 (b) any person who is or may be a person falling within section 1(1A)(c),
 may apply to the High Court or the county court for an injunction restraining the relevant person from pursuing any conduct which amounts to harassment in relation to any person or persons mentioned or described in the injunction.
(3) Sections 3(3) to (9) apply in relation to an injunction granted under subsection (2) above as they apply in relation to an injunction granted as mentioned in section 3(3)(a).

KEYNOTE

Anyone arrested under a warrant issued under s. 3(3)(b) may be dealt with by the court at the time of his/her appearance. Alternatively, the court may adjourn the proceedings and release the defendant, dealing with him/her within 14 days of his/her arrest provided the defendant is given not less than two days' notice of the adjourned hearing (Rules of the Supreme Court (Amendment) 1998 (SI 1998/1898) and the County Court (Amendment) Rules 1998 (SI 1998/1899)).

In a case involving an injunction restraining the actions of an anti-vivisection group, the Divisional Court held that the 1997 Act was not a means of preventing individuals from exercising their right to protest over issues of public interest. Such an extension of the law had clearly not been Parliament's intention and the courts would resist any attempts to interpret the Act widely (*Huntingdon Life Sciences Ltd* v *Curtin* (1997) *The Times*, 11 December).

The application for an injunction is essentially a private matter being pursued by an individual. The point at which the matter becomes of concern to policing is where the injunction is breached without reasonable excuse. The civil standard of proof (balance of probabilities) will apply to injunction applications (*Hipgrave* v *Jones* [2004] EWHC 2901 (QB)).

In harassment cases, the High Court can grant a provisional injunction under s. 37(1) of the Senior Courts Act 1981. This injunction can restrain conduct which is not in itself tortious or unlawful but is reasonably necessary to protect the legitimate interests of others. This includes the power to impose an exclusion zone when granting a non-molestation injunction (*Burris* v *Azadani* [1995] 1 WLR 1372). However, in *Hall* v *Save Newchurch Guinea Pigs (Campaign)* [2005] EWHC 372 (QB), the court held that a 200 km^2 exclusion zone was not reasonably necessary for the protection of the protected person's rights.

3.12.4.9 Breach of Injunctions

OFFENCE: **Breach of Injunction—*Protection from Harassment Act 1997, s. 3(6)***

- Triable either way • Five years' imprisonment and/or a fine on indictment
- Six months' imprisonment and/or a fine summarily

The Protection from Harassment Act 1997, s. 3 states:

(6) Where—
 (a) the High Court or a county court grants an injunction for the purpose mentioned in subsection (3)(a), and
 (b) without reasonable excuse the defendant does anything which he is prohibited from doing by the injunction,
 he is guilty of an offence.

KEYNOTE

Civil injunctions generally will only involve the police where a power of an arrest has been attached (e.g. under s. 3(3) above). In these cases, the role of the police will be to bring the defendant before the court in order that he/she can explain his/her behaviour. There is therefore no investigative or prosecuting function on the part of the officers. Section 3(6), however, creates a specific offence of breaching the terms of an injunction.

3.12.4.10 Civil Claims for Harassment

Under s. 3(1), conduct or apprehended conduct falling within s. 1(1) and (1A) may be the subject of a civil claim by the victim/intended victim. This creates a 'statutory tort' of harassment in addition to the criminal offence.

3.12.4.11 Restraining Orders

Section 5A of the Act enables the courts in England and Wales to impose a restraining order for the purpose of protecting a person from conduct which amounts to harassment or will cause a fear of violence (**see para. 3.12.5**) by the defendant. The court will be able to make a restraining order on acquittal for any offence where it considers it necessary to protect a person from harassment. The order can be made for a specified period or be indefinite (until further order). The prosecutor, the defendant or any other person mentioned in the order may apply to the court that made the order for it to be varied or discharged by a further order (s. 5A(2B)). Any person mentioned in the order is entitled to be heard on the hearing of such an application (s. 5A(2C)). It is a criminal offence to breach a restraining order. As an either way offence, it can be tried in the magistrates' court (where the maximum penalty upon conviction is six months' imprisonment) or in the Crown Court before a jury (where the maximum penalty on conviction is five years).

3.12.5 Putting People in Fear of Violence

OFFENCE: **Putting People in Fear of Violence—*Protection from Harassment Act 1997, s. 4***

- Triable either way • 10 years' imprisonment and/or a fine on indictment
- Six months' imprisonment and/or a fine summarily

OFFENCE: **Racially or Religiously Aggravated—*Crime and Disorder Act 1998, s. 32(1)(b)***

- Triable either way • 14 years' imprisonment and/or a fine on indictment
- Six months' imprisonment and/or a fine summarily

The Protection from Harassment Act 1997, s. 4 states:

> (1) A person whose course of conduct causes another to fear, on at least two occasions, that violence will be used against him is guilty of an offence if he knows or ought to know that his course of conduct will cause the other so to fear on each of those occasions.

KEYNOTE

'Course of conduct' is discussed at para. 3.12.4.2.

The defendant's course of conduct must cause the victim to fear that violence *will* (rather than might) be used against *him/her* (rather than someone else) so:

- showing that the conduct caused the victim to be seriously frightened of what *might happen* in the future is not enough (*R* v *Henley* [2000] Crim LR 582);

- causing a person to fear, on at least two occasions, that violence would be used against a member of their family is not enough (*Mohammed Ali Caurti* v *DPP* [2001] EWHC Admin 867).

The defendant must know, or ought to know that their conduct will cause the other person to fear violence. This may be shown by any previous conversations or communications between the defendant and the victim, together with the victim's response to the defendant's earlier behaviour (e.g. running away, calling the police etc.).

The fear of violence being used against the victim must be present on both occasions. If it is present on one occasion but not the other, the offence under s. 2 above may be appropriate. This is not necessarily as straightforward as it may seem. What if the defendant's conduct on the first occasion (e.g. a threat to burn the victim's house down) did not cause the victim undue concern, but a second threat some time later to do the same thing *did* put the victim in fear of violence, partly because this was the second time the threat had been made? These were the circumstances in *R (On the Application of A)* v *DPP* [2004] EWHC 2454 (Admin), where the defendant argued that the victim had only been put in fear of violence by his threats to burn her house down on the second occasion and that therefore the offence had not been made out. The Divisional Court disagreed and held that the magistrates were entitled to find as a matter of fact that the two incidents had put the victim in fear of violence, notwithstanding her admission that, on the first occasion, she had not been too concerned.

Unlike some of the other racially or religiously aggravated offences, provisions are specifically made for alternative verdicts in relation to harassment (s. 32(6) of the Crime and Disorder Act 1998). Where the racially or religiously aggravated form of the offence is charged, the aggravating element of the defendant's conduct must be shown in relation to both instances.

As with the s. 2 offence, a single instance of behaviour may be enough to support a charge for another offence.

This offence is not one of *intent* but one which is subject to a test of reasonableness against the standard of an ordinary person in possession of the same information as the defendant.

For the powers of a court to issue a restraining order in relation to this offence, see para. 3.12.4.11.

The Protection from Harassment Act 1997, s. 4 goes on to state:

(2) For the purposes of this section, the person whose course of conduct is in question ought to know that it will cause another to fear that violence will be used against him on any occasion if a reasonable person in possession of the same information would think the course of conduct would cause the other so to fear on that occasion.

Section 4(2) takes the same approach as s. 1(2)—whether a course of conduct is 'reasonable' will be a question of fact for a court to decide (an objective test).

3.12.5.1 Defence

The Protection from Harassment Act 1997, s. 4 states:

(3) It is a defence for a person charged with an offence under this section to show that—
  (a) his course of conduct was pursued for the purpose of preventing or detecting crime,
  (b) his course of conduct was pursued under any enactment or rule of law or to comply with any condition or requirement imposed by any person under any enactment, or
  (c) the pursuit of his course of conduct was reasonable for the protection of himself or another or for the protection of his or another's property.

KEYNOTE

There is a slight difference in the wording of the defence when compared with that under s. 1(3) above. There, the defendant may show that his/her conduct was reasonable in the particular circumstances. In relation to the offence under s. 4, the defendant must show that his/her conduct was reasonable *for the protection of him/herself, another person or his/her own/another's property.* These are the only grounds on which the defendant may argue reasonableness in answer to a charge under s. 4. He/she could not therefore argue, say, that the pursuit of the course of conduct was 'reasonable' in order to enforce a debt or to communicate with the victim.

In addition, s. 12 allows for the Secretary of State to certify that the conduct was carried out by a 'specified person' on a 'specified occasion' related to:

- national security;
- the economic well-being of the United Kingdom; or
- the prevention or detection of serious crime;

on behalf of the Crown. If such a certification is made, the conduct of the specified person will not be an offence under the 1997 Act.

3.12.6 Stalking Offences and Stalking Protection Orders

Offences of 'stalking' are set out under ss. 2A and 4A of the Protection from Harassment Act 1997.

3.12.6.1 The Offence of Stalking

OFFENCE: **Stalking—*Protection from Harassment Act 1997, s. 2A***

- Triable summarily • Six months' imprisonment and/or a fine

OFFENCE: **Racially or Religiously Aggravated Stalking—*Crime and Disorder Act 1998, s. 32(1)(a)***

- Triable either way • Two years' imprisonment and/or a fine on indictment
- Six months' imprisonment and/or a fine summarily

The Protection from Harassment Act 1997, s. 2A states:

> (1) A person is guilty of an offence if—
> (a) the person pursues a course of conduct in breach of s. 1(1), and
> (b) the course of conduct amounts to stalking.

For the purposes of the offence under s. 2A (and also the following offence under s. 4A below), a course of conduct amounts to stalking of another person if:

- it amounts to harassment of that person;
- the acts or omissions involved are ones associated with stalking; and
- the person whose course of conduct it is knows or ought to know that the course of conduct amounts to harassment of the other person.

KEYNOTE

What is 'Stalking'?

Section 2A(3) lists examples of behaviours associated with stalking. The list is not exhaustive but gives an indication of the types of behaviour that may be displayed in a stalking offence. The listed behaviours are:

- following a person;
- contacting, or attempting to contact, a person by any means;
- publishing any statement or other material (i) relating or purporting to relate to a person, or (ii) purporting to originate from a person;
- monitoring the use by a person of the internet, email or any other form of electronic communication;
- loitering in any place (whether public or private);
- interfering with any property in the possession of a person;
- watching or spying on a person.

Section 2A does not include a specific defence for stalking. However, because an offence of stalking can only be established where an offence of harassment has occurred, a person charged with an offence under s. 2A could rely on the defence to harassment under s. 1(3) (see para. 3.12.4.7)

Under s. 2B of the Act, the police have a power of entry in relation to the s. 2A stalking offence. A constable can apply to a justice of the peace, who may issue a warrant authorising entry and search of premises providing there are reasonable grounds to believe the conditions in s. 2B are met. A constable may seize and retain anything for which a search was authorised, and may use reasonable force, if necessary, in the exercise of any power conferred by s. 2B.

3.12.6.2 Stalking Involving Fear of Violence or Serious Alarm or Distress

OFFENCE: **Stalking Involving Fear of Violence or Serious Alarm or Distress—*Protection from Harassment Act 1997, s. 4A***

- Triable either way • 10 years' imprisonment and/or an unlimited fine on indictment
- Six months' imprisonment and/or a fine summarily

OFFENCE: **Racially or Religiously Aggravated Stalking Involving Fear of Violence or Serious Alarm or Distress—*Crime and Disorder Act 1998, s. 32(1)(b)***

- Triable either way • 14 years' imprisonment and/or a fine on indictment
- Six months' imprisonment and/or a fine summarily

The Protection from Harassment Act 1997, s. 4A states:

(1) A person ('A') whose course of conduct—
  (a) amounts to stalking, and
  (b) either—
    (i) causes another ('B') to fear, on at least two occasions, that violence will be used against B, or
    (ii) causes B serious alarm or distress which has a substantial adverse effect on B's usual day-to-day activities,

  is guilty of an offence if A knows or ought to know that A's conduct will cause B so to fear on each of those occasions or (as the case may be) will cause such alarm or distress.

(2) For the purposes of this section A ought to know that A's course of conduct will cause B to fear that violence will be used against B on any occasion if a reasonable person in possession of the same information would think the course of conduct would cause B so to fear on that occasion.

(3) For the purposes of this section A ought to know that A's course of conduct will cause B serious alarm or distress which has a substantial adverse effect on B's usual day-to-day activities if a reasonable person in possession of the same information would think the course of conduct would cause B such alarm or distress.

KEYNOTE

Section 4A(2) and (3) means that whether a course of conduct is 'reasonable' will be a question of fact for a court to decide (an objective test).

The phrase 'substantial adverse effect on the usual day-to-day activities' is not defined in s. 4A; however, the Home Office considers that evidence of a substantial adverse effect caused by the stalker may include:

- victims changing their routes to work, work patterns or employment;
- victims arranging for friends or family to pick up children from school (to avoid contact with the stalker);
- victims putting in place additional security measures in their home;
- victims moving home;
- physical or mental ill-health;
- victims' deterioration in performance at work due to stress;
- victims stopping or changing the way they socialise.

Although some victims try to continue their existing routines in defiance of a stalker, they may still be able to evidence substantial impact on their usual day-to-day activities, depending on the individual case.

Under s. 4A(4), there is a defence to the offence of stalking involving fear of violence or serious alarm or distress which is a mirror image of the defence to the offence under s. 4 (**see para. 3.12.5.1**).

3.12.6.3 Stalking Protection Orders

The Stalking Protection Act 2019, s. 1 states:

Applications for orders

(1) A chief officer of police may apply to a magistrates' court for an order (a 'stalking protection order') in respect of a person (the 'defendant') if it appears to the chief officer that—
   (a) the defendant has carried out acts associated with stalking,
   (b) the defendant poses a risk associated with stalking to another person, and
   (c) there is reasonable cause to believe the proposed order is necessary to protect another person from such a risk (whether or not the other person was the victim of the acts mentioned in paragraph (a)).

(2) A stalking protection order is an order which, for the purpose of preventing the defendant from carrying out acts associated with stalking—
   (a) prohibits the defendant from doing anything described in the order, or
   (b) requires the defendant to do anything described in the order.

KEYNOTE

A risk associated with stalking may be in respect of physical or psychological harm to the other person or may arise from acts which the defendant knows or ought to know are unwelcome to the other person even if, in other circumstances, the acts would appear harmless in themselves (s. 1(4)). It is irrelevant whether the acts mentioned in subs. (1)(a) are carried out in the UK or elsewhere (s. 1(5)).

The Protection from Harassment Act 1997, s. 2A provides examples of acts associated with stalking (see para. 3.12.6.1).

3.12.6.4 Power to Make Stalking Protection Orders

The Stalking Protection Act 2019, s. 2 states:

Power to make orders

(1) A magistrates' court may make a stalking protection order on an application under section 1(1) if satisfied that—
   (a) the defendant has carried out acts associated with stalking,
   (b) the defendant poses a risk associated with stalking to another person, and
   (c) the proposed order is necessary to protect another person from such a risk (whether or not the other person was the victim of the acts mentioned in paragraph (a)).

(2) A magistrates' court may include a prohibition or requirement in a stalking protection order only if satisfied that the prohibition or requirement is necessary to protect the other person from a risk associated with stalking.

(3) Prohibitions or requirements must, so far as practicable, be such as to avoid—
   (a) conflict with the defendant's religious beliefs, and
   (b) interference with any times at which the defendant normally works or attends an educational establishment.

KEYNOTE

A prohibition or requirement has effect in all parts of the UK unless expressly limited to a particular locality (s. 2(4)).

An order may be for a fixed period of at least two years or until a further order is made (s. 3(1) and (2)). Different periods may be specified in relation to different prohibitions or requirements (s. 3(3)).

A person who, without reasonable excuse, breaches a stalking protection order or an interim stalking protection order commits an offence (s. 8(1)) and is liable on summary conviction, to 12 months' imprisonment and/or a fine, and on conviction on indictment, to five years' imprisonment and/or a fine (s. 8(2)).

3.12.7 Police Direction to Prevent Intimidation or Harassment

The Criminal Justice and Police Act 2001 gives the police specific powers to prevent the intimidation or harassment of people in their own or others' homes. Situations envisaged by the legislation typically arise where protestors gather outside a house where a particular individual is believed to be. Under such circumstances, s. 42 provides a constable at the scene with discretionary powers to give directions to people in the vicinity. The Criminal Justice and Police Act 2001, s. 42 states:

> (1) Subject to the following provisions of this section, a constable who is at the scene may give a direction under this section to any person if—
> (a) that person is present outside or in the vicinity of any premises that are used by any individual ('the resident') as his dwelling;
> (b) that constable believes, on reasonable grounds, that that person is present there for the purpose (by his presence or otherwise) of representing to the resident or another individual (whether or not one who uses the premises as his dwelling), or of persuading the resident or such another individual—
> (i) that he should not do something that he is entitled or required to do; or
> (ii) that he should do something that he is not under any obligation to do;
> and
> (c) that constable also believes, on reasonable grounds, that the presence of that person (either alone or together with that of any other persons who are also present)—
> (i) amounts to, or is likely to result in, the harassment of the resident; or
> (ii) is likely to cause alarm or distress to the resident.

KEYNOTE

Although the premises involved may be in use by any 'individual' (e.g. not a company) and the purpose may be to persuade that or any other 'individual', the officer must believe that the ultimate effect will be harassment, alarm or distress of the resident.

The direction may be given orally and, where appropriate, may be given to a group of people together (s. 42(3)). There is no requirement that the officer giving the direction be in uniform.

A direction given under s. 42 requires the person(s) to do all such things as the officer specifies as being necessary to prevent the harassment, alarm or distress of the resident, including:

- a requirement to leave the vicinity of the premises in question (s. 42(4)(a)); and
- a requirement to leave that vicinity and not to return to it within such period as the constable may specify, not being longer than three months (s. 42(4)(b));

and (in either case) the requirement to leave the vicinity may be to do so immediately or after a specified period of time (s. 42(4)). Although s. 42(1) refers to 'a constable' giving the direction, this shall not include any power to give a direction at any time when there is a more senior-ranking police officer at the scene (s. 42(6)).

3.12.7.1 Contravening a s. 42 Direction

OFFENCE: **Knowingly Contravening a s. 42 Direction—*Criminal Justice and Police Act 2001, s. 42(7)***

- Triable summarily • Three months' imprisonment and/or a fine

The Criminal Justice and Police Act 2001, s. 42 states:

> (7) Any person who knowingly fails to comply with a requirement in a direction given to him under this section (other than a requirement under subsection (4)(b)) shall be guilty of an offence.

KEYNOTE

Generally, the best proof that the direction was 'given to them' will be to show that the person had received the direction (and the detail of its extent) personally and that he/she understood it. Therefore, although the section allows for directions to be given to groups, there may be practical benefits in giving personal directions where circumstances allow.

The reference to s. 42(4)(b) means a requirement to leave that vicinity and not to return to it within such period as the constable may specify, not being for a period longer than three months.

OFFENCE: **Unlawfully Returning to Vicinity—*Criminal Justice and Police Act 2001, s. 42(7A)***

- Triable summarily • Imprisonment for a term not exceeding six months and/or a fine

The Criminal Justice and Police Act 2001, s. 42 states:

(7A) Any person to whom a constable has given a direction including a requirement under subsection (4)(b) commits an offence if he—

(a) returns to the vicinity of the premises in question within the period specified in the direction beginning with the date on which the direction is given; and

(b) does so for the purpose described in subsection (1)(b).

KEYNOTE

The offence is committed where a person who is subject to a direction to leave the vicinity, returns within a period of up to three months (the precise length of time will be specified by the police officer) for the 'purposes' described at s. 42A(1)(b) (**see para. 3.12.7.2**)—representing to or persuading a person not to do something he/she is entitled to do, or to do something he/she is not obliged to do.

3.12.7.2 Harassment etc. of Person in their Home

OFFENCE: **Harassment of a Person in their Home—*Criminal Justice and Police Act 2001, s. 42A***

- Triable summarily • Imprisonment for a term not exceeding six months and/or a fine

The Criminal Justice and Police Act 2001, s. 42A states:

(1) A person commits an offence if—

(a) that person is present outside or in the vicinity of any premises that are used by any individual ('the resident') as his dwelling;

(b) that person is present there for the purpose (by his presence or otherwise) of representing to the resident or another individual (whether or not one who uses the premises as his dwelling), or of persuading the resident or such another individual—

(i) that he should not do something that he is entitled or required to do; or

(ii) that he should do something that he is not under any obligation to do;

(c) that person—

(i) intends his presence to amount to the harassment of, or to cause alarm or distress to, the resident; or

(ii) knows or ought to know that his presence is likely to result in the harassment of, or to cause alarm or distress to, the resident; and

(d) the presence of that person—

(i) amounts to the harassment of, or causes alarm or distress to, any person falling within subsection (2); or

(ii) is likely to result in the harassment of, or to cause alarm or distress to, any such person.

(2) A person falls within this subsection if he is—

(a) the resident,

(b) a person in the resident's dwelling, or

(c) a person in another dwelling in the vicinity of the resident's dwelling.

KEYNOTE

This offence has a number of elements, each of which must be proved if a successful prosecution is to be brought. The ingredients include:

- Place—the defendant must be shown to have been in the relevant place (outside or in the vicinity of a 'dwelling'). 'Dwelling' means any structure or part of a structure occupied as a person's home or as other living accommodation (whether the occupation is separate or shared with others) but does not include any part not so occupied (s. 42A(7)).
- Purpose—the defendant's purpose in being there must be to represent to, or persuade, the resident/another individual that he/she should not do something he/she is entitled/required to do or that he/she should do something that he/she is not under any obligation to do.
- Intention/knowledge—you must prove that the defendant intended his/her presence to amount to harassment of, or to cause alarm or distress to, the resident or that he/she knew/ought to have known that his/her presence was likely to have that result.
- Consequences—you must show that the defendant's presence amounted to/was likely to result in the harassment of, or causing alarm or distress to, any resident, person in the resident's dwelling or person in another dwelling in the vicinity of the resident's dwelling.

References in s. 42A(1)(c) and (d) to a person's presence are references either to his/her presence alone or together with that of any other people who are also present (s. 42A(3)).

For the purposes of this section, a person ought to know that his/her presence is likely to result in the harassment of, or to cause alarm or distress to, a resident if a reasonable person in possession of the same information would think that it was likely to have that effect (s. 42A(4)).

3.13 Offences and Powers Relating to Information and Communications

3.13.1 Introduction

This chapter examines the relevant provisions of the Computer Misuse Act 1990, Data Protection Act 2018, the Regulation of Investigatory Powers Act 2000, the Malicious Communications Act 1988, the Online Safety Act 2023, the Communications Act 2003 and the Fire and Rescue Services Act 2004.

Article 8 (Right to Respect for Private and Family Life, Home and Correspondence) of the European Convention on Human Rights has implications for the law in relation to all these areas, as well as other areas contained in this Manual.

3.13.2 Article 8—Right to Respect for Private and Family Life, Home and Correspondence

Article 8 of the Convention states:

1. Everyone has the right to respect for his private and family life, his home and his correspondence.
2. There shall be no interference by a public authority with the exercise of this right except such as is in accordance with the law and is necessary in a democratic society in the interests of national security, public safety or the economic well being of the country, for the prevention of disorder or crime, for the protection of health or morals, or for the protection of the rights and freedoms of others.

KEYNOTE

The provisions of Article 8 extend a right to respect for a person's private life, family life, home and correspondence.

This Article protects these features of a person's life from arbitrary interference by 'public authorities' (*Kroon* v *Netherlands* (1995) 19 EHRR 263). 'Public authorities' include a court, tribunal or groups which are concerned solely with discharging functions of a public nature or those which have some public functions (s. 6 of the Human Rights Act 1998). However, the Convention does allow for individuals to raise issues of unjustified interference with their private lives and the courts have held that even celebrities have a basic right to privacy which will be protected by Article 8 (*Campbell* v *Mirror Group Newspapers* [2004] UKHL 22); similar arguments can be found in *Theakston* v *Mirror Group Newspapers* [2002] EWHC 137 (QB).

The State is under a duty not to interfere with a person's life except in accordance with Article 8(2). Many police activities, such as entry onto premises, surveillance and the seizure of property, touch upon the features covered by Article 8.

Another reason why this Article is of importance to police services is that the State also has a positive obligation to prevent others from interfering with an individual's right to private life (*Stjerna* v *Finland* (1994) 24 EHRR 194). How far the police would have to go in order to discharge this obligation is unclear, but Article 8 will be relevant in many areas and in particular community safety.

It is here that the notion of balancing the rights and freedoms of individuals against each other and against those of the community at large can be seen most acutely.

3.13.3 Offences under the Computer Misuse Act 1990

The Computer Misuse Act 1990 was introduced to ensure that penalties relating to 'hacking' into computer systems, unauthorised access to computer material, the intentional serious hindering of a computer system and importing tools for cyber crime, reflect the seriousness of the criminal activities that can be involved in committing these offences.

3.13.3.1 Unauthorised Access to Computer Materials

OFFENCE: **Unauthorised Access to Computer Material ('Hacking')—*Computer Misuse Act 1990, s. 1***

- Triable either way • Two years' imprisonment and/or a fine on indictment
- Imprisonment for a term not exceeding the general limit in a magistrates' court and/or a fine summarily

The Computer Misuse Act 1990, s. 1 states:

(1) A person is guilty of an offence if—
  (a) he causes a computer to perform any function with intent to secure access to any program or data held in any computer;
  (b) the access he intends to secure is unauthorised; and
  (c) he knows at the time when he causes the computer to perform the function that that is the case.
(2) The intent a person has to have to commit an offence under this section need not be directed at—
  (a) any particular program or data;
  (b) a program or data of any particular kind; or
  (c) a program or data held in any particular computer.

KEYNOTE

'Computer' is not defined and therefore must be given its ordinary meaning. Given the multiple functions of many electronic devices such as mobile phones, this could arguably bring them within the ambit of the Act.

This offence involves 'causing a computer to perform any function', which means more than simply looking at material on a screen or having any physical contact with computer hardware. In the latter case, an offence of criminal damage may be appropriate. Any attempt to log on would involve getting the computer to perform a function (even if the function is to deny you access!).

In s. 17(5) of the Act (**see para. 3.13.3.2**), access is unauthorised where a person is not entitled to control access or does not have consent to access a program or data.

In the case of *DPP* v *Bignell* [1998] 1 Cr App R 1, two police officers obtained information from the Police National Computer (PNC) for their own personal use. A request was made by the officers in the proper form for an authorised computer operator to obtain the information from the PNC. The computer operator himself did not exceed his authority as he was permitted to access the data on the computer for the purpose of responding to such requests. Extracting data from a computer by a person who was otherwise generally authorised to use the computer, but in this case for an unauthorised purpose, does not constitute the offence of unlawful access.

In the case of *R* v *Bow Street Metropolitan Stipendiary Magistrates' Court, ex parte Government of the USA* [2000] 2 AC 216, the House of Lords considered whether an employee could commit an offence of securing 'unauthorised access' to a computer under this section. It was held that the employee clearly came within the provisions of s. 1 where a person intentionally caused a computer to give them entry to data which they knew they were not authorised to enter. An employee would only be guilty of an offence if the employer clearly defined the limits of the employee's authority to access a program or data.

The purpose of the Act was to criminalise the breaking into or hacking of computer systems to preserve the integrity of computer systems.

This is an offence of 'specific intent' and it must be show that a person intended to secure access to the program or data. It is also necessary to show that the person knew the access was unauthorised.

In *R* v *Coltman* [2018] EWCA Crim 2059, an NHS employee used the computer of a colleague to access a file to which he had no authorised access. The material from that file was later passed by the defendant to a newspaper. The Court of Appeal rejected the defence that the material was disclosed in the public interest.

Where a person had accessed programs on his own computer, these having been copied by him without payment and hence in breach of copyright, it was held that there was no offence in accessing programs in breach of copyright (*Bellencs* v *Hungary* [2023] EWHC 2235 (Admin)).

The Privacy and Electronic Communications (EC Directive) Regulations 2003 (SI 2003/2426) regulate the use of cookies and internet tracking devices, along with the use of unsolicited email and text messages. Guidance in their extent and practical effect is prepared by the Information Commissioner's Office (ICO).

The powers of entry, search and seizure under the Police and Criminal Evidence Act 1984 apply to this offence.

3.13.3.2 Definition of Terms

The 1990 Act defines a number of its terms at s. 17, which states:

(2) A person secures access to any program or data held in a computer if by causing a computer to perform any function he—
- (a) alters or erases the program or data;
- (b) copies or moves it to any storage medium other than that in which it is held or to a different location in the storage medium in which it is held;
- (c) uses it; or
- (d) has it output from the computer in which it is held (whether by having it displayed or in any other manner);

and references to access to a program or data (and to an intent to secure such access) shall be read accordingly.

(3) For the purposes of subsection (2)(c) above a person uses a program if the function he causes the computer to perform—
- (a) causes the program to be executed; or
- (b) is itself a function of the program.

(4) For the purposes of subsection (2)(d) above—
- (a) a program is output if the instructions of which it consists are output; and
- (b) the form in which any such instructions or any other data is output (and in particular whether or not it represents a form in which, in the case of instructions, they are capable of being executed or, in the case of data, it is capable of being processed by a computer) is immaterial.

(5) Access of any kind by any person to any program or data held in a computer is unauthorised if—
- (a) he is not himself entitled to control access of the kind in question to the program or data; and
- (b) he does not have consent to access by him of the kind in question to the program or data from any person who is so entitled,

but this subsection is subject to section 10.

(6) References to any program or data held in a computer include references to any program or data held in any removable storage medium which is for the time being in the computer; and a computer is to be regarded as containing any program or data held in any such medium.

. . .

(8) An act done in relation to a computer is unauthorised if the person doing the act (or causing it to be done)—
- (a) is not himself a person who has responsibility for the computer and is entitled to determine whether the act may be done; and
- (b) does not have consent to the act from any such person.

In this subsection 'act' includes a series of acts.

KEYNOTE

Securing access will therefore include:

- altering or erasing a program or data;
- copying or moving a program or data to a new storage medium;
- using data or having it displayed or 'output' in any form from the computer in which it is held.

Under s. 17(5), access is 'unauthorised' if the person is neither entitled to control that type of access to a program or data, nor does he/she have the consent of any person who is so entitled. The provision under s. 17(5)(a) was the basis for the decision in *Bow Street* (see para. 3.13.3.1). This definition does not affect the powers available to any 'enforcement officers', i.e. police officers or other people charged with a duty of investigating offences (s. 10).

3.13.3.3 Unauthorised Access to Computers with Intent

OFFENCE: **Unauthorised Access with Intent to Commit Further Offences—*Computer Misuse Act 1990, s. 2***

- Triable either way • Five years' imprisonment and/or a fine on indictment
- Imprisonment for a term not exceeding the general limit in a magistrates' court and/or a fine summarily

The Computer Misuse Act 1990, s. 2 states:

(1) A person is guilty of an offence under this section if he commits an offence under section 1 above ('the unauthorised access offence') with intent—
(a) to commit an offence to which this section applies; or
(b) to facilitate the commission of such an offence (whether by himself or by any other person); and the offence he intends to commit or facilitate is referred to below in this section as the further offence.
(2) This section applies to offences—
(a) for which the sentence is fixed by law; or
(b) for which a person of twenty-one years of age or over (not previously convicted) may be sentenced to imprisonment for a term of five years (or, in England and Wales, might be so sentenced but for the restrictions imposed by section 33 of the Magistrates' Courts Act 1980).
(3) It is immaterial for the purposes of this section whether the further offence is to be committed on the same occasion as the unauthorised access offence or on any future occasion.
(4) A person may be guilty of an offence under this section even though the facts are such that the commission of the further offence is impossible.

KEYNOTE

The defendant must be shown to have had the required intent at the time of the access or other *actus reus*.

The intended further offence does not have to be committed at the same time, but may be committed in future (e.g. where the data is used to commit an offence of blackmail or to secure the transfer of funds from a bank account).

The provision as to impossibility (s. 2(4)) means that a person would still commit the offence if he/she tried, say, to access the bank account of a person who did not in fact exist.

3.13.3.4 Unauthorised Acts with Intent to Impair Operation of Computer, etc.

OFFENCE: **Unauthorised Acts with Intent to Impair, or with Recklessness as to Impairing, Operation of Computer, etc.—*Computer Misuse Act 1990, s. 3***

- Triable either way • 10 years' imprisonment and/or a fine on indictment
- Imprisonment for a term not exceeding the general limit in a magistrates' court and/or a fine summarily

The Computer Misuse Act 1990, s. 3 states:

(1) A person is guilty of an offence if—
  (a) he does any unauthorised act in relation to a computer;
  (b) at the time when he does the act he knows that it is unauthorised; and
  (c) either subsection (2) or subsection (3) below applies.
(2) This subsection applies if the person intends by doing the act—
  (a) to impair the operation of any computer;
  (b) to prevent or hinder access to any program or data held in any computer; or
  (c) to impair the operation of any such program or the reliability of any such data.
(3) This subsection applies if the person is reckless as to whether the act will do any of the things mentioned in paragraphs (a) to (c) of subsection (2) above.

KEYNOTE

This section is designed to ensure that adequate provision is made to criminalise all forms of denial of service attacks in which the attacker denies the victim(s) access to a particular resource, typically by preventing legitimate users of a service from accessing that service. An example of this is where a former employee, acting on a grudge, impaired the operation of a company's computer by using a program to generate and send five million emails to the company (*DPP* v *Lennon* [2006] EWHC 1201 (Admin)).

The intention referred to in s. 3(2), or the recklessness referred to in s. 3(3), need not relate to any particular computer, any particular program or data, or a program or data of any particular kind (s. 3(4)). An 'unauthorised act' can include a series of acts, and a reference to impairing, preventing or hindering something includes a reference to doing so temporarily (s. 3(5)).

The 'hindering' provided by this section is intended to cover programs that generate denial of service attacks, such as by sending a virus or malware.

Causing a computer to record that information came from one source when it in fact came from another clearly affects the reliability of that information for the purposes of s. 3(2)(c) (*Zezev* v *USA*; *Yarimaka* v *Governor of HM Prison Brixton* [2002] EWHC 589 (Admin)).

3.13.3.5 Unauthorised Acts Causing, or Creating Risk of, Serious Damage

OFFENCE: **Unauthorised Acts Causing, or Creating Risk of, Serious Damage—*Computer Misuse Act 1990, s. 3ZA***

- Triable on indictment • 14 years' imprisonment and/or a fine

The Computer Misuse Act 1990, s. 3ZA states:

(1) A person is guilty of an offence if—
  (a) the person does any unauthorised act in relation to a computer;
  (b) at the time of doing the act the person knows that it is unauthorised;
  (c) the act causes, or creates a significant risk of, serious damage of a material kind; and
  (d) the person intends by doing the act to cause serious damage of a material kind or is reckless as to whether such damage is caused.
(2) Damage is of a 'material kind' for the purposes of this section if it is—
  (a) damage to human welfare in any place;
  (b) damage to the environment of any place;
  (c) damage to the economy of any country; or
  (d) damage to the national security of any country.
(3) For the purposes of subsection (2)(a) an act causes damage to human welfare only if it causes—
  (a) loss to human life;
  (b) human illness or injury;
  (c) disruption of a supply of money, food, water, energy or fuel;
  (d) disruption of a system of communication;
  (e) disruption of facilities for transport; or
  (f) disruption of services relating to health.

(4) It is immaterial for the purposes of subsection (2) whether or not an act causing damage—
   (a) does so directly;
   (b) is the only or main cause of the damage.

KEYNOTE

Reference to doing an act includes a reference to causing an act to be done, and 'act' includes a series of acts. In reference to a country, this includes a reference to a territory, and to any place in, or part or region of, a country or territory (s. 3ZA(5)).

Where an offence under this section is committed as a result of an act causing or creating a significant risk of serious damage to human welfare of the kind mentioned in s. 3ZA(3)(a) or (b), or serious damage to national security, a person guilty of the offence is liable, on conviction on indictment, to imprisonment for life, or to a fine, or to both (s. 3ZA(7)).

Section 3ZA(1) sets out the elements of the offence. The *actus reus* (or conduct element) is that the accused undertakes an unauthorised act in relation to a computer (as in s. 3(1)(a) of the 1990 Act) and that act causes, or creates a significant risk of causing, serious damage of a material kind. The *mens rea* (namely, the mental elements of the offence) is that the accused, at the time of committing the act, knows that it is unauthorised (as in s. 3(1)(b) of the 1990 Act) and intends the act to cause serious damage of a material kind or is reckless as to whether such damage is caused. An unauthorised act is defined in s. 17(8) of the 1990 Act as an act where the person doing the act does not have responsibility for the computer in question, which would thereby entitle him/her to determine whether the act is undertaken, and does not have the consent of the person responsible for the computer to commit the act.

3.13.3.6 Making, Supplying or Obtaining Articles for Use in Offences under s. 1, 3 or 3ZA

OFFENCE: **Making, Supplying or Obtaining Articles for Use in Offences under s. 1, 3 or 3ZA—*Computer Misuse Act 1990, s. 3A***

- Triable either way • Two years' imprisonment and/or a fine on indictment
- Imprisonment for a term not exceeding the general limit in a magistrates' court and/or a fine summarily

The Computer Misuse Act 1990, s. 3A states:

(1) A person is guilty of an offence if he makes, adapts, supplies or offers to supply any article intending it to be used to commit, or to assist in the commission of, an offence under section 1, 3 or 3ZA.
(2) A person is guilty of an offence if he supplies or offers to supply any article believing that it is likely to be used to commit, or to assist in the commission of, an offence under section 1, 3 or 3ZA.
(3) A person is guilty of an offence if he obtains any article—
   (a) intending to use it to commit, or to assist in the commission of, an offence under section 1, 3 or 3ZA, or
   (b) with a view to its being supplied for use to commit, or to assist in the commission, of, an offence under section 1, 3 or 3ZA.
(4) In this section 'article' includes any program or data held in electronic form.

KEYNOTE

This section creates three offences designed to combat the market in electronic tools, such as 'hacker tools' which can be used for hacking into computer systems, and the increase in the use of such tools in connection with organised crime.

3.13.4 The Data Protection Act 2018 and the UK General Data Protection Regulation

The Data Protection Act 2018 provides a comprehensive legal framework for data protection in the United Kingdom. The Act sets standards for protecting personal data in accordance with the UK General Data Protection Regulation (UK GDPR). The UK GDPR was adopted in 2021 to replace the European Union GDPR following the United Kingdom's exit from the EU (Data Protection, Privacy and Electronic Communications (Amendments etc) (EU Exit) Regulations 2019). The Data (Use and Access) Act 2025 reforms how the United Kingdom manages non-personal and personal data and aims to unlock the secure and effective use of data. It amends parts of the 2018 Act and the UK GDPR.

The Regulation applies to the automated or structured processing of personal data. It does not apply to:

(a) the processing of personal data by an individual in the course of a purely personal or household activity;
(b) the processing of personal data by a competent authority for any law enforcement purposes;
(c) the processing of personal data to which part 4 of the 2018 Act (intelligence services processing) applies.

(UK GDPR, Article 2)

The responsibility for compliance with the principles relating to processing of personal data rests on the shoulders of the 'controller', meaning an employer, public authority, agency or any other body which alone or jointly with others determines the purposes and means of the processing of personal data (Article 24).

The Information Commissioner is the lead enforcer of the Data Protection Act 2018 and the UK GDPR and is responsible for monitoring their application to protect the fundamental rights and freedoms of natural persons in relation to processing and to facilitate the free flow of personal data (Article 51).

3.13.4.1 Personal Data

The Data Protection Act 2018, s. 2 states:

Protection of personal data

(1) The UK GDPR and this Act protect individuals with regard to the processing of personal data, in particular by—
  (a) requiring personal data to be processed lawfully and fairly, on the basis of the data subject's consent or another specified basis,
  (b) conferring rights on the data subject to obtain information about the processing of personal data and to require inaccurate personal data to be rectified, and
  (c) conferring functions on the Commissioner, giving the holder of that office responsibility for monitoring and enforcing their provisions.

KEYNOTE

The UK GDPR, Article 4, provides the following definitions for the purpose of this Regulation:

1. 'personal data' means any information relating to an identified or identifiable natural person ('data subject'); an identifiable natural person is one who can be identified, directly or indirectly, in particular by reference to an identifier such as a name, an identification number, location data, an online identifier or to one or more factors specific to the physical, physiological, genetic, mental, economic, cultural or social identity of that natural person
2. 'processing' means any operation or set of operations which is performed on personal data or on sets of personal data, whether or not by automated means, such as collection, recording, organisation, structuring, storage, adaptation or alteration, retrieval, consultation, use, disclosure by transmission, dissemination or otherwise making available, alignment or combination, restriction, erasure or destruction;

The UK GDPR covers the processing of personal data in two ways: personal data processed wholly or partly by automated means (i.e. information in electronic form); and personal data processed in a non-automated manner which forms part of, or is intended to form part of, a 'filing system' (i.e. manual information in a filing system). The notion of processing means 'any operation or set of operations which is performed upon personal data, whether or not by automatic means, such as collection, recording, organization, storage, adaptation or alteration, retrieval, consultation, use, disclosure by transmission, dissemination or otherwise making available, alignment or combination, blocking, erasure or destruction' (Article 2).

The UK GDPR, Article 6, provides that processing is lawful only if and to the extent that at least one of the following applies:

(a) the data subject has given consent to the processing of his or her personal data for one or more specific purposes;
(b) processing is necessary for the performance of a contract to which the data subject is party or in order to take steps at the request of the data subject prior to entering into a contract;
(c) processing is necessary for compliance with a legal obligation to which the controller is subject;
(d) processing is necessary in order to protect the vital interests of the data subject or of another natural person;
(e) processing is necessary for the performance of a task of the controller carried out in the public interest or a task carried out in the exercise of official authority vested in the controller;
(ea) processing is necessary for the purposes of a recognised legitimate interest;
(f) processing is necessary for the purposes of the legitimate interests pursued by the controller or by a third party, except where such interests are overridden by the interests or fundamental rights and freedoms of the data subject which require protection of personal data, in particular where the data subject is a child.

According to Article 7: 'The data subject shall have the right to withdraw his or her consent at any time. The withdrawal of consent shall not affect the lawfulness of processing based on consent before its withdrawal. Prior to giving consent, the data subject shall be informed thereof. It shall be as easy to withdraw as to give consent.'

The data subject has the right to obtain from the controller confirmation as to whether or not personal data concerning him/her are being processed, and, where that is the case, access to the personal data and the following information:

- the purposes of the processing;
- the categories of personal data concerned;
- the recipients or categories of recipient to whom the personal data have been or will be disclosed, in particular recipients in third countries or international organisations;
- where possible, the envisaged period for which the personal data will be stored or, if not possible, the criteria used to determine that period;
- the existence of the right to request from the controller rectification or erasure of personal data or restriction of processing of personal data concerning the data subject or to object to such processing.

Under para. 1, the data subject is only entitled to such confirmation, personal data and other information as the controller is able to provide based on a reasonable and proportionate search for the personal data and other information described in that paragraph (Article 15).

3.13.4.2 Sensitive Personal Data

Some of the personal data that may be processed can be more sensitive in nature and therefore requires a higher level of protection. The UK GDPR refers to the processing of this data as 'special categories of personal data'.

The UK GDPR, Article 9, provides for the Processing of Special Categories of Personal Data:

1. Processing of personal data revealing racial or ethnic origin, political opinions, religious or philosophical beliefs, or trade union membership, and the processing of genetic data, biometric data for the purpose of uniquely identifying a natural person, data concerning health or data concerning a natural person's sex life or sexual orientation shall be prohibited.

However, Article 9(2) provides a number of exceptions to this prohibition, for example where the data subject has given explicit consent or where processing is necessary for reasons of substantial public interest, for the purposes of preventive or occupational medicine, for reasons of public interest in the area of public health, for archiving purposes in the public interest and for scientific or historical research purposes.

KEYNOTE

There must still be a lawful basis for processing special category data under Article 6, in exactly the same way as for any other personal data.

This type of data could create more significant risks to a person's fundamental rights and freedoms, for example by putting them at risk of unlawful discrimination. Additional specific conditions need to be satisfied in relation to this type of data (Article 9(2)).

Conditions applicable to children's consent in relation to information society services are provided by Article 8:

1. Where point (a) of Article 6(1) applies, in relation to the offer of information society services directly to a child, the processing of the personal data of a child shall be lawful where the child is at least 13 years old. Where the child is below the age of 13 years, such processing shall be lawful only if and to the extent that consent is given or authorised by the holder of parental responsibility over the child.
2. The controller shall make reasonable efforts to verify in such cases that consent is given or authorised by the holder of parental responsibility over the child, taking into consideration available technology.

3.13.4.3 Principles Relating to Processing of Personal Data

The six data protection principles are central to UK GDPR compliance and all organisations are required to comply and demonstrate privacy by design.

The GDPR requires an organisation to show how it complies with the principles, for example by documenting the decisions taken about a processing activity.

The principles relating to processing of personal data are provided by the UK GDPR, Article 5, which states:

1. Personal data shall be:
   (a) processed lawfully, fairly and in a transparent manner in relation to the data subject ('lawfulness, fairness and transparency');
   (b) collected (whether from the data subject or otherwise) for specified, explicit and legitimate purposes and not further processed by or on behalf of a controller in a manner that is incompatible with those purposes; further processing for archiving purposes in the public interest, scientific or historical research purposes or statistical purposes shall, in accordance with Article 89(1), not be considered to be incompatible with the initial purposes the purposes for which the controller collected the data ('purpose limitation');
   (c) adequate, relevant and limited to what is necessary in relation to the purposes for which they are processed ('data minimisation');
   (d) accurate and, where necessary, kept up to date; every reasonable step must be taken to ensure that personal data that are inaccurate, having regard to the purposes for which they are processed, are erased or rectified without delay ('accuracy');
   (e) kept in a form which permits identification of data subjects for no longer than is necessary for the purposes for which the personal data are processed; personal data may be stored for longer periods insofar as the personal data will be processed solely for archiving purposes in the public interest, scientific or historical research purposes or statistical purposes in accordance with Article 89(1) subject to implementation of the appropriate technical and organisational measures required by this Regulation in order to safeguard the rights and freedoms of the data subject ('storage limitation');
   (f) processed in a manner that ensures appropriate security of the personal data, including protection against unauthorised or unlawful processing and against accidental loss, destruction or damage, using appropriate technical or organisational measures ('integrity and confidentiality').

2. The controller shall be responsible for, and be able to demonstrate compliance with, paragraph 1 ('accountability').
3. For the avoidance of doubt, processing is not lawful by virtue only of being processing in a manner that is compatible with the purposes for which the personal data was collected.

3.13.4.4 Offences Relating to Personal Data

The 2018 Act creates a number of offences in relation to personal data, proceedings for which can only be instigated by the Commissioner, or with the consent of the Director of Public Prosecutions.

These offences include:

- Knowingly or recklessly obtaining or disclosing personal data without the consent of the controller (s. 170(1)).
- Selling personal data if the person obtained the data in circumstances in which an offence under subs. (1) was committed (s. 170(4)).
- Offering to sell personal data, etc. (s. 170(5)).
- Knowingly or recklessly re-identifying information that is de-identified personal data without the consent of the controller responsible for de-identifying the personal data (s. 171(1)).
- Knowingly or recklessly processing personal data that is information that has been re-identified where the person does so without the consent of the controller, etc. (s. 171(5)).
- The controller, or person employed by the controller, alters, defaces, blocks, erases, destroys or conceals information with the intention of preventing disclosure of all or part of the information that the person making the request would have been entitled to receive (s. 173(3)).

KEYNOTE

The s. 170 and s. 171 offences are triable either way (s. 196(2)). The s. 173 offence is summary only (s. 196(1)). Other indictable offences are contained within the Act that relate to the current or former ICO or a member of the ICO's staff.

3.13.5 The Regulation of Investigatory Powers Act 2000

The Regulation of Investigatory Powers Act 2000 (RIPA) is the Act governing the law in relation to the use of covert techniques by *public authorities* regarding the use of human intelligence sources and surveillance. It requires that when the police or other law enforcement bodies (e.g. the Serious Fraud Office or the National Crime Agency (NCA)), the security and intelligence services (MI5, MI6 and GCHQ) as well as a large number of other public bodies, including local government, need to use these covert techniques to obtain private information about a person, they do so in a way that is necessary, proportionate and compatible with human rights. Surveillance measures necessarily involve some interference with private life but have the legitimate aim of protecting national security and economic well-being (*Kennedy* v *United Kingdom* (2011) 52 EHRR 4).

In a policing context, any breach of the Act's provisions, or the provisions contained in the Codes of Practice, issued by the Secretary of State under s. 71, can have three main consequences:

- any evidence obtained may be excluded by a court or tribunal as being unfair;
- proceedings may be taken under the relevant police conduct regulations; or
- a person may make a claim before the Investigatory Powers Tribunal.

3.13.5.1 Surveillance and Covert Human Intelligence Sources

Part II of the Regulation of Investigatory Powers Act 2000, s. 26 states:

(1) This Part applies to the following conduct—
 (a) directed surveillance;
 (b) intrusive surveillance;
 (c) the conduct and use of covert human intelligence sources; and
 (d) criminal conduct in the course of or otherwise in connection with, the conduct of covert human intelligence sources.

KEYNOTE

Although only s. 26(1)(c) expressly uses the word 'covert' for the nature of the activity, it is relevant to *all four* of these areas. Part II is concerned with covert activity and so, as a general rule, if it is not covert, it is not covered. Similarly, the 'interception of communication' contained in parts 1 to 7 of the Investigatory Powers Act 2016 is also outside the scope of this Manual.

Some law enforcement activities fall outside the scope of the Act, e.g. 'property interference' which is a very intrusive form of intelligence gathering such as attaching listening devices within people's homes. This type of activity is covered by part III of the Police Act 1997 and is beyond the scope of this Manual.

3.13.5.2 Covert Human Intelligence Sources (CHIS): Definition

The following, which relates to s. 26, is an extract from the Covert Human Intelligence Sources Revised Code of Practice (December 2022), ch. 2, which states:

Definition of a covert human intelligence source (CHIS)

2.1 Under the 2000 Act, a person is a CHIS if:
- they establish or maintain a personal or other relationship with a person for the covert purpose of facilitating the doing of anything falling within paragraph 26(8)(b) or (c);
- they covertly use such a relationship to obtain information or to provide access to any information to another person; or
- they covertly disclose information obtained by the use of such a relationship or as a consequence of the existence of such a relationship.

See section 26(8) of the 2000 Act.

2.2 A relationship is established or maintained for a covert purpose if and only if it is conducted in a manner that is calculated to ensure that one of the parties to the relationship is unaware of the purpose.

See section 26(9)(b) of the 2000 Act for full definition.

2.3 A relationship is used covertly, and information obtained is disclosed covertly, if and only if the relationship is used or the information is disclosed in a manner that is calculated to ensure that one of the parties to the relationship is unaware of the use or disclosure in question.

See section 26(9)(c) of the 2000 Act for full definition.

2.4 The Regulation of Investigatory Powers (Covert Human Intelligence Sources: Relevant Source) Order 2013 ('the 2013 Relevant Sources Order') further defines a particular type of CHIS as a 'relevant source'. This is a source holding an office, rank or position with the public authorities listed in the Order and Annex B to this code. Enhanced authorisation arrangements are in place for this type of CHIS as detailed in this code. Such sources will be referred to as a 'relevant source' throughout this code.

2.5 Any police officer deployed as a 'relevant source' in England and Wales will be required to comply with and uphold the principles and standards of professional behaviour set out in the College of Policing Code of Ethics.

KEYNOTE

Covert

A purpose is 'covert' here only if the relationship (and the subsequent disclosure of information) is conducted in a manner that is calculated to ensure that one of the parties is unaware of that purpose. Therefore the definition would not usually apply to members of the public generally supplying information to the police. Similarly, people who have come across information in the ordinary course of their jobs who suspect criminal activity (such as bank staff, local authority employees etc.) do not have a covert relationship with the police simply by passing on information.

Great care will be needed, however, if the person supplying the information is asked by the police to do something further in order to develop or enhance it. Any form of direction or tasking by the police in this way could make the person a CHIS and thereby attract all the statutory provisions and safeguards.

Use and Conduct

There are two areas to be considered when considering covert human intelligence sources: the 'use' of a CHIS and 'conduct' as a CHIS. Both areas are strictly controlled by the legislation and require the relevant authorisation if they are to be lawful.

The 'use' of a CHIS involves any action on behalf of a public authority to induce, ask or assist a person to engage in the conduct of a CHIS, or to obtain information by means of the conduct of a CHIS (s. 26(7)(b)).

The conduct of a CHIS is any conduct of a CHIS which falls within para. 2.1 above, that is, steps taken by the CHIS on behalf, or at the request, of a public authority (s. 26(7)(a)). Most CHIS authorisations will be for both use and conduct as public authorities usually task the CHIS to undertake covert action, and because the CHIS will be expected to take action in relation to the public authority, such as responding to particular tasking.

Generally, covertly recording conversations and other personal information about a particular person will amount to some form of 'surveillance' (and therefore will be governed by the strict rules regulating such operations). However, such use of a CHIS will not amount to 'surveillance' (s. 48(3)).

Note that, apart from the many other considerations of using a CHIS, the police owe a duty to take reasonable care to avoid unnecessary disclosure to the general public of information provided by a CHIS (*Swinney v Chief Constable of Northumbria (No. 2)* (1999) 11 Admin LR 811).

3.13.5.3 CHIS: General Rules on Authorisations

In relation to the authorisation of a CHIS by the police, the Regulation of Investigatory Powers Act 2000, s. 29 states:

Authorisation of covert human intelligence sources.

(1) Subject to the following provisions of this Part, the persons designated for the purposes of this section shall each have power to grant authorisations for the conduct or the use of a covert human intelligence source.

(2) A person shall not grant an authorisation for the conduct or the use of a covert human intelligence source unless he believes—

(a) that the authorisation is necessary on grounds falling within subsection (3);

(b) that the authorised conduct or use is proportionate to what is sought to be achieved by that conduct or use; and

(c) that arrangements exist for the source's case that satisfy—

(i) the requirements of subsection (4A), in the case of a source of a relevant collaborative unit;

(ii) . . .

(iii) the requirements of subsection (5), in the case of any other source;

and that satisfy such other requirements as may be imposed by order made by the Secretary of State.

(2A) For the meaning of 'relevant collaborative unit' in subsection (2)(c)(i), see section 29A.

(3) An authorisation is necessary on grounds falling within this subsection if it is necessary—
(a) in the interests of national security;
(b) for the purpose of preventing or detecting crime or of preventing disorder;
(c) in the interests of the economic well-being of the United Kingdom;
(d) in the interests of public safety;
(e) for the purpose of protecting public health;
(f) for the purpose of assessing or collecting any tax, duty, levy or other imposition, contribution or charge payable to a government department; or
(g) for any purpose (not falling within paragraphs (a) to (f)) which is specified for the purposes of this subsection by an order made by the Secretary of State.

KEYNOTE

Note that in relation to s. 29(3)(b), preventing and detecting crime is defined in s. 81(5) and goes beyond the prosecution of offenders and includes actions taken to avert, end or disrupt the commission of criminal offences.

An authorisation under this section may not have the effect of authorising a covert human intelligence resource who is a person designated under s. 38 of the Police Reform Act 2002 to establish contact in person with another person (subs. (6A)). However, although a designated staff member or volunteer would not be able to work undercover face-to-face, they could do so online, for example as part of an online child sexual abuse investigation.

An authorisation for the conduct or the use of a covert human intelligence source does not authorise any criminal conduct in the course of, or otherwise in connection with, the conduct of a covert human intelligence source (s. 29(6ZA)). See s. 29B (**see para. 3.13.5.5**) for provision for the authorisation of such conduct.

For the purposes of section 29(2)(c)(i), a 'relevant collaborative unit' is a unit that either consists of two or more police forces whose chief officers of police have made an agreement under s. 22A of the Police Act 1996 (s. 29A(2)) or it consists of one or more police forces and the National Crime Agency by virtue of an agreement made under s. 22A (s. 29A(3)).

The following extract from the Covert Human Intelligence Sources Code of Practice, ch. 3, explains the terms 'necessary' and 'proportionate' contained within s. 29(2) and details the extent of authorisations:

Necessity and Proportionality—Section 29 use or conduct authorisations

3.2 The 2000 Act requires that the person granting a Section 29 authorisation believes that the use or conduct to be authorised is necessary on one or more of the statutory grounds listed in Section 29(3) of the 2000 Act.

3.3 If the use or conduct is deemed necessary on one or more of the statutory grounds, the person granting the authorisation must also believe that the use or conduct to be authorised is proportionate to what is sought to be achieved by it.

3.4 The degree of intrusiveness of the actions tasked or undertaken by a CHIS will vary from case to case, and therefore proportionality must be assessed on a case-by-case basis. This involves balancing the seriousness of the intrusion into the private or family life of the subject of the operation (and any other person who may be affected) against what is sought to be achieved by the proposed activity in investigative and operational terms.

3.5 The authorisation will not be proportionate if it is excessive in the overall circumstances of the case. Each action authorised should bring an expected benefit to the investigation or operation and should not be disproportionate or arbitrary. The fact that any activity under investigation may involve serious offences will not alone render the use or conduct of a CHIS proportionate. Similarly, the activity under investigation may involve an offence so minor that any use or conduct of a CHIS would be disproportionate. No activity should be considered proportionate if the information which is sought could reasonably be obtained by other less intrusive means.

3.6 The following elements of proportionality should therefore be considered:

- balancing the size and scope of the proposed activity against the gravity and extent of the perceived crime or harm;
- explaining how and why the methods to be adopted will cause the least possible intrusion on the subject and others;
- whether the conduct to be authorised will have any implications for the private and family life of others, and an explanation of why (if relevant) it is nevertheless proportionate to proceed with the operation;
- evidencing, as far as reasonably practicable, what other methods had been considered and why they were not implemented, or have been implemented unsuccessfully;
- considering whether the activity is an appropriate use of the legislation and a reasonable way, having considered all reasonable alternatives, of obtaining the information sought.

Extent of authorisations

3.16 A CHIS authorisation may authorise conduct that:

- involves the use or conduct of a CHIS, including criminal conduct by or in relation to that CHIS, as is specified or described in the authorisation;

- is carried out by or in relation to the person to whom the authorisation relates; and
- is carried out for the purposes of, or in connection with, the investigation or operation so described.

3.17 In the above context, it is important that those involved in the use of a CHIS are aware of the extent and limits of the authorisation in question and that the CHIS is made aware of the extent and limits of any conduct authorised (including criminal conduct).

KEYNOTE

Authorising officers are also required to take into account collateral intrusion; namely, the risk of any impact on persons who are not the intended subjects of the CHIS activity. Particular consideration should be given in cases where religious, medical, journalistic or legally privileged material may be involved. Where such collateral intrusion is unavoidable, the authorisation may still be granted, providing this collateral intrusion is considered proportionate to the aims of the intended intrusion. Any collateral intrusion should be kept to the minimum necessary to achieve the objective of the operation (Code of Practice, para. 3.18).

They are also required to be aware of any particular sensitivities in the local community and to any adverse impact on community confidence or safety (para. 3.27).

3.13.5.4 CHIS: Authorisation Procedures

The following extract from the Covert Human Intelligence Sources Code of Practice, ch. 5, outlines authorisation procedures for the use or conduct of a CHIS:

Authorisation Procedures

5.4 Responsibility for authorising the use or conduct of a CHIS rests with the authorising officer and all authorisations require the personal authority of the authorising officer. The 2010 CHIS Order sets out the seniority of prescribed office, rank and or position that an authorising officer must hold for each different public authority and the same in respect of those officers entitled to act only in urgent cases. In certain circumstances the Secretary of State will be the authorising officer (see section 30(2) of the 2000 Act).

5.5 The authorising officer must grant authorisations in writing, except in urgent cases, where they may be given orally. In such cases, a statement that the authorising officer has expressly authorised the action should be recorded in writing by the applicant (or the person with whom the authorising officer spoke) as a priority. This statement need not contain the full detail of the application, which should however subsequently be recorded in writing when reasonably practicable (generally the next working day).

5.6 Officers entitled to act only in urgent cases are empowered to grant authorisation in writing only e.g. written authorisation for use or conduct of a Relevant Source granted by a Superintendent.

5.7 A case is not normally to be regarded as urgent unless the time that would elapse before the authorising officer was available to grant the authorisation would, in the judgment of the person giving the authorisation, be likely to endanger life or jeopardise the operation or investigation for which the authorisation was being granted. An authorisation is not to be regarded as urgent where the need for an authorisation has been neglected or the urgency is of the applicant's or authorising officer's own making.

KEYNOTE

Authorising CHIS

Authorising officers should, where possible, be independent of the investigation. However, it is recognised that this is not always possible, especially in the cases of small organisations, or where it is necessary to act urgently or for security reasons.

The Regulation of Investigatory Powers (Directed Surveillance and Covert Human Intelligence Sources) Order 2010 (SI 2010/521, as amended by SI 2013/2788) prescribes the ranks of those within the police service in England and Wales who can authorise a CHIS. The ranks, mode of authorisation and associated time frames are summarised below:

Type of Authorisation	→	Ordinary CHIS	Urgent CHIS
		↓	↓
Minimum Rank	→	Superintendent or above	Inspector or above
		↓	↓
Form	→	In writing	Inspector—in writing Superintendent—in writing or oral
		↓	↓
Time Frame	→	12 months beginning on the day the authorisation is granted	72 hours beginning from the time authorisation is granted

The relevant rank of an authorising officer for a CHIS is a superintendent and above. However, in urgent cases where it is not reasonably practicable to have the application considered by someone of that rank in the same organisation, an inspector may generally give the relevant authorisation (sch. 1, part 1 to the 2010 Order). Unless it is renewed, the authorisation given by a superintendent will ordinarily cease to have effect after 12 months beginning on the day it was granted (s. 43(3)(b)). If that authorisation was given orally by a superintendent in an urgent case, it will only last for 72 hours unless renewed, and where the case is urgent and the authority was given by an inspector, it will cease to have effect 72 hours later unless renewed (s. 43(3)(a)).

Authorisations may also be made on an application made by a member of another police force where such a police force is party to a collaborative agreement that provides for this (s. 33(3ZA)–(3ZC)).

Long-term authorisations (those exceeding 12 months) can only be given by a chief constable/commissioner and are subject to approval by a Judicial Commissioner.

A single authorisation can combine two or more different authorisations (e.g. the use of surveillance and the use of a CHIS) but they operate independently of each other (s. 43(2)). This means that when one authorisation lapses, any other authorisations made at the same time do not necessarily end as well.

Authorising 'Relevant Sources'

The ranks, mode of authorisation and associated time frames are summarised below:

Type of Authorisation	→	Ordinary 'Relevant Source'	Urgent 'Relevant Source'
		↓	↓
Minimum Rank	→	ACC/Commander or above	Superintendent or above
		↓	↓
Form	→	In writing	In writing
		↓	↓
Time Frame	→	12 months beginning on the day the authorisation is granted	72 hours beginning from the time authorisation is granted

All deployments of undercover officers (referred to in the Order and Code as 'relevant sources') must be authorised by an assistant chief constable/commander or in urgent cases by a superintendent.

Authorisations lasting more than 12 months must be approved by a chief constable/commissioner and the Investigatory Powers Commissioner's Office must give prior approval (sch. 1, part 1A to the 2010 Order). The CHIS Code of Practice states that all police officers deployed as a relevant source must comply with the College of Policing Code of Ethics.

Authorising Juvenile/Vulnerable CHIS

The ranks, mode of authorisation and associated time frames are summarised below:

Type of Authorisation	→	Juvenile/Vulnerable CHIS
		↓
Minimum Rank	→	ACC/Commander
		↓
Form	→	In writing
		↓
Time Frame	→	Four months beginning on the day the authorisation is granted

Special safeguards apply in relation to juveniles and vulnerable individuals. Juveniles are those under 18 years of age. On no occasion should the use or conduct of a CHIS under 16 years of age be authorised to give information against his/her parents or any person who has parental responsibility for him/her. In other cases, authorisations should not be granted unless the special provisions contained within the Regulation of Investigatory Powers (Juveniles) (Amendment) Order 2018 (SI 2018/715) are satisfied.

A vulnerable individual is a person aged 18 or over who is or may be in need of community care services by reason of mental or other disability, age or illness and who is or may be unable to take care of him/herself, or unable to protect him/herself against significant harm or exploitation.

The authorisation levels for juveniles and vulnerable individuals are assistant chief constable/commander where they are to be used as sources. Regular reviews of authorisations are required to assess whether it remains necessary and proportionate to use a CHIS and whether the authorisation remains justified. An authorisation must be cancelled if the use or conduct of the CHIS no longer satisfies the criteria for authorisation.

In *R (On the Application of Just for Kids Law)* v *Secretary of State for the Home Department* [2019] EWHC 1772 (Admin), the court held that the scheme relating to the use of a juvenile CHIS adequately protects children's welfare and their Article 8 rights.

An enhanced authorisation regime exists when, through the use or conduct of a CHIS, it is likely that knowledge of legally privileged material or other confidential information will be required. The authorisation level where confidential information is likely to be acquired is a chief constable or assistant commissioner (the Regulation of Investigatory Powers (Covert Human Intelligence Sources: Matters Subject to Legal Privilege) Order 2010 (SI 2010/521, as amended by SI 2013/2788)).

3.13.5.5 CHIS: Criminal Conduct Authorisations

The Regulation of Investigatory Powers Act 2000, s. 29B states:

(1) Subject to the following provisions of this Part, the persons designated for the purposes of this section each have power to grant criminal conduct authorisations.

(2) A 'criminal conduct authorisation' is an authorisation for criminal conduct in the course of, or otherwise in connection with, the conduct of a covert human intelligence source.

(3) A criminal conduct authorisation may only be granted in relation to a covert human intelligence source after, or at the same time as, an authorisation under section 29 which authorises the conduct or the use of the covert human intelligence source concerned.

(4) A person may not grant a criminal conduct authorisation unless the person believes—
- (a) that the authorisation is necessary on grounds falling within subsection (5);
- (b) that the authorised conduct is proportionate to what is sought to be achieved by that conduct; and
- (c) that arrangements exist that satisfy such requirements as may be imposed by order made by the Secretary of State.

(5) A criminal conduct authorisation is necessary on grounds falling within this subsection if it is necessary—
- (a) in the interests of national security;
- (b) for the purpose of preventing or detecting crime or of preventing disorder; or
- (c) in the interests of the economic well-being of the United Kingdom.

KEYNOTE

In satisfying the requirements in subs. (4)(a) and (b), the person must take into account whether what is sought to be achieved by the authorised conduct could reasonably be achieved by other conduct which would not constitute crime (s. 29B(6)).

Section 29B(8) provides that the conduct that is authorised by a criminal conduct authorisation is any conduct that:

(a) is comprised in any activities—
   (i) which involve criminal conduct in the course of, or otherwise in connection with, the conduct of a covert human intelligence source, and
   (ii) are specified or described in the authorisation;

(b) consists in conduct by or in relation to the person who is so specified or described as the covert human intelligence source to whom the authorisation relates; and

(c) is carried out for the purposes of, or in connection with, the investigation or operation so specified or described.

Authorisation may be granted only where necessary and proportionate (e.g. because there are no other practicable means of preventing a more serious crime) and cannot include a licence to kill or torture.

The following is an extract from the Covert Human Intelligence Sources Revised Code of Practice (December 2022), ch. 6, in relation to applications for criminal conduct authorisations:

Notification to Judicial Commissioners—Criminal Conduct Authorisations

6.15 The Investigatory Powers Commissioner is required by statute to, in particular, keep under review the exercise of the power to grant Criminal Conduct Authorisations.

6.16 Where a person grants, renews or cancels a Criminal Conduct Authorisation under Section 29B of the 2000 Act, they must give notice to a Judicial Commissioner at the Investigatory Powers Commissioner's Office.

6.17 The notice must be given as soon as reasonably practicable and within seven days of the authorisation being granted, renewed, or cancelled.

6.18 The notice must set out the grounds on which the person giving the notice believes the authorisation to be necessary and proportionate and must specify what conduct is authorised.

6.19 In respect of the grant of an authorisation, the conduct that has been authorised can begin as soon as the authorisation has been granted by the Authorising Officer; there is no requirement to wait for comments from a Judicial Commissioner before commencing the activity.

6.20 Where a Judicial Commissioner makes observations in relation to a notification, it is for the Authorising Officer to determine what action should be taken. Having consulted with a more senior officer, they must, as soon as reasonably practicable, notify the Investigatory Powers Commissioner's Office of the intended action, or where action has been taken (for example in urgent cases) of the action.

Information to be provided in applications for authorisation of criminal conduct

6.21 An application for the authorisation of participation in criminal conduct by a CHIS should be in writing and record:

- the Section 29 authorisation to which it relates;
- the reasons why the authorisation is necessary in the particular case and on which of the grounds listed in Section 29B(5) of the 2000 Act;
- the purpose for which the CHIS will be tasked to participate in criminal conduct;
- the nature of what the criminal conduct will be;
- the reasons why the criminal conduct is considered proportionate to what it seeks to achieve;
- the details of any material subject to legal privilege or other confidential material that may be obtained as a consequence of the authorisation;
- where the intention is to acquire knowledge of matters subject to legal privilege, the exceptional and compelling circumstances that make the authorisation necessary;
- the level of authorisation required;
- a subsequent record of whether authorisation was given or refused, by whom and the time and date.

6.22 The authorisation should have clear parameters set out for the CHIS to ensure they are clear about the criminal conduct in which they are being authorised to participate.

6.23 Additionally, in urgent cases, the authorisation should record (as the case may be):

- the reasons why the Authorising Officer considered the case so urgent that an oral Instead of a written authorisation was granted; or
- the reasons why the officer entitled to act only in urgent cases considered the case so urgent and why it was not reasonably practicable for the application to be considered by the Authorising Officer.

6.24 Where the authorisation is oral, the detail referred to above should be recorded in writing by the applicant when reasonably practicable (generally the next working day).

6.25 When completing an application, the applicant must ensure that the case for the authorisation is presented in the application in a fair and balanced way. In particular, all reasonable efforts should be made to take account of information which weakens the case for the authorisation.

6.26 The criminal conduct that may be authorised is not limited to criminal conduct by a CHIS: a Criminal Conduct Authorisation may authorise conduct by someone else 'in relation to' a CHIS, namely those within a public authority that are involved in or affected by the authorisation.

Duration of authorisations

6.27 A written authorisation will, unless renewed or cancelled, cease to have effect at the end of a period of twelve months beginning with the day on which it took effect, except in the case of juvenile CHIS (four months—see paragraph 4.8) or where it is intended to obtain, provide access to or disclose knowledge of matters subject to legal privilege (three or six months—see paragraph 5.18 above).

6.28 A Criminal Conduct Authorisation can last no longer than the related Section 29 authorisation and will cease to have effect if the related Section 29 authorisation is cancelled or expires.

6.29 The duration of a Criminal Conduct Authorisation that is granted or renewed orally will last only for a period of seventy-two hours beginning when the grant of the authorisation or, as the case may be, its latest renewal takes effect.

6.30 A Criminal Conduct Authorisation should be cancelled as soon as reasonably practicable after the authorised conduct has been undertaken or if the conduct is no longer necessary or proportionate. The CHIS should be notified that their conduct is no longer authorised, and a full record should be kept of anything said to/by the CHIS on that issue.

KEYNOTE

The relevant source for authorising a criminal conduct CHIS is assistant chief constable (commander) and for long-term authorisations it is chief constable (assistant commissioner). A superintendent may give authorisation in urgent cases (Regulation of Investigatory Powers (Criminal Conduct Authorisations) (Amendment) Order 2021 (SI 2021/601)).

3.13.5.6 Criminal Conduct Authorisations: Safeguards for Juveniles

The Regulation of Investigatory Powers Act 2000, s. 29C states:

Criminal conduct authorisations: safeguards for juveniles

(1) This section applies in relation to the grant of a juvenile criminal conduct authorisation.

(2) 'A juvenile criminal conduct authorisation' is an authorisation under section 29B for criminal conduct in the course of, or otherwise in connection with, the conduct of a covert human intelligence source where that source is under the age of 18 ('the juvenile source').

(3) In addition to satisfying the requirements of section 29B, a person may grant a juvenile criminal conduct authorisation only if—
 (a) the person has considered the results of an appropriate risk assessment;
 (b) there are exceptional circumstances such that—
  (i) it is not reasonably foreseeable in the circumstances as the person believes them to be that any harm to the juvenile source would result from the grant of the authorisation, and
  (ii) the person believes the authorisation would be compatible with the need to safeguard and promote the best interests of the juvenile source; and
 (c) the person believes that appropriate arrangements for meetings are in force.

KEYNOTE

'An appropriate risk assessment' means an assessment which identifies and evaluates the nature and magnitude of the risks of harm to the juvenile source arising in the course of, or as result of, the conduct authorised by the authorisation (s. 29C(4)). 'Harm' means physical injury or psychological distress.

Authorisations for vulnerable adults are similar to those for juveniles. Vulnerable adults are persons aged 18 years or older and are vulnerable by reason of mental disorder or vulnerability, disability, age or illness, or who may be unable to take care of themselves or to protect themselves against significant harm or exploitation (s. 29D).

3.13.5.7 Covert Surveillance

The Covert Surveillance and Property Interference Revised Code of Practice (February 2024) provides:

2 Activity by public authorities to which this code applies

2.1 Part II of the 2000 Act provides for the *authorisation* of covert surveillance by *public authorities* listed at Schedule 1 of the 2000 Act where that surveillance is likely to result in the obtaining of *private information* about a person.

2.2 Surveillance, for the purpose of the 2000 Act, includes monitoring, observing or listening to persons, their movements, conversations or other activities and communications. It may be conducted with or without the assistance of a surveillance device and includes the recording of any information obtained.
(See section 48(2) of the 2000 Act)

2.3 Surveillance is covert if, and only if, it is carried out in a manner calculated to ensure that any persons who are subject to the surveillance are unaware that it is or may be taking place.
(As defined in section 26(9)(a) of the 2000 Act)

2.4 Specifically, covert surveillance may be authorised under the 2000 Act if it is either intrusive or directed:

- Directed surveillance is covert surveillance that is not intrusive but is carried out in relation to a specific investigation or operation in such a manner as is likely to result in the obtaining of *private information* about any person (other than by way of an immediate response to events or circumstances such that it is not reasonably practicable to seek *authorisation* under the 2000 Act);
- Intrusive surveillance is covert surveillance that is carried out in relation to anything taking place on residential premises or in any private vehicle (and that involves the presence of an individual on the premises or in the vehicle or is carried out by a means of a surveillance device).

KEYNOTE

Private Information

Private information includes any information relating to a person's private or family life (s. 26(10)). It should be taken generally to include any aspect of a person's private or personal relationship with others, including family. Family should be treated as extending beyond the formal relationships created by marriage or civil partnership and may include professional or business relationships. Private information may include personal data, such as names, telephone numbers and address details.

What DOES NOT Constitute Surveillance

Some surveillance activity does not constitute intrusive or directed surveillance for the purposes of part II of the 2000 Act and includes:

- covert surveillance by way of an immediate response to events, e.g. where police officers conceal themselves to observe suspicious persons that they come across in the course of a routine patrol;
- covert surveillance as part of general observation activities, e.g. where plain clothes police officers are on patrol to monitor a high street crime hotspot or prevent and detect shoplifting;
- covert surveillance not relating to specified grounds, e.g. where a specific investigation or operation does not relate to the grounds specified at s. 28(3) of the 2000 Act;
- overt use of CCTV and LFR (live facial recognition) where members of the public will be aware that such systems are in use. CCTV operation is covered by the Home Office Surveillance Camera Code of

Practice (2022) which sets out a framework of good practice. The use of LFR is subject to legal requirements and regulations to ensure compliance with human rights and privacy laws. The overt use of ANPR systems to monitor traffic flows or detect motoring offences does not require an authorisation under the 2000 Act;

- certain other specific situations, e.g. the use of a recording device by a CHIS in respect of whom an appropriate use or conduct authorisation has been granted permitting him/her to record any information obtained in his/her presence (s. 48(3));
- the recording, whether overt or covert, of an interview with a member of the public where it is made clear that the interview is entirely voluntary and that the interviewer is a member of a public authority.

3.13.5.8 Directed and Intrusive Surveillance

Chapter 3 of the Code of Practice provides guidance on directed surveillance and states:

Directed surveillance

3.1 Surveillance is directed surveillance if the following are all true:

- it is covert, but not intrusive surveillance;
- it is conducted for the purposes of a specific investigation or operation;
- it is likely to result in the obtaining of *private information* about a person (whether or not one specifically identified for the purposes of the investigation or operation);
- it is conducted otherwise than by way of an immediate response to events or circumstances the nature of which is such that it would not be reasonably practicable for an *authorisation* under Part II of the 2000 Act to be sought.

3.2 Thus, the planned covert surveillance of a specific person, where not intrusive, would constitute directed surveillance if such surveillance is likely to result in the obtaining of *private information* about that, or any other person.

KEYNOTE

Where private information is acquired by means of covert surveillance of a person having a reasonable expectation of privacy, a directed surveillance authorisation is appropriate. The fact that a directed surveillance authorisation is available does not mean it is required. There may be other lawful means of obtaining personal data that do not involve directed surveillance.

While a person may have a reduced expectation of privacy when in a public place, covert surveillance of that person's activities in public may still result in the obtaining of private information. This is likely to be the case where that person has a reasonable expectation of privacy even though acting in public and where a record is being made by a public authority of that person's activities for future consideration or analysis. Note also that a person in police custody will have certain expectations of privacy.

Authorising of Directed Surveillance

An authorisation for directed surveillance should not be granted unless it is believed to be proportionate to what is sought to be achieved and necessary on the specified grounds (see para. 3.13.5.3 in relation to 'necessary' and 'proportionate'). The specified grounds, contained in s. 28(3), are:

- in the interests of national security;
- for the purpose of preventing or detecting crime or of preventing disorder;
- in the interests of the economic well-being of the United Kingdom;
- in the interests of public safety;
- for the purpose of protecting public health;
- for the purpose of assessing or collecting any tax, duty, levy or other imposition, contribution or charge payable to a government department; or
- for any purpose (not falling within paras (a) to (f)) which is specified for the purposes of this subsection by an order made by the Secretary of State.

In *R* v *Bond* [2020] EWCA Crim 1596, where the authority to make a covert audio recording of two defendants speaking in the back of a police van was not necessary or proportionate under s. 28, the seriousness of the breach was mitigated by the fact that all the police officers concerned had acted in the genuine belief that the authority was necessary, proportionate and properly granted.

The Regulation of Investigatory Powers (Directed Surveillance and Covert Human Intelligence Sources) Order 2003 (SI 2003/3171), as amended, sets out the relevant roles and ranks for those who can authorise directed surveillance. The ranks, mode of authorisation and associated time frames are summarised below:

Type of Authorisation	→	Ordinary Directed Surveillance	Urgent Directed Surveillance
Minimum Rank	→	↓ Superintendent or above	↓ Inspector or above
Form	→	↓ In writing	↓ Inspector—in writing Superintendent—in writing or oral
Time Frame	→	↓ Three months beginning on the day the authorisation is granted	↓ 72 hours beginning from the time authorisation is granted

In the case of the police, the relevant rank will generally be at superintendent level and above, and the authorisation must be in writing except in urgent cases where oral authorisation may be given (s. 43(1)(a)). A written authorisation ceases to have effect after three months beginning on the day it was granted, and if given orally will only last 72 hours unless renewed (s. 43(3)). Where it is not reasonably practicable to have the application considered by a superintendent or above, having regard to the urgency of the case, then an inspector may give the relevant authorisation which will only last 72 hours unless renewed by a superintendent. For the NCA, the authorising officer is a Senior Manager (Grade 2) and for urgent cases a Principal Officer (Grade 3).

Authorisations may also be made on an application made by a member of another police force where such police forces are party to a collaborative agreement that provides for them (s. 33(3ZA)–(3ZC)).

As with a CHIS, the Codes of Practice provide additional procedural safeguards regarding where the material sought by the surveillance is subject to legal privilege, is confidential personal information or some journalistic material. It is of interest to note that the House of Lords has held that the 2000 Act permits covert surveillance of communications between lawyers and their clients even though these may be subject to legal professional privilege (*Re McE (Northern Ireland)* [2009] UKHL 15).

3.13.5.9 Intrusive Surveillance

Chapter 3 of the Code of Practice also provides guidance on intrusive surveillance and states:

Intrusive Surveillance

3.19 Intrusive surveillance is covert surveillance that is:

- carried out in relation to anything taking place on residential premises, or
- in any private vehicle, and
- involves the presence of an individual on the premises or in the vehicle, or
- is carried out by a means of a surveillance device.

3.21 The definition of surveillance as intrusive relates to the location of the surveillance, and not any other consideration of the nature of the information that is expected to be obtained, as it is assumed that intrusive surveillance will always be likely to result in the obtaining of private information. Accordingly, it is not necessary to consider whether or not intrusive surveillance is likely to result in the obtaining of private information.

KEYNOTE

Residential Premises

'Residential premises' are considered to be so much of any premises as is for the time being occupied or used by any person, however temporarily, for residential purposes or otherwise as living accommodation. This specifically includes hotel or prison accommodation that is so occupied or used (s. 48(1)). However, common areas (such as hotel dining areas) to which a person has access in connection with their use or occupation of accommodation are specifically excluded (s. 48(7)). The Act further states that the concept of premises should be taken to include any place whatsoever, including any vehicle or movable structure, whether or not occupied as land (s. 48(8)).

Private Vehicle

A 'private vehicle' is defined as any vehicle, including vessels, aircraft or hovercraft, which is used primarily for the private purposes of the person who owns it or a person otherwise having the right to use it. This would include, for example, a company car, owned by a leasing company and used for business and pleasure by the employee of a company (s. 48(1) and (7)).

In *R* v *Plunkett* [2013] EWCA Crim 261, in admitting evidence of statements and admissions by the accused in a police van which were covertly recorded, it was held that a police van is not a private vehicle for the purposes of s. 26(3) and that the authorisation given by a superintendent under s. 28 for directed surveillance was appropriate.

Surveillance is not intrusive if it is carried out by means only of a surveillance device designed or adapted principally for the purpose of providing information about the location of a vehicle (s. 26(4)(a)).

Consistent Quality

If the surveillance is carried out by means of a surveillance device in relation to anything taking place on the premises or private vehicle, but is carried out without that device being present on the premises or in the vehicle, it is not intrusive unless the device is such that it consistently provides information of the same quality and detail as might be expected to be obtained from a device actually present on the premises or in the vehicle (s. 25(5)).

Legal Consultations

The Regulation of Investigatory Powers (Extension of Authorisation Provisions: Legal Consultations) Order 2010 (SI 2010/461) provides that directed surveillance carried out in relation to anything taking place on any premises specified in the Order that is being used for the purpose of legal consultations shall be treated as 'intrusive surveillance'. The 'any premises' includes prisons, police stations, high-security psychiatric hospitals, the place of business of any professional legal adviser and any place used for the sittings and business of any court, tribunal, inquest or inquiry.

Authorising Intrusive Surveillance

As with the other authorisations under the Act, the authorising officer shall not grant an authorisation for the carrying out of intrusive surveillance unless he/she believes that the authorisation is necessary on the specified grounds and that the authorised surveillance is proportionate to what is sought to be achieved by carrying it out (s. 32(2)). The specified grounds, contained in s. 32(3) are:

- in the interests of national security;
- for the purpose of preventing or detecting serious crime;
- in the interests of the economic well-being of the United Kingdom.

In relation to 'national security', a senior authorising officer or designated deputy of a law enforcement agency shall not issue an authorisation for intrusive surveillance where the investigation or operation is within the responsibilities of one of the intelligence services and properly falls to be authorised by warrant issued by the Secretary of State.

'Serious crime' is defined in s. 81(2) and (3) as crime that comprises an offence for which a person who has attained the age of 21 and has no previous convictions could reasonably be expected to be sentenced to imprisonment for a term of three years or more, or which involves the use of violence, results in substantial financial gain or is conducted by a large number of persons in pursuit of a common purpose.

The ranks, mode of authorisation and associated time frames are summarised below:

Type of Authorisation	→	Ordinary Intrusive Surveillance	Urgent Intrusive Surveillance
		↓	↓
Minimum Rank	→	Chief constable/commissioner (or designated deputy)	Chief constable/commissioner (or designated deputy)
		↓	↓
Form	→	In writing	In writing or oral
		↓	↓
Time Frame	→	Three months beginning when the Judicial Commissioner approves the authorisation	72 hours beginning from the time authorised (provided notice is given to the Judicial Commissioner)

Authorisations for intrusive surveillance will generally be granted by chief constables/commissioners and the Director General of the NCA (s. 32), or in some cases designated deputies.

A written authorisation will cease to have effect (unless renewed) at the end of a period of three months. Oral authorisations given in urgent cases will cease to have effect (unless renewed) at the end of the period of 72 hours beginning with the time when they took effect.

Except in urgent cases, authorisation granted for intrusive surveillance will not take effect until a Judicial Commissioner has approved it and written notice of the Commissioner's decision has been given to the person who granted the authorisation. This means that the approval will not take effect until the notice has been received in the office of the person who granted the authorisation within the relevant force or organisation (s. 35(3)(a)). When the authorisation is urgent, it will take effect from the time it is granted provided notice is given to the Surveillance Commissioner (s. 35(3)(b)).

Authorisations may also be made on an application made by a member of another police force where such police forces are party to a collaborative agreement that provides for them (s. 33(3ZA)–(3ZC)).

3.13.6 Communications Offences

Offences relating to communication include the malicious communication offence under the Communications Act 1988, offences of false communications, threatening communications, sending or showing flashing images electronically and encouraging or assisting serious self-harm, all under the Online Safety Act 2023, the improper use of the public electronic communications network under the Communications Act 2003 and making false alarms of fires under the Fire and Rescue Services Act 2004.

3.13.7 Offence of Sending Letters etc. with Intent to Cause Distress or Anxiety

OFFENCE: **Sending letters etc. with Intent to Cause Distress or Anxiety—*Malicious Communications Act 1988, s. 1(1)***

- Triable either way • Two years' imprisonment and/or a fine on indictment
- 12 months' imprisonment and/or a fine summarily

The Malicious Communications Act 1988, s. 1 states:

Offence of sending letters etc. with intent to cause distress or anxiety

(1) Any person who sends to another person—

(a) a letter, electronic communication or article of any description which conveys—

(i) a message which is indecent or grossly offensive;

(b) any article or electronic communication which is, in whole or part, of an indecent or grossly offensive nature,

is guilty of an offence if his purpose, or one of his purposes, in sending it is that it should, so far as falling within paragraph (a) or (b) above, cause distress or anxiety to the recipient or to any other person to whom he intends that it or its contents or nature should be communicated.

KEYNOTE

'Sending' will include transmitting (note that this offence is complete as soon as the communication is sent).

'Purposes' is simply another way of saying 'intention'.

Section 1(1)(b) covers occasions where the article itself is indecent or grossly offensive (such as putting dog faeces through someone's letter box).

The relevant distress or anxiety may be intended towards the recipient or any other person.

Although the message must be sent to 'another person', that can include both an individual and a corporation and the content of the communication may be a statement of opinion just as much as a statement of fact (*R* v *BLC* [2024] EWCA Crim 1186).

In addition to letters, the above offence also covers any article; it also covers electronic communications which include any oral or other communication by means of an electronic communications network. This will extend to communications in electronic form such as emails, text messages, pager messages, social media etc. (s. 1(2A)). In *Ladbrook* v *R* [2022] EWCA Crim 113, after a married couple had separated, the husband sent a text message of foul abuse and threats to his wife.

Whether a communication is so grossly offensive that it amounts to a criminal offence and loses the protection of freedom of speech, depends on its content, the context in which it was sent and the purpose(s) of the sender. In *R* v *Casserly* [2024] EWCA Crim 25, the accused was in dispute with the town council and an email he sent was part of a series of communications between him and town councillors and therefore sent in a political context. The court commented that holding politicians to account is an important part of a democratic society. When people are expressing themselves in a political context, the law expects those who receive the communications to have a thicker skin than those who are ordinary citizens. The use of strong language, even that which is offensive, shocking or extremely rude, may not be enough to amount to the offence charge and, accordingly, the prosecution is required to meet a very high threshold. It would only be possible for the communication to be grossly offensive if, in the jury's judgement, it went well beyond robust scrutiny of an elected councillor. It was not enough for the prosecution to prove that an email was likely to have caused distress or anxiety and the defendant either knew it was likely to have that effect or did not give thought to whether it would. What mattered was what was the defendant's objective(s) in sending the email.

The content of the communication may be a statement of opinion just as much as a statement of fact (*R* v *BLC* [2024] EWCA Crim 1186).

The offence can be committed by using someone else to send, deliver or transmit a message (subs. (3)).

3.13.8 False Communications Offence

OFFENCE: **False Communication—*Online Safety Act 2023, s. 179***

- Imprisonment for a term not exceeding the maximum term for summary offences and/or a fine

The Online Safety Act 2023, s. 179 states:

False communication offence

(1) A person commits an offence if—

(a) the person sends a message (see section 182),

(b) the message conveys information that the person knows to be false,

(c) at the time of sending it, the person intended the message, or the information in it, to cause non-trivial psychological or physical harm to a likely audience, and

(d) the person has no reasonable excuse for sending the message.

(2) For the purposes of this offence an individual is a 'likely audience' of a message if, at the time the message is sent, it is reasonably foreseeable that the individual—

(a) would encounter the message, or

(b) in the online context, would encounter a subsequent message forwarding or sharing the content of the message.

(3) In a case where several or many individuals are a likely audience, it is not necessary for the purposes of subsection (1)(c) that the person intended to cause harm to any one of them in particular (or to all of them).

KEYNOTE

Section 180 of the Act provides that an offence under section 179 cannot be committed by:

- the holder of a licence under the Broadcasting Act 1990 or 1996 in connection with anything done under the authority of the licence;
- the holder of a multiplex licence in connection with anything done under the authority of the licence;
- the provider of an on-demand programme service in connection with anything done in the course of providing such a service;
- in connection with the showing of a film made for cinema to members of the public.

Proceedings for an offence under this section may be brought within the period of six months beginning with the date on which evidence sufficient in the opinion of the prosecutor to justify the proceedings comes to the prosecutor's knowledge but may not be brought more than three years after the commission of the offence (subss. (7) and (8)).

In relation to subs. (1)(a), s. 182 provides an interpretation of both s. 179 and s. 181 (below).

Section 182 states:

(2) A person 'sends a message' if the person—

(a) sends, transmits or publishes a communication (including an oral communication) by electronic means, or

(b) sends, or gives to an individual, a letter or a thing of any other description,

and references to a message are to be read accordingly.

(3) A person also 'sends a message' if the person—

(a) causes a communication (including an oral communication) to be sent, transmitted or published by electronic means, or

(b) causes a letter or a thing of any other description to be—

(i) sent, or

(ii) given to an individual.

A provider of an internet service by means of which a communication is sent, transmitted or published is not to be regarded as a person who sends a message (subs. (4)).

An 'encounter', in relation to a message, means read, view, hear or otherwise experience the message (subs. (5)).

It does not matter whether the content of a message is created by the person who sends it (so, e.g., in the online context, an offence may be committed by a person who forwards another person's direct message or shares another person's post) (subs. (6)).

In the online context, the date on which a person commits an offence in relation to a message is the date on which the message is first sent by the person (subs. (9)).

3.13.9 Threatening Communications

OFFENCE: **Threatening Communications—*Online Safety Act 2023, s. 181***

- Triable either way • Five years' imprisonment and/or a fine on indictment
- Imprisonment for a term not exceeding the general limit in a magistrates' court and/or a fine summarily

The Online Safety Act 2023, s. 181 states:

Threatening communications offence

(1) A person commits an offence if—

(a) person sends a message (see section 182),

(b) the message conveys a threat of death or serious harm, and

(c) at the time of sending it, the person—

(i) intended an individual encountering the message to fear that the threat would be carried out (whether or not by the person sending the message), or

(ii) was reckless as to whether an individual encountering the message would fear that the threat would be carried out (whether or not by the person sending the message).

(2) 'Serious harm' means—

(a) serious injury amounting to grievous bodily harm within the meaning of the Offences against the Person Act 1861,

(b) rape,

(c) assault by penetration within the meaning of section 2 of the Sexual Offences Act 2003, or

(d) serious financial loss.

KEYNOTE

In relation to subs. (2)(d), a threat of serious financial loss, it is a defence for the person to show that: (a) the threat was used to reinforce a reasonable demand, and (b) the person reasonably believed that the use of the threat was a proper means of reinforcing the demand (subs. (3)). This defence will be satisfied unless the prosecution proves beyond reasonable doubt that it is not (subs. (4)).

The threatening communication under this section is potentially much more serious than an offence under s. 179 and, to some extent, the offence overlaps with the offence of threats to kill under the Offences Against the Person Act 1861, s. 16 (see *Crime Manual*). However, in addition, this offence embraces threats to cause serious harm (s. 181(2)) as well as threats of death and it is satisfied by recklessness (s. 181(1)(c)) as well as intention.

3.13.10 Sending or Showing Flashing Images Electronically

OFFENCE: **Sending or Showing Flashing Images Electronically—*Online Safety Act 2023, s. 183***

- Triable either way • Five years' imprisonment and/or a fine on indictment
- Imprisonment for a term not exceeding the general limit in a magistrates' court and/or a fine summarily

The Online Safety Act 2023, s. 183 states:

Offences of sending or showing flashing images electronically

(1) A person (A) commits an offence if—

(a) A sends a communication by electronic means which consists of or includes flashing images (see subsection (13),

(b) either condition 1 or condition 2 is met, and

(c) A has no reasonable excuse for sending the communication.

(2) Condition 1 is that—
   (a) at the time the communication is sent, it is reasonably foreseeable that an individual with epilepsy would be among the individuals who would view it, and
   (b) A sends the communication with the intention that such an individual will suffer harm as a result of viewing the flashing images.
(3) Condition 2 is that, when sending the communication—
   (a) A believes that an individual (B)—
      (i) whom A knows to be an individual with epilepsy, or
      (ii) whom A suspects to be an individual with epilepsy,
   will, or might, view it, and
   (b) A intends that B will suffer harm as a result of viewing the flashing images.
(4) In subsections (2)(a) and (3)(a), references to viewing the communication are to be read as including references to viewing a subsequent communication forwarding or sharing the content of the communication.

KEYNOTE

The exemptions contained in s. 180 apply to an offence under subs. (1) as they apply to an offence under s. 179. According to s. 183:

(6) For the purposes of subsection (1), a provider of an internet service by means of which a communication is sent is not to be regarded as a person who sends a communication [subs. (6)].

Section 183(8) provides that a person (A) commits an offence if:

(a) A shows an individual (B) flashing images by means of an electronic communications device,
(b) when showing the images—
   (i) A knows that B is an individual with epilepsy, or
   (ii) A suspects that B is an individual with epilepsy,
(c) when showing the images, A intends that B will suffer harm as a result of viewing them, and
(d) A has no reasonable excuse for showing the images.

Offences under subs. (1) or (8) cannot be committed by a health care professional acting in that capacity (subs. (9)).

It does not matter whether flashing images may be viewed at once (e.g. a GIF that plays automatically) or only after some action is performed (e.g. pressing play) (subs. (11)).

Subsection (12) provides that references to sending a communication include references to causing a communication to be sent, and references to showing flashing images include references to causing flashing images to be shown.

In accordance with subs. (13):

'electronic communications device' means equipment or a device that is capable of transmitting images by electronic means;
'flashing images' means images which carry a risk that an individual with photosensitive epilepsy who viewed them would suffer a seizure as a result;
'harm' means (a) a seizure, or (b) alarm or distress.
'individual with epilepsy' includes, but is not limited to, an individual with photosensitive epilepsy;
'send' includes transmit and publish (and related expressions are to be read accordingly).

3.13.11 Encouraging or Assisting Serious Self-harm

OFFENCE: **Encouraging or Assisting Serious Self-harm—*Online Safety Act 2023, s. 184***

- Triable either way • Five years' imprisonment and/or a fine on indictment
- Imprisonment for a term not exceeding the general limit in a magistrates' court and/or a fine summarily

The Online Safety Act 2023, s. 184 states:

Offence of encouraging or assisting serious self-harm

(1) A person (D) commits an offence if—
   (a) D does a relevant act capable of encouraging or assisting the serious self-harm of another person, and
   (b) D's act was intended to encourage or assist the serious self-harm of another person.

(2) D 'does a relevant act' if D—
   (a) communicates in person,
   (b) sends, transmits or publishes a communication by electronic means,
   (c) shows a person such a communication,
   (d) publishes material by any means other than electronic means,
   (e) sends, gives, shows or makes available to a person—
      (i) material published as mentioned in paragraph (d), or
      (ii) any form of correspondence, or
   (f) sends, gives or makes available to a person an item on which data is stored electronically.

KEYNOTE

'Serious self-harm' means self-harm amounting to grievous bodily harm within the meaning of the Offences Against the Person Act 1861 and includes successive acts of self-harm which cumulatively reach that threshold (subs. (3)).

The person referred to in subs. (1)(a) and (b) need not be a specific person (or class of persons) known to, or identified by, D (subs. (4)) and D may commit an offence under this section whether or not serious self-harm occurs (subs. 5)).

If a person (D1) arranges for a person (D2) to do an act that is capable of encouraging or assisting the serious self-harm of another person and D2 does that act, D1 is to be treated as also having done it (subs. (6)).

Subsection (7) provides that in the application of subs. (1) to an act by D involving an electronic communication or a publication in physical form, it does not matter whether the content of the communication or publication is created by D (so, e.g., in the online context, the offence under this section may be committed by forwarding another person's direct message or sharing another person's post).

In the application of subs. (1) to an act by D involving an item on which data is stored electronically, the reference in subs. (2)(f) to the item is to be read as including a reference to content accessed by means of the item to which the person in receipt of the item is specifically directed by D (subs. (9)).

A provider of an internet service by means of which a communication is sent, transmitted or published is not to be regarded as a person who sends, transmits or publishes it (subs. 10)).

Any reference in this section to doing an act that is capable of encouraging the serious self-harm of another person includes a reference to doing so by threatening another person or otherwise putting pressure on another person to seriously self-harm.

'Seriously self-harm' is to be interpreted consistently with subs. (3) (subs. 11)).

Any reference to an act in this section, except in subs. (3), includes a reference to a course of conduct, and references to doing an act are to be read accordingly. In subs. (3), 'act' includes omission (subss. (12) and (13)).

3.13.12 Improper Use of Public Electronic Communications Network

OFFENCE: **Improper Use of Public Electronic Communications Network—*Communications Act 2003, s. 127***

- Triable summarily • Six months' imprisonment and/or a fine

The Communications Act 2003, s. 127 states:

(1) A person is guilty of an offence if he—
   (a) sends by means of a public electronic communications network a message or other matter that is grossly offensive or of an indecent, obscene or menacing character; or
   (b) causes any such message or matter to be so sent.

(2) A person is guilty of an offence if, for the purpose of causing annoyance, inconvenience or needless anxiety to another, he—

(a) . . .

(b) . . .

(c) persistently makes use of a public electronic communications network.

If the message sent is grossly offensive, indecent, obscene, menacing or false, it is irrelevant whether it was received. The offence is one of sending, so it is committed when the sending takes place.

KEYNOTE

These offences are designed to deal with 'nuisance' calls. They only apply to 'public' electronic communications networks. These are defined as an electronic communications network provided wholly or mainly for the purpose of making electronic communications services available to members of the public (s. 151) and would therefore not generally include internal calls in a workplace.

They would apply to sending messages (or tweets) on X (formerly Twitter) which are communicated and accessible via the internet (*Chambers* v *DPP* [2012] EWHC 2157 (Admin)). However, in *Scottow* v *CPS* [2020] EWHC 3421 (Admin), it was held that no offence was committed under s. 127(2(c) in relation to the posting of 'annoying tweets'.

There is no need to show a particular 'purpose' (intention) on the part of the defendant for the first offence under s. 127(1) and that offence is complete if the message is, as a matter of fact, grossly offensive, indecent, obscene or menacing.

The offence also covers actions which cause others to send such a message.

There is no need for any information passed to be 'false'.

In determining whether a message is 'grossly offensive', it is the message and not the content that is the basic ingredient of the offence. What constitutes 'grossly offensive' has to be judged by considering the reaction of reasonable people and the standards of an open and just multiracial society (*DPP* v *Collins* [2005] EWHC 1308 (Admin)).

In Cobban v DPP [2024] EWHC 1908 (Admin) the court considered how s. 127(1) applies to consensual messaging on WhatsApp between serving police officers (e.g. about vulnerable victims of crime). The court held that the messages concerned the appellants' policing duties and perspectives on those duties, and it was not an issue that their content was racist, misogynist, sexist, homophobic and disablist. The fact that the recipients of the messages did not find the messages grossly offensive was of no avail if those to whom the messages related would find them grossly offensive and if they were grossly offensive in the eyes of a reasonable member of the public judged by the standards of today's society. In relation to Article 10 of the ECHR and freedom of speech the court considered the convictions were a proportionate response to the legitimate aim of maintaining confidence in the police by expressing public disapproval of their actions through criminal liability. Considering Article 8 of the ECHR and the issue of the privacy of private consensual messaging the court considered that there could be no expectation of privacy given the defendants' position as police officers and the abhorrent nature of the messages.

The second offence, under s. 127(2), requires that the defendant is shown to have acted with the purpose of causing annoyance, inconvenience or needless anxiety.

A person is to be treated as 'persistently misusing' a network or service in any case in which his/her misuse is repeated on a sufficient number of occasions for it to be clear that the misuse represents a pattern of behaviour or practice, or recklessness as to whether persons suffer annoyance, inconvenience or anxiety (s. 128(6)).

In assessing these points, it is immaterial that the misuse was in relation to a 'network' on some occasions and in relation to a communications 'service' on others, that different networks or services were involved on different occasions or that the people likely to suffer annoyance, inconvenience or anxiety were different on different occasions (s. 128(7)).

This second offence is a 'penalty offence' for the purposes of s. 1 of the Criminal Justice and Police Act 2001.

Where a number of calls have been made to several different people within the community, the offence of public nuisance may also be considered (**see para. 3.9.9**).

3.13.13 False Alarms of Fire

OFFENCE: **Making False Alarm of Fire—*Fire and Rescue Services Act 2004, s. 49***
- Triable summarily • Three months' imprisonment and/or a fine

The Fire and Rescue Services Act 2004, s. 49 states:

(1) A person commits an offence if he knowingly gives or causes to be given a false alarm of fire to a person acting on behalf of a fire and rescue authority.

KEYNOTE

The offence requires proof that the defendant acted 'knowingly' (as opposed to, e.g., mistakenly). The offence clearly applies where someone makes a malicious call to a fire and rescue authority. However, the wording 'causes to be given' potentially covers the making of a false report to a body other than a fire and rescue authority, for example the police, if the person knew that this would result in the police passing that call to the relevant fire and rescue authority.

This offence is a 'penalty offence' for the purposes of s. 1 of the Criminal Justice and Police Act 2001.

3.14 Offences Against the Administration of Justice and Public Interest

3.14.1 Introduction

This chapter deals with a wide range of offences against the administration of justice and also the public interest. The first group of offences involve some form of interference with the machinery of justice such as perjury and witness intimidation, while others have an indirect effect on the process.

3.14.2 Perjury

OFFENCE: **Perjury—*Perjury Act 1911, s. 1***

• Triable on indictment • Seven years' imprisonment

The Perjury Act 1911, s. 1 states:

(1) If any person lawfully sworn as a witness or as an interpreter in a judicial proceeding wilfully makes a statement material in that proceeding, which he knows to be false or does not believe to be true, he shall be guilty of perjury ...

(2) The expression 'judicial proceeding' includes a proceeding before any court, tribunal, or person having by law power to hear, receive, and examine evidence on oath.

(3) Where a statement made for the purposes of a judicial proceeding is not made before the tribunal itself, but is made on oath before a person authorised by law to administer an oath to the person who makes the statement, and to record or authenticate the statement, it shall, for the purposes of this section, be treated as having been made in a judicial proceeding.

KEYNOTE

To commit this offence a defendant must have been *lawfully sworn*; this will include a person who makes a solemn affirmation in place of an oath (Evidence Act 1851, s. 16). The statement made in a 'judicial proceeding' can be one given orally before the court or tribunal, or in the form of an affidavit (sworn statement). If a witness tenders a false statement used under s. 89 of the Criminal Justice Act 1967, he/she commits a separate, lesser offence (see para. 3.14.3). Evidence given by live TV link under the provisions of the Criminal Justice Act 1988, s. 32 is also subject to the offence of perjury.

'Wilful' means deliberate or intentional (*R* v *Senior* [1899] 1 QB 283) and it must be proved that any alleged perjury was not the result of a misunderstanding or an accidental slip of the tongue (*R* v *Millward* [1985] QB 519). It could also involve being reckless as to whether or not the statement was true (*R (On the Application of Purvis)* v *DPP* [2020] EWHC 3573 (Admin)).

A 'statement material in that proceeding' means that the content of the evidence tendered in that case, although perhaps not crucial to the case, must have some importance to it and not just be of passing relevance. Whether something is material to a case is a question of law for a judge to decide. Whether a motorist had taken a drink between the time of having a road traffic accident and being breathalysed would be such a material issue, and to get a witness to provide false evidence about that matter would be a 'statement material in that proceeding' (*R* v *Lewins* (1979) 1 Cr App R (S) 246).

Evidence of an opinion provided by a witness who does not genuinely hold such an opinion may also be perjury.

Perjury may be proved by using a court transcript or the evidence of others who were present at the proceeding in question (Perjury Act 1911, s. 14).

Corroboration is required in cases of perjury (Perjury Act 1911, s. 13), solely in relation to the *falsity* of the defendant's statement. There is no requirement under s. 13 for corroboration of the fact that the defendant *actually made* the alleged statement, nor that he/she knew or believed it to be untrue. However, as that corroboration can be documentary and may even come from the defendant's earlier conduct (*R* v *Threlfall* (1914) 10 Cr App R 112) this requirement does not appear to present much of a hurdle to the prosecution.

A person also commits an offence who aids, abets, counsels, procures or suborns another person to commit an offence under the Act and may be liable to be proceeded against, indicted, tried and punished as if he/she were a principal offender (s. 7(1)). 'Suborning' in this context is simply another term for procuring. Additionally, a person who incites another person to commit an offence under the Act commits an offence and on conviction on indictment shall be liable to a maximum term of two years' imprisonment (s. 7(2)).

3.14.3 Offences Similar to Perjury

OFFENCE: **False Statements in Criminal Proceedings—*Criminal Justice Act 1967, s. 89***

- Triable either way • Two years' imprisonment and/or a fine on indictment
- 12 months' imprisonment and/or a fine summarily

The Criminal Justice Act 1967, s. 89 states:

(1) If any person in a written statement tendered in evidence in criminal proceedings by virtue of section 9 of this Act, wilfully makes a statement material in those proceedings which he knows to be false or does not believe to be true, he shall be liable ...

(2) The Perjury Act 1911 shall have effect as if this section were contained in that Act.

OFFENCE: **False Statements on Oath—*Perjury Act 1911, s. 2***

- Triable either way • Seven years' imprisonment and/or a fine on indictment
- 12 months' imprisonment and/or a fine summarily

The Perjury Act 1911, s. 2 states:

If any person—

(1) being required or authorised by law to make any statement on oath for any purpose, and being lawfully sworn (otherwise than in a judicial proceeding) wilfully makes a statement which is material for that purpose and which he knows to be false or does not believe to be true; ...

he shall be [guilty of an offence].

KEYNOTE

The first offence covers witnesses who tender false statements in criminal proceedings. The second offence covers the making of false statements under an oath which is not sworn in connection with a judicial proceeding.

3.14.4 Perverting the Course of Justice

OFFENCE: **Perverting the Course of Justice—*Common Law***

- Triable on indictment • Life imprisonment and/or a fine

It is an offence at common law to do an act tending and intended to pervert the course of public justice.

KEYNOTE

Although traditionally referred to as 'attempting' to pervert the course of justice, it is recognised that behaviour which is aimed at perverting the course of public justice does just that and the substantive offence should be charged (*R* v *Williams* (1991) 92 Cr App R 158).

'The course of public justice' includes the process of criminal investigation (*R* v *Rowell* (1978) 1 WLR 132).

Perverting the course of justice requires positive acts by the defendant, not merely standing by and allowing an injustice to take place, i.e. omissions. It could also involve being reckless as to whether or not the statement was true. Intent cannot be established by mere incompetence, muddle and the offender's failure to appreciate the significance of what he/she has done (*R (On the Application of Purvis)* v *DPP* [2020] EWHC 3573). In *R* v *Lalani* [1999] 1 Cr App R 481, the court stressed that the requisite intention needed to be proved and could not be implied even from admitted facts.

This offence can be committed in a wide variety of ways, including behaviour that could also be covered by other offences, e.g. intimidating witnesses (**see para. 3.14.5.1**). Such overlaps are not at all unusual in English law but, depending on the circumstances, it may be appropriate to charge with a more specific offence, e.g. perjury or witness intimidation.

Examples of perverting the course of justice include:

- Admitting to a crime to enable the offender to avoid prosecution (*R* v *Devito* [1975] Crim LR 175).
- A police officer abusing their authority to excuse someone of a criminal charge (*R* v *Coxhead* [1986] RTR 411).
- Making a false allegation of an offence (*R* v *Ahmed* [2021] EWCA Crim 1786 (rape); *R* v *Cotter* [2002] EWCA Crim 1033 (racist assault); *R* v *Beech* [2020] EWCA Crim 1580 (paedophile ring)).
- Giving a false identity when arrested (*R* v *Sookoo* [2002] EWCA Crim 800).
- Giving another person's details when being reported for an offence (*R* v *Hurst* (1990–1) 12 Cr App R (S) 373).
- Destroying and concealing evidence of a crime (*R* v *Kiffin* [1994] Crim LR 449); *R* v *Sidhu* [2019] EWCA Crim 1034).
- Completing an unpaid work requirement that has been imposed on another person (*DPP* v *SK* [2016] EWHC 837 (Admin)).
- Inducing witnesses to leave the court's jurisdiction before trial by paying them using cryptocurrency (*R* v *Mhasvi* [2024] EWCA Crim 1638).
- Emotionally blackmailing a rape victim to withdraw her complaint (*R* v *Fox* [2024] EWCA Crim 1667).

A charge of perverting the course of justice should not without good reason be added to cases in which a suspect has merely told lies when questioned (*Sookoo*).

3.14.5 Considerations Affecting Witnesses, Jurors and Others

There are several areas of law to consider in relation to offences involving witnesses. The main legislative provisions are set out below.

The Serious Organised Crime and Police Act 2005, chapter 5, sets out the provisions relating to the protection of witnesses and other persons. These arrangements stretch beyond witnesses and extend to a series of people involved in the criminal justice process, including people who are *or have been*:

- constables;
- employees accredited under the Police Reform Act 2002;
- jurors;
- magistrates (or their equivalent outside the United Kingdom);
- holders of judicial office (whether in the United Kingdom or elsewhere);
- the DPP, criminal prosecutors and staff of the Crown Prosecution Service.

The Act allows for the making of arrangements to protect these and other relevant people ordinarily resident in the United Kingdom where the 'protection provider' (usually the Chief Officer of Police or the Director General of the National Crime Agency) considers that the person's safety is at risk by virtue of being a witness, constable, juror etc. (s. 82(1)). A protection provider may vary or cancel any arrangements made by him/her under subs. (1) if the provider considers it appropriate to do so. Joint arrangements (e.g. between police forces) can be made where appropriate, and public authorities (other than courts and tribunals or parliament) are under a duty to take reasonable steps to assist protection providers where requested to do so (ss. 83 and 85).

3.14.5.1 Intimidation of, or Retaliation Against, Witnesses, Jurors or Others

OFFENCE: **Intimidating Witnesses and Jurors—*Criminal Justice and Public Order Act 1994, s. 51***

- Triable either way • Five years' imprisonment and/or a fine on indictment
- 12 months' imprisonment and/or a fine summarily

The Criminal Justice and Public Order Act 1994, s. 51 states:

(1) A person commits an offence if—
   (a) he does an act which intimidates, and is intended to intimidate, another person ('the victim'),
   (b) he does the act knowing or believing that the victim is assisting in the investigation of an offence or is a witness or potential witness or a juror or potential juror in proceedings for an offence, and
   (c) he does it intending thereby to cause the investigation or the course of justice to be obstructed, perverted or interfered with.
(2) A person commits an offence if—
   (a) he does an act which harms, and is intended to harm, another person or, intending to cause another person to fear harm, he threatens to do an act which would harm that other person,
   (b) he does or threatens to do the act knowing or believing that the person harmed or threatened to be harmed ('the victim'), or some other person, has assisted in an investigation into an offence or has given evidence or particular evidence in proceedings for an offence, or has acted as a juror or concurred in a particular verdict in proceedings for an offence, and
   (c) he does or threatens to do it because of that knowledge or belief.
(3) For the purposes of subsections (1) and (2) it is immaterial that the act is or would be done, or that the threat is made—
   (a) otherwise than in the presence of the victim, or
   (b) to a person other than the victim.
(4) The harm that may be done or threatened may be financial as well as physical (whether to the person or a person's property) and similarly as respects an intimidatory act which consists of threats.
(5) The intention required by subsection (1)(c) and the motive required by subsection (2)(c) above need not be the only or the predominating intention or motive with which the act is done or, in the case of subsection (2), threatened.

KEYNOTE

These offences are designed to exist alongside the common law offence of perverting the course of justice, and there will be circumstances which may fall under both the statutory and the common law offences.

Making a *threat* via a third person, knowing it will be passed on and that the ultimate recipient would be intimidated by it, amounts to an offence under s. 51(1) (*Attorney-General's Reference (No. 1 of 1999)* [2000] QB 365).

Where a person refuses to be deterred or intimidated, an offence under this section cannot be committed (*R* v *ZN* [2013] EWCA Crim 989). Nor can it be committed on the basis of an unshaken belief that an investigation is in progress (*R* v *Singh* [1999] Crim LR 681). However, in either of these cases a criminal attempt may be committed (**see *Crime Manual***).

'Harm' for the purposes of s. 51(2) means physical harm and not simply an assault or battery. Therefore spitting at a person does not amount to 'harm' for these purposes (*R* v *Normanton* [1998] Crim LR 220).

Section 51(2) provides a similar offence for acts done or threatened in the knowledge or belief that the person, *or another person*, has so assisted or taken part in proceedings. Doing acts to third parties in order to intimidate or harm the relevant person is also covered by this offence (s. 51(3)). Making threats by telephone will amount to 'doing an act to another' (*DPP* v *Mills* [1997] QB 300).

The intention to obstruct, pervert or interfere with the course of justice need not be the only or even the main intention (s. 51(5)).

Section 51(8) creates a statutory presumption under certain circumstances that the defendant had the required motive at the time of the actions or threats.

The Criminal Justice and Police Act 2001 makes similar provisions to protect witnesses in all proceedings other than proceedings for a criminal offence. Section 39 corresponds to s. 51(1) and s. 40 corresponds to s. 51(2). Similarly, both offences are triable either way with corresponding punishments.

3.14.6 Assisting Offenders

OFFENCE: **Assisting Offenders—*Criminal Law Act 1967, s. 4***

• Triable on indictment; either way if original offence is either way • Where sentence for original offence is fixed by law, 10 years' imprisonment and/or a fine on indictment; 12 months' imprisonment and/or a fine summarily • Where sentence for original offence is 14 years' imprisonment, seven years' imprisonment and/or a fine on indictment; 12 months' imprisonment and/or a fine summarily • Where sentence for original offence is 10 years' imprisonment, five years' imprisonment and/or a fine on indictment; 12 months' imprisonment and/or a fine summarily • Otherwise three years' imprisonment and/or a fine on indictment; 12 months' imprisonment and/or a fine summarily

The Criminal Law Act 1967, s. 4 states:

(1) Where a person has committed a relevant offence, any other person who, knowing or believing him to be guilty of the offence or of some other relevant offence, does without lawful authority or reasonable excuse any act with intent to impede his apprehension or prosecution shall be guilty of an offence.

(1A) In this section and section 5 below, 'relevant offence' means—
- (a) an offence for which the sentence is fixed by law,
- (b) an offence for which a person of 18 years or over (not previously convicted) may be sentenced to imprisonment for a term of five years (or might be so sentenced but for the restrictions imposed by section 33 of the Magistrates' Courts Act 1980).

KEYNOTE

For there to be an offence under s. 4 there must first have been a relevant offence committed by someone.

That relevant offence must, in the case of the above offence, have been committed by the 'assisted' person.

It must be shown that the defendant knew or believed the person to be guilty of that *or some other relevant* offence. Mere *suspicion*, however strong, that the 'assisted' person had committed a relevant offence will not be enough. Therefore, if the defendant believed that the 'assisted' person had committed a robbery when in fact he/she had committed a theft, that mistaken part of the defendant's belief will not prevent a conviction for this offence.

The defendant can commit the offence before the person assisted is convicted of committing the relevant offence.

This offence must involve some positive act by the defendant; doing or saying nothing will not suffice.

Although there is no duty on people to assist the police in their investigations generally, this offence and the one below create a negative duty not to interfere with investigations after an offence has taken place.

This offence requires the consent of the DPP before a prosecution is brought (s. 4(4)).

This offence cannot be 'attempted' (Criminal Attempts Act 1981, s. 1(4)).

3.14.7 Concealing Relevant Offences

OFFENCE: **Concealing Relevant Offences—*Criminal Law Act 1967, s. 5***

- Triable on indictment; either way if original offence is triable either way
- Two years' imprisonment on indictment • 12 months' imprisonment and/or a fine summarily

The Criminal Law Act 1967, s. 5 states:

(1) Where a person has committed a relevant offence, any other person who, knowing or believing that the offence or some other relevant offence has been committed, and that he has information which might be of material assistance in securing the prosecution or conviction of an offender for it, accepts or agrees to accept for not disclosing that information any consideration other than the making good of loss or injury caused by the offence, or the making of reasonable compensation for that loss or injury, shall be liable. ...

KEYNOTE

Again, someone must have committed a relevant offence before this particular offence can be committed. This offence requires proof, not only of the defendant's knowledge or belief that a relevant offence had been committed, but also that the defendant has information that might be of material assistance in securing the *prosecution or conviction of an offender* for it.

The main focus of this offence is:

- the acceptance of, or agreement to accept 'consideration' (i.e. anything of value);
- beyond reasonable compensation for loss/injury *caused by the relevant offence*;
- in exchange for not disclosing material information.

'Disclosure' does not appear to be confined to information passed to the police. It would probably extend to other agencies with a duty to investigate offences but is perhaps even wider than that.

This offence requires the consent of the DPP before a prosecution can be brought (s. 5(3)) and cannot be attempted (Criminal Attempts Act 1981, s. 1(4)).

The term 'relevant offence' is defined by s. 4(1A) (see para. 3.14.6).

3.14.8 Miscellaneous Offences Relating to Offenders

OFFENCE: **Escaping—*Common Law***

- Triable on indictment • Unlimited punishment

KEYNOTE

A person who, being in lawful custody either in prison or elsewhere on a criminal charge, escapes without the use of force commits the common law offence of Escape.

The 'custody' from which a person escapes must be shown to have been lawful. The offence applies to police custody or police detention (see the Police and Criminal Evidence Act 1984, s. 118) or custody following conviction. D is not lawfully confined if he/she has been mistakenly kept in prison after his/her proper release date (*R* v *O'Connor* [2010] EWCA Crim 2842) but note that it is irrelevant if he/she is guilty of the crime for which he/she was imprisoned.

Whether a person was 'in custody' is a question of fact and the word 'custody' is to be given its ordinary and natural meaning (*E* v *DPP* [2002] EWHC 433 (Admin) and *Richards* v *DPP* [1988] QB 701). In proving that a person was in custody at a particular time, it should be shown that his/her liberty was restricted in a way that meant that he/she was confined by another and that his/her freedom of movement was controlled; it is not necessary, however, to show that the person's actual ability to move around was physically impeded, e.g. in secure accommodation (*E* v *DPP*).

People may be in lawful custody even if not directly in the custody of a sworn police officer, for example those people who are being dealt with by an investigating officer or escort officers under sch. 4 to the Police Reform Act 2002.

People detained under the Mental Health Act 1983, s. 136, are also in lawful custody (**see para. 3.4.2**), and it is also an offence under s. 128 of the Mental Health Act 1983 to assist patients to absent themselves without leave (**see para. 3.4.5**).

Under the Armed Forces Act 2006, a civilian policeman may arrest without a warrant a person who is reasonably suspected of being a person subject to service law who has deserted or is absent without leave (s. 314), and a person who has been sentenced to service detention and who is unlawfully at large may be arrested without a warrant by a police officer (s. 318).

If a defendant uses force to *break out* of a prison or a police station, he/she commits an offence of prison breach, again at common law and attracting the same punishment and mode of trial as escaping.

Under the Prisoners (Return to Custody) Act 1995, s. 1, a person who has been temporarily released under the Prison Act 1952 commits a summary offence if he/she remains unlawfully at large or fails to respond to an order of recall to prison.

Escort officers designated under sch. 4 to the Police Reform Act 2002 have a duty to prevent the escape of people in their charge whom they are escorting in accordance with their statutory powers (Police Reform Act 2002, sch. 4, part 4, para. 35).

OFFENCE: **Assisting Escape—*Prison Act 1952, s. 39***

- Triable on indictment • 10 years' imprisonment

The Prison Act 1952, s. 39 states:

(1) Any person who
  (a) assists a prisoner in escaping or attempting to escape from a prison, or
  (b) intending to facilitate the escape of a prisoner—
    (i) brings, throws or otherwise conveys anything into prison,
    (ii) causes another person to bring, throw or otherwise convey anything into prison, or
    (iii) gives anything to a prisoner or leaves anything in any place (whether inside or outside a prison), is guilty of an offence.

KEYNOTE

Assisting escape can take many different forms. In *R* v *Williams* (1992) 13 Cr App R (S) 236, the offender committed the offence by changing places with a prisoner in an open prison for one night to allow the prisoner to spend the night at home. In *R* v *Walker* (1990–91) 12 Cr App R (S) 65, the offence was committed by an offender who aided a prisoner to escape by meeting him outside the prison and giving him a lift in his car.

The offence under s. 39 applies where the escape is from a prison, remand centre or young offender institution.

The offence under s. 39 does not apply to a prisoner who escapes while in transit to or from prison (*R* v *Moss and Harte* (1986) 82 Cr App R 116).

OFFENCE: **Harbouring Offenders—*Criminal Justice Act 1961, s. 22(2)***

- Triable either way • 10 years' imprisonment and/or a fine on indictment
- Six months' imprisonment and/or a fine summarily

The Criminal Justice Act 1961, s. 22 states:

(2) If any person knowingly harbours a person who has escaped from a prison or other institution to which the said section thirty-nine applies, or who, having been sentenced in any part of the United Kingdom or in any of the Channel Islands or the Isle of Man to imprisonment or detention, is otherwise unlawfully at large, or gives to any such person any assistance with intent to prevent, hinder or interfere with his being taken into custody, he shall be liable ...

KEYNOTE

The offence under s. 22(2) applies where the escape is from a prison, remand centre or young offender institution. This offence cannot be committed in respect of a person who escapes from custody while in transit to or from a prison or court etc. (*Nicoll* v *Catron* [1985] 81 Cr App R 339; *R* v *Moss* [1985] 82 Cr App R 116), nor can it be committed unless the person has already been sentenced to imprisonment or detention and is 'unlawfully at large'.

3.14.9 Wasting Police Time

OFFENCE: **Wasting Police Time—*Criminal Law Act 1967, s. 5(2)***

- Triable summarily • Six months' imprisonment and/or a fine

The Criminal Law Act 1967, s. 5 states:

(2) Where a person causes any wasteful employment of the police by knowingly making to any person a false report tending to show that an offence has been committed, or to give rise to apprehension for the safety of any persons or property, or tending to show that he has information material to any police inquiry, he shall be liable …

KEYNOTE

It is widely thought that there is a minimum number of hours which must be wasted before a prosecution can be brought for this offence. There is no reliable authority on this point.

It can be an offence under this section where a false allegation is made against another person even if, unknown to the offender, the subject of the allegation has died (*R* v *Brown* [2004] EWCA Crim 744).

No proceedings for this offence may be instituted except by or with the consent of the DPP (s. 5(3)). Under the Penalties for Disorderly Behaviour (Amount of Penalty) Order 2002 (SI 2013/1579), the offence under s. 5(2) is a penalty offence and the amount payable is £90.

3.15 Terrorism and Associated Offences

3.15.1 Introduction

The law on terrorism contained in this chapter relates to the Terrorism Act 2000, Anti-terrorism, Crime and Security Act 2001, Terrorism Act 2006 and the Counter-Terrorism and Border Security Act 2019. Also included are relevant offences under the Explosive Substances Act 1883.

3.15.2 Terrorism Defined

Terrorism is defined in the Terrorism Act 2000, s. 1 as:

(1) ... the use or threat of action where—
- (a) the action falls within subsection (2),
- (b) the use or threat is designed to influence the government or an international governmental organisation, or to intimidate the public or a section of the public, and
- (c) the use or threat is made for the purpose of advancing a political, religious, racial or ideological cause.

(2) Action falls within this subsection if it—
- (a) involves serious violence against a person,
- (b) involves serious damage to property,
- (c) endangers a person's life, other than that of the person committing the action,
- (d) creates a serious risk to the health or safety of the public or a section of the public, or
- (e) is designed seriously to interfere with or seriously to disrupt an electronic system.

(3) The use or threat of action falling within subsection (2) which involves the use of firearms or explosives is terrorism whether or not subsection (1)(b) is satisfied.

KEYNOTE

This definition includes domestic terrorism, and should be considered when dealing with other, more familiar offences such as blackmail, contamination of goods and threats to kill.

The definition recognises that terrorist activity may be motivated by religious, racial or fundamental reasons rather than simply political ones. It also encompasses broad activities (including threats) which, though potentially devastating in their impact on society, may not be overtly violent. Examples of such activity might be interference with domestic water and power supplies or serious disruption of computer networks.

The provision at s. 1(3) means that, where the relevant criminal activity involves the use of firearms or explosives, there is no further need to show that the behaviour was designed to influence the government or to intimidate the public or a section of the public. An example of such activity might be the shooting of a senior military or political figure. A 'firearm' for this purpose includes air weapons (s. 121).

The reference to 'action' here includes action outside the United Kingdom. Similarly, references to people, property, the public and governments apply to all those features whether in the United Kingdom or elsewhere (s. 1(4)).

3.15.2.1 Membership of a Proscribed Organisation

OFFENCE: **Membership of a Proscribed Organisation—*Terrorism Act 2000, s. 11***
- Triable either way • 14 years' imprisonment and/or a fine on indictment
- 12 months' imprisonment and/or a fine summarily

The Terrorism Act 2000, s. 11 states:

(1) A person commits an offence if he belongs or professes to belong to a proscribed organisation.
(2) It is a defence for a person charged with an offence under subsection (1) to prove—
  (a) that the organisation was not proscribed on the last (or only) occasion on which he became a member or began to profess to be a member, and
  (b) that he has not taken part in the activities of the organisation at any time while it was proscribed.

KEYNOTE

Specific organisations are proscribed by the Secretary of State and include some of the most active and widely known terrorist groups across the world, including Al-Qa'ida (sch. 2 to the Act). What amounts to membership is likely to depend on the nature of an organisation, e.g. membership of a loose and unstructured organisation may not need any formal steps or express process by which a person becomes a member (*R* v *Ahmed* [2011] EWCA Crim 184).

The reverse burden of proof contained in s. 11(2) has been held as imposing an evidential, as opposed to a persuasive, burden of proof (*Attorney-General's Reference* (*No. 4 of 2002*), *Sheldrake* v *DPP* [2004] UKHL 43).

Other offences relating to proscribed organisations are provided by s. 12 and include: inviting support; arranging or managing (or assisting in doing so) a meeting of three or more people in public or private, to support, further the activities or be addressed by a person belonging to a proscribed organisation; or addressing a meeting to encourage support or further the activities of the organisation. The offence may be committed by expressing an opinion or belief supportive of a proscribed organisation whilst being reckless as to whether a person to whom the expression is directed will be encouraged to support a proscribed organisation (s. 12(1A)). In *ABJ* v *R* [2024] EWCA Crim 1597, the court held that the defendant does not have to be aware that the organisation in question is proscribed. The court also held that this offence is compatible with Article 10 of the European Convention on Human Rights (freedom of expression).

The Act also created a summary offence of wearing an item of clothing, or wearing, carrying or displaying an article in such a way or in such circumstances as to arouse reasonable suspicion that the defendant is a member or supporter of a proscribed organisation (s. 13). In *Pwr* v *DPP* [2022] UKSC 2, it was held that s. 13(1) was a strict liability offence and, although Article 10 of the European Convention on Human Rights (freedom of expression) was engaged, s. 13(1) was a proportionate response. The offence can be committed by publishing an image of an item of clothing or other article in such a way or in such circumstances as to arouse 'reasonable suspicion' that the writer is a member of or supports a proscribed organisation (s. 13(1A)). Reference to an image is a reference to a still or moving image (produced by any means) (s. 13(1B)).

3.15.3 Terrorism Act 2000: Financial Measures

The main financial measures under the Terrorism Act 2000 relate to terrorist fundraising, possession of property and funding arrangements, and include:

- *inviting* another to provide money or other property (s. 15(1));
- *providing* money or other property (s. 15(3));
- *receiving* money or other property (s. 15(2));
- *possessing* money or other property (s. 16(2));
- *arranging* for money or other property to be made available (s. 17);

in each case intending that, or having reasonable cause to suspect that, it may be used for the purposes of terrorism (ss. 15, 16(2) and 17);

- *using* money or other property for the purposes of terrorism (s. 16(1));
- *concealing, moving or transferring* any terrorist property (s. 18).

Each of these offences is punishable by a maximum of 14 years' imprisonment on indictment (s. 22).

In relation to ss. 15, 16(2) and 17, 'having reasonable cause to suspect' does not mean that the accused must actually suspect that money may be used for the purpose of terrorism but from the information available to the accused, a reasonable person *would* (not might or could) suspect that the money might be used for terrorism (*R* v *Lane* [2018] UKSC 36).

3.15.4 Terrorism Act 2000: Duty of Disclosure and Tipping Off

The 2000 Act creates a number of offences in relation to the unlawful disclosure of information and provides where disclosure is permissible.

3.15.4.1 Disclosure of Information

OFFENCE: **Disclosure of Information—*Terrorism Act 2000, s. 19***

- Triable either way • Five years' imprisonment and/or a fine on indictment
- 12 months' imprisonment and/or a fine summarily

The Terrorism Act 2000, s. 19 states:

(1) This section applies where a person—
   (a) believes or suspects that another person has committed an offence under any of sections 15 to 18, and
   (b) bases his belief or suspicion on information which comes to his attention—
      (i) in the course of a trade, profession or business, or
      (ii) in the course of his employment (whether or not in the course of a trade, profession or business).

(1A) But this section does not apply if the information came to the person in the course of a business in the regulated sector.

(2) The person commits an offence if he does not disclose to a constable as soon as is reasonably practicable—
   (a) his belief or suspicion, and
   (b) the information on which it is based.

KEYNOTE

In relation to s. 19(2), a constable includes an authorised member of staff of the National Crime Agency (s. 19(7B)).

This section requires businesses to report any suspicions they may have that someone is laundering terrorist money or committing any of the other terrorist property offences in ss. 15 to 18. Section 19(1)(b) ensures the offence is focused on suspicions which arise at work.

'Employment' means any employment (paid or unpaid) including work under a contract for services or as an office holder, work experience provided pursuant to a training course or programme or in the course of training for employment, and voluntary work (s. 22A).

It is a defence for a person to prove that he/she had a reasonable excuse for not making the disclosure (s. 19(3)), or that the matters specified were disclosed in accordance with an established procedure for the making of disclosures (s. 19(4)). Disclosure by a professional legal adviser is not required if the information was obtained in privileged circumstances (s. 19(5)).

The Act also provides for offences of failure to disclose information by businesses in the 'regulated sector', i.e. accountancy firms, investment companies etc. (s. 21A) and tipping-off by businesses in the regulated sector (s. 21D). Businesses in the regulated sector are described in sch. 3A to the Act.

3.15.4.2 Disclosure of Information: Permission

The Terrorism Act 2000, s. 20 states:

> (1) A person may disclose to a constable—
> (a) a suspicion or belief that any money or other property is terrorist property or is derived from terrorist property;
> (b) any matter on which the suspicion or belief is based.
>
> (2) A person may make a disclosure to a constable in the circumstances mentioned in section 19(1) and (2).
>
> (3) Subsections (1) and (2) shall have effect notwithstanding any restriction on the disclosure of information imposed by statute or otherwise.
>
> (4) Where—
> (a) a person is in employment, and
> (b) his employer has established a procedure for the making of disclosures of the kinds mentioned in subsection (1) and section 19(2),
>
> subsections (1) and (2) shall have effect in relation to that person as if any reference to disclosure to a constable included a reference to disclosure in accordance with the procedure.

KEYNOTE

Section 20 ensures that businesses can disclose information to the police without fear of breaching legal restrictions.

References to a constable include references to an authorised National Crime Agency officer.

3.15.4.3 Information about Acts of Terrorism

OFFENCE: **Information about Acts of Terrorism—*Terrorism Act 2000, s. 38B***

- Triable either way • 10 years' imprisonment and/or a fine on indictment
- 12 months' imprisonment and/or a fine summarily

The Terrorism Act 2000, s. 38B states:

> (1) This section applies where a person has information which he knows or believes might be of material assistance—
> (a) in preventing the commission by another person of an act of terrorism, or
> (b) in securing the apprehension, prosecution or conviction of another person, in the United Kingdom, for an offence involving the commission, preparation or instigation of an act of terrorism.
>
> (2) The person commits an offence if he does not disclose the information as soon as reasonably practicable in accordance with subsection (3).
>
> (3) Disclosure is in accordance with this subsection if it is made—
> (a) in England and Wales, to a constable ...

KEYNOTE

This offence relates to any person who has information that he/she knows or believes might help prevent an act of terrorism or help bring terrorists to justice.

A person resident in the United Kingdom could be charged with this offence notwithstanding that he/she was outside the country when he/she became aware of the information (s. 38B(6)).

It is a defence for a person charged to prove that he/she had a reasonable excuse for not making the disclosure (s. 38B(4)).

3.15.4.4 Disclosure of and Interference with Information Offences

OFFENCE: **Disclosure of Information etc.—*Terrorism Act 2000, s. 39***

- Triable either way • Five years' imprisonment and/or a fine on indictment
- 12 months' imprisonment and/or a fine summarily

The Terrorism Act 2000, s. 39 states:

(1) Subsection (2) applies where a person knows or has reasonable cause to suspect that a constable is conducting or proposes to conduct a terrorist investigation.
(2) The person commits an offence if he—
 (a) discloses to another anything which is likely to prejudice the investigation, or
 (b) interferes with material which is likely to be relevant to the investigation.
(3) Subsection (4) applies where a person knows or has reasonable cause to suspect that a disclosure has been or will be made under any of sections 19 to 21B or 38B.
(4) The person commits an offence if he—
 (a) discloses to another anything which is likely to prejudice an investigation resulting from the disclosure under that section, or
 (b) interferes with material which is likely to be relevant to an investigation resulting from the disclosure under that section.

KEYNOTE

The offences within this section, including that at s. 39(2)(a), which is sometimes called 'tipping off', are essential to the disclosure regime and have a powerful deterrent effect. The defence at s. 39(5)(a) is listed in s. 118(5) and therefore imposes an evidential burden only on the defendant.

It is a defence for a person charged with an offence under s. 39(2) or (4) to prove that he/she did not know and had no reasonable cause to suspect that the disclosure or interference was likely to affect a terrorist investigation, or that he/she had a reasonable excuse for the disclosure or interference. The evidential burden of proof lies on the defendant.

If the disclosure is of a matter within s. 21D(2) or (3)(a) (terrorist property: tipping off), and the information on which the disclosure is based came to the person in the course of a business in the regulated sector, then subs. (2) and (4) above do not apply (s. 39(6A)).

3.15.5 Terrorism Act 2006: Offences

For the purposes of the 2006 Act the offences are grouped into three specific areas; encouragement etc. of terrorism; preparation of terrorist acts and terrorist training; offences involving radioactive devices and materials and nuclear facilities and sites. The offences relating to preparation of terrorist acts and offences involving radioactive devices are beyond the scope of this Manual.

3.15.5.1 Encouragement etc. of Terrorism

The offences within this group are:

- publishes a statement to encourage the commission, preparation or instigation of acts of terrorism or Convention offences (s. 1(2));
- engages in the dissemination of terrorist publications (s. 2(1)).

For the purpose of both these sections it is necessary to prove that the published statement(s) glorifies the act of terrorism and that a reasonable person would understand the statement as an encouragement or inducement to them to commit, prepare or instigate an act of terrorism. This 'reasonable person test' was introduced by the Counter-Terrorism and Border Security Act 2019.

'Glorification' includes any form of praise or celebration, and similar expressions are to be construed accordingly (s. 20(2)). The 'Convention offences' mentioned in s. 1(2) are those offences listed in sch. 1 to the Act and include offences in relation to explosives, biological weapons, chemical weapons, nuclear weapons, hostage-taking, hijacking, terrorist funds etc.

In relation to an offence under s. 2 of the Act, it was held that videos uploaded onto the internet of scenes showing attacks on soldiers of the Coalition forces in Iraq and Afghanistan by insurgents were depicting scenes of terrorism within the definition of s. 1 of the 2000 Act (*R* v *Gul* [2013] UKSC 64). Under this section, although the accused is free to argue that the prosecution constituted an unacceptable interference with the applicant's right to freedom of speech at common law, this defence is always a matter to be determined by the jury (*R* v *Brown* [2011] EWCA Crim 2751). In *Faraz* v *R* [2012] EWCA Crim 2820, it was held that evidence of possession of a publication cannot prove by itself that a person was encouraged by it to commit or instigate terrorist offences. This section does not prevent a person from holding offensive views or personally supporting a terrorist cause or communicating the fact that he/she supports such a cause. What this section prohibits is the intentional or reckless dissemination of a terrorist publication where the effect of an offender's conduct is a direct or indirect encouragement to the commission, preparation or instigation of acts of terrorism (*R* v *Ali (Humza)* [2018] EWCA Crim 547).

Section 3(1) provides that the offences under ss. 1 and 2 can be committed by publishing a statement electronically, i.e. via the internet. In *Iqbal* v *R* [2014] EWCA Crim 2650, the defendant posted and shared videos, articles and lectures that amounted to the glorification or encouragement of terrorism. 'Statement' includes a communication of any description, including a communication without words consisting of sounds or images or both (s. 20(6)). Section 3(3) provides for a notice to be served by a constable on the person electronically publishing the statement declaring that it is, in the constable's opinion, unlawfully terrorism-related and requiring its removal or modification (s. 3(3)). The methods for giving such a notice are provided in s. 4 of the Act. The offences under ss. 1 and 2 are punishable on indictment by a term of imprisonment not exceeding 15 years or a fine or both, and summarily by a term of imprisonment not exceeding six months or a fine or both.

3.15.6 Terrorism Act 2000: Police Powers

The Terrorism Act 2000 (Codes of Practice for the Exercise of Stop and Search Powers) Order 2012 (SI 2012/1794) sets out the basic principles for the use of powers by police officers.

3.15.6.1 Arrest without Warrant

The Terrorism Act 2000, s. 41 states:

(1) A constable may arrest without a warrant a person whom he reasonably suspects to be a terrorist.

KEYNOTE

The definition of a terrorist is broadly a person who has committed one of the main terrorism offences under the Act (including ss. 11, 12, 15 to 18, 54 and 56 to 63), or is or has been concerned in the commission, preparation or instigation of acts of terrorism (s. 40).

A magistrates' warrant may be obtained authorising any constable to enter and search the specified premises for the purpose of arresting the person to whom s. 41 applies (s. 42).

3.15.6.2 Search of Persons

The Terrorism Act 2000, s. 43 states:

(1) A constable may stop and search a person whom he reasonably suspects to be a terrorist to discover whether he has in his possession anything which may constitute evidence that he is a terrorist.

(2) A constable may search a person arrested under section 41 to discover whether he has in his possession anything which may constitute evidence that he is a terrorist.

(3) ...

(4) A constable may seize and retain anything which he discovers in the course of a search of a person under subsection (1) or (2) and which he reasonably suspects may constitute evidence that the person is a terrorist.

(4A) Subsection (4B) applies if a constable, in exercising the power under subsection (1) to stop a person whom the constable reasonably suspects to be a terrorist, stops a vehicle (see section 116(2)).

KEYNOTE

Where a vehicle is stopped the constable may search the vehicle, and anything in or on it, to discover whether there is anything which may constitute evidence that the person concerned is a terrorist, and may seize and retain anything which the constable discovers in the course of such a search, and reasonably suspects may constitute evidence that the person is a terrorist (s. 43(4B)). Nothing in s. 43(4B) confers a power to search any person but the power to search in that subsection is in addition to the power in subsection (1) to search a person whom the constable reasonably suspects to be a terrorist (s. 43(4C)).

In relation to s. 43(4A), s. 116(2) provides that the power to stop a person includes the power to stop a vehicle (other than an aircraft which is airborne).

Section 43C of the 2000 Act provides that a constable may stop and search a terrorist offender if the constable is satisfied that it is necessary to do so for purposes connected with protecting members of the public from a risk of terrorism (subs. (1)). This power applies where the offender has been released on licence (and not recalled), and the offender's licence includes a search condition (subs. (2)). The constable may search the vehicle and anything in or on it for purposes connected with protecting members of the public from a risk of terrorism (subs. (5)) (see the Terrorism Act 2000 (Alterations to the Search Powers Code for England, Wales and Scotland) Order 2022 (SI 2022/1087)).

3.15.6.3 Search of Vehicles

The Terrorism Act 2000, s. 43A states:

(1) Subsection (2) applies if a constable reasonably suspects that a vehicle is being used for the purposes of terrorism.

(2) The constable may stop and search—
- (a) the vehicle;
- (b) the driver of the vehicle;
- (c) a passenger in the vehicle;
- (d) anything in or on the vehicle or carried by the driver or a passenger;

to discover whether there is anything which may constitute evidence that the vehicle is being used for the purposes of terrorism.

KEYNOTE

A constable may seize and retain anything which the constable discovers in the course of a search under this section, and reasonably suspects may constitute evidence that the vehicle is being used for the purposes of terrorism (s. 43A(3)).

'Driver' in relation to an aircraft, hovercraft or vessel, means the captain, pilot or other person with control of the aircraft, hovercraft or vessel or any member of its crew and, in relation to a train, includes any member of its crew (s. 43A(5)).

3.15.6.4 Stop and Search in Specified Locations

The Terrorism Act 2000, s. 47A states:

(1) A senior police officer may give an authorisation under subsection (2) or (3) in relation to a specified area or place if the officer—
  (a) reasonably suspects that an act of terrorism will take place; and
  (b) reasonably considers that—
    (i) the authorisation is necessary to prevent such an act;
    (ii) the specified area or place is no greater than is necessary to prevent such an act; and
    (iii) the duration of the authorisation is no longer than is necessary to prevent such an act.

(2) An authorisation under this subsection authorises any constable in uniform to stop a vehicle in the specified area or place and to search—
  (a) the vehicle;
  (b) the driver of the vehicle;
  (c) a passenger in the vehicle;
  (d) anything in or on the vehicle or carried by the driver or a passenger.

(3) An authorisation under this subsection authorises any constable in uniform to stop a pedestrian in the specified area or place and to search—
  (a) the pedestrian;
  (b) anything carried by the pedestrian.

KEYNOTE

A constable in uniform may exercise the power conferred by an authorisation only for the purpose of discovering whether there is anything which may constitute evidence that the vehicle concerned is being used for the purposes of terrorism or (as the case may be) that the person concerned is a terrorist within the meaning of s. 40 (s. 47A(4)). However, the power conferred by such an authorisation may be exercised whether or not the constable reasonably suspects that there is such evidence (s. 47A(5)).

A constable may seize and retain anything which the constable discovers in the course of a search if he/she reasonably suspects that it may constitute evidence that the vehicle concerned is being used for the purposes of terrorism or (as the case may be) that the person is a terrorist (s. 47A(6)).

A 'senior police officer' who may give an authorisation is a police officer for the area who is of at least the rank of assistant chief constable (or commander) (sch. 6B).

Authorisation may also be given to prohibit or restrict parking on a specified road where it is considered expedient for the prevention of acts of terrorism (s. 48(1) and (2)). The power may be exercised by a constable placing a traffic sign on the road concerned (s. 49(1)).

3.15.7 Cordons

The 2000 Act gives the police the power, for a limited period, to designate or demarcate a specific area as a cordoned area for the purposes of a terrorist investigation, for instance, in the wake of a bomb.

3.15.7.1 Cordoned Areas

The Terrorism Act 2000, s. 33 states:

(1) An area is a cordoned area for the purposes of this Act if it is designated under this section.

(2) A designation may be made only if the person making it considers it expedient for the purposes of a terrorist investigation.

(3) If a designation is made orally, the person making it shall confirm it in writing as soon as is reasonably practicable.

KEYNOTE

Section 32 provides the meaning of 'terrorist investigation' as an investigation of:

- the commission, preparation or instigation of acts of terrorism;
- an act which appears to have been done for the purposes of terrorism;
- the resources of a proscribed organisation;
- the commission, preparation or instigation of an offence under this Act or under part 1 of the Terrorism Act 2006 other than an offence under s. 1 or 2 of that Act (terrorist publications).

The person making a designation shall arrange for the demarcation of the cordoned area, so far as is reasonably practicable, by means of tape marked with the word 'police', or in such other manner as a constable considers appropriate (s. 33(4)).

3.15.7.2 Power to Designate

The Terrorism Act 2000, s. 34 states:

(1) Subject to subsections (1A), (1B) and (2), a designation under section 33 may only be made—
  (a) where the area is outside Northern Ireland and is wholly or partly within a police area, by an officer for the police area who is of at least the rank of superintendent, and
  (b) ...
(1A)–(1C) ...
(2) A constable who is not of the rank required by subsection (1) may make a designation if he considers it necessary by reason of urgency.
(3) Where a constable makes a designation in reliance on subsection (2) he shall as soon as is reasonably practicable—
  (a) make a written record of the time at which the designation was made, and
  (b) ensure that a police officer of at least the rank of superintendent is informed.
(4) An officer who is informed of a designation in accordance with subsection (3)(b)—
  (a) shall confirm the designation or cancel it with effect from such time as he may direct, and
  (b) shall, if he cancels the designation, make a written record of the cancellation and the reason for it.

KEYNOTE

This power is designated to be investigatory in its nature.

Subsections (1A), (1B) and (1C) provide powers to designate to the Ministry of Defence and British Transport Police in relation to specified areas under their jurisdiction.

The period of designation begins at the time the order is made and ends on the date specified in the order. The initial designation cannot extend beyond 14 days (s. 35(2)). However, the period during which a designation has effect may be extended in writing from time to time by the person who made it, or an officer of at least superintendent rank (s. 35(3)). There is a time limit of 28 days on extended designations and this appears to mean an overall time limit of 28 days beginning with the day on which the order is made (s. 35(5)).

3.15.7.3 Police Powers

The Terrorism Act 2000, s. 36 states:

(1) A constable in uniform may—
  (a) order a person in a cordoned area to leave it immediately,
  (b) order a person immediately to leave premises which are wholly or partly in or adjacent to a cordoned area,
  (c) order the driver or person in charge of a vehicle in a cordoned area to move it from the area immediately,
  (d) arrange for the removal of a vehicle from a cordoned area,
  (e) arrange for the movement of a vehicle within a cordoned area,
  (f) prohibit or restrict access to a cordoned area by pedestrians or vehicles.

KEYNOTE

The officer giving the order or making the arrangements and prohibitions set out here must be in uniform. Therefore detectives or other plain clothes officers involved in the terrorist investigation will not have these powers available to them.

Failing to comply with an order, prohibition or restriction under this section is a summary offence punishable by three months' imprisonment and/or a fine (s. 36(2) and (4)).

This wording will presumably cover refusal. There is a defence if the person can show that he/she had a reasonable excuse for the failure.

A superintendent or above may request passenger, service and crew information from an owner or agent of a ship or aircraft which is arriving, or expected to arrive, at any place in the United Kingdom or is leaving, or expected to leave, from any place in the United Kingdom (Immigration, Asylum and Nationality Act 2006, s. 32(2)). There is a similar power to request freight information from the owners or agents of a ship or aircraft, and in the case of a vehicle, the owner or hirer (s. 33(2) and (3)).

It is an offence if without reasonable excuse a person fails to comply with a requirement imposed under ss. 32(2) or 33(2). The request must be for a police purpose, i.e. the prevention, detection, investigation or prosecution of criminal offences; safeguarding national security; and such other purposes as may be specified (s. 21(3) of the Immigration and Asylum Act 1999).

3.15.8 Offences Involving Explosive Substances

OFFENCE: **Causing Explosion Likely to Endanger Life or Property—*Explosive Substances Act 1883, s. 2***

- Triable on indictment • Life imprisonment

The Explosive Substances Act 1883, s. 2 states:

(1) A person who in the United Kingdom or (being a citizen of the United Kingdom and Colonies) in the Republic of Ireland unlawfully and maliciously causes by any explosive substance an explosion of a nature likely to endanger life or to cause serious injury to property shall, whether any injury to person or property has been actually caused or not, be guilty of an offence ...

KEYNOTE

This offence has as its purpose the protection of the public from serious harm, where the harm contemplated is of danger to life or serious harm to property from an explosion caused by an explosive substance. The broader context is the inherent dangerousness and unpredictability of explosive substances, and the potential risk they can pose (to life and property) if used, stored or manufactured, even in small quantities.

The consent of the Attorney-General (or Solicitor-General) is required before prosecuting this offence (s. 7(1) of the 1883 Act).

'Explosive substance' includes any materials for making any explosive substance; any implement or apparatus used, or intended or adapted to be used for causing or aiding any explosion (s. 9(1)).

The definition of 'explosive' under the Explosives Act 1875 also applies to this offence (*R* v *Wheatley* [1979] 1 WLR 144). Therefore, fireworks and petrol bombs will be covered (*R* v *Bouch* [1983] QB 246). Articles which have been held to amount to 'explosive substances' include:

- shotguns (*R* v *Downey* [1971] NI 224);
- electronic timers (*R* v *Berry (No. 3)* [1995] 1 WLR 7; *R* v *G* [2009] UKHL 13);
- gelignite with a fuse and detonator (*R* v *McCarthy* [1964] 1 WLR 196);
- a parcel sent through the post which would ignite and cause a fire when opened (*R* v *Margelis* [2021] EWCA Crim 1215).

An accused, who had an interest in chemicals and explosives, had turned an upstairs room in the family home into a makeshift laboratory where he stored chemicals and conducted experiments. One day, he mixed chemicals that resulted in an explosion causing damage to his home and serious injuries to himself. The defence was that he had not acted unlawfully or maliciously and had not intended or foreseen the risk of an explosion or its consequences. It submitted that the accused was 'a foolish and chaotic amateur' and the explosion was no more than an accident. The court held the accused had acted maliciously, stating that 'malice' means that nothing more needs to be proved for a s. 2 offence than an intention to cause an explosion or foresight that an explosion might be caused (*Haydon* v *R* [2026] EWCA Crim 12).

The Explosives Act 1975 provides a constable with the power to seize and detain any explosive or ingredient of an explosive or substance (s. 74).

OFFENCE: **Attempting to Cause Explosion or Keeping Explosive with Intent—*Explosive Substances Act 1883, s. 3***

- Triable on indictment • Life imprisonment

The Explosive Substances Act 1883, s. 3 states:

(1) A person who in the United Kingdom or a dependency or (being a citizen of the United Kingdom and Colonies) elsewhere unlawfully and maliciously—
   (a) does any act with intent to cause, or conspires to cause, by an explosive substance an explosion of a nature likely to endanger life, or cause serious injury to property, whether in the United Kingdom or elsewhere, or
   (b) makes or has in his possession or under his control an explosive substance with intent by means thereof to endanger life, or cause serious injury to property, whether in the United Kingdom or elsewhere, or to enable any other person so to do

shall, whether any explosion does or does not take place, and whether any injury to person or property is actually caused or not, be guilty of an offence ...

OFFENCE: **Making or Possessing Explosive under Suspicious Circumstances—*Explosive Substances Act 1883, s. 4***

- Triable on indictment • 14 years' imprisonment

The Explosive Substances Act 1883, s. 4 states:

(1) Any person who makes or knowingly has in his possession or under his control any explosive substance under such circumstances as to give rise to a reasonable suspicion that he is not making it or does not have it in his possession or under his control for a lawful object, shall, unless he can show that he made it or had it in his possession or under his control for a lawful object, be guilty of an offence.

KEYNOTE

The offence under s. 3 is one of specific intent.

Both of the offences under ss. 3 and 4 require the consent of the Attorney-General (or Solicitor-General) before a prosecution can be brought.

In cases of 'possession' the wording of these offences requires the prosecution to prove that a defendant *had* the relevant article in his/her possession and that he/she knew the nature of it (*R* v *Hallam* [1957] 1 QB 569). This should be contrasted with the usual approach to offences involving 'possession' where the second part (knowledge of the 'quality' of an item) does not need to be shown. However, the concept of 'in your possession' or 'under your control' is a wide one, as illustrated in a case where the defendant had moved out of his property and left homemade bombs and other articles in some boxes with a friend. New tenants in the property had discovered the boxes which later turned up on a rubbish tip. The defendant went to the police station after learning that he was a suspect and he claimed that he had collected the articles many years previously when he was too young to appreciate how dangerous they were. Although he had left the boxes with his friend he was nevertheless convicted of the offence under s. 4(1) as he still had the explosives under his control when he left the property (*R* v *Campbell* [2004] EWCA Crim 2309).

'Reasonable suspicion' in this case will be assessed *objectively*, that is, you must prove that the circumstances of the possession or making of the explosive substance would give rise to suspicion in a reasonable and objective bystander (*R* v *Fegan* (1971) 78 Cr App R 189; *R* v *G* [2009] UKHL 13).

Whether a person's purpose in having the items prohibited by these offences is a 'lawful object' will need to be determined in each case (*Fegan*). In *R* v *Riding* [2009] EWCA Crim 892, the defendant alleged he had made a pipe bomb out of mere curiosity, using explosives drained from a number of fireworks. The defence contended that 'lawful object' meant the absence of a criminal purpose rather than a positive object that was lawful. However, the court was satisfied it meant the latter and mere curiosity could not be a 'lawful object' in making a lethal pipe bomb. However, in *R* v *Copeland* [2020] UKSC 8 it was held that personal experimentation or self-education could be regarded as a 'lawful object'. In a further case considering the lawful object defence, it was held that given the obvious risks with using explosive substances, any experimentation involving them which gives rise to a risk of harm to other people or their property, or other unlawfulness such as causing a public nuisance, will not be capable of coming within the scope of the defence (*R* v *Flint* [2020] EWCA Crim 1266).

There is no need to show any criminal intent or an unlawful purpose on the part of the defendant (see *Campbell*).

In any proceeding against any person for a crime under s. 4, such person and his wife, or husband, as the case may be, may, if such person thinks fit, be called, sworn, examined and cross-examined as an ordinary witness in the case (s. 4(2)).

3.16 Diversity, Equality and Inclusion

3.16.1 Introduction

The Equality Act 2010 provides a framework of protection against direct and indirect discrimination, harassment and victimisation in services and public functions; premises; work; education; associations; and transport.

This chapter briefly sets out the key features of the 2010 Act together with Article 14 of the European Convention on Human Rights (ECHR) in relation to the 'prohibition of discrimination'.

3.16.2 Article 14—Prohibition of Discrimination

Article 14 of the ECHR states:

> The enjoyment of the rights and freedoms set forth in this Convention shall be secured without discrimination on any ground such as sex, race, colour, language, religion, political or other opinion, national or social origin, association with a national minority, property, birth or other status.

KEYNOTE

Article 14 simply provides a guarantee that access to the Convention's other provisions must be enjoyed equally by everyone under the jurisdiction of the particular State. The list set out in the Article is not exhaustive and other categories of people or grounds of discrimination may be added by the courts (and have been added by the European Court of Human Rights). A person claiming a breach of Article 14 must show that his/her own individual circumstances are similar to those of another person who has been treated differently in relation to the enjoyment of Convention rights.

The open-ended wording of Article 14 means that a wide range of categories of people who can be grouped by reference to their status may be protected. It makes express provision for indirect discrimination (see para. 3.16.4.7) and the Divisional Court has expressed considerable doubt as to whether Article 14 provides protection against indirect, as opposed to direct, discrimination (*R (On the Application of Barber)* v *Secretary of State for Work and Pensions* [2002] EWHC 1915 (Admin)).

3.16.3 Protected Characteristics

The protected characteristics covered by the Act are:

- Age
- Disability
- Gender reassignment
- Marriage and civil partnerships
- Race
- Religion or belief
- Sex
- Sexual orientation

KEYNOTE

Although Pregnancy and Maternity are also protected characteristics they are dealt with separately in the Act (see paras 3.16.4.5 and 3.16.4.6).

The Police and Criminal Evidence Act 1984, Code of Practice, Code C, para. 1.0 provides that the Equality Act 2010 makes it unlawful for police officers to discriminate against, harass or victimise any person on the grounds of the 'protected characteristics' of age, disability, gender reassignment, race, religion or belief, sex or sexual orientation, marriage or civil partnership, pregnancy and maternity, when using their powers.

3.16.3.1 Age

The Equality Act 2010, s. 5 states:

(1) In relation to the protected characteristic of age—
  (a) a reference to a person who has a particular protected characteristic is a reference to a person of a particular age group;
  (b) a reference to persons who share a protected characteristic is a reference to persons of the same age group.

(2) A reference to an age group is a reference to a group of persons defined by reference to age, whether by reference to a particular age or to a range of ages.

KEYNOTE

Where people fall in the same age group they share the protected characteristic of age, for example, an age group would include 'over fifties' or 21-year-olds.

In *Portelli* v *London Legal and Imaging Solutions Ltd* [2019] UKET Case No. 2201871/2205855, an employment tribunal held that the complainant had been subject to age discrimination based on a number of different behaviours by his employer. These included: promoting someone younger to his position while he was absent; showing unreasonable and hostile conduct towards him, for example, by dismissing him without a proper investigation and by not replying to his emails; writing him a letter that said he was 'finding it difficult to keep up with the pace of change' and suggesting that he should have basic-level remedial management training and that he had been employed for a long time and was set in his ways.

The Equality Act 2010 (Age Exceptions) Order 2012 (SI 2012/2466) provides the following exceptions:

- age-based concessions
- age-related holidays
- age verification
- clubs and associations concessions
- financial services
- immigration
- residential park homes
- sport.

There are no specific exceptions to the ban on age discrimination for health or social care services. This means that any age-based practices by the NHS and social care organisations need to be objectively justified, if challenged.

Persons aged under 18 or in school do not benefit from the protections in relation to goods, services and public functions.

3.16.3.2 Disability

The Equality Act 2010, s. 6 states:

(1) A person (P) has a disability if—
  (a) P has a physical or mental impairment, and
  (b) the impairment has a substantial and long-term adverse effect on P's ability to carry out normal day-to-day activities.

(2) A reference to a disabled person is a reference to a person who has a disability.
(3) In relation to the protected characteristic of disability—
  (a) a reference to a person who has a particular protected characteristic is a reference to a person who has a particular disability;
  (b) a reference to persons who share a protected characteristic is a reference to persons who have the same disability.

KEYNOTE

Schedule 1 to the Equality Act 2010 contains provisions of the Act relating to disability in employment and occupation. In relation to s. 6(1)(b), a person's ability to carry out normal day-to-day activities must be read as including a person's ability to participate fully and effectively in working life on an equal basis with other workers (sch. 1, para. 5A).

In *Hart* v *Chief Constable of Derbyshire Constabulary* [2008] EWCA Civ 929, confrontational duties were considered 'normal day-to-day activities'.

Physical or mental impairment includes sensory impairments such as sight and hearing and mental health issues. It also includes neurodivergent conditions such as ADHD (attention deficit hyperactivity disorder), autism (difficulties with social interaction and communication), dyspraxia (impaired coordination of physical movements) and dyslexia (reading disorder). Cancer, HIV infection and multiple sclerosis are each a disability. The focus of the Act is on the effect of impairment where there is evidence of a substantial long-term adverse effect. The effect of an impairment is long term if it has lasted for at least 12 months, it is likely to last for at least 12 months, or it is likely to last for the rest of the life of the person affected. If an impairment ceases to have a substantial adverse effect on a person's ability to carry out normal day-to-day activities, it is to be treated as continuing to have that effect if that effect is likely to recur (sch. 1, para. 2(1) and (2)).

A person's alcoholism is not an impairment for the purposes of this section (*R (On the Application of IXF)* v *Chief Constable of West Mercia Police* [2023] EWHC 2793 (Admin)).

3.16.3.3 Gender Reassignment

The Equality Act 2010, s. 7 states:

(1) A person has the protected characteristic of gender reassignment if the person is proposing to undergo, is undergoing or has undergone a process (or part of a process) for the purpose of reassigning the person's sex by changing physiological or other attributes of sex.
(2) A reference to a transsexual person is a reference to a person who has the protected characteristic of gender reassignment.
(3) In relation to the protected characteristic of gender reassignment—
  (a) a reference to a person who has a particular protected characteristic is a reference to a transsexual person;
  (b) a reference to persons who share a protected characteristic is a reference to transsexual persons.

KEYNOTE

Transgender people over the age of 18 have the right to change their legal gender so that it matches that of their gender identity. The Gender Recognition Act 2004 enables people who wish to change their legal gender to apply for a Gender Recognition Certificate (GRC) which shows that a person has satisfied the criteria for legal recognition in their acquired gender. The process only covers the gender identities of man and woman. Legal recognition comes in the form of a GRC and a new birth certificate. A GRC means that, from the date of issue, the individual will be considered in the eyes of the law to have the gender they identify with rather than the gender that accords with the sex that was recorded at birth.

The 2004 Act permits applications for a gender recognition certificate on the basis of having changed gender under the law of a country or territory outside the United Kingdom (s. 1(1)(b)). Applicants are required to provide evidence that they have changed gender under the law of an 'approved country or territory' outside the United Kingdom (s. 3(5)) (Gender Recognition (Approved Countries and Territories and Saving Provision) Order 2024 (SI 2024/401)).

In *R (On the Application of Castellucci)* v *Gender Recognition Panel* [2024] EWHC 54 (Admin), it was held that a fundamental legislative assumption of the Gender Recognition Act is that gender is binary and therefore it goes against the grain of the Act to interpret the word 'gender' as including non-binary gender. It therefore follows that the Act does not discriminate against a person contrary to Article 14 of the ECHR on the grounds of their status as a non-binary person.

It is a summary offence, punishable by a fine, for a person to disclose information acquired in an official capacity about a person's application for a gender recognition certificate or about the gender history of a successful applicant (s. 22(1) of the 2004 Act). This information is termed 'protected information' under the Act.

'Official capacity' means where a person acquires protected information in connection with the person's functions: as a member of the civil service, a constable or the holder of any other public office or in connection with the functions of a local or public authority or of a voluntary organisation; as an employer, or prospective employer, of the person to whom the information relates or as a person employed by such an employer or prospective employer; in the course of, or otherwise in connection with, the conduct of business or the supply of professional services (s. 22(3)).

Subsection (4) sets out exceptions to the general prohibition on disclosure, for example disclosure will not constitute an offence where the person to be identified had consented to the disclosure or where the disclosure is for the purposes of proceedings before a court or tribunal.

3.16.3.4 Marriage and Civil Partnerships

The Equality Act 2010, s. 8 states:

(1) A person has the protected characteristic of marriage and civil partnership if the person is married or is a civil partner.
(2) In relation to the protected characteristic of marriage and civil partnership—
  (a) a reference to a person who has a particular protected characteristic is a reference to a person who is married or is a civil partner;
  (b) a reference to persons who share a protected characteristic is a reference to persons who are married or are civil partners.

KEYNOTE

People who are not married or civil partners do not have this characteristic.

The Marriage (Same Sex Couples) Act 2013 extended marriage to same-sex couples and the Civil Partnership (Opposite-sex Couples) Regulations 2019 extended civil partnership to opposite sex couples.

3.16.3.5 Race

The Equality Act 2010, s. 9 states:

(1) Race includes—
  (a) colour;
  (b) nationality;
  (c) ethnic or national origins.
(2) In relation to the protected characteristic of race—
  (a) a reference to a person who has a particular protected characteristic is a reference to a person of a particular racial group;
  (b) a reference to persons who share a protected characteristic is a reference to persons of the same racial group.
(3) A racial group is a group of persons defined by reference to race; and a reference to a person's racial group is a reference to a racial group into which the person falls.
(4) The fact that a racial group comprises two or more distinct racial groups does not prevent it from constituting a particular racial group.

KEYNOTE

People who have or share characteristics of colour, nationality or ethnic or national origins can be described as belonging to a particular racial group. A racial group can be made up of two or more different racial groups.

'Nationality' has been held to include citizenship acquired by birth, and in *Souster* v *BBC Scotland* [2001] IRLR 150, it was held that an English applicant can be discriminated against by a Scottish employer.

'Ethnic group' may include any group with a shared culture or history (*Mandla* v *Dowell Lee* [1983] 2 AC 548). Sikhs (*Mandla* v *Dowell Lee* [1983] 2 AC 548), Jews (*Seide* v *Gillette Industries Ltd* [1980] IRLR 427), Romany Gypsies (*Commission for Racial Equality* v *Dutton* [1989] QB 783) and Irish Travellers (*O'Leary* v *Allied Domecq Inns Ltd*, CL 950275 July 2000, Central London County Court) have all been held to be ethnic groups but Scots, Welsh and English are, however, not an ethnic group (*Dawkins* v *Department of the Environment* [1993] IRLR 284).

'National origins' may overlap with nationality but the two concepts can be distinguished since 'nationality' is concerned with membership of a particular nation, and 'national origins' describes a person's connection by birth with a nation (*Ealing London Borough Council* v *Race Relations Board* [1972] AC 342).

'Racial group' includes a group of people who have or share a colour, ethnic, or national origin or nationality.

A Minister of the Crown may amend the Act so as to add 'caste' to the current definition of 'race' (s. 9(5)). The term 'caste' denotes a hereditary, endogamous (marrying within the group) community associated with a traditional occupation and ranked accordingly on a perceived scale of ritual purity, e.g. the four classes (varnas) of Hindu tradition (the Brahmin, Kshatriya, Vaishya and Shudra communities). In *Chandhok* v *Tirkey* [2014] UKEAT 0190/14/1912, it was considered that 'caste' might come within s. 9(1)(c) since 'ethnic origins' had a wide and flexible ambit, including characteristics determined by 'descent'.

3.16.3.6 Religion or Belief

The Equality Act 2010, s. 10 states:

(1) Religion means any religion and a reference to religion includes a reference to a lack of religion.
(2) Belief means any religious or philosophical belief and a reference to belief includes a reference to a lack of belief.
(3) In relation to the protected characteristic of religion or belief—
  (a) a reference to a person who has a particular protected characteristic is a reference to a person of a particular religion or belief;
  (b) a reference to persons who share a protected characteristic is a reference to persons who are of the same religion or belief.

KEYNOTE

The section provides a definition in line with the freedom of thought, conscience and religion guaranteed by Article 9 of the ECHR. The main limitation is that the religion must have a clear structure and belief system. Denominations or sects within a religion can be considered to be a religion or belief, such as Protestants and Catholics within Christianity.

In *Eweida* v *United Kingdom* (2013) 57 EHRR 8 it was held that prohibiting a woman from visibly wearing a cross at work amounted to an interference with her right to manifest her Christian religion and this was in breach of the positive obligation under Article 9 of the ECHR (Right to freedom of thought, conscience and religion). However, in three other applications in the same case, which related to practising Christians, there was held to be no breach of either Article 9 or Article 14. (The rights and freedoms set forth in the Convention shall be secured without discrimination on any ground such as religion.) These applications included: a nurse wearing a cross where the discrimination was based on health and safety rather than religious grounds; a registrar of births, deaths and marriages who believed that same-sex civil partnerships are contrary to God's law and refused to carry out civil partnerships; a Relate counsellor who refused to work with couples on same-sex sexual practices.

A religious police officer who regularly mentioned his faith at work was referred to by colleagues as 'Father Ted' (a priest portrayed in a TV comedy series) and other negative comments. He should not have been offended when other officers challenged his belief (*Roderick* v *Chief Constable of South Wales* [2021] UKET Case Nos 1601871/2018 and 1600511/2019).

Religious belief can vary from individual to individual within the same religion. Jewish people believe men should wear the Kippah (skull cap) at all times; and some Muslims believe women should cover their entire body and face with the Jilbab and Burqa (*R (On the Application of Begum)* v *Governors of Denbigh High School* [2006] UKHL 15). In *Power* v *Greater Manchester Police Authority* [2011] Eq LR 16, where a person was dismissed on grounds of his beliefs, it was not the belief itself but the expression of those beliefs which was in part the cause of his dismissal.

The criteria for determining what is a 'philosophical belief' are that it must be genuinely held; be a belief and not an opinion or viewpoint based on the present state of information available; be a belief as to a weighty and substantial aspect of human life and behaviour; attain a certain level of cogency, seriousness, cohesion and importance; and be worthy of respect in a democratic society, compatible with human dignity and not conflict with the fundamental rights of others. For example, a belief in 'climate change' affecting how a person lived his/her life is protected by the Act (*Grainger plc* v *Nicholson* [2010] 2 All ER 253).

A philosophical belief would only be excluded for failing to satisfy *Grainger plc* if it was the kind of belief the expression of which would be akin to Nazism or totalitarianism. The claimant held gender-critical beliefs, which included the belief that sex is immutable and not to be conflated with gender identity. Some transgender people found the claimant's remarks offensive and 'transphobic'. The tribunal held that the complainant's beliefs were widely shared and did not seek to destroy the rights of trans persons. The claimant's belief, whilst offensive to some, and notwithstanding its potential to result in the harassment of trans persons in some circumstances, fell within the protection of Article 9 of the ECHR and was therefore in line with s. 10 of the Equality Act 2010 (*Forstater* v *CGD Europe* [2021] UKEAT 0105 20 1006).

In *Cassamitjana* v *League Against Cruel Sports* [2020] UKET 3331129/2018 (21 January 2020) an employment tribunal judge ruled that ethical veganism was a philosophical belief.

Other cases where it was determined a philosophical belief was not protected by the Act included supporting Brexit where a person shared offensive posts on social media about immigrants (*Fairbanks* v *Change Grow Live* [2024] Case No. 2409700/2023) and a person's belief in English nationalism declaring that Muslims should be forcibly deported (*Thomas* v *Surrey and Borders Partnership NHS Foundation Trust* [2024] EAT 141).

3.16.3.7 Sex

The Equality Act 2010, s. 11 states:

In relation to the protected characteristic of sex—

(a) a reference to a person who has a particular protected characteristic is a reference to a man or to a woman;

(b) a reference to persons who share a protected characteristic is a reference to persons of the same sex.

KEYNOTE

This provision explains that references in the Act to people having the protected characteristic of sex are to mean being a man or a woman, and that men share this characteristic with other men, and women with other women.

In *Women Scotland Ltd* v *The Scottish Ministers* [2025] UKSC 16, the Supreme Court was concerned with establishing the correct interpretation of the Equality Act 2010 which seeks to give statutory protection to people who are at risk of suffering from unlawful discrimination directly affecting women and members of the trans community. The court held that the meaning of the terms, 'sex', 'man' and 'woman' in the 2010 Act is biological and not certificated sex and that any other interpretation would render this incoherent and impracticable to operate. Therefore, a person with a GRC in the female gender does not come within the definition of 'woman' for the purposes of sex discrimination in s. 11 of the Act. The ramifications of this case are to be considered by Parliament and the EHRC to determine if any amendments are required to the current legislation.

The Act contains provisions (ss. 66 to 70) designed to achieve equality between men and women in pay and other terms of employment where the work of an employee and his/her comparator, a person of the opposite sex, is equal. It does so by providing for a sex equality clause to be read into the employee's contract of employment. This is designed to ensure parity of terms between the employee and his/her comparator.

For work to be equal, a claimant must establish that he/she is doing like work, work rated as equivalent or work of equal value to a comparator's work (s. 65). For example, in *Blackburn* v *West Midlands Police* [2008] EWCA Civ 1208 it was held that where police officers needed to work hours compatible with their child care responsibilities they were not entitled to special payments received by officers working 24/7 shift patterns.

3.16.3.8 Sexual Orientation

The Equality Act 2010, s. 12 states:

(1) Sexual orientation means a person's sexual orientation towards—
  (a) persons of the same sex,
  (b) persons of the opposite sex, or
  (c) persons of either sex.
(2) In relation to the protected characteristic of sexual orientation—
  (a) a reference to a person who has a particular protected characteristic is a reference to a person who is of a particular sexual orientation;
  (b) a reference to persons who share a protected characteristic is a reference to persons who are of the same sexual orientation.

KEYNOTE

This section defines the protected characteristic of sexual orientation as being a person's sexual orientation towards: people of the same sex as him/her (the person is a gay man or a lesbian); people of the opposite sex from him/her (the person is heterosexual); people of both sexes (the person is bisexual).

3.16.4 Discrimination

The Equality Act 2010 provides for the following six different types of discrimination which are discussed within this section:

- **Direct discrimination**: discrimination because of a protected characteristic.
- **Associative discrimination**: direct discrimination against someone because he/she is associated with another person with a protected characteristic.
- **Indirect discrimination**: a rule or policy that applies to everyone but disadvantages a person with a protected characteristic.
- **Harassment**: behaviour deemed offensive by the recipient.
- **Victimisation**: discrimination against someone because he/she made or supported a complaint under Equality Act legislation.
- **Discrimination by perception**: direct discrimination against someone because others think he/she has a protected characteristic.

KEYNOTE

In proceedings relating to contraventions of the Act (save offences), the burden of proof rests initially with the complainant. Once the complainant establishes facts from which it might be presumed that there had been discrimination, the burden of proof shifts to the respondent to prove no breach of the principle of equal treatment (s. 136).

3.16.4.1 Direct Discrimination

The Equality Act 2010, s. 13 states:

(1) A person (A) discriminates against another (B) if, because of a protected characteristic, A treats B less favourably than A treats or would treat others.
(2) If the protected characteristic is age, A does not discriminate against B if A can show A's treatment of B to be a proportionate means of achieving a legitimate aim.
(3) If the protected characteristic is disability, and B is not a disabled person, A does not discriminate against B only because A treats or would treat disabled persons more favourably than A treats B.
(4) If the protected characteristic is marriage and civil partnership, this section applies to a contravention of Part 5 (work) only if the treatment is because it is B who is married or a civil partner.
(5) If the protected characteristic is race, less favourable treatment includes segregating B from others.
(6) If the protected characteristic is sex—
   (a) less favourable treatment of a woman includes less favourable treatment of her because she is breast-feeding;
   (b) in a case where B is a man, no account is to be taken of special treatment afforded to a woman in connection with pregnancy, childbirth or maternity.

KEYNOTE

To constitute direct discrimination the treatment experienced by B must be different from that of another person. This difference is often referred to as a 'comparator'. The treatment of B must be less favourable than the treatment afforded a comparator. The comparator can be hypothetical where B can establish direct discrimination by showing that if there was another person in similar circumstances, but without B's protected characteristic, that person would be treated more favourably (for an explanation of hypothetical comparators see *Shamoon* v *Chief Constable of the Royal Ulster Constabulary* [2003] UKHL 11).

Less favourable treatment is a broad concept and any disadvantage to which B has been subject will constitute such treatment. B need not have suffered a tangible or material loss (*Chief Constable of West Yorkshire Police* v *Khan* [2001] UKHL 48) but it is not enough merely to show unreasonable treatment (*Bahl* v *The Law Society* [2004] IRLR 799).

In *Earl Shilton Town Council* v *Miller* [2023] EAT, the employment tribunal held that the respondent's provision of inadequate toilet facilities for women subjected the claimant to direct sex discrimination.

The test of whether less favourable treatment was 'because of' a protected characteristic is an objective test of causation. The words 'because of' have the same meaning as the words 'on the grounds of' which were used in the previous legislation. This change in wording does not alter the legal meaning of the definition, but rather, is designed to make it more accessible to the ordinary user of the Act.

Less favourable treatment of a person because that person is associated with a protected characteristic, e.g. because the person has a friend or partner with a particular protected characteristic, or carries out work related to a protected characteristic, is within the scope of this section. This might include carers of disabled people and elderly relatives, who can claim they were treated unfairly because of duties that they had to carry out at home relating to their care work. For example, the non-disabled mother of a disabled child can be discriminated against because of the child's disability (*Coleman* v *Attridge Law* (Case C-303/06) [2008] IRLR 722). It also covers discrimination against someone because, for example, his/her partner is from another country. This is known as 'associative discrimination'.

The use of the words 'because of' are also wide enough to allow claims for direct discrimination where less favourable treatment is based on the claimant's perceived protected characteristics, i.e. where others think he/she has a protected characteristic (even if he/she does not). This is known as 'discrimination by perception'. For example, in *English* v *Thomas Sanderson Ltd* [2008] EWCA Civ 1421 it was held that homophobic banter amounts to unlawful harassment even when the victim's tormentors know the person is not gay.

3.16.4.2 Discrimination Arising from Disability

The Equality Act 2010, s. 15 states:

(1) A person (A) discriminates against a disabled person (B) if—
  (a) A treats B unfavourably because of something arising in consequence of B's disability, and
  (b) A cannot show that the treatment is a proportionate means of achieving a legitimate aim.
(2) Subsection (1) does not apply if A shows that A did not know, and could not reasonably have been expected to know, that B had the disability.

KEYNOTE

This section provides that it is discrimination to treat a disabled person unfavourably not because of the person's disability itself but because of something arising from, or in consequence of, that disability, such as the need to take a period of disability-related absence. It is, however, possible to justify such treatment if it can be shown to be a proportionate means of achieving a legitimate aim. In *Buchanan* v *The Commissioner of Police of the Metropolis* [2016] UKEAT 0112/16/RN, where a seriously injured police motor cyclist was subject to the 'Unsatisfactory Performance Procedure' it was held that he had received unfavourable treatment arising from a disability. The tribunal was required to consider whether the treatment was justified, as it was not sufficient to ask whether the underlying procedure was justified.

Where a disability places an employee at a substantial disadvantage such that they cannot continue in their present job, and are at risk of imminent dismissal, there is no rule of law that it cannot be a reasonable adjustment to give them a trial period in a new role. Nor is there any rule of law that it must be certain, or likely to some particular degree, that the employee will be successful in a trial (*Rentokil Initial UK Ltd* v *Miller (Disability Discrimination)* [2024] EAT 37).

For this type of discrimination to occur, the employer or other person must know, or reasonably be expected to know, that the disabled person has a disability.

In the judgment of *Lewisham London Borough Council* v *Malcolm* [2008] UKHL 43, it was held that the previous legislative provisions no longer provided the degree of protection from disability-related discrimination that is intended for disabled people. This section is aimed at re-establishing an appropriate balance between enabling a disabled person to make out a case of experiencing a detriment which arises because of his/her disability, and providing an opportunity for an employer or other person to defend the treatment.

3.16.4.3 Adjustments for Disabled Persons

The duty to make reasonable adjustments is a key element of a range of measures intended to eliminate barriers to access and participation for disabled people.

The Equality Act 2010, s. 20 states:

(1) Where this Act imposes a duty to make reasonable adjustments on a person, this section, sections 21 and 22 and the applicable Schedule apply; and for those purposes, a person on whom the duty is imposed is referred to as A.
(2) The duty comprises the following three requirements.
(3) The first requirement is a requirement, where a provision, criterion or practice of A's puts a disabled person at a substantial disadvantage in relation to a relevant matter in comparison with persons who are not disabled, to take such steps as it is reasonable to have to take to avoid the disadvantage.
(4) The second requirement is a requirement, where a physical feature puts a disabled person at a substantial disadvantage in relation to a relevant matter in comparison with persons who are not disabled, to take such steps as it is reasonable to have to take to avoid the disadvantage.
(5) The third requirement is a requirement, where a disabled person would, but for the provision of an auxiliary aid, be put at a substantial disadvantage in relation to a relevant matter in comparison with persons who are not disabled, to take such steps as it is reasonable to have to take to provide the auxiliary aid.

KEYNOTE

The duty to make reasonable adjustments comprises three requirements which apply where a disabled person is placed at a substantial disadvantage in comparison with non-disabled people.

The first requirement covers changing the way things are done (such as changing a practice), the second covers making changes to the built environment (such as providing access to a building), and the third covers providing auxiliary aids and services (such as providing special computer software or providing a different service). A claimant had a disability which caused her to suffer from migraines caused by computer software. The respondent unsuccessfully tried to address this by use of screen magnification software and eventually moved the claimant to a paper-based role. Although there was an unreasonable delay in making these adjustments, it was held that the respondent had complied with this section (*Department of Work and Pensions* v *Robinson* [2019] UKEAT 0021/19/2307).

Under the second requirement, taking steps to avoid the disadvantage will include removing, altering or providing a reasonable means of avoiding the physical feature, where it would be reasonable to do so (s. 209). Where the first or third requirements involve the way in which information is provided, a reasonable step includes providing that information in an accessible format (s. 20(6)). It also makes clear that, except where the Act states otherwise, it would never be reasonable for a person bound by the duty to pass on the costs of complying with it to an individual disabled person (s. 20(7)).

The section contains only one threshold for the reasonable adjustment duty, that of 'substantial disadvantage'. Section 212(1) defines 'substantial' as more than minor or trivial.

Section 21 provides that a failure to comply with any one of the reasonable adjustment requirements amounts to discrimination against a disabled person to whom the duty is owed. It also provides that, apart from under this Act, no other action can be taken for failure to comply with the duty. The test of reasonableness is an objective one (*Collins* v *Royal National Theatre Board Ltd* [2004] IRLR 395), and will always depend on the particular circumstances in an individual case (*Archibald* v *Fife County Council* [2004] IRLR 651).

Although accepting the difficult role the police are often called upon to play, in *ZH* v *Commissioner of Police for the Metropolis* [2012] EWHC 604 (QB) it was held that the police dealing with a person who was severely autistic had a duty to make reasonable adjustments in dealing with that person irrespective of the fact that they acted in a well-intentioned but misguided manner.

In *Chief Constable of South Yorkshire* v *Jelic* [2010] IRLR 744 it was determined that the force had not acted 'reasonably' when it failed to allow an officer suffering from chronic anxiety syndrome to swap jobs with another officer. Also, in *Hinsley* v *Chief Constable of West Mercia Constabulary* [2010] UKEAT 0200/10/0911, it was decided that there was a breach of duty to make reasonable adjustments where there was a failure to reinstate a probationary police officer who had resigned while depressed. However, where an officer was perceived to have a dangerous mental condition, the adjustments made to ensure he did not present a danger to colleagues or to the public were considered reasonable (*Aitken* v *Commissioner of Police of the Metropolis* [2011] EWCA Civ 582). In *Cordell* v *Foreign and Commonwealth Office* [2012] ICR 280, a tribunal dismissed claims of direct discrimination and discrimination by way of failure to make reasonable adjustments where the costs of providing an English-speaking lip-speaker support for a deaf employee were about £230,000 a year.

Taking a Psychiatric Assistance Dog to work was not considered a reasonable adjustment for an officer who suffered from a variety of disabilities including ASD (autistic spectrum disorder) (*Parker* v *Chief Constable of Hampshire* [2025] ET 1403767/2022).

It was held that police officers lawfully searching the home of a man whom they knew to be profoundly deaf did not have any effect on the ability of the man and the officers to communicate with each other effectively without a British Sign Language interpreter being present. Officers who had had previous dealings with the man were satisfied on the basis of these dealings that they could achieve a basic level of communication with him without the benefit of an interpreter (*Finnegan* v *Chief Constable of Northumbria* [2013] EWCA Civ 1191).

3.16.4.4 Gender Reassignment Discrimination: Cases of Absence from Work

The Equality Act 2010, s. 16 states:

(1) This section has effect for the purposes of the application of Part 5 (work) to the protected characteristic of gender reassignment.
(2) A person (A) discriminates against a transsexual person (B) if, in relation to an absence of B's that is because of gender reassignment, A treats B less favourably than A would treat B if—
  (a) B's absence was because of sickness or injury, or
  (b) B's absence was for some other reason and it is not reasonable for B to be treated less favourably.
(3) A person's absence is because of gender reassignment if it is because the person is proposing to undergo, is undergoing or has undergone the process (or part of the process) mentioned in section 7(1).

KEYNOTE

A person's absence is 'because of gender reassignment' if it is because the person is proposing to undergo, is undergoing, or has undergone gender reassignment. For example, where a female to male transgender person takes time off work to receive hormone treatment as part of his gender reassignment, his employer cannot discriminate against him because of his absence from work for this purpose.

3.16.4.5 Pregnancy and Maternity Discrimination: Non-work Cases

The Equality Act 2010, s. 17 states:

(1) This section has effect for the purposes of the application to the protected characteristic of pregnancy and maternity of—
  (a) Part 3 (services and public functions);
  (b) Part 4 (premises);
  (c) Part 6 (education);
  (d) Part 7 (associations).
(2) A person (A) discriminates against a woman if A treats her unfavourably because of a pregnancy of hers.
(3) A person (A) discriminates against a woman if, in the period of 26 weeks beginning with the day on which she gives birth, A treats her unfavourably because she has given birth.
(4) The reference in subsection (3) to treating a woman unfavourably because she has given birth includes, in particular, a reference to treating her unfavourably because she is breast-feeding.
(5) For the purposes of this section, the day on which a woman gives birth is the day on which—
  (a) she gives birth to a living child, or
  (b) she gives birth to a dead child (more than 24 weeks of the pregnancy having passed).

KEYNOTE

Note that pregnancy and maternity are 'protected characteristics' even though they are not grouped with the other protected characteristics in the Act.

Pregnancy and maternity discrimination is excluded from the definition of direct sex discrimination (s. 17(6)) and is dealt with under this separate provision and s. 18 (work situations, see para. 3.16.4.6).

3.16.4.6 Pregnancy and Maternity Discrimination: Work Cases

The Equality Act 2010, s. 18 states:

(1) This section has effect for the purposes of the application of Part 5 (work) to the protected characteristic of pregnancy and maternity.

(2) A person (A) discriminates against a woman if, in, or after, the protected period in relation to a pregnancy of hers, A treats her unfavourably—
  (a) because of the pregnancy, or
  (b) because of illness suffered by her in that protected period as a result of the pregnancy.
(3) A person (A) discriminates against a woman if A treats her unfavourably because she is on compulsory maternity leave or an equivalent compulsory maternity leave.
(4) A person (A) discriminates against a woman if A treats her unfavourably because she is exercising or seeking to exercise, or has exercised or sought to exercise, the right to ordinary or additional maternity leave or a right to equivalent maternity leave.

KEYNOTE

Section 18(6) provides that the protected period, in relation to a woman's pregnancy, begins when the pregnancy begins, and ends:

(a) if she has the right to ordinary and additional maternity leave, at the end of the additional maternity leave period or (if earlier) when she returns to work after the pregnancy;
(aa) if she does not have that right, but has a right to equivalent maternity leave, at the end of that leave period, or (if earlier) when she returns to work after the pregnancy;
(b) if she does not have a right as described in paragraph (a) or (aa), at the end of the period of 2 weeks beginning with the end of the pregnancy.

This section was amended by the Equality Act 2010 (Amendment) Regulations 2023 to reflect the principle in *Brown* v *Rentokil* (Case C-179/88) so that protection against discrimination on grounds of pregnancy and maternity covers unfavourable treatment after the 'protected period' as well as during it, where the treatment is because of the pregnancy or pregnancy-related illness during the protected period.

Section 13 (direct discrimination, **see para. 3.16.4.1**), so far as it relates to sex discrimination, does not apply to the treatment of a woman insofar as it is in or after the protected period in relation to her, and is for a reason mentioned in para. (a) or (b) of subs. (2), or it is for a reason mentioned in subs. (3) or (4) (subs. (7)). In *Maksymiuk* v *Bar Roma Partnership* [2012] Eq LR 917 an employee who was the only one of a number of bar staff who was selected for dismissal by reason of purported redundancy only a matter of days after she had announced that she was pregnant, had her claim of discrimination on the ground of pregnancy or sickness related to pregnancy dismissed.

In *The Commissioner of the City of London Police* v *Geldart* [2019] UKEAT 0032/19/2911, it was held to be direct sex discrimination where an officer on maternity leave was not given payment or partial payment of what is known as the London Allowance during her absence from duty.

Claims for direct pregnancy and maternity discrimination and unfair dismissal succeeded where an employee was dismissed after receiving a series of negative comments about her pregnancy concerning her performance at work. The type of conduct she had been guilty of in the eyes of her employer could not be considered as gross misconduct (*Sanderson* v *Bespoke Digital Agency Ltd*, ET 2405377/2018).

Pregnancy discrimination can include where the respondent: failed to adjust the claimant's hours; failed to redeploy the claimant or failed to explore the possibility thereof; raised issues regarding references previously accepted; breached the fundamental terms of trust and confidence due to discriminating against her because she was pregnant (causing the claimant to resign); failed to provide the claimant with a parking space; notifying the claimant that she would not be entitled to sick pay (*Ferguson* v *G4S Secure Solutions* [2021] UKET 2414102/2019).

The Police Regulations 2003 provide for pay and leave entitlement in relation to pregnant officers.

Pay

Regulation 24 states:

(1)–(2) ...
(3) For the purposes of this regulation in reckoning a member's service in any rank—
  (a)–(e) ...
  (f) in the case of a female member who has taken one or more periods of maternity leave, in respect of each maternity period—
    (i) where that leave has been for 52 weeks or more, account shall be taken of the first 52 weeks whilst on maternity leave;

(ii) where that leave has been for less than 52 weeks, account shall be taken of any period spent on maternity leave;

(g) account shall be taken of any period of parental leave taken in accordance with a determination under regulation 33(8)(b);

Leave

Regulation 33 states:

(1)–(5) ...

(6) A female member of a police force who is pregnant shall, in such circumstances as shall be determined by the Secretary of State, have the right not to be unreasonably refused special leave from duty to enable her to keep an appointment for the purpose of receiving antenatal care.

(7) A female member of a police force qualifies for maternity leave in such circumstances as shall be determined by the Secretary of State.

(8) A member of a police force shall, so far as the exigencies of duty permit, be granted such—

(a) maternity support leave;

(b) parental leave;

(c) adoption leave, and

(d) adoption support leave

in such circumstances, as the Secretary of State shall determine; and in this paragraph 'maternity support leave' means leave to enable support to be given to an expectant mother at or around the time of birth.

3.16.4.7 Indirect Discrimination

The Equality Act 2010, s. 19 states:

(1) A person (A) discriminates against another (B) if A applies to B a provision, criterion or practice which is discriminatory in relation to a relevant protected characteristic of B's.

(2) For the purposes of subsection (1), a provision, criterion or practice is discriminatory in relation to a relevant protected characteristic of B's if—

(a) A applies, or would apply, it to persons with whom B does not share the characteristic,

(b) it puts, or would put, persons with whom B shares the characteristic at a particular disadvantage when compared with persons with whom B does not share it,

(c) it puts, or would put, B at that disadvantage, and

(d) A cannot show it to be a proportionate means of achieving a legitimate aim.

KEYNOTE

Apart from pregnancy and maternity, indirect discrimination applies to all the protected characteristics.

Indirect discrimination occurs when a policy which applies in the same way for everybody has an effect which particularly disadvantages people with a protected characteristic. Where a particular group is disadvantaged in this way, a person in that group is indirectly discriminated against if he/she is put at that disadvantage, unless the person applying the policy can justify it.

When a policy would put a person at a disadvantage if it were applied, e.g. where a person is deterred from applying for a job or taking up an offer of service because a policy which would be applied would result in his/her disadvantage, this may also be indirect discrimination.

Examples of indirect discrimination have included:

- all employees to work within 'normal office hours' (*Bhudi* v *IMI Refiners* [1994] IRLR 204);
- all workers to have short hair thereby making it difficult for some groups such as Sikhs to comply (*Mandla* v *Dowell* [1983] 2 AC 548);
- 100 per cent of males but only 95 per cent of females could comply with a policy relating to rostering duties (*London Underground Ltd* v *Edwards (No. 2)* [1998] IRLR 364);
- BME and older candidates disproportionately failed to pass the Core Skills Assessment (CSA) compared to white and younger candidates. Passing the CSA was necessary to progress to higher grades in the Civil Service (*Home Office (UK Border Agency)* v *Essop* [2017] UKSC 27);
- a pregnant police officer required to transfer from an operational role to a non-operational role (*Town* v *Chief Constable of Devon and Cornwall* [2018] UKEAT 1401471/2018).

3.16.4.8 Indirect Discrimination: Same Disadvantage

The Equality Act 2010, s. 19A states:

(1) A person (A) discriminates against another (B) if—
  (a) A applies to B a provision, criterion or practice,
  (b) also applies, or would apply, the provision, criterion or practice to—
    (i) persons who share a relevant protected characteristic, and
    (ii) persons who do not share that relevant protected characteristic,
  (c) B does not share that relevant protected characteristic,
  (d) the provision, criterion or practice puts, or would put, persons with the relevant protected characteristic at a particular disadvantage when compared with persons who do not share the relevant protected characteristic,
  (e) the provision, criterion or practice puts, or would put, B at substantively the same disadvantage as persons who do share the relevant protected characteristic, and
  (f) A cannot show that the provision, criterion or practice is a proportionate means of achieving a legitimate aim.

(2) The relevant protected characteristics for the purposes of this section are—
  age;
  disability;
  gender reassignment;
  marriage and civil partnership;
  race;
  religion or belief;
  sex;
  sexual orientation.

> **KEYNOTE**
>
> This section was added by the Equality Act 2010 (Amendment) Regulations 2023 to reproduce the principle established in a European case (*'CHEZ Razpredelenie Bulgaria' AD* v *Komisia za zashtita ot diskriminatsia* (Case C-83/14)). A person without a relevant protected characteristic is indirectly discriminated against where he/she suffers alongside persons with a relevant protected characteristic from a particular disadvantage arising from a discriminatory provision, criterion or practice.

3.16.4.9 Harassment

The Equality Act 2010, s. 26 states:

(1) A person (A) harasses another (B) if—
  (a) A engages in unwanted conduct related to a relevant protected characteristic, and
  (b) the conduct has the purpose or effect of—
    (i) violating B's dignity, or
    (ii) creating an intimidating, hostile, degrading, humiliating or offensive environment for B.

(2) A also harasses B if—
  (a) A engages in unwanted conduct of a sexual nature, and
  (b) the conduct has the purpose or effect referred to in subsection (1)(b).

(3) A also harasses B if—
  (a) A or another person engages in unwanted conduct of a sexual nature or that is related to gender reassignment or sex,
  (b) the conduct has the purpose or effect referred to in subsection (1)(b), and
  (c) because of B's rejection of or submission to the conduct, A treats B less favourably than A would treat B if B had not rejected or submitted to the conduct.

> **KEYNOTE**
>
> This section defines three types of harassment.
>
> The first type, which applies to the protected characteristics apart from pregnancy and maternity, and marriage and civil partnership, involves unwanted conduct which is related to a relevant characteristic and has the purpose or effect of creating an intimidating, hostile, degrading, humiliating or offensive environment for

the complainant or of violating the complainant's dignity (*Richmond Pharmacology* v *Dhaliwal* [2009] IRLR 336). In deciding whether conduct has the effect referred to in s. 26(1)(b), the perception of B, the other circumstances of the case, and whether it is reasonable for the conduct to have that effect, must be taken into account (s. 26(4)).

The second type is sexual harassment which is unwanted conduct of a sexual nature where this has the same purpose or effect as the first type of harassment. In *Wadman* v *Carpenter Farrer Partnership* [1993] IRLR 374, sexual harassment was described as conduct of a sexual nature or other conduct based on sex affecting the dignity of women and men at work. This could include verbal remarks, written comments and physical contact. When a man calls another man 'mate' or 'lad' it is not demeaning. However, using words like 'chick, babes, bobs, honey, hun and sweetie' are all demeaning and infantilising ways of referring to women (*Hartley* v *D Hollowell & Sons Ltd* [2021] UKET Case No. 2405802/2020).

The third type is treating someone less favourably because he/she has either submitted to or rejected sexual harassment, or harassment related to sex or gender reassignment. Note that harassment related to sexual orientation and religion and belief is not unlawful outside a work context.

Whereas direct discrimination must be because of a protected characteristic, harassment need only be related to a protected characteristic (*Worcestershire Health and Care NHS Trust* v *Allen* [2024] EAT 40). In *Lockwood* v *Cheshire and Wirral NHS Foundation Trust* (2025) ET 2401211/2024 and 24071782024, an employment tribunal held that non-binary individuals in the workplace do not have the protected characteristic of gender reassignment, which means they are not entitled to protection against harassment based on their non-binary status.

3.16.4.10 Employees and Applicants: Harassment

The Equality Act 2010, s. 40 states:

(1) An employer (A) must not, in relation to employment by A, harass a person (B)—
   (a) who is an employee of A's;
   (b) who has applied to A for employment.

KEYNOTE

Apart from marriage and civil partnerships and pregnancy and maternity, this section extends to the other protected characteristics including the employer's liability for sexual harassment. This can include behaviour such as requests for sexual favours, lewd jokes, promises, and threats concerning a person's employment conditions in return for sexual favours.

In *Urso* v *Department for Work and Pensions* [2017] UKEAT 0045/16/DA, it was held that this section prohibits harassment at every stage of employment (before, during and after employment) and a submission that a dismissal may not be an affront to an employee's dignity was rejected.

In *Moore* v *Sean Pong Tyres Ltd* [2022] UKET 1803044/2021, the complainant and employer exchanged abusive language in what was described as a robust working environment. Initially there was no bad feeling towards each other but eventually the employer's language tipped over into aggression, persistently calling the complainant a lazy old English gay man. The court was of the view that the employer created a hostile and intimidating working environment that amounted to bullying and harassment. The complaint of harassment on the grounds of both age and race were upheld, together with a complaint of direct discrimination.

3.16.4.11 Employer's Duty to Prevent Sexual Harassment of Employees

The Equality Act 2010, s. 40A states:

(1) An employer (A) must take reasonable steps to prevent sexual harassment of employees of A in the course of their employment.
(2) 'Sexual harassment' in subsection (1) means harassment of the kind described in section 26(2) (unwanted conduct of a sexual nature).

KEYNOTE

With the introduction of this section, employers now have a legal duty to take reasonable steps to prevent sexual harassment and create a safe working environment.

If an employment tribunal has found an employer liable for sexual harassment, it can also consider whether the employer has failed in its duty to prevent it and, if so, the tribunal can order an uplift in compensation paid to the employee.

3.16.4.12 Victimisation

The Equality Act 2010, s. 27 states:

(1) A person (A) victimises another person (B) if A subjects B to a detriment because—
  (a) B does a protected act, or
  (b) A believes that B has done, or may do, a protected act.
(2) Each of the following is a protected act—
  (a) bringing proceedings under this Act;
  (b) giving evidence or information in connection with proceedings under this Act;
  (c) doing any other thing for the purposes of or in connection with this Act;
  (d) making an allegation (whether or not express) that A or another person has contravened this Act.
(3) Giving false evidence or information, or making a false allegation, is not a protected act if the evidence or information is given, or the allegation is made, in bad faith.

KEYNOTE

Victimisation takes place where one person treats another badly because he/she in good faith has done a 'protected act', e.g. taken or supported any action taken for the purpose of the Act, including in relation to any alleged breach of its provisions. In *Chief Constable of West Yorkshire Police* v *B & C* [2016] UKEAT 0306/15/RN, two former undercover police officers were found to have been subjected to detriments for making protected disclosures that related to the inadequate supervision and support of undercover operatives. Both officers had been removed from undercover duties and assigned civilian roles.

The test to be applied in assessing whether or not victimisation has taken place is, 'was the real reason for the victim's treatment the fact that they had carried out a protected act' (*Chief Constable of West Yorkshire Police* v *Khan* [2001] UKHL 48). In *Bayode* v *Chief Constable of Derbyshire* [2008] UKEAT 0499/07/2205, it was held that a police constable, who was black African and Nigerian by national origin, had not been victimised where his colleagues recorded any problems they encountered with him in their PNBs for fear of a race discrimination claim at some future date.

In *Wharburton* v *Northamptonshire Police* [2022] EAT 42, the tribunal considered the key test in relation to victimisation as 'Is the treatment of such a kind that a reasonable worker would or might take the view that in all the circumstances it was to his detriment?'

Only an individual can bring a claim for victimisation, and a person is not protected from victimisation where he/she maliciously makes or supports an untrue complaint.

3.16.5 Police Officers

The 2010 Act prohibits discrimination, victimisation and harassment in other non-employment work relationships and this specifically includes police officers.

The Equality Act 2010, s. 42 states:

(1) For the purposes of this Part, holding the office of constable is to be treated as employment—
  (a) by the chief officer, in respect of any act done by the chief officer in relation to a constable or appointment to the office of constable;
  (b) by the responsible authority, in respect of any act done by the authority in relation to a constable or appointment to the office of constable.

KEYNOTE

This section provides that police constables (and police cadets (s. 42(2))) are treated as employees. The relevant employer is either the chief officer or the responsible authority (local policing body or police authority) (s. 43), depending on who commits the act in question. For example, if a chief officer refused to allocate protective equipment to male and not female officers, he/she would be treated as the employer in a direct discrimination claim.

Subsection (1) does not apply to service with the Civil Nuclear Constabulary (as to which, see s. 55(2) of the Energy Act 2004) (s. 42(3)). It also does not apply to a constable at the NCA (s. 42(4)), who is to be treated as employed by it in respect of any act done by it in relation to the constable (s. 42(5)).

3.16.6 Employees and Applicants

The Equality Act 2010, s. 39 makes it unlawful for an employer to discriminate against or victimise employees and people seeking work. It applies where the employer is making arrangements to fill a job, and in respect of anything done in the course of a person's employment.

KEYNOTE

Examples of direct discrimination in relation to work have included: rescinding an officer's posting on the grounds of force policy that spouses should not work in the same Division because neither officer would be compellable as a witness against the other (*Graham* v *Chief Constable of Bedfordshire Constabulary* [2002] IRLR 239); treating a police officer of one racial group, who was under investigation for disciplinary matters, differently from another officer under such investigation belonging to a different racial group (*Virdi* v *Commissioner of Police for the Metropolis* (2000) LTL 5 February); acceding to a request by a customer not to be served by someone of a particular colour (*Eldridge & Barbican Car Hire Ltd* v *Zhang* (2001) LTL 10 May).

There are a number of exceptions and defences to the provisions of the Act but two of the more relevant defences in relation to discrimination or victimisation in employment are 'genuine occupational requirement' and 'positive action'.

The principle behind 'genuine occupational requirement' is that, in certain jobs and roles, there may well be a legitimate reason that an employee is of a particular sex or belongs to a particular racial group (sch. 1, part 1, para. 1(1)(a)). In reality, there are far more potential exceptions to discrimination on the grounds of sex and sexual orientation than for reasons of the other protected characteristics.

The concept of 'positive action' tends to confuse a great many people with most only seeing it as another form of discrimination. Although it is a form of discrimination that favours someone by treating them differently, it needs to be seen in a positive way. A key difference between positive action and positive discrimination is that positive action is lawful, provided that the employer meets the conditions set out in s. 158 or 159, whereas positive discrimination, generally, is not. 'Positive action' refers to measures to alleviate disadvantage experienced by people who share a protected characteristic, reduce their under-representation in relation to particular activities, and meet their particular needs (s. 158). It allows for measures to be targeted to particular groups, including training to enable them to gain employment, but any such measures must be a proportionate way of achieving the relevant aim.

An employer may to treat an applicant or employee with a protected characteristic more favourably in connection with recruitment or promotion than someone without that characteristic who is as qualified for the role (s. 159). The employer must reasonably think that people with the protected characteristic suffer a disadvantage or are under-represented in that particular activity. Taking the positive action must be a proportionate means of enabling or encouraging people to overcome the disadvantage or to take part in the activity. Employers must not have a policy of treating people who share a characteristic more favourably; they should decide whether or not to take positive action on a case-by-case basis. The position in relation to positive action in favour of disabled people is different because it is not unlawful to discriminate in favour of a disabled person and employers have a positive duty to make reasonable adjustments to compensate for disadvantages related to disability.

3.16.7 Liability for Discrimination in Employment

The Equality Act 2010, s. 109 states:

(1) Anything done by a person (A) in the course of A's employment must be treated as also done by the employer.

(2) ...

(3) It does not matter whether that thing is done with the employer's or principal's knowledge or approval.

KEYNOTE

This section makes employers and principals liable for acts of discrimination, harassment and victimisation carried out by their employees in the course of employment. It does not matter whether or not the employer or principal knows about or approves of those acts. For example, where police officers engage in inappropriate sexual behaviour towards a colleague at a work-related function, the chief officer may be liable for the acts of his/her officers at that function (*Chief Constable of Lincolnshire* v *Stubbs* [1999] IRLR 81).

Employers who can show that they took all reasonable steps to prevent their employees from acting unlawfully will not be held liable (s. 109(4)). An employer could not rely on this defence where training was stale and no longer effective to prevent harassment, and that there were further reasonable steps by way of refresher training that the employer should have taken (*Allay (UK) Ltd* v *Gehlen (Race Discrimination)* [2021] UKEAT 0031 20 0402).

An employee is also personally liable for unlawful acts committed in the course of employment where, because of s. 109, the employer is also liable (s. 110).

3.16.8 Public Sector Equality Duty (PSED)

3.16.8.1 Introduction

The Equality Act 2010, s. 149 states:

(1) A public authority must, in the exercise of its functions, have due regard to the need to—
   (a) eliminate discrimination, harassment, victimisation and any other conduct that is prohibited by or under this Act;
   (b) advance equality of opportunity between persons who share a relevant protected characteristic and persons who do not share it;
   (c) foster good relations between persons who share a relevant protected characteristic and persons who do not share it.

KEYNOTE

Public authorities are required, in carrying out their functions, to have due regard to the need to achieve the objectives set out under s. 149. *The Public Equality Duty: guidance for public authorities* (18 December 2023) is published by the government to help organisations to comply with the duty.

The following extract from PACE Code C relates to the public sector equality duty and states:

1 General

1.0 The powers and procedures in this Code must be used fairly, responsibly, with respect for the people to whom they apply and without unlawful discrimination. Under the Equality Act 2010, section 149 (Public sector Equality Duty), police forces must, in carrying out their functions, have due regard to the need to eliminate unlawful discrimination, harassment, victimisation and any other conduct which is prohibited by that Act, to advance equality of opportunity between people who share a relevant protected characteristic and people who do not share it, and to foster good relations between those persons. The Equality Act also makes it unlawful for police officers to discriminate against, harass or victimise any person on the grounds of the 'protected characteristics' of age, disability, gender reassignment, race, religion or belief, sex and sexual orientation, marriage and civil partnership, pregnancy and maternity, when using their powers.

Notes for Guidance

1AA In paragraph 1.0, under the Equality Act 2010, section 149, the 'relevant protected characteristics' are age, disability, gender reassignment, pregnancy and maternity, race, religion/belief and sex and sexual orientation.

3.16.8.2 PSED: Aims

The public sector equality duty, more commonly referred to as the general equality duty, requires organisations, including the police, to consider how they could positively contribute to the advancement of equality and good relations. It requires equality considerations to be reflected into the design of policies and the delivery of services, including internal policies, and for these issues to be kept under review.

The first aim of the general equality duty is to have due regard to the need to eliminate discrimination, harassment, victimisation and any other conduct prohibited by the Act because of any of the protected characteristics. However, the second and third aims of the duty (advancing equality of opportunity and fostering good relations) only apply in relation to persons who share a 'relevant protected characteristic'.

The broad aim of the general equality duty is to integrate consideration of the advancement of equality into the day-to-day business of all bodies subject to the duty. It is intended to accelerate progress towards equality for all, by placing a responsibility on bodies subject to the duty to consider how they can work to tackle systemic discrimination and disadvantage affecting people with particular protected characteristics.

The second aim of the duty requires relevant bodies to have due regard to the need to minimise or remove disadvantages; to take steps to meet the different needs of people with different protected characteristics; and by encouraging participation in activities by those whose participation is disproportionately low.

3.16.8.3 PSED: Have Due Regard

Bodies subject to the duty must have due regard to each of the three aims set out in the general equality duty in exercising their functions. To 'have due regard' means that in making decisions and in its other day-to-day activities a body subject to the duty must consciously consider the need to do the things set out in the general equality duty: eliminate discrimination, advance equality of opportunity and foster good relations.

In *R (On the Application of Brown)* v *Secretary of State for Work and Pensions* [2008] EWHC 3158 (Admin), the court considered what a relevant body has to do to fulfil its obligation to have due regard to the aims set out in the general equality duty. The six '*Brown* principles' it set out are that:

- In order to have due regard, those in a body subject to the duty who have to take decisions that do or might affect people with different protected characteristics must be made aware of their duty to have 'due regard' to the aims of the duty.
- Due regard is fulfilled before and at the time a particular policy that will or might affect people with protected characteristics is under consideration as well as at the time a decision is taken. Due regard involves a conscious approach and state of mind. A body subject to the duty cannot satisfy the duty by justifying a decision after it has been taken. Attempts to justify a decision as being consistent with the exercise of the duty when it was not, in fact, considered before the decision are not enough to discharge the duty.

- The duty must be exercised in substance, with rigour and with an open mind in such a way that it influences the final decision. The duty has to be integrated within the discharge of the public functions of the body subject to the duty. It is not a question of 'ticking boxes'. However, the fact that a body subject to the duty has not specifically mentioned s. 149 in carrying out the particular function where it is to have 'due regard' is not determinative of whether the duty has been performed. But it is good practice for the policy or decision-maker to make reference to s. 149 and any Code or other non-statutory guidance in all cases where s. 149 is in play. 'In that way the decision maker is more likely to ensure that the relevant factors are taken into account and the scope for argument as to whether the duty has been performed will be reduced.'
- The duty is a non-delegable one. The duty will always remain the responsibility of the body subject to the duty. In practice another body may actually carry out the practical steps to fulfil a policy stated by a body subject to the duty. In those circumstances, the duty to have 'due regard' to the needs identified will only be fulfilled by the body subject to the duty if: (1) it appoints a third party that is capable of fulfilling the 'due regard' duty and is willing to do so; (2) the body subject to the duty maintains a proper supervision over the third party to ensure it carries out its 'due regard' duty.
- The duty is a continuing one.
- It is good practice for those exercising public functions to keep an accurate record showing that they had actually considered the general equality duty and pondered relevant questions. Proper record-keeping encourages transparency and will discipline those carrying out the relevant function to undertake the duty conscientiously. If records are not kept, it may make it more difficult, evidentially, for a public authority to persuade a court that it has fulfilled the duty imposed by s. 149.

The equality duty in *Brown* was the Disability Equality Duty in s. 49A of the Disability Discrimination Act 1995. In *Bracking* v *Secretary of State for Work and Pensions* [2013] EWCA Civ 1345, the Court of Appeal approved the '*Brown* principles' as being applicable to s. 149, as well as setting out some additional principles that are relevant for a public body in fulfilling its duty to have 'due regard' to the aims set out in the general equality duty. These principles are that:

- The equality duty is an integral and important part of the mechanisms for ensuring the fulfilment of the aims of anti-discrimination legislation.
- The duty is upon the decision-maker personally. What matters is what he/she took into account and what he/she knew.
- A body must assess the risk and extent of any adverse impact and the ways in which such risk may be eliminated before the adoption of a proposed policy.

3.17 Complaints and Misconduct

3.17.1 Introduction

The complaints and misconduct framework is provided by primary legislation, a series of statutory instruments and both statutory and non-statutory guidance. This chapter focuses specifically on the following:

- The Police Reform Act 2002 (PRA) sets out the definitions for complaints, conduct matters and the procedures for the investigation of complaints and recordable conduct matters.
- The Police (Conduct) Regulations 2020 (SI 2020/4) (PCR), as amended, set out the procedures for investigating non-recordable conduct matters and the hearing of all misconduct proceedings, regardless of whether they concern complaints, recordable conduct matters or non-recordable conduct matters. They contain the 'Standards of Professional Behaviour', to which all police officers are required to adhere.
- The Police (Complaints and Misconduct) Regulations 2020 (SI 2020/2) (PCMR), as amended, augment the provisions in the Police Reform Act 2002 for the assessment of complaints and conduct matters and for the investigation of complaints and recordable (but not non-recordable) conduct matters.
- The Home Office Statutory Guidance on Professional Standards, Performance and Integrity in Policing (HoG) augments the Police (Conduct) Regulations 2020, but it is now out of date and great care should be taken when consulting it.
- The Independent Office for Police Complaints (IOPC) Statutory Guidance on the police complaints system augments the Police Reform Act 2002 and the Police (Complaints and Misconduct) Regulations 2020.
- The Police Appeals Tribunals Rules 2020 (SI 2020/1) (PAT Rules), as amended, set out the procedures for an appeal to a Police Appeals Tribunal and the grounds on which a police officer or special constable can appeal against a finding and/or a particular outcome from a misconduct hearing or a third stage performance meeting.

The Police (Conduct, Performance and Complaints and Misconduct) (Amendment) Regulations 2025 (SI 2025/558) clarify who can chair misconduct hearings, provide that a conviction for indicitable offence will now always amount to gross misconduct and that dismissal must now be imposed for all findings of gross misconduct unless exceptional circumstances apply. It is also intended that there should be an increased use of accelerated misconduct hearings, particularly for former officers.

3.17.2 The Standards of Professional Behaviour

The Standards of Professional Behaviour are stated at PCR, sch. 2 and provide the yardstick by which the conduct of police officers is judged. They apply to police officers of all ranks, special constables and to those subject to suspension. They are not intended to describe every situation but rather to set a framework which enables everybody to know what type of conduct by a police officer is acceptable and what is unacceptable.

The standards are:

- **Honesty and Integrity**: police officers are honest, act with integrity and do not compromise or abuse their position.
- **Authority, Respect and Courtesy**: police officers act with self-control and tolerance, treating members of the public and colleagues with respect and courtesy. Police officers do not abuse their powers or authority and respect the rights of all individuals.
- **Equality and Diversity**: police officers act with fairness and impartiality. They do not discriminate unlawfully or unfairly.
- **Use of Force**: police officers only use force to the extent that it is necessary, proportionate and reasonable in all the circumstances.
- **Orders and Instructions**: police officers only give and carry out lawful orders and instructions. Police officers abide by police regulations, force policies and lawful orders.
- **Duties and Responsibilities**: police officers are diligent in the exercise of their duties and responsibilities. Police officers have a responsibility to give appropriate cooperation during investigations, inquiries and formal proceedings, participating openly and professionally in line with the expectations of a police officer when identified as a witness.
- **Confidentiality**: police officers treat information with respect and access or disclose it only in the proper course of police duties.
- **Fitness for Duty**: police officers when on duty or presenting themselves for duty are fit to carry out their duties and responsibilities.
- **Discreditable Conduct**: police officers behave in a manner which does not discredit the police service or undermine public confidence, whether on or off duty. Police officers report any action taken against them for a criminal offence, conditions imposed by a court or the receipt of any penalty notice.
- **Challenging and Reporting Improper Conduct**: police officers report, challenge or take action against the conduct of colleagues which has fallen below the standards of professional behaviour.

The standard on Duties and Responsibilities provides that a police officer has a responsibility to cooperate in investigations when identified as a witness. This has no effect on the right to silence of an officer who is under investigation.

Misconduct is a breach of the Standards of Professional Behaviour that is so serious as to justify disciplinary action (at least a written warning). Gross misconduct is a breach that is so serious as to justify dismissal, and conduct which has resulted in conviction of an indictable-only offence is to be taken to constitute such a breach. Practice requiring improvement means underperformance or conduct not amounting to misconduct or gross misconduct, which falls short of the expectations of the public and the police service. These are defined at PCR, reg. 2. When a person assesses whether an officer's performance or conduct amounts to practice requiring improvement, they must have regard to the Code of Ethics: PCR, reg. 2(8).

3.17.2.1 Complaints

A complaint is any expression of dissatisfaction with a police force by or on behalf of a member of the public, whether or not it is expressed in writing: PRA, s. 12(1).

A complaint can be about the conduct of an individual or about something other than the conduct of an individual—such as an issue of police resources, standards, force initiatives or police policy.

A person may make a complaint that is an expression of dissatisfaction with a police force (but which is not about the conduct of an individual) where they are adversely affected by the matter or are acting on behalf of someone else who is adversely affected: PRA, s. 12(1A)(b), (4A).

A person may make a complaint about the conduct of a person serving with the police where they claim that the conduct took place in relation to them, they were adversely affected by it, they witnessed it or where they are acting on behalf of someone who meets those criteria: PRA, s. 12(1B).

In relation to either type of complaint, a person will be adversely affected if they have suffered loss, damage, distress or inconvenience by the matter complained about, or have been put in danger or unduly at risk by it: PRA, s. 29(5).

In relation to a complaint about a person serving with the police, a person will not be adversely affected by having heard or seen about the conduct or its effects unless they were sufficiently nearby to see and hear it or they already knew the person directly affected: PRA, s. 12(3), (4).

3.17.2.2 Conduct Matters

A conduct matter is any matter which is not and has not been the subject of a complaint where there is an indication that a person serving with the police may have committed a criminal offence or behaved in a manner that would justify the bringing of disciplinary proceedings: PRA, s. 12(2).

There is a distinction between conduct matters and recordable conduct matters (**see para. 3.17.5.3**).

3.17.2.3 Death or Serious Injury Matters

A death or serious injury (DSI) matter concerns any circumstances, other than those which arise from a complaint or amount to a conduct matter, where a person has died or sustained a serious injury whilst under arrest or during detention: PRA, s. 12(2A), (2B) or after having had contact with a person performing their policing duties where this may have caused or contributed to it: PRA, s. 12(2A), (2C). A serious injury means a fracture, deep cut, deep laceration or an injury causing damage to an internal organ or the impairment of any bodily function: PRA, s. 29(1).

Where there is an investigation into a DSI matter and there is no complaint or indication of any conduct matter, the investigation will focus on the circumstances of the incident. However, where during the course of the investigation there is an indication that a person serving with the police may have committed a criminal offence or behaved in a manner that would justify the bringing of disciplinary proceedings, the DSI matter will be reclassified as a recordable conduct matter (or complaint if appropriate) and dealt with accordingly: PRA, s. 21A.

3.17.3 The Appropriate Authority

The appropriate authority for matters concerning the chief officer or acting chief officer of police is the local policing body: PRA, s. 29(1). For the Commissioner of the Metropolitan Police, it is the Mayor's Office for Policing and Crime. For the Commissioner of the City of London Police, it is the Court of Common Council. For chief officers of all forces outside London, it is the Police and Crime Commissioner.

For every other officer, including senior officers (an officer above the rank of chief superintendent), the appropriate authority is the chief officer of police under whose direction they are serving at that present time: PRA, s. 29(1). A collaboration agreement may provide for direction and control to transfer from the home to the host chief officer.

In any recordable conduct matter or complaint concerning a senior officer, the chief officer of police may delegate any of their functions to another senior officer or police staff member of at least a similar level of seniority: PCMR, reg. 46(1)(a). In any other matter, the chief officer of police may delegate their functions to a police officer of at least the rank of inspector or police staff member of similar seniority: PCMR, reg. 46(1)(b).

The IOPC now has the power to present misconduct cases. In such instances, however, they do so on behalf of the appropriate authority: PCR, reg. 24(1).

3.17.4 The Role of the Police Friend

At all stages of misconduct processes or proceedings (including any interview during an investigation into misconduct), police officers have the right to consult with and be accompanied by a police friend: PCR, reg. 7; PCMR, reg. 18.

The police friend can be a police officer, a police staff member, or a person nominated by the police officer's staff association. A person asked to be a police friend is entitled to refuse and cannot be appointed to act if they have had any involvement in the case.

The police friend can:

- advise the police officer concerned throughout the investigation and proceedings under the Police (Conduct) Regulations 2020 and Police (Complaints and Misconduct) Regulations 2020;
- represent the police officer at misconduct proceedings whether an accelerated misconduct hearing, standard misconduct hearing, misconduct meeting, including an appeal meeting, or at a Police Appeals Tribunal unless the officer has the right to be legally represented and has chosen to be so represented;
- make representations to the appropriate authority concerning any aspect of proceedings under the Police (Conduct) Regulations 2020;
- accompany the police officer to any interview, meeting or hearing which forms part of any proceedings under the Police (Conduct) Regulations 2020 or Police (Complaints and Misconduct) Regulations 2020.

Where the police friend is a member of a police force, a special constable or a police staff member, the chief officer of the police friend must permit them to use a reasonable amount of duty time for these purposes: PCR, reg. 7(3); PCMR, reg. 18(4).

At a misconduct meeting, hearing or accelerated hearing where the police friend attends, they may (PCR, regs 41(6), 61(8)):

(a) put the case of the police officer concerned;
(b) sum up that case;
(c) respond on behalf of the police officer concerned to any view expressed at the meeting;
(d) make representations concerning any aspect of the proceedings;
(e) confer with the police officer concerned;
(f) in a misconduct meeting or hearing, ask questions of any witness, subject to the discretion of the person(s) conducting the proceedings.

A police officer is entitled to be legally represented at a misconduct hearing or accelerated misconduct hearing: PCR, reg. 8(1). Where they decide to be so represented, the police friend can also attend and may consult with the police officer concerned, but will not carry out functions (a)–(d) and (f) described above: PCR, reg. 41(8). A police officer is not permitted to be legally represented in any meetings held as part of the Reflective Practice Review process: PCR, reg. 8(4).

Where a police officer is arrested or interviewed in connection with a criminal offence committed while off duty that has no connection with their role as a serving police officer, the police friend has no right to attend the criminal interview.

3.17.5 Misconduct Procedures

The procedures are intended to provide a fair, open and proportionate method of dealing with alleged misconduct and to encourage a culture of learning and development.

Where the conduct is linked to a complaint, recordable conduct matter or DSI matter, the appropriate authority is required to follow the provisions in the Police Reform Act 2002, the accompanying Police (Complaints and Misconduct) Regulations 2020 and the IOPC Statutory Guidance, which set out how complaints by members of the public and recordable conduct matters are to be dealt with.

Probationer constables are not subject to the procedures for dealing with unsatisfactory performance, since there are separately established procedures for dealing with the performance of student police officers. However, they are subject to the misconduct procedures. The chief officer has discretion whether to use the misconduct procedures or the procedures set out at reg. 13 of the Police Regulations 2003 for discharge of a probationer as the most appropriate means of dealing with a misconduct matter. In exercising this discretion, regard should be had to whether the officer admits the conduct or not. Where the misconduct in question is not admitted then in most, if not all, cases the matter will fall to be determined under the misconduct procedures. If the reg. 13 procedure is used, the student police officer should be given a fair hearing (i.e. an opportunity to comment and present mitigation).

3.17.5.1 Suspension or Change of Duty

Suspension is not a formal misconduct outcome and does not suggest any prejudgement. The period of suspension should be as short as possible and any investigation into the conduct of a suspended police officer should be made a priority. The decision to suspend a police officer may be taken only where there is an allegation of misconduct/gross misconduct and where (PCR, reg. 11(4)(b)):

- an effective investigation may be prejudiced unless the police officer is suspended; or
- the public interest, having regard to the nature of the allegation and any other relevant considerations, requires that the police officer be suspended; and
- a temporary move to a new location or role has been considered but is not appropriate in the circumstances.

A temporary move to a new location or role must always be considered as an alternative to suspension: PCR, reg. 11(4)(a). While suspended, a police officer ceases to hold the office of constable and, in the case of a member of a police force, ceases to be a member of a police force, save for the purposes of the misconduct proceedings: PCR, reg. 11(1), (2).

The police officer or their police friend may make representations against the initial decision to suspend within seven working days beginning with the first working day after being suspended, and at any time during the course of the suspension if they believe the circumstances have changed and that the suspension is no longer appropriate: PCR, reg. 11(7).

The police officer should be told exactly why they are being suspended or being moved to other duties and this should be confirmed in writing: PCR, reg. 11(6). If suspension is on public interest grounds, it should be clearly explained, so far as possible, what those grounds are: HoG, para. 5.24. The use of suspension must be reviewed at least every four weeks, and sooner where facts have become known which suggest that suspension is no longer appropriate: PCR, reg. 11(8). In cases where the suspension has been reviewed and a decision has been made to continue that suspension, the police officer must be informed in writing of the reasons why: PCR, reg. 11(9). Suspension must be authorised by a senior officer (which is an officer holding a rank above that of chief superintendent) (PCR, reg. 2(4)(a)), although the decision can be communicated to the police officer by an appropriate manager (HoG, para. 5.28).

In cases where the IOPC has ordered a directed or independent investigation into a person serving with the police (**see para. 3.17.5.4**), the appropriate authority will consult with it before making a decision on whether or not to suspend them, although the decision remains that of the appropriate authority: PCR, reg. 11(11)(a). The appropriate authority must also consult the IOPC before making a decision to allow them to resume their duties following suspension (unless the suspension ends because there will be no misconduct or accelerated misconduct proceedings or because these have concluded): PCR, reg. 11(11)(b).

The Standards of Professional Behaviour continue to apply to police officers who are suspended from duty: PCR, reg. 11(2). The appropriate authority can impose such conditions or restrictions on the police officer concerned as are reasonable in the circumstances, e.g. restricting access to police premises or police social functions: HoG, para. 5.29.

3.17.5.2 Assessment of a Complaint

The appropriate authority must initially consider whether an allegation against an officer is a complaint or conduct matter.

If the matter is a complaint (**see para. 3.17.2.1**) and is made to a chief officer who is the appropriate authority, the chief officer must record it if either the complainant indicates that they want it to be recorded (PRA, sch. 3, para. 6A(a)) or it involves (PRA, sch. 3, paras 6A(b), 6B):

(i) an allegation that the conduct or matter has resulted in death or serious injury;
(ii) an allegation that there has been conduct by a person serving with the police which, if proved, might amount to a criminal offence or justify the bringing of misconduct proceedings;
(iii) a potential breach of Article 2 or 3 of the European Convention on Human Rights;
(iv) an allegation of conduct that constitutes a serious assault, a serious sexual offence, serious corruption, including abuse of position for a sexual purpose or pursuing an improper emotional relationship, a criminal offence or behaviour which is liable to lead to disciplinary proceedings and aggravated by discriminatory behaviour on the grounds of a person's protected characteristics, or a relevant offence.

The protected characteristics are age, disability, gender reassignment, marriage and civil partnership, race, religion or belief, sex and sexual orientation, as stated and defined in the Equality Act 2010: IOPC Guidance, paras 8.15, 9.24.

These criteria must be assessed on the factual basis of the allegations in the complaint—not on whether the allegations have any merit. There should be no pre-investigation scoping other than to ensure that the complaint is fully understood: IOPC Guidance, para. 6.28.

If the matter involves (i) or (iv) above, the appropriate authority must refer the complaint to the IOPC: PRA, sch. 3, para. 4(1); PCMR, reg. 4(1). If not, the appropriate authority may refer the complaint to the IOPC if it would be appropriate to do so by reason of the gravity of the complaint or any exceptional circumstances: PRA, sch. 3, para. 4(2). If the appropriate authority refers the complaint, the IOPC will determine whether the matter should be investigated: PRA, sch. 3, para. 5(1) and, if so, the manner of the investigation: PRA, sch. 3, para. 15(1)–(2). If the complaint is not referred but it appears from it that either the officer may have committed a criminal offence or behaved in a manner that would justify the bringing of disciplinary proceedings, or that there may have been a breach of a person's Article 2 or 3 Convention rights, the appropriate authority must investigate it locally pursuant to the Police Reform Act 2002 and Police (Complaints and Misconduct) Regulations 2020: PRA, sch. 3, paras 6(2A), (2C), 16(A1).

3.17.5.3 Assessment of a Conduct Matter

If the matter is not a complaint but amounts to a conduct matter, the appropriate authority must assess whether, if true (PRA, sch. 3, para. 11(2); PCMR, reg. 7(1)):

- it appears to have resulted in a person's death or serious injury;
- a member of the public has been adversely affected;
- it indicates a serious assault, a serious sexual offence, serious corruption, including abuse of position for a sexual purpose or pursuing an improper emotional relationship, a criminal offence or behaviour which is liable to lead to disciplinary proceedings and aggravated by discriminatory behaviour on the grounds of a person's protected characteristics, a relevant offence, or conduct whose gravity or exceptional circumstances make it appropriate to record the matter.

The protected characteristics are age, disability, gender reassignment, marriage and civil partnership, race, religion or belief, sex and sexual orientation, as stated and defined in the Equality Act 2010: IOPC Guidance, paras 8.15, 9.24.

If the matter does not fall within the above criteria, it is non-recordable conduct and is investigated under the Police (Conduct) Regulations 2020 (**see para. 3.17.1**).

If the matter does fall within the above criteria, the appropriate authority must refer it to the IOPC if (PRA, sch. 3, paras 11(3), 13(1); PCMR, reg. 7(3)):

- it relates to any incident or circumstances where a person has died or suffered serious injury;
- it indicates a serious assault, a serious sexual offence, serious corruption, including abuse of position for a sexual purpose or pursuing an improper emotional relationship, a criminal offence or behaviour which is liable to lead to disciplinary proceedings and aggravated by discriminatory behaviour on the grounds of a person's protected characteristics, or a relevant offence.

The appropriate authority may also refer a matter if it would be appropriate to do so by reason of its gravity or because of any exceptional circumstances: PRA, sch. 3, para. 13(2).

Any scoping should be purely to understand the nature of the conduct and whether it would justify a written warning or otherwise be suitable for referral to the Reflective Practice Review process. It should involve no detailed investigative activity: HoG, para. 6.27.

Where the appropriate authority refers a matter to the IOPC, it must also record it: PRA, sch. 3, para. 11(3A). If the conduct matter is not referred then, unless it involves substantially the same conduct as a previous complaint or conduct matter, there is no fresh indication that a person serving with the police may have committed a criminal offence or behaved in a way to justify disciplinary proceedings, there is no fresh evidence that was not reasonably available before, and the matter has been or is being investigated as a complaint or recordable conduct matter (PRA, sch. 3, para. 11(3B); PCMR, reg. 7(2)), it must be recorded (PRA, sch. 3, para. 11(3C)). Otherwise, the appropriate authority may, but need not, record it: PRA, sch. 3, para. 11(3D).

If the appropriate authority refers the conduct matter, the IOPC will determine whether it should be investigated and, if so, the manner of the investigation: PRA, sch. 3, para. 15(1)–(2). If the conduct matter is not referred, the appropriate authority may investigate it locally, pursuant to the Police Reform Act 2002 and Police (Complaints and Misconduct) Regulations 2020: PRA, sch. 3, paras 11(3E), 16(2).

Every recordable conduct investigation is investigated pursuant to the Police Reform Act 2002 and Police (Complaints and Misconduct) Regulations 2020 and not under the Police Conduct Regulations 2020: PCR, reg. 13.

3.17.5.4 Mode of Investigation and Selection of Investigator

If the IOPC determines that a complaint or recordable conduct matter must be investigated, it may direct a local investigation by the appropriate authority, an investigation by the appropriate authority under the direction of the IOPC or an independent IOPC investigation: PRA, sch. 3, para. 15(4). The investigator in a directed investigation acts under the direction and control of the IOPC Director General: PRA, sch. 3, para. 18(3).

In a local or a directed investigation, the appropriate authority must appoint an investigator: PRA, sch. 3, paras 16(3), 18(2). In a directed investigation, the IOPC may require that no investigator is appointed unless it has approved them or, if not satisfied with the investigator, require that the appropriate authority select another one: PRA, sch. 3, para. 18(2B). In an independent investigation, the IOPC selects the investigator: PRA, sch. 3, para. 19(2).

3.17.5.5 Special Procedure and Severity Assessments

The investigator for a local investigation of a complaint, or the IOPC in a directed or independent investigation of a complaint, must certify the investigation as being subject to special procedures at any point where it appears that a police officer may have committed a criminal offence or behaved in a manner which would justify bringing disciplinary proceedings: PRA, sch. 3, para. 19A(2), (3). The investigation of a recordable conduct matter is subject to special procedures from the outset: PRA, sch. 3, para. 19(4). This ensures that the same investigative processes apply to matters which would otherwise have been investigated as recordable conduct if they had not been the subject of a complaint.

Where an investigation is subject to special procedures, a severity assessment must be performed: PRA, sch. 3, para. 19(5); PCMR, reg. 16(1). In a local investigation, the investigator performs the initial severity assessment of the conduct after consulting with the appropriate authority: PCMR, reg. 16(4), (5). In a directed investigation, the investigator must form an opinion as to the severity of the conduct and what would be the appropriate form of disciplinary proceedings, and notify the IOPC for the Director General to make the assessment: PCMR, reg. 16(2). In an independent investigation, the investigator must refer the case back to the IOPC Director General to make the assessment: PCMR, reg. 19(3). On the completion of the severity assessment, the investigator must serve a written notice of it on the officer: PCMR, reg. 17 (**see para. 3.17.5.7**).

3.17.5.6 Non-recordable Conduct

Where a conduct matter is not recordable, it is investigated in accordance with the Police (Conduct) Regulations 2020. The appropriate authority performs the initial severity assessment (PCR, reg. 14) and then appoints an investigator (PCR, reg. 15) who must serve a written notice of the severity assessment on the officer (PCR, reg. 17) (**see para. 3.17.5.7**).

There is no special procedures assessment, as this applies only to investigations performed in accordance with the Police Reform Act 2002 and Police (Complaints and Misconduct) Regulations 2020.

3.17.5.7 Severity Assessments and Written Notification to Officer

The person performing the severity assessment of a non-recordable conduct matter must consider whether, if proved, the behaviour of the officer would amount to misconduct, gross misconduct or neither, or if it should be referred to be dealt with under the Police (Vetting) Regulations 2025: PCR, reg. 14(1). The assessment will also determine whether, if the matter was referred to misconduct proceedings, those proceedings would be likely to be a misconduct meeting (for cases of misconduct) or a misconduct hearing (for cases of gross misconduct or if the police officer concerned has a live final written warning at the time of the assessment and there is a further allegation of misconduct): PCR, reg. 14(5). If new evidence emerges or there is a change of circumstances or considerations, a fresh assessment can be made and the matter may be moved up to the level of gross misconduct or down to the level of misconduct: PCR, reg. 14(6).

Where the persons performing the above assessments decide that the matter falls below the level of misconduct, they must assess whether to take no further action or, after consulting with the line manager of the officer, it would amount to practice requiring improvement, or should be referred to be dealt with under the Police (Performance) Regulations 2020 or Police (Vetting) Regulations 2025: PCR, reg. 14(2)–(3). If the matter amounts to practice requiring improvement, it must be referred to the Reflective Practice Review process: PCR, reg. 14(4).

Written notification must be given to the police officer concerned by the investigator appointed to investigate the case, advising the officer that their conduct is under investigation: PCR, reg. 17.

The written notice must (PCR, reg. 17(1)):

- inform the police officer that there is to be an investigation of their potential breach of the Standards of Professional Behaviour;
- state the identity of the investigator;
- describe the conduct that is the subject of the investigation and how that conduct is alleged to have fallen below the Standards of Professional Behaviour;
- inform the police officer concerned of the result of the severity assessment, namely whether the conduct alleged, if proved, would amount to misconduct or gross misconduct;
- inform the police officer of whether, if the case were to be referred to misconduct proceedings, those would be likely to be a misconduct meeting or misconduct hearing;
- inform the police officer that if the likely form of any misconduct proceedings changes, the police officer will be notified of this together with the reasons for that change;
- inform the police officer of their right to seek advice from their staff association or any other body, and whom the police officer may choose to act as their police friend;
- inform the police officer that if their case is referred to a misconduct hearing or accelerated misconduct hearing, they have the right to be legally represented by a relevant lawyer. If the police officer elects not to be so represented, they may be represented by a police friend. The notice will also make clear that if they elect not to be legally represented they may be dismissed or receive any other disciplinary outcome without being so represented;
- inform the officer that if they are dismissed, their name and a description of the conduct which led to their dismissal will be added to the Police Barred List and may be subject to publication for up to five years;
- inform the police officer that within 10 working days of receipt of the notice (unless this period is extended by the investigator), they may provide a written or oral statement, including any document, relating to any matter under investigation to the investigator within this time;
- inform the police officer that while they do not have to say anything, it may harm their case if they do not mention when interviewed or when providing any information within the relevant time limits something which they later rely on in any misconduct proceedings or accelerated misconduct hearing or at an appeal meeting or Police Appeals Tribunal.

The written notification may be given to the officer in person or by email, given to the officer in person by his police friend where the police friend has agreed to this or given to the officer in any manner agreed with the officer. It may be left with a person at, or sent by first-class post by recorded delivery to, the officer's last known address where it is not reasonably practicable to supply it to the officer and there is no agreement that it can be given to a police friend: PCR, reg. 9(1)–(2).

Where a notice or document is sent by email on a working day before 4.30 pm, it is to be taken as having been given on that day, and otherwise on the next working day. If sent by post, it is to be taken as having been given on the second day after it was posted if a working day, and otherwise on the next working day after this: PCR, reg. 9(3)–(4).

3.17.5.8 Investigation

The purpose of an investigation that is subject to special procedures or of a non-recordable conduct matter is to (IOPC Guidance, para. 13.2; PCR, reg. 16(1)):

- gather evidence to establish the facts and circumstances of the alleged misconduct;
- assist the appropriate authority or IOPC to establish whether there is a case to answer in respect of either misconduct or gross misconduct or that there is no case to answer;
- identify any learning opportunities for the individual or the organisation.

In cases which are not being managed or dealt with by the IOPC, the appropriate authority should ensure that a proportionate and balanced investigation is carried out as soon as possible after any alleged misconduct comes to the appropriate authority's attention and that the investigation is carried out as efficiently as possible allowing for the complexity of the case: HoG, para. 7.53. It is therefore crucial that any investigation is kept proportionate to ensure that an overly lengthy investigation does not lead to grounds for challenge. Where the investigation identifies that the issue is one of performance rather than misconduct, the police officer should be informed as soon as possible that the matter is to be treated as a performance issue.

In an investigation of a complaint or recordable conduct matter, the Director General or appropriate authority, as the case may be, must inform the complainant and any interested persons of progress every four weeks from its start: PCMR, reg. 34(2). In an investigation of a non-recordable conduct matter, the investigator is required to notify the police officer of the progress every four weeks from its start: PCR, reg. 17(7).

The investigator has a duty to consider the suggestions submitted to them in response to a severity assessment notification: PCMR, reg. 20; PCR, reg. 18. The investigator should consider and document the reasons for following or not following any submissions made by the police officer or their police friend, with a view to ensuring that the investigation is as fair as possible. The suggestions may involve a further suggested line of investigation or further examination of a particular witness. The purpose is to enable a fair and balanced investigation report to be prepared and, where appropriate, made available for consideration at a misconduct meeting/hearing.

An investigation by the appropriate authority should be completed within 12 months of the date on which the allegation first came to its attention. Where it is not completed within this time, the appropriate authority must inform the local policing body, and the IOPC in the case of a recordable conduct matter or complaint, of the investigation's progress, an estimate of when it will be concluded and a report submitted, the reason for the time taken and a summary of the planned steps to bring it to a conclusion: PCMR, reg. 13(1); PCR, reg. 19(1). Where the investigation is conducted by the IOPC, whether independent or directed, it must provide the same information in writing to the local policing body and the chief officer of the investigated officer: PCMR, reg. 13(2).

If, during the investigation of a non-recordable conduct matter, the investigator believes that new evidence not previously considered by the appropriate authority means that it would likely decide that the alleged conduct, even if proved, would amount to neither misconduct nor gross misconduct, they must promptly inform the appropriate authority, provide their written report to that point and say whether the case should instead be dealt with under the Police (Vetting) Regulations 2025, Police (Performance) Regulations 2020 or Reflective Practice Review Process: PCR, reg. 21(4). The appropriate authority must then perform a further severity assessment under PCR, reg. 14 and refer the matter to be dealt with in accordance with it: PCR, reg. 21(5)–(7). This may require the appropriate authority to inform the officer that the misconduct notices are withdrawn, no further action will be taken and that the investigation has been concluded: PCR, reg. 21(7).

3.17.5.9 Interviews during Investigation

It will not always be necessary to conduct a formal interview with the police officer subject to the investigation. In some cases involving low-level misconduct, it may be more appropriate, proportionate and timely to request a written account from the police officer: HoG, para. 7.61. In an investigation for gross misconduct, however, an interview may be an essential protection to enable the officer to give an early account and to inform the investigator of further lines of inquiry. The police officer must attend the interview when required to do so (PCMR, reg. 21(7); PCR, reg. 20(8)) and it may be a further misconduct matter to fail to attend.

If the police officer concerned or their police friend is not available at the date or time specified by the investigator, the police officer may propose an alternative time. Provided that the alternative time is reasonable and falls within a period of five working days beginning with the first working day after that proposed by the investigator, the interview must be postponed to that time: PCMR, reg. 21(3)–(5); PCR, reg. 20(4)–(5).

Where a police officer is on certificated sick leave, the investigator should seek to establish when the police officer will be fit for interview. It may be that the police officer is not fit for ordinary police duty but is capable of being interviewed. Alternatively, the police officer concerned may be invited to provide a written response to the allegations within a specified period and may be sent the questions that the investigator wishes to be answered: HoG, para. 7.70.

Where a police officer is alleged to have committed a criminal offence, a normal criminal investigation will take place, with the police officer being cautioned in accordance with the Police and Criminal Evidence Act 1984. Where the matter to be investigated involves both criminal and misconduct allegations, it should be made clear to the police officer concerned at the start of the interview whether they are being interviewed in respect of the criminal or misconduct allegations: HoG, para. 7.72. This may be achieved by conducting two separate interviews, although this does not prevent the responses given in respect of the criminal interview being used in the misconduct investigation and, therefore, a separate misconduct interview may not be required: HoG, para. 7.73.

Care should be taken when conducting a misconduct interview where the police officer is also the subject of a criminal investigation in respect of the same behaviour, as anything said by the police officer concerned in the misconduct interview when not under criminal caution and then used in the criminal investigation could be subject to an inadmissibility ruling by the court at any subsequent trial: HoG, para. 7.74.

Prior to an interview with a police officer who is the subject of a misconduct investigation, the investigator must ensure that the police officer is provided with sufficient information and time to prepare for the interview. The information provided should always include full details of the allegations made against the police officer, including the relevant dates and places of the alleged misconduct if known: HoG, para. 7.68. The investigator should consider whether there are good reasons for withholding certain evidence obtained prior to the interview and, if there are no such reasons, the police officer should normally be provided with all the relevant evidence obtained. The police officer will then have the opportunity to provide their version of the events together with any supporting evidence: HoG, para. 7.69. The police officer should be reminded that a failure to provide any account or response to any questions at this stage of the investigation might lead to an adverse inference being drawn at a later stage: HoG, para. 7.75.

Interviews do not have to be electronically recorded but if they are, the person being interviewed must be given a copy upon request. If the interview is not electronically recorded, a written record or summary of the discussion must be given to the person being interviewed. The police officer concerned should be given the opportunity to check and sign that they agree with the summary as an accurate record of what was said and should sign and return a copy to the investigator: HoG, para. 7.76. Where a police officer refuses or fails to exercise their right to agree and sign a copy, this must be noted by the investigator. The police officer may make a note of the changes that they want to make to the record and a copy of this must be given to the person(s) conducting the hearing/meeting along with the investigator's account of the record: HoG, para. 7.77.

Other than for a joint criminal/misconduct investigation interview, it is not necessary for criminal-style witness statements to be taken. In misconduct investigations, an agreed and signed written record of the information supplied should be sufficient.

3.17.5.10 Investigation Report and Supporting Documents

At the conclusion of the investigation, the investigator must submit their investigation report, setting out an accurate summary of the evidence that has been gathered. In a non-recordable conduct matter, this must be as soon as practicable: PCR, reg. 21(1).

After a local investigation, the report must be submitted to the appropriate authority: PRA, sch. 3, para. 22(2); PCR, reg. 21(1). Where the investigation is of a non-recordable conduct matter, a recordable conduct matter or a complaint subject to special procedures, it must indicate the investigator's opinion as to whether there is a case to answer in respect of misconduct, gross misconduct or neither: PCMR, reg. 27(1)(c); PCR, reg. 21(2)(c). For a non-recordable conduct matter, misconduct for this purpose means a breach of the Standards of Professional Behaviour so serious as to justify disciplinary action, the lowest form of which is a written warning: PCR, reg. 2(1). For a recordable conduct matter or a complaint, misconduct means a breach of the Standards of Professional Behaviour: PRA, sch. 3, para. 29. Where it is neither, the report must indicate the investigator's opinion as to whether the matter should be dealt with by the Reflective Practice Review process or in performance proceedings under the Police (Performance) Regulations 2020 or, in a non-recordable conduct case, by the Police (Vetting) Regulations 2025: PCMR, reg. 27(3)(d), (e); PCR, reg. 21(2)(d). In respect of a directed investigation, the investigator must submit their report to the IOPC and send a copy to the appropriate authority (PRA, sch. 3, para. 22(3)) or, in respect of an independent investigation, just to the Director General (PRA, sch. 3, para. 22(5)). Such reports may not contain the investigator's opinion.

3.17.5.11 Final Assessments

On receipt of an investigation report into a non-recordable conduct matter, the appropriate authority must, as soon as practicable, determine whether the officer has a case to answer in respect of misconduct, gross misconduct or, if neither, whether the case amounts to practice requiring improvement to be dealt with by the Reflective Practice Review process, if it should be dealt with under the Police (Performance) Regulations 2020, if it should be dealt with under the Police (Vetting) Regulations 2025, or if no action should be taken: PCR, reg. 23.

On receipt of an investigation report into a recordable conduct matter or complaint after a local investigation, the appropriate authority must determine whether to send a copy of the report to the DPP, whether any person has a case to answer in misconduct or gross misconduct, whether any person's performance is unsatisfactory and what action to take in respect of the matters dealt with in the report: PRA, sch. 3, para. 24.

In matters involving a complaint, a complainant has a right of review, previously called an appeal: PCMR, reg. 29(1)(b). In such cases, the IOPC has the power to make recommendations and give directions as to whether there is a case to answer and/or what action should be taken: PRA, sch. 3, para. 28ZA. The appropriate authority, having made its decision on the outcome of the investigation into the complaint and whether there is a case to answer in respect of misconduct or gross misconduct, must notify the complainant of its determination and inform them of their right of appeal: PCMR, reg. 34. The police officer who is the subject of the investigation should be informed both of the determination of the appropriate authority and that this could be subject to an appeal to the IOPC. The appropriate authority should then wait for a period of 28 days plus two days, being the time in which the complainant may appeal, before confirming its decision to the officer. There is no requirement to wait where the appropriate authority determines that the case should be dealt with at a misconduct hearing or an accelerated misconduct hearing.

In respect of an IOPC-directed investigation or independent investigation, the IOPC must determine whether to send the DPP a copy of the report. The IOPC also seeks the view of the appropriate authority as to whether any person has a case to answer in misconduct or gross misconduct, whether any person's performance is unsatisfactory and on any other matters dealt with in the report. The IOPC must consider those views and then make the case to answer determinations itself: PRA, sch. 3, para. 23.

If, at any time before the proceedings start, the appropriate authority is no longer satisfied that there is a case to answer in misconduct or gross misconduct, it must direct that the case be withdrawn. It may then take no further action or, after consulting the officer's line manager, refer the matter to be dealt with under the Reflective Practice Review Process, the Police (Vetting) Regulations 2025 or Police (Performance) Regulations 2020: PCR, reg. 27(1)–(3). If the case concerns a complaint or recordable conduct matter, it may be withdrawn only on the Director General's direction where they had recommended or directed that proceedings be brought, or otherwise following consultation with them: PCR, reg. 27(4).

3.17.5.12 Action Prior to Misconduct Meetings/Hearings

Where a case is referred to misconduct proceedings, the appropriate authority must provide the police officer with a written notice of the referral, the particulars of the behaviour that is alleged to amount to misconduct/gross misconduct and the name of the person conducting or chairing the proceedings: PCR, reg. 30(1)(a), (1A). The officer must also be given as soon as practicable the name of the person appointed to advise the proceedings: PCR, reg. 30(2)–(2A). Subject to the harm test, the officer must be given a copy of the investigation report (or the part of the report which is relevant to them), any other relevant documents gathered during the course of the investigation and a copy of their statement to the investigator: PCR, reg. 30(1)(b), (c).

In determining which documents are relevant, the test to be applied is that stated in the Criminal Procedure and Investigations Act 1996 (CPIA), namely whether any document or other material undermines the case against the police officer concerned or would assist the police officer's case: HoG, para. 9.19. The CPIA does not, however, directly apply.

Where the IOPC has decided to present the misconduct proceedings, the appropriate authority must consult with it on the contents of the misconduct allegations, the application of the harm test and the documents to be provided. It must then comply with any direction on these that the IOPC gives and give them a copy of the notice: PCR, reg. 30(10).

Within 15 working days (unless this period is extended by the person conducting the misconduct meeting/hearing for exceptional circumstances) beginning with the first working day after being supplied with the investigator's report, relevant documents and written notice, the police officer will be required to submit in writing (PCR, reg. 31(1), (2)):

- whether or not they accept that the behaviour described in the particulars amounts to misconduct or gross misconduct as the case may be;

- where they accept that their conduct amounts to misconduct or gross misconduct, any written submission they wish to make in mitigation;
- where they do not accept that their conduct amounts to misconduct or gross misconduct, or they dispute part of the case, written notice of the particulars of the allegations that they dispute, their account of the relevant events and any arguments on points of law they wish the person conducting the meeting or hearing to consider.

The police officer concerned must also (within the same time limit) provide the appropriate authority and the person conducting the misconduct proceedings with a copy of any document that they intend to rely on at the proceedings: PCR, reg. 31(3).

The police officer shall be informed of the name of the person holding the misconduct proceedings with the name of any person appointed to advise them as soon as reasonably practicable after they have been appointed: PCR, reg. 30(2). The police officer may object to any person hearing or advising at a misconduct meeting or hearing within three working days, starting with the first working day after they are notified of the person's name: PCR, reg. 30(3).

If the police officer concerned submits a compelling reason why such a person should not be involved in the proceedings, which will usually have to relate to some form of bias, a replacement should be found and the police officer must be notified of the name of the replacement: PCR, reg. 30(6), (7). Although there is no statutory right to object to any replacement, standards of public law fairness may require the appropriate authority to consider any further such objections. The police officer concerned may object to a person conducting a misconduct meeting or hearing or advising at such proceedings if, for example, the person has been involved in the case in a way that would make it difficult for them to make an objective and impartial assessment of it.

Where the IOPC has decided to present the case, the officer must provide the above documents to the IOPC.

3.17.5.13 Documents for the Meeting/Hearing

The person conducting the misconduct meeting/hearing must be supplied with: (PCR, reg. 32(6)):

- a copy of the notice supplied to the police officer that sets out the fact that the case was to be referred to a misconduct meeting/hearing and details of the alleged misconduct etc.;
- a copy of the investigator's report or such parts of the report as relate to the police officer concerned, any other relevant documents gathered during the course of the investigation and a copy of any statement made by the officer;
- the notice provided by the police officer setting out whether or not the police officer accepts that their conduct amounts to misconduct or gross misconduct, any submission they wish to make in mitigation where the conduct is accepted and, where they do not accept that the alleged conduct amounts to misconduct or gross misconduct or they dispute part of the case, the allegations they dispute and their account of the relevant events;
- any arguments on points of law submitted by the police officer concerned as well as any documents on which they intend to rely at the meeting/hearing;
- where the police officer concerned does not accept that the alleged conduct amounts to misconduct or gross misconduct as the case may be or where they dispute any part of the case, any other documents that in the opinion of the appropriate authority should be considered at the meeting/hearing;
- any other documents that the persons conducting the meeting/hearing request that are relevant to the case.

3.17.5.14 Witnesses

A witness will be required to attend a misconduct meeting/hearing where it is necessary to resolve a disputed matter of fact either in their evidence or in relation to the evidence of another person: PCR, reg. 32(5); HoG, para. 10.20.

Before the end of three working days starting with the day after the officer concerned has provided their response, the appropriate authority (or the IOPC if it is presenting the misconduct proceedings) and the officer concerned shall inform each other of any witnesses they wish to attend, including brief details of the evidence those persons can provide: PCR, reg. 31(4).

The appropriate authority shall supply the person conducting the proceedings with a list of the witnesses. The person conducting a misconduct meeting or the chair of a misconduct hearing will decide whether to allow such witnesses: PCR, reg. 32. They may also decide that a witness other than one on such lists should be required to attend: HoG, para. 10.22.

In an accelerated misconduct hearing, only the officer concerned may give live evidence: PCR, reg. 61(6). Where there is a material, evidential dispute, the matter will not qualify as one to be heard in an accelerated misconduct hearing and must be heard in a standard misconduct hearing.

3.17.6 Misconduct Proceedings

There are two types of misconduct proceedings:

- A misconduct meeting for cases where there is a case to answer in respect of misconduct (PCR, reg. 23(10)(d)) and where the highest level of outcome is a final written warning.
- A misconduct hearing for cases where there is a case to answer in respect of gross misconduct, where the police officer has a live final written warning in force at the date of the initial severity assessment and there is a case to answer in respect of a further act of misconduct or where the officer was reduced in rank less than two years prior to the initial severity assessment: PCR, reg. 23(1)(a)–(c). The highest level of outcome at this hearing is dismissal from the police service without notice. An outcome of dismissal will result in the officer's name and the detail of the misconduct being added to the Barred List.

It is important that misconduct hearings are only used for those matters where the police officer has a live final written warning and has potentially committed a further act of misconduct that warrants misconduct proceedings or where the misconduct alleged is so serious that, if proven or admitted, dismissal from the police service would be justified.

3.17.6.1 Timing for Holding Meetings/Hearings

An officer has 15 working days to reply to misconduct allegations given to them under reg. 30 of the Police (Conduct) Regulations 2020. This begins with the first working day after the documents have been supplied to them unless the person chairing or conducting the proceedings extends this period: PCR, reg. 31(1).

A misconduct meeting must take place no later than 20 working days beginning with the first working day after the officer has replied to the misconduct allegations, or the last day on which they could have replied to them, as stated above: PCR, reg. 34(1).

Misconduct hearings must commence within 100 working days beginning with the first working day after service of the misconduct notice under reg. 30 of the Police (Conduct) Regulations 2020: PCR, reg. 29(2). The person conducting or chairing the misconduct proceedings may extend the time limit where they consider that this would be in the interests of justice: PCR, reg. 29(6).

3.17.6.2 Purpose of Misconduct Meeting/Hearing

The purpose of a formal misconduct meeting/hearing is to (HoG, para. 9.6):

- give the police officer a fair opportunity to make their case, having considered the investigation report, including supporting documents, and to put forward any factors the police officer wishes to be considered in mitigation;
- decide on the balance of probabilities if the conduct of the police officer fell below the standards set out in the Standards of Professional Behaviour, having regard to all of the evidence and circumstances;
- consider what outcome should be imposed if misconduct/gross misconduct is proven or admitted. Consideration must be given to any live written warnings or final written warnings (and any previous disciplinary outcomes that have not expired), the officer's culpability, the harm caused, and aggravating and mitigating factors.

3.17.6.3 Misconduct Meeting/Hearing

A misconduct meeting for non-senior officers (police officers up to and including the rank of chief superintendent) will be heard by a member of a police force of at least one rank above the police officer concerned: PCR, reg. 28(3)(a). A misconduct meeting for a special constable will be heard by a member of a police force of the rank of sergeant or above (regardless of the internal grade or 'rank' that the special constable holds) or a senior human resources professional: PCR, reg. 28(3)(b)(i)–(ii). Alternatively, a police staff member who, in the opinion of the appropriate authority, is a grade above that of the police officer or special constable concerned can be appointed, but not if the case substantially involves operational policing matters: PCR, reg. 28(3)(b)(iii).

A misconduct hearing for non-senior officers will consist of a three-person panel, chaired by the chief officer of police of the police force concerned and assisted by two independent members: PCR, reg. 28(4)–(4A). The chief officer may delegate the role of chairing the disciplinary proceedings to a senior officer or a former senior officer of no more than five years from the date of delegation: PCR, reg. 2(4A)–(4B)(a)–(b). This includes an officer who has been temporarily promoted to the rank of a senior officer, or an officer who held such a promotion on the date they retired: PCR, reg. 2(4D). If the matter does not substantially relate to operational policing matters, it can be to a police staff member who has a similar level of seniority to a senior officer: PCR, reg. 2(4B)(c).

The local policing body must appoint the two independent members, one of whom must have qualifications or experience relevant for the purpose of disciplinary proceedings and one of whom need not have such qualifications or experience: PCR, reg. 28(4)(b)–(c).

A misconduct hearing for a senior officer must be chaired by a more senior officer of a different police force: PCR, reg. 28(5). A misconduct hearing for a chief officer of police, or a Deputy or Assistant Commissioner of Metropolitan Police, must be chaired by His Majesty's Chief Inspector of Constabulary (HMCIC) or an inspector of constabulary who HMCIC nominates: PCR, reg. 28(5A).

The local policing body must also appoint a legally qualified person to advise the misconduct hearing: PCR, reg. 28(5B).

Where the IOPC Director General and the appropriate authority have expressed different views on whether a non-senior officer has a case to answer in gross misconduct and should face a misconduct hearing, the Director General may, within 10 working days from having made those decisions, make written representations to the chief officer of police as to whether the misconduct hearing should be chaired by a police officer of a different force: PCR, reg. 28(5E). The chief officer must determine that issue within 10 working days from having received those representations: PCR, reg. 28(5G).

3.17.6.4 Pre-hearings

A person chairing a misconduct hearing (but not a misconduct meeting) may decide to hold a misconduct pre-hearing: PCR, reg. 33(1). It is held in private (PCR, reg. 33(6)), can be held by video or telephone (PCR, reg. 33(7)) and does not have to be recorded. The officer, the officer's police friend, the officer's counsel and counsel representing the appropriate authority (or the IOPC if it is the presenting authority) are entitled to attend (PCR, reg. 33(5)).

Where a chair decides to hold a pre-hearing, he/she must inform the appropriate authority and the officer of this within 15 working days from the date he/she receives the case documents under reg. 32 of the Police (Conduct) Regulations 2020 (PCR, reg. 33(1)(a)) but may extend this period in the interests of justice (PCR, reg. 33(10)).

At the hearing, the chair must decide the date, time and duration of the misconduct hearing, consider the list of witnesses and decide which, if any, should attend the hearing, and consider any preliminary points of law, points of disclosure and the imposition of any conditions for the misconduct hearing: PCR, reg. 33(8).

At the pre-hearing, the chair may require the legally qualified person to provide any legal or procedural matters: PCR, reg. 33(8A).

Within five working days from the date of pre-hearing, the chair must serve on the presenting authority and the relevant officer a summary of the key matters discussed and a record of any directions issued: PCR, reg. 33(15). The misconduct hearing must be held within 30 days of the date of the pre-hearing, although the chair may extend this period in the interests of justice: PCR, reg. 33(9)–(10).

3.17.6.5 Misconduct Hearings in Public

Misconduct hearings, including accelerated misconduct hearings, are held in public, subject to any decision by the chair to hold part or all of it in private: PCR, reg. 39(1).

3.17.6.6 Joint Meetings/Hearings

Cases may arise where two or more police officers are to appear before a misconduct meeting or hearing in relation to apparent failures to meet the standards set out in the Standards of Professional Behaviour stemming from the same incident. In such cases, each police officer may have played a different part and any alleged misconduct may be different for each police officer involved. It will normally be considered necessary to deal with all the matters together in order to disentangle the various strands of action, and therefore a single meeting/hearing will normally be appropriate: HoG, para. 9.15.

A police officer may request a separate meeting/hearing if they can demonstrate that there would be a real risk of unfairness to them if their case was dealt with in a joint meeting/hearing: PCR, reg. 25(4). It is for the person conducting the proceedings to decide if a separate meeting or hearing is appropriate: PCR, reg. 25(5).

3.17.6.7 Meeting/Hearing in Absence of Officer Concerned

It is in the interests of fairness to ensure that the misconduct meeting/hearing is held as soon as possible. Thus a meeting/hearing may take place if the police officer fails to attend. In cases where the police officer is absent (e.g. through illness or injury), a short delay may be reasonable to allow for their attendance. If this is not possible or any delay is considered not appropriate in the circumstances, the persons conducting the meeting/hearing may allow the police officer to participate by telephone or video link: PCR, reg. 37(2). In these circumstances, a police friend will always be permitted to attend the meeting/hearing to represent the police officer in the normal way (and in the case of a misconduct hearing the police officer's legal representative where appointed): PCR, reg. 37(3)(a).

If a police officer is detained in prison or other institution by order of a court, there is no requirement on the appropriate authority to have them produced for the purposes of the misconduct meeting/hearing: HoG, para. 10.34. Fairness may require that they are able to attend by way of video link.

3.17.6.8 Conduct of Misconduct Meeting/Hearing

It will be for the persons conducting the meeting/chairing the hearing to determine the course of it in accordance with the principles of procedural fairness: PCR, reg. 41(1). They should have read the investigator's report together with any account given by the police officer concerned during the investigation or when submitting their response. They should also have had the opportunity to read any relevant documents attached to the investigator's report.

Any document or other material that is not submitted in advance of the meeting/hearing by the appropriate authority or the police officer concerned may still be considered at the discretion of the person conducting/chairing it: PCR, reg. 41(11). Where any such document or other material is permitted to be considered, a short adjournment may be necessary to enable the appropriate authority or police officer concerned to read or consider the document, or other material, and consider its implications: HoG, para. 11.112.

Where there is evidence at the meeting or hearing that the police officer concerned, at any time after being given written notification of a severity assessment, failed to mention when interviewed, or when making representations to the investigator, any fact relied on in their defence at the meeting/hearing, which in the circumstances existing at the time the police officer concerned could reasonably have been expected to mention when questioned or providing a written response, the persons conducting the meeting/hearing may draw such inferences from this failure as appear appropriate: PCR, reg. 41(14).

Any advice given by a legally qualified person in a misconduct hearing must be given to the misconduct hearing panel members, the presenting authority and the police officer concerned: PCR, reg. 41(14A)–(14B).

The persons conducting the misconduct meeting/hearing must consider the facts of the case and decide on the balance of probabilities whether the police officer's conduct amounted to misconduct, gross misconduct (in the case of a misconduct hearing) or neither: PCR, reg. 41(15)–(16)(a). Where proceedings are conducted by a panel, any decision shall be based on a majority: PCR, reg. 41(17). The chair of the misconduct proceedings may delegate the responsibility for writing the report on the finding and, as the case may be, outcome, to the legally qualified person: PCR, reg. 43(1B).

3.17.6.9 Standard of Proof

In deciding matters of fact misconduct meetings/hearings must apply the standard of proof required in civil cases—the balance of probabilities: PCR, reg. 41(16)(a). Conduct will be proved on the balance of probabilities if the persons conducting the meeting/hearing are satisfied that it is more likely than not that the conduct occurred: HoG, para. 9.10.

3.17.6.10 Outcomes of Meetings/Hearings

If the persons conducting the misconduct meeting/hearing find that the police officer's conduct amounts to neither misconduct nor gross misconduct, they must either direct that the matter be dealt with under the Reflective Practice Review process or take no further action. If they find that the conduct does amount to misconduct or gross misconduct, they must impose disciplinary action: PCR, reg. 42(1).

An officer whose conduct amounts to gross misconduct must be dismissed without notice unless there are exceptional circumstances which justify a final written warning or reduction in rank: PCR, reg. 42(3)(b).

Otherwise, the persons conducting the meeting/chairing the hearing should consider the College of Policing Guidance on Outcomes in Police Misconduct Proceedings: HoG, para. 10.44. This requires the person to assess the seriousness of the conduct, to keep in mind the purpose for imposing outcomes in police misconduct proceedings and then to choose the outcome which most appropriately fulfils that purpose.

The seriousness of conduct is assessed by reference to the officer's culpability for the misconduct, the harm caused by it, the existence of any aggravating factors and the existence of any mitigating factors. The purpose of imposing outcomes is threefold—to maintain public confidence in and the reputation of the police service, to uphold high standards in policing and deter misconduct and to protect the public.

The person will need to take into account any previous written warnings imposed under the Police (Conduct) Regulations 2020 or 2012 that were live at the time of the initial assessment of the conduct in question and have regard to the police officer's record of service, including any previous disciplinary outcomes that have not been expunged in accordance with reg. 15 of the Police Regulations 2003: HoG, para. 10.44. They may (only if deemed necessary and at their discretion) receive evidence from any witness whose evidence would assist them in this regard (PCR, reg. 42(14)) and are entitled to take account of any early admission of the conduct by the police officer concerned and attach whatever weight to this they consider appropriate in the circumstances of the case insofar as it demonstrates an officer's insight into their behaviour and the consequent lowering of any prospect of their misconducting themselves again.

The appropriate authority (or the IOPC Director General if presenting the misconduct proceedings) has the opportunity to make representations as to the most appropriate outcome: PCR, reg. 42(14)(c)(iii). Where a misconduct hearing considers the outcome of a reduction in rank, it must take into account the views of the appropriate authority in relation to the likely operational impact: PCR, reg. 42(12). The police officer concerned and their police friend (or where appropriate legal representative) must also be given the opportunity to make representations: PCR, reg. 42(14)(c)(i)–(ii).

3.17.6.11 Outcomes Available for Misconduct

On a finding of misconduct, the meeting/hearing must impose one of the following outcomes:

- **Written warning**: the police officer will be told the reason for the warning, that they have a right to appeal, the name of the person to whom the appeal should be sent and that the warning will be put on their personal file and remain live for a period of 18 months from the date that the warning is given. This is notified to the officer: PCR, reg. 42(4), (9)(a); Police Regulations 2003, reg. 15. It means that any misconduct in the following 18 months is likely to lead to (at least) a final written warning.
- **Final written warning**: where imposed by a misconduct meeting, the warning remains in force for a period of two years: PCR, reg. 42(9)(b). A misconduct hearing may impose it for up to five years: PCR, reg. 42(10). This means that only in exceptional circumstances will further misconduct not result in dismissal. The police officer will be told the reason for the warning, that any future misconduct may result in dismissal (Home Office Guidance, para. 10.52), that they have a right to appeal, the name of the person to whom the appeal should be sent and that the final written warning will be put on their personal file: PCR, reg. 43(2)–(4).

Where a misconduct hearing finds that the conduct of an officer amounts to misconduct (but not gross misconduct) and either there was a final written warning in force at the date of the initial severity assessment or the misconduct hearing finds that the officer's misconduct arises from two or more incidents which are not closely factually connected, then in addition to the two outcomes above, the person chairing the misconduct hearing will also have available the outcomes of:

- **Reduction in rank**: PCR, reg. 42(3)(a)(iii), (5), (6).
- **Dismissal without notice**, which will mean that the police officer is dismissed from the police service with immediate effect: PCR, reg. 42(3)(a)(iv), (5), (6).

3.17.6.12 Notification of the Outcome

In all cases, the person chairing the misconduct proceedings must send the report to the appropriate authority within five working days beginning with the first working day after their conclusion: PCR, reg. 43(1). In the case of a misconduct meeting it must include notification of the officer's right to appeal against the finding and/or outcome and the name of the person to whom any appeal should be sent: PCR, reg. 43(2), (3)(a)(i). In the case of a police officer who has attended a misconduct hearing, the notification must include their right of appeal against any finding and/or outcome imposed to a Police Appeals Tribunal: PCR, regs 43(2), 3(a)(ii). In cases involving a complainant where the complaint was the subject of a local investigation, the appropriate authority must send a copy of the report to the complainant and interested persons: PCR, reg. 43(5)(b). Police forces have five days to inform the College of Policing of dismissals for inclusion on the Police Barred List: Police Barred List and Police Advisory List Regulations 2017, reg. 5(1). Names placed on the Police Barred List, which is a publicly searchable database, will remain there for a minimum period of five years from the date of publication: Police Barred List and Police Advisory List Regulations 2017, reg. 6(10)(b).

3.17.6.13 Expiry of Warnings

Notification of written warnings issued, including the date issued and expiry date, will be recorded on the police officer's personal record, along with a copy of the written notification of the outcome and a summary of the matter: Police Regulations 2003, reg. 15. Where a police officer has a live written warning and transfers from one force to another, the live warning will transfer with the police officer and remain live until the expiry of the warning. It should be referred to as part of any reference before the police officer transfers: Police Regulations 2003, reg. 16.

Where a police officer who has a live written warning or final written warning takes a career break in accordance with Police Regulations, any time on such a break will not count towards the period for which the written warning or final written warning is live: PCR, reg. 42(11).

3.17.6.14 Attendance of Complainant or Interested Person at Misconduct Proceedings

Where misconduct proceedings are held as a result of a public complaint or a recordable conduct matter, complainants or interested persons have the right to attend them as an observer: PCR, reg. 40(3). This is subject to the right of the person conducting the meeting to exclude or impose conditions on persons' attendance to facilitate the proper conduct of proceedings, and to exclude them while evidence is being given, where disclosure to the complainant or interested party would be contrary to the harm test: PCR, reg. 39(3). They may, as of right, be accompanied by one other person and, if they have a special need, one further person to accommodate that need (e.g. an interpreter, sign language expert etc.): PCR, reg. 40(4).

The person conducting or chairing the misconduct proceedings may, at their discretion, put questions to the officer concerned that the complainant or interested person requests be put to them: PCR, reg. 40(5).

3.17.6.15 IOPC Attendance and Presentation at Meetings/Hearings

Where a misconduct meeting/hearing is to be held following:

- an investigation independently investigated or directed by the IOPC; or
- a local investigation where the IOPC has made a statutory recommendation that misconduct proceedings should be taken and the recommendation has been accepted by the appropriate authority; or
- the IOPC has given a statutory direction that misconduct proceedings shall be taken,

the IOPC Director General may attend the misconduct meeting/hearing to make representations: PCR, reg. 38(1). Such representations may be an explanation why the IOPC has directed particular misconduct proceedings to be brought or to comment on the investigation.

Where the IOPC is to attend a misconduct hearing, it may instruct a relevant lawyer to represent it: PCR, reg. 38(2)(a). The IOPC Director General may decide to present a case referred to a misconduct hearing or accelerated misconduct hearing where it has expressed a different view from the appropriate authority on whether there was a case to answer, where the appropriate authority did not accept a recommendation of there being a case to answer, where the appropriate authority agrees that it should do so or where the IOPC Director General considers that there is a compelling public interest for it to do so: PCR, reg. 24(1)–(3).

3.17.7 Right of Appeal

A police officer has a right of appeal against the finding and/or the outcome imposed at a misconduct meeting: PCR, reg. 45(1). The appeal is commenced by the police officer concerned giving written notice of appeal to the appropriate authority, setting out the grounds for the appeal within seven working days beginning with the first working day after the receipt of the notification of the outcome of the misconduct meeting (unless this period is extended by the appropriate authority for exceptional circumstances): PCR, reg. 45(3). The police officer has the right to be accompanied by a police friend: PCR, reg. 7(2).

The police officer concerned may only appeal on the grounds that (PCR, reg. 45(2)):

- the finding or disciplinary action imposed was unreasonable;
- there is evidence that could not reasonably have been considered at the misconduct meeting which could have materially affected the finding or decision on disciplinary action; or
- there was a serious breach of the procedures set out in the Regulations or other unfairness which could have materially affected the finding or decision on disciplinary action.

3.17.7.1 Appeal following Misconduct Meeting—Non-senior Officers

An appeal against the finding and/or the outcome of a misconduct meeting must be heard by a member of the police service of a higher rank or, unless the case substantially involves operational policing matters, a police staff manager who is considered to be more senior than the person who conducted the misconduct meeting: PCR, reg. 45(4). A police officer or police staff member may be present to advise the person conducting the appeal on procedural matters: PCR, reg. 8(6). The person determining the appeal must be provided with the following documents (PCR, reg. 45(13)):

- the notice of appeal from the police officer concerned setting out their grounds of appeal;
- the record of the original misconduct meeting;

- the documents that were given to the person who held the original misconduct meeting;
- any evidence that the police officer concerned wishes to submit in support of their appeal that was not considered at the misconduct meeting.

The person appointed to deal with the appeal must first decide whether the notice of appeal sets out arguable grounds of appeal. If they determine that there are no arguable grounds they must dismiss the appeal and inform the police officer concerned accordingly, setting out their reasons: PCR, reg. 45(14). Where the person appointed to hear the appeal determines that there are arguable grounds of appeal and the police officer concerned has requested to be present at the appeal meeting, the person appointed to conduct the proceedings must hold a meeting with the police officer concerned: PCR, reg. 46(2). Where the police officer fails to attend the meeting, the person conducting the appeal may proceed in their absence: PCR, regs 37(3)(b), 2(1).

The person conducting the appeal may consider:

- whether the finding of the original misconduct meeting was unreasonable having regard to all the evidence considered or if the finding could now be in doubt due to evidence which has emerged since the meeting;
- any outcome imposed by the misconduct meeting which may be considered as unreasonable, having regard to all the circumstances of the case;
- whether the finding or outcome could be unsafe due to procedural unfairness. The person conducting the appeal must consider whether there was unfairness and, if so, whether it could have materially influenced the outcome).

The person conducting the appeal must consider the grounds and may confirm or reverse the decision appealed against: PCR, reg. 47(1)(a). Where the person determining the appeal decides that the original disciplinary action imposed was too lenient, they may increase the outcome up to a maximum of a final written warning: PCR, reg. 47(1)(b). An appeal is not a rehearing of the misconduct meeting. Where the ground of appeal is unreasonableness, the person must consider whether the decision was within the band of reasonable responses open to the misconduct meeting chair rather than whether it would have made the same one. For a ground of fresh evidence or of breach of procedures or other unfairness, the person conducting the appeal must decide the substantive issue themselves.

The appeal will normally be heard within five working days beginning with the working day after the determination that the officer concerned has arguable grounds of appeal: PCR, reg. 46(2). The officer concerned can object to the person appointed to conduct the appeal: PCR, reg. 45(6)–(12).

3.17.7.2 Appeal Following Misconduct Hearing

Where a police officer has appeared before a misconduct hearing, any appeal against the finding or outcome is to the Police Appeals Tribunal (**see paras 3.17.9 to 3.17.9.9**). The police officer should be informed that the Police Appeals Tribunal can increase any outcome imposed as well as reduce or overturn the decision of the misconduct hearing or accelerated misconduct hearing.

Senior officers have the right to appeal against the finding and/or outcome of a misconduct meeting or hearing. The appeal in both cases will be made to the local policing body. The police officer should be informed that the Police Appeals Tribunal can increase any outcome imposed as well as reduce or overturn the decision of the misconduct hearing or accelerated misconduct hearing.

Where the IOPC presents the misconduct proceedings, it must appear as the respondent in the Police Appeals Tribunal: PAT Rules, r. 12.

3.17.8 Accelerated Misconduct Procedures

The operation of the accelerated misconduct procedures is set out in part 5 of the Police (Conduct) Regulations 2020. They can be used for a serving officer if the appropriate authority certifies the case as one where the 'special conditions' are satisfied (PCR, reg. 49(A1)–(1)) or if the IOPC has given a direction under the PRA, sch. 3, para. 20A.

The 'special conditions' are that there is sufficient evidence, in the form of written statements or other documents, without the need for further evidence, whether written or oral, to establish on the balance of probabilities that the conduct of the police officer concerned constitutes gross misconduct, and it is in the public interest for the police officer concerned to cease to be a police officer without delay: PCR, reg. 49(2). The first condition will be satisfied only where there is no material, evidential dispute.

These procedures are, therefore, designed to deal with cases where the evidence is incontrovertible in the form of statements, documents or other material (e.g. CCTV, DNA), such that this is sufficient to prove gross misconduct, and it is in the public interest if the case is found or admitted for the police officer to cease to be a member of the police service forthwith: HoG, para. 12.4. Even where the criteria for a special case are met, there may be circumstances where it would not be appropriate to certify it, for instance, where to do so might prematurely alert others (police officers or non-police officers) who are, or may be, the subject of an investigation: HoG, para. 12.7.

Where the appropriate authority determines that the special conditions are satisfied, and unless it considers that the circumstances are such as to make it inappropriate to do so, it must certify the case as one where the special conditions are satisfied and refer it to an accelerated misconduct hearing: PCR, reg. 49(4).

If, after certifying the case, the appropriate authority decides that the special case conditions are no longer satisfied, it must refer the case back to the investigator if further investigation is required or to misconduct proceedings under the standard procedures: PCR, reg. 50(1).

Where the appropriate authority determines that there should be disciplinary proceedings brought against a former officer, it must decide if it requires a misconduct hearing. If the decision is negative, the appropriate authority must give written notice to the former officer that his/her case will be referred to an accelerated misconduct hearing unless within 10 working days from the date of being notified he/she gives notice to the contrary: PCR, sch. 1, para. 14A, inserting reg. 21D. If the former officer gives notice within this period, the case must be referred to a misconduct hearing and not an accelerated misconduct hearing: reg. 21D(6) as inserted. Otherwise it must be referred to an accelerated misconduct hearing: reg. 21D(7) as inserted.

After the expiry of this period, the former officer can make a written request for a misconduct hearing, which must be received before the date of the accelerated misconduct hearing, explaining why he/she was unable to give notice within the required period and the reason for the delay in making the request: reg. 21E(1)–(2) as inserted. The person chairing the accelerated hearing must consider the request and may grant it only if satisfied that it was not reasonably practicable for the former officer to have given notice within the 10-working-day period and that the request was submitted a reasonable time after it expired: reg. 21E(4).

If the appropriate authority decides to refer the matter concerning a serving officer to an accelerated hearing, it will sign a special case certificate (HoG, para. 12.19) and will provide to the police officer or former officer concerned a written notice giving particulars of the conduct that is alleged to constitute gross misconduct and copies of the following (PCR, reg. 51(1)):

- the special case certificate (for a serving officer);
- any statement the police officer may have made to the investigator during the course of the investigation;

- subject to the harm test:
  - the investigator's report (if any) or such parts of that report as relate to the police officer concerned, together with any documents attached to that report; and
  - any relevant statement or documents gathered during the course of the investigation.

The police officer concerned must also be told the date, time and place of the hearing and of their right to legal representation and advice from a police friend: PCR, reg. 52(1). The date of the accelerated misconduct hearing must be not less than 10 working days and not more than 15 working days from the date on the special conditions certificate and other documents are provided to the police officer concerned: PCR, reg. 52(1).

Within seven working days of the first working day after the day on which the written notice and documents are supplied to the police officer concerned, the police officer must provide a written notice to the appropriate authority of (PCR, reg. 54(1)(a)–(c)):

- whether or not they accept that their conduct constituted gross misconduct;
- where they accept that the conduct constituted gross misconduct, any submission they wish to make in mitigation;
- where they do not accept that the conduct constituted gross misconduct:
  - the allegations they dispute and their version of the relevant events; and
  - any arguments on points of law they wish to be considered by the person or persons conducting the meeting.

At the same time, the police officer must provide the appropriate authority with copies of any documents they intend to rely on at the hearing: PCR, reg. 54(1)(d). Where the IOPC has decided to present the hearing, the documents must be provided to it instead of the appropriate authority: PCR, reg. 54(2).

3.17.8.1 Accelerated Misconduct Hearings

In the case of a senior officer, the case must be heard by a more senior officer from a different force (PCR, reg. 55(4)(a)(ii)), assisted by two independent members appointed by the local policing body, who must have relevant qualifications or experience for that purpose (PCR, reg. 55(1)(aa), (c)). In the case of non-senior officers, the case will be heard by the police officer's chief officer, who may delegate this to a senior officer, former senior officer of no more than five years or, if it does not substantially relate to operational policing matters, a police staff member of a similar level of seniority to a chief officer: PCR regs 55(1), 2(4A).

Where the IOPC Director General and the appropriate authority have expressed different views on whether a non-senior officer has a case to answer in gross misconduct and should face a misconduct hearing, the Director General may, within five working days from having made those decisions, make written representations to the chief officer of police as to whether the misconduct hearing should be chaired by a police officer of a different force: PCR, reg. 55(4D)–(4E). The chief officer must determine that issue within five working days from having received those representations: PCR, reg. 44(4F).

The local policing body must appoint a legally qualified person to advise the accelerated hearing: PCR, reg. 55(4A). As with a standard misconduct hearing, the legally qualified person must provide their advice to all the parties, and the chair of the hearing may delegate responsibility for writing the report on the finding and outcome: reg. 63(1B).

The police officer will have a right of appeal, in the same way as with a 'standard' hearing, to a Police Appeals Tribunal against any finding of gross misconduct and/or the disciplinary action imposed: PAT Rules, r. 3(1).

An accelerated misconduct hearing is held in public: PCR, reg. 59(1). There is no live witness evidence, other than from the police officer concerned: PCR, reg. 61(6).

The hearing may proceed in the absence of the police officer concerned (PCR, regs 37(3)(b), 2(1)), but the person conducting the hearing should ensure that the officer has been informed of their right to be legally represented at the hearing or to be represented by a police friend where they choose not to be legally represented.

3.17.8.2 Outcome of Accelerated Misconduct Hearing

Where the accelerated misconduct hearing finds that the conduct of the police officer concerned constituted gross misconduct, the person conducting it must dismiss the officer without notice unless satisfied that there are exceptional circumstances which justify a final written warning or reduction in rank: PCR, reg. 62(1).

Where the hearing determines that the conduct does not amount to gross misconduct, the person conducting or chairing it may either dismiss the case or return it to the appropriate authority to be dealt with at a misconduct meeting or hearing (where there is a live final written warning) under the standard procedures: PCR, reg. 62(8). This may be because the person conducting the hearing considers that the conduct is misconduct rather than gross misconduct. There is power under PCR, reg. 50 for the appropriate authority to remit the case to be dealt with under the standard procedures at any time prior to the start of the accelerated misconduct hearing, if it considers that the special conditions are no longer satisfied.

Where the police officer admits the allegation or the person conducting the hearing finds it proved on the balance of probabilities, the person conducting or chairing the hearing (PCR, reg. 62(10)):

- must have regard to the record of police service of the police officer concerned as shown on their personal record;
- may consider such documentary evidence as would, in their opinion, assist them in determining the question; and
- must give the police officer concerned, and their police friend or relevant lawyer, an opportunity to make oral or written representations.

The person conducting or chairing the accelerated misconduct hearing must submit a report of the outcome to the appropriate authority, including written reasons for their decisions, within five working days from its conclusion or, if this has been delegated to the legally qualified person, 10 working days from it: PCR, reg. 63(1C)–(1D). The appropriate authority must then provide a copy of the report to the officer as soon as practicable.

3.17.9 Appeals to the Police Appeals Tribunal

The Police Appeals Tribunal Rules 2020 govern the composition and operation of the Police Appeals Tribunal.

A police officer has a right of appeal to a Police Appeals Tribunal against any disciplinary finding and/or disciplinary outcome imposed at a misconduct hearing or accelerated misconduct hearing held under the Police (Conduct) Regulations 2020: PAT Rules, r. 4(1), (2)(a), (c). Senior police officers, in addition, have the right to appeal to a Police Appeals Tribunal against any disciplinary finding and/or outcome imposed at a misconduct meeting: PAT Rules, r. 4(2)(b). A police officer may not appeal to a tribunal against a finding of misconduct or gross misconduct where that finding was made following acceptance by them that their conduct amounted to this: PAT Rules, r. 4(3).

3.17.9.1 Composition and Timing of Police Appeals Tribunals

Where the appeal is made by a person who was, at the time of their dismissal, a non-senior officer or former officer and/or a special constable or former special constable, the Police Appeals Tribunal must consist of (Police Act 1996, sch. 6, para. 2):

- a legally qualified chair drawn from a list maintained by the Home Office;
- a serving senior officer;
- a lay person.

3.17.9.2 Grounds of Appeal

A Police Appeals Tribunal is not a re-hearing of the original matter; its role is to consider an appeal based on specific grounds.

In the case of matters dealt with under the Police (Conduct) Regulations 2020, the grounds for appeal are:

- the finding or disciplinary action imposed was unreasonable; or
- there is evidence that could not reasonably have been considered at the misconduct meeting (in the case of senior police officers), the misconduct hearing or accelerated misconduct hearing (as the case may be); or
- there was a breach of the procedures set out in the Police (Conduct) Regulations 2020, the Police (Complaints and Misconduct) Regulations 2020 or sch. 3 to the Police Reform Act 2002 or other unfairness which could have materially affected the finding or decision on disciplinary action.

In the case of matters dealt with under the Police (Performance) Regulations 2020, the grounds for appeal are:

- the finding of unsatisfactory performance or attendance or gross incompetence, or the outcome imposed, was unreasonable; or
- there is evidence that could not reasonably have been considered at the third stage meeting which could have materially affected the finding or decision on the outcome; or
- there was a breach of the procedures set out in the Police (Performance) Regulations 2020 or other unfairness which could have materially affected the finding or decision on the outcome; or
- where the police officer was required to attend a third stage meeting following a first and second stage meeting, the police officer concerned should not have been required to attend that meeting as their unsatisfactory performance or attendance was not similar to or connected with the unsatisfactory performance or attendance referred to in their final written improvement notice.

3.17.9.3 Notice of Appeal

Where a police officer wishes to appeal, they will need to give notice of their appeal in writing to the relevant local policing body: PAT Rules, r. 9(2). The notice of appeal must be given within 10 working days, beginning with the first working day after the police officer is supplied with a written copy of the decision that they are appealing against: PAT Rules, r. 9(1). In cases where the police officer fails to submit their notice of appeal within the 10-working-day period, they may, within a reasonable time after the end of that period, submit a notice of appeal accompanied by the reasons why it was not submitted within that period and the reasons for the officer's view that it was served within a reasonable time after that period: PAT Rules, r. 10(1)–(3). The tribunal chair must then determine whether the appeal could have reasonably and practicably been submitted within the time limit: PAT Rules, r. 10(5).

3.17.9.4 Procedure on Notice of Appeal

As soon as reasonably practicable after receipt of a copy of the notice of appeal and in any case within 15 working days (beginning with the first working day following the day of such receipt) the respondent to the appeal must provide to the relevant local policing body (PAT Rules, r. 13(3)):

- a copy of the decision appealed against (namely the written judgment of the original panel/person);
- any documents that were available to the panel/person conducting the original hearing; and

- the transcript or part of the transcript of the proceedings at the original hearing requested by the appellant (a copy of the transcript (if applicable) shall also at the same time be sent to the appellant).

The appellant, within 20 working days beginning with the first working day following the day on which they are supplied with a copy of the transcript or, where no transcript is requested, within 35 working days (beginning with the first working day following the day on which the appellant gave notice of their appeal), must provide to the relevant local policing body (PAT Rules, r. 13(7)–(9)):

- a notice setting out the finding, disciplinary action or outcome appealed against and of their grounds for the appeal;
- any supporting documents;
- where the appellant is allowed to call witnesses (for appeals made only on the ground of there being evidence that could not reasonably have been considered at the original hearing and which could have materially affected the finding or outcome):
  - a list of any proposed witnesses; and
  - a witness statement from each of the proposed witnesses;
- if they consent to the appeal being determined without a hearing (that is, on the basis of the papers alone), notice in writing that they so consent.

In relation to the appellant, a 'proposed witness' is a person whom the appellant wishes to call to give evidence at the hearing, whose evidence was not and could not reasonably have been considered at the hearing and whose evidence could have materially affected the decision being appealed against: PAT Rules, r. 13(10)(a).

3.17.9.5 Determination of an Appeal

Where the tribunal chair allows the appeal to go forward to a hearing, the local policing body will be responsible for making the administrative arrangements prior to and at the tribunal and for ensuring that the members of the tribunal appointed to deal with the appeal are sent the papers together with a schedule of the documents that each of the members should have.

The tribunal chair who made the determination as to whether to allow the notice of appeal to proceed to a tribunal need not necessarily be the same tribunal chair who hears the subsequent appeal. However, the chair who makes the decision as to whether the appeal should be dealt with at a hearing or on the papers should be the chair appointed to hear the appeal itself.

Where an appeal has not been dismissed at the review stage, the tribunal chair shall determine whether the appeal should be dealt with at a hearing: PAT Rules, r. 16(1). It is expected that this decision will be made by the tribunal chair within ten working days of receiving the papers. The tribunal chair may determine that the appeal shall be dealt with without a hearing only if the appellant has consented: PAT Rules, r. 16(2). If the appeal is to be dealt with at a hearing, the chair must give the appellant and the respondent their name and contact address: PAT Rules, r. 16(3).

3.17.9.6 Legal and Other Representation

The appellant can be represented at a hearing by a relevant lawyer or a police friend: PAT Rules, r. 19(1). Where the appellant is represented by a lawyer, the appellant's police friend may also attend: PAT Rules, r. 19(2).

3.17.9.7 Procedure at Hearing

Where the case is to be heard at a tribunal hearing, the chair of the tribunal shall cause the appellant and the respondent to be given written notice of the time, date and place of the hearing, at least 20 working days or such shorter period as may with the agreement of both parties be determined, before the hearing begins: PAT Rules, r. 18(1).

The tribunal chair will determine in advance of the tribunal whether to allow any witness that the appellant or respondent proposes to call to give evidence at the tribunal: PAT Rules, r. 18(2). Witnesses will only be permitted where the ground for appeal is that there is evidence which could not reasonably have been considered at the original hearing and which could have materially affected the finding or decision on outcome. No witnesses shall give evidence at the hearing unless the chair reasonably believes that it is necessary for the witness to do so: PAT Rules, r. 18(3). Any witness that does attend the tribunal may be subject to questioning and cross-examination: PAT Rules, r. 20(4). It is for the tribunal to decide on the admissibility of any evidence, or to determine whether or not any question should be put to a witness. A verbatim record of the evidence given at the hearing shall be taken; and the relevant local policing body shall keep such record for a period of not less than two years from the date of the end of the hearing: PAT Rules, r. 20(6).

The tribunal has discretion to proceed with the hearing in the absence of either party, whether represented or not, if it appears to be just and proper to do so: PAT Rules, r. 20(2).

Where it is decided to proceed in the absence of either party the tribunal should record its reasons for doing so. The tribunal may adjourn the appeal as necessary: PAT Rules, r. 20(2).

The hearing is held in public: PAT Rules, r. 22(1).

3.17.9.8 Attendance of Other Persons

Where the matter to be dealt with at the appeal is related directly to a complaint made against the appellant or a conduct matter involving an interested party, the chair of the tribunal shall cause any complainant or interested party to be given notice of the time, date and place of the tribunal: PAT Rules, r. 23(2).

3.17.9.9 Determination and Outcome of Appeal

A tribunal need not be unanimous in its determination of the appeal or of any other decision before it and may reach a decision based on a majority, but must not indicate this: PAT Rules, r. 26(4).

A tribunal, when determining any disciplinary or unsatisfactory performance outcome imposed, may impose any outcome that the original panel/person could have imposed; it has the power to increase as well as reduce the outcome: Police Act 1996, s. 85(2).

The tribunal chair shall, within three working days of the tribunal determining the appeal, give written notice to the appellant and respondent of the tribunal's decision: PAT Rules, r. 26(8).

A police officer ordered to be reinstated in their former force or rank will be deemed to have served in their force and/or rank continuously from the date of the original decision to the date of reinstatement: Police Act 1996, sch. 6, para. 7(2).

3.17.9.10 Reflective Practice Review Process

The Reflective Practice Review process comprises three stages: a fact-finding stage, a discussion stage and production of a reflective review development report, and monitoring of the officer in line with this.

The reviewer who conducts the process must be the line manager of or a police officer or staff member who is more senior to the officer: PCR, reg. 65(2). Where the reviewer considers that the officer is failing to engage with the process, they may refer the matter back to the appropriate authority for a renewed severity assessment: PCR, reg. 71.

The Reflective Practice Review process is considered to be a performance rather than a disciplinary process, so that an officer participating in it may continue to apply for and obtain promotion: PCR, reg. 66(3). Similarly, an officer may not be represented during it—whether by a lawyer or a police friend, and such persons may make no representations to the appropriate authority about any aspect of the process. There is, of course, nothing to prevent a police officer from seeking advice from their police friend, or a lawyer, at any point.

Where a matter is referred to the Reflective Practice Review process, the reviewer must provide the officer with details of the matter and invite them to provide their account of it: PCR, reg. 67(1). The officer must provide their account within five working days after the first working day on which the invitation is received, unless this is extended: PCR, reg. 67(2). The reviewer must then make inquiries which are reasonable, proportionate and relevant to establish the facts of the matter: PCR, regs 67(1), 68(1).

If evidence becomes available which was not available to the appropriate authority when it referred the matter, the reviewer must refer it back for a renewed severity assessment: PCR, reg. 68(3). If the matter is then referred to a misconduct investigation, any account that the officer has given is not admissible in subsequent disciplinary proceedings, unless it relates to something not referred: PCR, reg. 66(4).

Otherwise, or where the Reflective Practice Review process continues, after the fact-finding stage the reviewer must invite the officer to a Reflective Practice Review discussion: PCR, reg. 6(1). This must include a discussion both of the practice requiring improvement and related circumstances and the identification of any key lessons to be learnt by the officer, their line management or their police force, to address the matter and prevent a reoccurrence of it: PCR, reg. 69(3).

After the discussion has ended, the reviewer must produce a reflective review development report containing a summary of the issue and background circumstances, a summary of the discussion, the key actions to be taken within a specified period, the lessons identified for the officer, line management and/or police force and the period of time for reviewing the report and the actions to be taken: PCR, reg. 70(2). The reviewer must send a copy of the report to the appropriate authority (PCR, reg. 70(3)), which must ensure that any lessons for line management or the force are addressed (PCR, reg. 70(4)). The report and the review notes must then be discussed as part of the officer's PDR (performance and development review) during the 12-month period following the report: PCR, reg. 70(6).

3.18 Unsatisfactory Performance and Attendance

3.18.1 Introduction

The formal procedures to deal with unsatisfactory performance and attendance are set out in the Police (Performance) Regulations 2020. These are referred to as 'UPPs' (and are referred to by that abbreviation in this chapter).

The aim of the procedures is to provide a fair, open and proportionate method of dealing with performance and attendance issues and encouraging a culture of learning and development for individuals and the organisation. Early intervention via management action should achieve the desired effect of improving and maintaining a police officer's performance or attendance to an acceptable level; however, in some cases it will be appropriate for managers to take formal action under the procedures. The procedures in the UPPs are largely the same whether applied to unsatisfactory performance or attendance (the differences that do exist are set out below). However, the issues that arise in attendance cases may be different from those in performance cases.

Where a police officer's absence or poor performance is due to an underlying medical condition, which may amount to a disability for the purposes of the Equality Act 2010, consideration should be given as to whether the officer requires a referral to occupational health, the benefit of reasonable adjustments and/or if they are permanently medically unfit for performing the ordinary duties of a member of the police force, for the purposes of the Police Pensions Regulations 2015. If they are medically unfit and there are no reasonable adjustments that can be made to mitigate the disparate impact of their disability then the officer should be progressed through the ill-health retirement process and not the Police (Performance) Regulations 2020. Otherwise, such action may amount to unlawful disability discrimination.

There has been significant amendment to these procedures by the Police (Conduct, Performance and Complaints and Misconduct) (Amendment) Regulations 2025. Whereas the UPP process had previously involved three formal stages, these are now reduced to two. A gross incompetence meeting is now the equivalent of an accelerated stage two meeting.

3.18.2 Applicability

The procedures apply to police officers up to and including the rank of chief superintendent (PPR, reg. 2(1), (2)(a), including special constables (PPR, reg. 4(1)). However, given the nature of special constables as unpaid volunteers, initiation of such cases may be limited to those where the special constable either contests that his/her performance or attendance is unsatisfactory or agrees that it is unsatisfactory but expresses a desire to continue with his/her special constable duties. In other cases, the special constable may choose to resign from his/her role as a special constable. In setting meeting dates and establishing panels, regard should be had to the nature of special constables as volunteers.

> **KEYNOTE**
>
> The procedures *do not apply* to student police officers during their probationary period: PPR, reg. 2(1)(b). The procedures governing performance and attendance issues in respect of police students are determined locally by each force. These procedures are underpinned by reg. 13 of the Police Regulations 2003.

3.18.3 Ongoing Performance Assessment and Review

Every police officer should have some form of performance appraisal, commonly referred to as a 'performance and development review' (PDR). The PDR should be the principal method by which the police officer's performance and attendance are monitored and assessed. The activities and behaviours expected of a police officer in order to achieve his/her objectives should be in accordance with the relevant national framework which will form the basis of the police officer's role profile.

3.18.4 Sources of Information

Unsatisfactory performance or attendance will often be identified by the immediate line manager of the police officer as part of his/her normal management responsibilities. Where the police officer reports to a manager who has no line management responsibility for him/her, it is the responsibility of that manager to inform the police officer's line manager of any performance or attendance issues he/she has identified. It is possible that line managers may be alerted to unsatisfactory performance or attendance on the part of one of their police officers as a result of information or complaint from a member of the public. Such cases must be dealt with in accordance with the established procedures for the handling of complaints.

The outcome of an investigation into a complaint alleging misconduct may identify an issue of unsatisfactory performance or attendance. Consequently, the appropriate authority may determine that there is no case to answer in respect of misconduct or gross misconduct but that it may be appropriate to take action under the UPPs.

While the unsatisfactory performance and attendance procedures are internal management procedures, it may be necessary at times to inform public complainants of action taken with respect to the police officer about whom the complaint relates.

3.18.5 Informal Intervention Before Formal Proceedings

Managers should try to address poor performance informally before initiating formal performance action proceedings (Home Office Guidance, paras 14.8–14.13):

- the line manager should discuss any shortcoming(s) or concern(s) with the individual at the earliest possible opportunity. It would be wrong for the line manager to accumulate a list of concerns about the performance or attendance of an individual and delay telling him/her about them until the occasion of the police officer's annual or mid-term PDR meetings;
- the reason for dissatisfaction must be made clear to the individual as soon as possible and there must be a factual basis for discussing the issues, i.e. the discussion must relate to specific incidents or omissions that have occurred;
- line managers should seek to establish whether there are any underlying reasons for the unsatisfactory performance or attendance;

- consideration should be given as to whether there is any health or welfare issue that is or may be affecting performance or attendance;
- in cases where the difficulty appears to stem from a personality clash with a colleague or line manager, or where for other reasons a change of duties might be appropriate, the police officer's line management may, in consultation with the appropriate human resources adviser, consider redeployment if this provides an opportunity for the police officer to improve his/her performance or attendance. Where a police officer is redeployed in this way, the police officer and his/her new line management should be informed of the reasons for the move and of the assessment of his/her performance or attendance in the previous role;
- the line manager must make it clear to the police officer that he/she is available to give further advice and guidance if needed;
- depending on the circumstances, it may be appropriate to indicate to the police officer that if there is no, or insufficient, improvement, then the matter will be dealt with under the UPPs;
- line managers are expected to gather relevant evidence and keep a contemporaneous note of interactions with the police officer;
- challenging unsatisfactory performance or attendance in an appropriate manner does not constitute bullying.

The above principles cover the position when a line manager first becomes aware of some unsatisfactory aspect of the police officer's performance or attendance and is dealing with the issue as part of normal line management responsibilities: Home Office Guidance, para. 14.8.

Such management action should be put on record. Particularly, the line manager should record the nature of the performance or attendance issue, the advice given, and steps taken to address the problems identified: Home Office Guidance, para. 14.12. Such action ensures continuity in circumstances where one or more members of the management chain may move on to other duties or the police officer concerned moves to new duties.

Ideally performance or attendance will improve and continue to an acceptable level. Where there is insufficient or unsustained improvement, it will then be appropriate to use the UPPs: Home Office Guidance, para. 14.26. The period of time agreed or determined by the line manager for the police officer concerned to improve his/her performance or attendance prior to using the UPPs must be sufficient to provide a reasonable opportunity for the desired improvement or attendance to take place and must be time limited.

3.18.6 Performance Issues

Police officers should know what standard of performance is required of them and be given appropriate support to attain that standard. Managers should let a police officer know when he/she is doing well or, if the circumstances arise, when there are the first signs that there is a need for improvement in his/her performance.

KEYNOTE

Unsatisfactory performance (or attendance) is defined in reg. 4 of the UPPs as 'an inability or failure of a police officer to perform the duties of the role or rank he [or she] is currently undertaking to a satisfactory standard or level'.

There is no formula for determining the point at which a concern about a police officer's performance should lead to formal procedures under the UPPs being taken. Each case must be considered on its merits. However, the following points need to be emphasised:

- the intention of performance management, including formal action under the UPPs is to improve performance (Home Office Guidance, para. 14.3);

- occasional lapses should be dealt with in the course of normal management activity and should not involve the application of the UPPs, which are designed to cover repeated failures to meet such standards or more serious cases of unsatisfactory performance (Home Office Guidance, para. 14.8);
- managers should be able to demonstrate that they have considered whether management action is appropriate before using the UPPs (Home Office Guidance, para. 14.12).

3.18.7 Attendance Issues

Where the UPPs are used in relation to attendance matters, they will normally relate to periods of sickness absence such that the ability of the police officer to perform his/her duties is compromised. Other forms of absence unrelated to genuine sickness would normally be dealt with under the misconduct procedures, e.g. where a police officer's absence is unauthorised: Home Office Guidance, paras 19.2, 19.28. Except where a police officer fails to cooperate, appropriate supportive action must be taken before formal action is taken under the UPPs. A failure by a police officer to cooperate will not prevent formal action being taken or continued. If supportive action is taken, the police officer cooperates, and the attendance improves and is maintained at a satisfactory level, there will be no need to take formal action under the UPPs. Where police officers are injured or ill they should be treated fairly and compassionately. Managers should be able to demonstrate that they have acted reasonably in all actions taken at all stages of the attendance management process, including any action under the UPPs.

3.18.7.1 Monitoring Attendance

Line managers, in conjunction with the force's human resources department if necessary, are responsible for monitoring a police officer's attendance. A formal record of a police officer's period of illness will be kept in accordance with reg. 15 of the Police Regulations 2003. The force Occupational Health Service is an essential part of effective attendance management and should be involved as soon as any concerns about a police officer's attendance are identified. Where action is taken under the UPPs in respect of a police officer's attendance, the police officer may be referred to the Occupational Health Service for up-to-date information and advice at any stage within the procedure in accordance with force policy. This should enable the force to make an informed decision about a police officer's attendance. Where police officers do not attend appointments or otherwise fail to cooperate with the force's Occupational Health Service, an assessment will be made on the information available: Home Office Guidance, para. 19.29.

3.18.7.2 Action Under the UPPs

Formal action under the UPPs may be taken in cases of both unacceptable levels of persistent short-term absences and long-term absences due to sickness and/or injury. In deciding whether to take action under the procedures, managers must consider all of the facts available to them, including:

- the nature of the illness, injury or condition;
- the likelihood of the illness, injury or condition (or some other related illness, injury or condition) recurring;
- the pattern and length of absence(s) and the period of good health between them;
- the need for the work to be done, i.e. what impact on the force's performance and workload the absence is having;
- the extent to which a police officer has cooperated with supportive management action;

- whether the police officer was made aware, in the earlier supportive action, that unless an improvement was made, action under the UPPs might be taken;
- whether the selected medical practitioner (SMP) has been asked to consider the issue of permanent disablement and/or the police force is considering medical retirement;
- the impact of the Equality Act 2010 and the public sector equality duty.

Where an officer may be disabled pursuant to the Equality Act 2010, they should be referred to occupational health, who should be asked what reasonable adjustments could be made: Home Office Guidance, para. 14.15. Where the officer is medically unfit for performing the ordinary duties of a member of the police force, this should be addressed through the ill-health retirement process before any consideration of proceedings under the Police (Performance) Regulations 2020: Home Office Guidance, para. 14.17.

3.18.8 Multiple Instances of Unsatisfactory Performance

A police officer can move to a later stage of the UPPs only in relation to unsatisfactory performance or attendance that is similar to or connected with the unsatisfactory performance or attendance referred to in any previous written improvement notice. Where failings relate to different forms of unsatisfactory performance or attendance it will be necessary to commence the UPPs at the first stage (unless the failing constitutes gross incompetence). If more than one UPP is commenced, then, given that the procedures will relate to different failings and will have been identified at different times, the finding and outcome of each should be without prejudice to the others: Home Office Guidance, paras 14.37–14.38.

There may be circumstances where procedures have been initiated for a particular failing and an additional failing comes to light prior to the first stage meeting. In such circumstances, it is possible to consolidate the two issues at the first stage meeting provided that there is sufficient time prior to the meeting to comply with the notification requirements, explained in more detail below: Home Office Guidance, para. 14.39.

3.18.9 The First Stage

Where a line manager decides that the UPPs are the most appropriate way of addressing the performance or attendance matter, he/she will notify the police officer in writing that he/she is required to attend a first stage meeting (PPR, reg. 15) and include in that notification the following details (PPR, reg. 16(1)):

- details of the procedures for determining the date and time of the meeting;
- a summary of the reasons why the line manager considers the police officer's performance or attendance unsatisfactory;
- the possible outcomes of a first stage and second stage meeting;
- that a human resources professional or a police officer (who should have experience of UPPs and be independent from the line management chain) may attend the meeting to advise the line manager on the proceedings;
- that if the police officer agrees, any other person specified in the notice may attend the meeting;
- that prior to the meeting the police officer must provide the line manager with any documentation he/she intends to rely on in the meeting; and
- the police officer's rights, i.e. his/her right to seek advice from a representative of his/her staff association and to be accompanied and represented at the meeting by a police friend.

KEYNOTE

The notice shall be accompanied by copies of related documentation relied upon by the line manager in support of the view that the police officer's performance or attendance is unsatisfactory: PPR, reg. 16(2). In advance of the meeting, the police officer shall provide the line manager with any documents on which he/she intends to rely in support of his/her case: PPR, reg. 16(9). Any document or other material that was not submitted in advance of the meeting may be considered at the meeting at the discretion of the line manager, ensuring fairness to all parties: PPR, reg. 8(9). However the presumption should be that such documents or material will not be permitted unless it can be shown that they were not previously available to be submitted in advance: Home Office Guidance, para. 15.7. Where such a document or other material is permitted to be considered, a short adjournment may be necessary to enable the line manager or the police officer, as the case may be, to read or consider the document or other material and consider its implications. The length of the adjournment will depend upon the case: Home Office Guidance, para. 15.8.

Wherever possible, the meeting date and time should be agreed between the line manager and the police officer: PPR, reg. 16(4). However, where agreement cannot be reached the line manager must specify a time and date: PPR, reg. 16(5). If the police officer or his/her police friend is not available at the date or time specified by the line manager, the police officer may propose an alternative time. Provided that the alternative time is reasonable and falls within a period of five working days beginning with the first working day after that specified by the line manager, the meeting must be postponed to that time: PPR, reg. 16(6)–(7). Once the date for the meeting is fixed, the line manager should send to the police officer a notice in writing of the date, time and place of the first stage meeting: PPR, reg. 16(8).

3.18.9.1 First Stage Meeting

The meeting can take place in the absence of the officer, where they fail to attend: PPR, reg. 8(2). At the first stage meeting the line manager will (PPR, reg. 17(5)):

- explain to the police officer the reasons why the line manager considers that the performance or attendance of the police officer is unsatisfactory;
- provide the police officer with the opportunity to make representations in response;
- provide his/her police friend (if he/she has one) with an opportunity to make representations;
- listen to what the police officer (and/or his/her police friend) has to say, ask questions and comment as appropriate.

Where the line manager finds that the performance or attendance of the police officer has been satisfactory during the period in question, he/she will inform the police officer that no further action will be taken. Where having considered any representations by either the police officer and/or his/her police friend, the line manager finds that the performance or attendance of the police officer has been unsatisfactory he/she shall (PPR, reg. 17(6)):

- inform the police officer in what respects his/her performance or attendance is considered unsatisfactory;
- inform him/her of the improvement that is required in his/her performance or attendance;
- inform the police officer that, if a sufficient improvement is not made within the period specified by the line manager, he/she may be required to attend a second stage meeting;
- inform the police officer that he/she will receive a written improvement notice;
- inform the police officer that if the sufficient improvement in his/her performance or attendance is not maintained during the validity period of such notice, he/she may be required to attend a second stage meeting.

3.18.9.2 Procedure Following the First Stage Meeting

As soon as reasonably practicable following the meeting, the line manager shall cause to be prepared a written record of it and, where he/she found at the meeting that the performance or attendance of the police officer was unsatisfactory, a *written improvement notice*: PPR, reg. 18(1). The written record and any improvement notice shall be sent to the officer as soon as reasonably practicable after they have been prepared whether or not the officer attended the meeting: PPR, reg. 18(2), (5).

KEYNOTE

Improvement notices require a police officer to improve his/her performance or attendance and must state (PPR, reg. 18(3)):

- in what respect the police officer's performance or attendance is considered unsatisfactory;
- the improvement in performance or attendance required to bring the police officer to an acceptable standard;
- a 'specified period' within which improvement is expected to be made; and
- the 'validity period' of the written improvement notice.

Specified Period

The 'specified period' of an improvement notice is a period specified by the manager conducting the meeting (having considered any representations made by or on behalf of the police officer) within which the police officer must improve his/her performance or attendance: PPR, reg. 11(2). It is expected that the specified period for improvement would not normally exceed three months. On the application of the police officer or otherwise (e.g. on the application of his/her line manager), the appropriate authority may extend the specified period if it considers it appropriate to do so. In setting an extension to the specified period, consideration should be given to any known periods of extended absence from the police officer's normal role, e.g. if the police officer is going to be on long periods of pre-planned holiday leave, study leave, or is due to undergo an operation. The extension should not lead to the improvement period exceeding 12 months unless the appropriate authority is satisfied that there are exceptional circumstances making this appropriate: PPR, regs 17(6)(c), 10(3).

Validity Period

The 'validity period' of an improvement notice describes the period of 12 months from the date of the notice within which performance or attendance must be maintained (assuming improvement is made during the specified period): PPR, regs 11(2), 18(4). If the improvement is not maintained within this period the next stage of the procedures may be used. The period for improvement under an improvement notice and the validity period of an improvement notice do not include any time that the police officer is taking as a career break.

The written record supplied to the police officer should comprise a summary of the proceedings at that meeting. Any improvement notice must be accompanied by a notice informing the police officer of his/her right to appeal and the name of the appeal manager to whom the appeal should be sent: PPR, reg. 18(6)(b). The notice must also inform the police officer of his/her right to submit written comments on the written record of the meeting and of the procedure for doing so: PPR, reg. 18(6)(c).

The appeal manager is the person appointed by the appropriate authority to that role and must be a higher rank than the officer's line manager: PPR, reg. 4(1).

The police officer may submit written comments on the written record not later than the end of seven working days after the date that he/she received it (unless an extension has been granted by his/her line manager): PPR, reg. 18(7)–(8). However, if the police officer has exercised his/her right to appeal against the finding or outcome of the first stage meeting, the police officer may not submit comments on the written record: PPR, reg. 18(9). It is the responsibility of the line manager to ensure that the written record, written improvement notice and any written comments of the police officer regarding the written record are retained together and filed in accordance with force policies: PPR, reg. 18(10).

KEYNOTE

Action Plan

An improvement notice would normally be followed by an action plan which should:

- identify any weaknesses which may be the cause of unsatisfactory performance or attendance;
- describe what steps the police officer must take to improve performance and/or attendance and what support is available from the organisation, e.g. training;
- specify a period within which actions identified should be followed up; and
- set a date for a staged review of the police officer's performance or attendance.

The action plan will set out the actions which should assist the police officer to perform his/her duties to an acceptable standard. This may be agreed at the UPP meeting or at a later time specified by the line manager. It is expected that the police officer will cooperate with implementation of the action plan and take responsibility for his/her own development or improvement. Equally, the police officer's managers must ensure that any actions to support the police officer to improve are implemented.

3.18.9.3 Assessment of Performance or Attendance

It is expected that the police officer's performance or attendance will be actively monitored against the improvement notice and, where applicable, the action plan by the line manager throughout the specified period of the improvement notice. The line manager should discuss with the police officer any concerns that he/she has during this period as regards his/her performance or attendance and offer advice and guidance where appropriate: Home Office Guidance, para. 16.28.

As soon as possible after the improvement notice period comes to an end, the line manager must formally assess the performance or attendance of the police officer during that period: PPR, reg. 22(1)(a). If the line manager considers that the police officer's performance or attendance is satisfactory, he/she should notify the police officer in writing of this.

The notification should also inform the police officer that while the performance or attendance of the police officer is now satisfactory, the improvement notice is valid for a period of 12 months from the date printed on the notice so that it is possible for the second stage of the procedures to be initiated if the performance or attendance of the police officer falls below an acceptable level within the remaining period: Home Office Guidance, para. 16.30.

If the line manager considers that the police officer's performance or attendance is still unsatisfactory, he/she should notify the police officer in writing of this: PPR, reg. 22(1)(b). The line manager must also notify the police officer that he/she is required to attend a second stage meeting to consider these ongoing performance or attendance issues: PPR, reg. 22(2).

If the police officer has improved his/her performance or attendance to an acceptable standard within the specified improvement period, but then fails to maintain that standard within the 12-month validity period, it is open to the line manager to initiate stage two of the procedures: PPR, reg. 22(4). In such circumstances, the line manager must notify the police officer in writing of his/her view that the police officer's performance or attendance is unsatisfactory as the police officer has failed to maintain the improvement, and that as a consequence the police officer is required to attend a second stage meeting to discuss his/her failure to maintain a satisfactory standard of performance or attendance: PPR, reg. 22(5).

3.18.9.4 First Stage Appeals

A police officer has a right of appeal. However, any outcome of this first stage meeting will continue to apply up to the date that the appeal is determined. Therefore, where the police officer contests the finding or outcome, he/she should continue to follow the terms of the improvement notice and any accompanying action plan pending the determination of the appeal. The notice of appeal must set out the grounds and be accompanied by the evidence for it: PPR, reg. 19(6).

The grounds for appeal are (PPR, reg. 19(4)):

- the finding of unsatisfactory performance or attendance is unreasonable;
- any of the terms of the improvement notice are unreasonable;
- there is evidence that could not reasonably have been considered at the first stage meeting which could have materially affected the finding of unsatisfactory performance or attendance or any of the terms of the written improvement notice;
- there was a breach of the procedures set out in the UPPs or other unfairness which could have materially affected the finding of unsatisfactory performance or attendance or the terms of the improvement notice.

On the basis of the above grounds of appeal, the police officer may appeal against the finding of unsatisfactory performance or attendance or the terms of the written improvement notice, those being (PPR, reg. 19(3)):

- the respect in which the police officer's performance or attendance is considered unsatisfactory;
- the improvement which is required of the police officer; and/or
- the length of the period specified for improvement by the line manager at the first stage meeting.

KEYNOTE

At the first stage appeal meeting, the appeal manager will provide the police officer with the opportunity to make representations and provide his/her police friend (if he/she has one) with an opportunity to make representations: PPR, reg. 21(5). Having considered any representations by either the police officer and/or his/her police friend, the appeal manager may confirm or reverse the finding of unsatisfactory performance or attendance or endorse or vary the terms of the improvement notice appealed against: PPR, reg. 21(6).

The appeal manager may deal with the police officer in any manner in which the line manager could have dealt with him/her at the first stage meeting. Where the appeal manager has reversed the finding of unsatisfactory performance or attendance he/she must also revoke the written improvement notice: PPR, reg. 21(7).

Within three working days of the day following the conclusion of the appeal meeting, the police officer will be given written notice of the appeal manager's decision: PPR, reg. 21(9). If the appeal manager is in a position to send a written summary of the reasons for that decision, this may also accompany the written notice of the decision. Any decision made that changes the finding or outcome of the first stage meeting will take effect by way of substitution for the finding or terms appealed against and as from the date of the first stage meeting: PPR, reg. 21(10).

3.18.10 The Second Stage

Where, at the end of the period specified in the written improvement notice, the line manager finds that the police officer's performance or attendance has not improved to an acceptable standard during that period or that the police officer has not maintained an acceptable level of performance or attendance during the validity period of the notice, the line manager must notify the police officer in writing that he/she is required to attend a second stage meeting to discuss these issues: PPR, reg. 30(2). As soon as reasonably practicable thereafter, the senior manager (the person appointed to this role, who must be at least the same rank or level as the appeal manager) must give a notice to the officer informing him/her that (PPR, reg. 31(1)):

- the meeting will be with a panel appointed by the appropriate authority;
- the procedures for determining the date and time of the meeting;
- a summary of the reasons why the police officer's performance or attendance is considered unsatisfactory;
- the possible outcomes of a second stage meeting;
- if the outcome is dismissal, then the officer's name and a description of the conduct which led to their dismissal will be added to the barred list;
- a human resources professional or a police officer (who should have experience of UPPs and be independent from the line management chain) may attend to advise the panel on the proceedings;
- counsel or a solicitor may attend the meeting to advise the panel on the proceedings and on any question of law that may arise;
- where the police officer is a special constable, a member of the special constabulary will attend the meeting to advise the panel;
- if the police officer agrees, any other person specified in the notice may attend, e.g. a person attending for development reasons; and
- the police officer's rights, i.e. his/her right to seek advice from a representative of his/her staff association (in the case of a member of the police force) and to be accompanied and represented at the meeting by a police friend.

The notice must also include copies of related documentation relied upon by the line manager in support of the view that the police officer's performance or attendance continues to be unsatisfactory: PPR, reg. 31(2). It is important to note that a second stage meeting may not take place unless the officer has been notified of his/her right to representation by a police friend: PPR, reg. 31(3). The notice does not at this stage need to give the names of the panel members as these may not be known at the time of issue. However, as soon as the panel has been appointed by the appropriate authority, the appropriate authority should notify the police officer of the members' names: Home Office Guidance, para. 17.21.

The purpose of the meeting is for the panel to hear the evidence of the unsatisfactory performance or attendance and to give the police officer the opportunity to put forward his/her views: Home Office Guidance, para. 15.9. It will also be an opportunity to hear of any factors that are continuing to affect the police officer's performance or attendance and what the police officer considers can be done to address them.

Where the police officer has reached stage two following stage one (i.e. it is not a gross incompetence meeting), the possible outcomes of the meeting are as follows (PPR, reg. 46(1), (3)):

- redeployment;
- reduction in rank (in the case of a member of a police force and for performance cases only);
- dismissal (with a minimum of 28 days' notice); or
- extension of a written improvement notice (in exceptional circumstances).

Where the panel grants an extension to the written improvement notice, it will specify a new period within which improvement to performance or attendance must be made: PPR, reg. 46(8). The 12-month validity period of the extended written improvement notice will apply in full from the date of extension: PPR, reg. 46(8)(c). The panel may also vary any of the terms in the notice: PPR, reg. 46(8)(b).

3.18.10.1 Stage Two Gross Incompetence Meetings

There may be circumstances where the appropriate authority considers the performance (not attendance) of the police officer to be so unsatisfactory as to warrant the procedures being initiated at the second stage. This would be as a result of a single incident of 'gross incompetence': PPR, reg. 32(1)(a). It is not envisaged that an appropriate authority would initiate the procedures at the second stage in respect of a series of acts over a period of time.

KEYNOTE

'Gross incompetence' is defined in the Police (Performance) Regulations 2020 as 'a serious inability or serious failure of a police officer to perform the duties of the officer's rank or the role the officer is currently undertaking to a satisfactory standard or level, without taking into account the officer's attendance, to the extent that dismissal would be justified and "grossly incompetent" is to be construed accordingly': PPR, reg. 4(1).

Where the appropriate authority determines it is appropriate to initiate the procedures at this stage, the police officer must be informed in writing that he/she is required to attend a second stage meeting to discuss his/her performance: PPR, reg. 32(2). Where the appropriate authority has informed the police officer that he/she is to attend such a second stage meeting, it must, as soon as reasonably practicable, send the police officer a notice in writing which will include the following details (PPR, reg. 33(1)):

- the meeting will be with a panel appointed by the appropriate authority;
- the procedure for determining the date and time of the meeting;
- a summary of the reasons why the police officer's performance is considered to constitute gross incompetence;
- the possible outcomes of the second stage meeting;
- if the outcome is dismissal, the officer's name and a description of the conduct which led to their dismissal will be added to the barred list;
- a human resources professional and a police officer (who should have experience of UPPs and be independent from the line management chain) may attend to advise the panel on the proceedings;
- counsel or a solicitor may attend the meeting to advise the panel on the proceedings and on any question of law that may arise at the meeting;
- where the police officer is a special constable, a member of the special constabulary will attend the meeting to advise the panel;
- if the police officer agrees, any other person specified in the notice may attend, e.g. a person attending for development reasons; and
- the police officer's rights, i.e. his/her right to seek advice from a representative of his/her staff association (in the case of a member of the police force) and to be accompanied at the meeting by a police friend.

The purpose of the meeting is for the panel to hear the evidence of the gross incompetence and to give the police officer and his/her representative the opportunity to make representations on the matter.

The appropriate authority will explain that the police officer is required to attend the second stage meeting and that the possible outcomes of the stage two meeting are:

- redeployment to alternative duties;
- reduction in rank (with immediate effect);
- dismissal (with immediate effect); or
- the issue of a written improvement notice for three months or, if there are circumstances which justify a longer period, up to 12 months, if the panel considers that there has been unsatisfactory performance and not gross incompetence.

3.18.10.2 Panel Membership and Procedure

The panel will comprise a panel chair and two other members and be appointed by the appropriate authority of the force in which the police officer is a member: PPR, reg. 34(2).

At least one of the three panel members must be a police officer and one should be a human resources professional: PPR, reg. 34(2). Membership will be as follows:

- First panel member (chair): Senior police officer (holding a rank above that of chief superintendent) or senior human resources professional: PPR, reg. 34(3).
- Second panel member: Police officer of at least the rank of superintendent or human resources professional who in the opinion of the appropriate authority is at least equivalent to that rank: PPR, reg. 34(4).
- Third panel member: Police officer of at least the rank of superintendent or police staff member who in the opinion of the appropriate authority is at least equivalent to that rank: PPR, reg. 34(5).

KEYNOTE

Panel Membership

None of the panel members should be junior in rank to the police officer concerned: PPR, reg. 34(6). For the purposes of chairing a second stage meeting, the UPPs define a 'senior human resources professional' as 'a human resources professional who, in the opinion of the appropriate authority, has sufficient seniority, skills and experience to be a panel chair': PPR, reg. 34(10). The panel chair must hold a rank above that of chief superintendent: PPR, reg. 34(3).

The appropriate authority may appoint police officers or police staff managers from another police force to be members of a panel. No panel member should be an interested party, i.e. a person whose appointment could reasonably give rise to a concern as to whether he/she could act impartially.

As soon as the appropriate authority has appointed a second stage panel, it should arrange for copies of all relevant documentation to be sent to those members and, in particular, any document that (PPR, reg. 34(9)):

- was available to the line manager in relation to any first stage meeting;
- was available to the second line manager in relation to any second stage meeting;
- was prepared or submitted in advance of the second stage meeting;
- was prepared or submitted following those meetings, i.e. improvement notices, action plans and meeting notes;
- relates to any appeal.

As soon as the appropriate authority has appointed a second stage panel, it must send the police officer written confirmation of the names of panel members: PPR, reg. 34(8). The police officer has the right to object to any panel members appointed by the appropriate authority (PPR, reg. 35(1)) and any such objection must be made in writing to the appropriate authority no later than three working days after receipt of the notification of the names (PPR, reg. 35(2)). The police officer must include the ground of his/her objection to any panel member in that application. The appropriate authority must inform the police officer in writing whether it upholds or rejects an objection to a panel member: PPR, reg. 35(3). If the appropriate authority upholds the objection, a new panel member will be appointed as a replacement: PPR, reg. 35(4). As soon as practicable after any such appointment, the police officer must be informed in writing of the name of the new panel member: PPR, reg. 35(6). The appropriate authority must ensure that the requirements for the composition of the panel are met: PPR, reg. 35(9). The police officer may object to the newly appointed panel member in the same way whereupon the appropriate authority must follow the same procedure again: PPR, reg. 35(7).

3.18.10.3 Special Constables and Second Stage Meetings

In cases where the police officer is a special constable, as indicated above (**see para. 3.18.10**), the force will appoint a member of the special constabulary to attend the meeting to advise the panel (this is for the purpose of fairness): PPR, reg. 42(4). The special constable advising the panel must have sufficient seniority and experience of the special constabulary to be able to advise the panel. The special constable advising the panel can be a police officer serving in a different force. The special constable adviser does not form part of the panel and does not have a role in determining whether or not the police officer's performance or attendance is unsatisfactory. In arranging a second stage meeting that involves special constables, due consideration should be given to the fact that special constables are unpaid volunteers and may therefore have full-time employment or other personal commitments.

3.18.10.4 Second Stage Meeting Dates and Time Frames

Any second stage meeting should take place no later than 30 working days after the date that the notification has been sent to the police officer: PPR, reg. 38(1). Within that time frame, wherever possible, the meeting date and time should be agreed between the panel chair and the police officer: PPR, reg. 38(4). However, where agreement cannot be reached, the panel chair must specify a time and date: PPR, reg. 38(5). If the police officer or his/her police friend is not available at the date or time specified by the panel chair, the police officer may propose an alternative time: PPR, reg. 38(6). Provided that the alternative time is reasonable and falls within a period of five working days beginning with the first working day after that specified by the panel chair, the meeting must be postponed to that time: PPR, reg. 38(6)–(7). If the panel chair considers it to be in the interests of fairness to do so, he/she may extend the 30-working-day period within which the meeting should take place and the reasons for any such extension must be notified in writing to both the appropriate authority and the police officer: PPR, reg. 38(2)–(3). As soon as a date for the meeting is fixed, the panel chair should send the police officer notice in writing of the date, time and place of the second stage meeting: PPR, reg. 39(3).

3.18.10.5 Procedure on Receipt of Notice of Second Stage Meeting

Within 14 working days of the date on which a notice has been sent to the police officer (unless this period is extended by the panel chair for exceptional circumstances), the police officer must provide to the appropriate authority (PPR, reg. 36(1)):

- written notice of whether or not he/she accepts that his/her performance or attendance has been unsatisfactory or that he/she has been grossly incompetent, as the case may be;
- where he/she accepts that his/her performance or attendance has been unsatisfactory or that he/she has been grossly incompetent, any written submission he/she wishes to make in mitigation.

Where the police officer does not accept that his/her performance or attendance has been unsatisfactory or that he/she has been grossly incompetent, or where he/she disputes part of the matters referred to in the notice that he/she shall provide the appropriate authority with a written notice of (PPR, reg. 36(2)(c)):

- the matters he/she disputes and his/her account of the relevant events; and
- any arguments on points of law he/she wishes to be considered by the panel.

The police officer shall provide the appropriate authority and the panel with a copy of any document he/she intends to rely on at the second stage meeting: PPR, reg. 36(3).

Before the end of three working days following the officer's compliance, the senior manager and the officer shall each supply a list of proposed witnesses or give notice that they do not have any witnesses: PPR, reg. 36(4). Where witnesses are proposed, this must be accompanied by brief details of their evidence and their addresses. The officer should try to agree a list of witnesses with the senior manager: PPR, reg. 36(5). Where agreement has not been reached, the officer must send to the appropriate authority his/her list of witnesses: PPR, reg. 36(6). As soon as reasonably practicable after any list of witnesses has been agreed or, in the case where no agreement could be reached, supplied to the appropriate authority, the appropriate authority must send the lists to the panel chair together with, in the latter case, a list of its proposed witnesses: PPR, reg. 37(1). The panel chair will consider the list of proposed witnesses and will determine which, if any, should attend the second stage meeting: PPR, reg. 37(2).

The panel chair can determine that persons not named in the list should attend as witnesses: PPR, reg. 37(3). No witnesses should give evidence at a second stage meeting unless the panel chair reasonably believes that it is necessary in the interests of fairness for the witness to do so, in which case he/she will (PPR, reg. 37(4)):

- in the case of a police officer, cause him/her to be ordered to attend the second stage meeting;
- in any other case, cause him/her to be given notice that his/her attendance at the second stage meeting is necessary.

Such notices will include the date, time and place of the meeting.

Where a witness attends to give evidence, the panel chair must determine whether any question should be put to him/her: PPR, reg. 8(7). This would not prevent the panel chair allowing questions to be asked directly if he/she feels that this is appropriate.

The documents or other material to be relied upon at the meeting are required to be submitted in advance: PPR, reg. 36(3). Any document or other material that was not submitted in advance of the meeting may be considered at the meeting at the discretion of the panel chair: PPR, reg. 8(9). However, the presumption should be that such documents or other material will not be permitted unless it can be shown that they were not previously available to be submitted in advance (Home Office Guidance, para. 15.7) or that they relate to mitigation following a finding of unsatisfactory performance or attendance that was contested by the police officer.

3.18.10.6 At the Second Stage Meeting

At the second stage meeting, the panel chair will conduct the meeting, explain to the police officer the reasons why he/she has been required to attend and provide the police officer with the opportunity to make representations in response: PPR, reg. 44(2). Where the case is one of gross incompetence and the police officer has opted for legal representation, the chair will provide the police officer's legal representative with the opportunity to make representations: PPR, reg. 44(3)(b). If the officer has chosen not to be legally represented, they will provide the police officer's police friend (if they have one) with an opportunity to make representations. The panel chair has a duty to listen to what the police officer and/or police friend has to say and to ask questions as appropriate: Home Office Guidance, para. 17.45(e).

Having considered any representations by either the police officer and/or his/her police friend or (where applicable) the police officer's legal representative, the panel will come to a finding as to whether or not the performance or attendance of the police officer has been unsatisfactory, or whether or not his/her behaviour constitutes gross incompetence, as the case may be: PPR, reg. 45(1). If there is a difference of view between the three panel members, the finding or decision will be based on a simple majority vote, but it will not be indicated whether it was taken unanimously or by a majority: PPR, reg. 45(5).

The panel must prepare (or cause to be prepared) its decision in writing which must state its finding: PPR, reg. 45(2). Where the panel has found that the police officer's performance or attendance has been unsatisfactory or that he/she has been grossly incompetent, the decision must also state the panel's reasons and any outcome which it orders.

As soon as reasonably practicable after the conclusion of the meeting, the panel chair shall send a copy of the decision to the police officer and the line manager: PPR, reg. 45(3). However, the police officer must be given written notice of the finding of the panel within three working days after the conclusion of the meeting. Where the panel has made a finding of unsatisfactory performance or attendance, or gross incompetence, the copy of the decision sent to the police officer must also be accompanied by a notice informing him/her of the circumstances in which and the time frame within which he/she may appeal to a Police Appeals Tribunal: PPR, reg. 45(4). A verbatim record of the meeting must be taken: PPR, reg. 44(5). The police officer must, on request, be supplied with a copy of the recording.

3.18.10.7 Postponement and Adjournment of a Second Stage Meeting

If the panel chair considers it necessary or expedient, he/she may direct that the second stage meeting should take place at a different time from that originally notified to the police officer: PPR, reg. 39(1). The panel chair's alternative time may fall after the period of 30 working days: PPR, reg. 39(2). In the event that the panel chair postpones a second stage meeting, he/she should notify the following relevant parties in writing of his/her reasons and the revised time and place for it (PPR, reg. 39(3)):

- the police officer;
- other panel members; and
- the appropriate authority.

KEYNOTE

Video Link

If the police officer informs the panel chair in advance that he/she is unable to attend the second stage meeting on grounds which the panel chair considers reasonable, the panel chair may allow the police officer to participate in the meeting by video link or other means: PPR, reg. 38(9). In cases where the police officer is absent (e.g. through illness or injury), a short delay may be reasonable to allow him/her to attend. If this is not possible or any delay is considered not appropriate in the circumstances then the persons conducting the meeting/hearing may allow the police officer to participate by telephone or video link. In these circumstances, a police friend will always be permitted to attend the meeting/hearing to represent the police officer in the normal way (and, in the case of a gross incompetence meeting, the police officer's legal representative where appointed): PPR, reg. 8(1)(b).

3.18.10.8 Assessment of Written and Extended Written Improvement Notices Issued at the Second Stage

Where the police officer has been issued with a written improvement notice or, in exceptional cases, the panel has extended a written improvement notice period, it is expected that the police officer's performance or attendance will be actively monitored by the line manager throughout the specified period of the written/extended written improvement notice. The line manager should discuss with the police officer any concerns that the line manager has during this period as regards his/her performance or attendance and offer advice and guidance where appropriate: Home Office Guidance, para. 17.59.

As soon as reasonably practicable after the specified period of the written/extended written improvement notice comes to an end, the panel will assess the performance or attendance of the police officer during that period: PPR, reg. 48(1). The panel chair must then inform the police officer in writing of the panel's conclusion following assessment, i.e. whether there has been sufficient improvement in his/her performance or attendance during the specified period: PPR, reg. 48(2). If the panel considers that there has been insufficient improvement the panel chair shall also notify the officer that he/she is required to attend another second stage meeting.

If, at the end of the validity period of the written/extended written improvement notice, the panel considers that sufficient improvement to the police officer's performance or attendance has not been made or maintained during this period, the panel chair will inform the police officer of the panel's assessment. Any such notification to the police officer must also include notification that he/she is required to attend a further second stage meeting: PPR, reg. 48(4). Where an officer is required to attend a further second stage meeting, the UPPs shall apply as if he/she were required to attend that meeting for the first time and following a second stage meeting: PPR, reg. 48(7).

A further second stage meeting must relate to matters similar to or connected with the unsatisfactory performance or attendance or gross incompetence referred to in the written improvement notice extended or issued by the panel. The panel should (where possible) be composed of the same persons who conducted the previous second stage meeting: PPR, reg. 48(10). However, there may be cases where reconstitution of the panel is either inappropriate or not possible. In such circumstances, the appropriate authority may substitute members as it sees fit subject to the requirements in **para. 3.18.10.2**: PPR, reg. 48(11)-(12). As soon as reasonably practicable after the appointment of any new panel members, the police officer should be notified in writing of the changes in panel membership: PPR, reg. 48(13). The police officer will have the opportunity to object to any new panel members: PPR, reg. 48(14).

A police officer may only be given an extension to a written improvement notice on one occasion: PPR, reg. 49(2). Therefore, where the police officer is required to attend a reconvened second stage meeting and the panel finds that the police officer's performance or attendance continues to be unsatisfactory, the only outcomes available to the panel are redeployment, reduction in rank (only in performance cases) or dismissal (with notice).

3.18.10.9 Second Stage Appeals

Following a second stage meeting, a police officer may be able to appeal to a Police Appeals Tribunal: Police (Appeals) Tribunal Rules 2020, reg. 5(1). However, any finding and outcome of the second stage meeting will continue to apply up to the date that the appeal is determined.

3.18.11 Attendance at Each Stage of the Procedures and Ill-health

Attendance at a meeting is not subject to the same considerations as reporting for duty, and the provisions of reg. 33 (sick leave) of the Police Regulations 2003 *do not apply*. An illness or disability may render a police officer unfit for duty without affecting his/her ability to attend a meeting. However, if the police officer is incapacitated, the meeting may be deferred until he/she is sufficiently improved to attend. A meeting will not be deferred indefinitely because the police officer is unable to attend, although every effort should be made to make it possible for the police officer to attend if he/she wishes to be present. For example:

- the acute phase of a serious physical illness is usually fairly short-lived, and the meeting may be deferred until the police officer is well enough to attend;
- if the police officer suffers from a physical injury (for instance a broken leg) it may be possible to hold the meeting at a location convenient to him/her.

Where such circumstances apply at a stage two meeting, the force may wish to consider the use of video, telephone or other conferencing technology. Where, despite such efforts having been made and/or the meeting having been deferred, the police officer either persists in failing to attend the meeting or maintains his/her inability to attend, the person conducting the meeting will need to decide whether to continue to defer the meeting or to proceed with it in the absence of the police officer. The person conducting the meeting must judge the most appropriate course of action. Nothing in this paragraph should be taken to suggest that, where a police officer's medical condition is found to be such that he/she would normally be retired on medical grounds, the UPPs should prevent or delay retirement.

3.18.12 The Use of Records under UPPs

Records of any part of the UPPs should not be taken into account after an improvement notice has ceased to be valid. Equally, where a police officer appeals and that appeal is successful, the record of that procedure should not be taken into consideration in any future proceedings or for any other purpose.

3.18.13 Misconduct, Performance and Attendance Issues for Seconded Officers

The procedures set out in the UPPs cannot be applied by an organisation to which the police officer is seconded under s. 97 of the Police Act 1996. However, the procedures set out in the Regulations can be applied by the parent force in respect of conduct, performance or attendance while the officer is on secondment. Those responsible for managing police officers on secondment are expected to manage any issue of unsatisfactory performance or attendance or minor misconduct in a proportionate, fair and timely manner without returning an officer to his/her parent force. Only if it is necessary to institute the formal procedures should an officer be returned to force, in accordance with the principles and procedures expressed below.

Where an officer is on secondment under the Police (Overseas Service) Act 1945, with the Police Ombudsman for Northern Ireland or with the Police Service of Northern Ireland, he/she can be dealt with by the receiving organisation under its disciplinary arrangements. However, on return to his/her force, he/she can still be dealt with under the disciplinary arrangements in respect of the same matters.

It is important that police officers on secondment are clear about who has line management responsibility for them. The line managers for such police officers must ensure that the police officer continues to have a PDR and is made aware of these arrangements for dealing with issues of misconduct or unsatisfactory performance or attendance.

Where there is no or insufficient improvement in the performance or attendance of the police officer, the seconded police officer's line manager should prepare a written report which details the nature of the unsatisfactory performance or attendance together with the remedial and other measures taken, and send this report to the head of the organisation to which the police officer is seconded (or his/her nominated representative). The head of the organisation (or nominated representative), in conjunction with the appropriate authority for the police officer concerned, will decide whether it is appropriate for the police officer concerned to be returned to his/her parent force or whether the unsatisfactory performance or attendance can be addressed with the police officer remaining on secondment. Where a police officer who has been returned to his/her parent force under this procedure continues to demonstrate the same pattern of unsatisfactory performance or attendance, the details of the unsatisfactory performance or attendance while on secondment may be used to inform the decision whether it is appropriate to use the UPPs.

In cases of alleged misconduct by a secondee, the organisation to which the police officer has been seconded will need to make an initial assessment of the allegation of misconduct. If that assessment determines that the matter can be dealt with informally, the seconded officer's manager is expected to deal with the matter in this way. As part of this decision making process, it may be necessary for the line manager to contact the appropriate authority for the seconded officer to assist in determining the nature of the conduct and whether it should be investigated. In this regard, the appropriate authority will need to consider its obligations under the Police Reform Act 2002 and any requirement to refer a matter to the Independent Office for Police Conduct (IOPC).

However, where the line manager considers that an alleged breach of the Standards of Professional Behaviour is more serious and indicates that the police officer concerned may have committed a criminal offence, or behaved in a manner that would justify the bringing of disciplinary proceedings, the head of the organisation to which the police officer is seconded (or his/her nominated representative) will liaise with the appropriate authority from which the police officer concerned is seconded, to assess whether the officer should be returned to the force while a preliminary assessment into the matter is conducted by the parent force. If, as a result of that preliminary assessment, the parent force or the IOPC considers it appropriate to issue a notice according to reg. 17 of the Police (Conduct) Regulations 2020 or Police (Complaints and Misconduct) Regulations 2020 in relation to the matter, the officer must be returned to their force.

Where it is determined by the appropriate authority for the seconded officer and the organisation to which he/she is seconded, that the conduct, if proved or admitted, would not justify the bringing of disciplinary proceedings, informal action may still be taken where appropriate. At the conclusion of any disciplinary proceedings, where the police officer has been returned to the parent force, that force together with the organisation to which the police officer concerned was seconded will decide if it is appropriate for the police officer to be able to resume his/her secondment.

3.18.14 Vicarious Liability of Chief Officers

Section 88 of the Police Act 1996 originally provided that a chief officer will be vicariously liable for the 'torts' (civil wrongs) of his/her officers committed in the performance (or purported performance) of their duties. This meant that the chief officer was responsible for the payment of any damages arising out of a civil claim in respect of such a tort. The extent of this vicarious liability was wider than that imposed on employers generally (*Weir* v *Chief Constable of Merseyside Police* [2003] EWCA Civ 111).

However, despite the fact that the vicarious liability of chief officers was broader than that of any ordinary employer, its limitation to strictly actionable civil wrongs was felt to have led to some inequities, denying remedies to individuals while failing to impose full accountability on the relevant chief officers. The Police Reform Act 2002 clarified the position and amended s. 88 to provide that chief officers will be liable for the 'unlawful conduct' (as opposed to purely civil wrongs) of their officers and employees when acting as such (s. 102).

3.18.15 Other Regulations

In addition to the specific provisions for conduct, complaints and efficiency, there are several other sources of regulation that govern the employment and deployment of police officers.

3.18.15.1 Restrictions on Private Lives

The Police Regulations 2003 impose restrictions on the private lives of officers. Regulation 6 provides that the restrictions contained in sch. 1 shall apply to all members of a police force. It also provides that no restrictions other than those designed to secure the proper exercise of the functions of a constable shall be imposed by the chief officer of police on the private lives of members of a police force except such as may temporarily be necessary or such as may be approved by the Secretary of State after consultation with the Police Advisory Board for England and Wales.

Schedule 1

Schedule 1 provides that a member of a police force:

- shall at all times abstain from any activity which is likely to interfere with the impartial discharge of his/her duties or which is likely to give rise to the impression among members of the public that it may so interfere;
- shall in particular:
  - not take any active part in politics;
  - not belong to any organisation specified or described in a determination of the Secretary of State.

For this purpose the Secretary of State has determined that no member of a police force may be a member of the British National Party (BNP), Combat 18 or the National Front.

- shall not reside at premises which are not for the time being approved by the chief officer of police;
- shall not, without the previous consent of the chief officer of police, receive a lodger in a house or quarters with which he/she is provided, or sub-let any part of the house or quarters;
- shall not, unless he/she has previously given written notice to the chief officer of police, receive a lodger in a house in which he/she resides and in respect of which he/she receives an allowance under sch. 3, or sub-let any part of such a house;
- shall not wilfully refuse or neglect to discharge any lawful debt.

3.18.15.2 Business Interests

Some business interests preclude people from applying to be a police constable (reg. 7 of the Police Regulations 2003).

Regulation 8 provides that, if a member of a police force or a relative included in his/her family proposes to have, or has, a 'business interest', the member shall forthwith give written notice of that interest to the chief officer of police unless that business interest was disclosed at the time of the officer's appointment as a member of the force.

On receipt of such a notice, the chief officer shall determine whether or not the interest in question is compatible with the member concerned remaining a member of the force and shall notify the member in writing of his/her decision within 28 days.

If a business interest is felt to be incompatible, the chief officer may dispense with the member's services after giving him/her an opportunity to make representations. Regulation 7(2) provides that a member of a police force or relative has a business interest if:

- the member holds any office or employment for hire or gain or carries on any business;
- the member or a relative of the member has a pecuniary interest in any licence or permit granted in relation to alcohol licensing, refreshment houses or betting and gaming or regulating places of entertainment in the area of the police force in question.

'Relative' means a spouse or civil partner who is not separated from the member, a person living with the member as if they were their spouse or civil partner, or a parent, son, daughter, brother or sister who is included in the member's family.

A police officer must notify his/her chief officer of any changes in a business interest.

3.18.16 Offences

The following criminal offences relate to the general abuse of public office and specific offences relating to police officers or impersonation of officers or officials.

3.18.16.1 Misconduct in a Public Office

OFFENCE: **Misconduct in a Public Office—*Common Law***

- Triable on indictment • Imprisonment at large

It is a misdemeanour at common law for the holder of a public office to do anything that amounts to a malfeasance or a 'culpable' misfeasance (*R* v *Wyat* (1705) 1 Salk 380).

Where there is clear evidence of one or more statutory offences, they should usually form the basis of the case, with the 'public office' element being put forward as an aggravating factor for sentencing purposes.

The use of the common law offence should therefore be limited to the following situations:

- where there is no relevant statutory offence, but the behaviour or the circumstances are such that they should nevertheless be treated as criminal;
- where there is a statutory offence but it would be difficult or inappropriate to use it. This might arise because of evidential difficulties in proving the statutory offence in the particular circumstances;
- because the maximum sentence for the statutory offence would be entirely insufficient for the seriousness of the misconduct.

KEYNOTE

This offence has also been described as 'A man accepting an office of trust concerning the public is answerable criminally to the King for misbehaviour in his office ... by whomsoever and in whatever way the officer is appointed' (*R* v *Bembridge* (1783) 3 Dougl 327).

Such offences can only be tried on indictment and the court has a power of sentence 'at large', that is, there is no limit on the sentence that can be passed. This ancient common law oddity is both a civil wrong (tort) giving rise to an action for damages in the county and High Court, and a criminal offence which is triable on indictment and punishable by an unlimited term of imprisonment.

Given the wide scope of the 'offence' element, it can cover a multitude of transgressions by police officers, from mistreating prisoners to the improper use of criminal intelligence. The conduct can be separated into occasions of *mal*feasance and *mis*feasance. The first requires some degree of wrongful motive or intention on the part of the officer while the second is more likely to apply where there has been some form of wilful neglect of duty: both are difficult to prove.

The essence of both is generally an abuse of public power in bad faith (*Thomas* v *Secretary of State for the Home Office* [2000] Prison LR 188). There must at least be some real connection between the alleged misconduct and the public office, for instance where a man employed by a local council as a maintenance manager dishonestly caused his employees to carry out works on his girlfriend's premises (*R* v *Bowden* [1996] 1 WLR 98). Therefore, simply behaving badly while off duty would not of itself make a public office holder (such as a police officer) guilty of this offence (*Elliott* v *Chief Constable of Wiltshire* (1996) *The Times*, 5 December—disclosure of previous convictions from PNC to a newspaper capable of amounting to misfeasance). It may, however, make the relevant *chief officer* vicariously liable under other heads of law if the off-duty officer was purporting to rely on his/her status as a constable (*Weir* v *Chief Constable of Merseyside* [2003] EWCA Civ 111).

The key elements of the offence so far as it applies to public office holders (such as police officers) were set out by the Court of Appeal in *Attorney-General's Reference (No. 3 of 2003)* [2004] EWCA Crim 868. That case arose out of a death in police custody and the officers were charged with manslaughter by gross negligence, along with the alternative offence of misconduct in a public office. It was argued that misconduct in a public office is a 'conduct' crime, i.e. one where the acts (or omissions) themselves were the real consideration and not the consequences which those acts/omissions brought about (see *Crime*, chapter 1.2). Although reluctant to try to give an exhaustive definition of the offence, the Court of Appeal identified the elements of conduct and state of mind that must be proved in order to convict an officer of misfeasance, holding the main ingredients to be:

- Conduct (or omission) which involved the public office holder *acting as such*. In other words, this would need to arise from the actions (or omissions) of a police officer while acting in his/her capacity as a constable. A purely personal matter arising while the officer was off duty would not normally meet this first criterion.
- Evidence of wilful neglect and/or wilful misconduct. Simple inadvertence or accidental action/omission without more will not be enough.
- The degree of wilful neglect/misconduct must be such as to amount to an abuse of the public's trust in the office holder.
- Proof that the officer acted/omitted to act without any reasonable excuse or justification.

In the civil setting, even though there might be circumstances where officers could be criticised for failures, including incompetence, excess of zeal and even serious negligence, the absence of bad faith or deliberate misuse of power would generally mean that there is not enough to support an allegation of misfeasance (*Ashley* v *Chief Constable of Sussex* [2005] EWHC 415 (QB)).

The ingredients of the civil wrong are fully set out in *Three Rivers District Council* v *Governor and Company of the Bank of England (No. 3)* [2003] 2 AC 1. Their application, especially in the case of police officers, was discussed at length in *Cornelius* v *London Borough of Hackney* [2002] EWCA Civ 1073. In *Three Rivers*, Lord Steyn confirmed that the civil and criminal wrongs bore some resemblance. Although many of the earlier cases involved an element of corruption, this is not a requirement for the offence (*R* v *Dytham* [1979] QB 722). This offence might be committed where a police officer wilfully neglects to prevent a criminal assault (as in *Dytham*), or possibly where a supervisory officer fails to intervene in a situation where one of his/her officers is carrying out an unlawful act.

From the many authorities (especially *Bowden*) it is arguable that this offence could be extended in appropriate circumstances to misconduct of non-sworn employees such as those designated (or perhaps even those accredited) under the Police Reform Act 2002.

The Court of Appeal has held that, where the police wrote to the registered keepers of vehicles believed to have been stolen in another country, informing those keepers that they may not be the legal owners, the person who imported and sold the vehicles might be able to bring a claim for misfeasance—much would depend on the state of mind and intentions of the relevant individual in acting as they did (*R Cruickshank Ltd* v *Chief Constable of Kent* [2002] EWCA Civ 1840).

3.18.16.2 Offences Relating to Impersonation

OFFENCE: **Impersonating a Police Officer—*Police Act 1996, s. 90(1)***

- Triable summarily • Six months' imprisonment

The Police Act 1996, s. 90 states:

> (1) Any person who with intent to deceive impersonates a member of a police force or special constable, or makes any statement or does any act calculated falsely to suggest that he is such a member or constable, shall be guilty of an offence and liable ...

OFFENCE: **Wearing or Possessing Uniform—*Police Act 1996, s. 90(2) and (3)***

- Triable summarily • Fine *(No specific power of arrest)*

The Police Act 1996, s. 90 states:

> (2) Any person who, not being a constable, wears any article of police uniform in circumstances where it gives him an appearance so nearly resembling that of a member of a police force as to be calculated to deceive shall be guilty of an offence ...

(3) Any person who, not being a member of a police force or special constable, has in his possession any article of police uniform shall, unless he proves that he obtained possession of that article lawfully and has possession of it for a lawful purpose, be guilty of an offence ...

KEYNOTE

'Article of police uniform' means:

- any article of uniform, or
- any distinctive badge or mark, or
- any document of identification usually issued to members of police forces or special constables (s. 90(4)).

OFFENCE: **Impersonating Designated or Accredited Person—*Police Reform Act 2002, s. 46(3)***

- Triable summarily • Six months' imprisonment and/or a fine *(No specific power of arrest)*

The Police Reform Act 2002, s. 46 states:

(3) Any person who, with intent to deceive—
(a) impersonates a designated person, an accredited person or an accredited inspector,
(b) makes any statement or does any act calculated falsely to suggest that he is a designated person, that he is an accredited person or that he is an accredited inspector, or
(c) makes any statement or does any act calculated falsely to suggest that he has powers as a designated or accredited person or as an accredited inspector that exceed the powers he actually has,
is guilty of an offence.

KEYNOTE

These offences are based on the corresponding offences for police officers.

3.18.16.3 Causing Disaffection Among the Police

OFFENCE: **Causing Disaffection—*Police Act 1996, s. 91(1)***

- Triable either way • Two years' imprisonment on indictment • Six months' imprisonment and/or a fine summarily *(No specific power of arrest)*

The Police Act 1996, s. 91 states:

(1) Any person who causes, or attempts to cause, or does any act calculated to cause, disaffection amongst the members of any police force, or induces or attempts to induce, or does any act calculated to induce, any member of a police force to withhold his services, shall be guilty of an offence ...

3.18.16.4 Corrupt or Other Improper Exercise of Police Powers and Privileges

Section 26 of the Criminal Justice and Courts Act 2015 makes it an offence for a police officer and certain other persons to improperly exercise the powers and privileges of the office of constable. It supplements and expands upon the existing common law offence of misconduct in public office.

The definition of a constable includes a constable of a Home Office police force in England and Wales as well as the British Transport Police, a special constable of a police force or the British Transport Police, and National Crime Agency officers designated with the powers and privileges of a constable.

Subsection (1) provides that a police constable commits an offence if he/she exercises the powers and privileges of a constable improperly and the officer knows or ought to know that it is improper. A person guilty of the offence is liable on conviction on indictment to a sentence of imprisonment for 14 years or a fine, or both.

Subsection (4) provides that a police constable exercises the powers and privileges of a constable improperly if the exercise of a power or privilege is for the purpose of achieving a benefit to the officer, or a benefit or detriment for another person, and that a reasonable person would not expect the power or privilege to be exercised for the purpose of achieving that benefit or detriment. Subsection (9) defines 'benefit' or 'detriment' as meaning any benefit or detriment, whether or not in money and whether or not permanent.

The improper exercise of a power or privilege for the purpose of the offence can refer to cases in which there is a failure to exercise a power or privilege, or there is a threat to exercise a power or privilege or to fail to do so, in each case for the purpose of achieving a benefit or detriment and in any of these cases a reasonable person would not expect the power or privilege to be exercised for the purpose of achieving that benefit or detriment.

This new offence does not affect what constitutes the common law offence of misconduct in public office in England and Wales or Northern Ireland.

3.18.17 Health and Safety

Because police officers are not 'employees' (they are holders of the office of constable), many of the statutory provisions regulating the workplace do not apply directly to them. The health and safety regime created by the Health and Safety at Work etc. Act 1974 applies principally to 'employees' and therefore did not cover police officers (though it clearly covers their non-sworn support colleagues who *are* employees). However, the Police (Health and Safety) Act 1997 made changes to the legislation by treating police officers for certain purposes relating to health and safety as if they were employees. Briefly, these areas include:

- the application of part 1 of the 1974 Act to the police;
- the right of police officers not to be subjected to a detriment in relation to health and safety issues, e.g. not to be punished for raising appropriate health and safety issues or undertaking duties as health and safety representatives (s. 49A of the Employment Rights Act 1996);
- the right of police officers not to be unfairly dismissed in relation to health and safety issues (s. 134A of the Employment Rights Act 1996).

Under the Health and Safety at Work etc. Act 1974, any prosecution of a chief officer of police for an offence under that Act will be brought against the office of chief constable rather than against the individual him/herself. This change to the law (brought in by the Serious Organised Crime and Police Act 2005) brings the position of a chief officer into line with that of police authorities and their liability for breaches of health and safety legislation in respect of police staff (who are their employees). However, a chief officer may also be prosecuted in a personal capacity if it can be shown that he/she personally consented to the commission of an offence or personally connived in its commission or was personally negligent.

3.19 Road Policing Definitions and Principles

3.19.1 Introduction

The majority of definitions relevant to road policing offences and powers in this Manual are contained in the Road Traffic Act 1988. This chapter examines several of those fundamental statutory definitions such as 'motor vehicle', 'driver' and 'road', along with a large body of case law connected to those definitions. The chapter also considers associated definitions and behaviours such as 'public place' and 'using, causing and permitting'. Many of these definitions are intrinsically linked to the remaining chapters in this Manual; understanding the definitions in this chapter assists in understanding later chapters.

3.19.2 Key Definitions

The most commonly used road traffic definitions, such as 'motor vehicle', 'driver' and 'road', can be found in ss. 185 and 192 of the Road Traffic Act 1988. It is these and other frequently encountered definitions that this chapter deals with.

Sections 185 and 192 provide further definitions whose use is less frequent—where this is the case, the relevant definition is given and explained within the chapter dealing with that area of road policing law. This is also the case where legislation other than the Road Traffic Act 1988 provides a specific definition.

3.19.3 Vehicle

A 'vehicle' is not, of itself, defined in the Road Traffic Act 1988. The *Oxford English Dictionary* defines 'vehicle' as a 'carriage or conveyance of any kind used on land'. Virtually anything may be capable of amounting to a 'vehicle' under the right circumstances, even a chicken shed on wheels (*Garner* v *Burr* [1951] 1 KB 31) or a hut used as an office and being drawn along by a tractor (*Horn* v *Dobson* [1933] JC 1). In some circumstances, a pram may be a vehicle as may a scooter. A bicycle being ridden has been confirmed as a carriage which equates to a vehicle (*Crank* v *Brooks* [1980] RTR 441).

3.19.4 Mechanically Propelled Vehicle

The term 'mechanically propelled vehicle' is not defined in the Road Traffic Acts. It is ultimately a matter of fact and degree for the court to decide. At its most basic level, it is a vehicle which can be propelled by mechanical means. It can include electrical vehicles.

Case law decisions provide us with greater insight as to what this phrase actually means:

- The test as to whether a vehicle is 'mechanically propelled' is one of construction rather than use (*McEachran* v *Hurst* [1978] RTR 462). In this case, the defendant was pedalling a moped to a friend's house for repair. It was not taxed and there was no current test certificate in force for the moped. The justices held that it was not a mechanically propelled vehicle on the grounds that it was being used as a pedal cycle, the engine did not work and there was no petrol in the tank. The Divisional Court, reversing the justices' decision, held that the test to be applied to determine whether the moped was mechanically propelled was the same as any other motor vehicle; namely, *on its construction*. If it was constructed as a motor vehicle, it remained a mechanically propelled vehicle unless it could be said that there was no reasonable prospect of it again being mechanically propelled.

- The test will be an objective one which looks at what the vehicle was constructed to do; it does not look at the subjective intention of the owner (*Chief Constable of Avon and Somerset* v *Fleming* [1987] 1 All ER 318).
- The term 'mechanically propelled' not only includes petrol-driven and oil-driven vehicles, but also includes steam and electrically powered vehicles (*Elieson* v *Parker* (1917) 81 JP 265).
- A vehicle which has more than one source of power does not cease to be 'mechanically propelled', even though it is propelled by means other than an engine at the relevant time (*Floyd* v *Bush* [1953] 1 WLR 242).
- In *Newbury* v *Simmonds* [1961] 2 QB 354, it was held that a motor car from which the engine had been removed did not thereby cease to be a mechanically propelled vehicle if the evidence admitted the possibility that the engine might shortly be replaced and the motive power restored. It might be different if the motive power were permanently removed.
- The prosecution bears the burden of showing that a vehicle meets the requirements of being 'mechanically propelled' (*Reader* v *Bunyard* [1987] RTR 406).

3.19.5 Motor Vehicle

The term 'motor vehicle' is defined in s. 185(1) of the Road Traffic Act 1988 and s. 136(1) of the Road Traffic Regulation Act 1984 as 'a mechanically propelled vehicle (**see para. 3.19.4**), intended or adapted for use on roads'. The word 'adapted' means 'altered so as to make it fit' (*Maddox* v *Storer* [1963] 1 QB 451).

Although this is the legal definition, ultimately it is a matter of fact and degree for a court to interpret whether or not a vehicle is a motor vehicle.

The objective approach in deciding whether a vehicle is 'mechanically propelled' is also applied when deciding whether a vehicle is a 'motor vehicle', i.e. the test as to whether a vehicle is intended or adapted for use on roads is an objective one—would a reasonable person say that one of its uses would be general use on a road (*Burns* v *Currell* [1963] 2 QB 433)? It has nothing to do with the owner's or manufacturer's intention. An example of this approach can be seen in *Nichol* v *Leach* [1972] RTR 476, where the owner of a Mini car rebuilt it solely for 'auto-cross' racing, never intending it to be used on a road. Nevertheless, it was held to have retained its original intended road use character and remained a 'motor vehicle'.

If a vehicle is electrically powered but is not an e-bike (or a car, traditional motorcycle or mobility scooter), the government refers to it as a Powered Light Electric Vehicle (PLEV). This term covers all manner of personal transport including electric scooters, Segways, hoverboards, electric unicycles and electric skateboards. Over time, these vehicles have evolved and have tested the limits of existing legislation, most notably the Road Traffic Act 1988. There are no bespoke statutes dealing with PLEVs in general, but case law has clarified how they sit within the existing definitions.

Several cases involving 'personal transport' are worthy of note. In *Chief Constable of North Yorkshire Police* v *Saddington* [2001] RTR 15, a 'Go-Ped' (a motorised scooter) was sold with the specific instruction from the manufacturer that it was not to be used on a road. The Divisional Court emphasised the fact that the test was whether a reasonable person would say that one of its uses would be on the road. The court decided that the design and capabilities of the Go-Ped, allied with the fact that it offered an opportunity to get quickly through traffic, meant that general use on the road had to be contemplated. The Go-Ped had no lights, no suspension and no indicators. It was also marketed as an executive toy rather than a means of road transport. It was not useful as an off-road vehicle as it required a flat surface in order to move. Despite this, the court ruled on the facts that it was a vehicle likely to be used on the road and therefore the rider's conviction stood. The distributor's advice would, in practice, be ignored and its use on a road would not be an isolated occurrence—it was therefore a 'motor vehicle' and required insurance and registration, just like a normal motorcycle. Saddington was convicted of riding an unregistered and uninsured scooter on the road.

In *DPP* v *King* [2008] EWHC 447 (Admin), the defendant was stopped by the police while riding a 'City Mantis' electric scooter on a public road. The scooter looked like a bicycle except that it did not have any pedals or other means of manual propulsion and it was capable of speeds of up to 10 mph. The defendant was charged with driving a motor vehicle while disqualified and with no insurance. At trial, the issue arose regarding whether the scooter was a motor vehicle. The defendant was acquitted. However, following the case being passed to the High Court, it was remitted with a direction to convict. The court decided the scooter was a motor vehicle according to s. 185(1) of the Road Traffic Act 1988.

The Segway Personal Transporter is powered by electricity and transports a passenger standing on a platform, propelled on two or more wheels and able to steer and remain upright through the use of internal gyroscopes. In *Coates* v *CPS* [2011] EWHC 2032 (Admin) it was decided that the Segway was a 'motor vehicle'. The court highlighted that any user of the Segway would be tempted to ride on the road when convenient.

Two-wheeled e-scooters—the most popular type of PLEV—also fit the definition of a motorcycle, meaning that a helmet and driving licence with Compulsory Basic Motorcycle Training (CBT) are required.

'Self-balancing scooters' or 'personal transportation devices' (hoverboards) are illegal to ride on the road, because they do not meet the requirements to be registered under British schemes for road-legal vehicles. It is an offence under s. 72 of the Highway Act 1835 to ride on a pavement.

Case law shows that PLEVs fall between two stools. They cannot be driven on the road as they require insurance and registration. However, because they have a motor and can be mechanically propelled, they cannot be driven on the pavement either.

E-scooter trials enabled by the Department for Transport are underway in the United Kingdom. The trial period has recently been extended and is due to conclude in May 2028. This will inform and develop legislation and provide further guidance for criminal justice practitioners. Rental e-scooters formally approved by a relevant trial are currently the only way to lawfully ride an e-scooter on public roads or in other public places. These trials place restrictions on speed and location. The rider must hold a provisional or full driving licence. Insurance must be provided by the operator. Use of e-scooters outside an approved trial area or contrary to the trial conditions are illegal. Privately owned e-scooters or other powered transporters are not legal to use on public roads or public places.

Note that a motor vehicle continues to be such if it is towed by another vehicle (*Cobb* v *Whorton* [1971] RTR 392).

A diesel dumper truck used solely for road construction work and not intended to be driven along the parts of the highway open to the public has been held *not* to be a motor vehicle for insurance purposes (*MacDonald* v *Carmichael* [1941] JC 27). Dumper trucks intended for use solely on construction sites will not be 'motor vehicles' but, if you are able to adduce evidence that they *are suitable* for use on a road, they may be held to be motor vehicles (*Daley* v *Hargreaves* [1961] 1 WLR 487). They will, of course, still be 'mechanically propelled vehicles' even when used elsewhere than on a road.

Section 189 of the Road Traffic Act 1988 specifies which vehicles will *not* be treated as motor vehicles; they include pedestrian-controlled vehicles, some implements for cutting grass and electrically assisted pedal cycles.

3.19.6 Driver

Section 192(1) of the Road Traffic Act 1988 states that the 'driver' is a 'person engaged in the driving of the vehicle'.

It is possible for more than one person to be the 'driver' of a vehicle. In *Tyler* v *Whatmore* [1976] RTR 83, it was held that a girl in the front passenger seat of a car who leaned across the person in the driver's seat with both of her hands on the steering wheel, steering the car, with the ignition switch and handbrake within her reach, was 'actually driving'. Her companion in the driving seat whose view she obstructed and who was controlling the propulsion of the car but could not control the steering was also driving.

Whether a person supervising a driver from the passenger's seat is a driver will be defined by the degree of control exercised throughout by the supervisor. An instructor who retains simultaneous control of the car by keeping their hands on the brake and steering wheel may be the driver (*Langman* v *Valentine* [1952] 2 All ER 803); however, where the instructor was only in a position to assume control if necessary and therefore not in control at the material time, he was held not to be the 'driver' (*Evans* v *Walkden* [1956] 1 WLR 1019). These cases, of course, pre-date dual-control learner vehicles but would relate to non-dual-control vehicles.

For the purposes of some road traffic offences, the person who takes out the vehicle remains the 'driver' of it until that journey ends. Therefore, even if the vehicle is stationary and has been for some time, a person may still be the 'driver' of it if the journey has not ended (see *Jones* v *Prothero* [1952] 1 All ER 434, where the driver sitting in a parked car opened the offside door causing injury to a passing pedal cyclist). Another example is *Cawthorn (Jonathan)* v *DPP* [2000] RTR 45, where the defendant stopped his car on a hill to post a letter and activated the hazard warning lights. While he was away from the vehicle, it rolled down the hill and hit a wall that was damaged (the roll was started by a passenger releasing the handbrake). The defendant left the scene and was subsequently convicted of failing to stop and exchange details and failing to report an accident. The Divisional Court said that although there had been a break in the driving, the appellant was still making his journey (evidenced by the use of the hazard warning lights). The intervening act by the passenger did not make that passenger the driver. Both *Jones* and *Cawthorn* related to the obligations of a 'driver' under s. 170 of the Road Traffic Act 1988.

Whether a person was actually the driver of a vehicle at a particular time *cannot be inferred* from the fact that he/she is also the owner; more evidence of his/her actual involvement in the driving of the vehicle will be required (*R* v *Collins* [1994] RTR 216) and all evidence, including circumstantial evidence, can be considered (*McCombie* v *CPS* [2011] EWHC 758 (Admin)).

The term 'driver' also includes a separate person acting as a steersman of a motor vehicle under s. 192(1) of the 1988 Act (except for the purposes of an offence of causing death by dangerous driving under s. 1 of the 1988 Act (**see para. 3.21.2**)).

3.19.7 **Drive and Driving**

The Road Traffic Act 1988 does not define 'drive' but directs that 'drive' is to be interpreted according to the definition of 'driver' in s. 192(1) which simply refers to a person using the driver's controls for the purpose of directing the movement of the vehicle. This phrase has been enhanced by the decisions of the courts so that there are a number of different situations where a person can be said to be 'driving' a vehicle (even though they do not conjure up a picture of conventional driving).

The leading case is *R* v *MacDonagh* [1974] RTR 372. The circumstances related to whether a person who pushed a car along a road with both feet on the ground with one arm in the car to control the steering wheel could be said to be 'driving'—it was held that this *was not* driving (the behaviour was described as 'pushing'). This decision provides several determining factors to be considered when deciding if a person is 'driving':

- Whether a person is 'driving' or not is a question of fact, dependent on the degree and extent to which the person has control of the direction and movement of the vehicle.
- If the person is in control of the direction and movement of the vehicle, is that control 'in a substantial sense'?
- Even if the control of the direction and movement of the vehicle can be said to be 'in a substantial sense', it must still be considered whether the activity in question could fall within the ordinary meaning of the word 'driving' in the English language.

It was suggested (in *MacDonagh*) that it would be possible to find as a fact that a person was driving if a motorist pushing the vehicle had one foot in the car in order to make more effective use of the controls. This may seem like a fine distinction—two feet on the road is 'pushing', one foot on the road and the other in the car is potentially 'driving'—but then there must come a tipping point where 'driving' behaviour begins or ends and, wherever that may be, it is likely to be the slightest of actions that alters the balance one way or the other.

Later case law decisions have established additional tests to *MacDonagh*:

- Did the defendant deliberately set the vehicle in motion? In *Burgoyne* v *Phillips* [1983] RTR 49, the defendant was sitting behind the steering wheel of a car. Assuming he still had the keys in the ignition, he let the car roll forward to drive off carefully. He realised he had no keys in the ignition and put the brakes on quickly. The steering wheel was locked and the engine was not running. The car rolled a distance of 30 ft by gravity and collided with another vehicle. The defendant was held to be 'driving'.
- How long did the defendant have control of the direction and movement of the vehicle? In *Jones* v *Pratt* [1983] RTR 54, the Divisional Court held that the front seat passenger in a moving car who momentarily grabbed the steering wheel, pushing it in a clockwise direction causing the car to leave the road (behaviour carried out to prevent an accident), could not properly be described as 'driving' in the ordinary sense of the word.

It is also worth examining verdicts dealing with more specific circumstances.

Driving

- In *DPP* v *Alderton* [2003] EWHC 2917 (Admin), it was held that operating the controls of a car (accelerator, clutch and steering) which was parked on a grass verge and wheel spinning was 'driving' even though there was no movement of the vehicle.
- A person may be 'driving' even though he/she is only attempting to control the movement of the vehicle. In *Rowan* v *Merseyside Chief Constable* (1985), *The Times*, 10 December, the defendant knelt on the driving seat, released the handbrake and thereafter attempted to re-apply it to stop the movement of the vehicle—he was held to be 'driving'.

- A steersman in a motor vehicle towed by a rope or chain can properly be said to be 'driving'. In *McQuaid* v *Anderton* [1981] 1 WLR 154, the defendant sat in the driver's seat of a motor car while it was being towed by means of a tow rope connected to another vehicle. He steered the towed car and was able to use its brakes as and when required.
- In *Gunnel* v *DPP* [1994] RTR 151, the appellant was convicted of driving a motor vehicle, a moped, with excess alcohol. When he had attempted to start it, the engine did not fire and he set the moped in motion by sitting astride it and propelling it with his feet in a 'paddling' movement—this was held to be 'driving'. If he were not sitting astride it but pushing it while walking alongside it, then he would not have been 'driving' (*MacDonagh*).

Not Driving

- The Divisional Court has accepted a finding that a person sitting in the driver's seat of a car with the *engine running* had been 'driving' (*R (On the Application of Planton)* v *DPP* [2001] EWHC 450 (Admin)). This was extended in *Mason* v *DPP* [2010] RTR 120, where the Divisional Court suggested that 'driving' would occur when turning on the engine. This can be compared to the situation where the person sitting in the driving seat of a stationary motor vehicle with their hands on the steering wheel and the *engine off*, was held *not* to be 'driving' (*Leach* v *DPP* [1993] RTR 161).
- In *Blayney* v *Knight* [1975] RTR 279, a taxi driver left his taxi, which had automatic transmission, with the engine running. The defendant, who had no intention of driving, sat in the driver's seat. In the course of a struggle with the taxi driver, the defendant's foot touched the accelerator causing the taxi to drive along the road, mount a pavement and swerve back to the offside. The defendant was held *not* to be 'driving'.

Once the act of 'driving' has commenced, it continues until it terminates. This may sound obvious but the question for the court is precisely when does it terminate? A person may still be 'driving' although the vehicle is stationary, when he/she is buying a newspaper or changing a wheel (*Pinner* v *Everett* [1969] 1 WLR 1266; also consider *Cawthorn (Jonathan)* v *DPP* [2000] RTR 45 at **para. 3.19.6**). In *Edkins* v *Knowles* [1973] QB 748, it was emphasised that the reason for stopping is relevant, as it might be part of the journey, e.g. stopping at a set of traffic lights or a junction, or may mark a break in the journey, in which case the length of the break and whether the driver leaves the vehicle is important. The court must consider the period of time and the circumstances to decide whether the person still in the driver's seat (or not as the case may be) was 'driving'.

There must be admissible *evidence* of the features relating to 'driving'. Mere *suspicion* on the part of the arresting or reporting officer will not be sufficient to prove this aspect of the relevant offence (*R (On the Application of Huntley)* v *DPP* [2004] EWHC 870 (Admin)).

3.19.8 Attempting to Drive

The Criminal Attempts Act 1981 (s. 1) states that if a person does an act which is *more than merely preparatory* to the commission of an offence, then he/she is guilty of attempting to commit the offence. This approach is taken when deciding if someone is attempting to drive, i.e. is what this person is doing *more than merely preparatory to the act of driving*? Opening the door of a car is clearly preparatory (*Mason* v *DPP* [2010] RTR 120) but whether the person has done something that is more than merely preparatory to driving is a question of fact to be decided on the individual circumstances of the case.

The general approach to attempts under s. 1 of the Criminal Attempts Act 1981 is that one can attempt the impossible. This is also the case when considering whether someone is attempting to drive, so where the defendant was found revving the engine of a motor car which in fact could not be driven because the clutch had burnt out, he was still 'attempting to drive' (*R* v *Farrance* [1978] RTR 225). Likewise, when an unfit driver, who had no ignition key, sat in the driver's seat and attempted to insert other keys into the ignition, he was held to be properly convicted of attempting to drive (*Kelly* v *Hogan* [1982] RTR 352).

3.19.9 In Charge

The principles to be applied when considering whether a person is 'in charge' of a vehicle are set out in *DPP* v *Watkins* [1989] 2 WLR 966. Two different situations might arise:

- Where the defendant is the owner or lawful possessor of the vehicle or where the defendant has recently driven it. In these cases, it would be for the defendant to show that he/she was no longer in charge of it and that there was no likelihood of resuming control at the relevant time (e.g. while drunk).
- Where the defendant is not the owner, lawful possessor or has not recently driven the vehicle but is sitting in the vehicle or otherwise involved with it. In these cases, the prosecution must show that the defendant was in voluntary control of the vehicle or intended to become so in the immediate future.

The circumstances to be taken into account will vary, but the following would be relevant:

- whether the defendant was in possession of a key that fitted the ignition;
- where the defendant was in relation to the vehicle at the time and what he/she was doing;
- what evidence there is of the defendant's intention to take or assert control of the vehicle by driving or otherwise.

It is possible to be in charge of a motor vehicle even though it is immobile (*Drake* v *DPP* [1994] RTR 411).

In *DPP* v *Janman* [2004] EWHC 101 (Admin), the defendant was supervising his partner, a provisional licence holder, who was driving the car. He failed a breath test and was prosecuted for being in charge of the vehicle. He argued that he had no need to supervise the driver as she was able to drive. The Administrative Court concluded that although there might be circumstances in which a supervisor might be able to prove that there was no likelihood of driving, that was likely to be a difficult task. A supervisor was required because provisional licence holders are not yet deemed competent to drive on their own and a supervisor must be prepared at any time to take over responsibility for the vehicle—the defendant was manifestly 'in charge'.

3.19.10 Road

A road is defined under s. 192(1) of the Road Traffic Act 1988 as:

> ... any highway and any other road to which the public has access, and includes bridges over which a road passes.

This definition is applicable to most occasions where the expression 'road' is used in statutes.

Generally, a road stretches to the boundary fences adjacent to it, including any pavements and grass verges (*Worth* v *Brooks* [1959] Crim LR 855). In *Price* v *DPP* [1990] RTR 413, where the defendant drove across a pavement (part of which was maintained at public expense and part of which was privately owned) thereby causing a pedestrian to jump out of the way, it was held that the pavement as a whole constituted a road.

A useful description of a 'road' comes from the House of Lords in *Cutter* v *Eagle Star Insurance Co. Ltd* [1997] 1 WLR 1082. While it remained a question of fact in every case, a 'road' had the physical character of a defined or definable route or way, with ascertained or ascertainable edges, leading from one point to another with the function of serving as a means of access enabling travellers to move conveniently from one point to another along that route. The function of a car park was to enable stationary vehicles to stand and wait. In the ordinary use of language, a car park is not a road; they have separate and distinct characters. Where legislation referred to 'a road or other public place', the express addition of the words 'or other public place' clearly indicates that where the word 'road' stands alone, it bears its ordinary meaning and does not extend to places such as car parks. In the event of a carriageway being found to exist within its bounds which does so qualify, the remaining area will retain its integrity as a car park (*Clarke* v *Kato* [1998] 1 WLR 1647).

A 'highway' is a way over which the public has a right to pass and re-pass by foot, horse or vehicle, or with animals (*Lang* v *Hindhaugh* [1986] RTR 271). For a highway to exist, there must be some form of 'dedication' of the relevant land to the public and, once so dedicated, it is unlikely that the public status of a highway can be changed. A highway does not cease to be such when it is temporarily roped off or closed (*McCrone* v *J and L Rigby (Wigan) Ltd* (1950) 50 LGR 115). Highways include public bridleways and footpaths and include public bridges over which they pass. Bridleways are highways where the public have a right to ride or lead horses (and related animals) or to pass on foot.

Whether the public has access is a question of fact and degree (*R* v *Waterfield* [1964] 1 QB 164). In *Harrison* v *Hill* [1932] JC 13, a road leading off the public road to a farmhouse was held to be a road to which the public had access. The road had no gate and was maintained by the farmer, who sometimes turned away people using it, but at all other times it was used by people with no business at the farm at all.

In any case where use by the public may not be readily apparent, *Hallett* v *DPP* [2011] EWHC 488 (Admin) emphasises the need for the prosecution to adduce evidence of such. If only a restricted section of the public (such as members of a club) has access to a road, that is not enough to make it a 'road' (*Blackmore* v *Chief Constable of Devon and Cornwall* (1984) *The Times*, 6 December). Any access enjoyed by the public must be with the agreement of the landowner. So members of the public must not have obtained access 'either by overcoming a physical obstruction or in defiance of prohibition, express or implied'. Therefore roads are capable of being closed or cordoned off in a way that alters their status as such.

If a vehicle is partly on a road and partly on some other privately owned land, it can be treated as being 'on a road' for the purposes of road traffic legislation (*Randall* v *Motor Insurers' Bureau* [1968] 1 WLR 1900). A car supported by roller skates so that its wheels did not touch the surface of a road was held to be 'on a road' even though it was not in actual physical contact with the road (*Holliday* v *Henry* [1974] RTR 101). In *Avery* v *CPS* [2012] RTR 87, where the physical boundary of the road was in issue, it being asserted that the wheels of the vehicle driven by the defendant remained on a private driveway, the Divisional Court held that any material encroachment on the airspace vertically above the road was sufficient to justify a conclusion that the vehicle concerned was 'on a road'.

3.19.11 Public Place

In order to prove that a place is in fact a 'public place' for the purposes of road traffic offences, it must be shown by the prosecution that:

- those people who are admitted to the place in question are members of the public and are admitted as such, not as members of some special or particular class of the public (e.g.

people belonging to an exclusive club) or as a result of some special characteristic that is not shared by the public at large (e.g. those delivering goods or meter readers); *and*
- people are so admitted with the permission, express or implied, of the owner of the land in question.

(*DPP* v *Vivier* [1991] RTR 205.)

Whether a place is a 'public place' will be a question of fact for the court. Some examples of places which have been held to qualify as 'public places' are:

- a privately owned caravan site open to campers (*Vivier*);
- a school playground used outside school hours as a leisure park by members of the public (*Rodger* v *Normand* 1995 SLT 411);
- a field used in connection with an agricultural show (*Paterson* v *Ogilvy* 1957 SLT 354);
- a multi-storey car park (*Bowman* v *DPP* [1991] RTR 263);
- a car park attached to commercial premises intended only for the use of customers but accessible *from* a public place and with no restrictions placed on people entering the car park (*May* v *DPP* [2005] EWHC 1280 (Admin)).

For a place which is ostensibly *public* in its nature to become a *private* place, either permanently or temporarily, there needs to be some form of physical obstruction to be overcome in order to enter that place (*R* v *Waters* (1963) 47 Cr App R 149). Therefore a pub landlord, by ordering people to leave the car park of his pub, had not done enough to turn what was a public place (the car park during opening hours) into a private place.

In deciding whether or not a place is in fact a 'public place', magistrates may use their own local knowledge, but must be circumspect in doing so (*Clift* v *Long* [1961] Crim LR 121).

Police officers must provide enough evidence to show that a particular location is a public place. In *R* v *DPP, ex parte Taussik* [2001] ACD 10, the defendant was stopped as she drove out of an access road leading from a block of flats. The access road was a cul-de-sac leading off a highway and was maintained by the local housing department. At the entrance to it, there was a large sign saying 'Private Residents Only'. Following her conviction under s. 5(1)(b) of the Road Traffic Act 1988, the defendant appealed, alleging that the sign on the access road excluded anyone other than residents from using it and therefore it was not a 'public place'. The Divisional Court took the view that the evidence of the police officers as to the actual use of the access road by other people was very thin. As there was no evidence from the officers themselves that they had seen motorists (other than residents) using the road, the court was unable to conclude that the road was anything other than a private one. The court held that as the issue of whether a place is a 'public place' or not is largely a question of fact, it is essential that the prosecution presents clear evidence showing who uses the road, when and for what purpose.

However, in a case involving a motorist stopped in a pub car park, the police witness did not adduce specific evidence that the car park was in fact a public place at the time of the offence. Nevertheless, the Divisional Court went on to hold that it was clear from previous authorities that a car park was certainly *capable* of being a public place and this was more likely when its use was not restricted to a particular group of people. Therefore, it could properly be inferred that the car park, attached as it was to a pub to which members of the public were generally invited by the landlord, was in fact a public place. The court held that it was not necessary for the prosecution to adduce evidence to show that the car park was a public place and that the magistrates were entitled to reach the decision that they had (*R (On the Application of Lewis)* v *DPP* [2004] EWHC 3081 (Admin)).

In *Brown* v *Fisk* [2021] EWHC 2769 (QB), the High Court examined whether a privately-owned yard was a 'road or other public place'. The court emphasised that a location is public only if the public actually uses it in a real and significant way, beyond the owner's private purposes. Mere theoretical access or use linked solely to the occupier's private activities is insufficient.

3.19.12 Use, Cause or Permit

The concepts of using, causing or permitting are central to many road policing offences. If there is any doubt as to which offence is appropriate, it is acceptable to charge 'using' *or* 'causing' *or* 'permitting' as alternatives (*Ross Hillman Ltd* v *Bond* [1974] QB 435) but the advice of the local CPS should be sought.

3.19.12.1 Use

The term 'using' within the context of use, cause or permit has a restrictive meaning and must involve an element of controlling, managing or operating the vehicle by the person concerned (*Hatton* v *Hall* [1997] RTR 212).

The 'using' of a vehicle is generally, though not exclusively, restricted to:

- the driver;
- the driver's employer (when the driver is driving the vehicle on the employer's business).

In *West Yorkshire Trading Standards* v *Lex Vehicle Leasing Ltd* [1996] RTR 70, the Court of Appeal restricted the meaning of the word 'use' when it appears alongside 'cause' and 'permit'. In such circumstances, 'using' is restricted to the driver or owner of the vehicle and, in the case of the owner, only if he/she employed the driver under a contract of service and at the material time the vehicle was being driven on the owner's business.

Where the expression 'use' does not appear alongside 'cause' and 'permit', the concept is wider.

If a person driving a vehicle is doing so in the ordinary course of the employer's business, the employer is *using* the vehicle. In such a case, you must prove that:

- the defendant (employer) actually owned the vehicle;
- at the relevant time, the driver was employed by the defendant; and
- the driver was driving the vehicle in the ordinary course of his/her employment.

(*Jones* v *DPP* [1999] RTR 1)

It is immaterial that the employer has not specifically authorised the employee to use the vehicle in such a way (*Richardson* v *Baker* [1976] RTR 56).

If the driver is not an employee, then the employer is not using the vehicle, even if that driver is a partner of the firm or has been asked to drive the vehicle by the employer (*Crawford* v *Haughton* [1972] 1 WLR 572). The employer may, however, be shown to be 'causing' or 'permitting'.

If a garage lends one of its vehicles to a customer and the customer then uses the vehicle on his/her own business, the garage cannot be said to be 'using' the vehicle (*Dove (LF)* v *Tarvin* (1964) 108 SJ 404).

If a vehicle is shown to be a 'motor vehicle' and on a 'road', it may be said to be in 'use' even if it is in such a state that it cannot be driven (*Pumbien* v *Vines* [1996] RTR 37). There is no need to show some element of control or operation of the vehicle by the owner in order to prove 'use'.

Vehicles left unattended on a road can still be regarded as being used, as 'use' has been held to mean 'having some use of' for these purposes (*Eden* v *Mitchell* [1975] RTR 425). Accordingly, the mere fact of having two defective tyres did not preclude the vehicle's use and the owner's intention in relation to the vehicle was held to be irrelevant. Therefore, if a vehicle is not in a roadworthy condition it can still be available for the owner's use even though the owner has no intention of utilising it while it remains in that state.

It should be noted that the Divisional Court has applied a broader interpretation to the meaning of 'use' when considering offences involving *trailers*. The court held that the owner of a defective trailer who is responsible for putting it on a road should not be able to escape liability for its condition simply by arguing that it was being drawn and therefore 'used' by someone else (*NFC Forwarding Ltd* v *DPP* [1989] RTR 239).

3.19.12.2 Cause

'Causing' will involve some degree of 'control' or 'dominance' by, or some express mandate from, the *causer*.

Causing requires both positive action and knowledge by the defendant (*Price* v *Cromack* [1975] 1 WLR 988). If the owner of a vehicle is to be shown to have 'caused' an offence to be committed, he/she must be shown to have done something to contribute to it (e.g. by instructing another to drive it) *and also* to have known of any relevant facts (e.g. that it was overloaded) (*Ross Hillman Ltd* v *Bond* [1974] QB 435).

In cases involving employers' vehicles, it may be easier to prove 'use' of the vehicle (**see para. 3.19.12.1**).

Wilful blindness by employers to their employees' unlawful actions (e.g. not completing drivers' records) is not enough to amount to 'causing' the offence (*Redhead Freight Ltd* v *Shulman* [1989] RTR 1).

3.19.12.3 Permit

Permitting is less direct or explicit than causing. Permitting involves giving leave or licence to do something (*Houston* v *Buchanan* [1940] 2 All ER 179). The relevant permission (e.g. to use a vehicle in a certain way or subject to some proviso) can be express or it can be inferred by the relevant person (such as where someone is given the use of a friend's car without any conditions being stipulated by the friend).

Generally, in order to prove an offence of 'permitting', you will need to show knowledge by the defendant of the vehicle's *use*, and the *unlawful nature* of that use. However, it is necessary to consider the relevant piece of legislation in each case, together with its intended purpose.

You cannot 'permit' yourself to do something (*Keene* v *Muncaster* [1980] RTR 377).

3.19.13 Defences in Relation to Road Offences

3.19.13.1 Duress and Duress of Circumstances

The defence of duress applies where the defendant has been compelled to commit an offence having been threatened with death or serious physical injury, and duress of circumstances is where circumstances leave the defendant no real alternative but to commit an offence. Whatever the particular arguments for and against the defences, it is clear that they will generally apply to cases of dangerous, careless and inconsiderate driving (they also apply to the offences of driving while disqualified: *R* v *Martin* [1989] RTR 63 and confirmed in *R* v *Backshall* [1998] 1 WLR 1506).

Cases relating to these defences include where the driver was forced to commit the offence in order to avoid death or serious injury (*R* v *Conway* [1989] RTR 35). In *DPP* v *Bell* [1992] RTR 335, the defence was upheld where the defendant needed to drive a vehicle in order to escape serious physical harm, even though he had drunk a considerable amount of alcohol. However, where the defendant had driven a far greater distance than was necessary to escape the relevant danger, the Divisional Court was not prepared to accept the defence in answer to a charge of driving while over the prescribed limit (*DPP* v *Tomkinson* [2001] EWHC Admin 182).

In *DPP* v *Hicks* [2002] EWHC 1638 (Admin), a case arising out of driving while over the prescribed limit, the Administrative Court set out the following guidelines to be applied before the defences will generally be available to drivers:

- the defence is only available if the driving was undertaken to avoid consequences that could not otherwise have been avoided;

- those consequences must have both been inevitable and involved the risk of serious harm to the driver or someone else for whom the driver was responsible;
- the driver must do no more than is reasonably necessary to avoid the harm;
- the danger of so driving must not be disproportionate to the harm threatened.

In *R* v *Pearce* [2024] EWCA Crim 1557, the Court of Appeal held that duress did not arise because the defendant had reasonable, non-dangerous alternatives, such as locking his car doors rather than driving off with people clinging to the vehicle. The judgment emphasised that duress requires an immediate threat of death or serious injury and no reasonable avenue of escape.

In *DPP* v *Harris* [1995] RTR 100 (**see para. 3.19.13.3**), a case concerning an undercover police officer who proceeded through a red light while following a suspect, the Divisional Court rejected the defence of duress. Instead, officers must align actions within statutory police-purpose traffic exemptions.

3.19.13.2 Automatism

Where a person's movements are beyond his/her control or his/her actions are brought about involuntarily, he/she will not generally be liable at criminal law as the element of *actus reus* is not present.

A notable example of this is *automatism*. Where the defendant is deprived of the ability to control his/her movements, he/she may claim that the resulting consequences (e.g. the car swerving or colliding with something) were beyond his/her control and that the defence of automatism should apply. When this happens to the driver of a vehicle, it may remove his/her liability for certain offences such as careless driving. This is because there is no willed action or omission by the defendant. It is also highly unlikely that the defendant would have the required state of mind. Such a situation might be brought about by a swarm of bees flying in through the open window of a moving car or the driver lapsing into a coma (*Hill* v *Baxter* [1958] 1 QB 277).

There must, however, be a 'total destruction of voluntary control'; impaired or reduced control is not enough (*Attorney-General's Reference (No. 2 of 1992)* [1994] QB 91). The prosecution must establish the manner of the defendant's driving and then the defendant must adduce evidence that he/she was totally unable to control the car (*C* [2007] EWCA Crim 1862).

If a defendant is suffering from a particular medical condition or is prone to effects which are likely to impair driving ability (such as dizziness—*R* v *Sibbles* [1959] Crim LR 660), he/she has a duty to take reasonable steps to avoid driving when the symptoms are likely to arise. If a diabetic continues to drive while experiencing the start of a hypoglycaemic episode, it is unlikely that the defence of automatism would be available to a charge of careless driving; the diabetic should have stopped driving until the episode had passed (*Moses* v *Winder* [1981] RTR 37).

Similarly, where the loss of voluntary movement or control is brought about by self-induced measures (such as taking/failing to take medication or by drinking), automatism is not generally available as a defence (*R* v *Quick* [1973] QB 910).

Driving in a state of reduced awareness brought on by the continuous focusing on a long, featureless road (sometimes called 'motorway hypnosis') is not enough to raise the defence of automatism (*Attorney-General's Reference (No. 2 of 1992)* [1993] RTR 337).

3.19.13.3 Police Drivers

R v *Bannister* [2010] 2 All ER 841 held that when assessing dangerous or careless driving by a police officer, the officer's specialist training must be ignored and the standard is that of an ordinary, competent civilian driver. This position was decisively overturned by the Police, Crime, Sentencing and Courts Act 2022, which introduced a new statutory test requiring courts to judge police driving by reference to a 'competent and careful police driver with the same level of prescribed training'. The Act fundamentally reversed *Bannister* by making specialist training directly relevant to liability.

The Road Traffic Act 1988 (Police Driving: Prescribed Training) (Amendment) Regulations 2025 (SI 2025/792), which came into force in July 2025, complete this transformation by seeking out what counts as 'prescribed training'. Only a College of Policing-licensed provider qualifies. By standardising and legally defining police driver training, officers are judged against police-specific standards, rather than civilian ones, rendering *Bannister* obsolete both in principle and practice.

Sections 5 and 6 of the Police, Crime, Sentencing and Courts Act 2022 amended the 1988 Act tests for the offences of dangerous and careless driving respectively so that, in determining whether an offence has been committed, a designated person's standard of driving is compared to that of a competent and careful constable who has undertaken the prescribed training, and therefore has the same skills. The test applies where the designated person is driving for police purposes (or, in the case of the NCA, law enforcement purposes) and has undertaken the prescribed training.

Section 7 of the Police, Crime, Sentencing and Courts Act 2022 amended s. 195 of the 1988 Act to provide that the power to make regulations prescribing training for the purposes of the new comparator may make different provisions for different designated persons or areas.

The Road Traffic Act 1988 (Police Driving: Prescribed Training) Regulations 2022 made under ss. 192(1) and 195(7) of the Road Traffic Act 1988, set out the prescribed training that must have been completed by a police officer for the changes to the dangerous and careless driving offences to apply.

The training must meet the requirements set out in the regulations and is identified by the title, course length, the required ratio for the minimum number of trainers to the maximum number of students and the period for which the training is valid before refresher training is required. The necessary training standards of the instructor or trainer and the essential components of the training are also set out. The regulations additionally set out the requirements for training completed prior to the commencement of these regulations to be prescribed training.

The National Police Chiefs' Council (NPCC) has been working closely with the College of Policing and police forces to standardise police driver training across England and Wales. This will ensure that police drivers, depending on their role, are trained to a similar standard, and the legal test for police drivers will have a fairer comparator. This training will be aligned with the College of Policing's authorised professional practice and national police driver training curriculum.

The use of roadside cameras for detecting and prosecuting drivers for exceeding the applicable speed limit and passing through red lights has resulted in a significant increase in the number of emergency services vehicles being reported. As the vast majority of such cases fall within the legal parameters either for speed limits or for passing through lights at red, the government and NPCC (along with others) have signed up to a protocol. Part of the protocol operates by making assumptions that where the photograph shows flashing lights being displayed on the vehicle, the relevant exemption applied (in the absence of evidence to the contrary). This protocol is of practical effect in reducing the bureaucratic burden on the system of roadside cameras; it does not affect the substantive law which the rest of this paragraph addresses. However, police drivers are granted some exemptions from specific traffic regulation and there are several cases that help in identifying the relevant features that will be applied in determining the driver's liability.

It is also worth bearing in mind that while the particular circumstances under which the police driver was driving may not provide a specific defence, they may nevertheless provide mitigation and, where appropriate, special reasons for not disqualifying the driver (see e.g. *Agnew* v *DPP* [1991] RTR 144).

The Court of Appeal's review of the issues of civil liability arising from police drivers (*Keyse* v *Commissioner of the Metropolitan Police* [2001] EWCA Civ 715) held that:

- speed alone was not decisive of negligence by a police driver;
- emergency service vehicles on duty were expressly exempted from the statutory rules for speed limits, keep left signs and traffic lights (s. 87 of the Road Traffic Regulation Act 1984 and regs 15(2) and 33(2) of the Traffic Signs Regulations and General Directions 1994 (SI 1994/1519)) (note the relevant regulation is now sch. 14 (part 1, para. 5(4) of the Traffic Signs Regulations and General Directions 2016 (SI 2016/362)));
- police and other emergency service drivers were entitled to expect other road users to take note of the signs of their approach (e.g. sirens and flashing lights) and, where appropriate, react accordingly.

Consequently, the court held that a police driver who had accelerated through a green light at a road junction with the vehicle's visual and audible warning equipment in operation was not liable for the injuries to a pedestrian who stepped off the pavement into the path of the vehicle.

Appropriately trained drivers employed by the National Crime Agency will also be covered by emergency drivers' exemptions.

Regulation 33 (now sch. 14 (part 1, para. 5(4) of the Traffic Signs Regulations and General Directions 2016)) referred to above makes allowances for emergency services drivers to pass through red traffic lights under certain circumstances. The regulations set out the conditions under which a driver may proceed through a red light and failure to meet those conditions will render the driver liable to a charge under s. 2 or 3 of the 1988 Act. Consequently, the driver of a police surveillance vehicle following suspects to the scene of an intended armed robbery could not rely on the fact that he was required by the seriousness of the circumstances to go through a red light when he did so in a way which was not covered by the regulations (*DPP* v *Harris* [1995] RTR 100) (**see para. 3.19.13.1**). See also *R* v *Collins* [1997] RTR 439 at **para. 3.21.2.2, Keynote**.

In *Harris*, the Divisional Court held that the wording of the regulation meant that there was no scope for the defence of necessity where police drivers went through red traffic lights. It was held that the exemption for drivers of police vehicles in such circumstances was restricted to the extent that another driver should not be obliged to change speed or course to avoid a collision. The court held that all the driver in *Harris* need have done to avoid the accident was to have stopped for a couple of seconds or to have edged forward slowly.

This view was followed in the civil case of *Griffin* v *Merseyside Regional Ambulance* [1998] PIQR P34, where the Court of Appeal held that the duty of care required of a driver of any emergency vehicle is not to proceed 'in a manner likely to endanger any person' or cause them to change their speed or course of direction (per reg. 33(1)(b), now sch. 14 (part 1, para. 5(4) of the Traffic Signs Regulations and General Directions 2016)). It is the *manner* of the police officer's driving that must not cause the other driver to be endangered or to change speed or direction. The whole purpose of the audible and visual warning systems on emergency vehicles ('blues and twos') is to alert other drivers and, if necessary, to get them to change speed and/or direction. Similarly, rule 219 of the Highway Code tells drivers to look and listen for emergency vehicles and to make room for them, pulling over and stopping where necessary provided that does not endanger other road users.

It is perhaps worth noting that if a person drives in a way which creates a need for police officers to pursue that person and an officer is subsequently injured in that pursuit, that person may owe a duty of care to the police officer and may therefore be sued for damages. In *Langley* v *Dray* [1997] PIQR P508 (confirmed by the Court of Appeal [1998] PIQR P314), the court held that the driver of the stolen motor vehicle owed a duty of care to the police officer pursuing him. He knew or ought to have known that the police were in pursuit and should not have gone so fast on ice. He had a duty not to create such a risk. This decision suggests that there are times when the police can be placed under an obligation by a driver to pursue him/her.

KEYNOTE

The CPS has issued guidance in relation to charging offences arising from driving incidents involving emergency vehicles. These guidelines state:

> In the course of their duties, police officers, ambulance staff and fire-fighters may need to drive a vehicle in response to an emergency in a manner which would otherwise be considered unacceptable. Our starting point is that it is very unlikely to be appropriate to proceed with a prosecution on public interest grounds if a police officer, member of ambulance staff or fire-fighter commits a driving offence while responding to an emergency call.

However, every individual case must be considered on its own facts and merits, and when considering whether it is in the public interest to proceed with the case, prosecutors should have regard to the following factors:

- the nature of the emergency known to or reasonably perceived by the driver, e.g. whether the driver was responding to a 999 call in compliance with the agreed operating practice in that service;
- the level of culpability of the driver (including the nature of the driving); and
- whether there is evidence that the driver may be a continuing danger to others. For example, such evidence may include relevant convictions or internal disciplinary proceedings against the driver.

In all cases involving emergency vehicles or drivers in emergencies, which are referred by the investigator to the CPS for a prosecution decision, prosecutors will need to check that the following is provided by the investigator:

- evidence in the form of any police collision reports;
- advice provided by the NPCC pursuits lead where applicable;
- statements regarding the manner of the driving.

3.20 Key Police Powers Relating to Road Policing

3.20.1 Introduction

The Road Traffic Act 1988 provides police officers with numerous powers in respect of road policing matters. This chapter examines several powers that are at the core of many road policing issues—the *essential* power to stop a vehicle (s. 163), the powers to demand documentation and details from the driver (ss. 164 and 165), the associated powers of seizure and retention of vehicles (ss. 165A and 165B) and the duty to give information regarding the identity of the driver (s. 172). The chapter also examines the law regarding 'road checks' under s. 4 of the Police and Criminal Evidence Act 1984.

3.20.2 Power to Stop a Vehicle

The Road Traffic Act 1988, s. 163 states:

(1) A person driving a mechanically propelled vehicle on a road must stop the vehicle on being required to do so by a constable in uniform or a traffic officer.
(2) A person riding a cycle on a road must stop the cycle on being required to do so by a constable in uniform or a traffic officer.
(3) If a person fails to comply with this section he is guilty of an offence.

KEYNOTE

The offence of failing to stop is triable summarily and punishable by a fine.

'Stop' has been held to mean bringing the vehicle to a halt and remaining at rest for long enough for the officer to exercise whatever additional powers are appropriate (*Lodwick* v *Saunders* [1985] 1 WLR 382).

Section 163 is a 'Random' Power

The use of s. 163 is not restricted to road traffic matters only—a police officer in uniform may require a person driving a mechanically propelled vehicle on a road to stop the vehicle. This is a power for an officer in uniform to *randomly* stop vehicles.

That said, like any power available to the police, its use must be able to be justified. In *Stewart* v *Crowe* 1999 SLT 899, it was said that the power under s. 163 represented a necessary and proportionate response to the prevention of crime and that the only limit on the power is that it should not be used whimsically or oppressively.

Considering the use of the power from the road policing perspective, there may be a wide variety of reasons why a police officer in uniform would stop a vehicle, such as:

- to require the driver to produce his/her driving licence;
- to require the driver to give his/her name and address;
- to require the driver to give the name and address of the owner of the vehicle;
- to require the driver to produce his/her certificate of insurance and/or test certificate;
- to have the vehicle examined to see if it complies with construction and use regulations;
- to have the vehicle examined to see if it is in a dangerous condition.

The courts have accepted that the police are empowered to stop vehicles at random to inquire whether the driver has been drinking. Consider the annual drink/drive campaigns that take place over the Christmas/

New Year period—every vehicle passing through such a check-point might be randomly stopped by a police officer in uniform and drivers asked if they have been drinking. The requirement to stop the vehicle is a legal one and, as a result of a response given by the driver and/or the officer's observations, a suspicion may form in the officer's mind that the driver has alcohol in his/her body and the officer may require the driver to take a preliminary test. This is a random stop but not a random preliminary test (*Miller* v *Bell* 2004 SCCR 534).

In *Chief Constable of Gwent* v *Dash* [1986] RTR 41, vehicles were being randomly stopped in order to give a police officer further experience of the breath test procedure under the supervision of her senior officer. The court held that (what is now) s. 6(2) is concerned only with the provision of breath; it does not bear upon the circumstances in which the driver may be required to stop. The actions of the police were not an abuse of power and did not amount to malpractice; therefore, the requirement of a breath specimen and the subsequent procedure were lawful. Random stopping of cars for the purpose of ascertaining whether their drivers have alcohol in their bodies is perfectly permissible; random breath testing, however, is not. This case adds yet another reason for a police officer to stop a vehicle—to train newly appointed officers in traffic procedure.

Constable in Uniform

Whether a constable (which includes an officer of any rank, including special constables) was in uniform at the time is a matter of fact for a court to determine. What counts as 'uniform' is unclear but, if constables can be easily identified from their manner of dress as police officers, the requirement has probably been met (*Wallwork* v *Giles* [1970] RTR 117; officer without a helmet held to be 'in uniform'). The wearing of an 'ordinary' raincoat over a police uniform (*Taylor* v *Baldwin* [1976] RTR 265) did not affect the conclusion that the officer was still in uniform. Justices are also able to rely on their knowledge of how the local constabulary operates (*Cooper* v *Rowlands* [1971] RTR 291, in relation to a motorway patrol officer, and *Richards* v *West* [1980] RTR 215, in relation to special constables) and, in the absence of evidence to the contrary, they are entitled to infer or assume from the surrounding circumstances that a constable is in uniform (*Gage* v *Jones* [1983] RTR 508).

Power of Entry

Section 163 carries with it a power of entry under s. 17(1)(c)(iiia) of the Police and Criminal Evidence Act 1984 (hereafter referred to as 'PACE84') which states:

> Subject to the following provisions of this section, and without prejudice to any other enactment, a constable may enter and search any premises for the purpose of arresting a person for an offence under ...
>
> (iiia) section 4 (driving etc. when under the influence of drink or drugs or section 163 (failure to stop when required to do so by a constable in uniform) of the Road Traffic Act 1988.

The power of entry is only exercisable if the constable has reasonable grounds for believing that the person sought is on the premises (s. 17(2)(a)).

The power to stop vehicles is also available to 'Traffic Officers' (Highways England Traffic Officers and Welsh Government Traffic Officers).

There are further powers (under s. 35(1) and (2) of the Road Traffic Act 1988) for a police officer in uniform to stop a vehicle in connection with the regulation of traffic on a road or for the purposes of a road traffic survey carried out on or in the vicinity of a road.

3.20.3 Road Checks

The power to stop vehicles generally is provided under s. 163 of the Road Traffic Act 1988 (officers exercising the power must be in uniform). Having caused a vehicle to stop, there are then certain other powers which may be employed by a police officer (or other authorised people).

Among those powers are the powers set out in PACE84, s. 4, in relation to 'road checks'.

A road check is where the power under s. 163 of the Road Traffic Act 1988 is used in any locality in such a way as to stop all vehicles or vehicles selected by any criterion (s. 4(2) of PACE84). That general power for uniformed officers to stop vehicles might be used in a particular geographical area to stop all vehicles on the road or all vehicles of a certain make, model or colour, or only those vehicles containing a certain number of adult occupants. In all these cases, there would be a 'road check' for the purposes of s. 4.

The power to carry out road checks following the appropriate authorisation under s. 4 of PACE84 below is among those that can be conferred on a Police Community Support Officer designated under sch. 4 to the Police Reform Act 2002. In exercising this power, any such officer may also be given the power of a uniformed constable to stop vehicles (under s. 163 of the Road Traffic Act 1988).

PACE84, s. 4 states:

(1) This section shall have effect in relation to the conduct of road checks by police officers for the purpose of ascertaining whether a vehicle is carrying—
- (a) a person who has committed an offence other than a road traffic offence or a vehicle excise offence;
- (b) a person who is a witness to such an offence;
- (c) a person intending to commit such an offence; or
- (d) a person who is unlawfully at large.

(2) ...

(3) Subject to subsection (5) below, there may only be such a road check if a police officer of the rank of superintendent or above authorises it in writing.

(4) An officer may only authorise a road check under subsection (3) above—
- (a) for the purpose specified in subsection (1)(a) above, if he has reasonable grounds—
  - (i) for believing that the offence is an indictable offence; and
  - (ii) for suspecting that the person is, or is about to be, in the locality in which vehicles would be stopped if the road check were authorised;
- (b) for the purpose specified in subsection (1)(b) above, if he has reasonable grounds for believing that the offence is an indictable offence;
- (c) for the purpose specified in subsection (1)(c) above, if he has reasonable grounds—
  - (i) for believing that the offence would be an indictable offence; and
  - (ii) for suspecting that the person is, or is about to be, in the locality in which vehicles would be stopped if the road check were authorised;
- (d) for the purpose specified in subsection (1)(d) above, if he has reasonable grounds for suspecting that the person is, or is about to be, in that locality.

KEYNOTE

Road checks may only be authorised for the purposes set out at s. 4(4) and for the duration set out at s. 4(11) (see para. 3.20.3.1).

They must, subject to s. 4(5), be authorised in writing by an officer of superintendent rank or above (s. 4(3)). If it appears to an officer below the rank of superintendent that a road check is required as a matter of urgency for one of the purposes in s. 4(1), he/she may authorise such a road check (s. 4(5)). What amounts to 'urgency' is not defined, but it would appear to be a somewhat subjective requirement based on the apprehension of the officer concerned. Where such an urgent road check is authorised, the authorising officer must, *as soon as is practicable to do so*, make a written record of the time at which the authorisation was given and must cause an officer of superintendent rank or above to be informed of the authorisation (s. 4(6) and (7)). Where this occurs, the superintendent (or more senior officer) may authorise, *in writing*, that the road check continue (s. 4(8)). If the officer considers that the road check should not continue, he/she must make a written record that it took place as well as the purpose for which it took place (including the relevant 'indictable offence' (s. 4(9) and (14)).

The locality in which vehicles are to be stopped must also be specified (s. 4(10)).

Under s. 4(13), every written authorisation for a road check must include:

- the name of the authorising officer;
- the purpose of the road check—including any relevant 'indictable offence';
- the locality in which vehicles are to be stopped.

The road check authorisation also requires the duration of the check to be recorded.

3.20.3.1 Duration of a Road Check

PACE84, s. 4 goes on to state:

(11) An officer giving an authorisation under this section, other than an authorisation under subsection (5) above—
  (a) shall specify a period, not exceeding seven days, during which the road check may continue; and
  (b) may direct that the road check during the specified period—
    (i) shall be continuous; or
    (ii) shall be conducted at specified times.

(12) If it appears to an officer of the rank of superintendent or above that a road check ought to continue beyond the period for which it has been authorised he may, from time to time, in writing specify a further period, not exceeding seven days, during which it may continue.

KEYNOTE

The road check may be extended—in writing—any number of times for further periods up to a total of seven days by a superintendent if it appears to him/her that it 'ought' to continue. There is no restriction of 'reasonableness' or the requirement for the existence of particular grounds here, and it seems that the judgement may be an entirely subjective one by the superintendent.

Where a vehicle is stopped during a road check, the person in charge of it is entitled to a written statement of the purpose of that road check if he/she applies for one no later than the end of the 12-month period from the day on which the vehicle was stopped (s. 4(15)).

3.20.4 Power to Require the Production of a Driving Licence

The police have access to the DVLA database which allows them to check some aspects of driver records. However, the power to demand that a person, in certain circumstances (e.g. under the fixed penalty system), produce a licence is still valid.

3.20.4.1 Power to Require Production of Driving Licence

The Road Traffic Act 1988, s. 164 states:

(1) Any of the following persons—
  (a) a person driving a motor vehicle on a road,
  (b) a person whom a constable or vehicle examiner has reasonable cause to believe to have been the driver of a motor vehicle at a time when an accident occurred owing to its presence on a road,
  (c) a person whom a constable or vehicle examiner has reasonable cause to believe to have committed an offence in relation to the use of a motor vehicle on a road, or
  (d) a person—
    (i) who supervises the holder of a provisional licence while the holder is driving a motor vehicle on a road, or
    (ii) whom a constable or vehicle examiner has reasonable cause to believe was supervising the holder of a provisional licence while driving, at a time when an accident occurred owing to the presence of the vehicle on a road or at a time when an offence is suspected of having been committed by the holder of the provisional licence in relation to the use of the vehicle on a road,

  must, on being so required by a constable or vehicle examiner, produce his licence for examination, so as to enable the constable or vehicle examiner to ascertain the name and address of the holder of the licence, the date of issue, and the authority by which they were issued.

KEYNOTE

In order to have met the requirement to 'produce' a licence, the person must allow the constable (or vehicle examiner) a reasonable time to check the name and address of the holder, the date of issue and the authority under which the licence was issued (*Tremelling* v *Martin* [1971] RTR 196). Simply flashing the licence at a police officer or waving it under the officer's nose would not discharge the requirements of s. 164.

The requirement under s. 164(1)(a) is worded in the present tense. Therefore, the power to require a licence under this subsection ceases when the driver ceases 'driving' (as to which, **see chapter 3.19**) (*Boyce* v *Absalom* [1974] RTR 248). Unfortunately, the legislators did not use the same wording when drafting s. 164(1)(d)(i) in relation to supervisors of learner drivers. It is submitted, however, that the same restrictions would apply and that the power under this section would only apply if the relevant person were still supervising a learner at the time of the demand.

Clearly, if a driver is reasonably *believed* to have been driving under the circumstances described in s. 164(1)(b), (c) and (d)(ii), then the power to demand the relevant licence would not be restricted to the present tense. It also applies to Community licences (s. 164(11)).

A vehicle examiner is an examiner appointed under s. 66A of the 1988 Act for the purpose of carrying out the functions conferred on them in relation to the Goods Vehicles (Licensing of Operators) Act 1995, the Public Passenger Vehicles Act 1981, the Transport Act 1968 and any other enactment.

Driving licences must be produced in person.

3.20.4.2 Power to Require Date of Birth

The Road Traffic Act 1988, s. 164 states:

(2) A person required by a constable under subsection (1) above to produce his licence must in prescribed circumstances, on being so required by the constable, state his date of birth.

KEYNOTE

The 'prescribed circumstances' are set out under reg. 83 of the Motor Vehicles (Driving Licences) Regulations 1999 (SI 1999/2864) and are:

- where the person *fails* to produce the licence *forthwith*; or
- where the person *produces* a licence which the police officer has reason to suspect:
  - was not granted to that person;
  - was granted to that person in error;
  - contains an alteration to the particulars on the licence other than the driver number, made with intent to deceive; or
  - in which the driver number has been altered, removed or defaced; or
- where the person is/was a supervisor of a learner driver as specified under s. 164(1)(d) and the police officer has reason to suspect that the person is under 21 years of age.

Failing to state one's date of birth when lawfully required is a summary offence under s. 164(6).

Where a person does state his/her date of birth as required, the Secretary of State may serve a written notice on that person requiring evidence verifying that date of birth. If the person's name differs from his/her name at birth, the Secretary of State may also serve a similar notice requiring a statement from the person as to his/her name when born (s. 164(9)). Knowingly failing to do so is a summary offence (s. 164(9)).

3.20.4.3 Other Driving Licence Powers

Where a police officer has reasonable cause to believe that the holder of a driving licence has knowingly made a false statement to obtain it, the officer may require the production of that licence (s. 164(4)). Failure to do so is a summary offence under s. 164(6).

Where the rider of a motor bicycle produces a provisional driving licence to a police officer and that officer has reasonable cause to believe that the holder was not driving the motor bicycle as part of training on an approved course, the officer may require the production of a prescribed certificate in relation to the completion of, or exemption from, such a course (s. 164(4A)). Failure to produce such a certificate when lawfully required is a summary offence under s. 164(6).

3.20.4.4 Failure to Produce or Deliver Licence

Failing to produce a licence when lawfully required is a summary offence under s. 164(6) of the 1988 Act.

Where a person has had his/her licence revoked in relation to a disability or because it has expired and the licence has not been delivered to the DVLA, a police officer or vehicle examiner may require the licence to be produced and may then seize it (s. 164(3)). Similar powers apply where the licence holder has been ordered to produce his/her licence to a court (s. 164(5)). Failure to do so is a summary offence under s. 164(6).

Licences Surrendered under Fixed Penalty Procedure

If a person has surrendered his/her licence to a police officer in connection with a fixed penalty offence, it cannot be produced if required under s. 164. Therefore s. 164(7) provides that, if such a person produces:

- a *current* receipt (under s. 56 of the Road Traffic Offenders Act 1988) to that effect (either then and there or within seven days); and
- *if required to do so*, produces the licence on return to a police station;

that person does not commit an offence under s. 164(6).

Defence

The Road Traffic Act 1988, s. 164 states:

> (8) In proceedings against any person for the offence of failing to produce a licence it shall be a defence for him to show that—
> (a) within seven days after the production of his licence was required he produced them in person at a police station that was specified by him at the time their production was required, or
> (b) he produced them in person there as soon as was reasonably practicable, or
> (c) it was not reasonably practicable for him to produce them there before the day on which the proceedings were commenced,
> and for the purposes of this subsection the laying of the information ... shall be treated as the commencement of the proceedings.

KEYNOTE

This general defence allows for the issuing of an HORT/1 in respect of driving licences; it also applies to the certificate showing that a licence holder has completed compulsory training in relation to motor bicycles or that the licence holder is exempt from having to complete such a course (s. 164(8A)). Section 164(8) and (8A) also allow for occasions where the production of the relevant documents is not possible at the time.

3.20.5 Power to Require Name and Address/Insurance/Test Certificate

The Road Traffic Act 1988, s. 165 states:

> (1) Any of the following persons—
> (a) a person driving a motor vehicle (other than an invalid carriage) on a road, or
> (b) a person whom a constable or vehicle examiner has reasonable cause to believe to have been the driver of a motor vehicle (other than an invalid carriage) at a time when an accident occurred owing to its presence on a road or other public place, or

(c) a person whom a constable or vehicle examiner has reasonable cause to believe to have committed an offence in relation to the use on a road of a motor vehicle (other than an invalid carriage),

must, on being so required by a constable or vehicle examiner, give his name and address and the name and address of the owner of the vehicle and produce the following documents for examination.

(2) Those documents are—

(a) the relevant certificate of insurance (within the meaning of Part VI of this Act), or such other evidence that the vehicle is not or was not being driven in contravention of section 143 of this Act as may be prescribed by regulations made by the Secretary of State,

(b) in relation to a vehicle to which section 47 of this Act applies, a test certificate issued in respect of the vehicle as mentioned in subsection (1) of that section, and

(c) in relation to a goods vehicle the use of which on a road without a plating certificate or goods vehicle test certificate is an offence under section 53(1) or (2) of this Act, any such certificate issued in respect of that vehicle or any trailer drawn by it.

(2A) Subsections (2B) and (2C) below apply where a certificate of insurance is treated as having been delivered to a person under section 147(1) of this Act by virtue of section 147(1A) of this Act.

(2B) In the case of a certificate transmitted to a person as described in section 147(1A)(a) of this Act, the person is to be treated for the purposes of this section as producing the relevant certificate of insurance if—

(a) using electronic equipment ... he provides the constable or examiner with electronic access to a copy of the certificate, or

(b) he produces a legible printed copy of the certificate.

(2C) In the case of a certificate made available to a person as described in section 147(1A)(b) of this Act, the person is to be treated for the purposes of this section as producing the relevant certificate of insurance if—

(a) using electronic equipment ... he provides the constable or examiner with electronic access on the website in question to a copy of the certificate, or

(b) he produces a legible printed copy of the certificate.

(2D) Nothing in subsection (2B) or (2C) above requires a constable or examiner to provide a person with electronic equipment for the purpose of compliance with a requirement imposed on the person by this section.

(3) Subject to subsection (4) below, a person who fails to comply with a requirement under subsection (1) above is guilty of an offence.

(4) A person shall not be convicted of an offence under subsection (3) above by reason only of failure to produce any certificate or other evidence ... if in proceedings against him for the offence he shows that—

(a) within seven days after the date on which the production of the certificate or other evidence was required it was produced at a police station that was specified by him at the time when its production was required, or

(b) it was produced there as soon as was reasonably practicable, or

(c) it was not reasonably practicable for it to be produced there before the day on which the proceedings were commenced,

and for the purposes of this subsection the laying of the information ... shall be treated as the commencement of the proceedings.

(5) A person—

(a) who supervises the holder of a provisional licence granted under Part III of this Act while the holder is driving on a road a motor vehicle (other than an invalid carriage), or

(b) whom a constable or vehicle examiner has reasonable cause to believe was supervising the holder of such a licence while driving, at a time when an accident occurred owing to the presence of the vehicle on a road or at a time when an offence is suspected of having been committed by the holder of the provisional licence in relation to the use of the vehicle on a road,

must, on being so required by a constable or vehicle examiner, give his name and address and the name and address of the owner of the vehicle.

KEYNOTE

The power to require a name and address in s. 165(1) is among the powers that can be conferred on people (e.g. Police Community Support Officers) designated under schs 4 and 5 to the Police Reform Act 2002 where the suspected offence is one under s. 35 of the Road Traffic Act 1988 (drivers failing to comply with traffic directions).

Production of the certificate need not be in person but the certificate must be shown to the officer for long enough to allow proper inspection of it (as per *Tremelling* at **para. 3.20.4.1, Keynote**).

In cases where a requirement has been made under s. 165, s. 171 of the Road Traffic Act 1988 places a requirement on the owner of the vehicle to give such information as required by the police in order to determine whether the motor vehicle was being driven without insurance. Failure to comply with such a requirement is a summary offence.

The requirement under s. 165(1)(b) has been extended to 'public places' as well as roads by the Motor Vehicles (Compulsory Insurance) Regulations 2000 (SI 2000/726).

3.20.6 Power to Seize Vehicles Driven without a Licence or Insurance

The Road Traffic Act 1988 provides powers to seize vehicles in certain circumstances.

Section 165A states that, if *any* of the specified conditions are satisfied in relation to a vehicle, a constable may:

(a) seize the vehicle (in accordance with s. 165A(6) and (7));
(b) remove the vehicle; and (c) for the purpose of exercising the power, enter any premises other than a private dwelling house on which the constable has reasonable grounds for believing the vehicle to be (s. 165A(1) and (5)).

Note that the definition of 'private dwelling house' does *not* include any garage or other structure occupied with the dwelling house or land 'appurtenant' (belonging or relating) to it.

The first condition is that:

- a constable *in uniform* requires a person to produce his/her driving licence for examination (under s. 164);
- the person fails to produce them; and
- the constable has reasonable grounds for believing that:
  a motor vehicle
  is or was being driven
  by that person
  otherwise than in accordance with a licence (in contravention of s. 87(1)).

The second condition is that:

- a constable *in uniform* requires (under s. 165) a person to produce evidence that a motor vehicle is or was not being driven in contravention of s. 143 (requirement for insurance);
- the person fails to produce such evidence; and
- the constable has reasonable grounds for believing that the vehicle is or was being so driven.

The third condition is that:

- a constable *in uniform* requires a person driving a motor vehicle to stop the vehicle (under s. 163);
- the person fails to stop the vehicle, or to stop the vehicle long enough, for the constable to make such lawful inquiries as he/she considers appropriate; and
- the constable has reasonable grounds for believing that:
  that vehicle
  is or was
  being driven
  otherwise than in accordance with a licence (in contravention of s. 87(1)) or s. 143 (requirement for insurance).

In the exercise of any power to seize a vehicle under this provision or to enter relevant premises, a constable may use reasonable force, if necessary (s. 165A(5)(c)).

However, before seizing the motor vehicle, the constable must warn the person by whom it appears that the vehicle is or was being driven in contravention of s. 87(1) or s. 143 that it will be seized:

(a) in the case of s. 87(1) (driving otherwise than in accordance with a licence), if the person does not produce his/her licence *immediately*;
(b) in the case of s. 143 (no insurance), if the person does not provide the constable *immediately* with evidence that the vehicle is not or was not being driven in contravention of that section.

But the constable is not required to give such a warning if the circumstances make it impracticable to do so (s. 165A(6)).

Section 165A(7) provides that if the constable is unable to seize the vehicle immediately because the person driving the vehicle has failed to stop as requested or has driven off, it may be seized at any time within the period of 24 hours beginning with the time at which the condition in question is first satisfied. The wording of s. 165A(7) suggests (on one view) that the 24-hour 'window' within which to seize the vehicle only applies where the constable has been prevented from seizing the vehicle immediately owing to the person failing to stop or driving away: it does not, therefore, apply where some other reason prevented the officer from seizing the vehicle (e.g. by being called away to other duties) in which case there seems to be no restriction on the time during which the vehicle can be seized—ultimately, the courts will have to interpret the subsection.

In *Pryor* v *Chief Constable of Greater Manchester* [2011] EWCA Civ 749, the claimant (who did not have his own insurance policy for the vehicle) sued Greater Manchester Police for wrongful interference with goods following their seizure of his car which had been driven by a friend. The friend, who was driving the car with the claimant's permission, was relying on his own insurance policy which contained a clause allowing him to drive, with the consent of the owner, a motor car not owned by, and not hired under a hire purchase or self-drive agreement to, the policyholder. Nonetheless, the officers took the view that the vehicle was uninsured and seized it. The court held that they had been wrong to do so and Greater Manchester Police were liable for the wrongful seizure.

A reference to a motor vehicle does not include an invalid carriage (s. 165A(9)).

3.20.6.1 Retention etc. of Vehicles Seized under s. 165A

Under s. 165B, the Secretary of State may make regulations providing for the removal and retention of motor vehicles seized under s. 165A and for their release or disposal, together with any fees that may be payable. Those regulations may make different provisions for different cases and will apply to local authorities. So far as England is concerned, local authority means:

- a county council;
- the council of a district comprised in an area for which there is no county council;
- a London borough council;
- the Common Council of the City of London; or
- Transport for London.

In relation to Wales, it means the council of a county or county borough.

The relevant regulations are the Road Traffic Act 1988 (Retention and Disposal of Seized Motor Vehicles) Regulations 2005 (SI 2005/1606) and they set out the procedures to be followed by the police in exercising the seizure power.

In summary, the regulations provide that:

- When a vehicle has been seized, the appropriate police officer (or authorised agent) must take such steps as are reasonably necessary for its safe keeping until it is released or disposed of (reg. 3).
- On seizing a vehicle, the constable must give the driver a seizure notice unless it is impracticable to do so (reg. 4(1)).
- Where the driver is not the owner or registered keeper of the vehicle, the police officer or agent must take reasonably practicable steps to give a seizure notice to the keeper (and to the owner, if that is someone different) unless satisfied that this has already been done or the vehicle has been released in accordance with the regulations (reg. 4(2)).

The seizure notice must give specified details about the seizure and retention of the vehicle including:

- such information as can be (or could have been) ascertained from an inspection of the vehicle, or has been ascertained from any other source, relating to the registration mark and make of the vehicle;
- the place where the vehicle was seized and where it is being kept;
- a requirement that the owner (or keeper) claims it within a specified period of time not being less than seven working days from the day when the notice is given to the registered keeper or owner as the case may be;
- an indication that, unless the vehicle is claimed on or before that date, it may be disposed of; and
- an indication that a person must pay any relevant charges and must produce at a specified police station a valid licence and proof of insurance in respect of his/her use of the vehicle (or nominate a third person who can produce those documents in respect of that person's use of the vehicle to whom the vehicle can be released) (reg. 4(3)–(4)).

Regulation 5 deals with the procedure for releasing a vehicle. If, before a relevant motor vehicle is disposed of, someone:

- satisfies the authorised person that he/she is the registered keeper or the owner of that vehicle;
- pays to the authorised person such a charge in respect of its seizure and retention as provided for in reg. 6; and
- produces at a police station specified in the seizure notice a valid certificate of insurance covering his/her use of that vehicle *and* a valid licence authorising him/her to drive the vehicle,

the authorised person shall permit that person to remove the vehicle.

Specific provision is made for cases where the person claiming the vehicle can demonstrate that he/she is the owner and pays the required fee but nominates a third person who produces a valid certificate of insurance covering his/her use of that vehicle and a valid driving licence authorising him/her to drive that vehicle. In such circumstances, the authorised person must permit that person to remove the vehicle (reg. 5(2)).

Where a vehicle is not released, the conditions under which it can be disposed of are set out in reg. 7. In summary, the vehicle cannot be disposed of until at least 14 days after the date on which the vehicle was seized. If it is sold, the net proceeds are payable to the owner if claimed within a year.

The regulations also provide that the prescribed charges are not payable if the person claiming the vehicle was not driving it at the time of seizure, did not know it was being driven, had not consented to its being driven and could not reasonably have prevented its being driven (reg. 5(5)).

A key feature of the practical arrangements for enforcing the legislation in respect of uninsured drivers is the ability to get relevant information on vehicles and their insured status.

3.20.7 Duty to Give Information as to the Identity of the Driver

The Road Traffic Act 1988, s. 172 states:

(1) This section applies—
  (a) to any offence under the preceding provisions of this Act except—
    (i) an offence under Part V, or
    (ii) an offence under section 13, 16, 51(2), 61(4), 67(9), 68(4), 96 or 120,
  and to an offence under section 178 of this Act,
  (b) to any offence under sections 25, 26 or 27 of the Road Traffic Offenders Act 1988,
  (c) to any offence against any other enactment relating to the use of vehicles on roads, and
  (d) to manslaughter, or in Scotland culpable homicide, by the driver of a motor vehicle.

(2) Where the driver of a vehicle is alleged to be guilty of an offence to which this section applies—
  (a) the person keeping the vehicle shall give such information as to the identity of the driver as he may be required to give by or on behalf of a chief officer of police, and
  (b) any other person shall if required as stated above give any information which it is in his power to give and may lead to identification of the driver.

(3) Subject to the following provisions, a person who fails to comply with a requirement under subsection (2) above shall be guilty of an offence.

KEYNOTE

Section 172 applies to offences other than those listed at s. 172(1)(a)–(d). The excepted offences listed at s. 172(1)(a) and (b) are offences relating to:

- driving instructors;
- motoring events on public highways;
- protective headgear;
- testing of goods vehicles;
- regulations for 'type approval';
- obstruction of a vehicle examiner;
- requirements to proceed to a place of vehicle inspection;
- uncorrected eyesight;
- regulations for licensing of large goods vehicle/passenger carrying vehicle drivers;
- unlawful vehicle taking in Scotland; and
- post-conviction offences under the Road Traffic Offenders Act 1988.

Therefore, s. 172 will apply to regulations made under the applicable sections (e.g. the Road Vehicles (Construction and Use) Regulations 1986).

The requirement under s. 172 applies to the person keeping the vehicle and will apply to a person who is the keeper of the vehicle at the time the requirement is made even if he/she was not the keeper at the time of the alleged offence (*Hateley* v *Greenough* [1962] Crim LR 329). The second part of the power (s. 172(2)(b)) applies to *any other person*. Failing to give the information is a summary offence punishable by a fine and, in some circumstances, carrying a power for discretionary disqualification. Although it applies to both parts of the power set out earlier, the relevant offence (under s. 172(3)) creates one single offence (*Mohindra* v *DPP* [2004] EWHC 490 (Admin)).

There is no particular form of words to be used when making the requirement. It must be shown that the person making the requirement did so by, or on behalf of, the chief officer of police. A computerised form stating that the author is so acting has been held by the Divisional Court to be sufficient for this purpose (*Arnold* v *DPP* [1999] RTR 99).

Registered keepers of vehicles captured on roadside speed cameras are frequently served with a statutory notice under s. 172, along with a standard form. The form provides for details of the actual driver to be entered where the recipient of the form was not the driver at the time. If the recipient is unable to provide details of the driver, the form asks for reasons for that inability. Where a registered keeper returned the form with a covering letter stating that he had not completed the form because on the day of the alleged offence more than one person had used the vehicle, he was convicted of failing to comply with the requirement under s. 172. The defendant argued that he had complied with s. 172 because the form only required him to provide details of the actual driver, not a potential driver. The Divisional Court disagreed with him, holding that a notice issued pursuant to s. 172 requires an accurate response and not an inaccurate or misleading statement. That requirement under the notice is carried over to the form. The defendant's claim that he was only required to give details of an actual driver and not a potential driver was clearly contrary to the legislative intention as it would frequently be the case that the registered owner of a vehicle would at least suspect who the driver was, even if he/she did not know for certain, e.g. where the owner lent the vehicle to a friend but was not in the vehicle at the time of the alleged offence (*R (On the Application of Flegg)* v *Southampton and New Forest Justices* [2006] EWHC 396 (Admin)). The High Court has also held, where a husband and wife asserted that they did not know which of them drove their Aston Martin at speed through a static camera, that it was not 'on any view irrational for the Magistrates' Court to refuse to exclude the probability that a conscientious and determined enquiry by Mrs Marshall would have revealed whether it was Mrs Marshall or her husband who drove past the agreed camera' when upholding Mrs Marshall's conviction under s. 172(3) (*Marshall* v *CPS* [2015] EWHC 2333 (Admin)).

The information must be provided within a reasonable time which may, in the prevailing circumstances, mean immediately (*Lowe* v *Lester* [1987] RTR 30).

Note that is not necessary for the person to provide the required information on the specific form sent out by the police—it is enough that the relevant information is given in writing (*Jones* v *DPP* [2004] EWHC 236 (Admin)).

A chief officer is entitled to require the person providing the information to sign the relevant s. 172 form (*Francis* v *DPP* [2004] EWHC 591 (Admin)).

Where the requirement is made in writing and served by post, it shall have effect as a requirement to provide the information within 28 days beginning with the day on which it is served (s. 172(7)(a)) (see the defence at **para. 3.20.7.1**).

If a person falsely claims to have been the driver, an offence of perverting the course of justice may be appropriate.

Where the defendant is a company or corporate body, any director, secretary, manager or other officer of the company may also be prosecuted for the offence if it can be shown that the offence was committed with his/her 'consent or connivance' (s. 172(5)).

The Divisional Court for England and Wales has confirmed that an admission to being the driver of a particular vehicle given in response to a s. 172 requirement does not breach the defendant's privilege against self-incrimination under Article 6 of the European Convention on Human Rights (*DPP* v *Wilson* [2001] EWHC Admin 198). The court went on to say that where a defendant disputed the reliability of any such admission, a judge (or magistrate) ought to exercise his/her general discretion to exclude the written evidence and require the prosecution to adduce oral evidence which could then be tested by cross-examination. The court also held that there was no difference, so far as the effect of the Human Rights Act 1998 was concerned, between s. 172(2)(a) and (b).

3.20.7.1 Defence

Section 172(4) provides that a person shall not be convicted of an offence under s. 172(3) if that person can show that he/she did not know *and* could not have ascertained with reasonable diligence who the driver of the vehicle was.

Section 172(7)(b) provides that where the requirement is made in writing by post, the person shall not be guilty of an offence if that person can show that either he/she gave the information as soon as reasonably practicable after the end of the 28-day period or that it had not been reasonably practicable to give it.

In both of these cases, the evidential burden of proof lies on the defendant.

3.21 Offences Involving Standards of Driving

3.21.1 Introduction

The Road Traffic Act 1988 defines 'dangerous driving' (s. 2A) and 'careless and inconsiderate driving' (s. 3ZA). These behaviours and the offences directly associated with them (dangerous driving (s.1) and careless and inconsiderate driving (s. 3)) are examined in this chapter along with a series of offences connected to those behaviours that lead to death or serious injury. The chapter also considers the offences of causing death or serious injury by driving when unlicensed, disqualified or uninsured.

3.21.2 Causing Death by Dangerous Driving

OFFENCE: **Causing Death by Dangerous Driving—*Road Traffic Act 1988, s. 1***

• Triable on indictment • Life imprisonment • Obligatory disqualification—minimum five years • Compulsory re-test

The Road Traffic Act 1988, s. 1 states:

> A person who causes the death of another person by driving a mechanically propelled vehicle dangerously on a road or other public place is guilty of an offence.

KEYNOTE

For the purposes of this offence, the definition of 'driver' does not include a separate person acting as a steersman.

Note that this offence applies to a 'mechanically propelled vehicle' and can be committed on a road or public place.

Provided the basic elements (mechanically propelled vehicle on a road/public place) are met, you must prove that:

- the defendant caused the death of another person; and
- the defendant drove dangerously.

Where the defendant is charged under s. 1, evidence of drink will be admissible where the quantity of it may have adversely affected the quality of his/her driving (*R* v *Woodward* [1995] RTR 130).

Section 36 of the Road Traffic Offenders Act 1988 (requiring the court to disqualify a person convicted of certain offences until he/she has passed the relevant test) applies to this offence. This means that, if convicted of this offence, the defendant will have to take an extended driving test before getting his/her licence back.

Under the Powers of Criminal Courts (Sentencing) Act 2000, s. 143, forfeiture of the motor vehicle used for the purpose of this offence may be ordered.

3.21.2.1 Causes the Death of Another

The death must be that of a person other than the defendant. This would include a foetus which was later born alive but which subsequently died.

A driver causing the death of another in this way could still be indicted for homicide (*R* v *Governor of Holloway Prison, ex parte Jennings* [1983] 1 AC 624), however, a charge of manslaughter will rarely be brought in such cases.

The driving by the defendant must be shown to have been *a* cause of the death; it is not necessary to show that it was the sole or even a substantial cause of death (*R* v *Hennigan* [1971] 3 All ER 133). Therefore it is irrelevant whether or not the person killed contributed to the incident which resulted in his/her death or where it is alleged that a second collision was the immediate cause of death (*R* v *Girdler* [2009] EWCA Crim 2666).

The Court of Appeal has clarified that this offence relates to causing death *by* driving and not causing death *while* driving and therefore the 'driving' does not have to be coextensive with the collision that resulted in the death. In *R* v *Jenkins* [2012] EWCA Crim 2909, the court held that parking a van to make a delivery, leaving it in conditions of poor visibility where another vehicle collided with it, was certainly a causal link to the fatality that occurred.

In June 2022, under s. 86 of the Police, Crime, Sentencing and Courts Act 2022, the maximum penalty for causing death by dangerous driving (s. 1 of the Road Traffic Act 1988) was increased from 14 years' imprisonment to life imprisonment.

In *R* v *Gregory* [2024] EWCA Crim 749, the Court of Appeal reconsidered a nine-year sentence for causing death by dangerous driving after it was thought to be unduly lenient. Gregory, who was intoxicated, killed a vulnerable pedestrian and had relevant aggravating factors, including prior convictions and attempting to evade police. The Court of Appeal held that the sentence failed to properly reflect the seriousness of the offence, public protection and the Sentencing Guideline ranges. The court increased the sentence.

3.21.2.2 What is 'Dangerous Driving'?

The Road Traffic Act 1988, s. 2A states:

> (1) For the purposes of sections 1, 1A and 2 above a person is to be regarded as driving dangerously if (and, subject to subsection (2) below, only if)—
> (a) the way he drives falls far below what would be expected of a competent and careful driver, and
> (b) it would be obvious to a competent and careful driver that driving in that way would be dangerous.
> But this subsection does not apply where subsection (1B) applies.
> (1A) Subsection (1B) applies where a designated person—
> (a) is driving for police purposes (subject to subsections (1E) and (1F)), and
> (b) has undertaken prescribed training.
> (1B) For the purposes of sections 1, 1A and 2 above, the designated person is to be regarded as driving dangerously if (and, subject to subsection (2) below, only if)
> (a) the way the person drives falls far below what would be expected of a competent and careful constable who has undertaken the same prescribed training, and
> (b) it would be obvious to such a competent and careful constable that driving in that way would be dangerous.
> (1C) In subsections (1A) and (1B) 'designated person' means—
> (a) a constable,
> (b) a member of staff appointed by the chief officer of police of a police force in England and Wales,
> (c) a member of staff appointed by a local policing body and employed to assist a police force in England and Wales,
> (d) a member of staff appointed by the Scottish Police Authority under section 26(1) of the Police and Fire Reform (Scotland) Act 2012,

(e) an employee of the British Transport Police Authority appointed under section 27 of the Railways and Transport Safety Act 2003,
(f) a person employed or engaged by—
  (i) a chief officer of police,
  (ii) the British Transport Police Authority,
  (iii) the Civil Nuclear Police Authority,
  (iv) the chief constable for the Ministry of Defence Police, or
  (v) the Scottish Police Authority,
  to train a person within any of paragraphs (a) to (e) to drive for police purposes,
(g) a person employed or engaged by a person within paragraph (f)(i) to (v) to train another person to carry out training of the kind mentioned in that paragraph,
(h) a National Crime Agency officer, or
(i) a person engaged by the National Crime Agency—
  (i) to train a National Crime Agency officer to drive for law enforcement purposes, or
  (ii) to train another person to carry out training of the kind mentioned in sub-paragraph (i).

(1D) In subsection (1C) (a) 'constable' does not include a port constable within the meaning of section 7 of the Marine Navigation Act 2013 or a person appointed to act as a constable under provision made by virtue of section 16 of the Harbours Act 1964.

(1E) In the case of a National Crime Agency officer, the reference in subsection (1A)(a) to driving for police purposes is to be read as a reference to driving for law enforcement purposes.

(1F) In the case of a person within paragraph (i) of subsection (1C), the reference in subsection (1A)(a) to driving for police purposes is to be read as a reference to driving for the purpose of the training mentioned in that paragraph.

(2) A person is also to be regarded as driving dangerously for the purposes of sections 1, 1A and 2 above if it would be obvious to a competent and careful driver that driving the vehicle in its current state would be dangerous.

(3) In subsections (1) and (2) above 'dangerous' refers to danger either of injury to any person or of serious damage to property; and in determining for the purposes of those subsections what would be expected of, or obvious to, a competent and careful driver in a particular case, regard shall be had not only to the circumstances of which he could be expected to be aware but also to any circumstances shown to have been within the knowledge of the accused.

(4) In determining for the purposes of subsection (2) above the state of a vehicle, regard may be had to anything attached to or carried on or in it and to the manner in which it is attached or carried.

KEYNOTE

The courts have held that both elements of s. 2A(1)(a) and (b) must be demonstrated by the prosecution to prove this element of the offence (*R* v *Brooks* [2001] EWCA Crim 1944).

This is an objective test which focuses, at s. 2A(1)(a), on the manner of driving rather than the defendant's state of mind and, at s. 2A(1)(b), on what would have been obvious to a hypothetical 'competent and careful driver'. An example is where a diabetic driver drives on a road in the knowledge that he/she is likely to suffer a hypoglycaemic episode (*R* v *Marison* [1997] RTR 457).

In *Attorney-General's Reference (No. 4 of 2000)* [2001] EWCA Crim 780, the Court of Appeal reviewed the requirements of s. 2A. That case involved a bus driver who had inadvertently pressed the accelerator pedal instead of the brake, killing two pedestrians. The court held that under s. 2A the test is an objective one and there is no requirement to show any specific intent to drive dangerously. It is for the jury to determine what constitutes dangerous driving. The court held that the relevant *actus reus* is the act of driving in a manner which was either dangerous (in the case of a dangerous driving charge) or without due care and attention (in the case of the alternative offence). Where, as in this case, the driver had been conscious of the act he was performing, it was no defence to claim that he had not intended to press the accelerator. That was more a matter for mitigation than guilt. This view was approved by the Court of Appeal in *R* v *Shearing* [2012] EWCA Crim 842, where the court recognised that there is an overlap between this offence and that under s. 2B (causing death by careless driving; **see para. 3.21.6**).

The standard of driving must be shown to have fallen far below that expected of a competent and careful driver; minor driver errors would not amount to such behaviour.

In determining what would have been obvious to a competent and careful driver, s. 2A(3) and (4) introduces a subjective element by taking account of circumstances known to the defendant. This mixture of tests means that, although a defendant's behaviour will be judged against the ordinary standards of competent and careful drivers, the defendant's conduct will also be assessed in the light of facts personally known to him/her (such as knowledge of the risk of a load falling off the vehicle (*R* v *Crossman* [1986] RTR 49)). However, the test is a high one, as confirmed in *R* v *Conteh (Kondeh)* [2003] EWCA Crim 962. In that case, the defendant had caused the death of a pedestrian who was crossing the road at a pelican crossing. The lights were red for pedestrians and green for the defendant who was driving at 20 mph in a bus lane. It was shown that the driver of a vehicle in the outside lane had indicated to the pedestrian that she could cross the road. Quashing his conviction under s. 1, the Court of Appeal held that the threshold in s. 2A was a high one and it could not be said that the defendant's driving fell 'far below' the required standard, nor would it have been 'obvious' to a competent and careful driver that it was dangerous. Further, it was good practice expressly to remind a jury that a breach of the Highway Code did not necessarily mean that an offence had been committed.

If the vehicle involved was in a dangerous condition, it is important that you prove either:

- that the dangerous condition would itself have been obvious to a competent or careful driver; or
- that the defendant actually knew of its dangerous condition.

(*R* v *Strong* [1995] Crim LR 428)

In some circumstances, the condition of the driver will be relevant. There are specific offences involving driving while under the influence of drink and/or drugs (**see para. 3.21.5**) and there are several generic road policing offences dealing with drink and drugs (**see chapter 3.22**). However, the mere presence of a controlled drug (such as cocaine) in a driver's blood may of itself be relevant to the issue of whether a person drove dangerously—even if there is no specific evidence as to the drug's effect on the person's driving (*R* v *Pleydell* [2005] EWCA Crim 1447). The fact that a driver was adversely affected by alcohol is a circumstance relevant to the issue of dangerous driving, but is not in itself determinative to prove the offence (*R* v *Webster* [2006] 2 Cr App R 103). There is no requirement to prove whether the defendant was above or below the prescribed limit, as that is not an element of the offence (*R* v *Mari* [2009] EWCA Crim 2677); evidence of the amount of alcohol consumed and said to affect the defendant's ability to drive suffices.

The defendant's belief, however honestly held, as to the conditions surrounding his/her driving at the time is not relevant to the issue of whether he/she drove competently and carefully (*R* v *Collins* [1997] RTR 439). In *Collins*, a police driver went through a red traffic light at almost 100 mph colliding with another vehicle and killing two people. His belief that the traffic at the lights was being operated by other officers was not a relevant factor for the jury in considering whether or not his driving had been dangerous.

In *Dormer* v *Wilson & MIB* [2025] EWHC 523 (KB), the High Court confirmed that contravening a red light clearly amounted to dangerous driving under s. 2 of the Road Traffic Act 1988.

The CPS has provided examples of circumstances that are likely to be characterised as dangerous driving and are derived from decided cases. They include:

- racing or competitive driving;
- failing to have a proper and safe regard for vulnerable road users such as cyclists, motorcyclists, horse riders, the elderly and pedestrians or when in the vicinity of a pedestrian crossing, hospital, school or residential home;
- speed which is particularly inappropriate for the prevailing road or traffic conditions;
- aggressive driving, such as sudden lane changes, cutting into a line of vehicles or driving much too close to the vehicle in front;
- disregard of traffic lights and other road signs which, on an objective analysis, would appear to be deliberate;
- disregard of warnings from fellow passengers;

- overtaking which could not have been carried out safely;
- driving when knowingly suffering from a medical or physical condition that significantly and dangerously impairs the offender's driving skills, such as having an arm or leg in plaster or impaired eyesight. It can include failure to take prescribed medication;
- driving when knowingly deprived of adequate sleep or rest;
- driving a vehicle knowing it has a dangerous defect or is poorly maintained or is dangerously loaded;
- using a hand-held mobile phone or other hand-held electronic equipment whether as a phone or to compose or read text messages when the driver is avoidably and dangerously distracted by that use (*R* v *Browning* (2001) EWCA Crim 1831, *R* v *Payne* [2007] EWCA Crim 157);
- driving whilst avoidably and dangerously distracted, such as whilst reading a newspaper/map, talking to and looking at a passenger, selecting and lighting a cigarette or by adjusting the controls of electronic equipment such as a radio, hands-free mobile phone or satellite navigation equipment;
- a brief but obvious danger arising from a seriously dangerous manoeuvre. This covers situations where a driver has made a mistake or an error of judgement that was so substantial that it caused the driving to be dangerous even for only a short time. Cases that illustrate this principle include:
  - *Attorney-General's Reference (No. 32 of 2001)* [2002] 1 Cr App R (S) 121 (offender failed to stop at a junction where there was a give way sign, failing to see a taxi that was being driven across the junction perfectly properly and colliding with it);
  - *Attorney-General's Reference (No. 4 of 2000)* [2001] EWCA Crim 780 (offender unintentionally pressed the accelerator instead of the brake);
  - *Attorney-General's Reference (No. 76 of 2002) (Hodges)* [2003] 1 Cr App R (S) 100 (offender drove across a junction marked by a give way sign and collided with a car that was being driven along the major road and the driver had no explanation for his failure to see the other car)—'this was a single misjudgment. It was a bad misjudgment but nevertheless a single one.'

The dangers presented by dangerous driving mean that there will be many occasions where significant injury is caused to another person by the driving of the vehicle. The Court of Appeal has held that there is nothing wrong in principle in charging a driver with causing grievous bodily harm as well as dangerous driving, in appropriate circumstances, and that to do so did not amount to an abuse of process (*R* v *Bain* [2005] EWCA Crim 7). However, where a driver was charged with both offences, a court could not impose consecutive terms of imprisonment for both offences arising out of the same incident. With the introduction of the offence of causing serious injury by dangerous driving (**see para. 3.21.3**), the need to charge both offences may well be consigned to history.

The Court of Appeal gave judgment on the point of whether self-defence was capable of amounting to a defence to a charge of dangerous driving. It concluded that it was; albeit only rarely (*R* v *Tracey Riddell* [2017] EWCA Crim 392).

3.21.2.3 Meaning of Dangerous 'Current State'

The offence may also be committed if the state of a vehicle, including any attachment or load and the way in which it is attached or carried, would make driving it dangerous in the eyes of a 'competent and careful' driver. In relation to the dangerous state of a vehicle being 'obvious', no special definition is required and such an observation could arise from an inspection which is something between a fleeting glance and a long look (*R* v *Marsh* [2002] EWCA Crim 137).

The Court of Appeal has considered the meaning of the term 'current state' of the vehicle. In *R* v *Marchant and Muntz* [2003] EWCA Crim 2099, the court held that the term implied a state different from the original state of the vehicle. In that particular case, the vehicle involved had been a tractor fitted with a boom and grab for moving bales. The grab comprised a set of forward-pointing spikes on an upper and lower jaw. With the boom and grab set in the position recommended by the manufacturer, the defendant manoeuvred the tractor to make a turn and, while he waited to do so, a motorcyclist rode into the spikes and later died from his injuries. The defendants were charged with causing death by dangerous driving, with the prosecution relying on the s. 2A(2) provision that it would have been obvious to a competent and careful driver that driving the vehicle in its current state would have been dangerous. The defendants argued that the vehicle was an agricultural vehicle specially authorised by the Secretary of State under s. 44 of the Road Traffic Act 1988. The Court of Appeal held that there would be cases where, even though a vehicle was authorised in this way, its condition would allow a prosecution under s. 1 or 2. However, such cases would almost always involve allegations that the driver had created the danger by manoeuvring the vehicle, rather than simply relying on any danger caused by the vehicle's presence on a road (or other public place). Clearly, if the vehicle had been used in a built-up area or had been altered, allowed to deteriorate or used in a way that contravened the manufacturer's recommendations, the s. 2A argument would have had more force. In the circumstances of the particular case, however, the defendants' convictions were quashed.

In a further case involving another tractor, the Court of Appeal clarified the extent to which the practice of piling bales of straw onto a trailer would give rise to liability under s. 2. In that case, the defendant had been towing a semi-trailer with some 22 bales of straw on it, one of which fell off and seriously injured a pedestrian. The defendant maintained that this 'system of work' had been employed for 25 years without incident and that he had never been warned that it might be unsafe. On the evidence, the court held that it would be perverse to find that the system of carrying bales in this way was inherently 'dangerous' (*R* v *Few* [2005] EWCA Crim 728).

3.21.3 Causing Serious Injury by Dangerous Driving

OFFENCE: **Causing Serious Injury by Dangerous Driving—*Road Traffic Act 1988, s. 1A***

• Triable either way • Five years' imprisonment and/or a fine on indictment • Six months' imprisonment and/or fine summarily • Obligatory disqualification—minimum two years • Compulsory extended re-test

The Road Traffic Act 1988, s. 1A states:

> (1) A person who causes serious injury to another person by driving a mechanically propelled vehicle dangerously on a road or other public place is guilty of an offence.

KEYNOTE

This offence was introduced to the Road Traffic Act 1988 by s. 143 of the Legal Aid, Sentencing and Punishment of Offenders Act 2012. The elements of this offence ('dangerous' and 'dangerous driving') are the same as those under s. 1.

'Serious injury' means physical harm which amounts to grievous bodily harm for the purposes of the Offences Against the Person Act 1861. There may be cases where the injuries fall short of 'serious' by this definition. The CPS suggests that in these cases it may be appropriate to consider an additional assault charge of s. 47 of the Offences Against the Person Act 1861.

The Road Traffic Offenders Act 1988, s. 24, provides an alternative verdict to this offence under the Road Traffic Act 1988, s. 2 (dangerous driving) and s. 3 (careless, and inconsiderate, driving). A person convicted of the offence is subject to a minimum disqualification period of two years, unless the court considers that there are special reasons either not to disqualify or to disqualify for a shorter period. A person convicted of this offence will be disqualified until he/she passes an extended driving test (s. 36 of the Road Traffic Offenders Act 1988).

Under the Powers of Criminal Courts (Sentencing) Act 2000, s. 143, forfeiture of the motor vehicle used for the purpose of this offence may be ordered.

3.21.4 Dangerous Driving

OFFENCE: **Dangerous Driving—*Road Traffic Act 1988, s. 2***

• Triable either way • Two years' imprisonment and/or a fine on indictment
• Six months' imprisonment and/or statutory maximum summarily • Obligatory disqualification • Compulsory re-test

The Road Traffic Act 1988, s. 2 states:

> A person who drives a mechanically propelled vehicle dangerously on a road or other public place is guilty of an offence.

KEYNOTE

The elements of this offence are the same as those for s. 1.

Evidence showing how the particular vehicle was being driven before the incident itself may be given in support of the charge of dangerous driving. However, care needs to be taken by the prosecution not to seek to adduce inadmissible evidence about the defendant's past bad driving (*R* v *McKenzie* [2008] EWCA Crim 758). Where the dangerous driving leads to a collision, the court may allow a police officer who is an expert in the investigation of collisions to give evidence of opinion as to the cause of that collision (*R* v *Oakley* [1979] RTR 417).

In addition, there is a rarely used offence of causing bodily harm by wanton or furious driving or racing (Offences Against the Person Act 1861, s. 35) which is punishable by two years' imprisonment.

Section 36 of the Road Traffic Offenders Act 1988 (requiring the court to disqualify a person convicted of certain offences until the relevant test has been passed) applies to this offence. This means that, if convicted of this offence, the defendant will have to take an extended driving test before getting his/her licence back.

3.21.5 Causing Death by Careless Driving When Under the Influence of Drink or Drugs

OFFENCE: **Causing Death by Careless Driving When Under the Influence of Drink or Drugs—*Road Traffic Act 1988, s. 3A***

• Triable on indictment • Life imprisonment • Obligatory disqualification—minimum five years

The Road Traffic Act 1988, s. 3A states:

> (1) If a person causes the death of another person by driving a mechanically propelled vehicle on a road or other public place without due care and attention, or without reasonable consideration for other persons using the road or place, and—
> (a) he is, at the time when he is driving, unfit to drive through drink or drugs, or
> (b) he has consumed so much alcohol that the proportion of it in his breath, blood or urine at that time exceeds the prescribed limit, or
> (ba) he has in his body a specified controlled drug and the proportion of it in his blood or urine at that time exceeds the specified limit for that drug, or
> (c) he is, within 18 hours after that time, required to provide a specimen in pursuance of section 7 of this Act, but without reasonable excuse fails to provide it, or
> (d) he is required by a constable to give his permission for a laboratory test of a specimen of blood taken from him under section 7A of this Act, but without reasonable excuse fails to do so,
>
> he is guilty of an offence.
>
> (2) For the purposes of this section a person shall be taken to be unfit to drive at any time when his ability to drive properly is impaired.
>
> (3) Subsection (1)(b), (ba), (c) and (d) above shall not apply in relation to a person driving a mechanically propelled vehicle other than a motor vehicle.

KEYNOTE

There are a number of different ways that this offence can be committed. The prosecution needs to establish that:

- the driving has caused the death of another person;
- the driving was without due care and attention or without reasonable consideration for other road users; and
- the driver is either unfit through drink or drugs, or the alcohol concentration is over the prescribed limit, or there has been a failure to provide a specimen in pursuance of the Road Traffic Act 1988. This would include cases where the accused:
  - had consumed so much alcohol that the proportion of it in his/her breath, blood or urine at that time exceeded the prescribed limit; or
  - had in his/her body a specified controlled drug and the proportion of it in his/her blood or urine at that time exceeded the specified limit for that drug; or
  - within 18 hours after that time, the accused was required to provide a specimen in pursuance of s. 7 of the Road Traffic Act 1988 but without reasonable excuse fails to provide it; or
  - he/she is required by a constable to give his/her permission for a laboratory test of a specimen of blood taken from him/her under s. 7A of the 1988 Act, but without reasonable excuse fails to do so.

The elements in relation to 'causes the death of another person' are the same as those under s. 1.

The elements relating to 'due care and attention' and 'reasonable consideration' are discussed at **para. 3.21.6.1**.

The elements relating to unfitness to drive and being over the prescribed limit for alcohol or drugs are the same as those contained in drink drive legislation in **chapter 3.22**. For this offence, this means that s. 3A(1)(b), (ba), (c) and (d) apply only where the driving is of a 'motor vehicle', but the offence under s. 3A(1)(a) may be committed while driving any 'mechanically propelled vehicle'.

Effectively, the prosecution would therefore have to prove careless driving and the related 'drink/drug driving' offence in exactly the same way as if both offences had been charged, together with the requisite causal link to the death. The offence, however, does not require any causal connection between the alcohol or drugs and the death (*R* v *Shepherd* [1994] 1 WLR 530).

In applying the appropriate test to determine whether the defendant has driven without due care and attention, the jury are entitled to look at all the circumstances of the case, including evidence that the defendant had been affected by alcohol or had taken such an amount of alcohol as would be likely to affect a driver (*R* v *Millington* [1996] RTR 80).

The requirement under s. 3A(1)(c) is for the provision of a specimen for analysis under s. 7 of the Road Traffic Act 1988 and not a screening test under s. 6.

The wording in s. 3A(1)(c) seems to indicate that the request to provide a specimen must be made within 18 hours after the driving which caused the death and not after the death itself.

Section 36 of the Road Traffic Offenders Act 1988 (requiring the court to disqualify a person convicted of certain offences until the relevant test has been passed) applies to this offence. This means that if convicted of this offence, the defendant will have to take an extended driving test before getting his/her licence back.

3.21.6 Causing Death by Careless, or Inconsiderate, Driving

OFFENCE: **Causing Death by Careless, or Inconsiderate, Driving—*Road Traffic Act 1988, s. 2B***

- Triable either way • Five years' imprisonment and/or a fine on indictment
- 12 months' imprisonment (six months in Scotland) and/or statutory maximum summarily • Obligatory disqualification—minimum 12 months

The Road Traffic Act 1988, s. 2B states:

> A person who causes the death of another person by driving a mechanically propelled vehicle on a road or other public place without due care and attention, or without reasonable consideration for other persons using the road or place, is guilty of an offence.

KEYNOTE

The elements in relation to 'causes the death of another person' are the same as those under s. 1.

This section was added to bridge the large gap between causing death by dangerous driving and careless driving that resulted in a death. There will clearly be an overlap between the driving standards of this offence and those of causing death by dangerous driving, a fact the courts have recognised (see *Shearing* at para. 3.21.2.2, Keynote).

3.21.6.1 What is 'Careless and Inconsiderate' Driving?

3ZA Meaning of careless, or inconsiderate, driving

(1) This section has effect for the purposes of sections 2B, 2C and 3 above and section 3A below.

(2) A person is to be regarded as driving without due care and attention if (and only if) the way he drives falls below what would be expected of a competent and careful driver. But this subsection does not apply where subsection (2B) applies.

(2A) Subsection (2B) applies where a designated person—
- (a) is driving for police purposes (subject to subsections (2E) and (2F)), and
- (b) has undertaken prescribed training.

(2B) The designated person is to be regarded as driving without due care and attention if (and only if) the way the person drives falls below what would be expected of a competent and careful constable who has undertaken the same prescribed training.

(2C) In subsections (2A) and (2B) 'designated person' means—
- (a) a constable,
- (b) a member of staff appointed by the chief officer of police of a police force in England and Wales,
- (c) a member of staff appointed by a local policing body and employed to assist a police force in England and Wales,
- (d) a member of staff appointed by the Scottish Police Authority under section 26(1) of the Police and Fire Reform (Scotland) Act 2012,
- (e) an employee of the British Transport Police Authority appointed under section 27 of the Railways and Transport Safety Act 2003,
- (f) a person employed or engaged by—
  - (i) a chief officer of police,
  - (ii) the British Transport Police Authority,
  - (iii) the Civil Nuclear Police Authority,
  - (iv) the chief constable for the Ministry of Defence Police, or
  - (v) the Scottish Police Authority,

  to train a person within any of paragraphs (a) to (e) to drive for police purposes,
- (g) a person employed or engaged by a person within paragraph (f)(i) to (v) to train another person to carry out training of the kind mentioned in that paragraph,
- (h) a National Crime Agency officer, or
- (i) a person engaged by the National Crime Agency—
  - (i) to train a National Crime Agency officer to drive for law enforcement purposes, or
  - (ii) to train another person to carry out training of the kind mentioned in sub-paragraph (i).

(2D) In subsection (2C)(a) 'constable' does not include a port constable within the meaning of section 7 of the Marine Navigation Act 2013 or a person appointed to act as a constable under provision made by virtue of section 16 of the Harbours Act 1964.

(2E) In the case of a National Crime Agency officer, the reference in subsection (2A)(a) to driving for police purposes is to be read as a reference to driving for law enforcement purposes.

(2F) In the case of a person within paragraph (i) of subsection (2C), the reference in subsection (2A)(a) to driving for police purposes is to be read as a reference to driving for the purpose of the training mentioned in that paragraph.

(3) In determining for the purposes of subsection (2) or (2B) above what would be expected of a careful and competent driver or constable (as the case may be) in a particular case, regard shall be had not only to the circumstances of which he could be expected to be aware but also to any circumstances shown to have been within the knowledge of the accused.

(4) A person is to be regarded as driving without reasonable consideration for other persons only if those persons are inconvenienced by his driving.

In determining what is to be expected of a competent and careful driver, the following factors need to be considered:

- the circumstances of which the driver could be expected to be aware;
- any circumstances shown to have been within the driver's knowledge.

The test of whether the standard of driving has fallen below the required standard is objective. It applies both when the manner of driving in question is deliberate and when it occurs because of incompetence, inadvertence or inexperience.

In the absence of any explanation by the defendant as to the cause of the collision, a court may infer that the offence was committed. In *R* v *Warwickshire Police, ex parte Manjit Singh Mundi* [2001] EWHC Admin 448, the court held that crossing a central white line without explanation was, in itself, evidence of careless driving.

As with dangerous driving, the test is entirely objective in nature and focuses on the manner of driving rather than the defendant's state of mind. The element that distinguishes dangerous driving from careless driving is that the dangerous driver falls *far below* the required standard, while the careless driver merely falls *below* the required standard (**see para. 3.21.2.2, Keynote**).

Note also that if the defendant is alleged to have driven without reasonable consideration for another road user, that other road user must *actually* be inconvenienced by the defendant's driving; it is not enough that there was a potential for inconvenience (s. 3ZA(4)).

There is one *objective* standard of driving which is expected of all drivers, including learner drivers (*McCrone* v *Riding* [1938] 1 All ER 157) (**see para. 3.9.4**). Once you have proved that a defendant departed from that standard of driving, and that the defendant's actions were 'voluntary', the offence is complete. There is no need to prove any *knowledge* or *awareness* by the defendant that his/her driving fell below that standard (*R* v *Lawrence* [1982] AC 510).

The standard of driving that would be expected of a competent and careful driver will be a question of fact for the court to decide and, in so deciding, the magistrate(s) may take into account local factors such as the expected level of traffic, the time of day, peculiar hazards etc. (*Walker* v *Tolhurst* [1976] RTR 513).

KEYNOTE

CPS guidance as to the driving that courts will regard as careless or inconsiderate outlines examples that are typical of what is likely to be regarded as careless driving:

- overtaking on the inside;
- driving inappropriately close to another vehicle;
- inadvertently driving through a red light;
- emerging from a side road into the path of another vehicle;
- tuning a car radio (when the driver was avoidably distracted by this action);
- using a hand-held mobile phone or other hand-held electronic equipment when the driver was avoidably distracted by that use;
- selecting and lighting a cigarette or similar when the driver was avoidably distracted by that action.

3.21.7 Causing Serious Injury by Careless, or Inconsiderate, Driving

OFFENCE: **Causing Serious Injury by Careless, or Inconsiderate, Driving—*Road Traffic Act 1988, after s. 2C***

- Triable summarily • Two years' imprisonment and/or a fine on indictment

The Road Traffic Act 1988, s. 2C states:

> A person who causes serious injury to another person by driving a mechanically propelled vehicle on a road or other public place without due care and attention, or without reasonable consideration for other persons using the road or place, is guilty of an offence.
>
> In this section, 'serious injury' means, in England and Wales, physical harm which amounts to grievous bodily harm for the purposes of the Offences Against the Person Act 1861.

Section 3ZA(1) (meaning of careless, or inconsiderate, driving) of the Road Traffic Act 1998 has effect for the purposes of s. 2C.

3.21.8 Causing Death by Driving: Unlicensed, Disqualified or Uninsured Drivers

OFFENCE: **Causing Death by Driving: Unlicensed, Disqualified or Uninsured Drivers—*Road Traffic Act 1988, s. 3ZB***

- Triable either way • Two years' imprisonment and/or a fine on indictment
- 12 months' imprisonment and/or statutory maximum summarily
- Obligatory disqualification—minimum 12 months

The Road Traffic Act 1988, s. 3ZB states:

> A person is guilty of an offence under this section if he causes the death of another person by driving a motor vehicle on a road and, at the time when he is driving, the circumstances are such that he is committing an offence under—
>
> (a) section 87(1) of this Act (driving otherwise than in accordance with a licence), or
>
> (b) ...
>
> (c) section 143 of this Act (using motor vehicle while uninsured).

KEYNOTE

The elements in relation to 'causing the death of' and 'another person' are, generally, the same as those under s. 1.

This offence was initially construed as a 'but for' offence. It was considered that a person who should not have been on the road as they were disqualified, had no insurance or no driving licence ought to have their presence 'punished' where a fatality occurred. It was considered that 'but for' the presence of that person on that road, who indeed should not have been there at that time, a fatality may not have occurred and thus converted the basic offence into a far more serious one. This was confirmed by the Court of Appeal in *R* v *Williams* [2010] EWCA Crim 2552, where the deceased walked directly into the path of the uninsured defendant's car. The conviction was upheld despite the lack of any fault in the quality of the defendant's driving.

However, the Supreme Court has since ruled that there must be something more than 'but for' causation. In *R* v *Hughes* [2013] UKSC 56, their lordships made clear that the 'but for' interpretation 'confuses criminal responsibility for the serious offence of being uninsured with criminal responsibility for the infinitely more serious offence of killing another person'.

In terms of directions to the jury where such an offence is charged:

> ... it is not necessary for the Crown to prove careless or inconsiderate driving, but ... there must be something open to proper criticism in the driving of the defendant, beyond the mere presence of the vehicle on the road, and which contributes in some more than minimal way to the death.

An example of the 'but for' test is seen in *R* v *Wilson* [2019] RTR 24. The Court of Appeal said:

> s.3ZB is satisfied and the second limb of the test in *Hughes* is made out—'contributes in some more than minimal way to the death'—if the driving at the critical time was such as significantly or materially to increase the risk of death resulting from the appellant's culpable acts or omissions.

The judgment emphasised that the causal link was between the driving and the death rather than the driving and the collision. The defendant in that case had been travelling at 40 mph in a 30 mph zone and there was expert evidence to the effect that at this speed death was at least four times more likely than a collision at 30 mph.

This offence may only be committed by the driver of a motor vehicle (not a mechanically propelled vehicle unlike ss. 2, 2B and 3).

OFFENCE: **Causing Death by Driving: Disqualified Drivers—*Road Traffic Act 1988, s. 3ZC***

• Triable on indictment • 10 years' imprisonment and/or a fine • Obligatory disqualification

The Road Traffic Act 1988, s. 3ZC states:

A person is guilty of an offence under this section if he or she—

(a) causes the death of another person by driving a motor vehicle on a road, and

(b) at that time, is committing an offence under section 103(1)(b) of this Act (driving while disqualified).

OFFENCE: **Causing Serious Injury by Driving: Disqualified Drivers—*Road Traffic Act 1988, s. 3ZD***

• Triable either way • Four years' imprisonment and/or a fine on indictment • 12 months' imprisonment and/or fine summarily • Obligatory disqualification

The Road Traffic Act 1988, s. 3ZD states:

A person is guilty of an offence under this section if he or she—

(a) causes serious injury to another person by driving a motor vehicle on a road, and

(b) at that time, is committing an offence under section 103(1)(b) of this Act (driving while disqualified) . . .

KEYNOTE

The introduction of s. 3ZC is to increase the sentence for causing death while driving a vehicle whilst disqualified from two years to 10 years. The intention is to treat disqualified drivers differently from other illegal drivers.

This section, in relation to disqualified drivers who 'cause' death or serious injury, must be read in the light of the Supreme Court judgment in *Hughes* above.

Section 3ZD extends the offence under s. 1A of causing serious injury by dangerous driving specifically to disqualified drivers, increasing the sentence to four years' imprisonment from six months' imprisonment under s. 1A and removing the need to show 'dangerous' driving. In this section, 'serious injury' means physical harm which amounts to grievous bodily harm for the purposes of the Offences Against the Person Act 1861.

3.21.9 Careless and Inconsiderate Driving

OFFENCE: **Careless and Inconsiderate Driving—*Road Traffic Act 1988, s. 3***

• Triable summarily • Fine • Discretionary disqualification

The Road Traffic Act 1988, s. 3 states:

If a person drives a mechanically propelled vehicle on a road or other public place without due care and attention, or without reasonable consideration for other persons using the road or place, he is guilty of an offence.

KEYNOTE

The elements in relation to 'due care and attention' are discussed at **para. 3.21.6.1**.

Where a constable in uniform has reasonable grounds for believing that a mechanically propelled vehicle is being used or has been used on any occasion in a manner which contravenes s. 3 or 34 (off-road driving) and is causing (or is likely to cause) alarm, distress or annoyance to members of the public, the constable has the powers set out in the Police Reform Act 2002, s. 59 which states:

59 Vehicles used in manner causing alarm, distress or annoyance

(1) Where a constable in uniform has reasonable grounds for believing that a motor vehicle is being used on any occasion in a manner which—

(a) contravenes section 3 or 34 of the Road Traffic Act 1988 (c. 52) (careless and inconsiderate driving and prohibition of off-road driving), and

(b) is causing, or is likely to cause, alarm, distress or annoyance to members of the public,

he shall have the powers set out in subsection (3).

(2) A constable in uniform shall also have the powers set out in subsection (3) where he has reasonable grounds for believing that a motor vehicle has been used on any occasion in a manner falling within subsection (1).

(3) Those powers are—

(a) power, if the motor vehicle is moving, to order the person driving it to stop the vehicle;

(b) power to seize and remove the motor vehicle;

(c) power, for the purposes of exercising a power falling within paragraph (a) or (b), to enter any premises on which he has reasonable grounds for believing the motor vehicle to be;

(d) power to use reasonable force, if necessary, in the exercise of any power conferred by any of paragraphs to (a) to (c).

(4) A constable shall not seize a motor vehicle in the exercise of the powers conferred on him by this section unless—

(a) he has warned the person appearing to him to be the person whose use falls within subsection (1) that he will seize it, if that use continues or is repeated; and

(b) it appears to him that the use has continued or been repeated after the warning.

(5) Subsection (4) does not require a warning to be given by a constable on any occasion on which he would otherwise have the power to seize a motor vehicle under this section if—

(a) the circumstances make it impracticable for him to give the warning;

(b) the constable has already on that occasion given a warning under that subsection in respect of any use of that motor vehicle or of another motor vehicle by that person or any other person;

(c) the constable has reasonable grounds for believing that such a warning has been given on that occasion otherwise than by him; or

(d) the constable has reasonable grounds for believing that the person whose use of that motor vehicle on that occasion would justify the seizure is a person to whom a warning under that subsection has been given (whether or not by that constable or in respect the same vehicle or the same or a similar use) on a previous occasion in the previous twelve months.

(6) A person who fails to comply with an order under subsection (3)(a) is guilty of an offence and shall be liable, on summary conviction, to a fine not exceeding level 3 on the standard scale.

(7) Subsection (3)(c) does not authorise entry into a private dwelling house.

(8) The powers conferred on a constable by this section shall be exercisable only at a time when regulations under section 60 are in force.

(9) In this section—

'driving' has the same meaning as in the Road Traffic Act 1988 (c. 52);

'motor vehicle' means any mechanically propelled vehicle, whether or not it is intended or adapted for use on roads; and

'private dwelling house' does not include any garage or other structure occupied with the dwelling house, or any land appurtenant to the dwelling house.

3.21.9.1 Factors Affecting Offence of Careless Driving

Evidence of earlier incidents involving careless or inconsiderate driving around the same time as the offence charged may be admissible to support that charge under some circumstances (*Hallett* v *Warren* (1926) 93 JP 225) as it may if the offence is charged as one continuing offence (*Horrix* v *Malam* [1984] RTR 112).

If a witness reports the driver of an unidentified vehicle as having committed a driving offence, it is critical that the witness provides direct evidence of what he/she actually saw. It would not be enough to produce evidence from the police to show that they had received details of the vehicle which they subsequently traced back to the driver. Both vehicle *and* driver must be linked by admissible and relevant evidence (*Ahmed* v *DPP* [1998] RTR 90).

If a driver falls asleep at the wheel, he/she will be guilty of careless driving (*Henderson* v *Jones* (1955) 119 JP 304) but evidence of this fact from the driver alone will not be enough to support a charge under s. 3 (*Edwards* v *Clarke* (1951) 115 JPN 426).

Responding to an Emergency Situation

If a motorist takes action in response to an emergency situation, his/her actions are to be judged against what was a 'reasonable' course of action in those circumstances in assessing whether or not the driving amounted to an offence (*R* v *Bristol Crown Court, ex parte Jones* [1986] RTR 259).

Relevance of Breaching Road Traffic Regulations

Breaching certain road traffic regulations will always be potentially relevant evidence of poor driving but will not always be conclusive of the issue. For instance, although colliding with another vehicle has been held not to amount to sufficient evidence in itself of careless driving, crossing a central white line without explanation has done so (*Mundi* v *Warwickshire Police* [2001] EWHC 448 (Admin)). (See also *Bensley* v *Smith* [1972] Crim LR 239.) However, simply breaching the regulations at a pedestrian crossing is not of itself proof that the person's driving fell below the required standard (*Gibbons* v *Kahl* [1956] 1 QB 59). On the other hand, just because a traffic signal is showing a green light does not mean that a driver is entitled to assume that no other person or vehicle might be proceeding from another direction and it may be that, in the circumstances, a reasonably careful driver would have anticipated that a pedestrian or other road user might still move into his/her path (*Goddard and Walker* v *Greenwood* [2002] EWCA Civ 1590).

3.21.10 The Highway Code

One way of illustrating the standard of driving expected of a prudent and competent driver is through the Highway Code. Section 38 of the Road Traffic Act 1988 states:

> (7) A failure on the part of a person to observe a provision of the Highway Code shall not of itself render that person liable to criminal proceedings of any kind but any such failure may in any proceedings (whether civil or criminal, and including proceedings for an offence under the Traffic Acts, the Public Passenger Vehicles Act 1981 or sections 18 to 23 of the Transport Act 1985) be relied upon by any party to the proceedings as tending to establish or negative any liability which is in question in those proceedings.

KEYNOTE

The Highway Code gives motorists and road users guidance on all manner of practical and safety issues, and in particular advice in relation to considerate driving and the proper use of headlights, horns and indicators. The Code also gives advice on police stopping procedures. The provisions of the Highway Code, while certainly not conclusive, may still merit careful consideration as guidance as to the standards to be attributed to a competent and careful driver (*R* v *Taylor* [2004] EWCA Crim 213).

However, as the Court of Appeal has reminded us, breach of the Highway Code does not necessarily mean that an offence has been committed (*R* v *Conteh (Kondeh)* [2003] EWCA Crim 962).

The braking distances shown in the Highway Code, however, are not admissible in proving speeding cases as they amount to hearsay (*R* v *Chadwick* [1975] Crim LR 105).

3.21.10.1 The Highway Code Update

The Highway Code was updated in 2022. The update focuses on vulnerable groups with specific consideration on overtaking, passing distances, cyclist and pedestrian priority at junctions, opening vehicle doors and responsibility of road users. There are three main changes:

- introducing a hierarchy of road users which ensures that those road users who can do the greatest harm have the greatest responsibility to reduce the danger or threat they may pose to others;
- clarifying existing rules on pedestrian priority on pavements and that drivers and riders should give way to pedestrians crossing or waiting to cross the road;
- establishing guidance on safe passing distances and speeds when overtaking cyclists or horse riders, and ensuring that they have priority at junctions when travelling straight ahead.

Rule H1

- Rule H1: it is important that all road users are aware of the Highway Code, are considerate to other road users and understand their responsibility for the safety of others.
- 'Hierarchy of Road Users' ensures that those road users who can do the greatest harm have the greatest responsibility to reduce the danger or threat they may pose to other road users. The objective of the hierarchy is not to give priority to pedestrians, cyclists and horse riders in every situation, but rather to ensure a more mutually respectful and considerate culture of safe and effective road use that benefits all users.

Everyone suffers when road collisions occur, whether they are physically injured or not. But those in charge of vehicles that can cause the greatest harm in the event of a collision bear the greatest responsibility to take care and reduce the danger they pose to others. This principle applies most strongly to drivers of large goods and passenger vehicles, followed by vans/minibuses, cars/taxis and motorcycles.

Cyclists, horse riders and horse-drawn vehicles likewise have a responsibility to reduce danger to pedestrians. Road users must remember that the people they encounter may have impaired sight, hearing or mobility, and may not be able to see or hear them.

None of this detracts from the responsibility of all road users, including pedestrians, cyclists and horse riders, to have regard for their own and other road users' safety.

Rule H2

- Rule H2: this rule creates clearer and stronger priorities for pedestrians, particularly at junctions, and clarifies where pedestrians have right of way.

At a junction, drivers should give way to pedestrians crossing or waiting to cross a road into which or from which they are turning.

Drivers must give way to pedestrians on a zebra crossing and to pedestrians and cyclists on a parallel crossing.

Drivers should give way to pedestrians waiting to cross a zebra crossing and to pedestrians and cyclists waiting to cross a parallel crossing.

Pedestrians have priority when on a zebra crossing, on a parallel crossing or at light-controlled crossings when they have a green signal.

Cyclists should give way to pedestrians on shared-use cycle tracks. Only pedestrians may use the pavement. This includes people using wheelchairs and mobility scooters. Pedestrians may use any part of the road and use cycle tracks as well as the pavement, unless there are signs prohibiting pedestrians.

Rule H3

- Rule H3: this rule places a requirement on drivers to give priority to cyclists when they are turning into or out of a junction, or changing direction or lane, just as they would to other motor vehicles.

Drivers should not cut across cyclists going ahead when turning into or out of a junction or changing direction or lane, just as they would not turn across the path of another motor vehicle. This applies whether cyclists are using a cycle lane, a cycle track or riding ahead on the road and drivers should give way to them.

Drivers should not turn at a junction if to do so would cause the cyclist going straight ahead to stop or swerve, just as they would do with a motor vehicle.

Drivers should stop and wait for a safe gap in the flow of cyclists if necessary. This includes when cyclists are:

- approaching, passing or moving off from a junction;
- moving past or waiting alongside stationary or slow-moving traffic;
- travelling around a roundabout.

3.21.10.2 The Highway Code Update—Using the Road

The 'Using the road' chapter of the Highway Code has been updated to:

- reinforce the message that drivers have a duty of care towards cyclists, pedestrians and horse riders and should give way to these road users;
- establish clear priority rules at traffic signal junctions;
- provide advice on interactions between drivers and cyclists at roundabouts and at different types of junctions;
- introduce safe passing distances and speed limits when overtaking pedestrians, cyclists, horse riders, horse-drawn vehicles and motorcyclists.

The new text in the 'Using the road' chapter of the Highway Code updates:

- rule 160 to advise that drivers give way to cyclists when they are changing direction or lane;
- rule 163 on overtaking to advise that cyclists may pass slower moving or stationary traffic on the right or left, including at the approach to junctions.

Guidance is provided in respect of overtaking distance which requires motorcyclists, cyclists, horse riders and horse-drawn vehicles to leave at least as much room as they would when overtaking a car. As a guide they should:

- leave a minimum distance of 1.5 metres at speeds under 30 mph;
- leave a minimum distance of 2.0 metres at speeds over 30 mph;
- large vehicles should leave a minimum distance of 2.0 metres in all conditions;
- pass horse riders and horse-drawn vehicles at speeds under 15 mph and allow at least 2.0 metres of space;
- allow at least 2.0 metres of space where a pedestrian is walking in the road (e.g. where there is no pavement) and pass them at low speed;

- wait behind the motorcyclist, cyclist, horse rider, horse-drawn vehicle or pedestrian and not overtake if it is unsafe or not possible to meet these clearances;
- take extra care and give more space when overtaking motorcyclists, cyclists, horse riders, horse-drawn vehicles and pedestrians in bad weather (including high winds) and at night.

3.21.11 Road Safety Strategy

In January 2026, a consultation on a new Road Safety Strategy was launched by the government. The strategy proposes major reforms to improve road safety. Focus areas within the consultation include lowering the drink-drive limit, introducing alcohol-interlock devices and granting police new powers to suspend driving licences for suspected drink or drug drivers.

The consultation is proposed for a 12-month duration. However, there is no confirmation on any proposed changes in law or practice. Likewise, there is no confirmed implementation date.

3.22 Drink, Drugs and Driving

3.22.1 Introduction

This chapter examines offences, powers and procedures associated with drink, drugs and driving. Specifically, the chapter deals with offences of driving, attempting to drive and being in charge of a mechanically propelled vehicle/motor vehicle under ss. 4 to 5 of the Act, preliminary test powers, procedures, offences and powers of arrest and entry under s. 6 of the Act, obtaining evidential specimens and associated offences under ss. 7 and 9 of the Act and the power to detain a person in certain circumstances under s. 10 of the Act.

3.22.2 Unfit through Drink or Drugs

OFFENCE: **Driving or Attempting to Drive a Mechanically Propelled Vehicle when Unfit through Drink or Drugs—*Road Traffic Act 1988, s. 4(1)***

- Triable summarily • Six months' imprisonment and/or a fine
- Obligatory disqualification—minimum 12 months

The Road Traffic Act 1988, s. 4 states:

> (1) A person who, when driving or attempting to drive a mechanically propelled vehicle on a road or other public place, is unfit to drive through drink or drugs is guilty of an offence.

OFFENCE: **Being in Charge of a Mechanically Propelled Vehicle when Unfit through Drink or Drugs—*Road Traffic Act 1988, s. 4(2)***

- Triable summarily • Three months' imprisonment and/or a fine • Discretionary disqualification

The Road Traffic Act 1988, s. 4 states:

> (2) Without prejudice to subsection (1) above, a person who, when in charge of a mechanically propelled vehicle which is on a road or other public place, is unfit to drive through drink or drugs is guilty of an offence.

KEYNOTE

Section 4 creates three separate offences. For the definitions of 'driving', 'attempting to drive' and 'in charge' and the other relevant terms used in this offence, see chapter 3.19.

It will not be enough to rely on a suspicion that the defendant *had been driving* in order to prove the offence. Suspicion may be enough to trigger powers to require preliminary tests or powers of entry; it will not, however, be enough to prove the required element of driving/attempting to drive/being in charge for the purposes of prosecuting the relevant offence (*R (On the Application of Huntley)* v *DPP* [2004] EWHC 870 (Admin)).

The power of entry in connection with an offence under s. 4 is found in s. 17(1)(c)(iiia) of the Police and Criminal Evidence Act 1984 which states:

> Subject to the following provisions of this section, and without prejudice to any other enactment, a constable may enter and search any premises for the purpose of arresting a person for an offence under
>
> ...

(iiia) section 4 (driving etc. when under influence of drink or drugs) or s. 163 (failure to stop when required to do so by constable in uniform) of the Road Traffic Act 1988.

The power of entry is only exercisable if the constable has reasonable grounds for believing that the person sought is on the premises (s. 17(2)(a)).

Under s. 4:

(3) ... a person shall be deemed not to have been in charge of a mechanically propelled vehicle if he proves that at the material time the circumstances were such that there was no likelihood of his driving it so long as he remained unfit to drive through drink or drugs.

KEYNOTE

This is only a defence to 'being in charge' of the vehicle while unfit; it is not a defence to 'driving' or 'attempting to drive' while unfit. There is a need to distinguish between 'attempting to drive' and being 'in charge'. An attempt must be 'more than merely preparatory' to the act of driving. In *Mason* v *DPP* [2009] EWHC 2198 (Admin), the court held that opening a car door was merely preparatory to the act of driving and not an actual attempt to drive.

The onus is on the defendant to prove the fact that there was 'no likelihood' of driving. However, in determining whether the defendant was likely to drive the vehicle while unfit, a court may disregard any injury to the defendant or damage to the vehicle (s. 4(4)).

The likelihood of driving is not an element of the offence itself; the intention of the defendant is material only to the statutory defence, which the defendant is required to prove on a balance of probabilities (*CPS* v *Bate* [2004] EWHC 2811 (Admin)).

3.22.2.1 Drugs

'Drugs' will include any intoxicant other than alcohol (s. 11); toluene found in some glues will amount to such a drug (*Bradford* v *Wilson* (1984) 78 Cr App R 77) as would insulin (*Armstrong* v *Clark* [1957] 2 QB 391). In *R* v *Ealing Magistrates' Court, ex parte Woodman* [1994] RTR 189, the conviction of a diabetic suffering a hypoglycaemic attack was quashed because there was no evidence entitling the stipendiary magistrate to conclude that the presence of insulin in the applicant's blood was the real effective cause of the attack. The Divisional Court held that it would only be appropriate to rely on s. 4 in such cases where there is evidence of a clear overdose of insulin having been taken by the defendant.

3.22.2.2 Evidence of Impairment

A person shall be taken to be unfit to drive if his/her ability to drive properly is for the time being impaired (s. 4(5)).

Evidence of impairment is therefore essential and must be produced by the prosecution—this may be by expert opinion or by the evidence of a lay witness.

Impairment of ability to drive properly can be proved by evidence that a car was being driven erratically or had an accident at a spot where there was no hazard for a normal driver, provided, of course, that there is also evidence of drink or drugs. Opinion evidence of the defendant's state or the amount drunk by the defendant may be given by any 'lay' witness and does not require expert testimony, although such a witness cannot give evidence as to the defendant's ability to drive (*R* v *Lanfear* [1968] 2 QB 77). Witnesses who are not experts can give their general impression as to whether a person has had a drink (*R* v *Davies* [1962] 1 WLR 1111).

While it may be desirable (where unfitness to drive through drugs is at issue) that expert medical evidence is provided as to the defendant's degree of impairment, a lack of such evidence is not fatal to a prosecution. In *Leetham* v *DPP* [1999] RTR 29, the Divisional Court upheld a conviction under s. 4(1) based on the defendant's fast and erratic driving, his admitted consumption of cannabis, the presence of cannabis in his blood on subsequent analysis, the known effects of the drug and the evidence of the officers who stopped him that his eyes were red and glazed and that his speech was slow and slurred.

Evidence of impairment may be provided by the opinion evidence of an expert witness, normally a doctor, who has examined the defendant, even if the defendant has refused to be examined, and the expert's testimony should be treated as that of any 'independent expert witness giving evidence to assist the court', whether a police surgeon or anyone else (*Lanfear*).

It is not necessary to show what quantity of alcohol or drug the defendant had in his/her system for this offence. Therefore there is no need for any form of breath test, although the prosecution may adduce evidence of the amount of alcohol or a drug in a specimen properly provided by the defendant under s. 7 of the Road Traffic Act 1988.

However, the police powers under s. 4 do not 'fall away' if you do embark on the procedure under s. 6 (e.g. requiring a breath sample: **see para. 3.22.4**). This was made clear in the decision of the Administrative Court in *DPP* v *Robertson* [2002] EWHC 542 (Admin). In that case, the officers had breathalysed the defendant who produced a negative result. However, on talking to the officers further, the defendant slurred his speech when giving the name of his solicitor. The officers then arrested the defendant under s. 4 (**see para. 3.22.2**) and took him to a police station where he provided an evidential sample of breath which was over the prescribed limit. The magistrates held that the defendant had been unlawfully arrested and the prosecutor appealed on a number of grounds. The Administrative Court held that it was quite conceivable to have a case where, notwithstanding that a driver had given a negative screening breath test, he/she was seen moments later staggering in a way that gave rise to a suspicion of unfitness. In such a case, the law (s. 4) clearly gave a constable a power to arrest if what the constable had witnessed amounted to reasonable cause to suspect that the person was impaired.

3.22.3 Over Prescribed Limit

OFFENCE: **Driving or Attempting to Drive a Motor Vehicle while Over the Prescribed Limit—*Road Traffic Act 1988, s. 5(1)(a)***

- Triable summarily • Six months' imprisonment and/or a fine
- Obligatory disqualification—minimum 12 months

The Road Traffic Act 1988, s. 5 states:

(1) If a person—
(a) drives or attempts to drive a motor vehicle on a road or other public place,
...
after consuming so much alcohol that the proportion of it in his breath, blood or urine exceeds the prescribed limit he is guilty of an offence.

OFFENCE: **Being in Charge of a Motor Vehicle while Over the Prescribed Limit—*Road Traffic Act 1988, s. 5(1)(b)***

- Triable summarily • Three months' imprisonment and/or a fine
- Discretionary disqualification

The Road Traffic Act 1988, s. 5 states:

(1) If a person—
(a) ...
(b) is in charge of a motor vehicle on a road or other public place,
after consuming so much alcohol that the proportion of it in his breath, blood or urine exceeds the prescribed limit he is guilty of an offence.

OFFENCE: **Driving or Attempting to Drive a Motor Vehicle with Concentration of Specified Controlled Drug above Specified Limit—*Road Traffic Act 1988, s. 5A(1)(a)***

- Triable summarily • Six months' imprisonment and/or a fine
- Obligatory disqualification—minimum 12 months

The Road Traffic Act 1988, s. 5A states:

> (1) This section applies where a person ('D')—
> (a) drives or attempts to drive a motor vehicle on a road or other public place, or
> ...
> and there is in D's body a specified controlled drug.
> (2) D is guilty of an offence if the proportion of the drug in D's blood or urine exceeds the specified limit for that drug ...

OFFENCE: **Being in Charge of a Motor Vehicle with Concentration of Specified Controlled Drug above Specified Limit—*Road Traffic Act 1988, s. 5A(1)(b)***

- Triable summarily • Three months' imprisonment and/or a fine
- Discretionary disqualification

The Road Traffic Act 1988, s. 5A states:

> (1) This section applies where a person ('D')—
> ...
> (b) is in charge of a motor vehicle on a road or other public place,
> and there is in D's body a specified controlled drug.
> (2) D is guilty of an offence if the proportion of the drug in D's blood or urine exceeds the specified limit for that drug ...

KEYNOTE

These offences apply to *motor vehicles* as defined in chapter 3.19.

Driving etc. Exceeding the Prescribed Limit—Alcohol

'Consuming' is not restricted to drinking and will encompass other methods of getting alcohol into the bloodstream (*DPP* v *Johnson* [1995] RTR 9).

The prescribed limit is:

- 35 microgrammes of alcohol in 100 millilitres of breath;
- 80 milligrammes of alcohol in 100 millilitres of blood;
- 107 milligrammes of alcohol in 100 millilitres of urine.

Section 11(2) which sets out these limits also allows for the levels to be changed.

The prosecution has to establish that the defendant's breath-alcohol content exceeded the permitted maximum; it does not have to establish a specific figure (*Gordon* v *Thorpe* [1986] RTR 358). The meaning of the word 'breath' in s. 5(1) of the 1988 Act is not confined to 'deep lung' air and should be given its dictionary definition of 'air exhaled from any thing' (*Zafar* v *DPP* [2004] EWHC 2468 (Admin)).

When dealing with the offence under s. 5(1)(b), it will be important to remember the statutory defence (see para. 3.22.3.1). The effect of this is that police officers investigating offences of being 'in charge' will have to ensure that a defendant is interviewed properly and fully as to all the circumstances, taking particular care to establish that the defendant is fully sober at the time of interview and establishing that there was a real risk of the defendant driving the vehicle while still over the prescribed limit.

The Divisional Court has held that there is some positive duty on a person to inquire whether a drink contains alcohol before drinking it if that person intends to drive afterwards (*Robinson* v *DPP* [2003] EWHC 2718 (Admin)).

The prescribed limits for drugs are inserted by the Drug Driving (Specified Limits) (England and Wales) Regulations 2014 (SI 2014/2868).

Driving etc. Exceeding the Specified Limit—Drugs

Drug	Limit (microgrammes per litre of blood)
Amphetamine	250
Benzoylecgonine	50
Clonazepam	50
Cocaine	10
Delta-9-Tetrahydrocannabinol	2
Diazepam	550
Flunitrazepam	300
Ketamine	20
Lorazepam	100
Lysergic Acid Diethylamide	1
Methadone	500
Methylamphetamine	10
Methylenedioxymethamphetamine	10
6-Monoacetylmorphine	5
Morphine	80
Oxazepam	300
Temazepam	1000

These are the limits described in s. 5A as 'specified limit for that drug'.

A device known as 'Drugwipe' is the first portable device that can detect the presence of cannabis (delta-9-tetrahydrocannabinol) and cocaine—two of the most common substances used by drug drivers. This would be the device that would be used when conducting a preliminary drug test (see para. 3.22.4).

3.22.3.1 Defences

The Road Traffic Act 1988, s. 5 states:

(2) It is a defence for a person charged with an offence under subsection (1)(b) above to prove that at the time he is alleged to have committed the offence the circumstances were such that there was no likelihood of his driving the vehicle whilst the proportion of alcohol in his breath, blood or urine remained likely to exceed the prescribed limit.

(3) The court may, in determining whether there was such a likelihood as is mentioned in subsection (2) above, disregard any injury to him and any damage to the vehicle.

The Road Traffic Act 1988, s. 5A states:

(6) It is a defence for a person ('D') charged with an offence by virtue of subsection (1)(b) to prove that at the time D is alleged to have committed the offence the circumstances were such that there was no likelihood of D driving the vehicle whilst the proportion of the specified controlled drug in D's blood or urine remained likely to exceed the specified limit for that drug.

(7) The court may, in determining whether there was such a likelihood, disregard any injury to D and any damage to the vehicle.

KEYNOTE

This is effectively the same defence based around the likelihood of driving as it relates to driving whilst the alcohol in breath, blood or urine remained likely to exceed the prescribed limit or whilst the proportion of a specified controlled drug in blood or urine remained likely to exceed the specified limit for that drug.

There is existing case law, decided at the time for alcohol only, but as the details relate to the essentials of 'likelihood of driving' this case law should be arguable in relation to the drug-driving offence.

A good example of this defence in operation is the case of *CPS* v *Bate* [2004] EWHC 2811 (Admin). In that case, the defendant had been found in a car with the keys to the ignition in his hand. Following a positive breath test, he appeared at court charged under s. 5(1)(b). The defendant argued that he had only been in the car for the purpose of retrieving a disabled permit before ringing his wife to arrange a taxi for him to get home. Although the magistrates' court accepted this account, the CPS argued that they were wrong to do so. The Divisional Court held that the magistrates had treated the likelihood of driving as an element of the offence itself. The court held that this was the wrong approach; that the defendant had manifestly been 'in charge' of the vehicle and had also been over the prescribed limit. Therefore the likelihood of the defendant driving the vehicle while still over the limit was only relevant if and when he raised the statutory defence. If he chose to rely on that defence, the usual considerations with regard to standards of proof (set out later) would then apply.

The presence of a wheel clamp on a motor vehicle could not be discounted by the Divisional Court when considering the likelihood of the person being able to drive it while over the limit. The defendant had refused to pay the fee to have the wheel clamp on his car removed and, while this did not constitute damage to the vehicle (as the clamp did not intrude on the integrity of the vehicle), the court held that there was no likelihood of him driving the vehicle (*Drake* v *DPP* [1994] Crim LR 855).

This defence was subjected to considerable scrutiny in a case where a defendant was found asleep in a van and, on being breathalysed, provided a reading that showed his alcohol-to-breath ratio to be four times the legal limit. The defendant claimed that there had been no likelihood of him driving while over the prescribed limit but the magistrates did not accept that he had proved the point sufficiently. The defendant then argued that the application of s. 5(2) was contrary to Article 6(2) of the European Convention on Human Rights (the presumption of innocence). Although the Divisional Court failed to agree at the first hearing and were still not unanimous on the second occasion, the majority decision was that the defence could be read as follows: 'It is a defence for a person charged with an offence under s. 5(1)(b) *to demonstrate from the evidence an arguable case that* at the time he is alleged to have committed the offence etc.' (emphasis added). Therefore, once the prosecution proves the elements of the offence beyond a reasonable doubt, the defendant must demonstrate an arguable case that there was no likelihood of his/her driving the vehicle while still over the prescribed limit. Once the defendant does this, the prosecution must then prove beyond a reasonable doubt that there was such a likelihood (*Sheldrake* v *DPP* [2003] EWHC 273 (Admin)). This case came before the House of Lords as *Attorney-General's Reference (No. 4 of 2002) (Sheldrake v DPP)* [2004] UKHL 43. There it was held that although the subsection did in fact infringe the presumption of innocence, the burden placed on the defendant was reasonable because it was in pursuance of a legitimate aim. The likelihood of the defendant driving was a matter that was so closely linked to his/her own knowledge at the relevant time that it made it much more appropriate for the defendant to prove, on the balance of probabilities, that he/she would not have been likely to drive (as opposed to requiring the prosecution to prove the opposite, beyond a reasonable doubt).

The Road Traffic Act 1988, s. 5A states:

(3) It is a defence for a person ('D') charged with an offence under this section to show that—
- (a) the specified controlled drug had been prescribed or supplied to D for medical or dental purposes,
- (b) D took the drug in accordance with any directions given by the person by whom the drug was prescribed or supplied, and with any accompanying instructions (so far as consistent with any such directions) given by the manufacturer or distributor of the drug, and
- (c) D's possession of the drug immediately before taking it was not unlawful under section 5(1) of the Misuse of Drugs Act 1971 (restriction of possession of controlled drugs) because of an exemption in regulations made under section 7 of that Act (authorisation of activities otherwise unlawful under foregoing provisions) ...

(4) The defence in subsection (3) is not available if D's actions were—
- (a) contrary to any advice, given by the person by whom the drug was prescribed or supplied, about the amount of time that should elapse between taking the drug and driving a motor vehicle, or
- (b) contrary to any accompanying instructions about that matter (so far as consistent with any such advice) given by the manufacturer or distributor of the drug.

(5) If evidence is adduced that is sufficient to raise an issue with respect to the defence in subsection (3), the court must assume that the defence is satisfied unless the prosecution proves beyond reasonable doubt that it is not ...

KEYNOTE

This 'medical defence' will be available where:

- the drug was lawfully prescribed, supplied, or purchased over the counter, for medical or dental purposes; and
- the drug was taken in accordance with advice given by the person who prescribed or supplied the drug, and in accordance with any accompanying written instructions (so far as the latter are consistent with any advice of the prescriber).

The effect of s. 5A(4) is that prescribers and suppliers of medicines should give suitable clinical advice to patients regarding the time that should elapse after taking the drug supplied and before driving, and drivers should be aware of any instructions provided with the medication in relation to this. Failing to adhere to this advice/instructions means the defence at s. 5A(3) is not available.

Once raised, the court will assume the defence is satisfied unless the prosecution proves that it is not to criminal standards.

3.22.4 Preliminary Tests

The relevant police powers now provide for three different types of preliminary test, set out under ss. 6A, 6B and 6C of the Road Traffic Act 1988.

The Road Traffic Act 1988, s. 6 states:

(1) If any of subsections (2) to (5) applies a constable may require a person to co-operate with any one or more preliminary tests administered to the person by that constable or another constable.

(2) This subsection applies if a constable reasonably suspects that the person—
  (a) is driving, is attempting to drive or is in charge of a motor vehicle on a road or other public place, and
  (b) has alcohol or a drug in his body or is under the influence of a drug.

(3) This subsection applies if a constable reasonably suspects that the person—
  (a) has been driving, attempting to drive or in charge of a motor vehicle on a road or other public place while having alcohol or a drug in his body or while unfit to drive because of a drug, and
  (b) still has alcohol or a drug in his body or is still under the influence of a drug.

(4) This subsection applies if a constable reasonably suspects that the person—
  (a) is or has been driving, attempting to drive or in charge of a motor vehicle on a road or other public place, and
  (b) has committed a traffic offence while the vehicle was in motion.

KEYNOTE

These powers allow the police to administer three preliminary tests: a breathalyser test, a test indicating whether a person is unfit to drive due to drink or drugs and a test (a 'drug-wipe') to detect the presence of drugs in the person's body.

As s. 6(1) refers to 'any one or more preliminary tests', it is clear that they are not mutually exclusive and the constable could require cooperation with each of the tests in turn, if only to eliminate any suspicion in relation to alcohol or a drug.

The requirement must be made using words of sufficient clarity although there is no set format for any particular words to be uttered.

Although the *requesting* police officer does not have to be in uniform, the officer *administering* a preliminary test under s. 6(2)–(4) *must be in uniform* (s. 6(7)). This means that the officer administering the test must be in uniform whatever test is being administered (preliminary breath test, impairment test or drug test).

The circumstances fall into the three main categories set out at s. 6(2)–(4), with the final category (under s. 6(5)) relating to accidents (**see para. 3.22.4.3**). It can be seen from the previous categories that they involve:

- the present—someone who is reasonably suspected to be driving, attempting to drive or being in charge of a motor vehicle on a road or other public place, and of having alcohol or a drug in his/her body or being under the influence of a drug;
- the past—someone reasonably suspected of having been driving, attempting to drive or being in charge of a motor vehicle on a road or other public place while having alcohol or a drug in his/her body or while unfit to drive because of a drug, and who still has alcohol or a drug in his/her body or is still under the influence of a drug; and
- a combination of the past and present—someone who it is reasonably suspected is or has been driving, attempting to drive or in charge of a motor vehicle on a road or other public place, and who is reasonably suspected to have committed a traffic offence while the vehicle was in motion. 'Traffic offence' here means an offence under any provision of the Road Traffic Act 1988 (other than part V—driving instruction), the Road Traffic Offenders Act 1988, the Road Traffic Regulation Act 1984 and part II of the Public Passenger Vehicles Act 1981. Such offences, which include offences under any regulations made under those Acts, must have been committed while the vehicle was moving.

Random Tests

Although the police can use their powers to stop vehicles at random, the law in England and Wales does not permit entirely random testing of drivers for drink or drugs (**see para. 3.20.2** for an explanation of this area of law).

3.22.4.1 'Reasonably Suspects'

There is a distinction between 'reasonably suspects' and 'reasonably believes' and whether the constable reasonably suspected or believed a fact in issue will be determined in the light of all the available evidence. The distinction between the two expressions has been held to be a significant one, intended by Parliament (*Baker* v *Oxford* [1980] RTR 315). In that case, it was held that the deliberate use of the word 'believe' in the Act imposed a requirement for a greater degree of certainty in the mind of the officers concerned. While an officer might reasonably suspect someone has been drinking or taking drugs, a single error of judgement or carelessness on the part of a driver will not necessarily justify such a suspicion (see e.g. *Williams* v *Jones* [1972] RTR 4).

The importance of whether or not such suspicion or belief existed lies not only in triggering the relevant powers, it also has the potential to affect the nature of any conversation that might take place between the officer and a suspected driver. A good example of this can be seen in *R (On the Application of Ortega)* v *DPP* [2001] EWHC Admin 143. In that case, the officers were held not to have had reasonable grounds to suspect that any offence had been committed at the time they questioned the defendant about his ownership and driving of a particular car. The absence of such reasonable grounds to suspect an offence meant that the doorstep conversation, which was not contemporaneously recorded and some of which took place without caution, was nevertheless admissible.

The important factor to consider when examining cases such as *Ortega* is that there is a huge difference between *reasonably suspecting that a person has alcohol or a drug in his/her body or is under the influence of a drug* and *reasonably suspecting a person of committing an offence*—they are not the same thing. Reasonably suspecting that someone has alcohol/drug in his/her body does not trigger a requirement to caution a person before speaking to him/her in such circumstances. The reasonable suspicion in relation to the alcohol/drug may trigger the power to require a person to take part in a preliminary test. The result of that preliminary test, e.g. by providing a positive breath test, may then, in turn, provide the reasonable suspicion that the person has committed an offence and this suspicion triggers the need to caution along with other powers (such as the power of arrest and/or a power of entry). The screening test is indicative only and is only relevant as to whether a constable should arrest the suspect with a view to securing an evidential specimen thereafter.

With the above in mind, you can now understand why the Divisional Court has held that a 'roadside confession' before any caution was given is admissible where it was made prior to the driver being given a breath test (*Whelehan* v *DPP* [1995] RTR 177). In that case, the defendant was found sitting in the driver's seat of a car at the roadside with the keys in the ignition. On being approached by a police officer, he admitted that he had been drinking and was then asked if he had driven to that location. The driver replied that he had and was required to provide a roadside screening breath test which was positive. The driver was convicted of driving while over the prescribed limit. Dismissing his appeal, the court held that the time, place and circumstances in which he had been found afforded sufficient evidence to infer that he had driven to the scene, quite apart from the admission. The magistrates' court had been entitled to find that it was only *after* the roadside breath test that the police officer suspected an offence had been committed and therefore it was only then that the need to caution arose. This is exactly the situation described earlier—reasonable suspicion regarding the presence of alcohol/drug is not reasonable suspicion that someone has committed an offence.

Of course, if officers do reasonably suspect that someone has committed an offence in relation to drink/drive matters, they should caution the suspect as they would do in any other circumstances.

In addition to first-hand observation of a driver's behaviour, reasonable suspicion may arise from the observations of another officer (*Erskine* v *Hollin* [1971] RTR 199) and this is clearly provided for now in the extended wording of s. 6. Reasonable suspicion may even arise from information provided by a member of the public (*DPP* v *Wilson* [1991] RTR 284). An officer receiving a radio message that a driver had been seen driving erratically may thereby acquire enough reasonable suspicion to require the administering of one of the three preliminary tests on that basis.

3.22.4.2 The Tests

The Road Traffic Act 1988 states:

6A Preliminary breath test

(1) A preliminary breath test is a procedure whereby the person to whom the test is administered provides a specimen of breath to be used for the purpose of obtaining, by means of a device of a type approved by the Secretary of State, an indication whether the proportion of alcohol in the person's breath or blood is likely to exceed the prescribed limit.

(2) A preliminary breath test administered in reliance on section 6(2) to (4) may be administered only at or near the place where the requirement to co-operate with the test is imposed.

6B Preliminary impairment test

(1) A preliminary impairment test is a procedure whereby the constable administering the test—
  (a) observes the person to whom the test is administered in his performance of tasks specified by the constable, and
  (b) makes such other observations of the person's physical state as the constable thinks expedient.

...

(4) A preliminary impairment test may be administered—
  (a) at or near the place where the requirement to co-operate with the test is imposed, or
  (b) if the constable who imposes the requirement thinks it expedient, at a police station specified by him.

6C Preliminary drug test

(1) A preliminary drug test is a procedure by which a specimen of sweat or saliva is—

(a) obtained, and

(b) used for the purpose of obtaining, by means of a device of a type approved by the Secretary of State, an indication whether the person to whom the test is administered has a drug in his body and if so—

(i) whether it is a specified controlled drug;

(ii) if it is, whether the proportion of it in the person's blood or urine is likely to exceed the specified limit for that drug.

(2) A preliminary drug test may be administered—

(a) at or near the place where the requirement to co-operate with the test is imposed, or

(b) if the constable who imposes the requirement thinks it expedient, at a police station specified by him.

(3) Up to three preliminary drug tests may be administered.

KEYNOTE

The officer administering any of the tests above must be in uniform (s. 6(7)) (**see para. 3.20.2**). This uniform requirement does not apply in the case of preliminary tests following an accident (as to which, **see para. 3.22.4.3**).

The tests referred to at ss. 6A and 6C are for the purpose of obtaining, by means of a device of a type approved by the Secretary of State, an indication of whether the proportion of either alcohol or drugs in a person's breath or blood is likely to exceed the prescribed limit as it relates to alcohol or the specific drug. This is an important distinction as the preliminary test is undertaken only to give an indication to the officer administering it of the likelihood of the offence, not for proving the relevant offence. This is evident from the fact that the prosecution is not obliged to disclose to the defence the results in figures from a roadside test (*Smith* v *DPP* [2007] 4 All ER 1135).

Failure to comply with the manufacturer's instructions on the use of approved devices has always raised contentious points and will no doubt continue to do so. Generally, failing to follow the key instructions of the manufacturer, such as assembling the tube on a breathalyser or allowing the driver to smoke immediately before taking the test, has meant that the person has not provided a preliminary test and he/she may be asked to provide another; refusing to do so will be an offence (**see para. 3.22.4.4**) (*DPP* v *Carey* [1970] AC 1072). The Divisional Court also decided that an innocent failure by a police officer to follow the manufacturer's instructions should not be deemed to render either the test or any subsequent arrest unlawful (*DPP* v *Kay* [1999] RTR 109).

Evidential Breath Testing Instruments are computers. The law relating to them is the common law position which presumes that any mechanical or other device is working properly unless the contrary is proved (affirmed in *Clarke* v *CPS* [2013] EWHC 366 (Admin)).

Note that the legislation for preliminary breath tests prevents drivers from claiming an extra 20 minutes' grace by pretending that they have just had a drink (*Grant* v *DPP* [2003] EWHC 130 (Admin)). Similar efforts to manipulate the circumstances in the light of the relevant manufacturer's instructions for the other tests can be expected to receive similar treatment from the courts.

A preliminary breath test under s. 6A may only be administered at or near the place where the requirement to cooperate with the test is imposed unless it is made under the provisions relating to accidents (**see para. 3.22.4.3**). The other two tests, under ss. 6B and 6C, may be administered at or near the place where the requirement to cooperate is imposed or, if the constable imposing it thinks it expedient, at a police station specified by the constable. A preliminary impairment test under s. 6B is a completely different procedure from the other two and involves an appropriately trained police officer authorised by his/her chief officer observing the person performing specified tasks and that officer making such other observations of the person's physical state as he/she thinks 'expedient'. The types of tests are set out in a Code of Practice published by the Secretary of State and include pupillary examination, walk-and-turn tests and finger-to-nose tests. The police officer administering a preliminary impairment test must have regard to the Code of Practice (s. 6B(5)) and can only administer such a test if approved for that purpose by his/her chief officer (s. 6B(6)).

The preliminary drug test under s. 6C is introduced to enable officers to carry out a roadside test that detects drugs in the driver's body and up to three preliminary drug tests may be administered to ascertain whether the person has a specified controlled drug in his/her body and, if so, whether it is likely that it exceeds the specified limit.

3.22.4.3 Procedure Following an Accident

The Road Traffic Act 1988, s. 6 states:

(5) This subsection applies if—
  (a) an accident occurs owing to the presence of a motor vehicle on a road or other public place, and
  (b) a constable reasonably believes that the person was driving, attempting to drive or in charge of the vehicle at the time of the accident.

KEYNOTE

In relying on this section, you must show that an accident had 'occurred', i.e. it has in fact taken place, not simply that you suspected or even believed that to be the case (*Chief Constable of West Midlands Police* v *Billingham* [1979] RTR 446). It is important to emphasise that the meaning is not restricted to that given to a 'reportable' accident under s. 170.

The requirement here is for the officer to have a 'reasonable belief' that the person was driving, attempting to drive or in charge of a relevant vehicle at the time of an accident (for 'reasonable belief', **see para. 3.22.4.1**).

There is no need for the police officer making the requirement to believe or even suspect that the person has been drinking or that he/she has committed any offence; reasonable belief in his/her involvement (as a person driving, attempting to drive or being in charge of a vehicle) in the accident is enough. *Nor is there a need for the officer making the requirement or administering the preliminary test to be in uniform.*

A preliminary breath test (under s. 6A) administered under the previous provisions may be administered:

(a) at or near the place where the requirement to cooperate with the test is imposed; or
(b) if the constable who imposes the requirement thinks it expedient, at a police station specified by the constable (s. 6A(3)).

Note that there is no general power of entry in order to administer preliminary breath tests; however, there is a specific power of entry in relation to the above subsection (**see para. 3.22.4.6**).

Where an officer has imposed a requirement to cooperate with a preliminary breath test in circumstances where s. 6(5) applies, he/she may also require an evidential breath specimen under s. 7 (as to which, **see para. 3.22.5.1**) at or near the place where the preliminary breath test has been administered or would have been but for the person's failure to cooperate.

Where a constable imposes a requirement to cooperate with a preliminary breath test at any place, he/she is entitled to remain at or near that place in order to impose on the person a requirement for an evidential specimen under s. 7 (s. 7(2C)) there.

3.22.4.4 Failure to Cooperate with Preliminary Test

OFFENCE: **Failing to Co-operate with a Preliminary Test—*Road Traffic Act 1988, s. 6(6)***

- Triable summarily • Fine • Discretionary disqualification

The Road Traffic Act 1988, s. 6 states:

(6) A person commits an offence if without reasonable excuse he fails to co-operate with a preliminary test in pursuance of a requirement imposed under this section.

KEYNOTE

As with any requirement carrying a sanction for failure to comply, you must show that the requirement for the preliminary test was properly made in accordance with the relevant conditions set out earlier. It will also need to be shown that the person both heard and understood the requirement.

In *DPP* v *Crofton* (1994) RTR 265, it was held that the court should consider the following matters where 'reasonable excuse' is raised as a defence:

- medical evidence of physical or mental inability to provide the specimen;
- the causative link between the physical or mental condition and the failure to provide the specimen.

An example of 'reasonable excuse' would be where the defendant is physically unable to cooperate with the requirement or where to do so would entail a substantial risk to the defendant's health (see e.g. *R* v *Lennard* [1973] 1 WLR 483).

Failing includes a refusal (s. 11(2)).

A person does not cooperate with a preliminary test or provide a specimen of breath for analysis unless his/her cooperation or the specimen:

(a) is sufficient to allow the test or the analysis to be carried out; and
(b) is provided in such a way as to enable the objective of the test or analysis to be satisfactorily achieved (s. 11(3)).

Therefore, if the person does not follow the instructions given or does something which purports to fulfil the requirement made by the officer but which does not meet the criteria in s. 11(3), he/she has 'failed' to cooperate. However, it is not necessary for the officer to produce a breath test device before this offence can be committed. The person's attitude and conduct after being required to give a breath specimen under s. 6A may be sufficient to make out the offence above and the evidence of the officer witnessing this attitude or conduct may suffice as proof that it amounted to a failure or refusal. In the event that a person clearly does something which amounts to a refusal to provide a preliminary breath test, the offence will be made out even though the officer did not produce a device for doing so (*DPP* v *Swan* [2004] EWHC 2432 (Admin)).

Having been required to provide a specimen of breath, a person may also be required to wait until a device is brought to the scene; failing to wait for a reasonable time, or doing anything which demonstrates an intention not to provide the specimen, can amount to a 'failure' (*R* v *Wagner* [1970] Crim LR 535).

Simply producing enough breath to enable the device to give a positive reading does not necessarily mean the defendant has 'provided a specimen'; he/she must produce sufficient breath in the manner required to enable the device to give a reliable reading—positive or negative (*DPP* v *Heywood* [1998] RTR 1).

3.22.4.5 Powers of Arrest

The Road Traffic Act 1988, s. 6D states:

(1) A constable may arrest a person without warrant if as a result of a preliminary breath test or preliminary drug test the constable reasonably suspects that—
  (a) the proportion of alcohol in the person's breath or blood exceeds the prescribed limit, or
  (b) the person has a specified controlled drug in his body and the proportion of it in the person's blood or urine exceeds the specified limit for that drug.

(1A) ...

(2) A constable may arrest a person without warrant if—
  (a) the person fails to co-operate with a preliminary test in pursuance of a requirement imposed under section 6, and
  (b) the constable reasonably suspects that the person has alcohol or a drug in his body or is under the influence of a drug.

(2A) A person arrested under this section may, instead of being taken to a police station, be detained at or near the place where the preliminary test was, or would have been, administered, with a view to imposing on him there a requirement under section 7 of this Act.

(3) A person may not be arrested under this section while at a hospital as a patient.

KEYNOTE

The power of arrest is divided into two parts, neither of which requires the officer to be in uniform.

The first part relates to the situation where an officer (not necessarily the arresting officer) has administered a preliminary breath test under s. 6A or a preliminary drug test under s. 6C. If any officer reasonably suspects, as a result of that preliminary test, that the proportion of alcohol in the person's breath or blood exceeds the prescribed limit or a specified controlled drug in the person's blood or urine exceeds the specified limit for that drug, the officer may arrest the person without warrant. However, there is no obligation to do so.

Note that even where evidential specimens have been provided under s. 7, this does not prevent the power of arrest under s. 6D(1) from having effect (**see para. 3.22.5.1**).

The second part of the section allows any officer to arrest a person who fails to cooperate with any preliminary test imposed under s. 6 provided the officer reasonably suspects that the person has alcohol or a drug in his/her body or is under the influence of a drug. Without this reasonable suspicion, s. 6D(2) provides no power of arrest for failing to cooperate with a preliminary test.

Instead of, or before, arresting a person under this section, a constable may detain the person at or near the place where the preliminary test was, or would have been, administered with a view to imposing on the person there a requirement under s. 7.

3.22.4.6 Powers of Entry

There is a specific power of entry provided by the Road Traffic Act 1988, s. 6E as follows:

(1) A constable may enter any place (using reasonable force if necessary) for the purpose of—
   (a) imposing a requirement by virtue of section 6(5) following an accident in a case where the constable reasonably suspects that the accident involved injury of any person, or
   (b) arresting a person under section 6D following an accident in a case where the constable reasonably suspects that the accident involved injury of any person.

KEYNOTE

The wording of this subsection limits the purposes of entry to:

- Imposing a requirement for a preliminary test after an accident (s. 6(5)). To enter you must *know* there has been an accident, *suspect* that accident involved an injury to any person and *believe* that the person was driving/attempting to drive/in charge at the time of the accident.
- Arresting the person if, as a result of a preliminary breath or drug test, the officer reasonably suspects that the proportion of alcohol in the person's breath or blood exceeds the prescribed limit or the proportion of a specified drug in the person's blood or urine exceeds the specified limit (arrest under s. 6D(1)). To enter, you must *know* there has been an accident, *suspect* that the accident involved an injury to any person and *suspect* that the proportion of alcohol in the person's breath or blood exceeds the prescribed limit or the proportion of a specified drug in the person's blood or urine exceeds the specified limit.
- Arresting the person for failing to cooperate with a preliminary test where the officer reasonably suspects that the person has alcohol or a drug in his/her body or is under the influence of a drug (arrest under s. 6D(2)). To enter, you must *know* there has been an accident, *suspect* that the accident involved an injury to any person (the person must have failed to cooperate with any preliminary test) and you must *suspect* that the person has alcohol or a drug in his/her body or is under the influence of a drug.

3.22.4.7 Trespassing

Many legal arguments have raged over the legitimacy of a breath test carried out or requested where the officers concerned are in fact trespassing on the property of another. The results of these deliberations are:

- if police officers are trespassing *on the defendant's property*, they are not entitled to require a breath test (*R* v *Fox* [1986] AC 281);

- if the officers are trespassing at the time they make the requirement, any subsequent arrest made by them is unlawful (*Clowser* v *Chaplin* [1981] RTR 317);
- although the entry and the arrest may be unlawful, this will only affect the offence under s. 6(6) and not any other offences detected at the police station;
- any requirement for a sample of breath properly made, and any subsequent arrest, remains lawful *until* the officers become trespassers. A police officer, like any other member of the public, has an implied licence to go onto certain parts of someone's property (e.g. the front doorstep) unless and until that licence is withdrawn. If police officers go onto such a part of the defendant's property, they are not trespassing until told to leave and any requirement for a breath test, or any arrest made before this happens, will be lawful. (See *Pamplin* v *Fraser* [1981] RTR 494 where the defendant drove onto his own land and locked himself in his car. It was held that the officers' licence to enter the land had not been withdrawn at that stage.) Telling officers to 'fuck off' is not necessarily enough to withdraw this implied licence (*Snook* v *Mannion* [1982] RTR 321);
- a person cannot seek refuge on someone else's land as a trespasser; a requirement for a breath test and any subsequent arrest may be lawful if the person is a trespasser (*Morris* v *Beardmore* [1980] RTR 321);
- if a person has been lawfully arrested on his/her own land, officers may remain on the land and enter premises to recapture that person, even if asked to leave (*Hart* v *Chief Constable of Kent* [1983] Crim LR 117);
- although the provisions of s. 15(2) of the Road Traffic Offenders Act 1988 may render evidence from a specimen taken after an unlawful arrest admissible, any finding that the officer(s) concerned acted in a way that he/she knew to be unlawful or unwarranted may lead to that evidence being excluded under s. 78 of the Police and Criminal Evidence Act 1984 (*DPP* v *Godwin* [1991] RTR 303).

3.22.5 Evidential Specimens

Sections 7 to 9 of the Road Traffic Act 1988 govern the procedure for obtaining specimens for analysis, or evidential specimens. Unlike the preliminary breath tests discussed earlier, specimens taken under this part of the Act are retained for evidential purposes in subsequent hearings. Such specimens will either be by breath samples taken on an approved machine (e.g. the Lion Intoximeter or the Camic Breath Analyser) or by blood/urine samples.

Minor errors in the printing functions of such machines will not necessarily invalidate the evidence produced by the machine, provided it can be shown that the analytical function of the machine was calibrated and working properly (*Reid* v *DPP* [1999] RTR 357).

Many of the difficulties which have been encountered during the police station process have now been addressed by police forces adopting a national pro-forma and strict adherence to those forms will significantly reduce the likelihood of convictions being quashed.

3.22.5.1 Provision of Specimens for Analysis

The Road Traffic Act 1988, s. 7 states:

(1) In the course of an investigation into whether a person has committed an offence under section 3A, 4 or 5 of this Act a constable may, subject to the following provisions of this section and section 9 of this Act, require him—
  (a) to provide two specimens of breath for analysis by means of a device of a type approved by the Secretary of State, or
  (b) to provide a specimen of blood or urine for a laboratory test.

(1A) In the course of an investigation into whether a person has committed an offence under section 5A of this Act a constable may, subject to subsections (3) to (7) of this section and section 9 of this Act, require the person to provide a specimen of blood or urine for a laboratory test.

(2) A constable may make a requirement under this section to provide specimens of breath only if—
(a) the requirement is made at a police station or a hospital,
(b) the requirement is imposed in circumstances where section 6(5) of this Act applies, or
(c) the constable is in uniform.

. . .

(2C) Where a constable has imposed a requirement on the person concerned to co-operate with a relevant breath test at any place, he is entitled to remain at or near that place in order to impose on him there a requirement under this section.

(2CA) For the purposes of subsection (2C) 'a relevant breath test' is a procedure involving the provision by the person concerned of a specimen of breath to be used for the purpose of obtaining an indication whether the proportion of alcohol in his breath or blood is likely to exceed the prescribed limit.

(2D) If a requirement under subsection (1)(a) above has been made at a place other than at a police station, such a requirement may subsequently be made at a police station if (but only if)—
(a) a device or a reliable device of the type mentioned in subsection (1)(a) above was not available at that place or it was for any other reason not practicable to use such a device there, or
(b) the constable who made the previous requirement has reasonable cause to believe that the device used there has not produced a reliable indication of the proportion of alcohol in the breath of the person concerned.

(3) A requirement under this section to provide a specimen of blood or urine can only be made at a police station or at a hospital; and it cannot be made at a police station unless—
(a) the constable making the requirement has reasonable cause to believe that for medical reasons a specimen of breath cannot be provided or should not be required, or
(b) specimens of breath have not been provided elsewhere and at the time the requirement is made a device or a reliable device of the type mentioned in subsection (1)(a) above is not available at the police station or it is then for any other reason not practicable to use such a device there, or
(bb) a device of the type mentioned in subsection (1)(a) above has been used (at the police station or elsewhere) but the constable who required the specimens of breath has reasonable cause to believe that the device has not produced a reliable indication of the proportion of alcohol in the breath of the person concerned, or
(bc) as a result of the administration of a preliminary drug test, the constable making the requirement has reasonable cause to believe that the person required to provide a specimen of blood or urine has a drug in his body, or
(c) the suspected offence is one under section 3A, 4 or 5A of this Act and the constable making the requirement has been advised by a medical practitioner or a registered health care professional that the condition of the person required to provide the specimen might be due to some drug;

but may then be made notwithstanding that the person required to provide the specimen has already provided or been required to provide two specimens of breath.

(4) . . .

(5) A specimen of urine shall be provided within one hour of the requirement for its provision being made and after the provision of a previous specimen of urine.

(5A) A constable may arrest a person without warrant if—
(a) the person fails to provide a specimen of breath when required to do so in pursuance of this section, and
(b) the constable reasonably suspects that the person has alcohol in his body.

(6) A person who, without reasonable excuse, fails to provide a specimen when required to do so in pursuance of this section is guilty of an offence.

(7) A constable must, on requiring any person to provide a specimen in pursuance of this section, warn him that a failure to provide it may render him liable to prosecution.

KEYNOTE

As the evidential samples taken will form part of the case against a defendant, a lot of attention is paid to the device that was used and the extent to which its readings can be relied upon, as well as the due process to obtain such samples. To assist with this, a series of MG DD forms are used to assist the police officer in following due procedure. In *Afolayan* v *CPS* [2012] EWHC 1322 (Admin), although Form MG DD/A had not been properly completed, the Divisional Court concluded that the justices had evidence from the police and from what the analyst said about the specimen she received entitling them to prefer that evidence to the defendant's evidence that the blood sample taken from him had not been sealed, as required, in his presence.

There are detailed guidelines available to operators conducting evidential tests to ensure the reliability of the results produced. Just as a failure to follow the key requirements by the *defendant* can amount to a failure/refusal to provide, similarly a failure by the *operator* to follow such a requirement can allow the procedure to be challenged. However, in the latter case any failure must be such as to affect the *reliability* of the test. It is common for device manufacturers to issue guidelines that require a 20-minute period free from consumption of alcohol or other substances prior to the administration of the test. In *DPP* v *Carey* [1970] AC 1072, the House of Lords ruled that if an officer has no knowledge or reason to suspect consumption of any substances within the relevant 20-minute period, the test remains valid even if it later transpires that some substance was actually consumed during that 20-minute period. If the officer *does* have knowledge or reason to suspect such consumption, then 20 minutes should be allowed to elapse before administering the test. In *Coulter* v *DPP* [2005] EWHC 1533 (Admin), the defendant had provided a positive breath specimen during a roadside screening test. During the police station procedure to obtain an evidential specimen, the police officer asked if he had eaten anything. The defendant said he might have had a 'tic-tac' sweet. The officer nevertheless continued with the procedure and required a specimen of breath. The defendant refused and was charged under s. 7(6) of the Road Traffic Act 1988 (and the Road Traffic Offenders Act 1988, sch. 2). The police officer had been unaware of the guidelines recommending a 20-minute wait before testing a driver who had recently eaten before continuing with the procedure. The magistrates' court held that there was no case to answer as the officer should have waited 20 minutes before requiring a breath specimen and because the officer had been unable to show that the waiting period was not mandatory. On appeal by the DPP, the Divisional Court held that there was nothing in s. 7 to indicate that a requirement to produce a breath specimen was unlawful if the particular police guidelines were not followed. While it is possible for a failure to follow the guidelines to affect the reliability of a specimen, the court held that that was not relevant in the instant case as no specimen of breath was ever provided.

While the reliability of a reading made by any device in any particular case is always open to challenge by way of admissible evidence, a defendant does not have an automatic right to challenge the Secretary of State's approval of devices every time they are used (*DPP* v *Memery* [2002] EWHC 1720 (Admin)).

In the case of a breath specimen, it is presumed that the machine used was reliable; if that presumption is challenged by relevant evidence, the magistrates will have to be satisfied that the machine had provided a reading on which they could rely before they make the assumption (*DPP* v *Brown and Teixeira* [2001] EWHC 931 (Admin); *Cracknell* v *Willis* [1988] AC 450). This rebuttable presumption was tested by a well-known rugby player who argued on the grounds of only drinking an expresso martini that the machine was not reliable. The senior District Judge at Westminster Magistrates' Court disagreed and supported the decision in *Cracknell*. In *R (On the Application of Hassani)* v *West London Magistrates' Court* [2017] EWHC 1270 (Admin), the court affirmed and restated the decision of the Chief Magistrate and Senior District Judge in *CPS* v *Cipriani* [2016] giving extensive guidance in relation to the conduct of drink drive cases including case management at the first hearing, disclosure, expert witnesses and challenging the reliability of breath machines.

Where there are reasons to believe that a type of device is generally unreliable (as opposed to the specific device used in a particular case), representations should be made to the Secretary of State (*R* v *Skegness Magistrates' Court, ex parte Cardy* [1985] RTR 49); it is not open to magistrates to consider whether the type of device should be on the list of 'approved devices' because of some alleged general design flaw (*DPP* v *Brown and Teixeira*).

The Queen's Bench Division examined two cases where the machine gave an 'ambient fail' yet went on to give a positive result for a further, fresh sample. In the first case, the court held the sample was reliable despite the 'ambient fail' and allowed the roadside result to support the positive reading. In the second case, the appeal was allowed; however, this appears to be more linked to the drafting of the questions by the examining magistrate and the inconsistencies of the officers' evidence than the reliability of the machine. It seems the courts are unwilling to allow technical defences but remain strong on the actual procedure carried out (*DPP* v *Vince* [2016] EWHC 3014 (Admin)).

The fact that specimens of breath have been provided under s. 7 does not prevent the power of arrest (under s. 6D(1)—**see para. 3.22.4.6**) having effect if the constable who imposed the requirement to provide the specimens has reasonable cause to believe that the device used to analyse the specimens has not produced a reliable indication of the proportion of alcohol in the breath of the person (s. 6D(1A)).

Urine samples do not need to be taken by a medical practitioner. The samples will be admissible as long as they are provided within the time set out under s. 7(5) and there are two distinct samples (as opposed to two samples taken during the same act of urinating) (*Prosser* v *Dickeson* [1982] RTR 96). In *Ryder* v *CPS* [2011] EWHC 4003 (Admin), the Administrative Court held that obtaining the urine sample from a catheterised patient amounted to more than one sample. The court held that if someone had to drain their urine into a catheter, and this was treated as a single sample, the person on a catheter would never be able to supply a specimen of urine for analysis. This would usurp due process. This conclusion is consistent with the guidance offered by May LJ in *Nugent* v *Ridley* [1987] RTR 412 that the specimen to be analysed must be 'a fresh specimen and properly reflects the bodily condition of the person from whom it is taken'.

The hour within which the specimens must be produced starts from the time the request is made. However, the defendant must be given the opportunity to provide the urine within the one-hour period (*Robertson* v *DPP* [2004] EWHC 517 (Admin)).

It would appear by the wording of s. 7(3)(bc) and (c) that, where a preliminary drug test has been carried out, the officer can require a specimen of blood/urine without the advice of a medical practitioner or a registered health care professional. However, in s. 3, 4 or 5A offences where a preliminary drug test has not been carried out, the advice of a medical practitioner or a registered health care professional must be sought before the power to request blood/urine can be made. When such medical advice is sought, the doctor or a registered health care professional must give the officer a clear verbal statement to the effect that the driver's condition was due to some drug before the power arises (*Cole* v *DPP* [1988] RTR 224); however, the doctor is not limited to the findings of his/her own examination at the police station, but is entitled to take into account all relevant information, including what he/she has been told by police officers (*Angel* v *Chief Constable of South Yorkshire* [2010] EWHC 883 (Admin)).

It should be noted that s. 5A of the Road Traffic Act 1988 makes reference to the availability *in law* of a device enabling what is termed as a 'roadside *evidential* specimen of breath' (not to be confused with a preliminary roadside *screening* test) to be obtained. The idea is that an evidential specimen could be obtained by an approved device *at the roadside or even at a hospital* rather than at a police station. This might also occur, for example, immediately after a positive screening test has taken place (see s. 7(2)(c)). This would limit the opportunity to escape a conviction for an offence committed under s. 5 (over the prescribed limit) because of the amount of time elapsed between the positive screening test and the evidential specimen being obtained at a police station. While the legislation that created and governs the use of such a device (the Serious Organised Crime and Police Act 2005) has been in force for some time, it is important to stress that no device is currently available for operational use. The only devices currently used to obtain an evidential specimen of breath are those situated at a police station (Lion or Camic device). However, as the provisions relating to these devices are an integral part of the Road Traffic Act 1988, they are dealt with in this chapter in order to provide the reader with the most complete picture of the current *legislative framework* that exists in relation to drink/drive matters.

3.22.5.2 The Requirement

Unlike the requirement for specimens of blood or urine, a requirement under s. 7 to provide evidential *breath* specimens can be made:

(a) at a police station;
(b) at a hospital; or
(c) at or near a place where a preliminary breath test has been administered to that person or would have been but for his/her failure to cooperate with it.

That requirement can be made of more than one person in respect of the same vehicle (e.g. if it is believed that one of three defendants was driving the vehicle) (*Pearson* v *Metropolitan Police Commissioner* [1988] RTR 276). A requirement under s. 7 to provide specimens of breath cannot be made at or near the place where a preliminary breath test has been administered to the person (or would have been but for his/her failure to cooperate) unless the constable making it:

- is in uniform; or
- has imposed a requirement on the person concerned to cooperate with a preliminary breath test in circumstances where s. 6(5) applies (i.e. following an accident).

Note that where a constable has imposed a requirement on the person concerned to cooperate with a preliminary breath test at any place, the constable is entitled to remain at or near that place in order to impose on the person a requirement for an evidential specimen under s. 7 there (s. 7(2C)).

If a requirement for an evidential breath specimen is made under s. 7(1)(a) at a place other than at a police station, such a requirement can still be made later *at* a police station but only if:

- a device or a reliable device was not available at that place or it was for any other reason not practicable to use such a device there; or
- the constable who made the previous requirement has reasonable cause to believe that the device used there has not produced a reliable indication of the proportion of alcohol in the breath of the person concerned (s. 7(2D)).

A requirement for blood or urine can be made at a police station or hospital if the conditions under s. 7(3)(a)–(c) are met.

3.22.5.3 Medical Reasons

For the officer making the requirement to have 'reasonable cause to *believe*' that medical reasons exist, there is no need to seek medical advice first (*Dempsey* v *Catton* [1986] RTR 194). It is the objective *cause* of that belief which will be considered by the courts, not whether the officer actually did believe that a medical reason existed (*Davis* v *DPP* [1988] RTR 156). This was demonstrated in *Bodhaniya* v *CPS* [2013] EWHC 1743 (Admin), where the officer made this requirement after five failed attempts by the defendant to provide an evidential breath sample. The defendant appealed the conviction, stating that the request for blood was unlawful. The officer contended that by failing to provide an evidential breath sample five times, the only reasonable inference was that there had been a medical reason for the defendant not doing so; the appeal was dismissed.

In *Kinsella* v *DPP* [2002] EWHC 545 (QB), the Divisional Court held that just because the defendant had a mouth spray (for angina) and tablets at the time of arrest, that did not of itself impose an obligation on the relevant police officer to consult a doctor before deciding that any specimen to be provided would be blood. In that case, the officer had asked the defendant if there were any medical reasons why blood should not be taken and he had said that there were not.

Where an officer specifically asks whether there are any medical reasons for not taking a blood sample, the officer is entitled to rely on the answer given unless it is obvious that such reasons exist (*Jubb* v *DPP* [2002] EWHC 2317 (Admin)).

If a person is too drunk to provide a breath specimen, that may be regarded as a 'medical' reason for requiring a sample of blood/urine (*Young* v *DPP* [1992] RTR 328).

3.22.5.4 Device 'Available'?

If the relevant machine at a police station will not calibrate or is in some other way unreliable, this would appear to make it 'unavailable'. In such a case, however, the driver may be taken to another police station where such a machine is 'available'; this may be done *even if the driver has already provided two samples on the inaccurate machine* (*Denny* v *DPP* [1990] RTR 417).

Whether a machine is 'available' if it produces an accurate reading of the analysis of the driver's breath but cannot, for some reason, produce a hard copy printout of that reading, is open to some doubt. In one case (*Morgan* v *Lee* [1985] RTR 409) where the officer did not know of the machine's defect, his subsequent request for a blood sample was held to have been unlawful. However, in a later case the Divisional Court held that if the officer knew at the time that the machine had any form of malfunction, he/she could require a specimen of blood/urine under s. 7(3)(b) (*Thompson* v *Thynne* [1986] Crim LR 629) and this *subjective* approach has been followed and approved many times since.

Where the requirement for blood/urine is made under s. 7(3)(b), that sample must be used and the prosecution cannot revert to evidence produced by the breath sample (*Badkin* v *Chief Constable of South Yorkshire* [1988] RTR 401).

If the option to provide a blood sample is chosen, then, again, the driver may be taken to another police station where a doctor is available (*Chief Constable of Kent* v *Berry* [1986] Crim LR 748).

Section 7(3)(b) also allows the officer (**see para. 3.22.5.1**) the option of a blood/urine specimen when 'for any other reason' it is not practicable to use a breath-testing device at the police station. This would clearly include the situation where no trained operator is available to work the machine (*Chief Constable of Avon and Somerset* v *Kelliher* [1986] Crim LR 635).

3.22.5.5 Warning

The warning required by s. 7(7) is critical to a successful prosecution for failing to provide a specimen when required under s. 7(3). It is not needed when a driver elects to give an alternative sample under s. 8 (**see para. 3.22.5.10**) (see *Hayes* v *DPP* [1993] Crim LR 966 and also *DPP* v *Jackson*; *Stanley* v *DPP* [1999] 1 AC 406 at **para. 3.22.5.6, Keynote**).

3.22.5.6 Choice by Officer

The Road Traffic Act 1988, s. 7 states:

> (4) If the provision of a specimen other than a specimen of breath may be required in pursuance of this section the question whether it is to be a specimen of blood or a specimen of urine and, in the case of a specimen of blood, the question who is to be asked to take it shall be decided (subject to subsection (4A)) by the constable making the requirement.
>
> (4A) Where a constable decides for the purposes of subsection (4) to require the provision of a specimen of blood, there shall be no requirement to provide such a specimen if—
>
> (a) the medical practitioner who is asked to take the specimen is of the opinion that, for medical reasons, it cannot or should not be taken; or
>
> (b) the registered health care professional who is asked to take it is of that opinion and there is no contrary opinion from a medical practitioner;
>
> and, where by virtue of this subsection there can be no requirement to provide a specimen of blood, the constable may require a specimen of urine instead.

KEYNOTE

In exercising the power under s. 7(3), the decision as to whether the specimen will be blood or urine will be made *by the officer*.

In *DPP* v *Warren* [1993] AC 319, the House of Lords stated unequivocally that the decision, in both situations, is to be made by the officer. However, that is not to say that the officer can simply assume that blood should be taken unless medical reasons prevent it or that the officer should take no notice of any information given by the driver. The statutory discretion given to the officer by s. 7(4), although wide, has to be exercised reasonably (*Joseph* v *DPP* [2003] EWHC 3078 (Admin)). In *Joseph*, the driver told the officer that he was a

Rastafarian and therefore could not give blood. The officer's insistence that the driver give blood anyway, even though there was no reason not to take urine instead, was held to be so unreasonable as to make it unlawful.

Following the decision in *Warren*, many forces adapted their pro-formas in order to close what Lord Bridge called *a variety of wholly unmeritorious avenues of escape from conviction*. This has not stopped cases being argued in relation to choice and when it must be given to a defendant when explaining the choices available under s. 7(4).

In *Fraser* v *DPP* [1997] RTR 373, Lord Bingham CJ examined many of the other authorities since *Warren*. In his judgment, he endorsed the pro-forma used by Northumbria Police and said that there was a danger of putting *a new and heretical gloss* on the statute itself. His lordship held that there were many things which drivers ought to be told, but they need not be told them all at once. In addition, there was no requirement for an officer to explain to a defendant *at the time of making a decision under s. 7(4)* that any blood sample taken would only be so taken by a doctor.

In *DPP v Jackson*; *Stanley v DPP* [1999] 1 AC 406, the House of Lords stressed the distinction between the roles of the police officer and the doctor. The police officer decides *which* evidential sample(s) should be obtained and the medical practitioner decides *on the validity of the reasons put forward by the defendant* as to why a specimen of blood should not be taken. With three exceptions, the rules laid down in *Warren* were not mandatory elements of the procedure for taking evidential specimens but were guidelines indicating matters which should be brought to a defendant's attention before he/she exercised any choice that might be available.

The two elements that are mandatory are:

- in a s. 7(3) case **(see para. 3.22.5.1)**, the warning required under s. 7(7) **(see para. 3.22.5.5)**; and
- a statement as to why, in a case under s. 7(3), a breath specimen could not be used.

The Divisional Court's decision in *Bobin* v *DPP* [1999] RTR 375 found that, as long as the information set out above is provided by a police officer, it does not matter *which* police officer. Therefore, the warning under s. 7(7) can be given by the arresting officer, the custody officer or any officer who makes the requirement for the relevant specimen.

3.22.5.7 What Information Should Be Given to a Defendant?

As with other decisions involving when and where to give information to a defendant, there are probably fewer dangers in giving more than is required, sooner than required, than vice versa. Many of the cases before and since *Warren* have turned on the fact that drivers claim that they were not given the chance to reveal medical reasons as to why they could not give blood or that they were not told that it would be a doctor who took the blood rather than a police officer. Such opportunity and information need not be given out as a general requirement although there seems to be little harm in following an approach that errs on the side of caution.

The officer should explain what the options are and that the decision as to which will be chosen is the officer's; the driver should also be given the opportunity to state any reasons why blood should not be taken so that the officer may take the appropriate advice (*Edge* v *DPP* [1993] RTR 146).

3.22.5.8 Requesting Medical Practitioners to Take a Specimen

The Road Traffic Act 1988, s. 7A states:

> (1) A constable may make a request to a medical or health care practitioner for him to take a specimen of blood from a person ('the person concerned') irrespective of whether that person consents if—
>
> (a) that person is a person from whom the constable would (in the absence of any incapacity of that person and of any objection under section 9) be entitled under section 7 to require the provision of a specimen of blood for a laboratory test;

(b) it appears to that constable that that person has been involved in an accident that constitutes or is comprised in the matter that is under investigation or the circumstances of that matter;

(c) it appears to that constable that that person is or may be incapable (whether or not he has purported to do so) of giving a valid consent to the taking of a specimen of blood; and

(d) it appears to that constable that that person's incapacity is attributable to medical reasons.

(2) A request under this section—

(a) shall not be made to a medical or health care practitioner who for the time being has any responsibility (apart from the request) for the clinical care of the person concerned; and

(b) shall not be made to a practitioner other than a police medical or health care practitioner unless—

(i) it is not reasonably practicable for the request to be made to a police medical or health care practitioner; or

(ii) it is not reasonably practicable for such a practitioner (assuming him to be willing to do so) to take the specimen.

(3) It shall be lawful for a medical or health care practitioner to whom a request is made under this section, if he thinks fit—

(a) to take a specimen of blood from the person concerned irrespective of whether that person consents; and

(b) to provide the sample to a constable.

KEYNOTE

This legislation came about as a result of the procedural difficulties encountered where suspected drivers are injured in an accident and, as a result, are incapable of giving their consent to the taking of a blood sample.

In order to prevent such drivers escaping conviction where they would otherwise have had to provide a blood sample, the legislation allows for the sample to be taken lawfully without consent at the time. Thereafter, the system relies on the driver giving his/her permission for the sample to be tested in a laboratory. It must appear to the constable that the person has been 'involved' in an accident, which is a far wider term than suspecting that the person was driving, attempting to drive or in charge of a vehicle at the time. However, the reason for the test will be important in determining the penalty available in the event that the person fails to give his/her consent (**see para. 3.22.5.9**).

It must also appear to the officer that the person is or may be *incapable* (as opposed to simply unwilling) of giving valid consent and that this incapacity is attributable to medical reasons (rather than other issues such as language or ethical objections).

As a general rule, the doctor approached should be a police medical or health care practitioner. If it is not reasonably practicable either to make the request to the police medical or health care practitioner, or for the police medical or health care practitioner to take the sample, another medical or health care practitioner can be approached but not the medical or health care practitioner who has responsibility for the person's clinical care. The medical or health care practitioner is then empowered both to take the sample and to provide it to the officer without the person's consent if the medical or health care practitioner thinks fit; however, there is no obligation to do so.

A 'medical or health care practitioner' means a medical practitioner or a registered health care professional and 'police medical or health care practitioner' means a medical practitioner, or a registered health care professional, who is engaged under any agreement to provide medical or health care services for purposes connected with the activities of a police force.

The Road Traffic Act 1988, s. 7A goes on to state:

(4) If a specimen is taken in pursuance of a request under this section, the specimen shall not be subjected to a laboratory test unless the person from whom it was taken—

(a) has been informed that it was taken; and

(b) has been required by a constable to give his permission for a laboratory test of the specimen; and

(c) has given his permission.

(5) A constable must, on requiring a person to give his permission for the purposes of this section for a laboratory test of a specimen, warn that person that a failure to give the permission may render him liable to prosecution.

KEYNOTE

The above requirements are critical if the analysis of any sample lawfully taken is to be of any evidential value. By implication, the requirement that the person give his/her permission to the sample being sent to a laboratory means that he/she should only be informed of the above matters and given the statutory warning once capable of understanding what is going on.

3.22.5.9 Failing to Give Permission for Test or Provide Specimen

OFFENCE: **Failing to Give Permission for Laboratory Test of Specimen—*Road Traffic Act 1988, s. 7A(6)***

• Triable summarily • If the test was for ascertaining ability to drive or the proportion of alcohol at the time the offender was driving or attempting to drive—six months' imprisonment and/or a fine and obligatory disqualification—minimum 12 months • In any other case, three months' imprisonment and/or a fine and discretionary disqualification

The Road Traffic Act 1988, s. 7A states:

(6) A person who, without reasonable excuse, fails to give his permission for a laboratory test of a specimen of blood taken from him under this section is guilty of an offence.

KEYNOTE

For a discussion of what may amount to reasonable excuse, **see para. 3.22.5.11**. However, there should be far fewer opportunities for claiming reasonable excuses here given that there is no technical equipment involved. The permission being given (or not) is for the laboratory analysis, not the taking of the specimen. Therefore delaying the giving of permission in order to obtain legal advice may be acceptable, particularly as once the specimen has been taken and properly stored, there is not the same urgency as there is with the taking of a specimen before the alcohol/drugs dissipate. 'Failing' includes refusing (s. 11(2)).

3.22.5.10 Breath Specimen Showing Higher Alcohol Level to be Disregarded

The Road Traffic Act 1988, s. 8 states:

(1) Of any two specimens of breath provided by any person in pursuance of section 7 of this Act that with the lower proportion of alcohol in the breath shall be used and the other shall be disregarded.

KEYNOTE

It is standard practice that a driver provides two evidential breath samples. For charging and court purposes, the higher reading will be disregarded and the lower used.

3.22.5.11 Failing to Provide an Evidential Specimen

OFFENCE: **Failing to Provide Evidential Specimen—*Road Traffic Act 1988, s. 7(6)***

• Triable summarily • Six months' imprisonment and/or a fine • Obligatory disqualification—minimum 12 months

The Road Traffic Act 1988, s. 7 states:

(6) A person who, without reasonable excuse, fails to provide a specimen when required to do so in pursuance of this section is guilty of an offence.

KEYNOTE

Section 11(3) of the Road Traffic Act 1988 states that a breath specimen must be provided in such a way as to enable the analysis to be carried out. If a driver produces it in any other way, he/she will have 'failed to provide'. Provision of only one specimen of breath is a 'failure to provide' (*Cracknell* v *Willis* [1988] AC 450).

As with preliminary breath tests, 'fail' will include a refusal.

A person's general conduct in answer to a lawful requirement to provide a specimen, or a conditional response (e.g. 'I'm only providing a specimen if ...'), can amount to a refusal. The Court of Appeal has held that any such conduct or any such 'condition' does not need to be outrageous (cf. *R* v *Mackey* [1977] RTR 146). The key issue when considering any condition imposed by a driver before compliance is whether it amounted to a reasonable excuse for failure to comply with the test.

Reasonable Excuse

What amounts to a 'reasonable excuse' is a matter of law (see *Falzarano* later); whether the defendant actually *had* such an excuse is a question of fact for the court to determine having regard to the particular circumstances in each case.

In *DPP* v *Furby* [2000] RTR 181, it was held that if a police officer required a motorist to provide a breath specimen at the police station and the motorist made no effort at all to blow into the machine, he/she could not subsequently argue that he/she had a reasonable excuse for failing to do so. This principle was restated by the Administrative Court in a case where the driver alleged at the roadside that he suffered from bronchitis and therefore could not provide a breath sample. The arresting officer did not tell the custody officer of this alleged condition, neither did the motorist himself. As a result, the court held that no objective observer could say that the custody officer had 'reasonable cause to believe that for medical reasons a specimen of breath should not be required' and therefore the defendant should have been convicted for failing to provide a specimen (*DPP* v *Lonsdale* [2001] EWHC 95 (Admin)).

Although the choice under s. 7(4) is to be made by the requesting officer, the possibility of medical reasons for not giving blood must still be considered. An alleged fear of needles by the driver is a relevant consideration when making a decision as to whether a blood sample should be taken (*DPP* v *Jackson*; *Stanley* v *DPP* [1999] 1 AC 406 at **para. 3.22.5.6, Keynote** and also *Johnson* v *West Yorkshire Metropolitan Police* [1986] RTR 167). The driver should be given the opportunity to state any medical reasons why blood should not be taken but failure to give the driver that opportunity will not necessarily be fatal to an ensuing prosecution (*DPP* v *Orchard* [2000] All ER (D) 1457). However, any such reasons should be raised promptly. Where a driver clearly declined the option of replacing the breath specimen with a blood or urine sample, he was not permitted to claim later that a phobia of needles had caused him to decline the opportunity (*R (On the Application of Ijaz)* v *DPP* [2004] EWHC 2635 (Admin)).

The issues arising where a defendant claims to have had a 'reasonable excuse' for failing to provide a specimen of breath were reviewed by the Divisional Court in *DPP* v *Falzarano* [2001] RTR 14.

In *Falzarano*, magistrates had accepted the defendant's claim that she was physically unable to provide the specimen as she was suffering from a panic attack. The defendant proved that she had a history of such attacks and that she was receiving medical treatment for the condition. Despite evidence from her own doctor that the condition and her failure to take her medication on the day in question should not have prevented her from providing a specimen of breath, the magistrates found that she did in fact have a reasonable excuse. On appeal by way of case stated, the Divisional Court held that:

- the 'reasonable excuse' had to arise out of a physical or mental inability to provide a specimen or a substantial risk to health in its provision (*R* v *Lennard* [1973] RTR 252);
- the evidence in support of the 'reasonable excuse' normally had to be medical but the defendant could provide it him/herself;
- there had to be a causative link between the excuse and the failure to provide a specimen (*DPP* v *Pearman* [1992] RTR 407);
- being drunk or under stress was not in itself enough to provide a 'reasonable excuse' for failing to provide a specimen;
- having considered the medical evidence, legal advice from their clerk and the demeanour of the defendant when testifying, the magistrates had been entitled on the evidence to find that Falzarano had a reasonable excuse for failing to provide breath specimens.

This decision does *not* mean that shortness of breath caused by panic attacks or stress will always amount to a reasonable excuse.

In assessing a highly unusual and creative defence to s. 7(6), the Divisional Court was not prepared to accept that seeing blood would have sent the defendant, a registered member of the Zimbabwe National Traditional Healers Association, into a trance whereby he could be violent to himself and others. A refusal to provide a blood specimen for such 'spiritual reasons' was not a reasonable excuse on the facts of this case (*DPP* v *Mukandiwa* [2005] EWHC 2977 (Admin)).

There have been many cases where 'excuses' have been put forward. The following is a brief summary:

Not Reasonable

- Refusal until legal advice has been sought (*Campbell* v *DPP* [2002] EWHC 1314 (Admin)). This was reiterated by the Divisional Court in *Kennedy* v *DPP* [2002] EWHC 2297 (Admin), where it was held that the public interest required that the obtaining of specimens should not be delayed in this way. It would seem that this would include where a solicitor was ready and immediately available (*Chalupa* v *CPS* [2009] EWHC 3082 (Admin)).
- The absence of an appropriate adult where the defendant is a juvenile (*DPP* v *Evans* [2002] EWHC 2976 (Admin)).
- Refusal until a solicitor is present.
- Refusal on advice by a solicitor.
- Refusal until the driver had read the Codes of Practice under PACE.
- Mistaken belief by the defendant.
- Belief that the officer did not have the authority to make the requirement.
- Religious beliefs.
- Self-induced intoxication.
- Mental anguish caused by the custody officer's behaviour.

Reasonable

- Mental incapacity.
- Physical incapacity.
- Inability to understand the requirement caused by factors other than drink or drugs (e.g. language barrier).

Where any physical or mental incapacity (to provide the specimen or to understand the warning which accompanies it) is put forward, there will need to be clear, independent support for the claim being genuine (e.g. from a medical practitioner). Where a defendant's mental capacity to understand the warning is impaired by drunkenness, this is not a 'reasonable' excuse (*DPP* v *Beech* [1992] RTR 239).

The courts have warned of the need for caution when accepting a defendant's claim of such incapacity, particularly given the generally stressful nature of the police station procedure, together with the possible effects following an accident or motoring incident leading up to the request.

3.22.6 Hospital Procedure

The Road Traffic Act 1988, s. 9 states:

(1) While a person is at a hospital as a patient he shall not be required to co-operate with a preliminary test or to provide a specimen under section 7 of this Act unless the medical practitioner in immediate charge of his case has been notified of the proposal to make the requirement; and—
  (a) if the requirement is then made, it shall be for the provision of a specimen at the hospital, but
  (b) if the medical practitioner objects on the ground specified in subsection (2) below, the requirement shall not be made.

(1A) While a person is at a hospital as a patient, no specimen of blood shall be taken from him under section 7A of this Act and he shall not be required to give his permission for a laboratory test of a specimen taken under that section unless the medical practitioner in immediate charge of his case—
  (a) has been notified of the proposal to take the specimen or to make the requirement; and
  (b) has not objected on the ground specified in subsection (2).

(2) The ground on which the medical practitioner may object is—
  (a) in a case falling within subsection (1), that the requirement or the provision of the specimen or (if one is required) the warning required by section 7(7) of this Act would be prejudicial to the proper care and treatment of the patient; and
  (b) in a case falling within subsection (1A), that the taking of the specimen, the requirement or the warning required by section 7A(5) of this Act would be so prejudicial.

KEYNOTE

Note that a requirement to provide evidential breath specimens can be made at a hospital (**see para. 3.22.5.2**). A 'hospital' is an institution which provides medical and surgical treatment for in-patients or out-patients (s. 11(2) of the Road Traffic Act 1988). It will also include anywhere within the precincts of that hospital, e.g. the hospital car park (*Attorney-General's Reference (No. 1 of 1976)* [1977] RTR 284).

Whether the person is there as a 'patient' or in another capacity will be a question of fact. In assessing this fact, the courts will be helped by reference to hospital records which show names of patients, together with their times of admission and discharge (*Askew* v *DPP* [1988] RTR 303), although these records will not be conclusive.

If a person has been treated and then discharged from the hospital, he/she ceases to be a 'patient' for these purposes even if he/she has to return at a future date for further, related treatment (e.g. to have stitches removed).

Section 9(1A) was inserted in order to deal with the situations where a doctor has taken a blood specimen from the patient without his/her consent (under s. 7A, **see para. 3.22.5.8**). The overall effect of s. 7A and the above provision is that both the doctor taking the sample and the doctor in immediate charge of the patient need to be two separate people, both of whom will have to agree to the taking of the specimen. The 'medical practitioner in immediate charge of his case' was examined in *Cherpion* v *DPP* [2013] EWHC 615 (Admin), where the defence sought to claim that the doctor who gave permission for the specimen to be taken could not have been in immediate charge as she was a specialist. Although the doctor was not an A&E doctor, she was the doctor the officer first saw at the hospital. The High Court held that the magistrates were right to take a common-sense view that this doctor was in immediate charge even though she was an orthopaedic surgeon.

In *Webber* v *DPP* [1998] RTR 111, the driver of a vehicle involved in an accident was taken to a hospital and registered as a patient. At the hospital, she was requested to provide a preliminary breath test under s. 6.

She refused and was therefore required to provide a blood sample but, before she was able to provide the specimen, she was discharged. She was then arrested under s. 6 as a result of her earlier refusal. The driver was taken to a police station where she provided a specimen of blood on the strength of which she was subsequently convicted of driving while over the prescribed limit. She appealed, by way of case stated, on the ground that s. 9(1)(a) required the blood specimen to be taken *at the hospital*, which in this case it was not. The Divisional Court held that once the obligation to provide a specimen for analysis has been made, it is not to be discharged simply by an 'irrelevant change of *locus*'. The court went on to say that by making the requirement, the police officer set in train a procedure which carries a sanction (s. 7(6)), a procedure that was not to be altered by the mere fact that the defendant, for whatever reason, had left the hospital before complying with the requirement.

The restriction applies to both preliminary breath tests and evidential tests.

If the patient provides a positive reading or fails to provide a specimen of breath, he/she cannot then be arrested while still a 'patient' (s. 6D(3)).

3.22.7 Detention of Person Affected

The Road Traffic Act 1988, s. 10 states:

(1) Subject to subsections (2) and (3) below, a person required under section 7 or 7A to provide a specimen of breath, blood or urine may afterwards be detained at a police station (or, if the specimen was provided otherwise than at a police station, arrested and taken to and detained at a police station) if a constable has reasonable grounds for believing that, were that person then driving or attempting to drive a mechanically propelled vehicle on a road, he would commit an offence under section 4, 5 or 5A of this Act.

(2) Subsection (1) above does not apply to the person if it ought reasonably to appear to the constable that there is no likelihood of his driving or attempting to drive a mechanically propelled vehicle whilst—
- (a) the person's ability to drive properly is impaired,
- (b) the proportion of alcohol in the person's breath, blood or urine exceeds the prescribed limit, or
- (c) the proportion of a specified controlled drug in the person's blood or urine exceeds the specified limit for that drug.

(2A) A person who is at a hospital as a patient shall not be arrested and taken from there to a police station in pursuance of this section if it would be prejudicial to his proper care and treatment as a patient.

(3) A constable must consult a medical practitioner on any question arising under this section whether a person's ability to drive properly is or might be impaired through drugs and must act on the medical practitioner's advice.

KEYNOTE

The wording of this section means that this is a *subjective* test and the officer must be able to point to the 'reasonable grounds' for his/her belief. It is possible that a further screening test might provide such grounds but there is no specific requirement or power for this test to take place.

If it ought reasonably to appear to the officer (another *subjective* test) that there is no likelihood of the person driving/attempting to drive such a vehicle while impaired or over the prescribed limit, the power to arrest and/or detain under s. 10(1) does *not apply* and the person cannot be further detained under this section.

While effective, the practice of retaining the person's car keys after their release is not authorised by s. 10.

Index

A

B

D

E

I

J

K

L

M

N

O

P

T

U

V

W

Y